AF269632

Nicolae Iorga
A Biography

Nicholas Nagy-Talavera

Nicolae Iorga
A Biography

The Center for Romanian Studies
Las Vegas ◊ Oxford ◊ Palm Beach

Published in the United States of America by
Histria Books, a division of Histria LLC
7181 N. Hualapai Way
Las Vegas, NV 89166 USA
HistriaBooks.com

The Center for Romanian Studies is an imprint of Histria Books. Titles published under the imprints of Histria Books are distributed worldwide.

All rights reserved. No part of this book may be reprinted or reproduced or utilized in any form or by any electronic, mechanical or other means, now known or hereafter invented, including photocopying and recording, or in any information storage or retrieval system, without the permission in writing from the Publisher.

Library of Congress Control Number: 2020938094

ISBN 978-973-98091-7-7 (hardcover)
ISBN 978-1-59211-075-9 (paperback)

Copyright © 1998, 2021 by Histria Books

Table of Contents

Dedication

I dedicate my work to the memory of Professor Nicolae Iorga, and that in the twenty-first century his cultural nationalism will be interpreted correctly. Thus, it will be possible to build a better future for mankind.

— Nicholas M. Nagy-Talavera

Introduction

As the title indicates, this study is a biography of Nicolae Iorga, not the last word. Perhaps it is more inclusive than previous studies about his life; it is certainly more inclusive than anything written about Iorga in English or other languages of international circulation.

I undertook the task of writing Iorga's biography, I had to confront the 1,200 books and 20,000 articles written by him, and consider not only Iorga the historian, the politician, the journalist, the literary critic, the playwright, writer, poet, and linguist, but also Iorga the orator, the teacher, and last, but not least, Iorga the human being. I was overwhelmed. The immensity of this titan, this truly Goethean "Tatmensch" made it clear to me that I could use only Rembrantian methods: to paint the picture, and throw light on the important action within the whole tableau. I can only hope that I have succeeded to some degree.

I undertook this project because, up to now, there seems to be a lacuna about Iorga's life as a whole and, as Vasile Râpeanu correctly observed, Iorga's life can only be considered as a whole, in its entirety. I hope that my work will help to fill this gap.

My study touches on a sensitive subject: nationalism in general, and Romanian nationalism (as well as Balkan nationalism) in particular. Iorga's life is inseparable from it. This is a sensitive issue, because — according to some present-day intellectuals — nationalism is only "a passing phase of adolescence." In the vocabulary of these intellectuals, the nation belongs to "nationalists," that is to extremist radicals.

I do not believe this to be true. Nationalism is often exaggerated, but one must not dismiss it or condemn it outright, despite its sometimes tragic implications, especially in the Balkans. I have tried to explain nationalism in Southeastern Europe with some understanding — even sympathy. Following the course of Iorga's life and work, I tried to rectify some erroneous concepts about nationalism in general, and Iorga's nationalism in particular. Like Iorga, I believe that national feelings are natural manifestations of human nature. Like Iorga, I believe that there is a nationalism which is compatible with humanity, and there is a nationalism which is not. Iorga was murdered by such nationalists.

Nevertheless, the key to the history of the region (and, perhaps, of the world as a whole) remains centered around national identity. This is not only true in Romania, as Iorga's life demonstrates, but, as the last decade of the twentieth century has proven, also in six or seven countries of the former Eastern Bloc, in the former Soviet Union, and elsewhere.

I do not wish anyone to become teary-eyed about the abuses of nationalist extremists, whose nationalism is incompatible with humanity. Still, I hope that my study will encourage other historians to investigate further the life and work of Iorga, and nationalism in the region so that it can be better understood.

When considering Iorga's biography, one should keep in mind that for 50 years (1890-1940) his life was interwoven with Romanian history. Thus, I had to discuss this history at considerable length.

I was the first Westerner to have had access to numerous primary sources, including Iorga's correspondence, interviews with his family, and family archives. In addition, I also conducted personal interviews with many people who knew him (including the Romanian Iron Guardists who murdered him).

I have also included some materials relevant to the present tragedy in the Balkans. This is because the importance of Iorga's life in our days is that he was a nationalist historian-politician, deeply rooted in Balkan tradition. One should approach the twenty-first century with a comprehension of the past.

Nicolae Iorga
A Biography

It was the spring of 1932. The unfortunate Prime-Ministership of Nicolae Iorga was nearing its end. He was sitting on the porch of his home in Vălenii-de-Munte, silently looking into the sunset, with the peaks of the Transylvanian Alps, the Carpathians, shimmering in the distance. The son of his faithful political lieutenant, Professor Dimitrie Munteanu-Râmnic, a distant relative, then in his late teens, was at his side. Everything around them submerged in the solemn silence of sunset, so characteristic of rural Romania in the spring.

Suddenly, he turned to the young man: "Frasine, what do people think of me?" The youngster was taken aback by the unexpected confidence of Professor Iorga; even more by the question. He did not wish to risk too great a familiarity, nor was he anxious to answer the question. Iorga understood this, but did not relent, "Hai, dragă!" ("Come on, dear one!"), don't hesitate — give me a frank answer! What do people think of me?" The young man finally answered, timidly: "Well, people say you should have remained the great historian you are and never gotten mixed up in politics."

Iorga's answer erupted instantly: "But then I would have deserted the cause! I would have become a traitor!"

— Mr. Frasin Munteanu-Râmnic,
former curator of the Iorga Museum at Vălenii-de-Munte,
to the author in 1983

Chapter I

Nationalism and the Writing of History

"The historian is a social phenomenon, both the product and the conscious or unconscious spokesman of the society to which he belongs. It is in this capacity that he approaches the historical facts."

— E.H. Carr, *What Is History?*

"The new times are here again...," the Serbian writer A. Beljak commented recently, adding: "We just plain have no luck." From 1914 to our days, the Balkans (and Europe) have traveled full cycle: from Sarajevo back to Sarajevo. The writing of history is hardly static, and there is no last word, even where nationalist passions are less paramount than in East Central Europe. If Carr is right, widespread changes in the writing of history are in order from one generation to another. We call these changes revisionism; an inadequate term, even if history has a penchant for it.

Considering the spectacular changes in East Central Europe since 1989, there is little doubt that there will be formidable revisions in writing the history of the region. Much of it will be inspired by nationalist passion.

We are witnessing the rebirth and return of the revenge of nations in this region. Today, it is fashionable to read the headlines this way. But revenge, return, and rebirth rarely bring about resurrection. The national rebirths of our days take place against a different background than those after 1914.

Nothing of the legacy of the French Revolution is so fateful as nationalism, which during the nineteenth and the first half of the twentieth centuries created a school of nationalist history-writing. There have been two types of nationalist historians: those of the great powers (in the West and in Russia), who have often attempted to lend moral or ideological support to expansion — or to justify absolutism and expansion with Messianism, and those of small countries like those in Central Europe and the Balkans.

The role of the nationalist historian in the Balkans and in Central Europe was different from those of the great powers. The small nations, at the focal point of three supernational empires (Ottoman, Hapsburg, and Russian), lacked strength to assert their claims (just or otherwise). Therefore, historical arguments became very important in this region, making up for the lack of military force.

Dimitrije 'has pointed out that "Two factors determine the relationship between historians and politics in the Balkans: the role which historiography performed in modern nationalism, and the part which the fairly thin layer of intelligentsia played in the public and political lives of Balkan peoples. From the eighteenth century on, the national (political; renaissance of Balkan society found its ideological foundations in historical works and writings. In contrast to the Enlightenment in Western Europe, a similar movement in the Balkans was based on history. Its function was to legitimize the revolutionary birth of nineteenth century Balkan national societies, to reveal to them their perspectives, and to justify the aggressiveness of the young nationalists. It was by way of history these links were established between the past and the present, between the historian and the politician.

The second factor which stimulated the historian's role in politics was the prestige which scholars enjoyed among the Balkan public. In a predominantly peasant society, where the far from numerous intelligentsia was still in the early stages of development, the word science had a mystical, even magical resonance. Scientific was *eo ipso* genuine: the scholar was considered the apostle of Truth."[1] These factors all too often predestined the historian for a political role.

---

[1]Dimitrije Djordjevic: "Historians in Politics: Slobodan Jovanovic," *Journal of Contemporary History*, Vol. 8, No. 1 (January 1973).

Nicolae Iorga placed, in his evocative way, these words into the mouth of that champion of small nations, Edgar Quinet: "Whenever I raised my voice, I tried to speak up for the cause of weak nations — or those nations hoping for resurrection. True, I died with such words on my lips. But I am now buried in Italy, in Venice, in Poland, and with the Hungarians and Romanians. If there will be talk about my fatherland or my resting place, people of good faith should remember me so...."[2]

Although Iorga idealized (with this interpretation) the rebirth of the nation, his words were not devoid of a romantic nationalist reality. Such sentiments are deeply embedded in the psyche of the region, and almost always present in the writing of nationalist historians.

What is nationalist history? Are there distinctions between nationalist histories? Above all, should a historian engage in politics?

Until the nineteenth century, history was a private affair; but soon it became a prestigious discipline due to Leopold von Ranke's historical methodology, strongly supported by biological theories of evolution. According to him, the study of history could determine sound political judgment.[3] The state made documents available to the historian, who, in his turn, supplied the government with answers. Today such roles have been taken over by economists or social scientists.

Under such circumstances, can the historian remain faithful to scholarly impartiality (in Ranke's sense)? Or, should he remain in his Ivory tower? Goethe

---

[2]Barbu Theodorescu, *Nicolae Iorga* (Bucureşti, 1968) p. 317.

[3]The education of the elite was different at the turn of the century. Bismarck remembered the demands of his gymnasium's curriculum — hall of his class flunked out, and the other half ruled Germany. Today we often dismiss such emphasis contemptuously as elitist, but Harold MacMillan remembered how in his liberal arts college freshman were greeted by the Dean: "Gentlemen, you are embarking on a four-year adventure, and I can assure you that when it is over you will not be able to make a penny out of what you learn here; except when someone talks rot, you will be able to recognize it and expose him. And that is what education is all about!" Bismarck and MacMillan had in mind liberal studies, and the study of history.

told Eckermann, "One is always unjust in deeds; justice belongs to the observer." This would be inconceivable for nationalists in East Central Europe, and an anathema to the nationalist historian.

Ranke founded in the West the scientific impartiality of historical studies (as he said, to present history me *wie es gewsen ist*). Yet, reading him, one feels his admiration for the Hohenzollerns and Prussian institutions, their sense of duty and incorruptibility, creating the great Prussian state out of nothing. Ranke's history of the Reformation portrays Luther as a German national hero.

Jules Michelet was the best the French spirit could offer, but he was no politician, rather "a poet of history." Much less attractive are the historian-politicians A. Thiers and E. Guizot. The ideals they espoused seemed to have little relation to their policies. Historical erudition seemed encourage their arrogance and contempt for their own nation and humanity, and often to serve their personal ambitions.

In the United States, Henry Adams, John Fiske, and especially George Bancroft did not hide their nationalism. Critical reception of Bancroft's position has changed drastically.[4] T.B. Macaulay rhapsodized about the British Empire and people, their achievements, sciences, arts, and political institutions, past and present.[5]

In Germany, there were also aggressive nationalist historians like Heinrich von Treitschke and his followers. Maybe his history of Germany during the nineteenth century is more a literary work than a historical yet it had great influence. Cles, the founder of the ultra-chauvinistic Pan-German League, attended Treitschke's lectures. So did Admiral A. von Tirpitz. (Like Admiral A.T. Mahan, he had close relations with George Bancroft and his school of thought.)

---

[4] "The damage done to a sane perspective in American history by (Bancroft's) works was almost incalculable, if not irreparable." H.E. Barnes, *History of Historical Writing* (New York, 1962), p. 232.

[5] *Ibid.*, pp. 232-234.

N.M. Karamzin, who worked in Russia before the arrival of nationalist historiography there, justified the unlimited arbitrary power of the Russian autocrat. His arguments were based on Russian history.

These historians participated little in the politics of their countries, yet their lectures and writings exerted a powerful influence. Their Delphic and oracular predictions, along with reasoned justifications showed the way for statesmen. During wartime, they cheered the decisions of their leaders, emphasizing the past. They were inclined to justify conquests of the past or of the future. Often these moral and intellectual justifications were disguised ambitions. Statesmen welcomed these underpinnings.

Where does this leave historical objectivity? Tacitus wished to write history "without fear or favor." Ranke followed him by writing history *wie es gewesen ist*. We see a different situation in East Central Europe and Romania. On the crossroads of the German, Austrian, and Russian military monarchies, this "no man's land" is part of Europe only geographically. Some intellectuals refer to it contemptuously as the "dark side of Europe" (which, like the moon's dark side, is never seen). True, there was as much in common Dutch or a Danish village and the unsanitary villages of Poland or Moldavia, as there is between Oxford and the Gobi Desert. In this unfortunate end of Europe, the historian had another role — that of justifying conquests. As Nicolae Iorga saw it *in extremis*: "We demand life for ourselves!" [6] This presents contrasts to Admiral Mahan's sense of Manifest Destiny, to the British superiority presented by Macaulay (or Rudyard Kipling), or to the German idea of *an den deutschen Wesen, soll die Welt gensen*. There is no "Austrian Mission" here as proposed by Austrian historians. Not even the *mission civilisatrice* of the French, or Russian Messianism, always the moral justification of Russian expansionism.

This area is different from the West culturally. Dr. Samuel Johnson would hardly make sense for historians here, neither would Descartes, nor even Voltaire. Under the compulsions mentioned, for a major historian not to assume a

---

[6]*Neamul Românesc*, 21 August 1916.

political role, to withdraw into an Ivory Tower for the sake of abstract objectivity would often have been tantamount to treason. Did Iorga want a choice? Did he have a choice?

The Enlightenment led to the French Revolution, to liberty, equality, and fraternity. But another idea also emerged: nationalism. After the Napoleonic wars, which acquainted the rest of Europe with it, a disillusioned West embraced Romanticism. Romanticism has two aspects: the reactionary one, a disillusionment with Napoleon's *more geometrico*. Europe rediscovered the Middle Ages; the romantic medieval "alliance between throne and altar." But something else was emerging: finding in Romanticism an ally. Nationalist historians, especially in small nations, inspired by Romanticism, scoured the archives and, studying old parchments, discovered the past, the forgotten greatness of their nations. This rediscovered past greatness became a battle cry in the struggle to resurrect it. In this period, Romanticism, democracy, and nationalism became inseparable. This was the "Vormärz spirit" in Germany. Elsewhere in the West, the nationalism of Giuseppe Mazzini and Jules Michelet exalted their nations. Michelet's lectures inspired a whole generation from Adam Mizkiewicz to the generation that would achieve Romanian independence: Brătianu the Elder, Nicolae Bălcescu, and others.

The paramount need for national self-assertion was expressed by Bălcescu, the Romanian revolutionary democrat and historian-politician: "The question of nationality is more important than liberty. Liberty, when lost, can be easily recovered, but not nationality." Another great twentieth century nationalist, the historian-politician Charles De Gaulle (who taught, wrote, but mostly made history), was the type of leader about whom Corneille would say: "Our destinies are an open book for him." While a professor of history at the Military Academy of Saint-Cyr, he defined the role of the nation: "All human activity is ordered around the nation. The nation, shaped by history, is the supreme collective, armed by the state, with roots on a certain territory, molded by common interest, inspired by its heroes. Nothing can prevail against the force of the nation rising out of the depths of the ages, a force as elemental as it is tangible."

Both De Gaulle and Iorga would feel at ease nowadays. Iorga always considered the Soviet Union "...a nationalist hegemony with social pretensions," and did not believe it could long endure in the face of the only true reality: the nation. De Gaulle treated communism with equal disdain, considering it a bright but transitory tinsel, a pretense for imperial hegemony. And the mighty communist superpower broke apart, along the lines of its real components: national and religious ones. As De Gaulle predicted, Germany was reunited. East Central Europe is free, and the road is open for a "Europe from the Atlantic to the Urals."

Neither De Gaulle nor Iorga believed in a "melting-pot" of a European nation, least of all in a supernational Aeropagus. Both of them instead looked forward to a "Spring of Nations."[7]

But the Spring of Nations in 1848 was a failure. Realism, Bismarck, and Marx followed Schiller and Heine. Yet, Italy was united with the help of Romantic nationalism. Germany would be united, not by Romanticism, but by "iron and blood" through the *Realpolitik* of Bismarck. Nevertheless, in the new German Empire, nationalist historiography would rise through Heinrich von Treitschke and German historians who followed in Treitschke's footsteps: Max Lenz, Gustav Schmoller, Dietrich Schaffer, Hans Delbruck, and others.

Romantic nationalism arrived in East Central Europe in the first half of the nineteenth century, and rose to prominence during that century's second half, when it was over in the West. It would bring a tremendous nationalist sentiment, which would become a more fundamental feature of life here than in Western Europe, proving itself, thanks to geopolitics (and the meddling of the Great Powers), a highly combustible substance. This nationalism challenged the three supernational empires, crushing two (the Hapsburg and the Ottoman empires), and administering a temporary setback to the third — the Russian Empire. But Rus-

---

[7] Jean Lacouture, *Citations du Président De Gaulle* (Paris, Seuil, 1968), p. 21. Iorga's disparaging definition of the U.S.S.R. (among many similar ones) can be found in *Neamul Românesc*, 2 July 1940.

sia under Stalin managed to establish a tough nationalist dictatorship and modernized their military and police forces to reestablish their "national hegemony with social pretensions."

After the Second World War, East Central Europe became the defense perimeter of the Soviet superpower, and for almost half a century was directed by a sort of Monroe Doctrine from Moscow.

Yet, nationalism was by no means dead here. The Soviets had to act more than once to crush it. Finally, the historic year 1989 proved the Gaullist maxim: "No nation can be ruled against the will of the majority forever." But the Soviets acted for half a century as a kind of a refrigerator here, freezing political, social, and cultural evolution. They left post-Second World War problems unresolved, and they accumulated deep economic and social frustrations. But let us not forget that already in 1948 the communist monolith foundered on Tito's nationalism.

Today we are witnessing a tragic, bloody spectacle in the former Soviet Union and Yugoslavia. But this is not the fault of democratization, rather the consequence of the failure of communism.

The liberty of a citizen is unimaginable without the self-determination of the collective. Such self-determination is called: *Independence*. Those who fancied a democratic revival without a national rebirth were dreaming of sunshine without warmth, or dry water. When considering the present upheaval in Eastern and Southeastern Europe, there is no reason for astonishment: these disorders signal the return of life and liberty.

Lenin, an enlightened true internationalist and a realist, considered nations, as he put it, "stubborn facts." He did not like them (perhaps he did not really understand them), but he recognized their existence and learned to live with the nation.

At present many intellectuals consider the nation the domain of the "nationalists." These revisionist schools of thought try to enter even into historiography, rejecting the importance of national characteristics.[8] They forget the difference between chauvinism and being aware of national characteristics. As a consequence of the excesses of certain *racial* nationalisms during the twentieth century, some intellectuals disregard and disparage these realities, refusing to differentiate between different national aspirations, and they belittle the existence of national (that is, cultural) differences. Yet, in historical writing, such tendencies, together with the ubiquitous ideologues and bureaucrats, cannot obscure national differences, even with the aid of their appalling ignorance of geography and history. They try to establish a pattern of academic (and bureaucratic) thinking which dismisses national characteristics as a reactionary nineteenth century *myth*.

Such tendencies were (not surprisingly) present at the fiftieth anniversary of the defeat of the most malignant nationalism of all, German Naziism. An editorial in *Time* magazine made an interesting comment: the tendencies responsible for Naziism were "nationalistic war whoops, the egotism and sentimentality of nineteenth century European romanticism, having found its deadly end in Naziism and Fascism."[9]

Such an analysis is, in our days, not particularly helpful. National characteristics will not disappear regardless of how much some intellectuals, situated comfortably (sometimes arrogantly) in their Ivory Towers, would wish for it.[10] The most formidable and deepest boundaries are not marked on the map; they are not rivers or mountain ranges. These boundaries exist between nations and cultures. Such a global condemnation of nationalism — instead of a selective, pondered analysis — attacks the whole world.

---

[8] In the United States, I have the so-called Wisconsin school in mind.

[9] *Time*, 29 April 1985, p. 29.

[10] George Orwell assessed the abstract self-centeredness of some intellectuals during the Second World War in 1942 in England. They brought up four or five irrefutable arguments predicting Nazi and Japanese victory. Orwell commented that no common person thought so at that time. "Such absurdities were only believed by intellectuals."

With immense respect, this author asks: is any intellectual compromise possible? Could intellectuals elaborate a nationalism that is compatible with humanity? One should not think of becoming conscious of one's national characteristics as a passing phase, like adolescence, for example. The manifestations of nationalism are often quite objectionable, especially in East Central Europe. But, above all, these national feelings demand an understanding.

Since the reawakening nations try now to find their way, one should offer them credible acceptance into the framework of European solidarity. One should assist them in every possible way, above all, to help them turn their attention from their detested neighbor; to help them look to the West instead, which will have to assume a heavy responsibility, to become the (imperfect) model. Joseph De Maestre said that "the nation is a convenient concept — one can make out of it anything (one wishes)." Those modern statesmen who did not "make something out of it" did not achieve much.

Working out an answer to the realities of national sentiments on the one hand, and humanity on the other, is like walking a tightrope, and there will be pitfalls along the way. But it is not too late. Many past (and future) mistakes can be avoided or rectified. But first, one must accept a reconciliation with reality. Events in Yugoslavia should be a warning. As the pacifist Serbian writer Mirko Kovac (*La vie de Malvina Trifkovic*) cried out in despair: "Here (in Yugoslavia) nationalism has turned into an ideology. Because of that, it cannot be considered a national feeling anymore!..." What Mirko Kovac said is true about the whole region. Is there an answer?

Nicolae Iorga's life and his activities — up to his tragic end — were an attempt to find an answer to this dilemma. Did he fail because of the times in which he lived? Or because of his personal inadequacies as a politician? Is there any way to assimilate nationalism with humanity?

Nationalism, like socialism, capitalism, and fascism, was born in Europe. From there, it found its way to the rest of the world. During the Cold War, many people feared a nuclear Munich. Nowadays there is a much greater chance of danger from an inadvertent Sarajevo (possibly a nuclear one) because of the non-recognition of the identity of a nation.[11] But before we turn to the nationalist historian-politician of East Central Europe, let us say some words about this confused region between German and Russian imperialism and the Hapsburg Empire (the ally of German ambitions, opposing Russian policies). Bismarck put it fittingly: "if the Hapsburg Empire did not exist, one would have to invent it." What he meant was that it was needed for a balance of power favorable to the Reich. Hugh Seton-Watson called this area the "middle zone," and this author referred to it as the "No Man's Land of Europe." A torturous history created here a world very different from the West, both in form and content. There we see clearly defined nation-states, with few insoluble problems. But here, on roughly 570,000 square miles (little more than twice the size of France, with its unitary political, ethnic, and religion structure, and its secure national identity, in addition to its stable borders we find a conglomeration of two dozen national identities of more than one hundred million people, and every subdivision of Christianity, Islam, and Judaism.

These nation-states are the relatively recent product of the disintegration of the Hapsburg, Ottoman and Russian Empires. All these peoples have a tragic past and a menacing present. They all have had tragic histories of lost freedom, submerged identities, massacres, and shifting boundaries. Many people will consider the drama of this region — as Mircea Eliade did — a "historical fatality." But, then, some people show more interest for the *sense* of history than they do for history's *weight*. If in the West one Alsace-Lorraine problem was a burden, the "No Man's Land" is confronted with at least a dozen such disputes of

---

[11]How deep this misunderstanding can get, the remarks of two great statesmen. B. Disraeli, and W.S. Churchill show. Disraeli — it is alleged — brought home in 1878 "a peace with honor." His well-documented contempt for the sufferings or national aspirations of "the Balkan X-tians," (sic!) is known. But the settlement of 1878, it would seem, opened up the road to the fatal shots in Sarajevo in 1914. Churchill dwells long on the beauty of the world as it existed before 1914. Then he proceeds to describe Gavrilo Prinčip as a kind of a monster, rising out of the depths of the Balkans, to disrupt this pre-World War I perfection with his shots. No consideration is given to Serbian national aspirations — just or unjust. To this writer, the inscription on the Gavrilo Prinčip Museum (in Sarajevo) rings more true: "(The shots)... were a violent protest against tyranny — and (they) expressed a centuries-old yearning of a people — for freedom..."

an equal or greater magnitude. After the rise of nationalism, here the nation was to become the only reality, in the sense De Gaulle has defined it.

National rights and demands of these little nations are often based on history. But in these arguments we find very little similarity to those of a Macaulay or Manifest Destiny. The Slavophile V. Soloviev said: "History is a witness; when history takes the witness stand, its deposition is decisive during the process when there is litigation between nations." Iorga commented: "No wonder there are people who try to corrupt such an important witness." Another expert on the history of the "No Man's Land," Robert Lee Wolff observed that "In the Balkans, medieval data accumulated by scholars are often regarded as providing strong arguments for the settlement of present-day controversies."[12] Thus, historians not only interpreted their findings had to influence — oracularly, one almost thinks – the present and the future as well. It was proper for historians to assume a political role. Therefore, we find here a phenomenon not paralleled in the West: the emergence of the historian who became a politician in his own right.

In Bohemia, Frantisek Palacky (with his history of Jan Hus), more than anyone else championed Czech nationalism. His political role is known. J. Rački's role was as important in the Croat *Preporod* as Ludjevit Gaj's. The Serbians had their venerable historian-politician in Slobodan Jovanović. Hungary had its share of historian-politicians: Mihály Horváth, Gyula Szegfü, and Bálint Hóman. After 1989, so many historians entered politics and the foreign service that some Hungarians began to speak about a "Dictatorship of History Professors..." Poland has Oskar Halecki. In Austria, H. Redlich and H. Friedjung defended the "Austrian Mission." In Bulgaria, Father Paisie's and Father Sophroni's role does not equal that of the "Apostles," yet their part was important in searching the holdings of Mount Athos about the Bulgarian past and championing the vernacular. And there was the ill-fated World War II Prime Minister, the archeologist B. Filov.

---

[12]R.L. Wolf, "The Second Bulgarian Empire: Its Origins and History to 1204," in *Speculum* (Cambridge, Mass., April 1949) Vol. XXIV, No. 2, p. 175.

Of all these nations, no country produced so many historian-politicians as Romania did. Perhaps, no nationalism was so frustrated as Romanian nationalism was and is.[13] Romania has Nicolae Bălcescu, Mihail Kogălniceanu, Titu Maiorescu, Gheorghe Brătianu, even the communists had their own historian-politician: Lucrețiu Pătrășcanu. Without doubt the greatest among them was Nicolae Iorga. He was the historian-politician, "par excellence," not only for Romania, but for the whole "No Man's Land."

Iorga was the first intellectual of international stature of the newly-independent Romanian state. Romanians always mention him together with the poet laureate Mihai Eminescu, the composer George Enescu, and the sculptor Constantin Brâncuși as the bearers of Romanian culture. None of the historian-politicians mentioned before could match Iorga's stature as a historian or an intellectual, nor his commitment to romantic nationalism. Nor could other historian-politicians match his determination to carry his ideals over into practical politics.[14] He represented the most extraordinary mind ever given to the Romanian nation. The greatness of Iorga originated from his talents; but the source of his proverbial energy, turning into a Goethean *Tatmensch,* was fueled by his nationalism. He was a figure larger than life. During his life, his genius was reflected in many activities. He went through many changes, but there was one unbroken consistency: he remained faithful to Romania, and tried to serve his nation unselfishly. One must consider his activities as a whole. But this is not an easy task: about 1,200 volumes and 20,000 articles comprise Nicolae Iorga's oeuvre; he was a prolific political journalist and pamphleteer; a playwright, essayist, a poet, a militant literary historian and critic; an orator, a linguist, and a memorialist; also a first-rare university professor, mesmerizing his audiences. Then, there are his political activities, lectures, extensive travels, and the volumes of his travel descriptions.

---

[13] When I mention to my Romanian friends justice, reason, or equity in international relations, their reaction is bitter laughter: "We know by experience how justice and equity prevailed in our history."

[14] When Iorga received his honorary degree at Oxford, the Public Orator called him "the Livy of Romania."

To paint an integral picture of an almost superhuman phenomenon is difficult. One can only hope to achieve proper discretion, trying to paint the picture in a Rembrandtian fashion, presenting the whole picture as a backdrop, and trying to throw the light on what he considers important.

One of Iorga's detractors, George Călinescu, said that "(Iorga's) activities in their cumulative sense seem to be great, yet, in details, each one of his activities is of minor significance."[15] To begin, we must turn Călinescu's maxim on its head. One can criticize some of Iorga's activities in detail, but cannot deny the overall greatness of Iorga's accomplishments. Between 1890 and 1940 Iorga's life and events in Romania were interwoven and inseparable. So his political, cultural, literary, and intellectual role must be considered. It would be perhaps impossible for Iorga to remain consistently wise through the hundreds of thousands, of pages he produced, being at the focal point of a turbulent history. In the final balance, he seems to be one of the last representatives of the nineteenth century, in the spirit of 1848, and the type we shall analyze later: the East European intellectual. And this is a cause for sadness: Iorga was, as he so often and so proudly affirmed, a "man of the nineteenth century."[16] Somerset Maugham wrote somewhere: "Sometimes a man survives a considerable time from an era in which he had his place into one of which is strange to him, and then the curious are offered one of the most singular spectacles in the human comedy." In the last decade of his life, Iorga offered such a spectacle many times. They used to refer to him as the "Apostle;" at other times as "the teacher of the nation." Ultimately this nineteenth century nationalist-intellectual found his bloody doom at the hands of those who were very much twentieth century nationalists.

---

[15]G. Călinescu, *Istoria Literaturii Române* (Bucharest, 1941), pp. 542-545. Yet Călinescu proceeds in the same breath to call Iorga the very motor of Romanian culture, comparing his role with that of Voltaire on the French scene. *Ibid.*

[16]*Neamul Românesc*, 9 September 1939. De Gaulle was often referred to as "the last survivor of the 19th century."

Nationalism is often misunderstood because there are two kinds. One is backward nationalism, like the one in the Athens of antiquity, or during the Middle Ages, where belonging depended on race or heredity. The other nation, the progressive one, emerged from the French Revolution. It was based on a voluntary adherence to a commonwealth: a nation of choice. Those who confuse these two nations confuse the France of Deroulède and of the Action Française with that of Valmy; Vichy with De Gaulle; Heine with Hitler; Mazzini with Mussolini; the Legion with Iorga; and chauvinism (or racism) with nationalism.

These differences were one of the major issues of the Second World War. These concepts are as incompatible as barbarism is with civilization, as the "mores" of the Teutonic "Urwald" are with our Bill of Rights. A Gaullist, Mme. Germaine Tillon said: "A Frenchman is one who wishes to become one." And Iorga said (about Jewish assimilation): "In Romania only those will remain strangers who wish to remain so."

E.H. Carr said: "Before you study a historian, study his historical and social environment." The origins of the Romanians were laid out by A.D. Xenopol, and later by Iorga and other historians. According to them, a continuity can be identified from the Geto-Dacians, throng the Romans, to the Romanians of today. This continuity is especially relevant in Transylvania.

This claim brought forth Hungarian, Russian, and even Bulgarian counterclaims that the Romanians were not present in Transylvania, or for that matter, in present-day Romania, before the twelfth century. Rather, they infiltrated Transylvania (and the area) during the twelfth and thirteenth centuries, as semi-nomadic shepherds. Many Western historians accept a continuous Latin presence here.

The modern answer is based less on the historical arguments than on linguistic and ethnic homogeneity and the right of self-determination. It was Iorga more than anyone else who tried to give to Romania powerful historical arguments in addition to the obvious right of self-determination.

During the great migrations, nearly a dozen barbarian hordes swept over this area. The Romanians also had contact with the Byzantine Greeks, yet they preserved much of their Latin character. Then the Hungarians moved into the mountainous Romanian stronghold of Transylvania: the Romanians saw them and survived. Around the thirteenth and fourteenth centuries, the waves of barbarian hordes subsided, and two Romanian principalities arose: Wallachia and Moldavia (which included Bessarabia and Bucovina).

The Romanians became Christians early on. Because of geography, they adopted Christianity from Byzantium, becoming the only Latins not of the Latin Christian rite. Once Constantinople fell, many Byzantine Greeks fled to the Romanian Principalities, which, coming to terms with the Turks, preserved a degree of independence. The Romanian principalities fought the Turks, but seeing the odds, Wallachia, and later Moldavia, accepted Turkish suzerainty. They were treated more advantageously than any other Balkan country. The Romanians were considered allies under Turkish suzerainty rather than conquered territories. With no protective power to defend them, the Romanians were realists. This does not mean that they liked the Turks; whenever there was a chance, they asserted themselves. Nobody did that so successfully as the mighty prince, Michael the Brave, who established his power over Transylvania, uniting Wallachia and Moldavia with it. Ever since, he became a symbol for those who still believed in a better future for the Romanian nation. But as soon as he departed the scene, his achievement fell apart.

By the end of the seventeenth century, the Ottoman Empire was in decline two great powers appeared on the boundaries of the Romanian Principalities: Austria, which acquired Transylvania, and the Banat. More fateful for Romania was the arrival of Peter the Great. The long series of Russian-Turkish wars started. The Ottoman Empire considered the Romanian Principalities a periphery; for the ever-expanding Russian Empire, it became a roadblock. Their ambitions would cross the Romanian lands. When Peter the Great approached the Balkans with their Orthodox population, he issued an appeal to all Orthodox Christians to rise against the "infidel." The Romanian princes hesitated; they would have liked to get rid of the Turks, but they were not certain that the Russians were the best means to accomplish that. Ultimately, they sided with Peter the Great. But his Orthodox cause was defeated. The consequence was the loss of the sultan's confidence in Romanian princes, who were substituted by Phanariot Greek puppets. The coming 120 years, the Phanariot Period, would bring well-known consequences for Romania.[17]

Russia always needed a Messianistic ideology to conquer. Her mission was to lead the world into a state of holiness, justified by an exceptional religious or ideological insight. Appeals for Orthodox solidarity were often followed by annexation. Replaced by Marxism, the Russians had the confidence that others were willing to be as holy as the Russians thought themselves to be. The Romanians, not being Slavs, would awaken from their dashed hopes first.[18] During the eighteenth century Russian expansionism continued under Catherine the Great. Beginning with her reign, the Russians would march a dozen times across the principalities towards Constantinople, the unobtainable goal of *Tsargorod*, the first teacher of the Eastern Slavs, and the dream of celebrating a *Te Deum* in the Hagia-Sophia Cathedral — by that time cleansed from the infidels. Every time they passed, they left behind a trail of plunder, death, disease, and ruin. Since the time of Ivan the Terrible, a centralized Russian state had been expanding, a remarkable and unique phenomenon in history. Although during this long process they suffered setbacks, they soon recouped their losses with interest. The Russians call this incessant drive a quest for security. But this instills a sense of insecurity in all of their neighbors. Pan-Slavic never evoked sympathy in Poland. It only had an appeal in Slavic areas not bordering on Russia, to the Czechs, Serbians, and Bulgarians. Once the Russians reached these areas, enthusiasm for Pan-Slavism decreased. All this must be emphasized if one wishes to understand Romanian nationalism, and the meaning Iorga gave to his life.

---

[17]Iorga showed with some success that the Phanariot Regime had not been so barren an episode as it had been considered, because, above all, it did not disrupt "organic development." Despite his persuasive arguments, this writer (along with other historians) maintains that the Phanariot period in Romanian history was disastrous.

[18]Nicolae Iorga, *Histoire des relations russo-roumaines* (Iaşi, 1917). During the Second World War even Slavic illusions would be dissipated. No Slavic people was so pro-Russian as the Montenegrins. Yet by 1948 their hopes were also dashed. See Milovan Djilas, *Conservations with Stalin*, (New York, 1962), passim.

By the end of the eighteenth century, the Ottoman Empire became even weaker. In 1775, Austria reached the borders of Moldavia and wrenched Bucovina from the Porte. Austrians settled Ukrainians, Germans, and Jews there during the next 120-150 years. In 1812, the Russian took the eastern half of Moldavia, Bessarabia. A brutal Russification followed. The Romanians withdrew into their historical experience: passive resistance. After the 1829 Adrianople Peace Treaty, the Romanian principalities became Russian protectorates. Russian consuls ruled supreme in Iaşi and Bucharest and treated the Romanian boyars "like dogs," making it clear: Russia was not a neighbor, but a master. Although there were exceptional Russian governors, such as Pavel Kisseleff, who tried to case the sufferings of the Romanians,[19] Tsar Nicholas I forced the so-called *Organic Regulations* on Romania, which perpetuated the exploitation of the peasant. With more than half of historic Moldavia lost, what was left became the holy land of Romanian nationalism.

Amid suffering and degradation, Romanian national awakening came from the outside, as in Greece, Serbia, and Bulgaria. It came from Transylvania, wherefrom they adopted the Latin alphabet in substitute of the Cyrillic Church Slavonic one. The Uniate Church of Transylvania gave the Romanians a chance to go to Rome to look at the Forum and Trajan's Column and to reestablish their national identity.

In 1848, there were two revolutions; in Wallachia and in Transylvania. The Russians and the Austrians thwarted both, darkness descended again. Yet, with the start of the Crimean War, there was light at the end of the tunnel. The Paris Peace Treaty brought parts of Bessarabia back under Romanian rule. Amidst the widespread euphoria of the late 1850s, with the help of Louis Napoleon III (the self-appointed defender of nationalism everywhere), Romania achieved nationhood, despite the opposition of many great powers. Prince Alexandru Ioan Cuza of Moldavia became the first new Romanian State.

The 1877 "War of Independence" (as it was called in Romania) was fought during Iorga's childhood. He distinctly remembered this unfortunate milestone

---

[19]Nicolae Iorga, *op.cit.*, passim.

in Russian-Romanian relations. Russia, needing to march through Romania, enlisted it as an ally. When Russia's armies faced a difficult situation at Plevna, they needed help fast, which the Romanian army rendered. The Russians, once victorious, forced the Romanians to surrender southern Bessarabia.

The history of this Romanian-Russian alliance is known. Consider Gorchakov's assurances, and his later declaration (in private) that: "The military situation presses us to make promises to Romania which we have no intention of keeping anyhow." Thus, he gave a new dimension to Russian diplomacy — breaking an agreement *in anticipando*. Take Tsar Alexander II's vulgarities uttered about an ally; the threats issued to Mihail Kogălniceanu that, in case of Romanian noncompliance concerning Bessarabia, the Russians would disarm the Romanian army. Kogălniceanu's answer was: "You may crush us, but you will never disarm us." Bismarck embarrassedly disapproved of Russian behavior; and R. Poincaré, a friend of Russia, said: "My face turns red when I think how you were forced to surrender Bessarabia in order to buy your liberty."[20]

What happened afterwards did not strengthen Romanian faith in their eastern neighbor. Iorga believed in the Napoleonic dictum that the foreign policy of a country is determined by its geography. No messianistic ideology would change the nature of the organism he considered a nation to be.[21]

Many Romanians complain about double standards when a great power's policies are judged in one way and the policies of small countries in another. If a great power does something reprehensible, this is considered *raison d'état, renversement des alliances, Realpolitik,* or a "great design," a great diplomatic coup — or (at worst) "flexibility." If a small nation fights for its survival, it is treachery, cowardice, opportunism, pusillanimousness, etc.

---

[20]Nicolae Iorga, *Războiul pentru independenţa României (acţiuni diplomatice şi stări de spirit)* (Bucureşti, 1927), passim, and *Correspondance diplomatique Roumaine sous le roi Charles I (1866-1880), publiće sous les auspices du Ministère des Affaires Étrangères de Roumanie* (Paris, 1923), passim; finally, *Revue Slave,* Vol. 2, (April 1928), p. 141.

[21]Iorga called Kerensky a demagogue who "believes that the new world can be created with the help of a few speeches." *Supt Trei Regi* (Bucureşti, 1932) p. 242.

In Transylvania, after reconquering the province from the Ottoman Empire, the Hapsburgs practically handed the Romanians over to me Hungarian landlords. What this meant for the Romanians there was witnessed by the future Emperor Joseph II, who traveled through this province in disguise. Only the Uniate Church could offer some relief, serving to uphold Romanian national spirits. In 1783-1784 Joseph, now emperor, issued decrees to remedy the plight of Romanian serfs. His good intensions, coupled with the people's ignorance and sufferings, resulted in the bloody peasant uprising led by Horia, Cloşca, and Crişan. Imperial troops restored order and things went on as before. The next Romanian uprising came in 1848, when Louis Kossuth united Transylvania with Hungary without taking the Romanian majority into consideration. Now the Romanians rose in a bloody uprising led by Avram Iancu. But neither Romanian nor Hungarian nationalism had a place in Prince Felix Schwarzenberg's plans for a united, centralized Austria. During the coming Austro-Hungarian Compromise in 1867, the Romanians of Transylvania were handed over without ado to the new centralized Hungarian state. Bishop Andrei Şaguna, the spiritual leader of the Romanians, advised passive resistance.

But young Romanians did not want to live as their fathers did. With an increasingly harsh Hungarian Magyarization campaign underway, they would try an old remedy: they turned to the emperor for help, but he was not in a position to challenge his partners. The "Memorandists" (because they handed a Memorandum to the emperor listing their complaints) were treated administratively by the Hungarians, and sentenced in 1894 to long jail terms.[22] During the first decade of the twentieth century the Magyarization campaign reached its peak. The educational laws established Hungarian state control even over the educational curriculum of the denominational schools. The rise of nationalism

---

[22]R.W. Seton-Watson (an admirer of Kossuth, and a friend of the Hungarians) came to Hungary at the beginning of the century in order to refute the charges levelled against Hungary of oppressing the other nationalities. When he saw the situation in Transylvania and elsewhere, he changed his mind radically, and he let Britain and the world know the reality of the situation. R.W. Seton-Watson, *A History of the Roumanians* (Cambridge, 1934), pp. 394, 395, 401, and 428.

and that of the nation-state (after 1867) made the problem of Transylvania intractable. Refused by the Hungarian state during the nineteenth century, the Romanians in Transylvania chose the either/or solution: Transylvania would be either Romanian or Hungarian. The Hungarians thought in the same way — with all the might of the state and the bureaucracy on their side. After that, there was little room for ethnic plurality there. Thus, when Iorga entered the Romanian political scene, almost half of the Romanian people lived under foreign rule, and quite unhappily.

Iorga and the nationalists referred to independent Romania as "Free Romania," but life was neither free nor rosy there. Because of Romanian cooperation with the Ottomans here, the nobility was not exterminated.

Romanians boyars, very much alive, made sure that peasant misery should hit a rock bottom. Many of them were not Romanians. Thanks to the Phanariot rule, we see Greeks among them, as their names — Cantacuzino, Mavrocordat, Lahovary, Sturdza, Ghică — show. If one wishes to understand their despotic Oriental philosophy, one must look across the Dniester for examples. Despite the Constitution, peasants were effectively excluded from representation through the "Electoral Colleges."[23]

The achievements of 1848, 1859, and 1866 were the subject of much debate afterwards. The "Bonjourists" (mostly identified with the Liberals) subjected Romania to a kind of "shock treatment," grafting a Belgian constitution, Napoleonic code, French administrative structures, French philosophy and fashions, French architecture and manners, even a French theater (and the novels of Dumas père) on semi-barbaric foundations.

The institutional alienation of the elite was followed by cultural alienation, opening an abyss between the upper classes and Romanian masses. The reaction

---

[23]A British consul during the nineteenth century reported: "There does not, perhaps, exist a people laboring under a greater degree of oppression from the effect of despotic power and more heavily burdened with impositions and taxes than the peasants of Wallachia and Moldavia." W. Wilkinson, *An Account of the Principalities of Wallachia and Moldavia* (London, 1820), p. 155.

to this cultural rape was the devastating Junimist criticism of Titu Maiorescu and Mihai Eminescu, in which Iorga also joined.

In retrospect, it is hard to see what else could have been done. How could the Brătianus otherwise have formed a state? The Junimists did not recognize that those "forms without foundations" (i.e., the Western institutions) were absolutely necessary to start Romania's national, social and cultural integration into the European concern of nations. Iorga hated the Liberals and their policies. Yet, this Liberal intelligentsia considered itself progressive enough — more so than they considered the socialists to be! It saw itself remodeling Romanian society into a modern one: on the model of France.[24] The inevitable result was a great alienation. Later the cultural rape would find its nemesis in the Iron Guard. But the Liberal revolution of 1848 in Wallachia was an urban phenomenon, leaving the village cold.

When the modern, pseudo-Western state was grafted on the Oriental foundations, it was the peasants who had to pay for it. Taxes more than doubled by 1900; Constantin Dobrogeanu-Gherea called their misery *Neoiobăgia* (New Serfdom). The recruiting sergeant appeared at the doorstep of the peasant hut, taking away their sons to the new army.

Beyond this, there were the untouchable vested foreign interests. Oil production began by the end of the century. It was owned and operated mainly by foreigners. They were instrumental in railroad ownership and construction, and there were government loans. The Romanian government borrowed freely, and loans were available if the government was pliant. Thus, by the end of the century, capitalism and imperialism were in full swing, with foreigners or non-ethnic Romanians in many key positions. There were large numbers of Greeks, Armenians, and Jews. Romania had other nationalities, yet for nationalists the Jews were the most numerous and noxious.

____

[24]Ştefan Zeletin, staunchly defended Liberal economic policies during the forced industrialization of the 1920s. This policy placed the burden of this "necessary process" squarely on the peasantry. Zeletin dismissed Marxist pretensions. "Since capitalism was in its formative stage in Romania, a proletariat pursuing its own revolutionary goals was nonsense." Ştefan Zeletin: *Burghezia română şi rolul ei istoric* (Bucureşti, 1925), passim.

As this author will voice some unorthodox views about the Jewish problem in Romania, he has to state (unwillingly) some autobiographical information. He is Jewish, from one of the old Sephardic Jewish (but assimilated Hungarian) families in Transylvania. He suffered every Nazi persecution possible, except death. On the question of anti-Semitism in East Central Europe (and in Romania), he would like to go on record as being in agreement with the opinion of Hugh Seton-Watson: "Thus, anti-Semitism is a most noxious disease, incompatible with peace and civilization, for three reasons. It victimizes a large number of innocents. If some guilty suffer among them, they suffer on account of their race and not because of their guilt. It demoralizes the persecuting nation. If (like in Romania!) a young generation is educated by their professors and the police that the beating up of an old man or a female student is an act of chivalry or heroism, this will have grave consequences on the morals of the nation. Then, use of Jews as scapegoats for every existing evil (a process carefully fostered from "above"), might give a temporary respite to the rulers. But real problems remain unresolved, thus everybody suffers."[25]

This statement, though irrefutable, is not exhaustive. Seton-Watson states a few pages before: "The mentality of the Jews is entirely alien to the romantic nationalism which spread throughout Eastern Europe from the second half of the last century onwards." The British Envoy in Bucharest, Sir William White — by no means an anti-Semite (in 1879 he tried to intervene on behalf of Jewish civil rights in Romania, according to the decision of the Berlin Congress, and the British Government) — commented in a letter to Lord Salisbury: "A Romanian might become a Jew — yet, it was quite impossible for a Jew to become a Romanian."[26]

The fate of the Jews in the Diaspora is known; the Roman Empire, tired of the incessant rebellions in that minuscule corner of their empire (Judea), expelled most of the Jews. The Jews reacted by forming a spiritual nationhood of

---

[25]Hugh Seton-Watson, *Eastern Europe Between the Wars* (New York, 1962), p. 293.

[26]*Ibid.* p. 290, and William O. Oldson, *A Providential Anti-Semitism, Nationalism and Polity in Nineteenth Century Romania* (Philadelphia, 1991), p. 82.

the toughest kind: their religion and nationhood became identical. They always followed the routes of commerce, enriching themselves with what one in the soil commerce always seems to find: culture. Commerce demands security. Until the nineteenth century, the Romanian lands were one of the most insecure parts of Europe. Consequently, there was a minuscule Jewish community, mostly of Sephardic Jews who came to Romania during Ottoman times. During the Late Middle Ages, many German ("Ashkenazi") Jews migrated to the *Reczypoczpolita*, the territories of the elective Polish kingdom. Gabriel Bethlen, the enlightened Protestant prince of Transylvania, invited a Sephardic Jewish community into that region. There they were involved in ordering the finances and participated in the meetings of the Princely Council. They were also the physicians of the Princely family. How did the presence of such a relatively small Jewish community grow into a major problem?

We must seek the answer in the *Polish Reczypuczpolita*, partitioned by Russia, Austria, and Prussia. Jews were better off in Prussia and the Austrian part; in Russia they were restricted to a "Pale of Settlement." Barred from guilds, they were forced to make a living in professions which were needed, but in which no respectable Christian would engage. The confinement of the Jews to these professions, and the degrading humiliations, massacres, and expulsions to which they fell victim, contributed to the development of a Jewish "Pale of Settlement" type. Yet the Jews preferred degradation, persecution, and even death to giving up their peculiar religious nationhood. In such a situation only their God (identical with their nationhood) and their survival along with the family mattered. Historically, the family is the stronghold in a hostile land; its honor must not be tarnished. In the Pale of Settlement the Jews obeyed a double standard. Within the family they demonstrated all qualities usually not attributed to them by superficial observers: they were reliable, honest, obedient, generous, brave, and disciplined; outside their families, they often employed the tactics of underground fighters in an enemy-occupied territory.

During the nineteenth and twentieth centuries, a tremendous population explosion touched the Jews before it touched the local populations.[27] Population growth on top of persecution filled the lives of the Jews with a feeling of economic hopelessness. At this time the local people — Poles, Ukrainians, Russians, or Baltic — were touched by a nationalist awakening. This, in addition to their miserable lives, turned them, in their despair, against a minority neither willing nor able to assimilate. In the Austrian part, Jews felt only economic and demographic pressures. In the Russian part, Jews felt increasing persecution. They answered brutality as always; they submitted to it, tried to alleviate it, but refused to assimilate into the nation which brutalized them. By the nineteenth century, many Jews tried to escape these conditions through emigration. In the 1820s, during the rule of Ioniţă Sturdza, we see a rapid increase of Jews in Moldavia, bordering on the Pale of Settlement.

Religious intolerance and persecution were almost unknown in the principalities. The Romanian lands knew no St. Bartholomew's Nights, no Inquisition, and no Joan of Arc was burned at the stake. In Huşi (as the name shows), a substantial Hussite community flourished as late as 1500. Before the 1820s, the few Jews living there were never forced into ghettos within the Romanian lands; their synagogues were never attacked.

If the Romanians remained Orthodox Christians, this was to prevent Polish and Hungarian cultural, that is, national encroachments. Even conversions to the Uniate Church in Transylvania served the purpose of gaining Hapsburg support for preserving Romanian identity.

Jewish immigrants remained mainly in Moldavia, and were most unwelcomed in such great numbers. But this antipathy had no racial or motivation; its roots were cultural and economic. Put simply, the rising Romanian nationalism clashed with rising numbers of Jews. Romanian governments demonstrated an

---

[27]In the area of historical Poland there were 617,000 Jews in 1788 (some estimates put it at 900,000); within a century this figure increased roughly tenfold. S.M. Dubnow, *Die neueste Geschichte des jüdischen Volkes* (Berlin, 1920), vol. I, p. 90.

incapacity in dealing with the problem — it was the corruption of local officials that was responsible for letting the Jews enter Moldavia in large numbers.

And once they were there and their struggle for survival began to cause grave problems, to corruption, brutality was added. For most Romanians there was never any question of accepting such a large number of Jews.[28] The Romanian government, following Seton-Watson's maxim, tried to use the Jews as scapegoats for the existing social and economic problems, counting on the despair and the ignorance of the peasantry. All this created a complex situation, and represented a very real danger to frustrated Romanian nationalists, especially in Moldavia.

The Romanian situation cannot be judged by Western standards. In more fortunate Western countries (contrary to the closed world and society of Romania and Eastern Europe), such conflicts do not explode. Social, economic, and political mobility allows them to be bypassed. Mobility is still possible. Such elbow-room was in short supply in Romania.

According to a Zionist formula: anti-Semitism = the number of Jews x social dislocations and misery /assimilation of the Jews (The formula refers to the old, pre-Hitlerian type of anti-Semitism). If one accepts this formula, anti-Semitism in Romania would reach tremendous proportions.

Not every form of anti-Semitism has the same roots or manifestations. There is the medieval type, a reaction of the primitive masses against a rather primitive Jewish community living in their midst, unwilling or unable to assimilate, and engaging in professions where it is bound to come into conflict with the majority. Such anti-Semitism prevailed in Eastern Europe and in Romania. The second type is known in the West. There, anti-Semitism is mostly a social manifestation, a vestige of medieval contempt toward the "despicable" Jew.

---

[28]Until 1829, the number of Jews was small. After that their number increased. By 1859, there were 180,000 Jews in Moldavia and only 9,200 in Wallachia; by 1901, 201,000 Jews in Moldavia and 68,000 in Wallachia. A quarter of a million Jews in a population of five million would not seem so numerous, but they were predominantly middle class city-dwellers (more than 40% of the city population) L.S. Stavrianos, *The Balkans since 1453* (New York: 1965), pp. 484-485.

This kind of anti-Semitism has almost disappeared during the last 20 or 30 years. During the twentieth century, a very different type of anti-Semitism emerged, directed against an almost completely assimilated, useful, patriotic Jewish community. Unable to demand assimilation or patriotism anymore (even intermarriage and conversion to Christianity becoming commonplace), anti-Semites based their hatred on *race*. Adapted by the two Germanic countries, Austria and Germany, its brutality was unprecedented in recorded history; outside the German ethnic block, only Hungary (with its "sub-German culture," as Iorga would call it) adopted it. Remarking on this phenomenon in fin-de-siècle Vienna, its cultural flourishing, due greatly to its assimilated Jews, Carl Schorske wrote: "If civilization is a domesticating force, directed by the few with the compliance of the many, it is reasonable to suppose that the business of the few is to keep the damper on such dark, irrational emotions and energies which periodically effect the many."

The relevance of Schorske's observation goes beyond Vienna, and to a certain extent is applicable to Romania. But in Romania there was minimal Jewish assimilation, it was not encouraged. Jews could be naturalized only in exceptional cases, but were required to perform military service. There were many disabilities and restrictions. Constant persecution and prevailing corruption all demonstrated that the Romanian government tried to make their position intolerable. Brătianu the Elder illustrated this with a Romanian folk tale about a fox which sneaks into an orchard through a hole in the fence and grows so fat that he cannot fit through the hole to make his escape. The gardener throws the fox into a corner and starves him until he loses enough weight to allow him to fit through the hole. "This is exactly what we are doing with our Jews," said Brătianu.[29] By 1910, a total of 70,217 emigrants left the old Romanian kingdom for the New World, of which 67,301 were Jews.[30]

---

[29]Dubnow, *op. cit.*, vol. 3, p. 275. The Romanian Jews had all the rights and privileges which follow from this analogy.

[30]Stavrianos, *op. cit.*, p. 491.

But if the Jews were brutalized, one should remember that life in Romania was generally despotic and brutal, not only for Jews, who were considered unwelcome, aggressive, and disloyal. All great honest Romanians took stands against Jewish presence there during the nineteenth Century, just as all great statesmen in Hungary and the West (Bismarck, Clemenceau) were for the acceptance of Jews.[31]

It was the intervention of the Powers on behalf of the Jews during the Berlin Conference (in 1878) — an intervention which was skillfully delayed by the Romanians — which increased anti-Semitism tremendously. From then on, being a nationalist became synonymous with being an anti-Semite in Romania.

Jews tend to assimilate only to a culture they find attractive. It is unjust and even dangerous to consider one culture superior to another. But the Germans (Saxons) in Transylvania rarely assimilated to the peoples around them; nor did the English assimilate to their surroundings in their colonies; one could continue in this vein throughout world history. This was not a Jewish peculiarity.

But Jews were needed in Romania. Some high Romanian functionaries explained to an American journalist in 1940: "The Jews were too important in the economic life of Romania to be liquidated in a hurry. Moreover, though we are anti-Semites, we are somehow unable to live without the Jews. A Romanian never trusts another Romanian. Only to the Jew can he confide his sordid little affairs."[32] And there was something else: the traditional Romanian state and way of life was being transformed inevitably and painfully into a capitalist economy, governed by impersonal, employer-employee relationships, replacing relationships which (at least theoretically) were warm and patriarchal. These changes

---

[31]When there was talk at the 1878 Berlin conference of giving the Jews the right of citizenship, Mihail Kogălniceanu (a very moderate anti-Semite) protested: "The Romanian Jews have nothing in common with the French, English, or German Jews. Here they want rights before they become Romanians!" Charles Klauss, *Die Eiserne Garde* (Berlin/Vienna, 1939), p. 87.

[32]R.G. Waldeck, *Athene Palace* (New York, 1942). This writer cannot help but remember the Philippines, where the Chinese fulfill the role of a non-native middle class. A leading intellectual told me in Manila in 1983: "We Filipinos cannot live with the Chinese, and cannot live without them."

occurred within a few decades and devastated a social order that had endured since time immemorial. Suffering people did not understand what was happening to their world. Suspended between the past and an unknown future, they felt frustrated and insecure. Capitalist amorality and rationalization were anathema to the peasantry and to romantic nationalist intellectuals. To make things worse, capitalist transformation was often spearheaded by a non-assimilated Jewish middle class and other foreign interests. In the West, the Jews were part (and only a small part) of this process. Resentment could not be directed against them alone. (Let us remember — among others — the words of W.H. Vanderbilt: "The public be damned!"). In Romania, the transition from a traditional economy to the capitalist one could be easily identified with the unassimilated and unwanted minority. Problems arising from the presence of an alien middle class wedged in between the upper classes and the peasantry have parallels outside Romania. The best example is the difficulties faced by the Chinese in Southeast Asia. Chinese merchant and middle classes encounter many difficulties in the Philippines and Vietnam, and even more in Indonesia, Cambodia, and Thailand. (In Thailand, one of the kings enacting laws against the Chinese middle classes called them "the Jews of Thailand...”). Yet the Chinese stubbornly preserve their culture.

With decolonization and rising nationalism in Africa (and elsewhere), Indians and Pakistanis in East Africa, representing alien middle classes, are much disliked. In South Africa, their shops were violently attacked by native Africans. In West Africa, the Lebanese play such a role, to the displeasure of local nationalists. Nasser's nationalists removed the Greeks, Italians, Jews, and the (Christian) Syrians from Alexandria — turning the city into a monotonous, sterile shadow of its former self, where despair now reigns.

To the Fiji Archipelago, the British brought indentured workers from India. There is a lot of tension between the subcontinentals and the native Fijians, since the Indians nowadays play the role of an alien professional and merchant class. Finally, in May 1987, these tensions exploded.

Thus, conflicts arising from such a situation are no Romanian invention. The Jewish influx into Romania during the nineteenth century was especially offensive to nationalists because the Jews overflowed the cities. The historical capital of Moldavia, Iaşi, was inhabited by more than 50% Jews.[33] That Moldavia became the hotbed of Romanian anti-Semitism is not an accident: after the loss of more than half of historical Moldavia to Russia and Austria, now the remainder was flooded with an alien (and, according to some — and not only nationalists...), unassimilable minority.

Here, the nationalists sensed a real danger!

At the turn of the century, Romania was not a country for mass-immigration like the United States, not even like England or France. The country lived through great social and economic difficulties, shortly after its painful birth as a nation-state. The Romanians were full of insecurities and frustrations. Barred from owning land for centuries, Jews engaged in professions which did not endear them to the population (in practice, owning the village inn, money-lending, usury, little shops, and renting out land from an absentee landlord). The peasant concluded that an alien creature, dressed differently, unable to speak his language decently, "who crucified his Savior," got hold of the little cash he needed to buy some of the consumer goods sold as government monopolies. The peasant had little understanding of the miserable profit margin the Jew made in his grocery store! He only knew that the little cash he had disappeared into the hands of this disgusting alien. The result was a ferocious anti-Semitism. The big capitalist interests were in untouchable foreign hands. There were few big Jewish banks (like the Marmarosch-Blanc, or Blank). There was no Jewish domination in the Romanian economy on the industrial and banking level (as happened in Hungary) because such a level was nonexistent, (The all-important result for Hungary was that east of Vienna only Budapest was capable of accumulating capital. Neither St. Petersburg nor Constantinople, much less Warsaw, were able to accomplish such a feat).

---

[33]Stavrianos, *op. cit.*, pp. 484-485. When the movement started in Iaşi in 1848, the rebels found no response among the numerous Jews of the city. The Jews, being relative newcomers, had no interest in provoking the wrath of the local authorities for the sake of Romanian nationalism. Lukinich-Gáldi Makkai, *Geschichte der Rumanen*, p. 360. But these Romanian nationalists were not inclined to dig into the reasons for the Jewish attitudes. They flatly credited the Jews with the responsibility for their failure.

An interesting novel illustrates this lack of communication between the Jewish middle class and Romanian nationalism: *The Balkan Trilogy*[34] the book which became a successful television serial. It is a *roman à clef* and is Mrs. Manning's autobiographical note (she is "Harriet Pringle" in the book). She lived in Bucharest in 1939 and 1940 with her husband, a British teacher working for the British Cultural Mission, Reggie Smith. Of leftist and anti-Nazi sympathies, her husband ("Guy Pringle" in the novel) remains in Bucharest to help Jewish students trying to emigrate, learning English to prepare themselves for their new life. This writer spent those years as a youngster in Transylvania and Bucharest. Rarely has he seen a novel which recreates (like Mrs. Manning's) the atmosphere of those days. Recently, the memoirs of Archie Gibson, correspondent for the *Times* of London (more than once personified in Mrs. Manning's book), confirmed many of the happenings related in the *Trilogy*.[35] To anyone who knows the Bucharest scene, the personalities (whom Mrs. Manning mentions under pseudonyms) can be recognized, such as the Jewish industrialist, Max Auschnit, under the fictive name "Drucker," and others.

The "Druckers" (Auschnit) invite the English leftist intellectuals, "Guy and Harriet Pringle" (Mr. and Mrs. Manning) to their Bucharest apartment. Guy is their son's professor at the university; and they want to keep in social contact with the English instructor. The visit takes place in the fall of 1939. The Pringles arrive to spend the afternoon in Drucker's apartment, who receive them in overwhelmingly friendly manner. Drucker's sisters are there, speaking French and English.

Guy told Harriet beforehand about Drucker's brothers-in-law. Only Drucker had a Romanian passport, evidence of his power. The others — one German, one Austrian, and one Polish — had only been granted *permis de séjour*. They (like the whole family) existed in Drucker's shadow.

---

[34]Olivia Manning, *The Balkan Trilogy* (London, 1981).

[35]Dennis Deletant: "Archie Gibson: the 'Times' Correspondent in Romania 1928-1940," in *Anuarul Institutului de Istorie și Arheologie*, A.D. Xenopol, vol. XXII (1985), pp. 135-149.

The conversation turns to a former British diplomat who was a man of the left. They ask Guy: "What would he think of this German-Soviet friendship treaty?" Everyone looks to Guy (who was also a man of the left). He says "I imagine Russia has a plan; she knows what she is doing."

Then they talk about the Romanian countryside. One of the Drucker sisters cuts in: "All these Balkan countries are wild. They have dangerous wild beasts. I wouldn't travel here. In Germany it was different. There, Willy and I would take out walking sticks, and..." She talked affectionately of life in Germany.

By this time lunch is served. At the lunch table, someone brings up the war, which had broken our just a few weeks before. "Ah, the war! (...) What folly ever to start it. The great nations think only of power. They do not think of the ones who suffer for such a war." In a conciliatory way, Guv predicts a German financial collapse. (Guy was innocent enough not to know that, although Drucker's heart was in London, his pocketbook was in Berlin.) He looked around for applause but saw alarm. Drucker, lifting his head, said: "That is a rumor started by the British. There will be no collapse." His firm assurance brought immediate calm. Harriet looked at Guy, who was unaware of the disturbance he had created. Drucker noticed this, and said quietly: "It is true our business depends on German prosperity. But we made our connections long ago. We do not love the Germans any more than you do. Nevertheless, we did not cause the war. We must wait." Drucker's sister's husband broke in: "A banker," he said, "upholds the existing order. He's an important man. He has the country behind him." "Suppose the Nazis come here?" Drucker's brother-in-law retorted with a swaggering air: "It wouldn't be in their interests to do so. They do not want a financial debacle. Already if it were not for us, Romania would be on her knees." The other brother-in-law added somberly: "We could a dozen times buy and sell this country." Drucker, the only one who understood that such remarks were far from impressing Harriet and Guy, tried now to check the turn of conversation, but his younger sister said: "We work, we save, we bring them prosperity and yet they persecute us. In Germany my husband was a clever lawyer. He had a big office. He comes here and he is forbidden to practice. Why? Because he's a Jew. He must work for my brother. Why must they hate us? Even the coachman, when he is angry with his horse, will shout, 'Go on you Jew!' Why is it, why is it so?" As the conversation continues, Harriet tries to comfort: "You are not in danger here." "It is not the danger," answered Drucker's sister. "There is danger everywhere. It is the feeling, a very ancient feeling. In Bucovina, you will see the Jews wear fox fur around their heads. So it was ordered hundreds of years ago to say that they are crafty as a fox. Today they laugh, and wear it still. They are clever, it is true, but they live apart: They harm no one." "Perhaps that's the trouble," said Harriet, "that they live apart. Your first loyalty is to your own race. And you all grow rich. The Romanians feel that you rake from the country and give nothing back."

Harriet had merely offered this as a basis for discussion, and was stunned by the turmoil it gave rise to. With a cacophony of voices, everybody accused the Romanians with racism, greed, laziness, etc. Drucker (when he could be heard) said: "There is room for all here, there is food and work for all. The Romanians are content to do nothing but eat, sleep, and make love. Such is their nature. The Jews and the foreigners run the country. Those who do the work make the money — isn't it so? One may rather say of the Romanians that they take all and give nothing back." His statement was greeted with nods and exclamations of agreement.

The brother-in-law said: "But we are generous, we Jews, we always give them what they ask of us. When the Iron Guard was powerful in 1937, the Green Shirt boys came to the offices collecting for party funds. The Jewish firms gave twice, even three times more than the Romanians. And what was the gratitude?" His wife added: "At the university, our boy was thrown out of the window. His spine was broken. Now he is in a sanatorium in Switzerland. Our daughter was a medical student. In the laboratory, the young men took off her clothing and beat her. She went to America. She is ashamed to come back. So you see we have lost both our children." Harriet looked helplessly across to Guy, who, shocked by the racist atrocities, had grown pale. He suddenly said that a Soviet takeover will bring justice. These leftist remarks were not appreciated. Drucker's brother-in-law accused Russia of dumping and ruining Europe's trade. Guy explained the economic reasons for the depression in Europe, but he was hooted down. But the conversation calmed. The younger sister smiled at Harriet and said: "Still, you will enjoy life here. It is pleasant. It is cheap. There is much food. It is — you understand — comfortable."[36]

Many of these opinions emphasize the problem, yet more than 99% of Romanian Jews were not in the privileged position of the banker "Drucker"/Auschnit and tried to stay alive amidst the exceptionally difficult circumstances. Auschnit's attitude was similar to attitudes of capitalist amorality and rationalizations in the West, Jewish or otherwise. Yet, in the West, they could not be identified by their religion.

Mommsen said that anti-Semitism is the mentality of the *canaille*. Since under Naziism the excesses committed led to the greatest failure of civilization on our planet, it is difficult to discuss the issue with detachment. Jews are very sensitive. After all, their experiences during the twentieth century did not strengthen their faith in humanity. Those who have not known the assembly-line killings of the Hitlerian genocide do not experience that death-anguish which fills Jewish hearts and makes them fear that it will start again. But without explaining the Jewish issue, Romanian history during Iorga's lifetime becomes incomprehensible. Both the Romanians and the Jews suffered throughout their history. Both became virtuosi of national and ethnic survival. There was a real problem then, and this infuriated romantic nationalists. After the Holocaust, many civilized people became cautious in their anti-Jewish attitudes, because they perceived what unheard of excesses the encouragement of such attitudes may lead to. Yet, everything which occurred in Romania during our story ruefully lacked the post-Auschwitz caution that settled upon Western civilization.

Iorga's life began in Botoşani, the city, in his own words, where his "horizons were shaped."[37] Botoşani was a microcosm of all the problems mentioned before. The town's geographical position was precarious: it was about ten miles from the Austrian border and a little more distance from the Russian border. Iorga would many times refer to these borders as "our miserable, torn, bleeding

---

[36] Manning, *op. cit.*, pp. 94-106

[37] Nicolae Iorga, *O viață de om așa cum a fost* (Bucharest, 1934), p. 1.

borders."[38] In the villages around Botoşani, young Iorga had evidence of the crushing problems which burdened society. The misery and mistreatment of peasants and the abuses of land tenure deeply impinged on his consciousness. He was similarly aware of the vanishing beauty of traditional, patriarchal relations — a dream of which he would try to recapitulate during his lifetime. Iorga was a Moldavian, who spoke the Romanian language with an unmistakable Moldavian accent. In Botoşani, by the time Iorga was born, Jews constituted almost half of the population, their numbers increasing. There were also Greeks, Armenians, Gypsies, Tartars, Russo-Ukrainians, even some Poles, Germans, and even Lipoveni.[39]

Small wonder then that the other great son of Botoşani, Mihai Eminescu, the national poet laureate, cried out:

> *From Tisa to Dniester's tide*
>
> *All Romanians to me cried,*
>
> *That they could no longer dwell*
>
> *Amidst the foreign swell*[40]

Is it an accident that two great Romanians, Iorga and Eminescu (Eminescu's nationalism would become a great inspiration for Iorga), both came from Botoşani? It was here where Nicolae Iorga was born on 5 June 1871.

---

[38]Nicolae Iorga, *Românismul in trecutul Bucovinei* (Vălenii-de-Munte, 1939), p. 261.

[39]The Lipoveni were sectarian Orthodox Russians, cruelly persecuted there, who escaped to Moldavia.

[40]"Doina" in Kurt W. Treptow, ed. *Poems of Mihai Eminescu: A Bilingual Edition* (Iasi, 1992), p. 11.

Chapter II

The Making of a Historian-Politician: Iorga's Origins, Childhood, and Adolescence

"So! (Even) in Moldavia some (real) men are born...!"

— Miron Costin

"I was taught at home to look people straight in the eyes, and to leave no insult unanswered."

— Nicolae Iorga's motto[41]

The Iorgas originated from the healthy Greek peasant world of the island of Kefalonia, although this is not unequivocally clear. They may have come from the mainland facing the Ionian islands.[42] The earliest recorded ancestor's name was *Galeongiul,* suggesting Albanian ancestry, but Aromanian and Macedonian traces are also possible in a family coming from this mixed region. Galeongiul was a Greek (or Orthodox) sailor in the Ottoman Navy. His descendants came to Botoşani around 1750 and opened a grocery store. He was Galeon-

---

[41]Nicolae Iorga's lifelong principle. The family repeated it to the writer during the encounters they kindly granted to him.

[42]Barbu Theodorescu, *Contribuţiuni la cunoaşterea strămoşilor lui Nicolae Iorga* (Bucharest, 1947), pp. 6-7.

giul Gheorghiu, "Cupetul" (merchant). *Gheorghiu* in time became *Iorgu* and finally *Iorga*.[43] He did not follow the trend of Greek settlers who came to the Romanian lands for hundreds of years. They found the atmosphere congenial in the *Byzance après Byzance*. Because Greek influence was so predominant in the upper echelons of society, they were in no hurry to assimilate or to intermarry, and kept contact only with Greeks. After acquiring riches, they often returned to Greece.[44] Not Galeongiul Gheorghiu. Marrying a Romanian woman, the family quickly assimilated, becoming attorneys, and participating in Moldavian politics.

On his mother's, Zulnia Arghiropol's side, Iorga originates from the Fanar. His mother's grandfather, Christophorovich (or Ioan) Arghiropol, was an Ottoman *dragoman* for Russian officials in Iaşi. The Arghiropols' ancestry included Byzantine nobility, and maybe even royalty. They intermarried with Romanians, and became Romanianized to the point that one of them somehow got lost, as a well-to-do peasant, in a Moldavian village.[45] But the rest of the Arghiropols kept their status.

Gheorghe Arghiropol married Elena Drăghici, and from this marriage Iorga's mother, Zulnia, was born. The marriage was unhappy. Elena Drăghici was a well-educated girl who spoke several languages. The daughter of the vornic,[46] Iordache Drăghici, she had little in common with her husband. The marriage ended in divorce, but not before two boys, Costache and Manole, and a girl, Zulnia, were born.

---

[43]The Iorga family preserves a silver icon, brought by the family from Greece, with the original name engraved on its back.

[44]The aversion to Greeks in Oltenia was as strong as so Jews in Moldavia, for the same reason: they formed an alien middle class. Vasile Alecsandri's "Bloodsucker of the Village" had two exploiters, a Greek and a Jew. Eminescu's hatred for Greeks was, in his own words, "twenty times stronger than for the Jews."

[45]Theodorescu, *Contribuţiuni,* pp. 66-70. One of them came to see Iorga during his Premiership, asking his famous nephew to make him a village chief.

[46]One of the highest dignitaries of the feudal court of Moldova.

The Drăghicis originated in Wallachia and intermarried with the renowned Filipescu family, although some members of the Iorga family consider this rather a genealogical myth. During the eighteenth century, they moved to Iaşi.[47]

Since Iorga was to become "the Apostle" of Romanian nationalism, his opponents investigated his family tree, not only in Romania, but in the whole region. A great deal of political capital can be gained if a nationalist does not originate 100% from the nation he champions. Little attention is given to his sincerity. His foreign origins and the formal names of his family are held up to ridicule. The basis for speculating over Iorga's nationality was unwittingly laid by C. Sion. In his *Arhondologia Moldovei*, Sion, a disgruntled boyar and the first Romanian pamphleteer, expressed anger at Vornic Drăghici, who had risen from the lower ranks to become a high official and the confidant of Prince Sturdza. He was an honest farsighted official. In *Arhondologia Moldovei*, Sion provided the Drăghicis (and many other nobles) with a spurious Armenian or even Jewish ancestry. He also wrote unkind things about the Arghiropols.[48] Sion's allegations were unfounded. As a political pamphleteer he had to exaggerate. Once Iorga entered the political scene, Sion's exaggerations were taken up by his opponents in the most vicious fashion.[49] They called him the "Albanian Galeongiul," "Jewish," "Armenian," etc. Observing his rule that no attack should be left unanswered, Iorga initiated legal proceedings against some of the perpetrators.[50]

---

[47]Theodorescu, *Contribuţiuni*, pp. 38-65.

[48]*Op. cit.*, p. 10.

[49]Iorga dismissed these malingerings as "typical Oriental and barbaric mudslinging" (Theodorescu, *Contribuţiuni*, p. 35), yet he would resort to such tactics dealing with his opponents, belaboring their former family names and origins.

[50]In 1940, Pamfil Şeicaru, editor of the Bucharest daily *Curentul*, asked Iorga to write a foreword to a work about Romanian pamphleteers. Iorga agreed, but when he discovered that C. Sion was mentioned, he refused: "Why did Şeicaru not tell him that that swine Sion, slanderer of his family, figures in the book?" Şeicaru explained in vain that Sion was the first Romanian pamphleteer, and the task of a pamphleteer was to exaggerate. Iorga remained firm in his refusal unless Şeicaru excluded Sion. Pamfil Şeicaru, *Nicolae Iorga* (Madrid, 1956), pp. 106-107.

Such a campaign of words, the vulgarity of which equaled its futility, is instructive. Since these countries did not offer immigration "with unlimited opportunities," their indigenous inhabitants saw too many foreigners pass as hosts, refugees, or unwanted intruders. Their contributions (especially in Romania) were less than constructive. Even foreigners living as assimilated Romanians could revive bad memories and inflame nationalism. Intolerance was never far beneath the surface.

Iorga's father, Nicu, was a successful young attorney. Uncommonly strong, he had a very violent temper. He gambled and drank, vices he could not master, despite the risk they presented to his health. His marriage with Zulnia Arghiropol, 17, started with a romantic elopement. The Iorgas opposed the union, but later forgave them, and received Zulnia into the family. However Nicu Iorga could not stay away from cards. The consequences were fatal. He was stricken by paralysis. Unable to speak or move, he became deranged (fancying, for example, that his head was full of rabbits...). In 1876 he suffered a painful death, in his late thirties.

Beyond his explosive temper, Iorga inherited little from his father. He was shaped by his mother, Zulnia Arghiropol, a well-bred girl, who spoke perfect French, and showed a great interest in literature up to her death at 92. Zulnia started every day with a reading of her son's *Neamul Românesc* and read many of his 1,200 books. Strong-willed to the point of being dominating, she was nevertheless kind. Madame Zulnia, together with Iorga's second wife, Madame Catinca, had a determining influence on his life and activities.[51] In view of the contributions Iorga made to Romanian culture, much credit goes to these two women.

He inherited from his mother her intellectuality and her gift for languages. More importantly, Iorga knew he originated from a line of (as they say in closed societies) "better people" — high court officials, chroniclers, attorneys, writers, journalists, and other intellectuals. A line from which even women undertook intellectual efforts. Thus "Iorga was the descendent of boyars."

After Nicolae, his brother Gheorghe was born in 1873. Gheorghe Iorga attended the Military Academy and graduated as an artillery officer. He went

---

[51]Mme. Lilliana Pippidi-Iorga to the writer.

abroad to study in Belgium, and settled down in an executive position with the Ministry of Agriculture and Commerce. Gheorghe's life ran parallel with that of his brother, yet their lives rarely met. One could see Iorga walking briskly, with his attaché case under his arm, while Gheorghe was walking elegantly and slowly. Iorga dressed casually; Gheorghe with great elegance. Iorga showed little interest in women beside his wife, while Gheorghe showed a tremendous interest. Only when Gheorghe died in 1934 did Nicolae Iorga feel the loss.

Iorga vividly remembered his father's agony. The loss was also a severe economic blow as his father left only an inadequate pension. Madame Zulnia, still only 33 years of age, and beautiful, would never remarry. She dedicated her life to her two children. In practice this meant hard work as a private seamstress sewing dresses for the ladies of society. It meant poverty and privations. It also meant moving from one place to another, as Iorga remembered: "driven by the whip of need," trying to find lower rent, and taking in tenants to make ends meet.[52] Madame Zulnia tried constantly to preserve her dignity, status, and not to sink even lower (such a struggle can be understood by those familiar with the atmosphere of Botoşani and the demands such a town might make on a widow like Zulnia Iorga). Fortunately, family ties are strong there. The Arghiropols, Drăghicis, and also the Iorgas helped both financially and morally, supporting the education of Nicolae Iorga.[53]

His education began at home. At the age of four or five he became literate. He acquired French before entering grade school, without grammar or dictionary. The Romanian language Iorga learned was the Romanian of Kogălniceanu. In a book describing the severing of Bucovina from Moldavia, Iorga first encountered Romanian history before he entered grade school. He learned geography and history from books and novels, mainly in French.[54] His world was

---

[52]Nicolae Iorga, *O viaţă de om aşa cum a fost*, 3 vols. (Bucharest, 1934), vol. I, pp. 44-45.

[53]*Op. cit.*, vol. I, p. 42.

[54]*Op. cit.*, pp. 10-17. Iorga describes passing through India and the streets of Havana with an English guidebook. George Sand took him through the Venice of Orio Soranzo; Daniel Stern to the superstitious Alsacian Jews, Emile Souvestre opened French provincial life; and with Victor Hugo's *Orientale,* Iorga experienced the firestorm of Sodom and Gomorrah, entering the palace of Ali Pasha

formed through his readings during grade and high school, like a parallel education. Iorga's relationship with books would become a lifetime romance. Nothing would be so dear to him as his library. He spent his life in archives and with books. In Romania and abroad, a considerable share of his time would be spent in used book shops, searching, exchanging, and trading books. One should not be surprised that grade and high school imbued him "neither love nor pride."[55] He was far ahead his peers and perpetually lonely. He enrolled in grade school literate, with a good command of the French language, submerged in a dream world acquired from his continually expanding readings. This loneliness and paucity of friendships continued into his high school years, and during the time he spent at Romanian (and foreign) universities.[56] After graduating from university, early fame catapulted him even further ahead of his contemporaries. He became a university professor in his mid-twenties. A university professor has a special status in the Balkans. He is in his loftiness, surrounded with rigid respect, and loneliness, isolating him from the mainstream of life. This meant more loneliness for Iorga, despite his public activities.[57] He had warm relations with his family, but Iorga had no youth; there were no pranks, no foolish mistakes. His mistakes proceeded from stubborn principle, committed deliberately and never regretted afterwards. Did he have a childhood like most of us? Perhaps this was the reason that he conveyed, in his utterances and in some of his actions, the impression of an eternal student — even in his advanced age. He was trying perhaps to recapitulate something he never had, and he missed. Iorga never re-

---

[55] *Op. cit.*, p. 61.

[56] *Op. cit.*, p. 79.

[57] Şeicaru, *op. cit.*, pp. 92-93. Şeicaru was Iorga's student, keeping close contact with him during the Great War and after. Writes Şeicaru: "I remember an infinite sadness in Nicolae Iorga's eyes. Perhaps he drowned questions of existence and fear of death in his uninterrupted work, revising any rest. This was the reason for the fact that, like every romantic, Iorga preferred the plastic to music. Music is abstract by definition, sensibilizing the infinite, and this is the reason and the explanation of Iorga's almost integral disinterest in music."

ally grew out of his eternal studenthood. In a sense, he remained an eternal teen-ager.[58] Keeping this in mind, we can better understand Iorga's contempt for much of his formal education. He did not consider his history classes and text-books responsible for turning him into a historian, but cited "the books of those of Kogălniceanu, who saw history for themselves, and *made* history. It was these books and these witnesses that turned (Iorga) into a historian."[59] Typically for somebody shaped in the humanities, Iorga had no interest in physics, mathemat-ics, or biology. As he put it, "not everybody is made for sciences."[60]

The Botoșani of his childhood appears to have been a miserable backdrop into which the child unwillingly emerged from his books and dream world, and the protection of his modest home. The depravity of the lower classes, even his schoolmates (both Romanian and Jewish) were vivid memories for him,[61] as was the anti-Semitic demagoguery of Polihroniade, who found in Botoșani a fertile

---

[58]Karl Göllner, professor at the University of Sibiu, Iorga's student both in Romania and in France, vividly remembered Iorga's eternal student attitudes, and four-letter word aphorisms. Many others who knew him confirmed the same to the writer. I should point out that Iorga displayed these attitudes only before men. If any women were around, not only did he refrain from student language, but did not hesitate to use physical force on someone who forgot decorum.

[59]*O viață de om așa cum a fost*, vol. I, pp. 13 and 93.

[60]*Ibidem*

[61]*Op. cit.*, pp. 37 and 79.

ground. These were the days of the Berlin Conference (1878). Foreign intervention on behalf of the Romanian Jews was received less than kindly in Moldavia.[62]

What did Iorga read before his entry into the formal school system? Travelogues, Victor Hugo, Lamartine, the tragedy of Abélard and Héloïse, English love poems, the novels of Dumas Père, books dealing with the age of Napoleonic, and so on.[63] The school curriculum was quite easy, but he remained lonely. Living in his world, he came constantly into conflict as hypocrisy or sheer injustice. Once he contradicted his teacher. He was punished for his audacity, a punishment he resented even sixty years later.[64]

From grade school, Iorga enrolled in high school (Gymnasium). The trends we saw before continued: case in completing the curriculum, reaping fruits from a parallel education. Now he became acquainted with writings about the Haiducs, the nationalist guerilla-highwaymen, presented in a Romantic fashion. And there was more loneliness.[65] Prime Minister Ion Brătianu the Elder (whom Iorga called "the old, tyrannical Vizier")[66] visited the school. His visit showed reality to those who (like Iorga) were educated in a nationalist spirit.

---

[62]*Op. cit.*, pp. 69-70. As the research of Carol Iancu into the correspondence between A.I. Crémieux (French Minister of Justice and President of the Alliance Israelite) and G. Bleichröder (the confidant of Bismarck) shows, the Powers insisted in Berlin that Romania should treat the Jews, like they were treated in the West — granting them full equality. The Romanian delegation opposed this ferociously. Bismarck pressured the Romanians on behalf of the Jews. Since the Ruler of Romania was a Hohenzollern, Bismarck's stand was decisive. Then the question of the unprofitable Romanian railroad network (built with German capital) came up. In order to prevent catastrophic losses for German shareholders, the Romanian state was ready to buy up the shares — at a price nine times their value — it only Bismarck would relent his pressure about the Jews! Bismarck's Realpolitik put Bleichröder "in his place," allowing the provision about the civil rights of Jews to lapse. Carol Iancu, *Bleichröder et Crémieux: Le combat pour l'émancipation des Juifs de Roumanie devant le Congrès de Berlin (1878-1880)* (Montpellier, 1988).

[63]*O viață de om așa cum a fost*, vol. I, pp. 17-18.

[64]*Op. cit.*, pp. 37-38.

[65]*Op. cit.*, pp. 79. Iorga remembers ruefully, "I do not remember any of my student colleagues ever entering my home."

[66]*Op. cit.*, pp. 72-75.

He spent summer vacations usually with his uncle Manole, Madame Zulnia's brother, the modest editor of a provincial newspaper *Românul*, who had a good library, including editions of *Contemporanul*, a socialist periodical of Ion Nădejde. It is here that he, at the age of 12 or 13, began his journalistic career, in his uncle's newspaper. More importantly, in Manole's library he familiarized himself with Zola, reading about (as Iorga put it) the "infamous world of Nana," traveling with Frédéric Mistral through French provincial life; reading Daudet, Baudelaire, Maupassant, and many others.[67] When school started, Iorga returned to his studies in Botoşani, once again managing to get into confrontations with the established high school order. It is not easy to imagine what the Gymnasium curriculum demanded from students at the time, nor the discipline it imposed. Students were obliged to salute their professors, within the school or on the outside. On one occasion Iorga accidently failed to salute. The professor tried to force him to salute repeatedly in public.

Iorga, considering such a punishment humiliating, refused. He was suspended from classes, assuring his failure at the examinations. Fortunately, his family got him accepted with a scholarship at the *Lyceum* in Iaşi.[68] The scholarship included room and board, offered him in a hostel near the *Lyceum*. Iorga also had family in Iaşi to keep him company. Gheorghe, Iorga's brother, was also in Iaşi, attending a military school. The departure of her two sons made life easier for Madame Zulnia.

Studies came easy, but life was difficult at the hostel for Iorga. The dormitory facilities were crowded. For a change, he managed to make some friends.[69] Here he met one of his two life-long friends, Petre Liciu, who became a famous actor. The other friend Iorga had outside his family was Vasile Bogrea. Besides Liciu and Bogrea, Iorga never had any relationship resembling friendship.[70]

As time progressed, he came into conflict with the supervisor of the dormitory. The supervisor forbade Iorga (very arbitrarily, no doubt) to go out on a

---

[67]*Op. cit.*, pp. 137-139.

[68]*Op. cit.*, pp. 101-102.

[69]*Op. cit.*, p. 137.

[70]*Op. cit.*, p. 115. Iorga had only one man within family whom he could call a friend, his brother-in-law, Professor Ioan Bogdan.

Sunday morning. Iorga questioned the decision. The supervisor considered this as an unprecedented arrogance. Iorga, unrepentant, was called before the director of the school. When the director asked what he would do if suspended, he answered defiantly, "Well, if I am suspended I will try to make a future either as a water carrier or as minister in Bulgaria." After this, the decision was a foregone conclusion; he was suspended again.[71] He became neither a water carrier, nor did anyone invite him to Bulgaria to become a minister. He faced great hardships instead; he was homeless, wandering about Iaşi. Finally, one of his professors took pity on him, assuring him shelter. Later, the professor managed to get him a salaried job in a private school so that Iorga could graduate from high school, and have the opportunity to earn his baccalaureate. He passed the examination at the age of $17^{1/2}$, earning himself a baccalaureate and qualifying for university study.

What were the influences on Iorga during the first eighteen years of his life? First, the poverty and the humiliations inherent in it. In his early years at the Gymnasium, Iorga had to supplement the family income as a tutor for wealthier schoolmates. On one occasion, he wrote an examination that manifested so much maturity that the professor believed Iorga's pupil must have plagiarized it, and reprimanded the pupil. The mother of his pupil did not want to believe that Iorga had written the examination on his own. Considering Iorga a cheat, she expelled him from her home. And there was an even more painful incident: once he acquired another tutoring position with a schoolmate, but arriving for the first session, the family took one look at his ragged clothes, and they were afraid, as Iorga put it, "that (he) would infect the offspring of the family. They gave him a coin and terminating his employment, ordered him out of the house.[72] There were other painful incidents inherent in his poverty which did not leave the young Iorga's sensitive soul untouched.

During these years he must have developed some durable ideas about religion and Orthodoxy. Iorga considered all experiences with the Orthodox Church during his childhood and adolescence as proof that Orthodoxy is little but form

---

[71]*Op. cit.* pp. 121-122.

[72]*Op. cit.*, pp. 80-81.

without content. He bitterly mocked Orthodoxy for the differences that existed between the Scriptures, the realities of the Church, and the behavior of the priests. Iorga referred to it as "Orthodoxy without soul, from which nothing prospered into our being."[73] In his later teens, Iorga refused to go to church because he was "a militant socialist," reading Marx and Prince Kropotkin's writings.[74] He never failed to remember the formalism and emptiness of religious instruction in the *Lyceum*. He ridiculed the instructor, a priest, using a book written by the priest's brother, the bishop of Roman.[75] In his works, Iorga rarely missed an opportunity to express his hostility toward organized religion. Reading the seven volumes of his *Memorii*, the three volumes of his *O viață de om așa cum a fost*, and his political memoirs *Supt trei regi*, it is difficult to find any metaphysical experience or reference to divinity — except when he speaks about the Nation. A distant family member, Frasin Munteanu-Râmnic, remembers Easter Sunday, 1932, toward the end of Iorga's premiership. Iorga was in Bucharest, where he remained because of his duties. With him were his mother (90 at the time), young Frasin Munteanu-Râmnic, and the family's cook Baba Burta ("Baba Burta" meant "old woman with a paunch" — she was almost a family member). Despite being an agnostic at best, Iorga somehow felt the impact of Orthodox Easter. Madame Zulnia waited for her son's government limousine to take her to church. Iorga had no intention of going. His mother, below in the living room, sat down at the piano and began to play. Iorga was upstairs in the bedroom. Madame Zulnia called her son down to the piano to listen to her play. "Niculae!" At that point the limousine arrived and the old lady left. Iorga remained alone, and called out from the bedroom to Frasin Munteanu-Râmnic: "Be with me! I don't wish to be alone." Young Frasin felt ill at ease as Iorga poured his heart out: "I was always an unbeliever. When I was young, my mother forced me to go to Church. I don't believe today either. Some of the Iorga family believe that the outburst was due rather to Iorga's anger about the

---

[73] *Op. cit.*, p. 49.

[74] *Op. cit.*, p. 124.

[75] *Op.cit.*, p. 117.

disorderly conduct of the clergy during the Easter Services." And then changing the subject: "And I have a wife who is a mother to me, and a mother who acts to me like a wife."[76]

In 1940, when the Royal Dictatorship was competing with a fanatically Orthodox Iron Guard, sentiments were firmly religious. Iorga addressed the Association of Orthodox Women. In this definitive speech on religion, he pointed out that religion for him had only a national role; its function being to strengthen the organic being, the nation, through raising morale, coming to the aid of the family, etc. He recalled the Church distributing Bibles in the trenches to the Romanian army in 1917. Without such a function, the Church would become just an over-decorated Pharaoh cult, the Church is complementary to the nation, it can only grow in proportion and in the interests of the nation. "I am someone who has always had my nationalist faith on the margins of my theological knowledge." Iorga continued, "Orthodoxy is for the nation, not the other way around." He went on to praise the Uniate Church in Transylvania for its nationalist role, but he claimed to care only about the Romanian Orthodox Church, advising his audience to change the name of their association to "Romanian Orthodox Association of Women." Such statements were considered daring. In his conclusion, he asserted "until the last man has been lifted into a Christian and nationalist consciousness, the Orthodox Church has not fulfilled its role," ending defiantly, "I had the courage to say this."[77]

What shaped Iorga's nationalism during his first eighteen years? He conceded that his school education (like all education in Romania at that time) was strongly nationalistic. Yet his nationalistic education suffered several jolts. We saw the visit of Ion Brătianu the Elder. An even greater disappointment was the visit of King Carol I in Iaşi. With disgust, he remembered the mob of Romanians and Jews, instigated by the political opposition, enacting the ugliest scenes, throwing rotten tomatoes, onions, and eggs on the royal cortege. The Royal

---

[76]The reminiscences of Frasin Munteanu-Râmnic to the writer in 1983.

[77]Nicolae Iorga, "Concepţia Româna a Ortodoxiei," Conferinţa ţinută in ziua de 13 ianuarie 1940, "La Societatea Femeilor Ortodoxe," Bucureşti, 1940.

Guard and the army made moves to protect the symbol of the nation in that political outbreak.[78] Iorga also remembered his visits to the estate of one of his relatives. He saw the peasants beaten by the supervising foreman for arriving a few minutes late. Iorga recalled how he clenched his teeth in fury at the sight. He remembered how the beautiful peasant girls were the prey of the foreman and supervisors, even to his own relations; they had to come at night, out of fear rather than out of desire. This was considered, almost idyllically, a way of life. As Iorga put it, "I left from there a determined enemy of a society which rested on such a base."[79] Iorga's role in the literary political movement around *Sămănătorul* is clearly foreshadowed here.

In his last years at the *Lyceum,* Iorga turned for answers to Marxian Socialism. At the end of the nineteenth century, Marxian Socialism was popular among the intelligentsia in Iaşi, even in Bucharest. Iorga was introduced to Marx's ideas by an English minister in Iaşi, Mayers, and his family. The minister and his son Edward (Iorga's classmate in the *Lyceum*) conducted a Marxist debating circle, and Iorga was welcomed. Fifty years later, Iorga chastened, ruefully remembered how impressed he was by *Das Kapital*. He left his studies "in order to read the abstractions and the naked stone road of syllogisms and sophisms in Marx's arguments: the laws of supply and demand, of surplus value which belongs to the worker, and of greedy exploiting capital and the theft it perpetrates every day," of the coming proletarian revolution, and, at the end of the road, salvation: a classless society He even accepted "missionary work": "to go to the people, to return to Botoşani during the summer vacation, to agitate, to spread the creed." Iorga made one convert: a former classmate whose conversion to Marxism did not keep him from becoming the proprietor of the town's most luxurious hotel. The university was to change his convictions altogether. What remained in Iorga from this short brush with Marxism was "the need to be kind to humans, to every

---

[78]*O viaţă de om aşa cum a fost*, vol. 1, pp. 100-133.

[79]*Op. cit.*, pp. 142-143.

human without exception, and to show more kindness to them the more unfortunate they are."[80] Later, Iorga, in his long political activity, took an anti-Marxist, an even stronger anti-Soviet stand. But in attacking communism or the Soviets, he rarely attacks them as socialists. He fulminates against "Maximalists," Bolsheviks, Communists, against the Soviets, or against "Rakovskiists," or "Rakovskiism,"[81] but rarely do we see Iorga put socialism to the pillory. Here is a passage from an article written in 1920: "While there are many good things in Marxian Socialism, there are also many exaggerations. There are different socialisms. There is the one of Constantin Dobrogeanu-Gherea, who came to us about 30 years ago with Carol Mayer, and also the booklets; Kropotkin — *Revista Socială*. He explains that he received from it the warm love for the people and peasants. After these people left the scene, the workers remained leaderless. Then came Christian Rakovski's ideas, and where his ideas would lead one can see in his third fatherland: When a doctrine arrives at its last practical conclusions, as in the case of Rakovskiism, across the Dniester, there is no need to define it, or to judge it; the spectacle speaks for itself. Do we wish to arrive at this? Not only the state, but also the society must defend itself. But in defense, one should not refer to socialism. Whoever the sectarian may be, socialism is much more noble than he."[82] Iorga was not so much against socialism than against the "sectarian' (Soviet) abuse of the "noble ideas" of socialism.

During his childhood and adolescence, he developed a complex about poverty. Even half a century later, Iorga remembered that during his youth he was

---

[80] *Op.cit.*, pp. 133-135.

[81] This refers to Christian Rakovski, who lived in Romania before joining the Soviets. Rakovski was somebody whom Iorga particularly "loved to hate." Personalizing his hatred, Iorga often called the Soviet Union and system "Rakovskiism."

[82] *Neamul Românesc*, 14 February 1920.

"always living out of alms."[83] During the fall of 1888, at the age of $17^{1/2}$, Iorga entered the Faculty of Letters at the University of Iaşi, the subdivision of History and Literature, on scholarship.[84] Iorga established close relationships with Ştefan Vîrgolici, professor of Romance literature. Educated in Madrid, Vîrgolici, was the first translator of *Don Quixote* into Romanian history: A.D. Xenopol. His multi-volume history of the Romanians was just beginning to appear. Xenopol was to become a protector of Iorga and, despite ups and downs in their relationship, a sincere friend.

Iorga concentrated on foreign languages, intensifying his study of German, French, Greek, Latin, Italian, and other Romance languages. He continued his readings. In these readings, as Iorga remembered, "the good Emanuil Hayman," a Jew, was his support, lending the poor student many books from his book shop for a few pennies. He also allowed Iorga to borrow without charge uncut books on condition that he not cut the pages. What were these books? The novels of the great Russians, Tolstoy, Dostoyevsky, and Turgeniev. He pored through the works of Schiller, Mommsen, Karl Wundt's work in psychology, and Hegel's *Aesthetics*. More importantly: the aesthetics of Paul Bourget, J.M. Guyau and E. Hennequi, Hippolyte Taine's history of the French Revolution, also the classics of antiquity. He read John Stuart Mill's *Logic* and many of Carlyle's works; and practically every book he could lay his hands upon.

Iorga wrote articles for *Lupta, Convorbiri Literare* (the magazine of the Junimea Society), the socialist periodical *Contemporanul*, and the Iaşi literary magazine *Arhiva*. During his student years, Iorga wrote more about literature than history. Sometimes it is not the courses that we study, or even the books

---

[83] *O viaţă de om aşa cum a fost*, vol. I, p. 146. In 1919, during the electoral campaign, Iorga remembered "how we experienced even' possible human misery" in his childhood and adolescence. He recalled a conversation with Ion Brătianu: "So I asked him 'Do you know what human poverty and human suffering is like?' Brătianu answered, 'I do know'," Iorga said: "Leave me at least that superiority." He told Brătianu how he suffered from rheumatism, contracted ill-housed and ill-fed in unheated dormitories. He went on to remember the sufferings of his family. "So one cannot say that I do not understand the sufferings of the people better than those who have the fortune of the Brătianus." *Partidul Naţionalist Democrat, Cuvântarea lui Nicolae Iorga, Candidat pentru Senat in judeţul Ilfov* (Bucureşti, Tipografia "Cultura Neamului Românesc," 1919).

[84] Nicolae Grigoraş, *Nicolae Iorga ca student al Universităţii din Iaşi* (Iaşi, 1941), p. 16.

that we read, that exercise the greatest influence on the shaping of our intellectual horizon. It is the people that we encounter. In Iorga's case it was a young Jew, from a German intellectual family. Iorga describes him as "a noble and righteous soul, passionately interested in Romanian philology and about everything concerning our people, (...) spoke Romanian without the ugly accent of his co-religionists who had lived among us for generations." Young H. Tiktin introduced Iorga "to the atmosphere of the West" and disciplined, methodical approach to studies. Tiktin helped in printing the fledgling scholar's first works. Their friendship lasted for a lifetime.[85]

In his formal studies Iorga showed excellence and passed with case. Difficulties came from the dormitories where he was forced to live. Iorga's great superiority and failure to communicate with his colleagues bred conflicts. He made no effort to make friends. All he wished was to be left alone, which is easier said than done. Fortunately, there was an older student, physically strong, who took Iorga under his wing. Thus the others left him alone.[86] Iorga did not look for company in the university dormitories, not even in the classrooms. He sought it in the intellectual circles of Iaşi, where he would be accepted because of the articles he wrote and the debates he conducted.

During these student years Iorga met A.C. Cuza, with whom he would be associated as friend (or foe) for the rest of his lifetime. Cuza had just returned from Brussels, where he studied. Still young, elegant, pronouncing his aphorisms and epigrams, charming women about him, and debating with Iorga on the pages of *Lupta*, he propounded his single-minded, sterile, pathological, anti-Semitic credo.

When Caragiale was attacked for his newest play, Iorga rushed to his defense, establishing thus a valuable contact.[87]

Attending the University of Iaşi for little more than one year, Iorga presented his thesis (under the guidance of Xenopol) on the policies of Michael the Brave. Two professors opposed awarding the degree, considering him too young. Despite intrigues from many quarters, Iorga and his protectors managed

---

[85] *O viaţă de om aşa cum a fost*, vol. I, p. 174

[86] Theodorescu, *op. cit.*, p. 50.

[87] *O viaţă de om aşa cum a fost*, vol. I, p.178.

to ensure his triumphant graduation in December 1889. They organized a banquet for someone referred to in Iaşi intellectual circles as the "Iorga phenomenon."[88]

When his scholarship ended, his perennial financial difficulties returned.[89] His protectors got a professorship of Latin at the lycée of Ploieşti for him. He would not teach there but he had an income. For many years he shared his salary with another professor doing the actual teaching, which would be a great help to him in his endeavors. His protectors, Professors Vîrgolici and Xenopol, Jacob Negruzzi, and I. Caragiani, undertook every effort to get Iorga a post-graduate travel scholarship. By chance, Prime Minister Teodor Rosetti visited Iaşi. A direct personal intervention to Rosetti was made on behalf of the "young genius." Thus Iorga received a scholarship to visit Italy for two months.[90] His protectors – who now included the Academician Alexandru Odobescu – were working to obtain a major scholarship to a foreign university, from which he would return with a doctorate.

How much did Iorga's formal education contribute to his formation? As we saw, he acquired most of his education from his voracious reading. By the very amount, we can attribute a decisive influence to it. Iorga, through his unusual memory and evocative imagination could insert himself into the very heart of any situation about which he read, These readings, and the contacts he made at the university, and later in France and Germany (and during his travels connected with his research) had a much more enduring impact on his formation than his formal studies.

Barely $18^{1/2}$, in November 1889, he met a girl in Iaşi called Maria Tasu, whom a few months later he foolishly married. In his autobiography, Iorga dedicated only a few painful lines to his first marriage, saying that for the precipitate decision he "paid later with a lot of suffering and pain."[91] The encounter between Iorga and Maria Tasu, barely 17 at the time, was a romantic one. Iorga noticed

---

[88] *Lupta*, 23 Dec. 1889.

[89] *Corespondenţa lui Nicolae Iorga*, Holdings in the Library of the Romanian Academy (cited henceforth as *BAR, Corespondenţa lui Iorga*), Volume I, Letters from 5 Jan and 8 Feb 1890.

[90] *O viaţă de om aşa cum a fost*, vol. 1, p.184.

[91] Op. cit., p. 181.

the girl, the daughter of the respected president of the Iaşi Court of Appeals, Vasile Tasu, leaving a photo workshop. He was overwhelmed by her extraordinary beauty, and impulsively entered the photo workshop, where he learned that the girl had had her picture taken; he obtained a copy of the photograph and placed it on his desk. Iorga was living with his uncle, Iancu Iorga, who noticed the picture on his desk. Recognizing the girl he intervened with Judge Vasile Tasu whom he knew well (he was a well-known member of the Iaşi Junimea Society). Soon the young girl was allowed to spend time with Iorga, and in January 1890 they exchanged engagement rings. Finally, in April 1890, a wedding between Nicolae Iorga and Maria Tasu was celebrated in Iaşi.[92] Shortly after, the newlywed couple left for Italy.

The Iorgas would spend two months of the late spring and early summer travelling up and down Italy. Nowadays, people with prepackaged tours travel through Italy in one or two weeks. In Iorga's time, a trip to Italy was part and parcel of every intellectual's education. As the writer's grandfather — Iorga's contemporary — used to say: he went to Italy to spend two years; and those two years were meant to last a lifetime. Iorga was so well prepared from his readings for what he would see, that this trip was one of recognition rather than of study. He would return to Italy constantly for the rest of his life. He was very frugal in order to see more. They went first to Venice, that city of dreamlike, mystical qualities, with its canals and palaces, its sunsets and omnipresent past. Particularly for the Romantic — such as Nicolae Iorga — Venice is deeply interesting. For him it was the beginning of a love affair. Later he would found a school there. But he loved Venice, not with the love of Nietzsche, Ruskin, Liszt, or Wagner! Nicolae Iorga, the Eastern Latin nationalist of Greek origins, the future Byzantinist of world renown, found in Venice the classical link between Byzantium and the Latin world, the West and the Levant. Later, as he grew to mistrust great urban agglomerations, he loved the splendid time he spent in Venice, weeks without hearing the horn of an automobile and the other "pretentious vulgarities of ultra-modernism," as he would call it. Iorga the Byzantinist could not ignore the bitter Greco-Latin controversy during the Middle Ages, especially on

---

[92]The story of Iorga's first marriage and the events leading to it were recounted to the writer by the Iorga family.

the Balkans for, above all, Iorga was a medievalist. Perhaps it was in Venice that he found the best synthesis between the two cultures.

From Venice they went to Padua, where he began his fruitful research about Şerban Vodă Cantacuzino. Then on to Vicenza, Verona, and the imperial capital, Rome. For him (as for anyone else), the past always dwarfed the present in Rome. For the anti-religious agnostic he was, the riches of the Church were an affront. He would never miss out on a pun that could be made on the Church. Milan, the only modern city Italy had in those days, by and large repelled him. Naples was the southernmost point of Iorga's travels, and he found much time for study in the archives and libraries. By this time he spoke Italian well, and proudly stated his knowledge of the Italian language and his readiness to make contact with the people assured that "he should not be confused with the contemptible masses of strangers in Italy, whom the natives exploit, laughing behind their backs."[93]

Iorga always kept a meticulous diary of his travel impressions which would be published later.[94] He showed interest in a contemporary poet, Giosue Carducci, who began his career as an anti-religious revolutionary, later becoming a nationalist, glorifying the reigning House of Savoy. Carducci had close relations with the nationalist Prime Minister Crispi, and with Queen Marguerita, and greatly inspired Mussolini later.

After his return from Italy, Iorga frequented the intellectual circles in Bucharest. He was introduced by his father-in-law, Vasile Tasu of the Junimea Society, but by now many people had read Iorga's articles. He was known.

A few words about the Romanian elite, or the intellectual leadership. They were in those years (perhaps even today) synonymous, forming a kind of Romanian establishment. This is such a narrow upper-crust, that everything that happens within it, even opposition within the establishment — is something like a family affair. Once you are "in," you are in. (Sometimes one is under the impression that even the *Siguranţa* makes its arrest in a family fashion.)

Iorga was introduced to the great satirist, Caragiale, and his close companions: the Transylvanian poet Vlahuţă and the writer Delavrancea. Before (in

---

[93] *O viaţă de om aşa cum a fost*, vol. I, p. 186.

[94] Nicolae Iorga, *Amintiri din Italia, Giosue Carducci* (Bucureşti, 1895), passim.

Iaşi), he had made a fleeting acquaintance with Vasile Alecsandri. Iorga would have liked to meet the aging Mihail Kogălniceanu, but he could not bring himself to pay a visit to the venerable architect of Romanian independence. He was too shy. Of more consequence was Iorga's meeting with the intellectual of Romanian Marxism, Constantin Dobrogeanu-Gherea. A Russian Jewish refugee, Gherea's original name was Solomon Katz. Let Iorga describe him: "... a persecuted, haunted (man) incarcerated in sinister Tsarist Russia, carrying in his sick chest a memory of the Siberian bullet (he received) but (himself) of unlimited goodness. (He was) ready to dedicate his soul to the doctrine (of Marxism) interpreting without the hate present in the violent and narrow-minded manifestations (of Marxism) of others. My nationalism was never repelled by his Jewish origins." Making a living from running the restaurant of the Ploieşti railway station Iorga often visited Gherea there. Gherea expressed desire to establish a literary periodical *Literatura şi Ştiinţa* to which Iorga would contribute in the future.[95] But despite Iorga's high school brushing with Marxism, the Junimist criticism of the Romanian system had much more influence on his outlook.

Junimism originated from the discontent of the Moldavian "Protipendata" Boyars, who felt their decreasing role in running the new united Romanian state. This diminishing role was the result of the new (Western) Constitution and of the moving of the capital from Iaşi to Bucharest. By the 1860s some intellectuals in Iaşi formulated a pertinent criticism of the changes. No one voiced them more lucidly than Titu Maiorescu. He pointed out the lack of organic development; that the men of 1848 grafted Western institutions and political culture onto foundations of semi-Oriental barbarism. According to him, all this improvisation corresponded neither to the Romanian past, nor to the present. No wonder it was a failure! These improvisations resulted in "pretensions without foundation," "a body without a soul," and "illusions without truth," touching only the upper classes in a meaningless way. Because: "There is only one reality in Romania: the peasant. It was their sweat and suffering which made it possible to maintain this artificial structure which some people call Romanian political culture."[96]

---

[95] *O viaţă de om aşa cum a fost*, vol. I, pp. 198-199.

[96] Ştefan Zeletin considered Titu Maiorescu the most important Junimist thinker. *Burghezia Română şi rolul ei istoric* (Bucureşti, 1925), p. 27.

Yet, this phenomenon was hardly an exclusively Romanian one. None of these peoples of Eastern Europe had a chance of modern autonomous (as Iorga would call it: an "organic") development, which by its nature would shield the native cultures from rupture.

According to the Junimists, this system of "form without foundations" was maintained with the help of *Politicianism*.[97] *Politicianism* was, according to the Junimists, only the instrument to prove that the politicians and politically-engaged attorneys were indispensable for the existence of the Romanian state. The Junimists understood that there was no return to the days of the Organic Regulations, but Titu Maiorescu and Constantin Rădulescu-Motru did not wish any new changes until Romania adjusted psychologically to the existing reforms. Until then, only carefully weighed concessions should be granted to avoid social explosion.[98] Not surprisingly these conservatives never gained any mass support; their political demise would come with the introduction of universal suffrage. But other political parties had no mass support until 1918 either. Junimism was opposed to anti-Semitism, considering it to be a barbarous affront to human intelligence.[99] Maiorescu's literary' views were expressed characteristically: "Since the Romanian public reached maturity in literary taste and selectiveness, there is no more need for literary reviews, let alone literary criticism." Maybe Maiorescu's conservatism had the literary' reviews of V. Belinsky in mind, which were much more than literary reviews. The Junimists wanted literature to be separated from politics; to remain *l'art pour l'art*, with no social content desirable. Emphasizing the difference between civilization and culture, Romania remained, as far as Rădulescu-Motru was concerned, a gigantic caricature of the West, a situation which *Politicianism* perpetuated for its selfish interests, creating a "pseudo-culture."[100]

---

[97]Meaning "politicking," where politics served the profit of those who engaged in it.

[98]See E. Lovinescu's works on the Junimea Society and the works of the movement's ideologue, Constantin Rădulescu-Motru, *Cultura Română şi Politicianismul* (Bucureşti, 1904), p. 156.

[99]Zigu Ornea, *Junimismul: Contribuţii La Studierea Curentului*, Bucureşti, 1966, p. 43.

[100]Rădulescu-Motru, *op. cit.*, p. 144.

Iorga (like Eminescu) was strongly influenced by Junimist criticism, not unlike Rădulescu-Motru or Simion Mehedinți. But Iorga had some important reservations: first, the Junimist insistence on the complete separation of art and politics; secondly, the Junimists' belief that no individual should relinquish his identity for the sake of the nation.

In those years Iorga had some contact with Populism, widespread in Romania, called the equivalent of the Russian Narodniki — *Poporanism* in Romanian. For its origins (as in so many instances in Romania), one must look across the Prut. Not surprisingly one of its most important representatives, Constantin Stere, came from Bessarabia. Populism was a reaction to Marxism, which had little to offer the peasantry'. Many Eastern European intellectuals thought that Marxism was only valid for Western industrial countries. No worker's movement made sense without a working class deserving of the name. Marxism was very ambiguous about the peasantry. The peasants were a class with a petit-bourgeois mentality; yet, Marxists made stern efforts to win the landless agrarian proletariat over. Some solution had to be found for the burning problems of countries with a peasant majority, with miserable agrarian population. Stere and other important Populist ideologues rejected Western industrialization. Like their Russian counterparts, they did not wish to lead the peasants through a "Capitalist Cavalry." The model for Stere or Garabet Ibrăileanu was the Danish, Dutch, or Swiss village, and Stere considered the goals of nationalism superior to social revolution. A moderate anti-Semite, he considered the Jews to be the representatives of "vagabond capital." The Populists did not blame Romanian problems on Western institutions, but on social and structural causes, proposing to confront and remove these causes.

In art and literature, the Populists did not recognize the impartiality of the writer or the artist. Stere (like his counterparts in Russia) thought that the writer must make everyone love the people (that is: the peasantry), helping to disseminate knowledge about them. The writer was supposed to contribute to the enlightenment and the uplifting of the people through a popular literature. This meant the establishment of political and social criteria for gauging artistic works. As Nikolai Nekrasov put it, "One does not have to be a poet, but one is under the obligation to be a citizen."

Iorga subscribed to the Populist theory on art and literature, although he rejected most of its political ideas. Junimism was closer to Iorga's political ideas, but he opposed its notion of *l'art pour l'art*. He wanted to put political commitment into the service of Emincscu's nationalism — as Şeicaru called it — to create a sort of "Nationalist Realism."[101] The political ideas and goals of Populism were unacceptable to Iorga: "Populism makes no sense in this domain." Because one cannot lift the people up through literature, "if there is anything which can accomplish the task of uplifting, it is only nationalism, because, as it happens to be, a nation has a soul; but an international, vulgar mob, the 'people,' which only works and suffers, has none."[102] For Populists, it was irrelevant whether the landlord or exploiters were of Romanian or of other ethnic-origins. Their only interest was to help the peasants and the workers. For them, only the peasants and the workers constituted more than just them; and the nation was more important than class. Yet ultimately, neither Marxism nor Junimism would be adopted by Iorga as his political philosophy, but the nationalism of the poet laureate, Mihai Eminescu.

Iorga did not embrace Eminescu immediately. Eminescu came after Iorga had familiarized himself with a whole spectrum of thought. But Eminescu would become the decisive influence, shaping his political, literary, and (to a certain extent) historical work. Above all: Eminescu's ideas formed Iorga's concept of the nation. Accordingly, comprehending Eminescu's message was like "a lightning bolt of revelation, a transcendental experience, as though it had come from another world." He continued to praise Eminescu's language: "Triumphing over the inherent difficulties of making use of a language only recently resurrected." Eminescu sounded like "a religious organ, tearing the soul apart." He freely admitted that it took time for him (and his generation) to make the realization. But "suddenly we found ourselves confronted with a kind of poetry which ruled out

---

[101]How this "nationalist realism" propounded during the "Literary Struggle" by Iorga came close to socialist realist ideas on art in the Soviet Union one can see, if one compares Iorga's ideas with those of Maxim Gorki. Gorki always maintained that "one must not bring despair to the masses." This intentional optimism, a certain vocabulary, and a redundancy in the forms of expression is what Chekhov condemned so vehemently! But this became a dogma for Gorki, and was the basis of his friendship with Lenin. Gorki maintained that literature had a social and moral role to play, that is: literature must be committed to certain goals. Literature must make a contribution to the shaping of a "new man," shaped according to an ideal, regardless of individual aspirations Thus, Gorki willingly joined Lenin's and later Stalin's progress. See the recent work of Henri Trovat on the subject: *Gorki* (Paris, 1986).

[102]Şeicaru, *op. cit.* p. 30.

the snickering and smiles of the drawing room. Either there is total incomprehension, or there is unconditional submission to his message. We fretted and struggled before; I myself passed through this identity crisis. In the beginning, his books seemed to be scaled with seven seals for us; then, suddenly, our soul opened completely to his message, and we wondered why did we not understand Eminescu from the beginning? As if we would have tread on the road to Damascus, like Saul, the one who did not understand the Word. Suddenly, an inexorable light shone so powerfully that we fell to the ground before the demi-god's passage; and this demi-god never left our soul afterwards. Our entire generation wishes to identify with him. We speak Eminescu's language, we think his thoughts and wish to live his clean life, dedicated to our country alone, a life full of sacrifices, (a life) which felt nothing but contempt for material gratifications, a life disdainful of self-interest. This kind of life we wish to live."

The nationalist message of the "demi-god" (Eminescu) determined Iorga's nationalism and Iorga's life. Eminescu's goal — he identifies it as his "supreme law" — was the preservation of his country and its ethnic identity. Because, if Romanians would lose their unique national characteristics, they would also lose their right to survive. For Eminescu this ethnicity transcended everything. Any means were justified for its preservation; values, individuals — even facts! — were important only as long as they contributed to the fundamental goal: the preservation of the nation and safeguarding of the national interest. This was so paramount of a significance to Eminescu that it was to be protected even at the cost of employing methods of duplicity, and sacrificing one's integrity of humaneness. Consequently, the national interest must determine every political, cultural, and educational decision.

Thus, in Eminescu's eyes, what he called "American liberalism" (or Western humanitarian values) might imperil the uniqueness of the Romanian ethnic character, and should therefore be rejected.[103]

Eminescu, Romania's greatest poet, was also a native of Botoşani. Like Iorga, he was of non-Romanian ethnic origins, the family's original name being *Eminovici*, of Polish-Ukrainian, Serbian, Armenian or other roots.

---

[103]Nicolae Iorga, "În amintirea lui Eminescu," *Neamul Românesc Literar*, 1909, pp. 503-507; and Mihai Eminescu, *Opera politică*, vol. 1 (1880-1883) (Bucureşti, 1941), passim.

He rejected the incomplete and superficial Westernization of 1848. Eminescu recognized only two positive classes in Romania: the nobility and, above all, the peasantry. Any development must be based on the peasant, and it must be an organic one. His nationalism is associated with Junimist thought, but he was less of an elitist than the likes of Petre P. Carp. Eminescu was closer to the peasants than to the boyars.[104] It should not be surprising that Eminescu was the literary discovery and protege of Titu Maiorescu. He permanently published in *Convorbiri Literare*, taking part in many a Iaşi Junimea session. His short life — he lived 39 years — was full of suffering. Educated in Cernăuţi, Vienna, and Berlin, he was familiar with world literature, that of Antiquity and of the Orient, especially with German literature, and with works of German philosophy. German literature meant for him above all the *Spä-Romantik* (Heine, Hölderlin, Novalis, et al.), and the atmosphere of Jena. It was from here that Eminescu received his sentimental, religious, metaphysical pessimism, as well as his romantic nationalism. He would always be fascinated by history and folklore. Eminescu took a strong stand against the many foreigners despoiling Romania. They — according to Eminescu — passed through the Romanian lands, conquered, robbed, pillaged, and raped, and more often than not, stayed to exploit and to rule.[105]

By his late twenties and early thirties, Eminescu fell gravely ill, mainly because of the strains of his great efforts. He died at the age of thirty-nine. Amongst his writings were over three hundred political articles for *Timpul*, in which he attacked the political establishment and the realities of pseudo-Westernization. He hammered away at *Politicianism*, which, according to him, "through a ruthless political machine distributes miserably paid bureaucratic jobs, creating a proletariat of the pen!" He called such a democracy a budgetary

---

[104]During the war of 1877-1878, Eminescu described how soldiers, gravely wounded, returned to Romania from Bulgaria. Arriving at night, they asked for shelter at a boyar estate. They received crude insults from the servants, chasing them away, despite their bleeding wounds. *Timpul*, 28 December 1877.

[105]The anti-Junimists (especially the Liberals) would accuse Eminescu of "philo-Germanism" Germanism, acquired thanks to his education and "spiritual formative process." See Zoe Dumitrescu-Buşuleanga, *Eminescu şi Romantismul German* (Bucureşti, 1986). Ştefan Zeletin considered Eminescu "the greatest figure of the Romanian reaction against the Romanian middle class." Zeletin, *Neoliberalismul* (Bucureşti, 1927), p. 127.

democracy, as opposed to a real one: a democracy of work. The patriotism of *Politicianism* is the love of the country's budget, rather than of the country; exploiting the country's dwindling resources to the utmost.[106] Like Carp, he criticized the Liberals for preventing the advent of a real democracy. He demanded respect for the existing laws, which called for free elections. According to Eminescu, Liberal policies delivered the country' into foreign hands that dominated the economy, as well as cultural and public life. He elegantly referred to them as a "Xenocracy."

Iorga always considered the Western democratic message to be respectable. Many aspects of it could be adapted, but not copied in the manner of the "odious" Liberals! Because Romania had a different past, its development could only be organic. Solutions to problems would have to grow out of Romanian tradition.

Although Iorga adapted Eminescu's nationalist creed — practically without reservation — yet, the sad metaphysical pessimism omnipresent in the works of the poet laureate is absent from that of Iorga. Perhaps because Iorga was above all a fighter. Thus, pessimist resignation, so Eminescian, was out of the question.

After introductory rounds within the Bucharest intellectual establishment, Iorga left with his wife, in the fall of 1890, to spend three years abroad, in study and research. He obtained a scholarship with the help of Odobescu and Xenopol, to help him learn the Greek language to perfection. Later, he changed his major to history.

The Iorgas arrived in Paris, where he enrolled at the Ecole Practique des Hautes Etudes, settling down in the "Quartier" (in the Latin Quarter). They lived in the Paris of the *fin-de-siècle*, but Iorga was too much engaged in his studies to have time for the lively delights of the times. He was completely isolated. Financial insufficiencies of his scholarship also imposed restraints. He lived austerely, friendless, never visiting the home of any colleague. The Iorgas went to the theater, sometimes even to the Opera, and on Sundays went on excursions.

---

[106]Caragiale immortalized the type, creating the fictive person "Rică Venturiano."

Concerning his studies at the Ecole des Hautes Etudes, we are back to square one: "I find nothing in school which interests me."[107] As usual, his readings and personal experiences were responsible for widening his horizons. He acquainted himself with the magnificent holdings of the Bibliothèque Nationale, the greatest library he had seen in his life (he would contract a lifelong relationship with it); he spent much time in the archives of the Arsenal; and purchased every book his budget would allow in used book stores. What did Iorga read? Montaigne, Ronsard, Boileau, Florian, Béranger, Diderot, Chénier, Rousseau, Chateaubriand, Voltaire and other philosophers, all the Romantics, Hugo, Lamartine, Champfleury, Stendhal, Mérimée. He read Balzac with appreciation, and Zola, who carried Balzac's realism much further; Dumas, also Mallarme (whom he considered decadent). He read some contemporaries, Ohnet, Feuillet, Bourget, Loti, and Vallès, the writers and poets of antiquity. Virgil, Pindar, and the dramatists, like Euripides. He steeped himself in Shakespeare and other English writers; but his information on English literature came from Taine. Of German authors he read Heine, Lenau, Körner, Ruckert, Uhland, Murger. Iorga admired Goethe for his equilibrium and self-control. He read also Kant and Schopenhauer. He could read the great Russian novelists and poets Tolstoy, Turgeniev, Dostoyevsky, as well as Pushkin and Lermontov only in French translation. And there was Desiderius Erasmus, whom he considered one of the deepest philosophical spirits who ever lived, placing him on the same level as Voltaire, and claiming that Erasmus's humor made perhaps as great a contribution to the Reformation as Luther himself. In Romanian literature, he re-read Eminescu more deeply and profoundly than before, his admiration for the man and the Romanian peasantry increasing ever more.[108]

But the *fin-de-siècle* Paris did penetrate the isolated world in which the scholar Iorga had withdrawn: the Paris of Ravachol and Anarchist bombs, exploding around him; that of President Saadi Carnot; the cortege of the good-willed, unhappy Emperor of Brazil, Dom Pedro, passing through the Place de la Concorde into exile; the blunt, anti-Republican General Boulanger, and that of

---

[107] *O viață de om așa cum a fost*, vol. I, p. 208.

[108] *Op. cit.*, p.209.

Paul Déroulède, whom Iorga qualified as "nationalistic"[109]; and the periodic demonstrations at Strasbourg's statue. These were the years of the Franco-Russian Entente Cordiale, and Iorga, a subject of a Hohenzollern ruler, did not have it easy. On one occasion, an insolent French student asked: "Why don't you let yourself be annexed to the Russians?"[110]

Of all his professors at the Ecole, Iorga was somewhat impressed by Professor Duchesne who, with Professor Gabriel Monod, edited *Revue Historique*, but it was Charles Bémont who would remain a friend and associate for the rest of his life. Iorga contributed several articles to *Revue Historique, Revue Critique,* and *Revue D'Orient Latin.* Charles Langlois played a cardinal role in Iorga's studies, advising him to undertake his study of Philippe de Mézieres. At the Institute, Iorga encountered the spirits of Renan and of Jules Michelet. He learned to appreciate the latter not so much for his method as for his interest in every small nation's history, and his arrival at the contours of universal history on the basis of detailed study of small nations.

Reading Iorga's *Life of Philippe de Mézieres* shows how he wrote history, what history meant to him, and how he would write history. Through his search in the Arsenal archives, Iorga felt able to write about a man "whom I knew personally, with whom I lived, whose painful aspirations and ideals I shared, whom I accompanied on long journeys, and with whom I spent time in the cell of the Celestine monastery in Paris, where he retreated, in supreme disillusion, with one desire, that death should redeem him from all his sufferings."[111] Thus the history of the last chancellor of Cyprus was born, somebody who preached a crusade during the fourteenth century. He would have been a great leader had he only been born three hundred years before.

---

[109]In Iorga's contemporary thinking, nationalism equated with anti-Semitism, but he would learn better. One may ask: if Déroulède was a nationalist, then what can people like Jeanne d'Arc, Danton, or Clémenceau be? (He could not get closer acquainted with Charles De Gaulle.) Iorga never mentions the Dreyfus Affair in his memoirs, since that affair fell flat. In 1895, Cuza and Iorga joined the *Alliance Anti-Sémite Internationale,* created for exploiting the consequences of the Dreyfus Affair. Carol Iancu, *Les Juifs en Roumanie — 1866-1919: De l'exclusion à l'émancipation* (Aix-en-Provence, 1978), p. 222.

[110]*O viață de om așa cum a fost,* vol. I, p. 211.

[111]Teodorescu, *op. cit.,* p. 102.

Meanwhile, Iorga continued reading English literature, Bulwer-Lytton, Dickens, and Thackeray. He read (in Portuguese) *O Parnaso Lusitano*, Luis Camoes, and Gil Vicente, and fought his way through the original Dano-Norwegian of Bjornsterne Bjoernson. He could get along in any language except the Slavic and Turanic ones. This was unfortunate, since Romanian documents until the seventeenth century were written in Church Slavonic — a handicap Iorga freely recognized.[112] His research on Philippe de Mézieres took him to the Vatican Archives and to England. Iorga was impressed by London: "The Avenue d'Opera in Paris seems provincial compared to the life and traffic of London." He visited Oxford's Bodleian Library, where he read the correspondence between Mézieres and Richard II, Carlyle on Fredrick II and on Cromwell, who always fascinated Iorga. Iorga's wife accompanied him, taking notes and transcribing documents. This was the beginning of the family teamwork Iorga would expand in his second marriage. Both his wife and his children cooperated in his scholarly and political efforts.[113]

The Ecole des Hautes Etudes did not award degrees, only a diploma witnessing the student's attendance. After his examinations, Iorga transferred to the University of Berlin, the condition of his scholarship being that he obtain a doctorate. After his examinations, Professor Monod wrote a letter to Iorga's mentor, A.D. Xenopol, pointing out symptoms that would mark Iorga's career. Conceding the excellence of Iorga's scholarship, Monod remarked that Iorga "improvises in learning, and by undertaking too much, is overlooking the school's tradition."[114]

In early 1893, the Iorgas traveled to Berlin. Berlin was becoming a modern Weltstadt, but not in an organic fashion. It was a swollen growth completed after the Industrial Revolution. He was received in Berlin in a friendly way; after all, he came from a country ruled by a Hohenzollern. Yet, the Prussian "Soldateska" irritated Iorga. He describes the army officers in their uniforms, with their arms and decorations, helmets with (or without) eagles, forcing everyone to clear out of the way, the *Drill und Exerzizien*, and contrasted them with "the easygoing

---

[112]*O viață de om așa cum a fost*, vol. I, pp. 220 and 259.

[113]Teodorescu, *op. cit.*, p. 127.

[114]*O viață de om așa cum a fost*, vol. I, p. 213.

red caps of the French officers."[115] Iorga enrolled in the Fridericus-Wilhelmina University, where he immediately noticed how the bells rang the start of classes, something unimaginable in France.

The Iorgas took a room in a boarding house owned by a Jewish lady. In the house there was a truly international atmosphere. Besides Iorga, there were Americans, Greeks, Japanese, Hungarians, and other Romanian students.

But Iorga did not feel himself at home in Berlin. He made only one friend, Richard Sternfeld, a poor Jew, an admirer of French culture and of music. Sternfeld helped Iorga much in his research on Thomas III, the Marquis of *Saluzzo*. The Marquis was an important personality around 1400, a political thinker with great moral values, and author of books which fascinated contemporary princes. In Iorga's study of Thomas III, we can identify his approach to history. The study was not undertaken in a rigid scientific spirit, dominated by dates and names. Iorga tried to reconstruct the life and times of his subject. All this was presented in a literary form.[116] But a technicality loomed over Iorga. He had to swear that he wrote his thesis without the help of anyone. But Iorga did not master the German language to write his dissertation without help. So he had to transfer to Leipzig, where no such regulations existed in order to receive his doctorate. After five months Iorga went to Leipzig. As he remarked: "I leave Berlin without regret."[117]

He had not wasted the time in Berlin, for he collected many documents concerning Romanian history in the archives and libraries. He found even more in Leipzig. Iorga felt better in Leipzig. As he later explained: "Here life was born, not made." Leipzig merchants had longstanding trade relations with Romania (after whom the Strada Lipscani in Bucharest was named). It was not "the solemn precise life of Berlin." Iorga worked feverishly in the archives, where he found quite a few documents on sixteenth and seventeenth century Romanian history. He wrote about them to Xenopol happily, naively unaware that he was intruding upon the turf of his protector. Xenopol's answer disabused him: "It is I who wrote the history of Romania and there is no need to write further about

---

[115]*Op.cit.*, pp. 224-225.

[116]Thomas III, *Marquis de Saluces* (Saint Denis, 1893).

[117]*O viață de om așa cum a fost*, vol. I, pp. 230-233.

it." Xenopol urged him to concentrate on universal history, because the Chair of Universal History awaited him at the University of Iaşi. Fortunately, Iorga was not discouraged and continued his research, patiently gathering all the material he could find about Romania.[118]

At the University of Leipzig, Iorga made a life-long friend: Professor Karl Lamprecht. Lamprecht helped him publish some of his studies on Romanian and Ottoman history. Since his transfer to the University of Leipzig was a technicality, he graduated in August 1893 with honors. With time and money left, he traveled to other European libraries and archives to gather materials on Romanian history. In spite of the hard work he would also absorb the sights. He always observed people first, then the sights, both man-made and natural, finally distilling these impressions into the history of the place. But, as Iorga put it: "There is no city and no country which would possibly awaken my interest if it does not have libraries or archives."[119] The materials gathered in Germany mostly concerned the history of the late Middle Ages up to the sixteenth and seventeenth centuries. They provided details of connections between German courts and Constantinople, relating to the Principalities. Iorga remained a medievalist. He tried to get to the roots of Romanian history. He evidently wrote a lot of modern history but according to his concept, modern events were continuations or consequences of older historical situations. They were therefore of secondary status. In searching for documents, Iorga was guided by the concept of Romanian history being indivisible; events occurring in Transylvania or Bessarabia were also the subject of his research. He was fortunate enough to see Dresden and Nuremberg before their destruction. Afterwards he traveled to Munich, to see another face of Germany — that of the Catholic South — where he discovered many Romanian historical treasures. He continued towards the Alps, to Tyrol, where

---

[118]*Op. cit.*, pp. 233-235.

[119]The Iorga family to the writer.

the south of this province seemed completely Italian to him. The Tyroleans impressed him. Their nature-child peasant ways offered a refreshing contrast to the "rotten, bureaucratized Vienna."[120]

From Innsbruck Iorga proceeded to Venice, to the Frari Archives, then to the state archives of Milan. In Milan he angrily discovered how Hungarians had falsified a reference to John Hunyadi. Original documents referred to him as "Ioan Hunyadi Vallaco" (the Wallachian), but Hungarians referred to him as "Ioan Hunyadi *Transilvano*" (the Transylvanian). Fruitful research followed in Florentine archives, and in those of Genoa about Genoese outposts in the Pontus, and the Crimea. So Iorga began to reconstruct the obliterated Romanian history piece by piece, as one would work on a Byzantine mosaic. As he put it, "With these treasures, which awaited only elaboration and a broader base to establish the history of my people, during the summer of 1894, I returned to Romania after years of assiduous studies."[121] One cannot escape from the Romantic image of the *Vormärz* period: a gifted, nationalist historian searching patiently in the dusty archives, emerging thence with the long forgotten history of his nation.

In Romania, Iorga turned to literature, an interest which he could not sufficiently cultivate during his absence abroad.[122] For him, literature was both inseparable from history, and both inseparable from nationalism, having an interdetermining effect on each other.

In Bucharest, he found the general intellectual upheaval which characterized the Romanian scene in the last decade of the nineteenth century. Iorga managed to get into a quarrel with *Convorbiri Literare* about Romanian phonetics

---

[120] *O viață de om așa cum a fost*, vol. I, pp. 244-245. Iorga casually remarks that if "one is frugal with a scholarship, it will cover a lot of expenses." Iorga had an organic antipathy for "Schmelztägel-Wien," rarely missing an occasion to point out what he saw behind the impressive facade of Viennese culture. This facade might delight many Westerners, but rarely someone from the Balkans, who dealt with it for centuries. These people knew Vienna on a different level than those who spent only pleasant evenings at the Vienna Opera or Alpine holidays. Iorga writes sarcastically about the "almost unlimited dimensions and measure of Viennese deviousness." *Op. cit.*, vol. I, pp. 294-295. According to him, this deviousness apparently upset even Michael the Brave, who, descending from Byzantium, should have known something of Byzantine treachery.

[121] *Op. cit.*, vol. I, p. 248.

[122] *Op. cit.*, vol. I, p. 258. "I have not forgotten the love, a love which has not abandoned me for a moment, namely the love which I felt for literature."

and spelling, clashing even with B.P. Haşdeu.[123] His ties with other literary magazines like *Revista Nouă* or *Lupta*, worsened. The Caragiale-Vlahuţă-Delavrancea literary triangle underwent several upheavals. When Iorga presented Caragiale a novel, he received such sarcastic comments that he tossed his work into the fire.[124] At this time Iorga wrote in *Adevărul Ilustrat* that "Literary criticism has no value if not through the symbiosis between the critic and the one who creates the piece of literature, even more important is love, a naive, childlike, consuming love of art."[125] We can see here the contours of *Sămănătorism* emerging. His relation to Caragiale turned sour. The great satirist was too uncommitted for Iorga; Caragiale would not identify with any political current, or party. His aesthetic criticism of the Romanian scene was so acidic and unredeeming that the young, idealistically nationalist Iorga considered it evidence of an outright hatred for Romania. The relationship between Iorga and Gherea (and his *Literatura şi Ştiinţa*) went awry when Gherea demanded an ideological commitment which Iorga was neither willing nor able to give. Gherea interpreted one of Iorga's poems as revolutionary, although he had expressed only personal disillusionment. Iorga made further literary attempts in periodicals like *Timpul*, and others.

He made a historical contribution based on documents he had so assiduously collected. His *Contribution to the History of Wallachia during the Sixteenth Century* was accepted for publication by the Romanian Academy of Sciences. Between 1895 and 1897 Iorga published the three-volume *Acte şi fragmente privitoare la istoria românilor* (*Acts and Fragments about the History of the Romanians*), containing more than two thousand documents from the period between 1839 and 1786. Thus, the obstacles were removed before his appointment to a chair in history; but he was not to be appointed at the University of Iaşi. The position to which Iorga sought appointment was the vacant chair of Universal History at the University of Bucharest. Both Xenopol and Odobescu supported him with their recommendations. The examination was a competitive

---

[123] *Op. cit.*, vol. I, pp. 249-250.

[124] *Op. cit.*, vol. I, p. 252.

[125] *Adevărul Ilustrat*, 1895, No. 2133.

one; in October 1894, Iorga narrowly won the competition and temporary appointment to the chair.[126]

The debutante Iorga was confronted with the intense hostility of three powerful Bucharest history professors: Professor Tocilescu; Professor Urechia; above all, with the hostility of Professor Maiorescu, the most formidable ideologue of the Junimea Society, who had an unchallenged influence over the university. Iorga was close to Junimist ideas, nevertheless the conflict between Maiorescu and him went beyond ideology. In Maiorescu's eyes Iorga was "the pupil of Gherea, the protege of Haşdeu and Odobescu, the Iorga who wrote for the journals of the competition, a man of the left, and worst of all, an intruder from Iaşi," for, according to Maiorescu (as Iorga saw it), "within the faculties all positions were to be filled by his students, one after the other, after all, he has prepared them philosophically for the task." Iorga would see an "edgy rudeness of the soul hiding behind this former pupil of the Viennese *Theresianum*."[127]

But the great clash between Maiorescu and Iorga was a conflict of personalities. For the last twenty years, Maiorescu had been the dominating personality at the University of Bucharest, retaining the unanimous respect of the student body, even when most of the students had considered themselves socialists. He was a sort of *arbiter elegantiarum*. It is difficult to imagine a greater contrast than the one that existed between Iorga and Maiorescu. Maiorescu was cold and measured, Iorga full of passion and exaggeration. Maiorescu made his point with the harmony of his sentences and balanced arguments, Iorga with the unexpected dialectical *pari* and colorful expressions. If Maiorescu resembled Goethe's *Conversations With Eckermann*, there was no parallel or prototype for Nicolae Iorga, or perhaps, for his lecturing, Michelet, as a writer, Victor Hugo. Those professors trying to follow in Maiorescu's footsteps arrived at lectures and finished them exactly on the hour, since everything (the length and delivery of the lecture) had been strictly timed. Nothing foreseen could occur. Into this atmosphere of harmony (as some witnesses, including Şeicaru, pointed out), Iorga introduced an unexpected contrast, as though one had interrupted a Mozart

---

[126]*O viaţă de om aşa cum a fost*, vol. I, pp. 254-255.

[127]*Op. cit.*, vol. I, p. 267.

Sonata or a Haydn symphony by inserting a Wagnerian prelude. Since Maiorescu had more than a few supporters, this personality conflict gave rise to intrigues with which anyone having spent in academe will be familiar. They were aggravated by Iorga's youth, talent, and inflexibility, ensuring that professional jealousy would erupt into power struggles. Most of us know only too well these demoralizing intrigues. It would give us only dubious comfort that the University of Bucharest at the *fin-de-siècle* was not very different from our present academies. Iorga freely recognized his own attitudes: "In face of insults I could never rest calm like those who could have inherited a different kind of blood."[128] These intrigues would stop only when those who spun them tired of doing so. What made these connivances so protracted? Perhaps because usually so little was at stake. Sometimes petty financial stakes or politics were involved, but the central issue was generally ego.

Iorga made a close friendship with Ioan Bogdan, a professor of Slavistic from Braşov (who would become his brother-in-law), whom he characterized as a European, with orderly, clear thinking. He mockingly described how his older colleagues looked on with incredulity as he dared to establish a friendship with young Bogdan, without feeling "what dangers he risked by associating with a man who stated openly his position about people and things."[129] Understandably, the older Byzantine foxes of the faculty must have felt menaced by the sincerity of Professor Bogdan. Iorga's other young faculty friend was D. Onciul from Cernăuţi. He had an Austrian sense of strict philological method. The Iorga-Bogdan-Onciul trio brought youth, a new Western scientific method and responsibility, and close friendly relations to the students.

It was Maiorescu's dubious pleasure to introduce Iorga before his first lecture, done with a style that Europeans call "correct." Its brevity allowed for a

---

[128]Op. cit., vol. I, p. 317. Which does not mean at all that Iorga was ignorant of rational philosophy. He held a series of lectures on Descartes, models of penetrating clarity. The philosophical revolution by the man of the *Discours de la méthode* was presented with richness of reference. Much later, many professors of philosophy at Bucharest (like Vasile Gheţu) remembered the lecture with emotional admiration. Of course nothing could be further from Iorga's thinking than the methodical doubt of Descartes. The Bucharest faculty thought that by this series of lectures Iorga presented a reminder to Titu Maiorescu that the history of philosophy was not his *chansse réscevée*. Şeicaru, *op. cit.*, p. 20.

[129]*O viaţă de om aşa cum a fost*, vol. I, p. 317.

cold hostility: "I recommend to you Mr. Iorga, who will lecture you on history."[130] Iorga's opening lecture was entitled "The Present Concept of the Genesis of History." Within ten years, Iorga had won over the student body. The slogan bandied about was brief: "With Iorga or with Maiorescu!" If by 1904 most students became Iorghists that was due to the "apostolic" role, as it was later known, that Iorga assumed for himself in politics. During the coming years, especially in 1897 and 1898, he lectured on "the general outline of the history of the Middle Ages," and he held a seminar on "the sources of the Crusades during the fifteenth century,"[131] conducting the seminar in his home.

Meanwhile, never attracted by luxury or comfort, the Iorgas lived in modesty, but still happily. His first marriage still gave him a "steadying influence and happiness."[132] His success in digging up unknown documents on Romania's past made it possible for him to go abroad on his university salary, on research leaves. Thus during 1895-96 he left again for Venice working in the *Archivo Notarile*. He traveled again to Milan, Genoa, Rome, Florence, Naples, Ferrara, and Bologna. In Bologna, as in Padua before, it was Iorga who discovered the correspondence of Constantin Cantacuzino. Until then considered the work of anonymous writers, this correspondence elevated Cantacuzino to the level of Dimitrie Cantemir, giving him his place in Romanian history, the real power behind Constantin Brâncoveanu.

Iorga visited Assisi, Orvieto, and Urbino, descended to Ancona and from there he crossed the sea to Zara. From there it was on to Ragusa, where he worked for a long period in the archives and was overwhelmed by the beauty of the city. As he said, "In Dalmatia I feel myself in Italy, and yet I am not in Italy." From Ragusa he returned to Bari, then on to Northern Germany, to Danzig, working in the archives of the Teutonic Order; then through Lwow and Cracow (whose beautiful historical center Iorga called "Polish Ragusa.") In Königsberg, Iorga had conversations with Germans and sensed that dangerous naivete of Wilhelminian Germany. Germans lectured him about Germany's destiny "being on the sea, on the oceans." In 1899, Iorga went to Vienna where his disgust for

---

[130]*Op. cit.*, vol. I, p. 268.

[131]*Anuarul Universității din București, 1897-1898*, p. 8.

[132]*O viață de om așa cum a fost*, vol. I, p. 280.

the Viennese was compensated by the emporium of documents (on the history of Transylvania and Michael the Brave) in the archives. Then he went to Innsbruck, where he wrote "practically in one breath" the history of Chilia and Cetatea-Albă, unraveling the medieval history of the mouth of the Danube.[133] From Innsbruck, Iorga proceeded to The Hague. He paid a visit to the archives of Braşov across the border. The result of this research was also a major work: *The Romanians and Braşov.*

By this time, Iorga began to publish, establishing a firm reputation. In 1893 he published his work on Thomas III of Saluzzo, and finally in 1896 his work on Philippe de Mézieres.[134] His *Annotated Acts and Fragments Concerning Romanian History*, with other anthologies of Romanian documents discovered in European libraries were published in the Hurmuzaki collection as volumes Ten and Eleven.[135] His work on the medieval history about the mouth of the Danube also appeared during this period.[136] Iorga's writing was accepted for publication by the Romanian Academy of Sciences, although no payment was made to him. But the Liberals and Politicianism stepped in. It was said, "We should not publish such Junimist trifles." Indeed, the Iorga-Bogdan-Onciul alliance continued to cause professional jealousies.

Intrigues were mixed with Politicianism, Iorga was accused of slandering Michael the Brave and adulating the Phanariots. Soon his position at the university was endangered. He went to see Take Ionescu, the Minister of Education. Their meeting was confrontational. Take Ionescu assured him that, while he was

---

[133] *Op. cit.,* vol. I, pp. 291-293.

[134] *Philippe de Mézières (1327-1405) et la croisade au XIV siècle* (Paris, 1896).

[135] *Colecţia de Eudoxiu de Hurmuzaki,* vol. X, "Rapoarte Consulare Prusiene din Iaşi şi Bucureşti 1763-1844," and vol. XI, XII, and parts of vol. XIV, XV, Bucureşti, 1897. "Acte şi fragmente cu privire la istoria românilor," — Adunate din depozite de manuscrise ale apusului şi publicate cu sprijinul ministerului de instrucţie publică. The first volume (1895) deals with documents from 1389-1772; the second (1896) with documents 1768-1839, and the third (1897) with documents 1367-1497. Then there is *Manuscripte din biblioteci străine relative la istoria românilor* (Bucureşti, 1899).

[136] His *Studii istorice asupra Chiliei şi Cetăţii-Albe* was published in Bucharest in 1899.

the Minister of Education, Iorga would not be a university professor. Iorga answered, "It doesn't matter. Sir, I can wait."[137] These intrigues were gravely damaging to Romanian scholarship. By this time, Haşdeu, set off balance by the death of his daughter, also turned against Iorga. Luckily, the government changed. Take Ionescu was no longer Minister of Education, and Iorga received tenure. Iorga had no intriguing nature, preferring direct confrontation to connivances. While this mixture of Politicianism and intrigues delayed the publication of his works, Iorga remembered how he had collected the documents, stretching his financial means to the point where (in Venice) he had to buy Polenta and eat it standing on the street to sustain himself.[138]

In 1897, Iorga, 26, became a Corresponding Member of the Romanian Academy of Sciences. Iorga complained "of the resolute intention of some of the members to leave him outside the Academy's door for a long time coming."[139] He continued his lectures, having financial difficulties, writing several articles for *Arhiva*, *Revue Historique*, and *Revue Critique*. The intrigues continued, degenerating into insults and press attacks. Professor Tocilescu — according to Iorga — plagiarized some of Iorga's works, which he managed to stop from being published.[140]

In 1899, Iorga wrote an article in *Indépendence Roumaine*. From then on he became the focal point in the cultural and political life of Romania, a position he maintained until his tragic death.

---

[137] *O viaţă de cum aşa cum a fost*, vol. I, pp. 302-303.

[138] *Op. cit.*, vol. I, p. 307.

[139] *Ibid.*

[140] *Op. cit.* vol. I, p. 316.

Chapter III

The Struggle Begins

"We are a land of peasants. We should run our land (and its household) like peasants."

— Eminescu

"...To enter public service must not become a means for advantage or for notoriety, but (rather) for the fulfillment of a formidable and portentous duty towards (one's) country, expecting no reward."

— Nicolae Iorga

Reluctantly, Iorga entitled the second volume of his autobiography "The Struggle."[141] He devoted a book to the subject, *Thoughts and Counsel of a Man like Any Other*[142] refuting charges that he was attempting to become an apostle. How fitting to call this volume "The Struggle!" Iorga was above all a fighter for the ideas for which he lived. This is how his personality and manifold activities must be understood. Struggle was the principal manifestation of Iorga's "system," his messianistic complexes concerning his dignity can only be understood in the light of his pugnacity. Iorga the historian, the playwright, the orator, the university lecturer; above all, Iorga the journalist and the literary critic; and even

---

[141]Iorga considered struggle and light something vulgar, like a gladiator. *O viață de om așa cum a fost*, Vol. II., pp. 106-107.

[142]*Gânduri și sfaturi ale unui om ca oriecare altul* (București, 1905).

Iorga the memorialist, throughout his amazing range of activities the might of his struggle shows clear. He was a fighter and animator, passive about nothing. Dr. Samuel Johnson said once, "Intentions must be gathered from actions." For Iorga, even in history, ideas were inseparable from action, and that meant struggle. Action and ideas formed a unity, his actions should be considered in the light of his ideas, his ideals guided his actions.

It is unfair to single out any one point as marking a turning in a life, or any one step, always consistent in direction and even in pace as more decisive than any other. But an article Iorga published in *L'Indépendence Roumaine* in 1899 was a truly decisive step.[143] With it he abandoned the ivory tower. That article carried Iorga past the dividing line, from a respected historian, who is untouchable and entitled to respect even from those who hate him,[144] to a belligerent politician who, if defeated, in this part of the world (more often than not), is at the mercy of the victor. He entered the political struggle well known through his many accomplishments and well-armed, with immense historical and literary erudition, a knowledge of classical and modern languages, endowed with a formidable memory and with deep convictions. But Iorga was also endowed with personal qualities which, though mostly commendable, made political activities problematic. With all the ups and downs, he would not abandon politics; the consequences of defeat would eventually cost him his life.

Concerning Romania's political situation at the *fin-de-siècle*, Professor Z. Barbu said of the mutation in Romanian political psychology (taking into account "the limitations of psychological vocabulary"), that the period was "a transition from a predominantly schizoid to a predominantly paranoid version of the Romanian world outlook; more specifically, from a mental structure dominated by mechanisms of withdrawal and avoidance, to a mental structure dominated

---

[143] *La vie intéllectuelle des roumains en 1899* (Bucarest, 1899).

[144] Iorga recalled that once in Transylvania he had trouble with the Hungarian gendarmerie, until a Szeckler gendarme officer, who was otherwise "eating the Romanians alive," quickly relented when he learned that Iorga was a university professor. He said: "A university' professor is a big shot, one doesn't fool around with him." *O viață de om așa cum a fost,* vol. II, p. 169.

by mechanisms of attack, and a moral system based on aggressive assertion and power."[145] All things considered, this analysis is not exhaustive.

Romania was the not-so-secret ally of the Austro-Hungarian Empire and Germany Its king, Carol I of the House of Hohenzollern, was strongly set against revisionism. All politicians made revisionist noises before attaining power; in office, however, all revisionist action was forgotten, in deference to the king's feelings.

The king put a distance between Romanian society and himself. As Prince Barbu Știrbey remarked to Iorga, "For the king one German is not (automatically) like another German — but all Romanians are for him like water!"[146] Yet, half of all Romanians were under foreign domination. In Transylvania and the Banat, after the uprisings of 1785 and 1848, the discontent of the Romanians erupted in 1890 in the "Memorandum" struggle. Their leader, Ion Rațiu, during his trial in 1894, proclaimed: "The existence of a people cannot be disputed, it can only be affirmed." Later the Hungarians increased the pressure of Magyarization. The nationalist struggle for Transylvania was conducted without quarter. Mysteriously, both Hungarians and Romanians consider Transylvania vital to the very existence of their respective peoples.[147] Iorga called Transylvania "the heart of the Romanian people!" Romanians consider Transylvania more important than Bessarabia, and by 1900 the acquisition of Transylvania seemed more practicable than the liberation of Bessarabia. Unfortunately, the problem is insoluble at present. A constructive solution can only be attained by changing the minds of one's opponents; and for this purpose, both Romanians and Hungarians would have to place themselves in the position of each other. This is unlikely to happen soon. Bucovina under Austrian rule had been flooded by Ukrainians, Germans, and Jews. Iorga considered Bessarabia the most hopeless irredenta, the "Land of the Dead" — Romanians buried in the cemeteries, and

---

[145]Arnim Heinen, *Die Legion des Erzangel Michaels in Rumanien* (München, 1986), p. 96.

[146]*O viață de om așa cum a fost*, vol. II, p. 32.

[147]In Berlin, Iorga clashed with a Hungarian girl student over Transylvania. They concluded that "only blood can decide this issue..." *O viață de om așa cum a fost*, vol. I, p. 228.

that of the living dead.[148] Many Romanians considered Russia's annexation of Bessarabia only the first step towards dismembering and devouring the rest of Moldavia — and more. Iorga often thought of Romania as a living body whose "bloody borders" were "tugged across the bleeding national body."[149]

But conditions in the so-called "Free Romania" left a lot to be desired. The population of "Free Romania" consisted of more than 80% peasants. There are few words which could describe the miser)' of their lives,[150] but the congress of the Romanian Socialist Party can convey some idea. During this Fifth Congress (Spring, 1898), Dobrogeanu-Gherea considered the misery of the peasants overwhelming. "The peasants are so desperate that they are ready to follow a fool." Yet, he explained that the Socialist Party would mean something (in Romania) only if it considered the peasants along with the workers. He warned that Socialists must be careful with propaganda, for "one may, with careless propaganda, provoke a danger for the peasantry as well as for the Socialist Party." He suggested gradual civic and political education for peasants, the only way of preventing a bloody, sterile explosion. Ion Nădejde agreed with Dobrogeanu-Gherea's analysis; recalling how the despairing, starving peasants in Iaşi and elsewhere approached him, looking for salvation, "as though I were God." This had frightened Nădejde. "One cannot reason with such people. They fell on their knees before us, and begged us to save them from the black poverty in which they lived."[151] At the rum of the century Romania's political life was dominated by the peasant problem. Both political parties tried to hide it, yet the conscience

---

[148]*Op.cit.*, vol. II, p. 2.

[149]*Op.cit.*, vol. II, p. 48.

[150]BAR, *Corespondenţa lui Nicole Iorga*, volume 65, documents 109 and 110. After the peasant uprising, in an interview with the *Frankfurter Zeitung* (29 March 1907), the then Minister of the Interior, the Liberal Vasile Lascăr, explained that four-fifths of the peasant population was suffering from hunger and condemned to beg. Land tenure rates in Moldavia were quadrupled and the tithes to be paid to landowners in Muntenia and Oltenia increased inordinately.

[151]*Lumea Nouă*, 14 April 1898.

of the intellectuals kept it to the fore. A wild peasant uprising in 1888 was something of a dress rehearsal for the one in 1907, but nothing happened to improve the peasant's lot. Political rights for peasants were effectively denied by the notorious Electoral Colleges.

Romania's elite was not worthy of the name. Despotic, exploitative, hedonistic, many of them were of non-Romanian origin, and like colonial elites who feel greater contempt for their own people than for the colonizing power, the Romanian elite had no feeling for the peasantry. Iorga remarked that, for this elite, Romania was but a few hundred miles of track seen from their comfortable railway coaches while on their way to Paris.[152] Before the nineteenth century many of them spoke Greek. Now they exchanged it for French. Their culture was French: they staged a French theater in Bucharest; sent their diplomatic dispatches in French; and more than once they addressed the Romanian National Assembly in French. Educated by French governesses, they went to foreign universities.[153] As for Romanian literature, they had as much interest in it as the French had in Algerian literature, or the English in Indian. Many Romanians of intellect would rightfully ask: what Romanian leadership could arise from all this? Alienated oriental despots with sound political instincts characteristic of Romanians, but what political program? Politicianism. The Conservative and Liberal parties alternated, but the labels were cover for the elite's will to monopolize power.

---

[152]*O viață de om așa cum a fost*, vol. II, pp. 2-3.

[153]Crown Prince Ferdinand explained to Iorga that he intended to send his sons to Potsdam and to the Royal Navy. Iorga replied that such education would be proper for the sons of the King of Annam, not for the sons of the Romanian Crown Prince. They should be educated in Romania. *Op. cit.*, vol. II. 179. In his study of Iorga, Oldson, pointing out that Iorga was educated in foreign universities, reproached him for wanting to deny Romanians the same benefits (Oldson, *op. cit.*, p. 96). Oldson misses Iorga's point. Iorga suffered no estrangement from Romania on account of his foreign education; he employed the knowledge he acquired to revive Romanian culture. But he had little reason to believe that the same would happen to other Romanians exposed to Western culture.

For Iorga and for the nationalists, this conservative and liberal two-party system was reminiscent of the twin settlement, Sodom and Gomorrah.[154] Indeed, the elite attempted to make Bucharest a Paris of the Orient; one could witness all manner of corruption, since the elite broke every written and unwritten moral law.

What was the economy like? Beyond the large-landed estates and peasant miser); foreign interests provided badly needed loans to the government.[155] Internally, Maurice and Aristide Blank's bank represented Romanian capital; but their banking house was more like the moneylenders of an Oriental despotism, than a modern banking system. Both foreign and domestic financial interests were tied in a sinister fashion to the system. Romania needed a Western-style middle class, yet it was still a two-class society A surrogate was found in a portion of the Jewish population — (only a portion because the overwhelming majority of Jews were living in misery). This portion of Jews fulfilling the function of the middle class belonged to the twentieth century: they were professionals, merchants, and middlemen in the leasing of land. Unfortunately, Romanians were interested only in administrative and bureaucratic jobs, officer's commissions, and the priesthood — preferences for which Iorga chastened his countrymen. It became the lot of the Jews to carry out the country's modernization. It is they who (to quote Max Weber) "brought capitalist rationalization" to Romania, often after the fashion of Caiman and Mochi Fischer. Perhaps in the long run even they had accomplished more than the landlords. The overwhelming majority of Jews could neither *faire nor passer*. The towns in Moldavia were flooded by Jews. In "Holy Iaşi," according to Iorga, even the *stones* were anti-Semitic.[156] By 1890. the Jewish birthrate began to decrease. Reasons for Jewish emigration must be sought in the restrictions under which Jews, within the Russian Empire, lived. At the time when Iorga entered politics, Pobedonostsev, tutor

---

[154]Iorga wrote: "Now Sodom is out of power; but when Gomorrah governs again..." *Neamul Românesc*, 25 June 1906.

[155]*Supt trei regi*, pp. 9-21. Also, *O viaţă de om aşa cum a fost*, vol. II, p. 11.

[156]*O viaţă de om aşa cum a fost*, vol. I, pp. 159 and 180.

to the scions of the imperial family (until 1905 *de facto* ruler of the scene), persistently issued new legislation which took away the livelihood of Jews. He proclaimed that (as a result of his policy) one-third of the Jews would die out, another third would leave the country, and the remaining third would disappear, assimilated by the Russians. From 1881, those ghastly and incredible mass lynchings of Jews, which gave the word *pogrom* to every language, started. These pogroms became an official policy, a safety-valve against discontent, turning Russian Jews into scapegoats; it was the Ministry of the Interior which organized them. By 1900 the Russian system of autocracy through bureaucracy could not handle social discontent. So, the Minister of Interior, Count Vyacheslav Plehve, gave the order: "We shall draw the revolution into Jewish blood!" Thus, the theory of Hugh Seton-Watson was carried out to the letter.

The Jews in the Russian Pale of Settlement saw no hope in the future. Many of them tried to leave.

The continuing influx of Jews aggravated an already grave situation, and was bad news for Romanian nationalism; most of these unfortunate Jews were not greeted by Emma Lazarus's comforting words. They got only as far as Moldavia, pressing from the Northeast in a Southwestern direction.

Even legal mass immigrations result in tensions. Think of the arrival of Vietnamese and Latin Americans (especially Mexicans) in the United States or people from the Third World or Eastern Europeans to Western Europe. But these are no comparison to the Jewish influx to Moldavia. The West has a democratic tradition, and its economy is more capable of absorbing arrivals. Turn of the century Romania was no land for immigrants. Jews were not seasonal agricultural workers. Thus, what was going to happen?

There was practically no assimilation — nor could there be. Iorga remarked that these Jews which flooded Moldavian towns were practically inassimilable.[157]

---

[157] *Op. cit.*, vol. II, p. 1.

In Eastern Europe, few Gentiles considered the Jew a human being; at best, he was known through the lenses of anti-Semitic distortions and caricatures; all too often a diabolical quality was attributed to him. Jews responded by isolating themselves, and becoming indifferent to what Gentiles thought of them. Their own prejudices reinforced those of the Romanians about them. Jews in the West assimilated and brought immense contributions to their host nations. The same cannot be said about the Iaşi ghetto. For Jews, Moldavia was only a stop on the sad millennial road.[158] A deadlock developed that foreshadowed tragedy. Such a social situation did not endear the Jews in Romania either to peasants or to nationalists in the towns. Neither did the fashion in which they spoke Romanian. The numerous foreign interventions on behalf of the Jews only exacerbated the situation. Metternich used to say, "Every country has the kind of Jews it deserves."[159] Iorga's paper disputed this statement, which is food for thought, but not the last word.

Let us examine two contemporary arguments: one by Dr. Moses Gaster, a Romanian Jew who in Britain made a name as a philologist, pleading the case of the Jews; then Iorga, during these years strongly against the Jews. Interestingly, Moses Gaster, an admirer of Eminescu and everything Romanian, and Iorga became very close. Iorga invited Gaster to his Summer School in Vălenii-de-Munte to hold lectures; when Dr. Gaster died in 1939, Iorga braved the violently anti-Semitic atmosphere in Romania, writing a moving obituary. In 1907, however, they were opponents. Speaking during the anti-Jewish excesses of 1907, to the Hebrew Romanian Association in England, Professor Gaster laid out the Jewish problem in Romania as follows: pointing out that the directives

---

[158]Iorga answered his demand that the Jews should assimilate forcibly, in the 4 May 1903 *Semănătorul*, "Cu prilejul dispariţiei *Tribunei*," writing about the mistreatment of Transylvanian Romanians who, in addition, were expected to participate in fraudulent elections which they declined to do, Iorga said: "Romanians in Transylvania have but one duty: to allow the furious waters of the times to flow by and above the old, inflexible marble of their national existence, and not to participate in such comedy." Iorga would not admit comparison between Jews in Moldavia, and Romanians in Transylvania. The Romanians, there for two millennia, had organic rights, while recently resident Jews did not. But if one wants to assimilate a nationality, one must make assimilation attractive.

[159]*Neamul Românesc*, 20 April 1914.

of the Berlin Congress on Jewish citizenship were not enforced (although Jews paid taxes and were forced to serve in the Army), he described Romanian corruption. Looking at the liberal and conservative governments, he warned the English not to be deceived; they were a cover only for oriental despotism and the will to power. Gaster cited the non-negligible contemporary figure of 60 million pounds that had Romania acquired in foreign loans, and inquired: where had it gone? Not to solve the social ills which beset the country!

He explained that the Jews were scapegoats for the unbearable situation, and said that "the Jews love their country (Romania) as a child loves his mother." He himself, proud to be a British subject, "would love to tread native soil again," and said the Jews had a deep-seated affection for the peasantry, who wished no harm to them. The problem seemed to be the government. He concluded that the Jews were too poor to be moneylenders; if they had had money, they would have left Romania long ago.

The first halt of Gaster's expose concerning Romanian corruption, despotism, the hypocrisy of the existing political system, and the misappropriation of foreign loans is not exceptional. But on the Jewish attitude towards Romania, Dr. Gaster's statement idealized reality.

Responding to Christian Rakovski's socialist arguments, and answering a French newspaper, Iorga presented his version of the situation. Accordingly, five million Romanians had created a national state, and wished to create a Romanian national ideal. Hundreds of thousands of Jews, most of them concentrated in Moldavia, took over cities, villages, land, and gardens. As land-tenure holders, they treated the peasants like slaves. It was against this that the revolt of 1907 broke out. The Jews did not speak Romanian, but German; they dressed differently and had an implacable hatred for Gentiles. They were foreigners and conquerors, with no feelings for Romania and made no sacrifices for it whatsoever. Iorga did not consider this a religious or a racial persecution, which he personally abhorred. For him, at stake was the national existence, and the Romanian character of Romania.[160] Iorga (even Cuza) and many other Romanians, had sympathy for the Sephardic Jews in Romania.

Iorga always shows a preference towards them considering them Latins and endowing them with positive qualities.[161] Should this writer, from an old Sephardic family, and who prides himself with ties to "La Madre España" and Latindom consider this flattery? He would rather like to point out that for every Sephardic Jew in Romania there were approximately thirty Ashkenazy Jews from the Pale of Settlement. This should explain the phenomenon.

The new Romanian state, amidst crushing internal and external problems, was searching to find its identity and place. Modernization is a difficult task; even in the West, where it was a homemade product. But here we do not deal with a homemade product (or an organic process, as Iorga would say). The beautiful patriarchal relationships Iorga idealized in his *Sămănătorist* ideal were to be demolished either from within or without. Idealization of this old Romania was what *Sămănătorism* was all about. Iorga described his view of the *Sămănătorist* village in 1933: "I tried to reconstruct the patriarchal environment, and tried to give an example to our own times which had broken away from these natural ties, the memories of the valleys of Dorohoi; however now they rose in my mind, the villages and their nobles, the manors of my adolescence, with all the profoundly human relations they represented. (...) All this was contrary to a prevalent mistaken spirit, which must be destroyed in order to encourage growth of the healthy spirit."[162]

However, Romania was fatefully tied to the twentieth century. Unwillingness to change was unwillingness to survive. Jews caught up in this process were sometimes innocent and helpless witnesses, sometimes scapegoats. Professor

---

[160]For Dr. Gaster's statement, see the 2 April 1907 edition of *London s Morning Post*. Iorga's opinions are in *Neamul Românesc*, 24 June 1909.

[161]Iancu, *op. cit.*, p. 135 and *Neamul Românesc*, 18 January 1908. Iorga's opinion about the Sephardic Jews can be found often in *Neamul Românesc*, until 16 March 1939.

[162]*O viață de om așa cum a fost*, vol. II, p. 104 and 113.

Barbu spoke of a transition from schizophrenia to paranoia; but for Romanian patriots the Romanian nation, culture, and economy were falling apart in three different directions. Intellectuals looked for an answer. They seemed to find it (in the 1890s) in socialist currents; during the 1900s, many of them would become Iorghists. And because Iorghism was no answer either, after the First World War, many of them would look for very different answers. Such was the situation when Iorga opened his struggle with the article in *L'Indépendence Roumaine*.

He started his "Struggle" in his early thirties. His personality, views about history, literature, art, poetry, and morality were formed; so were his nature and attitudes; there was remarkably little change afterwards. (Any significant change in his attitudes was on the Jewish question.) A rather determined anti-Semite, Iorga would abandon anti-Semitism after the Great War. Otherwise, he called this first decade of the twentieth century "the completion of my political and social creed," a creed from which he never parted. It is time that we should get acquainted with Iorga in his incarnations: his nationalism; his historical thought; his journalism; and his aesthetic and critical ideals; with his way of working and his family life; with his ideas about morality and money; with Nicolae Iorga, the human being.

Nationalism is basic to an understanding of Iorga. Nationalism, culture, and history are interwoven in his mind; ultimately, they constitute his life's work.[163] Iorga became a historian through nationalist impulses. Nationalism and history would remain inseparable for the rest of his life. His nationalism determined that whatever Iorga undertook in public life would be a struggle. Despite that he considered nationalism and history to be spiritual and intellectual endeavors.

Iorga's nationalism was a "cultural nationalism." It was concerned basically with culture; with "the soul," the "spirit," and the "culture"; thus, with the

---

[163] See Iorga's *Generalități cu privire la studii istorice* (București, 1911, 1933, 1944). I used the 1944 edition, identical to the one of 1911. This work is the most concise explanation of Iorga's cultural nationalism and concepts of history.

mentality of the nation. Though difficult to define, these characteristics are important. For him, the conception of nation was decisive for interpreting the world and understanding one's own and other countries. Like von Ranke, to whom he refers often, the fundamentals of Iorga's understanding and his interpretations were determined by moving from the history of small nations to an understanding of world history, and vice versa.

Iorga's nationalism was that of Eminescu — in the sense of the "Supreme Law" we tried to explain before. In a way, Eminescu's (and Iorga's) nationalist struggle showed regard for the advice of von Clausewitz, who considered that the one who won the main battle also won the campaign. Thus, those who followed the "Supreme Law" could not possibly go wrong on anything. Iorga believed that the history of any nation can only be understood in the context of world history (and its permanent characteristics). Thus, national and universal histories should not only be studied in parallel, but they should also be considered complementary. He found his way from world literature back to Romanian literature; he traveled doing research all over Europe. After his travels and studies abroad, he spent years searching through Romanian collections: church inscriptions, Romanian monasteries, and private holdings.

According to Iorga, a nationalist should know that his nation (like any other nation) is a product of history. History has permanent characteristics, instructive, organic manifestations. These are not laws; laws are too inflexible, and universal histories too complex. Often, for the historian, materials which would render irrefutable proof for law-like development of historical processes are either incomplete or nonexistent. But Iorga saw similarities between patterns of different nations, and he drew conclusions from similar patterns when definite materials were lacking. Analyzing these similarities, he sought to understand and reconstruct history — events and processes which generated it. Patterns emerging from the life of other nations were helpful hints, sometimes even keys. But they were not laws (as in natural sciences). They were permanence (permanent characteristics and qualities of history) allowing historians to make judgements. Where did these permanent characteristics come from? From the "soil," "race," and "idea." "Soil" for Iorga meant the land where the group of people that becomes a nation has its roots, and was shaped through the organic process. "Race" was a breed in the sense of the Spanish *raza*. He abhorred racism in any form, and he rejected it categorically.

Iorga's nationalism was a cultural nationalism like that of Ernest Renan, who held that the nation was the soul of a people who knew a common glory in the past and feel a common will in the present; the pride in having done great things together and the desire to do them again. I his common knowledge, will, pride, and desire are the conditions for the existence of a nation. Renan's (and Iorga's) French concept of cultural nationalism stands opposed to the German concept of *Blut und Boden*. It is from Renan's concept of a nation that Iorga's permanent characteristic of the nation, the "idea," emerges. Through the idea people express their way of life, thoughts and feelings; it is an instinctive behavior, coming from the depth of the soil and race. These things are organic, spontaneous manifestations, beyond reason, and cannot be altered by it. These emerging ideas become sentiments which are resistant to change. After a while they become the mentality of the nation, forming its culture. They also determine the choices for the nation's future. Inasmuch as the culture is the nation's soul it underwrites the nation's unity. To neglect or abandon it in favor of another culture is not only a mistake, but moral wrongdoing. Thus, a nation is born, developing organically through an original process which provides it with an organic life and energy. Tradition derives from it, encompassing the long historical experiences, all-important in the life of a people. The national spirit, born within specific climatic and geographic conditions on its soil, endows a people with a folk psychology and a pattern of action manifesting itself spontaneously. Art and literature deriving from it, in turn, refine the expression of the national spirit.

For Iorga these permanent qualities were the connecting link between the universal processes of forming groups, and the historical experience from which the culture and the national consciousness arose. Any nation — Romania in particular — has the natural right to remain where the organic life of that "gigantic being" (as Iorga called the nation) originated and developed.[164] Iorga was not much of an Orthodox believer, but these ideas of hierarchical order and nation in it are close to the Orthodox Church's concepts. For him, this process forming the nation is a force of nature, and, as such, immutable and indestructible. According to Iorga, civilization maintains itself through the freedom it allows to this organic process to develop a national soul and mentality, because these different national spirits are the basis for international harmony. Since the nation rests on these ideas, international harmony rests on the recognition of the nation. For Iorga, this is not contradictory, but complementary, based on the constitution of man and the world. His world is of such inclusive diversity. The nation is a basic component of humanity. This organic process is a natural development, because nations have missions and only nations can fulfill such "historic missions." If they deviate from it or are forced to deviate from it, the natural (organic) order of the world will be disrupted (just as the ecological balance of the natural world can be disrupted through industrial or other forceful interventions in an ecological niche). Pressures may destroy the nation, but they will never alter or modify it. Since it is organic, it cannot be transformed into something else.

The Romanians are, above all, Latins, but they are Eastern Latins. They are Orthodox, yet it is the Romanian nation that dominates relations with Orthodoxy, not the other way around. (Interestingly, Iorga never went to Mount Athos in spite of the research possibilities there. In his writings, he wrote that Mount Athos (and the establishment of the cult of Saint Nicodem) had had a negative influence on Romanian history.[165]

---

[164]*Ramuri*, 1 January 1912. The Orthodox Church, although subscribing to Christian doctrine, is less universal in its concepts about humanity than Catholicism or other Christian religions are. According to Orthodox concepts, nations form part of a hierarchical order established by God. In his *Neamul Românesc*, Iorga constantly repeated his belief that nations are indestructible. During the crisis years from 1938 to 1940, in the face of Hitler's and Stalin's pretenses, Iorga repeated his dictum even more emphatically. It would seem that for Iorga, churches or monasteries served but one purpose: as a source for historical inscriptions needing deciphering, images needing evaluation, and historical documents awaiting discovery and transcription.

[165]*Le mont Athos et les Pays Roumains* (Bucharest, 1914).

On what is this "gigantic being" based in Romania? With Eminescu, Iorga claims char this "gigantic being" is based on the peasant. He is the authentic product of this organic process ("the holy peasant," as he sometimes called him). Yet, Iorga is essentially paternalistic (realistic) towards the peasantry: proposing a strong government to treat the peasant justly and well, he always wished to give guidance to him. This authentic Romanian (the peasant) is the source of the Romanian language and tradition, the mainstay for Iorga's cultural nationalism. Iorga's whole life was dedicated to safeguarding him as the link to Romanian tradition. The vernacular is the most pregnant expression of nationalism. It is the peasant who is the repository of it. Romanian literature is very important for Iorga's cultural nationalism. Romanian culture is original and Latin. Being the very expression of the peasantry, literature is the soul of the people. Like Eminescu, Iorga believes also that it is this culture that justifies the existence of the Romanian people, consequently it must be protected. Literature must become its expression. Iorga hoped that this literature would establish a truly Romanian way of life. The Romanian nation might be divided by borders which Imperial Powers dug into the flesh of this "gigantic organic being," but for Iorga, there was but one Romanian culture. And this cultural unity should mean national solidarity. The unification of Romania would come if and when all Romanians were made conscious of their national heritage and their cultural nationalism. Then they would unite, not by violent revolution.[166]

Culture was so important for Iorga that he believed that even national disunity, the denial of national self-determination, corruption, and social injustice could be remedied by it. He believed in fundamental change through cultural nationalism, this being his version of the cultural revolution.

Iorga's nationalism was a moral concept. Thus, one could be liberal or a nationalist; conservative or a nationalist; and so on. Nationalism excluded all

---

[166]In an article about "non-free" Romanians in Transylvania, Iorga contrasted the "heroic" Innocentiu Micu to his nephew, Samuil Micu. Innocentiu Micu, despite his heroism, failed to help Romanian serfs. His non-revolutionary cousin, Samuil Micu, using patience and perseverance, contributed to the cultural consciousness and self-preservation of the dejected Romanian serfs. "Politica şi cultura la Românii ncliberi," *Sămănătorul*, 20 July 1903.

other political parties or doctrines.[167] Iorga felt in the 1900s respect for democracy, but later he lost faith in it (at least as far as Romanian realities were concerned). As he saw it — like Eminescu — it interfered with Romanian cultural nationalism, thus, with the "Supreme Law." Like Nicolae Bălcescu, speaking about "Free Romania," Iorga meant national freedom from foreign domination. He abhorred the abstract, but had his own national mystiques. There is no nationalism without it. He wrote once that there was a breath arising from the native Romanian soil, containing all elements in Romanian national culture. These elements represent not only the present, but also the spirit of Romania's past, rising from native earth to influence present and future generations.[168] He hoped that the Romanian national ideal for national solidarity would become a "common religion," because national solidarity signified national culture. This national culture should be based on virtues of which Nicolae Iorga was the incarnation: work, study, and sacrifices.

Iorga was an agnostic at best, and respected Orthodoxy only in proportion to its services to the Romanian nation; he respected the Uniate Church in Transylvania more than Orthodoxy; yet, he hoped always that a new common religion based on cultural nationalism would become the best pledge for human fellowship,[169] because, according to Iorga, Romanian politics (around the 1900s) represented a historical anomaly. Since society is organic, political parties are self-seeking and they divide. As Iorga's newspaper elegantly put it, they give a choice only between Sodom and Gomorrah. But Romanian society was too egotistic to realize national unity through cultural nationalism and to arrive at national solidarity. In the 1900s, Romania did not have significant nationalities. The problem for him was the presence of great numbers of Jews (and the cultural alienation of the elite). Iorga differentiated between national and nationalistic

---

[167]The disdain of Charles De Gaulle exceeded all bounds when he spoke about political parties. He forbade any movement in his support to use the word party in designating themselves.

[168]*Neamul Românesc*, 3 April 1938.

[169]*Neamul Românesc*, 24 November 1936.

policies. National policies mean conquest and plunder. On the other hand, nationalistic policies strive only so that all Romanians should live under Romanian rule. The only interference in foreign sovereignty is the redemption of Romanians who are "unfree." Cultural unity and the national solidarity it created were for Iorga more important than political boundaries.

By the width and scope of his culture and interests, Iorga was a universal Renaissance man. Yet, he found his way to this kind of universality through his cultural nationalism. His world was a world of nations in harmony. He looked to the nation as to an icon, which represents truth for an Orthodox Christian. And Iorga, the follower of Eminescu, was a Romanian historian deeply convinced of the truth of Romanian cultural nationalism. Thus, if one wants to ask Iorga's solution to any problem, one should ask first: what was the Romanian interest (as he discerned it) in that moment? He saw this interest in the framework of his *Sămănătorist* cultural nationalism. He always placed himself modestly behind the Romanian national interest. After asking about this Romanian national interest, one may ask many other questions concerning his position, but one must not forget to return to Romanian interests. Some people have called Iorga inconsistent; he seems to be consistent within the framework of his cultural nationalism. His inconsistencies were tactics, other times they were due to his personality, or to the times he lived in — but not to his lack of sincerity However sincerity's intrinsic value is politically insufficient. As Churchill said once, "It is a fine thing to be honest, but it is also very important to be right."

Iorga rejected charges of chauvinism. For him, they referred to the extremes of the Napoleonic warrior Chauvin (or Chalet), "whose words came out of the brain, not out of the heart.... He tried to aggrandize himself through his words... There is where I come from; it is a better, a bigger place — even the sun shines brighter here! Nothing is lacking where I come from; it is a great country, a great nation. Down with your hat — before me!" Iorga found such nationalists among Hungarians, Jews, and Frenchmen. "But real nationalism is the love of one's nation above every other nation. To love what is good and natural in a nation; not the nation's sins and evils. Patriotism is love and defense of one's country; the nationalist and patriot loves his land and nation because it is a moral duty to do so. He loves his nation as he loves his parents or children. Love of his nation is a lofty moral law of nature for him. He does not consider his nation more beautiful or better than it is. All the existing shortcomings hurt him. He does not act as a propagandist for his nation. Nor does he strive for it. A true nationalist does not wish to despoil other nations. But God save the one who comes with hostile thoughts of conquest — into his house, where his beloved arc! God save the one who mocks his country within the reach of his car! Because against such one all his might will rise." He explains under the title "What is Nationalist?": "Nationalists are people of understanding, conscientious and diligent; (they are) men of character. They realize that the nation is an organic being and a living fact of the world. One can allow a nation to live or one may kill it, but one cannot transform it into another organic being. Consequently, it has but one purpose: to fulfill its role within the framework of universal civilization. The nation must be itself. It is this universal civilization which presides over humanity and the happiness of any nation, a goal best served within the framework of it. The national soil is inseparable from the nation, the very root from which the nation's spirit and actions originated.

Here is where we are, where we live; here is where we think for those who live here. All this is simple and positive."[170] Iorga rejected the contemporary (ridiculous) current, "Romanianism," which explained modern Romania's small size with the Romanians' studied modesty and prudence. If these qualities did not exist, there would be no limits on Romania's impact in world affairs.[171]

Are nationalists conservatives? Was Iorga an inveterate conservative?

True nationalism by definition includes the whole of the nation, which in Romania was in its majority poor. True nationalists hold that the nation encompasses all classes. At the end of the twentieth century, let us consider some Messianistic dreams of the millennium: how did they turn out in reality? Which way did the Russian Revolution go? Did not proletarian internationalism become a

---

[170]*Neamul Românesc*, 24 November 1936.

[171]*Cuvinte Adevărate* (Bucureşti, 1904). pp. 104-106.

one-way street? Was Tito a communist or a nationalist, or both? Were the absurdities of Albanian Communism motivated by Marxism — or previous national experiences? Was Ho Chi Minh a nationalist, or does communism explain him? What motivations were decisive in Fidel Castro's policies, nationalist or Marxist ones? What were the motivations of the Sandinistas? In China, the Cultural Revolution condemned 'Confucius, but in the attitudes of Mao, Deng, and those of Chou En Lai one can recognize many of his thoughts.

Chekhov considered every label a prejudice. Drieu la Rochelle took a stand against identifying political movements as *right or left*: "The right and the left, two of the most outworn of the least truthful and the stupidest of words." At the end of the twentieth century one cannot help but note the imbecility of categories, even if some intellectuals, ideologues, and bureaucrats appreciate them. Many Conservative regimes have called their systems nationalist. Yet, they were only keeping a privileged class in power (at times with foreign financial and military support), unlike the rebels which were called leftists or communists.

De Gaulle rebelled against the conservative French military establishment in the name of the French Nation. He carried out a "coup de nation" (like others a coup d'état), choosing legitimacy over legality. During his second presidency, he was forced to govern with the Conservatives, who (as the newest research shows) got rid of him in 1969, because, after the events of May 1968, he wanted sweeping nationalizations, giving the French worker an effective voice in the management of industry.[172]

Iorga and Eminescu championed the peasantry, opposing Marxism. In 1917, Iorga would be instrumental in the proclamation of land reform and universal suffrage. But many of Iorga's concepts (especially of art and literature) were arch-conservative; can someone who champions the welfare of 80 or 90% of the people be labelled without qualification as a conservative?

---

[172]Jean Lacouture, vol. 1 "Le Rebelle," vol. 2 "Le Politique," vol. 3 "Le Souverain." Lecaunet pointed out to Lacouture: "De Gaulle's mistake was picking his Prime Minister straight from a bank's safe deposit box," referring to Pompidou and his tenuous relations with the Patronat and Rothschild's bank.

Iorga also disliked big modern industrial cities and modern art. As the saying goes, he who looks like a duck, walks like a duck, and quacks like a duck — is a duck. Yet, something seems to be missing here. Was he a conservative, or a Romantic nationalist of the nineteenth century, who believed in the organic development of society? For him, there was no more organic entity than the nation. Revolutions tended to disrupt and to destroy this organic process, as he pointed out during his American lectures.[173] Iorga tried to minimize such ruptures. But it was here where "the man of the nineteenth century" ignored the impact of industrialization. Generalizations are meant to be sweeping; they do not serve their purpose if, like a broom, they are left in a corner. Yet, if one calls a nationalist a conservative without qualification, one is apt to degrade truth into a tact, with truth losing all intellectual content.

As the story of the Irish lady who gossiped about her neighbors goes, someone protested: "This cannot be true!" She replied: "It isn't true, but it is true enough!" The point can be reversed: calling every nationalist a conservative is not true enough. In the last decade of the twentieth century, one has some doubts about assimilating nationalism to conservatism. Concerning Iorga's anti-Semitism up to the First World War, we see the complex nature of the Jewish question in Romania. For Iorga, the Jews were an alien element flooding the towns. In the villages he saw their single-minded efforts to survive. The peasants needed protection. He was angry because of the Jews' unwillingness to assimilate as they had in Hungary. But Jewish assimilation was not encouraged by circumstances. After the First World War, Iorga would recognize that. As he said: "In Romania only that one remains a foreigner who wants to remain so."[174]

For a number of reasons, the Jews in Romania wanted to remain foreigners. Iorga (like Eminescu) considered the Jews a product of history, and did not exclude a solution through assimilation. But he also worried about the future of the Romanian people. Iorga saw Jews in Transylvania as Hungarian chauvinists. In Bucovina, if the Hapsburg Emperor had devoted subjects, they were Jews.

---

[173] *Americani şi Români din America* (Vălenii de Munte, 1930) p. 214.

[174] *Neamul Românesc*, 29 November 1926.

Even Bessarabia was flooded by Jews. But during Iorga's anti-Semitic period, we see little personal hatred against Jews. He had excellent personal relations with them (even with the Jewish Marxist, Dobrogeanu-Gherea, and many other Jews, Byzantinist historians, etc.). Characteristically, in his anti-Semitic period, his newspaper announced almost triumphantly that Dreyfus was innocent: "No traitor," and styled Colonel Piquart, "a noble character."[175]

Iorga liked Sephardic Jews better. He had harsh words for the emigres, however, whom he called *Mahalaua* (a word of Turkish origin meaning "the scum of skid row"). Well, oppression demoralizes, and not only Jews get demoralized. If a Jew showed the slightest interest in Romanian culture, Iorga held him up as a shining example before Romanians and Jews, hoping he would be followed by other Jews. Later, he would call for full acceptance of the Jews. Did Iorga not look across the border to Hungary and see the Jews' willingness to become Hungarians? He saw it, and saw also that in Transylvania (and in Bucovina) the Jews were the most determined enemies of Romanian nationalism. And he was envious too; he observed that even after Transylvania was annexed by Romania, the Jews asked for the maintenance of Hungarian language schools for themselves, rejecting Romania's offer to provide Jewish schools. He asked angrily: "Why don't the Romanian Jews follow the example of the Hungarian Jews in Transylvania, and show the same loyalty towards Romania as they do towards Hungary even after the Hungarian administration has departed?"[176] Did Iorga not understand the reasons for Jewish loyalty? He did, but it concerned Hungary, it was difficult for him to admit it. He also understood the reasons for Jewish loyalty and willingness to assimilate in the West. Before his Party's Congress in 1935 he said: "In those countries, different circumstances created a very different type of Jew." And he wrote an article in his paper, asking: "Why do the Jews not dominate America?" He observed that American mentality and work morale, the Puritan spirit, prevented the rise of such a situation. Romanians

---

[175]*Neamul Românesc*, 11 June 1906 and 9 July 1906.

[176]*Neumul Românesc*, 20 September 1923.

should look at the American example and draw pertinent conclusions.[177] Once more we should remember Metternich's maxim, "Every country has the kind of Jew it deserves."

Then there was Professor A.C. Cuza. We can place Cuza's life as an instructive contrast to that of Iorga's. He was the most reprehensible of Iorga's associates, but the fact is that Iorga broke with Cuza because he found Cuza's "doctrine" (a term Iorga used in contempt to describe Cuza's anti-Semitism) unacceptable. Cuza wore a different pair of shoes than Iorga, especially on the Jewish question. In Cuza's case, there was no ambiguity or qualifications about anti-Semitism. It was obsessive.

Professor of Political Economy at the University of Iaşi, educated in Dresden and Brussels, Cuza was also a Junimist. Although excluded from the party because of his excessive anti-Semitism, he remained a part of Iaşi intellectual circles. Iorga and Cuza started their struggle together. Both were intellectuals formed in Iaşi, ex-Socialists, atheists, and had close connections with the Junimea Society Cuza's motto was: "Nationalism is the creative force of culture; and culture is the creative force of nationalism." Cuza was close to Iorga, writing articles for *Neamul Românesc*, and helping him found the Nationalist Democratic Party. But Cuza's tunnel-minded anti-Semitism revolted Iorga even then, and more after. In his espousal of anti-Semitism, Cuza gradually abandoned atheism, and returned to the Church. Not only was Cuza's anti-Semitism different from Iorga's, it was different from the general Romanian anti-Semitism. His hatred towards Jews was *pathological* — like the Austro-German anti-Semitism which emerges during the twenties. Cuza preceded this by many years, giving anti-Semitic speeches when Hitler was still a youngster, brandishing the swastika before the First World War (as a symbol of international anti-Semitism). No

---

[177]*Neamul Românesc*, 25 March 1907. See also Nicolae Iorga, *Cuvântarea ţinută la întrunirea comitetului executiv al Partidului Nationalist Democrat de la 11 August 1935 la Vălenii de Munte* (Bucureşti, 1935), p. 19.

other problems existed for Cuza.[178] In his articles on the Jewish question (he rarely touched upon anything else), he worried about the imminent foundation of a Jewish state "in Dacia," referred to Iaşi as *Municipium Judaeorum*. Jean Jaurès, Briand, Viviani, Clemenceau and Millerand were too close to Jews for Cuza's taste; they were referred to as *Jidoviţi* (the hirelings of the Jews). Socialism was for him a Jewish invention. His discussions of the Jewish religion are full of blasphemies and falsehoods. He rejected Heine, Borne, and other Jewish poets or intellectuals with arguments resembling those of Dr. Joseph Goebbels; attacked "Halevy's opera" about the Huguenots as an attempt (by a Jewish composer) to foment hatred between Protestants and Catholics.[179] Cuza should not have fretted. His *Municipium Judaeorum* bore no Heines or Bornes, Halevys, or Meyerbeers for that matter. No Karl Marxs, Einsteins or Freuds emerged from the kind of atmosphere Cuza helped create. Even if such a Jew had come from Moldavia, his ten pound ideas would not have fit into Cuza's hate-filled one pound mind.

He rejected any idea of Jewish assimilation. When Iorga invited Cuza to lecture at his Summer University in Vălenii-de-Munte in 1909, he embarrassed Iorga by lecturing exclusively on the Jewish question. Their paths began to diverge. Later, the distance between them became wider when Iorga renounced anti-Semitism. At that point Cuza started a campaign of slander and defamation. As we saw, Iorga was in constant personal and friendly contact with Jews even during his anti-Semitic period. We don't know of a single Jew who had personal

---

[178]In Iorga's correspondence, this writer found hard to believe several of Cuza's letters to Iorga. Cuza describes every trivial incident between Jews and Gentiles in Iaşi, asking Iorga to publish these accounts. In one letter, he described a spitting contest between uncouth Jewish and Romanian louts. It is difficult to accept that a university professor could write a world-renowned historian about such non-events and ask him to publish them. BAR, *Corespondenţa lui Iorga*, vol. 62 (1907), Doc. 84, et. al.

[179]*Neamul Românesc*, 22 June 1906, 22 February and 1 March 1907, and 18 February 1908. Cuza confused Halevy, a Jewish composer with Meyerbeer — the author of *The Hugenots*.

contact with Cuza (if we do not consider a "personal contact" when an enraged Jew slapped Cuza's face on a Iași street).[180]

Iorga and Cuza would drift further apart despite sentimental memories and early common struggle. Cuza established close contact with Hitler.[181] His contacts were closer with the Nazis than those of the Iron Guard; Iorga, on the other hand, was the very embodiment of animosity towards Germany and Hitler. But during forty years of Cuza's anti-Semitic tirades, he rarely mentioned the names of Maurice or Aristide Blank, or Max Auschnit, let alone that of Mme. Lupescu! Iorga never mentioned Mme. Lupescu and the others either. Must there be some height which criticism never reaches?

Even as an anti-Semite Iorga demanded assimilation, always rejecting anti-Jewish violence; he held these views forty years before the Holocaust. When it came to pass, Iorga was dead. The Holocaust was a product not of his nationalism, but of a twentieth century "New Nationalism." Was this political naiveté on his part? Iorga was often accused of "releasing the nationalist 'Djenee' from the bottle." But how could a nineteenth century nationalist foresee (while trying to remedy many *legitimate* grievances!) where a twentieth century nationalism would lead? Either way Iorga paid a high price. And when it came to the payment, the price turned out to be higher than his nineteenth century naiveté and his nationalist good faith warranted it to be.

---

[180]C.Z. Codreanu, *Eiserne Garde* (Berlin, 1939), p. 214. Although Cuza made exceptions for beautiful Jewish women, excusing himself with a Talmudist argument that "women are not to be considered Jewish." Pamfil Șeicaru, *Un Junimist Anti-Semit: A.C. Cuza* (Madrid, 1956), passim.

[181]The Romanian academician, Andrei Oțetea, recalled in 1969 to this writer that Professor Cuza greeted him in 1933 (after Hitler took power), saying "My LANC (the League of National Christian Defense, Professor Cuza's political party) has taken power in Germany."

History always dominated Iorga's activities. Even his social sensibilities impress us as the feelings of a historian.[182] Iorga was meant to be a historian.[183] His historical work established a place for Romanian history in the world. His cultural nationalism emanated from it. It determined his historical work, literary criticism, and his other activities, and drove Iorga into politics. In this sense his life forms a whole, which can be understood only as such. Modern rights of self-determination were helpful for Romanians. Iorga gave them historical arguments — historical rights. Until the "New School" emerged during the 1930s,[184] his interpretation of Romanian history went unchallenged. Yet, even after, he remained the Romanian historian par excellence.

Iorga considered historical studies the most humane study. He thought history could educate, "re-integrate" the student into humanity. But it was a formidable undertaking: a historian must have encyclopedic knowledge. Iorga was endowed with the capacities of historical research and thinking; he had intuition, capacity to analyze facts, and documents. In his opinion the historian must have "a vision of the past," a hallucinatory capacity to reconstruct the times and enter into the spirit of them, visualize events and sites, and familiarize himself with the psychology of the persons involved. But this vision must be based on rigorous research and irrefutable facts. Although this reconstructive historical vision differs from the historical novelist's work, Iorga demands the historian have a good literary style. The beauty of the historian's text is almost as important for

---

[182]The *Generalități cu privire la studii istorice* is also the best repository of Iorga's historical thought. Most of the ideas and the passages I cite are to be found there.

[183]Șeicaru records a characteristic incident. The League of Nations voted sanctions on Italy because of Ethiopia. Romanian policy supported the sanctions. Iorga, however, firmly opposed them. Soon after, Iorga traveled to the Hague. The Romanian Ambassador was anxious to keep Iorga from disavowing the official Romanian position. He could think of no better way than to arrange for the historian access to the archives of the House of Orange. The plan succeeded; during his whole visit, Iorga, submerged himself in the Royal Archives, emerging only to return to Bucharest. Iorga said: "That cunning Oltean (the Romanian Ambassador) hid me in the Archives, but I got the best of it! I have profited handsomely for history." Șeicaru, *op. cit.*, pp. 85-87.

[184]The "Noua Școală," ("New School of History") will be an attempt by younger Romanian historians to introduce a less romanticized version into Romanian historiography.

him, as reliable facts.[185] The historian must not become a telephone directory, recording names, numbers, and addresses.[186] He thought it necessary for the historian to have suffered in life, to have spiritual and psychological characteristics that generate sympathy for the human character of history. Only by critically analyzing rigorously organized facts and writing literary prose can the historian reconstruct the historical event, which even when based on documentation, cannot be completely transcended.

For Iorga, if history is a science, it is a synthesis of all human experiences in their manifestations. Thus, the historian must enter museums and theaters, know both traditional and contemporary literature, and study architecture; for history is not only factual, scientific record; it cannot be. History opens perspectives and makes valuable suggestions.

He had a superhuman memory and erudition, and was a follower of Michelet, for whom history was "la résurrection intégrale de la vie." He spent much of his life in libraries and in archives in research, submerged in the silence there,

---

[185]Iorga explained to an American audience that "the only way to give a tolerable lecture about history is to do it as an historian and not as a professor of history. If one does it as a professor of history, the cause is lost at the outset. But if one undertakes the task as an historian, the lecture will become endurable; it may even become interesting." *Americani și Românii din America*, p. 213.

[186]The Iorga family to the writer.

and his romantic nature found opportunity for reconstructing the past. Iorga's prodigious memory was very helpful here.[187]

Iorga had a good command of modern European languages; a fine knowledge of Latin and Greek. His one deficiency was his ignorance of Slavonic languages and of Hungarian and Turkish.

Mme. Catinca (his second wife), being Transylvanian, helped Iorga read nineteenth century Hungarian documents written in Hungarian; most Hungarian documents prior to that were written in Latin. Iorga's brother-in-law and colleague, Ioan Bogdan, provided help with documents in the Slavonic languages.[188]

He did not belong to any historical school, for he was an impressionist who concentrated on the particular, interpreting historical phenomena in the context of it. He arrived at his conclusions from a family of notions which he sought to define constantly: soil, nation, religion, instinct, organism, soul, idea, race — terms of a nineteenth century romantic nationalist. Like Michelet, Iorga found it essential to define the nation and the "spirit" shaping it, which became the nation's consciousness and endured in art, artifacts, behaviors, social structures and outlook, turning into factors which establish a nation's continuity. The continuous, organic development of the "race" and of the "idea" on the "soil," as-

---

[187]In 1985, Professor Karl Göllner, a former student of Iorga now of the Sibiu University, told a story to this writer: Iorga sent one of his best students to his school in France. Soon Iorga promoted his voting Transylvanian Saxon student to research-assistant. Göllner received a note from Iorga indicating his arrival in Paris. Göllner was waiting at the Gare de l'Est, Iorga arrived in the company of Dr. C. Angelescu. He introduced young Göllner to Dr. Angelescu, making a point: "I hope that this student of mine will not betray me, like my former students C.C. Giurescu and P.P. Panaitescu did." Exiting the station, Iorga proceeded directly to the Bibliothèque Nationale, to conduct research in preparation for his next lecture. When he finished, he gave his notes to Göllner, asking him to check his quotations. "Ei dragă," Iorga said, "my dear friend, check it for possible mistakes, because you know..." (Göllner recalled how Iorga made horrible four letter words from the initials of the first names of his opponents in the Noua Școală) "you know, they will pick on it!" Göllner remembers that out of the 160 quotations Iorga had written down from memory, he had found 158 correct, only two footnotes contained minor errors.

[188]*O viață de om așa cum a fost,* vol. I, p. 259, and vol. II, p. 59.

sured for Iorga that the future of a nation would be no repetition of past experiences, *but rather a natural sequence* of it. A nation's original genius must be free to develop; foreign interference can only damage it. If this consciousness (this "spirit") is held captive, it must be liberated. An obvious conclusion: every nation must be independent. Once every nation becomes independent, these national states will join in an amiable system of international harmony (based on the voluntary recognition of this inclusive diversity), and live in peace. Here one has a touch of Mazzini's nationalist optimism. Almost a century later one may only comment: if only the success of the first phase could assure the second! It would seem that for Iorga, *his* sense of history was more paramount than the tremendous weight of history of the region, but utopia is an indispensable projection of creative imagination — as an opposite pole to ideology. And Iorga, always full of new ideas, was not lacking creative imagination.

Deadly set against imperial ventures and empires (Romania was victimized by at least four of them, during his lifetime), he rejected them also on the basis of his historical theories. Believing the nation to be the most natural, organic society, he condemned "the nefarious role which these large non-organic formations (empires) play in history." According to Iorga, on one hand you have the natural yearnings of organic entities for development and fulfillment — on the other, these natural strivings are forcefully submerged into large, abstract, non-organic units, "superstates" or "supranational" empires. This will not happen! Because "empires are transitory, but the nations are indestructible; empires are merely a form, but nations are an organism."

For Iorga, history taught but one thing: these unnatural, inorganic formations carry in themselves the germ of their own destruction. It could not be otherwise, since there is but one historical organic reality: the nation. If a nation moves out from its organic, natural confines and establishes domination over other organic entities by founding an empire, such an unnatural move "will make this nation exhausted" and lead it to decline.

Iorga brought up many historical examples: the Greeks under Alexander the Great conquered the Middle East and brought Hellenism to it, but they killed their ancient spirit. It has been dead ever since. Attila's empire, like the one of

Genghis Khan, fell apart. Napoleon's mistake was using the best French resources ("tiring France out") for his attempt at world domination. To avoid this, Iorga suggests "for each nation, the first rule must be to exercise self-restraint," respect other organic entities, other nations, and not to undertake expansionist, empire-building ventures.[189] Once more, one cannot help remarking that Iorga would feel comfortable in our days.

He based his work on documentation gathered in and outside Romania during a lifetime. He was the first to dig up the half-forgotten Romanian past and to reconstruct it out of forgotten documents, a compilation larger than any made by any other Romanian historian, which Iorga's detractors regarded with envy. Even friends (like Şeicaru) considered it "a disorderly file card drawer which has been turned over."[190] No historian of Southeastern Europe can fail to be grateful for what Iorga accomplished. He saved many historians travel, confrontation with bureaucrats, and long hours in dusty, unheated archives. His annotations may be "confusing" or "chaotic," but it is easier to read them than to undertake the effort to discover the documents.[191]

Iorga felt that only selective use of documentation could help the historian penetrate and succeed in reconstructing past events; only great historical knowledge could guide this selection. Documents helped the historian acquire the insight leading to truth. But facts are subject to interpretation. "Certitude" (as Iorga called it) is an approximation of the truth. He looked for the significant, but he knew the difference between the significant and the important. He is

---

[189]In all his works, Iorga repeated that real peace can be achieved only if "each nation restricts its domination to the geographical limits of the territory it inhabits." His strong stand against "supranational" states and empires can be found in many of his works, among them is his *Generalităţi*, this statement came in a radio address on 24 March 1939, a few days after Hitler marched into Prague. *Luceafărul*, 23 November 1985.

[190]E. Lovinescu called it "an informative chaos." Florin Mihăilescu, ed., *N. Iorga* (Bucureşti, 1979), p. 151; Şeicaru, *op. cit.*, p. 76.

[191]Iorga dug up about 50,000 half-forgotten documents concerning Romanian history. As he used to say, he "brought them to life." The family remembers that once Romanians became aware of Iorga's efforts, practically the whole country supplied him with historical documents.

sometimes superficial, but never shallow. He felt that analysis of documents, events, and personalities as products of the culture's spirit was all-important. Individuals in history were important; yet they should be understood in the context of their time.

Although he did not belong to any historical school, Iorga did believe in his historical method which he called *historiology*. Accordingly, since mankind's history forms a unity, one should look for representative common characteristics. Once they are found, the historian should evaluate them. But these common characteristics were not laws. Iorga recognized no metaphysical interpretation of history. He looked within mankind's experience for parallels, repetitions, and how these were resolved. But he believed in the dictum: "History repeats itself" only in a very qualified fashion. History (according to Iorga) "does not repeat itself"; history continues. To divine the future of a country, one should not expect repetitions, but a natural sequence of the nation's past. The historian should also look for similarities and parallels within the chronology of mankind's experience. Such "permanent characteristics" (*permanenţe*) should be found. The historian should look for the point where the parallels between these causes and effects (from which the historical event emerges) intersect. For Iorga, the ability to find these points of intersection is what makes the difference between a clerk (or a chronicler) on one hand, and a historian on the other. He always tried to discover the relationships between human experiences and the institutions which emerged from these experiences. Discovery of such relationships depends upon the reliability of one's facts: they should be thoroughly examined. More important is the interpretation of the relationships between different sources of evidence. Such scrutiny helps to determine history's direction; but the historian must master world history. Iorga argued that history deals with the nature and the unity of mankind. A culture is the product of soil, race, and idea. Human society is an organic unit; should a group of people feel the nation (this "gigantic being") must reform itself, they can always refer to these organically determinative factors. Iorga did not seek to understand Romanians in the abstract, but through their vitality and essential characteristics which helped them survive through history; his Romania was a product of these processes. Only by understanding these common characteristics and experiences could one write true Romanian history. If one writes something other than universal history, one merely describes an organic process forming an organic entity.

Understanding this organic process and its manifestations (e.g., national psychology) are even more important than primary sources. Since for the early Middle Ages documentary evidence about Romanian history was lacking, Iorga tried to reconstruct the uninterrupted nature of Romanian life and presence in Dacia from the permanent manifestations of soil, race, and idea, that is: the culture, the mentality of Romanians. He concluded that, during the Middle Ages, many "Popular Romanias" existed; these "Popular Romanias" (with the cessation of barbaric onslaughts) later coalesced along the main trade routes. According to his historical method, such permanent manifestations — drawing on historical parallels from the past of other nations — permit the historian to draw conclusions about the nation. Such reconstructions on the basis of permanent, organic cultural manifestations fill documentary voids, and explain the continuity of the Romanian people in Dacia: a study of popular life is always the best recourse for the historian when documents are unavailable.

Iorga's historical work followed three concentric circles: Romanian history was in the center; the next circle consisted of the history of Romania's neighbors; finally, the outer circle was a universal history.

This method raised the following questions for him: how strictly should the historian adhere to available documentary evidence? Does strict adherence to documents insure "objectivity?" Ranke and Michelet depended upon imagination and instinct to aid them in their work. Iorga's ideas in this direction are prudent. He argued that as history is not a science, and precise verification on the basis of deductive reasoning not always possible, there could be no philosophy of history. He believed philosophy makes people intransigent, and intolerant of other opinions, Iorga never pretended to be a deductive thinker; he remained an impressionist and a Romantic nationalist, depending on instincts and the spontaneity of his genius; being an example of *Pascal's esprit de finesse* rather than *Descartes' esprit de géometrie*. Of his own historical work, Iorga maintained that "he was a more severe judge of it than any of his professors ever were."[192]

By which criteria did Iorga judge his work? How did Iorga interpret history? What were his biases? Iorga became a nationalist politician and he was by nature very temperamental. The further Iorga's studies moved from his contemporaries and his own times, the better his historical works arc. How fortunate it is that he was (mainly) a medievalist! His works about the Middle Ages and Byzantium are priceless; but when he discussed contemporary issues (especially his work on the history of contemporary literature), Iorga, the temperamental politician, was of no help. His studies on literature after the Junimea Society are not literary histories, but lampoons. According to Barbu Teodorescu, himself a flatterer of Iorga, when giving historical background to some of his articles, or writing many political-historical works relating to contemporary events, "Iorga confounded political action with historical work."[193]

His enemies attacked him for the numerous inaccuracies, but when one considers the immense body of Iorga's accomplishments, his errors become relatively insignificant. Although his early works are accurate, his later works show the strains of Iorga's human limitations. His errors resulted mostly from haste. Often political pressures caused him to rush the publication of a book insufficiently corrected; all too often sending a hastily written work with one proof-reading (or without it) to his publisher. Iorga considered the correctness of the horizon and that of the leitmotif sufficient.

He had a wonderfully organized brain, and memory. Knowing how to keep the welter of facts from blurring his main ideas, he could organize his material so that his "horizons" showed clear. The message and the structure of his work were bright and sensible. Iorga's admirers respectfully drew his attention to his many minor errors, his detractors pounced upon them with ghoulish glee.

---

[192] *O viață de om așa cum a fost*, vol. I, p. 300.

[193] Theodorescu, *op. cit.*, p. 321.

Iorga was mightily angered by a lack of a sense of proportion in those who emphasized such minor errors. He used to say: "Why do these people not teach mathematics or physics rather?" Later he remarked with resignation: "Someday a cultural establishment of grave and worthy scholars and accurate researchers will organize what I have collected, and make something smoother and more brilliant than I have been capable of. In doing this, they will point out my mistakes and shortcomings, forgetting the strenuous efforts I made, and the heart I put into my work. God should forgive them, because I forgave them already."[194] These minor inaccuracies do not invalidate the historical conclusions Iorga drew. The detractions resemble a dinosaur whose overgrown body is supported by a pea-sized brain. The quantity of these (minor) errors is large; reflections on the significance of them is superficial. If one must recognize significant faults in his work, it should be (as his own family points out) the declining overall quality. His earlier works were his best. Later, Iorga tried to open the "horizons" — much else became of secondary importance. Iorga always held that the Phanariot period was not barren. What was most important: it did not disrupt the organic process.

Dr. Samuel Johnson would not have approved of Iorga's personality or his historical theories, for he would have regarded him as a man whose deepest convictions were in conflict with law and order. (Dr. Johnson had said of Wesley that his inner Methodist "light" was incompatible with law and order.) Nor would have Descartes or Voltaire and Iorga understood each other. Iorga was a distinctly individual figure.

He was more than a Medievalist and Byzantinist of world renown. His work on the Middle Ages was impressive because he drew upon his belief in the organic development of humanity through history. His political arguments defending and explaining Romanian continuity drew upon his account of the organic

---

[194]*O viață de om așa cum a fost*, vol. I, pp. 312-313, and Teodorescu, *op. cit.*, p. 259. Iorga's report on his visit to America contains errors that are typical. Describing the journey across the Sierra to California he casually remarks that "we bypassed the capital city of California, Colorado." He confuses the sinking of the Luisitania with that of the Titanic. *Americani și Români din America*, pp. 108 and 160.

development of the early medieval Romanian society. His strongest account of the origins and continuity of the Romanian people is the celebrated "Daco-Romanian Theory." Developing some of Xenopol's findings, he argued that the Geto-Dacians were the ancestors of the Romanians, intermarrying with their Roman conquerors; his overall arguments establish the place of the Romanian people in European culture. The Junimist tendencies in Iorga's historiography were pronounced. He maintained that Feudalism was not an organic product of Romanian society based on free peasants, but was adapted under the disruptive influence of Hungary, Poland, and Byzantium. It was none other than Michael the Brave who established serfdom in Romania, and Iorga was quite unhappy with it. He disparaged all historical processes in Romania after 1800, since he felt that foreign influences had disrupted organic patterns and processes. Iorga rejected "Nicolae-Pavlovich's" — Tsar Nicholas I — "Regulamentul Organic" as a hateful foreign institution.[195] Only Nicolae Bălcescu — a romantic nationalist — escaped Iorga's nearly universal censure of the 1848 leaders.[196] Iorga maintained that the Brătianus disrupted Romania's organic development; they were indifferent to Romania's peasants.

He dismissed some modern sciences, calling sociology an "insane asylum." He felt no personal animosity towards the great Romanian sociologist Dr. Dimitrie Gusti, but was given to sarcastic remarks about him. He also dismissed psychiatry as "Freud's nonsense"[197]; but that does not mean that Iorga did not think individual or mass psychology important — such factors play a large role in Iorga's writing; he merely thought that there could be no scientific and systematic treatment of psychology in the manner of Freud.

His history writing and his politics show even more his lack of understanding for the dynamic changes of twentieth century economics. Since his historical understanding was based on rather inflexible "permanent" elements of cultural

---

[195]*Op. cit.*, p. 104. As Iorga put it: "I rejected it *like every nationalist did.*"

[196]On Bălcescu, see *Originile naționalismului român* (Vălenii de Munte, 1908).

[197]Șeicaru, *op. cit.*, p. 86. *Americani și Români din America*, p. 71.

development, Iorga could not discern the shifts that Toynbee called "acceleration of history." He did not think that his poor grasp of economics was a handicap; as he said in 1934, "It has been my country's and my own good luck (sic!)
that I have not yet become an economist!"[198] Iorga did not think that the economy or finances are of cardinal importance in statesmanship — since he never
separated the state from the nation — nor from the historical circumstances in
which the nation was conceived. He did write several economic histories, with
massive documentation and thousands of facts, geographic and paternalistic interpretation. An acute understanding of technological and economic changes
was exactly what would have helped Iorga in his political incarnation.

Iorga's sense of the all pervasive influence of history almost automatically
imposed the various political roles he played as journalist, literary critic, playwright, university professor, orator, and statesman. But at the core of his political concept and activity was that, without understanding the past, the present
cannot be interpreted properly. And without a correct understanding of the present there is no way of deriving a viable policy for the future. Thus, the historian
has an important role in foreseeing the future. The nationalist historian was also
an educator.[199] He evaluated Romanian life from the earliest anthropological

---

[198]"Necesitatea unei enciclopedii a științelor economice," Conferința ținută la 1 November
1934; *Academia Înaltă de Studii Comerciale și Industriale din București* (București 1934).

[199]Șeicaru remembers Iorga was sometimes prematurely worried if the halls where he was to
lecture did not fill up. "Nobody wishes to listen anymore to what I have to say" And realizing
he had relatively few readers he commented: "Nobody wants to read my works anymore,
nobody's interested in what I have to say." Șeicaru joked with Iorga: "You know. Professor,
what they will say about you after 200 years? Nicolae Iorga was a most prolific writer,
nobody will be able to believe that one man could possibly write so many books in so many
fields." Whereupon Iorga, with great sadness, answered: "And his work was fared to go
unread by his contemporaries and by his posterity — such was to be his fate." Șeicaru, *op.
cit.* pp 73, 90. But Iorga sometimes said to his family, "Well, if they don't read me, it is their
loss." *Neamul Românesc*, 16 Jan 1921. G. Călinescu wrote: "It is impossible to pass on any
Romanian historical subject — however obscure or narrow it may be — without noting that
Iorga was previously there..." Călinescu, *op. cit.*, p. 542.

documents to the present, making splendid use of the 50,000 documents he discovered because "The historian must be tireless in reminding people of their traditions, and become an advocate of national solidarity.[200]

Iorga may have been motivated (as he claimed) by his wish not "to become a deserter and traitor," but he was not suited to politics. Someone surveying his life cannot help feeling relief when Iorga leaves the political scene (which he himself more than once contemptuously referred to as "Suprafanar"[201] and returns to his work as a historian! A poetic and conjectural passage Iorga wrote about Miron Costin, the father of Romanian historiography, could be applied to him. Recounting Miron Costin's arrest, being dragged away from his family, and his murder by Dimitrie Cantemir's henchman, Iorga suggests: "Possibly Cantemir's henchmen did not permit him a last prayer; but (Costin) could lift up his soul above his old age and say a good prayer with (submitting) his service to his nation and with his historical writings as his chief merit." Iorga biographers have wondered: Could he possibly have had a premonition of the similar fate awaiting him?[202]

Starting in his teens, Iorga wrote about twenty thousand articles, mainly on literature and history. Now we shall shift attention front his professional activities to his political journalism (although with him it is difficult to draw the line between the two). Iorga, the fighter, the animator, carried out his "struggle" through political journalism. He considered historical work and literary criticism to be the strategic aspect of his struggle. The tactical aspect was his daily political journalism. In his mouthpiece, *Neamul Românesc*, contributors often discussed whether journalism was a profession or a vocation; Iorga was not resigned to judge events "without fear or favor." Never indifferent to the subjects he discussed, his journalistic role often overshadowed his roles as a historian and internationally known intellectual, even his role as a politician. His powerful

---

[200]*Neamul Românesc*, 16 Jan 1921.

[201]One can find this epithet many times in *Neamul Românesc*, especially during the political conflicts of the year 1933.

[202]Şeicaru, *op. cit.*, p. 78.

affirmations, the pathos of his negations, his thundering incomparable anathemas, resounded. Iorga rarely expressed skepticism or relativism — attitudes strangely absent in a historian. He wrote his articles with such spontaneous emotion, that even today they read like outcries of pain. Whether he was right or wrong, Iorga's sincerity and total lack of artificiality give his journalism a human tone. His hundreds of articles still seem as burning actualities. Tudor Vianu remembered Iorga's writing as "an absolutely individual literary work; it is impossible to confound it with the work of any other pen."[203]

In 1899, *L'indépendence Roumaine* published Iorga's articles on Romania's intellectual life; in these he transformed himself from a rather timid historian and literary critic into a terrifying polemicist. In 1903 he began his contributions to *Sămămătorul*; he would formally take over the paper later.

It was not easy to collaborate with Iorga. He had a tremendous ego, and his nature demanded that he become "first among (by no means) equals." On the Romanian national holiday, 10 May 1906, Iorga started *Neamul Românesc* ("The Romanian Nation"), which he would direct until the end of his life. The paper enjoyed varied fortunes, in the beginning appearing twice weekly, then daily, dropping to a weekly, climbing to a daily again.

Editing his own paper was not enough for Iorga. In 1908 (wishing to avoid previous difficulties with getting published), he acquired his own printing press. Iorga called his press *Datina Românească* ("Romanian tradition"), and many of his books would bear its imprint. His political journalism was a link between the historian and the politician.

Newspapers and journalism in Eastern and Southeastern Europe were traditionally below Western standards. Taking into account that the passage of nearly a century makes earlier journalism appear unsophisticated, we may still ask whether East European (or Balkan) newspapers at the turn of the century differed so greatly from their Western counterparts. The struggles between the Hearst and the Pulitzer presses in the United States, ("You supply me the news and I will supply the war!") were typical. German and Austrian newspapers

---

[203]Tudor Vianu, *Arta prozatorilor români* (Bucureşti, 1941), p. 153.

(during the Boer War), French newspapers (during the Fashoda crisis), and even the English popular press notably lacked reserve and reasonableness (with which the British justly pride themselves). The differences between Western and East European press were then of degree rather than kind.[204] The differences would become more pronounced; Western newspapers improved themselves after 1910, with exception of the unsavory journalistic practices of the Nazis and Fascists. Tabloids do not observe the standards of the legitimate press, but there is nothing that resembles *fin-de-siècle* European journalism at present.

Yet, *Neamul Românesc* was never meant to be a tabloid! It was the mouthpiece of Nicolae Iorga, the Romanian intellectual "par excellence," which served Iorga in the frontline in his struggle for Romanian cultural nationalism.[205] He infused his spirit into the paper, and few of its pages were serene. For Iorga it was hardly a choice between journalistic ethics or justice; rather: "Us — or them!" He once observed: "One can make peace with death but once: while dying!" He wanted to continue the political journalistic tradition of Mihai Eminescu, but without resembling Eminescu's more even temper.

Iorga addressed his *Neamul Românesc* to a select intellectual circle; he never meant it to be a mass newspaper but hoped to steer Romania's intellectual elite towards (what he considered) the right direction, "on a day-by-day basis," by which Iorga had in mind the daily needs of Romania. Thus, his journalism often does not consider truth or facts to be something absolute — and he frequently contradicts himself in positions previously taken. Iorga's opinions were expressed in a violent, emotional manner, with little reflection before he wrote them down. There is however a consistent, inflexible fidelity to Romania's interests (as Iorga saw them) within the framework of his cultural nationalism. There are great differences between opinions Iorga expresses as a historian, or even in his diary *Memorii*, (seven volumes) and the articles he wrote about the same subjects as a political journalist. Even greater are the differences between

---

[204]In 1911, a French newspaper criticized the Romanian press saying: "The Romanians have an unrivalled talent for insulting each other through the press." Iorga retorted, citing French examples of press insults and lawsuits emanating from it *Neamul Românesc*, 2 August 1911.

[205]*Neamul Românesc*, 10 May 1906.

his historical writings and his opinions on the same subjects, expressed verbally to his family or to his associates.

Later, Iorga wished to reach broader segments of Romania. He published a popular edition of *Neamul Românesc, Neamul Românesc pentru Popor (Neamul Românesc for the People)*, to appeal to the peasantry. And considering literature so important, he published *Neamul Românesc Literar*.

Neamul Românesc was not exactly serene. How could it be, if Cuza, in an article dismissed with one of his epithets Jewish claims to being *Am Kodesh* ("Holy People," or "the People of the Book"), calling them *Am Kodosh ("am codoş"* — "a Nation of *pimps*") instead?[206] Iorga never expressed himself calmly on any subject; he maintained that "a convinced polemicist is a soldier; a corrupt polemicist is a henchman; and a dilettante polemicist is a pervert."[207] Neverthe-less, *Neamul Românesc* seemed to be restrained compared to the mass circula-tion press associated with Strada Sărindarilor (the Elect Street of Bucharest). Romanian presses (during the "constitutional period" of Carol I's reign) enjoyed much freedom, mainly because 90% of the population either could not read, or could not afford daily newspapers. However, Strada Sărindarilor used its limited freedom in the most repulsive fashion: they were untruthful and irresponsible; blackmailing and smearing public figures was common; it was yellow journal-ism at its most yellow. Caragiale often described Bucharest journalism in his satires.[208]

Iorga's paper did not include such journalism. He wrote almost all the edi-torials and during some periods proofread and corrected the paper daily. During critical times, Iorga wrote two or more editorials daily; dramatic pressures

---

[206]*Neamul Românesc*, 18 January 1908.

[207]Nicolae Iorga, *Cugetări* (Bucureşti, 1970), p. 251.

[208]The standards of the Strada Sărindarilor were legendary even in the Bucharest of the interwar period. The general epithet used for the moral and intellectual standards there was "şantaj-etaj." Describing the activities of Şeicaru's *Curentul*, this meant that you carry out a blackmail operation and from the money you can add a floor to the editorial offices of the corresponding newspaper. But prevailing corruption differed in degree rather than in kind. The *Adevărul* and *Dimineaţa* were vulgar enough; none of the newspapers was as bad as that bulwark of Cuzist bourgeoisie, the *Porunca-Vremii* and its editor, Ilie Rădulescu.

brought our Iorga's most sensitive journalism. As a historian he increased his activities and his writing gained in power and clarity. In 1907, 1912, 1913, during the war years (especially between 1916 and 1919), and through the 1930s, the most politically crucial decade of this century, Iorga worked feverishly His output is of uneven quality and intensity, as should be expected from someone of his diverse reactions, romantic philosophy, impressionistic style, and vast intellect; had he maintained an even intensity over the course of thirty years, he would have been no more than an automaton. Often he collected his articles and published them in book form.[209]

But Iorga was no ordinary journalist; the historian's vision molded his articles, and historical arguments bolstered his political observations. He used paradoxical titles to emphasize his message. "Dictatorships and dictatorships," "Theaters and theaters," "Führer and Verführer," "Democracy and Democracy," "Propaganda and Propaganda," "Student Homes and Student Homes," and so on. His journalism was, even in its shortcomings, that of an East European intellectual. Many times Iorga printed his main points in an arresting boldface. Because of these idiosyncrasies, *Neamul Românesc* bore little resemblance to the London or New York *Times*, the *Christian Science Monitor*, *Le Monde*, or the Swiss press. But then, conditions in Romania differed from conditions in Western countries.

When Iorga saw his principles challenged, he mixed his erudition with a capacity for vituperation which only the best traditions of East European journalism can offer. He anathematized Romania's detractors thunderously, and delighted in casting aspersions on his opponent's family name (even though he was a victim of the same practice). Jewish Bolshevik leaders are referred to only by their former names: Trotsky "Bronstein," Maxim Litvinov "Meier Wallach." But Iron Guard Captain Codreanu also becomes Zelinschi (the name of his al-

---

[209]Cuvinte adevărate; *Războiul nostru în note zilnice*, 3 volumes; *O luptă literară*, 2 volumes; *Oameni care au fost*, 4 volumes, etc.

leged Ukrainian ancestors); Hungarian revisionists, politicians, and even Hungarian historians are called by their former German (Swabian) or Slavonic names, Iorga reserved special vituperation for Hungarians ostensibly of Romanian ancestry: he called Miklós Kozma (Cosma) an "Armenian-Romanian renegade," etc. Although an outspoken anti-Marxist, Iorga never abused Marxists when they showed sincere interest in the Romanian people. He never refers to Constantin Dobrogeanu-Gherea as Solomon Katz; and Iorga spared those Jews who showed interest in Romanian culture: Dr. Moses Gaster, Rabbi Nemierower, or Hayman Tiktin. He answered all attacks, usually with a greater force than that of the provocation; he took even trivial matters to court. His ego and temperament did not differentiate between legitimate challenges and those cheap publicity seekers hoping to gain notoriety. In all too many instances he dignified them by devoting editorial space in *Neamul Românesc* his provoker did not deserve; his erudition suggested to him ironical remarks, and for the sake of exercising his biting wit, Iorga would make space for a sarcastic response, forgetting the higher wisdom of leaving certain wisecracks unsaid. His tremendous ego gave the impression that he felt nearly infallible, and he alone knew the truth in historical, political, and literary matters. Iorga seemed to identify himself with the Romanian nation in the names of his newspapers and printing press. He claimed the intellectual virtues by the names of his other publications: he called his literary newspaper *Drum Drept* ("The Right Road"), the forum for his cultural nationalism *Cuget Clar* ("Clarity of Thought"). His collected articles for the newspaper *Epoca* into book form were entitled *Cuvinte Adevărate* ("True Words").

Why was it that *Neamul Românesc* never became a widely circulated newspaper?[210] Iorga's personality, temperament, and lack of practical sense contributed to this. Even though he wished to address the intellectual elite, as a politician, he should have been interested in selling more than the 90 issues per edition. Pamfil Şeicaru, later editor of *Curentul,* one of the largest dailies, recalled an incident that goes a long way towards explaining both Iorga's failure as a

---

[210]*Neamul Românesc* was sometimes reduced to appearing twice weekly; at its lowest, it appeared weekly and sold 90 issues. Şeicaru, *op.cit.*, p. 82.

politician and that of his paper. In 1924, *Neamul Românesc* was selling 90 issues per edition. Iorga left for France to give lectures at the Sorbonne. During his absence, Şeicaru directed the newspaper and determined to give it a large circulation. He obtained endowments from party members and Iorga's wealthy adherents; Titus Enacovici (from Botoşani) contributed the most, asking to be kept anonymous to prevent intrigues by Iorga's "inner circle." Şeicaru hired poets and journalists. Circulation swiftly rose to 2,000. Only one incident occurred: G. Vlădescu-Răcoasa, who felt a nearness to the "inner circle," brutally assaulted one of the editors. Şeicaru promptly discharged him. When Iorga returned, Şeicaru's changes pleased him. He did learn of Titus Enacovici's contributions, and thanked him effusively; he also learned of G. Vlădescu-Răcoasa's discharge.

The intrigues of the "inner circle" Enacovici feared began in earnest. Iorga reacted childishly, refusing to descend to the redaction, sending his articles in by messenger; and asking — indirectly, no doubt — Şeicaru to reinstate Vlădescu-Răcoasa. Şeicaru refused adamantly. Finally Iorga came to the offices, declaring to Şeicaru that he wanted "all the people with those 'Calabrian hats' (meaning Bohemians) out of the redaction. This is a political paper!" Şeicaru asked, "Do you think, Professor, that Vlădescu-Răcoasa could replace them?" Iorga answered: "Oh no, that's not what I meant! I don't want that dog Răcoasa back! I just want those Calabrian hats out!" Şeicaru drew the pertinent conclusions and left, taking the most talented journalists with him, and founded his own paper.[211] This incident goes a long way explaining the failure of Iorga's political career.

Culture, according to Iorga, represented the nation's spirit, developing parallel to the organic historical process of the nation's experiences. In it, as in a

---

[211]Şeicaru, *op.cit.*, pp. 82-85. Considering this incident typical and Şeicaru's credibility less than fool-proof, *when he was involved personally*, the writer reconfirmed the story with the Iorga family. They confirmed every see detail.

mirror, the historical process was reflected. Culture determined the nation's vitality, worth, and place among other nations.[212] Of all its manifestations, literature was the most original, but his quest for a "pure" art was not such a natural companion as he would have liked it to be. Before his political "struggle" started, Iorga was more open-minded about literature.[213] After 1900, Iorga closed his mind to literary innovation. Călinescu noted: "Nothing modern in literature impinged upon his mind anymore."[214] Nonetheless, Iorga reviewed all the works on Romanian literary history and culture. Had he been simply a historian, he could not have exercised such influence.

Iorga felt that the historian of Romanian literature should have a superb knowledge of Romanian history, and he "had no sympathy for the Romanian historian without thorough knowledge of the history of the Romanian soul — how this soul is reflected in Romanian literary history." He did not understand the art historian who "didn't know the life of the society where this art developed."[215] He always treated his literary criticism as contributions to his "struggle," calling his most important work about it "Literary Struggle."[216] Iorga was a kind of commander of a political party, he demanded obedience, discipline, and loyalty from his subordinates during the struggle towards the triumph of his

---

[212]*Neamul Românesc*, 7 March 1937.

[213]See Nicolae Iorga, *Pagini de critică din tinerețe* (Craiova, 1921), passim.

[214]Călinescu, *op. cit.*, p. 541.

[215] Nicolae Iorga, Istoria literaturii românești: introducere sintetică (București, 1929) p. 7.

[216]*O luptă literară* in two volumes, published in 1914 and 1916, in Vălenii-de-Munte. Republished in Bucharest in 1979, the edition this writer used for reference. *O luptă literară*, together with the *Generalități* are the cardinal tools in understanding Iorga's artistic and historical concepts. But *O luptă literară* represents his analysis of the social and cultural situation in Romania at the beginning of the century. It is a manifestation of Iorga's doctrines and ideals.

cultural nationalism.[217] Unfortunately, Iorga confused the aesthetic with the ethical and the ethnic, ensuring that his cultural struggle turned into a political one. He believed that aesthetics function ethically, restoring the soul's harmony, while calming and purifying men. Iorga's combativeness, intolerances, and inveterate political tone in literary criticism derived from this belief.

More objective in his historical work, he was tolerant because he thought history bore out his claims. Maybe this explains why his style as a history writer was less rigid and more spontaneous. Analytic thinking dominated his historical work, synthetic thinking his literary productions. He distinguished historical truth based on precise documentation from artistic expression, phenomena amidst which Iorga lived. For him only art could reveal the reality of these phenomena. Unfortunately, all too often Iorga's historical concepts determined also his aesthetics. Since he adopted a theory explaining the rise of the Romanian boyars as a non-organic, foreign phenomenon, he embraced C. Sandu Aldea's *Două Neamuri* because it presented a village resembling Iorga's historical descriptions, regardless of its literary value.

Although Iorga felt history and literature inter-determined each other, literature was vaguer than history, with its documents. According to him, Romania's organic development was disrupted by Liberal political mistakes following independence. As a consequence, Romania embraced foreign cultural models, poisoning its soul. Her art became full of *"hidre odioase"* (odious hydras), whose numerous ugly heads, Iorga, dressed in full combat gear, set out to destroy. His historical and aesthetic views form a consistent whole, and his literary criticism became politicized. Iorga stood above other Romanian literary critics because of his erudition. Neither Maiorescu nor Gherea equaled him. We should remember that Iorga was reading world literature since the age of five — and in

---

[217]He warned the kindly Transylvanian poet, Ştefan Octavian Iosif, because he saw him in the company of Ilarie Chendi with whom Iorga was at odds. About one of the editorial staff members of *Neamul Românesc*, Răcoasa, he couldn't say anything more damning than that he frequents Dimitrie Gusti's circles! Şeicaru, *op. cit.*, pp. 21 and 86.

a critical fashion. During these formative years his cultural values were developing on Western lines — mainly French, and classical literary values — but not restricted to those.

He derived most of his critical ideas from five French authors: Paul Bourget, J.M. Guyau, G. Séailles, E. Hennequin, and from H. Paine. These critics distinguished themselves with the century's scientific discoveries in discussing art, often invoking Spenser, Darwin, and Karl Wundt. Iorga did not follow them entirely, but modified ideas he could use.

Paul Bourget was a *revanchard,* a distinguished figure of Republican reaction during the Third Republic. He maintained that the Church must be the source of cohesion, and could counter the anarchy plaguing society. Iorga (a non-believer) thought that just such a national and social function was appropriate for the Church, accepting it even from "re-converts" like Bourget. He also found Bourget's *"nous n'acceptons que les doctrines dont nous portons déjà le principe en nous"* attractive.

Bourget analyzed in his work the causes of the prevailing social and intellectual crisis (*Essais de psychologie contemporaine,* 1883) and fought the cult of science and that of naturalism, advocating established middle class values in aesthetics (*Drames de famine,* 1900). He preferred the psychological novel to the moralizing one (*Le Disciple,* 1899).

Séailles's Essai sur le gènie influenced Iorga, but not as much as Guyau's *Problèmes de l'esthétique contemporaine* on judging what beauty is. Guyau expounded aesthetic vitalism, and emphasized intuition in literature. This put Iorga into Guyau's camp. Iorga attacked naturalist writers like Zola (invoking Guyau), arguing that seeing nothing in the world but vice and filth was simplistic and unrealistic. Guyau maintained that a genius's work is harmonious and unitary in describing the objective and subjective worlds. He valued simplicity in literature. Iorga came to detest the worship of beautiful form. He argued that the writer must exercise imagination permitting the reader to identify with characters; even the historian must write in such a way, thus the importance for him of writing history *evocatively.*

Hennequin represented a psychological school, and Iorga, following him, believed that no "impersonal novel" was possible. An author's personality is involved in selecting material for his subject. Hennequin emphasized aesthetic, psychological, and sociological analysis of a work.

As a philosopher and literary critic, Taine had a profound influence on Iorga's views about art and even history. He accepted many (but by no means all) of Taine's criteria, especially on the connections between nature and literature (*L'intélligence and Histoire de la littérature anglaise*). Harmony in development must not be disrupted. Both Iorga and Taine whole-heartedly hated the French Revolution, the Jacobins, and Robespierre (*Origines de la France contemporaine*). Taine judged a writer according to the "moral environment" of society. He was a determinist: the race, the environment, the historical moment had determining effects. Hennequin opposed this idea. Only primitive societies are monolithic; the more developed and complex the society, the less the environmental forces shape the writer.

Any relativity was difficult to conceive for Iorga, and he interpreted these ideas to suit his cultural nationalism. In 1890 (at the age of nineteen), Iorga wrote "The Artist and the Public." He maintained that contemporary authors must make concessions since they wrote for a large public and not only for "stray literary mandarins." Nevertheless, the writer's concepts and taste are superior to the public's. He must not allow the manipulation of his art by it, but understand his art's social function.[218] For Iorga, the artist exercised social leadership through a "nationalist realism."

When *Tribuna* (a literary paper for Transylvanian Romanians) ceased publication, Iorga published an article in *Sămănătorul*.[219] In *Tribuna*, Ioan Slavici had pleaded always for "*realismul poporal*" realism about the peasantry, "novels inspired by national realities," which should inspire the peasantry and deal with its fate. *Sămănătorism* maintains that the nation is the natural society. As Iorga

---

[218]Theodorescu, *op. cit.*, p. 85.

[219]Iorga started to write in the *Sămănătorul* on 4 May 1903.

wrote: "...there is no more natural entity in the world than the nation."[220] Literature must elevate the reader. According to Iorga, it "cannot resemble a coffee-house where anybody who can pay may enter. Such kind of literature may be acceptable there, where it has no great mission to guide and elevate morality. In our country literature must recognize that mission and fulfill it proudly."[221] For Iorga, literature was a "social command" in the spirit of Eminescian nationalism, a kind of "nationalistic realism." He delivered the criteria of his literary criticism from his political and social concepts. During the 1900s, we witness the formation of the dogmatic Iorga. He would never abandon his concept of an *"engage"* for a "nationalist-realist" literature and art. If it were not based on Eminescu's concepts of aesthetics, it would be based on Eminescian nationalism.

He dismissed *l'art pour l'art* with the question, "You desire art for art's sake; why do you not desire rather people who live not for living's sake?"[222] The study of literature and of artistic currents were nothing else for Iorga but dialectical relations within an organic system. He believed that promoting organic development required a cultural revolution, not the disruptive sort he and Taine deplored, but one that would achieve national unity and internal reform, even the change of political ethics through culture and not the other way around.[223] Since art and literature were the truly important manifestations of Romanian culture, they were the most pregnant manifestations of Romanian originality, nationalism, and life. They should get inspiration from Romanian national life, not be borrowed from French or any other culture!

Iorga was intransigent when it came to the writer's position: "A poet not fully dedicated to his people is no poet at all." He was sympathetic with writers whose public did not respond: "There where people have no interest in literature,

---

[220]Şeicaru, *op. cit.*, p. 26.

[221]*Op. cit.*, p. 25.

[222]*Cugetări*, p. 162.

[223]We saw Iorga's preference for the patient, evolutionary cultural nationalist Samuil Klein (Micu) instead of his rebellious, senior relative Inocenţie Klein (Micu).

the writer must feel like the spark does when it has fallen under snow."[224] After his *Sămănătorism* period he would become inflexibly and completely dogmatic in his "nationalist-realism."[225]

It is difficult to understand that somebody acquainted with world literature like Iorga should adopt such aesthetic views! His cultural nationalism explains his violent rejection of modern trends, and his acrimonious criticism of symbolism, etc.[226] Iorga's hatred of futurism led him to prevent the Romanian Academy of Sciences from receiving Marinetti (even though Iorga would try to maintain a good relationship with Mussolini).[227] Iorga considered Shaw's plays "hideous" and branded Mark Twain a "nihilist." He accused Zola of creating "a world of infamy" in his novels.[228] He would reach the zenith of his rejections of modern literary trends after the First World War. He urged the classical Latin ideal on writers inasmuch as the Latins "bring logic, clarity, harmony, and measure to civilization." Iorga's classicism was identical to Winckelmann's description of ancient Greece: "*edle Einfalt, stille Grosse*" a description which Iorga found fit the *Sămănătorist* village. He was a romantic who espoused classicism. His literary histories are pioneering works scrupulously written until his involvement with the Junimea Society. Thereafter he simply attacked those deviating from his cultural nationalism, especially those who treated the erotic, dubbing it "pornography."

Iorga was criticized for reworking literary reviews of others into literary histories under his own name; he worked also here with haste under pressure, and the accuracy of his work suffered. In his literary reviews and criticisms,

---

[224]*Cugetări*, pp. 83 and 228.

[225]Even in 1929, Iorga unflinchingly defined his concepts about art and politics: "We were, we are, and we shall remain supporters of the peasantry. We were, we are, and we shall remain supporters of the ethnic idea. We were, we are, and we shall remain ethically motivated." Theodorescu, *op. cit.*, p. 165.

[226]*Op. cit.*, p. 161. The cosmopolitan, decadent current of symbolism."

[227]*Nicolae Iorga*, p. 82.

[228]*Americani şi Români din America*, p. 271, and *O viaţă aşa cum a fost*, vol. I, p. 136.

Iorga tried to be above all a psychologist, then a sociologist, an aesthete, and a historian — in that order.

His prose could be beautiful, even his historical writings. The prose of his biography, *O viață de om așa cum a fost*, rates among the most beautiful written in the Romanian language. Iorga could be an excellent portraitist, although his portraits were more historical, humane, and psychological, than artistic. His journalism could be movingly beautiful. His poetry was of indifferent literary value.

Iorga wrote numerous plays and nourished ambitions to become a playwright of dramatic and popular theater, but aspects of his relationship with the stage show naivete, for he wrote without being familiar with theatrical matters, staging of plays, etc. Iorga's numerous plays fall into four categories: 1) historical, 2) contemporary, 3) themes for "modest people," and 4) "living scenes," making some educational point in the framework of cultural nationalism. He even wrote political allegories: "Against the Fatherland," written in the early 1920s, portrays French emigres stepping out from occupation army bandwagons (after Napoleon's defeat). Iorga's allegory castigates German collaborators of the Great War: Marghiloman, Stere, Slavici, and Arghezi. He also wrote many *romans à clef* and allegorical pieces, but none of his work was very good. Iorga was vain, and became somewhat obsessed by his "Popular Theater," and its importance in educating people for his "cultural nationalism." Șeicaru recalls that the empty amphitheater of his *Teatru Popular* caused Iorga to despair. He hired professional director Victor Ion Popa, who assembled an excellent troupe and a good program. When the season's program was presented to Iorga, he objected that only two of his plays were included. "Are the others not good enough?" Victor Ion Popa left his job. Like many others, he was not able to work with Iorga.[229] The theater would linger on in Vălenii-de-Munte under the leadership of Iorga's brother Gheorghe. Iorga sincerely believed that a theater at his disposal (like Molière and Shakespeare) was in the interests of Romanian cultural

---

[229]Șeicaru, *op. cit.*, p. 98.

nationalism. Although he lacked talent to justify it, funds from Aristide Blank financed the theatre. The consequences for Iorga were grave.

In painting, Nicolae Grigorescu's suave, harmonious rural landscapes and peasant scenes impressed him most.[230] Iorga had little interest in music, and he does not say much about it. He was in Paris at the same time as Enescu. He supported popular music and contributed to the support of popular choirs.[231]

Iorga encouraged organizing public libraries and made donations to them from his personal library. He also promoted folkloric crafts; in his house at Vălenii one can admire a beautiful collection of Romanian folklore. He decorated the walls of his schools in Venice and France with Romanian popular art, and organized folkloric exhibitions.

Iorga's output was astounding. He published 700 titles on Romanian history alone, and there was no aspect of the Romanian past too trivial for him to devote intellectual energy. This vast work is of uneven quality, yet much is a real contribution to history and to the history of literature. When Iorga was abducted from his desk by the Legionary terror squad, he was working on his Universal History. He was 69 years old then; the thought of how much more he could have accomplished had he lived is awe-inspiring.

How did Iorga manage to produce so much? Such diverse types of works: scholarly books, articles, monographs on history and literature, plays, poetry; novels, and articles? Some of his books were re-issued (depending on actuality), sometimes heavily revised and often under different titles. Iorga published volumes that were collections of his articles and editorials; entire chapters of his histories of literature were often partly condensed reviews written by others (as Lovinescu, one of Iorga's detractors, reminded him).[232] Then, he published his lectures, especially political ones, in book form. Iorga's many travels provided

---

[230]*O viață de om*, vol. II, p. 10.

[231]Theodorescu, *op. cit.*, p. 167.

[232]*Nicolae Iorga*, p. 153. Lovinescu's opinions about the merits of Iorga's literary criticism were less than positive. This writer had opportunity to judge the plausibility of this using less prejudiced sources than E. Lovinescu.

material for travelogues — he managed to distill almost all of his experiences into books. There are Iorga's memoirs, both personal and political. He also published his political speeches and polemics. Finally, his parliamentary contributions were collected into volumes. His works also appeared in translations in eleven languages.

Iorga established his own printing press and published many of his books himself, often in not more than 500 copies. He always complained that he did not have enough readers.[233] Some people claimed that Iorga's style was "too hot for consumption." He angrily dismissed the idea that his passionate style could offend.[234] He wrote complicated sentences and coined words. As Tudor Vianu commented: "...the difficulty of Iorga's phrases comes from their density. The concentration of a great number of ideas, facts, data, and images does not remain isolated, but always demands parallels and differentiations."[235] He always seemed to hold the thread throughout his convoluted advance through the maze of facts he presented, but his readers (and audience) were often lost. Although Iorga's published prose was difficult, he was a captivating lecturer. Şeicaru claimed that it was Iorga's impressionist Romanticism that conquered audiences overflowing the lecture halls, sometimes sitting on the floor. Iorga participated in the events he recounted. He concentrated mightily, and lectured under great pressure, admonishing students for the slightest noises. Vet everyone complied and listened rapturously. He did not prepare his lectures, but scribbled only a few words on a piece of paper (sometimes on calling cards), and depended on his prodigious memory. His lectures were not easy to follow: Iorga piled fact on fact, often digressing to point out parallels with contemporary events. However, he never lost sight of his goal, and his lectures formed unities. Călinescu recalls the different tones Iorga used while lecturing: sometimes flattering, other times secretive (as if spies eavesdropped); he could become friendly, then bitter, and

---

[233]Şeicaru, *op. cit.*, pp. 72-75. Writing about his quite interesting book about the History of Eastern Slavs, he remarks ruefully: "I wonder whether one single soul has ever read it." *O viață de om*, vol. III, p. 7.

[234]*Op. cit.*, vol. II, p. 83.

[235]Tudor Vianu, *op. cit.*, vol. 2, pp. 147-148.

then suddenly change to a calm and matter-of-fact tone. His conclusions were memorable: "He seemed to be pronouncing Biblical sentences that transcended petty passions"; he "wound his lecture up as if enveloped in black smoke, like Moses who, after bringing the Ten Commandments down to a worthless people, smashes the tablets and pronounces thundering prophecies with righteous anger over the hall; and departed amidst the audience's thunderous applause."[236] Iorga constantly digressed from the historical topic to point out parallels with contemporary events and situations.[237] He often addressed the Romanian Academy, and even more often social gatherings. Even detractors conceded that "if he was not read, he was certainly listened to." Iorga drew a great deal from his oratorical talents. Tudor Vianu calls Iorga a "rhetorical talent *par excellence.*"[238] He made regular broadcasts during the 1930s as the European crisis deepened."[239]

Iorga's correspondence is immense, he wrote over 10,000 letters. Certainly Iorga was a workaholic.[240] Frasin Munteanu-Râmnic remembered a conversation between Iorga and Nicolae Titulescu. Titulescu, visiting Iorga, said: "Well, now I go to the 'Lido' and take two days of good rest. Tell me, *Domnu* Iorga,

---

[236]Şeicaru, *op. cit.*, pp. 17-19. Also, Călinescu, *op. cit.*, pp. 542-543. And Professor Eliza Campus, a former student of Iorga, to the writer.

[237]Professor Göllner recalls that Professor Iorga returned from Bucharest to his Summer University at Vălenii, directly from an audience in the Royal Palace. By that time Mme. Lupescu and Colonel Ernest Urdăreanu's influence in the Royal Palace was all-pervasive. Iorga seemed to be very upset. He set the scheduled lecture (about Romanian medieval history) aside, and, to the incomprehension of the students, in furious tones, he delivered a lecture on the court of Louis XV and Mme. Pompadour. Recalling that Mme. Pompadour said: "Aprés nous le déluge," and the deluge "accepted the invitation..." Such none too subtle parallels with contemporary events abound through Iorga's lectures and editorials.

[238]*Nicolae Iorga*, p. 85. Pompiliu Constantinescu was an articulate critic of Iorga. Tudor Vianu, *op. cit.*, p. 146.

[239]He delivered political commentaries *Sfaturi în întuneric*, ("Advices into the Darkness") weekly on *Radio Romania*. Mme. Lia Brătianu told Frasin Munteanu-Râmnic: Despite the Brătianu clan's hostility towards Iorga, Dinu or Gheorghe Brătianu sent the servants away to have absolute quiet. When the broadcast started they sat down, listening to even' word Iorga had to say.

[240]Şerban Cioculescu: "N. Iorga Corespondenţă," *Romania Literară*, 26 March 1987.

do you know the meaning of two days of rest, doing nothing?!" Iorga was intolerant of idleness and laziness. "God likes strange negative things like *not* working on Sundays, *not* eating on fasting days, *not* loving in life, like monks do, that is: *not* living." And: "An unused talent is a theft." Or: "Isn't it strange how people can think of death when there is so much to do during a lifetime?" Then: "Why rest before death if (eternal) rest waits for you after death?" Also: "Money is only worth something if it is earned by work; otherwise it is only dirty metal with a worn image on it."[241]

Not many people could accept Iorga for somebody larger than life. Enemies and detractors envied him; his temper and scathing style only encouraged inferiority complexes. Further, he said (perhaps not necessarily referring to himself), "A giant in the land of dwarfs is considered a public enemy."[242]

Some have maintained that Iorga did not write all his books himself. Surely he had research assistants and secretaries. Anyone of his stature would, but his highly individualistic style precludes that someone else could have penned some of the volumes bearing his name, even Romanians believed that others helped write his books, since a man with a large family "could not possibly have time to accomplish what he claims to have accomplished." Iorga ironically thanked his detractors for their delicate feelings concerning the troubles of the neglected Iorga family.[243] How did Iorga accomplish his life's work? What were his techniques and motivations? He once said, "Fame gets rusty if not polished by daily work."[244] Even Titu Maiorescu remarked: "Iorga resembles a spider, spinning his nets, constantly working on something." He had determination, discipline, vitality, and energy, and application that belied his impulsiveness. Iorga wrote: "In the face of death, one should have only one thought: work faster, because there's a deadline." And again: "Idleness is a render, soft suicide." And: "A learned man has two duties: to continue to learn constantly, and to teach others

---

[241]Iorga, *Cugetări*, pp. 17, 21, 50, 99, and 188.

[242]*Op. cit.*, p. 156.

[243]*O viață de om*, vol. II, pp. 42-43.

[244]*Cugetări*, p. 84.

constantly." Finally: "Laziness is the daughter of injustice."[245] We see something resembling the Puritan "work ethic" — coming from an Eastern Latin.

Yet, Iorga did not accomplish his work alone. We have mentioned the help he got from his family. His first wife helped him with research and his doctorate. If we agree with Dr. Samuel Johnson, that re-marriage is the triumph of hope over experience, then Iorga was lucky. His second wife, Mme. Catinca helped Iorga flourish throughout his life. A true companion, unselfish, self-effacing, she stood by tirelessly helping her husband. A newspaper featured her, entitled "Mr. Iorga's Secretary." It explained that Mme. Catinca was discussed more by Europeans than she was known in Romania. Those unappreciative of her should take note: in her modesty she was Professor Iorga's "perpetual secretary." First, she fulfilled her duty as mother of seven children and cared for Iorga's elderly mother, securing food, clothes, and watching the health of all, tending twelve pairs of shoes every morning. She did everything to accommodate "Nicu" when he returned from Bucharest to Vălenii after lectures, speeches, and conferences. She never tired. Mme. Catinca also proofread Iorga's works and helped in translating Hungarian and Italian. A true friend, sacrificing herself, she assisted Professor Iorga with his thousands of books. So Mme. Catinca received her distinct place among the women of Romania.[246] Without Mme. Catinca, Iorga could not have accomplished what he did. Indeed, he had his entire family working for him; his daughter remembered: "Father was very demanding."[247]

Any visitor who arrived to see Iorga usually found him reading in his study, surrounded by books piled on the floor up to the ceiling, and all the shelves overloaded (though Iorga knew his inventory well). Iorga would carefully mark the page, rise to greet the visitor. So jealous was he of his time, that with intimate acquaintances he permitted himself to continue reading (or taking notes) during

---

[245]*Op. cit.*, pp. 50, 73, 230 and 265.

[246]*Vremea Nouă*, (Craiova, 26 February 1923).

[247]Mme. Liliana Pippidi-Iorga to the writer. Iorga always referred to her as "*slăbiciunea slăbiciunilor mele*" (weakness of all of my weaknesses).

the conversation. With the visitor gone, he resumed his work. His reading techniques were phenomenal. In order to catch the leit motif he often read only every fourth page, sometimes not even bothering to cut the pages. He always took notes, whether aboard a train or in restaurants; he dictated to his secretary, or jotted notes onto napkins and menus.[248] Iorga more than once alighted from the train with a book outline or an article or two written during the journey. To record his flashes of ideas he used even' possible surface: bottle stickers, wrapping paper, cigarette packs, even his white cuffs. Iorga later turned these into books, articles, lectures, plays, reviews, etc.[249]

Șeicaru remembers that in 1919 the Armenian colony in Bucharest asked Iorga to write a history of the Armenian nation for presentation at the Peace Conference. He agreed, but pointed out that he would require a high fee. The Armenian delegation thought he was asking for an honorarium; he quickly explained that he would work gratis, but he needed an experienced shorthand secretary since he did not have the time to write it out by hand. Dictating a four hundred page history of the Armenian people three hours daily for three weeks, he astonished Armenian intellectuals. As late as 1954, Șeicaru encountered an Armenian student of history who spoke of that "miraculous book" Iorga, so nobly disinterested, had written.[250] Șeicaru recalled an example of Iorga, the historian, at work. Șeicaru made many excursions with Iorga. Once they passed a church built by the Argetoianu family. Iorga entered the church and went to work. He discovered an old Evangelium containing centuries-old notes a priest had written about a Turkish raid, copied the priest's remarks without taking his eves from the page of the Evangelium. Afterwards he found a candle and began looking for inscriptions, which he copied from walls and columns. Everything

---

[248]The volumes of Iorga's correspondence give a curious proof of the very different form and quality of the papers gathered through a lifetime.

[249]The family of Professor Iorga to the writer.

[250]Șeicaru, *op. cit.*, pp. 76-77. It appeared in French, under the title *Brève histoire de la Petite Arménie* (Paris, 1930).

was accomplished in a quarter of an hour. Şeicaru witnessed such scenes a dozen times more during their trips.[251]

Henri Stahl, former student and stenographer, remembered how he wrote a Romanian history for high schools. Iorga dictated the 350-page book in 28 hours (during four Sundays, afternoons between 2 and 5, and from 9 at night until 2 in the morning). While dictating, he walked around his desk, rarely interrupting his dictation; Stahl considered it, "a captivatingly interesting lecture." According to Stahl, had he not dictated his book, Iorga would have needed 150 hours to write.[252] His family helped with his correspondence with adherents to his party, political figures at home and abroad, scholars, and ordinary citizens who sought his help. Iorga left no piece of mail unanswered. A story still circulates in which he reads a book while pacing before three stenographers, stopping occasionally to dictate a book, a play, and an editorial simultaneously. The apocryphal incident captures the spirit of Stahl's story. Without the aid of tape recorders, word processors, computers, airplanes, or other "high-tech" help, Iorga depended on his work-ethic, brain and exceptional memory. One may wonder what he might have accomplished with the help of "high tech!" Commuting daily between Bucharest and Vălenii-de-Munte, almost always he emerged (on both ends of the line) with an article or with an outline. To give some feeling for Iorga's output, we might choose one of Iorga's average, years: in 1928 Iorga wrote 46 volumes, gave 370 lectures, participated in 64 conferences, visited 5 countries, and contributed to 11 periodicals.[253] It would be interesting but difficult to describe one day in Iorga's life. Few of his days passed without activity. He constantly traveled in and outside Romania (as far as America), attending political meetings and congresses, or lecturing at his schools in France, Venice, and Rome.

---

[251]*Ibid.*

[252]Theodorescu, *op. cit.*, p. 266.

[253]The Iorga family kindly gave this writer access to the family archives where he copied material concerning Iorga's activities during the year 1928.

Where did he get inspiration for such an effort? He did not work for the benefits he reaped; his motivation was his sense of duty to Romania. As Professor Mihai Berza remembered, Iorga reflected one day: "I did today my duty, nor did I bring harm to Romania either..."[254] What he meant was that he had served Romania well. Only through untiring work in realizing his ideals of cultural nationalism could Iorga feel he did justice to his ideals.

In his memoirs, Iorga says little about his wife, children, and other members of his family. He was the public figure of old Europe, whose public and private lives run parallel and do not meet. Only through reminiscence. of friends, relations, and contemporaries can a private portrait of Iorga be drawn.

Iorga's divorce from his first wife was his first great personal trial. After their romantic meeting, courtship, and nuptial journeys, difficulties arose. Iorga's father-in-law died in 1894, his moderating influence passing away with him. The Iorgas lived with their young children Petru and Florica (they also had two daughters, born 1895 and 1896, who died 1897 and 1899 respectively) in Bucharest. The source of trouble was Maria's acquaintance with a handsome officers, Strǎjescu. Strǎjescu began sending Maria Tasu-Iorga flowers and cards. Iorga discovered one of Strǎjescu's gifts and without accepting her explanations moved into another apartment, taking a modest lodging for himself. He sent his children to Mme. Zulnia in Botoşani, obstinately rejected all reconciliation, and initiated divorce proceedings, formalized in June 1900. Maria Tasu worked in the Ministry of Health as a modest functionary and Iorga maintained impersonal, but friendly relations with the mother of his children. Petru became an officer and died in 1965. Florica lived until 1956. The real reason for the marriage's failure was probably the pressures Iorga's lifestyle put on two extremely young people, who married more out of romanticism, walking on air and magic, than any assessment of their compatibility.

Iorga married a second time (on 4 February 1904), to Catinca Bogdan, the sister of his friend and colleague, Professor Ioan Bogdan, a Slavist of the University of Bucharest. The Bogdans were a typical Romanian intellectual family

---

[254]*O viaţă de om* (1972 edition). Professor V Râpeanu's introduction, p. xxxv.

from Transylvania. Iorga moved with his new wife into a modest apartment in Bucharest, remaining there until 1907, when he established himself at Vălenii-de-Munte. The second marriage was based on maturity: the couple did things together. Furthermore, it was founded on mutual compatibility and trust, which can develop only through long years. The couple had seven children: Mircea (1901-1966) became an engineer; Magdalena (1905-1994); Ştefan (1907-1976) was a physician; Adriana (1904-1912) died after a tragic illness; Liliana (1910-1985), Iorga's favorite, became the wife of the renowned Professor Dionisie Pippidi; Valentin (1912-1977) became an architect; and Alina (1914-1979).

The central feature of Iorga's personality was his "ego." Even his family agreed that his ego was immense, and many people spoke of Iorga's "exaggerated morality complex" or his "persecution complexes."[255]

His emphatic sense of moral rectitude was not a product of an impoverished and unhappy childhood (after all, one could have drawn different conclusions from the trials of poverty). It is perhaps unfortunate that few in public life seemed to have such a sense, when Romania needed more of it. One may understand his "persecution complexes" upon recognizing the number of Iorga's enemies — even paranoiacs have enemies. His talents and accomplishments made people envious, and his political, historical, and literary stances irritated others; when we add Iorga's temperament — which was not a conciliatory one — and the many conflicts in which he engaged, his awareness of others' animosity seems reasonable. His identification with Romania led him to react more sharply. In his eyes personal attacks against him were all too many times synonymous with an attack against his country. The conviction he was fighting for Romania no doubt caused him to lose perspective. Iorga never acted without the sense that he was carrying on a struggle for his country. He considered himself a discoverer of the means of Romania's salvation: his "cultural nationalism." He dedicated his life and sacrificed himself to define, assess, and explore its potentialities. If he was impatient with his follower's shortcomings, and dismissive of

---

[255] *Op. cit.*, p. vii.

distractions, it was because any let-up in his struggles might mean that his "cultural nationalism" might perish. The message of his life was that he maintained his position until the bitter end, and he paid the ultimate measure of devotion to it. Pioneers and crusaders are difficult companions. Iorga was no exception. He demanded from his less gifted and devoted followers the same he demanded from himself: principle and discipline, plus their loyalty and submission. Many people mocked Iorga's "Apostolmania" when he demanded acceptance of his leadership and suggested any dissent was treason. He was not modest and did not feel he had reason to be. Famous for his vanity, his flatterers had a field day; unfortunately. Iorga appreciated flatterers more than sincere friends who dared to contradict him: hence his conflicts with V. Pârvan, I. Chendi, Mircea Eliade, and even such admirers like Pamfil Şeicaru. Şeicaru once compared Iorga to "an immense oak in whose deep broad shadow nothing could grow."[256] Iorga resented those who felt that his pride was insufferable.[257] Of a suspicious and somewhat unstable nature, he was easily influenced; his quick changes in attitudes and the nefarious influences under which he fell meant that he was neither steadfast in his friendships nor unyielding in his hostilities. His troubles with his mentor Xenopol, and with his literary discovery, the writer Mihail Sadoveanu, illustrate this point. Iorga tried to justify this instability: "I cannot afford to worry long about personalities; the succession of events interests me much more, this being natural for a historian."[258]

His violent temper was an additional source of trouble. In politics, violent outbursts carry penalties as great as inconsistencies do. Iorga's political opponents criticized him for his romantic, violent temperament. The Populist leader G. Ibrăileanu said Iorga had "a woman's sensibility,"[259] and the literary critic H.

---

[256]Şeicaru, *op. cit.*, pp. 81-82.

[257]*O viaţă de om*, vol. II, p. 160. He was angry that "his inherited pride, to which he gave even more weight through erudition and his position as university professor" was considered "insufferable."

[258]*Op. cit.*, vol. III, p. 106.

[259]*Op. cit.*, vol. II, p. 150. *Nicolae Iorga*, p. 125. Sanielevici was no great fan of Iorga.

Sanielevici called him a "cultured woman with sensibility." Romanian Parliamentary diaries contain some memorably vulgar epithets. Iorga was known as a "bearded woman" or worse (A.C. Cuza talked about Iorga's "menopauses").

Iorga lived in relative isolation. Ironically, his worst enemies were his colleagues in literature and nationalist politics who trespassed on his cultural nationalist terrain. Iorga would never be reconciled with National Peasant leader Iuliu Maniu, or worse, Populist leader Constantin Stere. His hatred for Corneliu Zelea Codreanu, Captain of the Iron Guard, and for modernist writers like Tudor Arghezi was boundless. Nor could he forgive collaborators with the Germans during World War I like Alexandru Tzigara-Samurcaş, and others. Perhaps he was so easily influenced by some of his associates because of an almost childish idealism and naivete.[260] He certainly lacked realism for politics; his vanity, temper, and naivete almost guaranteed his political failures.

Besides his dedication to Romania, Iorga was devoted to his wife and family. Şeicaru remembers discussing his plays with him, and asked how he expected to write good plays having known only two women in his life? Iorga agreed, but confessed that he could not look at other women, for this would pain Mme. Catinca. Şeicaru also recounted the story of an actress's attempt to seduce Iorga. On the pretext of discussing a play, she invited him to dinner. She had everything prepared: dinner, drinks, an attractive gown; she opened the door... to find Iorga and his wife bidding her good evening. In yet another incident, he told Şeicaru his horror at discovering, — as he was helping a young lady down from a tree — that beneath her skirt she was naked.[261] According to Frasin Munteanu-Râmnic, Iorga once politely but firmly rejected a pass made by the wife of a Yugoslav diplomat. Iorga noticed the beauty of females, but only platonic relations with them interested him.[262]

---

[260]Iorga himself admitted so much: "They tell me that I was and I remained a child. Yes, I have a part in me of the soul of a child which allows himself to be guided by unseen powers towards the good!" Teodorescu, *op. cit.*, p. 359.

[261]Şeicaru, *op. cit.*, pp. 98-100.

[262]The incident occurred in the presence of Frasin Munteanu-Râmnic on the platform of the Ploieşti railroad station.

Iorga was austere and modest in his tastes and life-style, he could be foul-mouthed in the company of men, though (like a traditional Latin) he did not tolerate vulgarity in the presence of ladies.[263] He was always formal and stiff in public. He never appeared before visitors in pajamas. Since he did not have a normal childhood, perhaps the adult Iorga tried to recapture, in vain, a childhood he never really had. Mme. Zulnia was the head of the Iorga household. Everybody called her *Grand'maman*; Mme. Catinca resented her mother-in-law's attitudes slightly, although there was great love between them. Mme. Zulnia always addressed her letters: "Dear Catinca and Nicu."[264]

Of the children, the girls fared better than the boys. Mme. Zulnia always stressed her descent from the Draghici family, and wished her granddaughters to marry well. Mircea was vain, self-centered, with ambitions to take over Iorga's party and newspaper; he maintained relations with the Legionaries. Valentin lived an unambitious life. Ştefan wrote verses which were not appreciated by everybody.

Iorga's moral sensibility was uncommon in Bucharest. He often used his editorials to bring his countrymen to their senses. Even in private he spoke constantly of the corruption plaguing the country, with little effect. Iorga's behavior was always beyond reproach; he lived modestly, spartanly, and seemed impervious to luxury. But his political naivete undermined his moral crusading; Aristide Blank, King Carol II, and the assistants, all took advantage of it. Because Iorga was not interested in earning money unscrupulously, he had to conduct baccalaureate examinations past 1900; he would never give into unsavory schemes for the sake of money.[265]

Mme. Catinca handled family finances, for Iorga gave little thought to money: often he could not pay a restaurant tab because he had neglected to bring

---

[263]Professor Mihai Dragomirescu, a literary historian, used foul language in Iorga's presence before ladies. Iorga promptly hit him with an umbrella. Dragomirescu filed a complaint, but nothing came of it.

[264]BAR, *Corespondenţa lui N. Iorga,* vol. 41, Document 80. Several dozens of Mme. Zulnia's letters begin "Dragă Catinca and Nicu."

[265]*O viaţă de om,* vol. II, p. 83.

sufficient money for higher prices.[266] Only when buying books from antiquarians did he intend to get his money's worth. Iorga was very charitable. Mme. Catinca made hefty contributions to hospitals.

When Transylvania became Romanian, Mme. Catinca tried to use her husband's influence as the Speaker of the First National Assembly, to find jobs for her old Hungarian schoolmates seeking work as schoolteachers.[267]

Iorga was always at the disposal of common people, making special efforts to help veterans of the Great War. His manifold charities were carried out discreetly — rarely did they become public knowledge. He seldom accepted honoraria for his lectures; in driving with his chauffeur (sitting next to him) he always offered rides to peasants walking along the roads. When he was elected deputy in Iași in 1907, he donated 3,000 of his books to the city to found a public library.

He was approachable and gladly talked with his students. He held informal seminars in his home and students accompanied him on the streets. Despite this, Iorga remained distant and reserved. Amongst his thousands of associates, even close ones, only a very few used the familiar *tu* with him. Despite his readiness to associate with people, he preferred small groups, or solitude. He always felt isolated and misunderstood; as Șeicaru put it, Iorga remained a monk devoted to one cult: Romanian history.[268]

Writing in French, Iorga addressed an article appearing in *L'Indépendence Roumaine*[269] to Romania's elite (writing in French assured a restricted public), expecting — as always — leadership from them. He argued that only the elite's

---

[266]Mme. Liliana Pippidi-Iorga to the writer.

[267]BAR, *Corespondența lui N. Iorga*, vol. 35, Doc. 3. This letter thanks Mme. Catinca (in 1907) for the contribution of 2,000 Lei (a very considerable sum then) to the tuberculosis fund of the Colțea Hospital in Bucharest. Also, vol. 289, Doc. 558, expresses thanks (in Hungarian) to Mme. Catinca for having obtained a position for a Hungarian schoolteacher despite her inability to speak Romanian. The author of the letter greets her "Dragă Katicám!" (My dear Kathy!).

[268]Șeicaru, *op. cit.*, p. 109.

[269]*La vie intellectuelle des roumains en 1890* (Bucharest, 1899).

return to national ("healthy") culture can restore Romania's national health. Since Iorga was well-known, his article caused a stir, catapulting him onto the center stage of political and intellectual controversy. (Academicians reacted pettily, denying him premiums and creating difficulties for him as a corresponding member of their Academy).[270] And no wonder. Iorga attacked the alienation of the elite, their lack of interest in Romanian literature and culture, their cosmopolitanism, and pseudo-French culture. He had much to say about the corrupt state of Romanian intellectual life and its domination by the Liberal political establishment. Further, he deplored the quality of courses which were offered at the university; the low preparedness of faculty, the prevailing favoritism, and other shortcomings in academe (like thinly disguised power-struggles within the faculty). Iorga had aired many of these charges in an 1899 article entitled "Mutual Admiration Circles," written with devastating candor, without euphemisms, because "hypocrisy does no good and euphemisms do not conceal anything."

Counterattacks followed. Iorga responded with a series of articles, "Pernicious Opinions of a Bad Patriot."[271] It was typical of Iorga-journalistic "one-upsmanship." The battle was on. The metamorphosis, transforming a historian and literary critic into a fearless polemicist was accomplished. He continued teaching, gaining student support. Romania was a Third World country. There, universities were an important forum for political discussions. He also continued his researches abroad: in Holland and Galicia, where he visited the Czartoriski Archives. After the turn of the century, Iorga concentrated on "greater" Romania proper — in the sense of *Dacia Traiana*, travelling from one end of it to the other, investigating and copying church inscriptions and the holdings of monastic libraries. He confessed that he stole some documents he felt imperiled and deposited them in Bucharest Academy's archives.[272] Iorga visited Blaj, Transylvania's Uniate center of culture, religion, and national sentiment. Always a friend of the Transylvanian Uniate Church, Iorga appreciated what it had done

---

[270] *O viață de om*, vol. I, pp. 318-319.

[271] *Opinions pernicieuses d'un mauvais patriot* (Bucarest, 1900).

[272] *O viață de om*, vol. II. p. 42.

for the survival of the Romanian nation. But a Romanian Catholic world was strangely new for Iorga. "Here this trip was the revelation of a Romania whose existence until now was unknown to me." Iorga did find the leadership of the Blaj cultural center too old and moderate.[273] He aired his disdain for religion: "Innocențiu Clain was a bad priest, a bad monk, a bad convert, but exactly because of that he was a good Romanian." Or: "I did not come to Catholic Oradea, or to Catholic Blaj, but to Romanian Blaj and Oradea."[274]

Upon his return, Iorga published two books: *Legăturile Principatelor Române cu Ardealul* treated the historical relations of the Romanians on both sides of the Carpathian Mountains. *Sate și Preoți in Ardeal* describes village life and the miserable serfdom of the Transylvanian Romanians. As Iorga put it, "living on their knees," but under the leadership of their priests, who had helped preserve their national identity during the ages.[275] He returned to Transylvania often, publishing *Neamul Românesc în Ardeal și în Țara Ungurească* and *Scrisori și înscripții ardelene și maramureșene*.[276] Iorga was known to Romanians in Transylvania. A young peasant girl recognized him (as the author of a book on Transylvania she had read), and said: "If you are the author of this book, I kiss your soul." He drove with Mme. Catinca on horse-drawn carriages from holding to holding (also for reasons of economy).[277]

---

[273]*Op. cit.*, vol. II. pp. 17 and 37.

[274]Theodorescu, *op. cit.*, pp. 146 and 154.

[275]*Legăturile Principatelor Române cu Ardealul* (București, 1902) and *Sate și preoți din Ardeal* (București, 1902). In the latter volume, Iorga emphasized how the peasants, led by their priests, struggled to maintain Romanian nationality. His argument was strikingly similar to the ill-fated "Vive Quebec Libre!" speech of De Gaulle in French Canada. De Gaulle described the survival of Canadian French, led by their priests in their villages, helping them maintain their identity.

[276]*Neamul Românesc în Ardeal și Țara Ungurească* (București, 1906) and *Scrisori și înscripții ardelene și maramureșene* (București, 1906).

[277]*O viață de om*, vol. II, pp. 22 and 36-37, 47.

In 1901 he traveled to Budapest and addressed Transylvanian Romanians studying there: "You are in a struggle. Fight!"[278] He inspired the Romanian student body to publish the literary journal *Luceafărul*, in which young Octavian Goga made a name for himself. In 1903, after the overthrow of King Alexander Obrenovich, Iorga traveled to Belgrade, and although a steadfast friend of the Serbians he was shocked by the violence of the coup d'état.[279]

The year 1904 was important to Iorga the Moldavian. It marked the 400th anniversary of the death of Prince Stephen the Great. He traveled to Austrian-ruled Bucovina, and talked with Romanians high and low. The anniversary celebration was held at the Monastery of Putna, Stephen's burial place. Iorga succeeded in establishing firm ties with Romanian intellectuals in Bucovina. He wrote a book about his experiences, *Neamul Românesc în Bucovina*. In Romania, he published a book on Stephen the Great's rule that later also appeared in German.[280]

Iorga had deep feelings for Stephen the Great and the plight of Bucovina's peasants. These feelings provoked an almost religious vision. Good Friday and the night of Resurrection are more important in Orthodox countries than Christmas. Iorga attended Mass of the Resurrection next to Stephen the Great's grave. He heard Romanian peasants praying for "our Emperor Franz Joseph I," then suddenly "the song of Resurrection over death," and: "amidst the darkness, illuminated by nothing but the stars alone" and "for the worthy and the unworthy, for believers and for those without faith, suddenly he was (there) with us, Stephen, our Prince and rightful Emperor, not Franz Joseph I! Appearing amid shadows of the night, amid the sky's and the land's light; carrying the darkness away with wings, reaching to the mountains and across Romania's bleeding borders. Holy and Imperial for all those who speak Romanian! Songs resounded and bells tolled as he, Stephen the Great, carried word about the Resurrection of

---

[278]Theodorescu, *op. cit.*, p. 62 and *Scrisori către Nicolae Iorga*, vol. 2, p. 617.

[279]*O viață de om*, vol. II, pp. 55-57.

[280]*Neamul Românesc în Bucovina* (Bucureşti, 1905), *Istoria lui Ştefan cel Mare* (Bucureşti, 1904) and Kurze Geschichte *Stephan des Grossen* (Gotha, 1904).

the Almighty and that of Justice!" Iorga saw him return through the Church's locked door to rest, but was assured of Romania's future.[281] Such vision was the only religious experience Iorga could have; he used it to produce one of his better dramas, "The Resurrection of Stephen the Great."

In 1905 he traveled to the "Land of the Dead": Bessarabia. Russia was suffering from its defeat by the Japanese and internal disorders; Iorga wanted to visit the historical Moldavian fortresses in Tighina and in Hotin. The Russian bureaucracy kept him waiting, and the answer was "Nyet!" A gendarme escorted him to a train and forced him to leave. Seeing Romanian border guards was the happiest moment in his life.[282] In his *Neamul Românesc în Basarabia*, Iorga wrote devastatingly about the non-Romanian minorities of Bessarabia.[283]

Iorga undertook numerous journeys to Transylvania, and traveled in 1906 through Bulgaria to Constantinople, during the last years of Abdul Hamid's sinister rule.

From 1900 Iorga examined private collections of boyar families: the Ştirbey, Calimachi, Bibescu, Ghică, Carp, Cantacuzino, and the Brâncoveanu. Being a conservative, they readily gave him access. Using this material, he not only published many works but established important personal ties. Iorga had completed a body of work in all parts of *Dacia Traiana*, and touching upon all classes. He announced his future motto: "There is but one Romanian culture!"[284]

In February 1902, a conservative politician, Nicolae Filipescu, invited Iorga to write for *Epoca*, a conservative paper. Iorga's *Epoca* articles were collected to form *Cuvinte adevărate*.[285] Filipescu wished to renew the Conservative Party with new blood, just as in 1898 the Liberals renewed themselves with the influx of many socialists. Iorga had a special place in Filipescu's plan. Iorga had

---

[281] *Românismul în trecutul Bucovinei* (Vălenii de Munte, 1939), pp. 259-261.

[282] *O viață de om*, vol. II, pp. 66-68.

[283] *Neamul Românesc în Basarabia* (Bucureşti, 1905).

[284] *O luptă literară*, p. xii.

[285] *Cuvinte adevărate* (Bucureşti, 1904).

some conservative ideas, but he was essentially a nationalist; nevertheless, he kept close contact with conservatives, and in February 1906 he addressed the Conservative Party Congress in Bucharest. He called upon the boyars and the leaders of the party to resume natural relations with their traditional base, the peasantry, as their leaders. For only through such a collaboration could Romania solve its problems. No Liberal improvisations or urban dwellers could replace such a symbiosis.[286]

But Iorga's future in the Conservative Party was doomed. He clashed with party leaders like Take Ionescu and Titu Maiorescu. Maiorescu used some ideological rift within the conservatives to block Iorga's entry into the Junimea Society (as the Iorga family remembers), maybe out of pettiness or for political and ideological reasons. Yet, in much of Maiorescu's Junimist criticism Iorga concurred to the point that some considered him to be "a Maiorescu who descended from Olympus." Personal and ideological conflicts do not explain all. Undoubtedly, Iorga's individualism, his refusal to follow anyone's leadership, made adherence to a party difficult.

His extreme nationalism and his proposals to ameliorate conditions of the peasantry made him an antagonist to the conservatives. Iorga hated the Liberals, and he did not believe in class struggle. He explained that class struggle destroyed national unity, and so dismissed both socialists and populists. Iorga's rejection of their egalitarianism and his own anti-Semitism (at this time) made him an opponent of the socialists, who he believed offered no solution for Romania's peasants. For him, only nationalism offered a comprehensive solution for the problems of Romanian society. Iorga considered himself first of all a nationalist, secondly a democrat, and thirdly a champion of the peasantry — not even social justice was of higher value for him than the nation.[287] But his emphasis on social justice within a nationalist framework confused conservatives, even the great Bismarckian, Petre P. Carp. Iorga broke with the conservatives

---

[286] *O viață de om*, vol. II, p. 119.

[287] *Neamul Românesc*, 16 January 1915.

after the Conservative Party Congress in February 1906, realizing his nationalism was irreconcilable with the party platform. By then, he had developed a program based on his cultural nationalism, and literary-cultural struggles which would go under the name *Sămănătorism*. All this becoming *Luptă Literară*, the "literary struggle."

In 1903 Iorga became the leader of a literary movement named after the literary journal *Sămănătorul*. In 1933 he wrote: "In my articles (in *Sămănătorul*) I expressed the faith I shall maintain my whole life through." Like Kogălniceanu, he tried to harmonize tradition with evolution. *Sămănătorism* had an undeniable influence on Romanian literature. Eugen Lovinescu called it the "great cemetery of Romanian literature."[288] It did not hold sway for long, but for Iorga it provided lifelong critical standards.

It originated around the turn of the century. Spiru C. Haret (a mathematician), the Minister of Education, tied to the Liberal establishment, wished to educate the peasantry. He used Ministry of Education funds for a literary paper called *Albina (The Bee)* which addressed village teachers, who were to become the "apostles" of the new creed, ordering them to lift up the peasants. Haret's collaborators in *Albina* founded *Sămănătorul* on 2 December 1901. *Sămănătorul (The Sower)* was the name of a painting by Nicolae Grigorescu (who designed the journal's cover). Grigorescu had been inspired by the Transylvanian poet Alexandru Vlahuță, who hoped that the seeds sown by the sower would take root, blossom, and bear fruit.

Between 500 and 2000 copies of *Sămănătorul* appeared weekly. Until 1903 it followed a Haretist line; after Iorga joined the staff (at the invitation of Ilarie Chendi), he began to impose Eminescian nationalism and a combative spirit with his article "On the Occasion of the Disappearance of *Tribuna*.[289] Only in June 1905 did Iorga formally take over the journal. Even before, his influence was decisive. If not for him, *Sămănătorul* would have been just another *Albina*. After 1903, the journal did not receive state subsidies. Iorga moved editorial

---

[288]*O luptă literară*, p. xxviii.

[289]"Cu prilejul dispariției Tribunei," in *Sămănătorismul*, 4 May 1903.

offices to his home. He resigned the editorship in October 1906 because of financial difficulties. For the most part, Iorga's resignation was due to the conflicts which had arisen between him and members of the *Sămănătorul* staff. Dimitrie Anghel, a friend, claimed that it was impossible to collaborate with Iorga.[290] Even Iorga's protege, Mihail Sadoveanu, denounced his imperial attitudes, as did I. Scurtu.[291] After Iorga's departure, *Sămănătorul* was never the same. It lingered on (under Scurtu's leadership) until June 1910.

Let us consider Iorga's collaborators and the *Sămănătorul's* audience and goals. Almost all of the journal's collaborators were Transylvanian: George Coşbuc, Ion Gorun, Ilarie Chendi, Botiş-Ciolanu, Ştefan O. Iosif, Alexandru Vlahuţă (who withdrew in 1902), Sextil Puşcariu, Dimitrie Anghel, Zaharia Bârsan, Elena Farago, Ovid Densuşianu, and Ion Agărbiceanu. (The only significant non-Transylvanian was Sadoveanu, the Moldavian.) The predominance of Transylvanians should not surprise anyone, for they were the most stubbornly Romanian. It is difficult for a writer not to write on the national soil without addressing a receptive national public. Even in those areas of Transylvania where Romanians were a majority (and Transylvanian Romanians were often more cultured than Romanians of the Regat), writers and poets were hindered in their endeavors, and flocked to Bucharest. Goga said: "For us, the sun rises in Bucharest." *Sămănătorul* was directed at village teachers. Iorga would become the apostle of the new creed, which would emerge from the *fin-de-siècle* intellectual confusion. Intellectual alienation and the low prestige of Romanian literature disturbed young intellectuals. Romania's literary language was only recently reconstructed; this made the creation of important works difficult. Intellectuals were impatient. The cry "We need a Romanian novel!" was heard. Iorga felt that the new literature had to depict the organic harmony of village life and avoid topics from "odious" twentieth century cities: industrial slums, their "pestilential breath"; and "vulgarity of slum dwellers" with their "horrible accents" could not inspire such a novel. He thought literature should not focus on "the

---

[290]Theodorescu, *op.cit.*, p. 169.

[291]*O viaţă de om*, vol. II, pp. 146-147.

struggles or pleasures of pathetic, unfortunate human beings" or "miserable, weak, and mutilated souls." Because of his "nationalist realism," Iorga condemned all realist literature.

Vlahuță described *Sămănătorul's* goals: he claimed the journal's writers felt they had lost too much time in their absorption with their own bitterness and petty pains. They had become "estranged from the great current of life lived by the people; the people's great sufferings and aspirations that should have filled and warmed our hearts from the very start."[292] In another editorial, Vlahuță wrote: "It is about time our writers, and especially them, turned their minds and loving hearts towards other people." Noble actions on the part of priests, teachers, or landlords could show the way to the peasants. "Books to and for the people; a great soul searches for life. Hidden geniuses await awakening, like a spring which demands light. From this spring hidden geniuses will sprout forth as though struck by the stick of Moses. There is our strength and future."[293]

The program must be understood as a social propagandistic appeal to bring culture to the peasantry. Little consideration was given to aesthetics, expressing patriotic pride, exalting the past and love of the peasantry. It would affirm a national ideal, offering cultural and social criticism.

Iorga envisioned a social goal: emergence of the "*Sămănătorist* Village" and a "*Sămănătorist* Man." This vision coincided with the popularity of *haiduci* as espoused in the poetry of Coşbuc, and as described by *Bucura Dumbravă*. The *haiduci* village — like the *Sămănătorist* Village — represented tradition and organic development. Priest, teacher, and boyar were integrated in this world; foreign infiltrators, the *ciocoi*, Jews, and Greeks lived by greed; the "*Sămănătorist* Man" was contrasted with inhabitants of big cities and industrial suburbs. In the *Sămănătorist* village there was organic harmony, as envisaged by Eminescu. Iorga wished to realize this ideal.

---

[292]*Sămănătorul*, 1 December 1901.

[293]*Sămănătorul*, 9 December 1901.

Thus, he imposed an Eminescian line on *Sămănătorism*. While Eminescu believed in the same political ideals as Iorga, he never confused the aesthetic with the ethical — let alone with the ethnic! Eminescu was a great poet — while Iorga proclaimed that "literature was not a coffeehouse where everybody who can pay can come in." It was to have a social function.

Starting with *Sămănătorul*, Iorga would accord a literary work value to the extent it served his cultural nationalism. Only social and moral criteria, much less aesthetic ones, were appropriate to judging a work of art. For him, the nation, "the most natural of all human societies," rested on the peasant: "the defender and worker of the Romanian land," a task he fulfilled under all temporary foreign rule or unjust exploitation. He was "the most honorable and moral and the most hardworking of all inhabitants of this country, and he has always been." Peasants remained honest, in contrast to the deceitful boyars, who were steeped in luxury, and obscene games, orgies with Gypsies, and with the *ciocoi*. Peasant life was 'the eternal divine spectacle of rosy sunrises, red sunsets, quiet summer noons, mysterious evenings and clear winter nights, the frozen earth and the sky with diamond-like stars." "Peasants live such poetic lives, and will continue to lead such lives, remaining magnificent and clean 'savages' in this country of ours."[294] Iorga elaborated such harmony and contrasted it with the standard topics of *fin de siècle* literary alienation. Eminescu began but did not finish a novel, *Barren Genius*, dealing with the alienated man from the village, uprooted from his traditions in the big city.

Iorga pointed out that society was essentially spiritual, and required harmony in thought and feeling. Romania sorely lacked the moral climate that the elevation of the peasantry could provide. Romanians had to become the masters of their commerce and industry.[295]

With hindsight, we can say that the *Sămănătorist* village was no solution to Romania's problems, or to the peasant problem. But Iorga believed in the force of his cultural nationalism, and the cultural revolution it would unleash. If

---

[294]Theodorescu, *op. cit.*, pp. 146-147.

[295]"Şcoala lui Ştefan cel Mare," *Sămănătorul*, 25 April 1904.

only Romania could face the fact that the peasantry was its sole hope, it could join humanity as a nation renewed.[296] Hence literature, the most important cultural expression, must be for the entire people; and it must be a national literature. Iorga demanded "healthy currents," and abandonment of decadent foreign models so popular in some circles.[297] Only Romania's past could provide the organic model for the development of a healthy literature. He was not opposed to cultural interchange; but he decried the slavish adherence to foreign models, to the exclusion of the indigenous product. Cultural interchange must not disrupt.[298] During these years, he even proposed heavy taxes for imported foreign books, newspapers, even foreign education.[299] He exhorted the elite and teachers to turn to Romanian cultural nationalism, creating an aristocracy of merit and eliminating the "aristocracy of calculations."[300] His nationalism, temper, and vanity led him to adopt distortions, promoting works of non-entities because they were compatible with his cultural nationalism. Iorga's ideas on literature are the least valuable of his contributions. But he would steadfastly adhere to these principles, and struggle, as Don Quixote with the windmills, for the rest of his life. He liked to repeat the words of Cambronne: "The guard is ready to die, but the guard does not surrender!"

In the fall of 1940 his world was crumbling around him: the Swastika was floating down the Eiffel tower, France had collapsed; red flags were fluttering over Chișinău and Cernăuți; half of Transylvania was lost, Bulgarians marched into Dobrogea and the Legionaries were in power. Iorga had to cease the publication of his *Neamul Românesc*. He said farewell to his readers with the words: "When there is a defeat, the flag is not surrendered; it is used to dress the

---

[296]*O viață de om*, vol. II, p. 7.

[297]*O luptă literară*, p. vi.

[298]"Boierimea Franceza din Romania," *Sămănătorul*, 22 February 1904.

[299]*Ibid*. Cf. Professor Oldson's remarks about Iorga's lack of equity, (Iorga who benefited from foreign education) in wanting to impose taxes on foreign books and newspapers, Oldson, *Iorga*, 1973, p. 96. One must observe that Western equity applies only to equitable situations.

[300]Theodorescu, *op. cit.*, p. 154.

wounded heart." And his closing words were: "In the heart of our struggle stood the idea of national culture! The founder and publisher of *Neamul Românesc*: Nicolae Iorga."[301]

In view of all this, the events of 13 March 1906 were inevitable. Iorga entitled his chronicle: *Struggle for the Romanian Language*.[302] By 1906, he condemned the staging of plays in French on the Romanian stage several times and fulminated against the frivolous Madame Flirt.[303] He opposed frivolity as much as the adoption of French culture instead of Romanian. In the beginning of March, the Obolul (a charity to which all high-ranking *protipendata* boyars belonged) announced the staging of a play in French at Bucharest's National Theater. Boyar amateurs would perform, and the proceeds would go to charity. Iorga recognized the elite's contempt for Romanian language, literature, and the peasantry. The French language maintained barriers between the ruling classes and the rest. Indeed, Iorga considered the staging of a play in French at the National Theater an obvious show of contempt for his *Sămănătorist* movement. A few days before, he had published an article in *Epoca* entitled, "A Request," which had the sound of a command, calling the staging of a play in French on the National Theater stage "an act of spiritual treason against the Fatherland and the nation."[304] On the 13th (performance day), Iorga addressed students. After that, he went home. The students, however, gathered before the National Theater and attempted to halt the performance. The play in French was only a pretext for the student demonstration against the elite and prevailing social injustice. Students

---

[301]*Neamul Românesc*, 11 October 1940.

[302]*Lupta pentru limba românească* (Bucureşti, 1906).

[303]Iorga's article "Boierimea Franceză din România," in *Sămănătorul*, pointed out the importance of the vernacular, that even children mock Jews for not speaking Romanian correctly, adding that the Boyarime speak an even more offensive Romanian because they communicate with each other only in French. Romanians cling strongly to their language. Iorga pointed out to Mussolini that even medieval Italian travelers noted the tenacity with which Romanians clung to the language. *Nicholas Iorga, Former Prime Minister of Romania to His Excellency Benito Mussolini, Head of the Italian Government* (Bucharest, 1937).

[304]"O rugăminte," *Epoca*, 12 March 1906.

had started the demonstration as shock troops, and later the mob joined the fracas. Crown Prince Ferdinand and the elite understood the real reason for the demonstration. As the scene got uglier, Crown Prince Ferdinand and Princess Marie came to see some of their friends, who belonged to their circle at Cotroceni Palace, perform. They called the army out. King Carol was abroad. A violent clash ensued and many were wounded. The situation inspired nearly revolutionary fervor during the evening. Had Iorga arrived, he might have led a coup; the crowd was waiting for him. But they waited for him in vain; far from entertaining revolutionary thoughts, Iorga sat in his apartment frightened by what had developed under his influence. As his family remembered, he feared being called to account. He was eventually called to the police station two days after. He arrived in the carriage of Alexandru Calimachi. Although Iorga knew that police officials would be impressed with this university professor escorted by a nobleman, he nevertheless brought with him some reading in Byzantine history in case he was arrested.[305]

He received a great deal of correspondence about the riot. Bucharest high society was outraged. A great lady, a kind of "Dowager Duchess," knew no end to her outrage, reminding Iorga that even though Frederick the Great staged French plays, Goethe and Schiller were born and nourished during his reign. She held Iorga responsible, saying: "You are the apostle for the majority of students and they follow you blindly." She felt: "My only crime is having been raised with French culture." Alexandru Marghiloman sent a cautious letter of disapproval.[306] Predictably, the student body acclaimed the events. Their notes and letters overwhelmed about 20 to 1 those from the nobility They sent poems entitled "The Romanian Language." Donations arrived. Goga sent a letter for Romanian students in Budapest in the name of *Luceafărul;* the Transylvanians were enthusiastic and addressed Iorga as *Apostol* and *Magnificenţie.*[307] The

---

[305]*O viaţă de om,* vol. II, p. 132.

[306]BAR, *Corespondenţa lui N. Iorga,* vol. 32 (1906), document 59, 63.

[307]Volumes 37, 38, 39, 40 and 41 of Iorga's correspondence from 1906 include dozens of letters expressing enthusiastic praise and approval of his action before the National Theater.

French were sympathetic; the French press understood that Iorga was neither anti-French, nor a rabble-rouser. As he explained, "French culture is too great and proud to be subjected to such superficial aping."[308] Iorga published translations from "healthy currents" of foreign literature (even of Emerson), in his *Floarea Darurilor.*

What resulted from the furor? As Professor Eugen Weber said: *Parturiunt montes, nascetur ridiculus mus.*[309] Later events seemed anticlimactic; but Iorga could not offer what he did not have. He believed in organic progress and based his criticism on his cultural nationalism. As he pointed out, "There are some who regret revolutions, but welcome good results; there are others that welcome revolution regardless of its results."[310] Shortly after, he left Bucharest with Sadoveanu, E. Gârleanu, and Iosif to carry the "new faith" to the countryside. In Iaşi, Liberals and Junimists united in their opposition to the government and demonstrated in the streets. As a result, *Frăţia Bunilor Romani* (The Brotherhood of Good Romanians), in Bălcescu's tradition, was formed "to give a voice to those Romanians without voice or rights: the peasants."[311] Iorga pointed out that the Brotherhood was formed "in defense of Romanian language and literature, and the lofty interest of the Romanian people, which should be considered one spiritual being."[312]

During the meetings in Iaşi, Iorga conceived the idea of a newspaper that would become the mouthpiece of the new spirit. Shortly afterwards *Neamul Românesc* would appear. The aristocracy in part financed the paper: Nicolae Filipescu, Gheorghe and Barbu Ştirbey, and other scions of historical families

---

[308] *Le Temps,* (Paris, 15 April 1906), and *O viaţă de om* vol. II, p. 130.

[309] *The European Right: An Historical Profile,* H. Roger and E. Weber, Editors, Berkeley/Los Angeles 1965, p. 511.

[310] *Americani şi Romani din America* (Vălenii-de-Munte, 1930) p. 214.

[311] *O viaţă de om,* vol. II, pp. 134-135.

[312] Theodorescu, *op. cit.,* p. 175.

made contributions. Iorga referred to the Ştirbeys as "resolute friends of the peasants."[313]

More likely, *Politicianism* was at work: the establishment intended to manipulate Iorga, whose naivete, anti-revolutionary cultural nationalism, and popularity with students could serve their interests. Later, Iorga would many times be the victim of such co-option.

Neamul Românesc first appeared on 10 May 1906, a royal and national holiday, during the fortieth jubilee year of King Carol I's reign. Iorga dedicated the first number to King Carol I.[314]

A.C. Cuza and other like-minded nationalists were part of his staff. Iorga left *Sămănătorul* the following October, having his own paper now. He planned other organs for his cultural nationalism: arriving at conclusions from past experiences Iorga started his pattern of "One-Man-Shows." He would always be in such a commanding position, that there would be little question of collaboration — much less of opposition to his views. He founded *Floarea Darurilor* ("Flower of Gifts") in January 1907, as a *Sămănătorist* branch of *Neamul Românesc*: in December 1908 started a literary supplement, *Neamul Românesc Literar*; and, in January 1910, he published a popular edition of his paper, *Neamul Românesc pentru Popor*. Iorga had a decisive role in *Făt Frumos* (Prince Charming) (from 1904-1906, and again in 1909) with H. Gârleanu, and others. Finally, in Craiova, with the help of C. Saban Făgăţel, and D. Tomescu, he transformed his *Drum Drept into Ramuri* ("Branches"), a *Sămănătorist* literary paper. These periodicals had various fortunes, appearing weekly, bi-weekly, monthly, and then after a few years ceasing publication. All propounded the *Sămănătorist* creed.

During the fortieth anniversary celebrations of Carol I's reign in 1906, Bucharest glittered before the many Romanian and foreign guests, among whom

---

[313]*O viaţă de om*, vol. II, p. 33.

[314]*Neamul Românesc*, 10 May 1906.

was Karl Lueger, the anti-Semitic and anti-Hungarian mayor of Vienna.[315] Transylvanian and Bucovinian Romanians also flocked to Bucharest. What was behind this facade became clear with the Peasant Revolt of February 1907.

Romanian peasants continued to suffer, despite the protests of intellectuals and decent Romanians. Beyond economic exploitation they were subjected to daily humiliations. Iorga had intimate knowledge of the abuses. His trips and correspondence kept him informed. A few months before the revolt, he wrote a shattering article: "Keep The Peasant Out Of Sight, Hide Him!"[316] Some of his correspondents witnessed police on trains forcing peasants to give the seats (scats they had paid for) to people of higher classes.[317] Correspondents had also informed Iorga of Mochi Fischer's abuses on the lands he tenured, long before the revolt which would erupt on these lands.[318] The peasant-rising broke out in Flămânzi, in northern Moldavia, whose name means "starving people," on lands that Mochi Fischer's banking trust controlled. Mochi Fischer financed land tenure in northern Moldavia using capital from Galician banks. Travelling in a rented railroad car, from which he did not find it necessary to descend, he decided the fate of tens of thousands of people.[319] He found it expedient to hike the land tenure fourfold. Other land tenants followed suit.[320] This was the beginning of capitalism's less attractive face. Max Weber would have said that Mochi Fischer had rationalized land tenure. Iorga does not seem to have had any contact with Weber (he failed to appreciate sociology), and his understanding of Fischer was contained in the comment that he "was no improvement over the

---

[315]Iorga greeted the Mayor of Vienna, the enemy of "Judeo-Magyars."

[316]*Neamul Românesc*, 1 October 1906.

[317]BAR, *Corespondenţa lui N. Iorga*, volume 44 (1906), Document 41.

[318]*Ibid.*, volume 43, Document 55. A letter, dated 3 August 1906, reported to Iorga the manifold abuses of Mochi Fischer. The same year, Iorga wrote a symbolic book about the defender (in the Haiduc spirit) of poor peasants: *Un Apărător al Săracilor — Domnul Tudor din Vladimir*, ("The Defender of the Poor: Lord Tudor of Vladimir") (Bucureşti, 1906).

[319]*O viaţă de om*, vol. II, p. 156-157.

[320]*New York Herald*, 24 March 1907.

tricksters and the hucksters I remember from my childhood."[321] Thus he shows his lack of understanding of twentieth century economics; how Fischer's doings were transforming the traditional society into a modern one, even with quite objectionable methods. In Romania the transformation was no uglier than it was in England a century before, when large amounts of land were enclosed, English yeomanry destroyed, and thefts to appease hunger were punished with deportation to Australia. In France, when workers were massacred in Lyon in 1831, Prime Minister Casimir Périer proposed an epitaph for them: "The workers have to get one thing through their head; their only remedies are patience and resignation."[322] When reminded that some of his actions countered public interest, W.H. Vanderbilt answered: "The public be damned!"

Mochi Fischer was no worse. Wherever Western nations introduced industry and capitalism — in China, in India, in Dutch East India — grave injustices were inflicted. Iorga himself wrote that "capitalist industrial societies contain gigantic injustices."[323] All Western industrialization was pallid compared to the horrors accompanying Stalin's forced industrialization of Russia, for which the peasantry paid such a horrible price. Yet, that painful process could not be identified with one unassimilated and, under the circumstances, inassimilable minority.

Starting in northern Moldavia the Peasant Revolt quickly spread to Wallachia and Oltenia where the land-tenure abuses were perpetrated by Greeks, not "hateful" Jews. Iorga wrote an editorial: "God Forgives," claiming that God forgives the Army for shooting peasants in his native Botoșani, but not those who caused them to revolt.[324] The worst anti-Semitic excesses were caused by Lipoveni; they massacred and levelled blood libel charges against Jews, and

---

[321] *O viață de om*, vol. II, p. 157.

[322] Gordon Wright, *France in Modern Times* (London and Chicago, 1966), p.218.

[323] *Neamul Românesc*, 6 January 1908.

[324] *Neamul Românesc*, 8 March 1907. Iorga organized campaigns to collect money and other donations for the victims of the peasant rising *Neamul Românesc*, 5 April 1907.

faithfully emulated the example set by their country of origin.[325] *Neamul Românesc* chronicled the horrors, taking a squarely pro-peasant stand. Jews left in droves. Iorga angrily reported that the boyars asked for Austro-Hungarian intervention to restore order.[326] But Romania's General Averescu quickly restored order by killing about ten thousand peasants. Repression defied description; the army opened artillery fire indiscriminately on rebellious villages.

Iorga's editorializing soon made police protection necessary. In *Czernovitzer Tageblatt*, Take Ionescu designated "Cuza's anti-Semitic agitation" and "Iorga's anarchist instigations" chiefly responsible for the peasant uprising.[327] Iorga responded by coining the name "Tachi-Mochi." He received many letters of support, but voluminous was his hate mail. He appealed to the Minister of Education to stop attacks against him; the Minister preferred "not to become embroiled with the press." Cuza begged Iorga from Iași: "to take good care of yourself."[328] The American, English, Trench, German, and Austrian presses (in far-fetched ways) credited Iorga and Cuza with instigating the revolt.[329] The hate mail Iorga received was remarkable for its quantity and quality. A landlord called him an "infamous hound," swearing vengeance over the dead bodies of

---

[325] According to the *Frankfurter Zeitung* and almost unanimous reports in the foreign press, the Lipoveni distinguished themselves once again in anti-Jewish violence, especially in Târgu Frumos. *Frankfurter Zeitung*, 24 March 1907.

[326] *O viață de om*, vol. II, p. 158.

[327] *Czernovitzer Tageblatt*, 10 April 1907. Also, BAR, *Corespondența lui N. Iorga* (1907), volume 68, Document 21. A young school-teacher in Topoloveni-Muscel would become Iorga's student in his Summer University in Vălenii (in 1912) the future peasant leader Ion Mihalache sent a very different explanation to Iorga entitled: "Invățător-Instigator." Mihalache's analyses do not contain any anti-Semitism; he sees the prevailing exploitation, ignorance, and lack of education. Much of the insufferable abuses of the peasantry are exposed. Mihalache rejects the charges of "anarchy." "If schoolteachers, people with conscience and education expose evils, they are considered "instigators" instigating a revolt. But history will establish who the real instigators were." vol. 67 (1907), Doc. 13.

[328] The Minister of Education's answer is dated 26 March, 1907. BAR, *Corespondența lui N. Iorga* (1907), Vol. 63, Document 42. Professor Cuza's warning letter ("Be careful, don't go out alone") to Iorga, dared on March 17, 1907, derails the "Terror of Politicianism." In BAR, *Corespondența lui N. Iorga* (1907), see vol. 64-69.

[329] BAR, *Corespondența lui N. Iorga* (1907), see vol. 64-69.

his family; in another letter, one of Iorga's articles arrived, covered, penned by an elegant hand, and as a contrast, by a virtuoso collection of obscenities which are hard to read without turning red, and also threats;[330] notice came that forty landlords had collected a 10,000 lei reward for Iorga's head. His university lectures were suspended, and he spent his time at home guarded by student volunteers and police.[331] New elections were held, with prisons full and bodies floating down the Danube; on 21 May 1907, Iorga was elected deputy by the "Electoral College" in Iaşi.[332] Cuza failed in his bid in Iaşi, but Iorga as always demanded assimilation from the Jews.[333] He entered Parliament with a show of the temper he would brandish as a member of that body for 30 years; attacked both political parties, preached cultural nationalism and defended the peasantry. He still hoped to establish a peasant-boyar collaboration within the framework of a *Sămănătorist* village. During the Socialist Congress in Iaşi, he called Marxism: "What will not be."[334]

---

[330]BAR, *Corespondenţa lui N. Iorga* (1907), vol. 65, Doc. 115, and vol. 68, Doc. 89.

[331]*Scrisori către N. Iorga*, p. 623.

[332]*O viaţă de om*, vol. II, p. 159.

[333]*Neamul Românesc*, 25 November 1907; Wrote Iorga about Zionism: "One cannot welcome (in Romania) anybody, except (those) who wish to become Romanian sincerely!"

[334]Wrote Iorga about the International Socialist Conference in Bucharest, calling socialism "the dream which cannot be," attacking the participants. His special targets were Christian Rakovski, and the Bucovinan Pole Grigorowitz, and Auerbach, a Saxon calling them contemptuously; "erring louts who went astray" (i.e., from their own nations); he poked fun at Gelehrter and Păcurariu: "They are trying to speak Romanian." Iorga concluded: "All honest youth understands, that constructive solution can come only if every nation cleans his own holy national premises resolutely." *Neamul Românesc*, 20 August 1906. Two years later, Iorga commented on Romanian participation at a Hungarian Socialist gathering: "Time passed long ago over the abstract, metaphysical economic ideals of Karl Marx." Yet he made it clear that one cannot forbid the workers to have their own trade union organizations, because capitalist societies have gigantic injustices. According to Iorga, the solution does not lie in outmoded metaphysical internationalism, but in recognition of the needs of the organic entity, the nation. Only in the framework of it can people live, develop, progress, and solve problems. *Neamul Românesc*, 6 January 1908.

By the spring of 1907 Iorga grew restless in Bucharest; the hate campaign made his stay uncomfortable, his residence placed a strain on his resources. Fortunately, Iorga and his brother-in-law visited friends in Vălenii-de-Munte, sitting at the foothills of the Carpathians. There was no railway to Vălenii yet at that time, and they reached it by carriage whose bells "scared wolves and warned thieves"; Iorga was enthusiastic: the village was unspoiled and situated near monasteries with "inscriptions yet to be deciphered." Vălenii was blessed with a *Sămănătorist* atmosphere. "There was peace and good Romanian understanding, a harmony of old days, undisturbed by the foreign elements that destroyed it elsewhere." Iorga found Vălenii's only Jew, the smith Moses, to be a very sympathetic fellow, who mixed well with Romanians. He found a shelter here and always referred to it so. It became the center for his activities for the rest of his life. He sought Vălenii's *Sămănătorist* atmosphere, fleeing Bucharest to return to Mother Earth, whose touch was life to him. Here he could live among his books, for, without books, "such a retreat in the countryside would be suicide."[335] But Iorga could not afford to buy a home. Fortunately, Spiru Haret commissioned him to write a history of the Church in Romania. Not particularly interested in the subject, the money spurred him on.[336] Public subscription and the assistance of friends helped make up the difference, and Iorga established a press at Vălenii. His followers became stockholders. *Neamul Românesc*'s original backers financed machinery and construction costs, and villagers supplied enthusiastic labor. Everyone involved participated in the inauguration in the spring of 1908.[337] That summer, Iorga would open his Summer University. But before discussing Iorga's Summer University, let us examine Austria-Hungary's progressive deterioration.

Magyarization pressures in Transylvania (and elsewhere) reached their peak during this decade, directed not only against Romanians but against other

---

[335]*O viață de om*, vol. II, pp. 72-75

[336]*Istoria bisericii Românești*, in two volumes (Vălenii-de-Munte, vol. 1, 1908 and vol. 2, 1909).

[337]*O viață de om*, vol. II, pp. 72-77.

nationalities. Count Albert Apponyi, Hungarian Minister of Education, instituted the "Apponyi Laws," undoing Francis Deàk and Josef Eötvös's far-sighted educational policies. His measures meant the Magyarization of grade school education. When the seat of the Uniate Church was removed from Blaj to Hajdùorog, a purely Hungarian region, Iorga spoke about the "absurdity of the Hungarian ideal of an exclusively Hungarian state, which now these feudal Lords, megalomaniac lawyers, and Jews try to establish by moving against the last redoubt of Romanian nationalism, the Romanian Uniate Church." The Vatican bowed to pressure, appointing a Hungarian bishop at Hajdùorog. Iorga considered this forced denationalization. The Romanian Uniate hierarchy was not consulted; Romanian students from the Theological Seminary in Oradea were expelled for speaking Romanian, Blaj had to be called "Balàzsfalva." Iorga said that though he admired the Hungarians, he would not be surprised if a revolution broke out.[338] The measures affected 73,225 Romanians: 20,000 demonstrated against it in Alba Iulia in 1912.[339] Iorga protested against the census of 1910, and electoral abuses. The number of Hungarian inhabitants of historic Hungary had increased since the previous census in 1900 from 8,742,000 to 10,050,000; Iorga called this "a true blessing from heaven."[340]

Austria governed its part of the Dual Monarchy more tolerantly than Hungary, but Austrians were not patient with the Romanians of Bucovina. The anational Hapsburgs had managed to overwhelm the autochthonous Romanian population with Ukrainians, Jews, Germans, even Poles, and the Austrians acted harshly against manifestations of Romanian nationalism. Iorga considered Bu-

---

[338]*L'évéché de Hajdú-Dorogh et les droits de l'Eglise roumaine unie en Hongrie* (Bucarest, 1913), passim.

[339]V. Neta and C. Gh. Marinescu, *Liga culturală şi unirea Transilvaniei cu Romania* (Iaşi, 1978), p. 244.

[340]*Les dernières élections en Hongrie et les Roumains* (Vălenii-de-Munte, 1910). The violence dining Hungary's 1910 elections caused negative Western reaction. Clemenceau condemned the "free Hungarian nation" for repressing their nationalities. Garibaldi's own son (despite his father's admiration for Hungary) condemned the Hungarians for oppressing the "Latin Romanians."

covina a part of Moldavia. When he visited the University of Cernăuți, the Rector Adler, a Jew, received him with "perfect Viennese hypocrisy." When he attempted to return in 1909, the Austrian authorities (under partial influence of Mochi Fischer) expelled Iorga without ceremony.[341]

By now, the majority of Romanian politicians decided to seek revision in Transylvania and Bucovina, excepting Bessarabia, where revision was impractical. When the anti-Hungarian Archduke Franz Ferdinand visited Romania, Dr. Aurel Popovici, a reactionary Romanian nationalist was rapturous. He had sought an Austro-German solution to Romania's problems, by the establishment of a united Austro-Romanian monarchy, after Franz Ferdinand's ascension to the Austrian throne "with or without the (Romanian) king."[342] Iorga was repelled by Popovici's ideas, for he could not accept an Austrian solution, much less a German one.[343] No longer was Iorga prepared to recognize any compromise. Like every Southeast European nationalist he was determined to redraw the map. He wrote: "We shall go forward straight towards national unity."[344] Nor was Iorga impressed by the democratic-minded Hungarian intellectual Dr. Oszkàr Jàszi, who proposed a conciliatory policy towards the nationalities, not forced Magyarization. When in 1913 the Hungarian Socialist Party proposed measures to stop Magyarization, Iorga responded: "One can reconcile oneself with death but once — while dying."[345] He felt no personal animosity towards Hungarians. When the Hungarians brought the body of the national hero, Fran-

---

[341]*O viață de om*, vol. II, pp. 172-175.

[342]*Op. cit.*, vol. 13, p. 144. See also: Count Ottokar Czernin, *Im Weltkriege* (Wien-Berlin, 1919), p. 64.

[343]In his *Oameni care au fost*, volume II (București, 1935), Iorga inveighs against Dr. Aurel Popovici's "Grossösterreich" solution, and ridicules Popovici's racist ideas. Iorga found especially obnoxious Chamberlain's claim that "everything good in mankind must be of German origin," pp. 264-267.

[344]*O viață de om*, vol. II, p. 175.

[345]For Iorga, socialists were not much better in Hungary than nationalists were. He considered Dr. Oszkàr Jàszi a "white Raven." *Neamul Românesc*, 10 October 1913.

cisc Ràkòczi, home from Turkey, Iorga remarked: "The Hungarians did not forget him under Austrian rule or now. These bold and unflinching people recognized a chivalrous fighter, who did not surrender his rights or bow before anyone.... Today we Romanians bow our heads before Ràkòczi's coffin; tomorrow we can speak again of *Us* and *Them*."[346]

And when Count Bellegarde, Governor of Bucovina who signed the order of Iorga's expulsion, died in battle during the First World War, Iorga remembered his kindness to the abject Romanian peasants. Iorga imagined (with his evocative powers) that maybe Bellegarde met death next to some of Bucovina's Romanian peasants, drafted into the Austro-Hungarian Army against their will.[347] It was unfortunate that he could not transcend his nationalism and see Bellegarde's humanism motivating his kindness; Bellegarde promoted the anti-national "Austrian Mission," he also executed his Christian duty as other Hapsburg bureaucrats often did.

Practicable or not, Iorga the Moldavian never gave up Bessarabia. He corresponded with Bessarabian intellectuals, one of whom was particularly sympathetic: the historian Paul Gore. Iorga sent some books on Moldavian history Gore requested, but they never arrived. As Gore wrote: "censorship is not dead here."[348] Bessarabian intellectuals notified Iorga of the discovery of a police informer in their organization, whom they promptly expelled.[349] Rakovski, in 1912, addressed the Socialists, pointing out: "The Russians have no right to remain in Eastern Moldavia."[350] In 1912 Russia ordered celebrations in Bessarabia

---

[346]*Neamul Românesc*, 19 October 1906.

[347]*Oameni care au fost*, vol. II, p. 176.

[348]Remarkably, young Paul Gore was introduced to Iorga by one of those Iorga "loved to hate," Constantin Stere. BAR, *Corespondenţa lui N. Iorga*, volume 30 (1906), Documents 23 and 24, and volume 31 (1906) Document 11. Gore wrote his letters to Iorga in Romanian in Latin script.

[349]The letter was sent without signature. BAR, *Corespondenţa lui N. Iorga*, (1907) volume 64, Document 46.

[350]Supt trei regi, p. 163.

observing the 100th anniversary of its annexation; Iorga commented: "Bessarabia celebrates the 100th anniversary of its enslavement," and published several books on the Romanian history of the province. He organized an exhibit on Bessarabia's Romanian character, and founded a student-home in Iaşi for Bessarabians wishing to study in "Free Romania." In a festive issue of *Neamul Românesc* dedicated to Bessarabia, Iorga wrote: "We know that Romanians live between the Prut and the Dniester; nobody can take their ancient rights away, and the Moldavian glory is inscribed on every stone."[351]

But the real struggle was conducted in Transylvania, where two decades before the Memorialists had made an abortive move for Romanian national rights. In order to understand it, we must examine Iorga's work with the *Liga Culturală* and his Summer University at Vălenii-de-Munte. Iorga spent many summers prior to 1907 in foreign countries doing research; he worked in "Unfree" Romania as much he did in the Regat. After 1908, he would spend his summers at his summer university. When the Bucovinian intellectual Gheorghe Tofan asked him in 1904 to organize a summer course for students from *dincolo*,[352] to promote the advent of national unity through national cultural studies, Iorga was unable to take up the idea. By 1908 the political atmosphere changed, and he was established in Vălenii. In the 11 June 1908 edition of *Neamul Românesc* Iorga announced the opening of the "Popular University of Vălenii-de-Munte" and the participation of renowned faculty as lecturers.[353] The Summer University was formally opened on 2 July 1908.

It was organized for Transylvanian, Bucovinian, and (to a lesser extent) Bessarabian youth, and was meant to become a catalyst of cultural solidarity for

---

[351]*Neamul Românesc*, 8 May 1912 and *Basarabia noastră scrisă după 100 de ani* (Vălenii-de-Munte, 1912); *O genealogie a Basarabilor* (Vălenii-de-Munte, 1912); *Însemnătatea ţinuturilor de peste Prut*, (Bucureşti, 1912); *Pagini despre Basarabia de astăzi* (Vălenii-de-Munte, 1912); *O viaţa de om*, vol. II, p. 176; *Neamul Românesc*, 18 May 1912.

[352]"From over there." The people of the Regat use the term to refer to Transylvanians.

[353]Iorga was not enthusiastic about Cuza preaching unbridled anti-Semitism. It was not the image Iorga wished to convey — not even in this period — to the youth of Transylvania or Bucovina. Iorga confesses as much in *O viaţă de om*, vol. II, p. 175. He expressed his disapproval to his family in much more emotional terms, as they recalled to this writer.

Romanians everywhere.[354] His inaugural lecture, "Cuza Vodă and His Foes Two Days after His Dethronement," was an act of political vengeance recounting the role of Dimitrie Sturdza (leader of the Liberal Party) in Cuza Vodă's dethronement. Support for the university came from subscriptions and donations; the state did not help.

Iorga charged modest fees for dormitory accommodations and board. All this complemented the work of the reinvigorated *Liga Culturală*. He never deviated from the Summer University's goals: "We believe that we are one nation of an admirable unity with an original culture common to all. We must never forget our cultural traditions. Based upon this foundation, we must offer the Romanian nation a modern culture of appropriate value. Out of this culture will rise an overwhelming energy; and one day our descendants will draw the appropriate conclusions from all of this."[355]

Austro-Hungarian authorities discouraged Romanians from over there" from attending.[356] After 1908, the Summer University held sessions every summer, except 1913, and after 1914. By 1922 it became "Nicolae Iorga Popular University." Iorga's press, *Datina Românească*, would function uninterruptedly. Foreign scholars visiting Romania made ritual visits there. Iorga's prestige guaranteed that lecturers were of quality, and the subjects covered history, cultural history, literature, geography, national economy, even shorthand. Students and faculty debated these subjects. There were excursions through the picturesque surroundings; visiting monasteries. Students staged works by Caragiale and Vasile Alecsandri; sometimes Iorga invited Bucharest professionals. There were poetry readings, concerts of popular music, and performances of folkloric

---

[354]Young Prince Carol (the future King Carol II) also took courses at the Summer University, as did future peasant leader Ion Mihalache.

[355]*Neamul Românesc Literar*, 10 July 1911.

[356]Theodorescu, *op. cit.*, p. 223.

dances — all conforming to Iorga's *Sămănătorist* artistic conservatism.[357] Bucharest high society poked fun at this "villagieture" saying it was "*Neamul Românesc of Nicolae Iorga.*"[358]

Iorga was an active member of the *Liga Culturală*, founded in 1891 to maintain cultural contacts between Romanians under different foreign masters and those who were "free," and as a response to the movement of the Memorandists in Hungary. Nevertheless, activity in the *Liga* declined; by 1907, the original 52 chapters had dwindled to six.[359] When Iorga and his followers revitalized the *Liga*, it signaled an unofficial change in Romanian policy towards Transylvania and Bucovina. Even before, Iorga placed *Neamul Românesc* at the *Liga's* disposal. On 10 June 1907, Iorga entered the *Liga's* Central Committee; on 2 June 1908, he became Secretary General. Each year a beautiful calendar was published, containing portraits and life stories of national heroes and writers, as well as folklore and pictures of costumes. Iorga considered it "the calendar of Romanian idealism."[360]

The *Liga* published on patriotic and social themes, and held conferences, attempting to win sympathy for the Romanian peasantry. Its publications were smuggled into Austria-Hungary using innocuous covers like *New Methods in Cultivating Potatoes*, and spread among the Romanians there. The *Liga* also sought to purify the culture of the upper classes, especially of those beyond the political borders.[361]

Iorga founded a library in Iaşi, directed mainly towards the Bessarabian Romanians, donating over 5,000 of his own books; he organized libraries in other Romanian towns, and in military hospitals, and organized the library of

---

[357]Neta-Marinescu, *op. cit.*, p. 236.

[358]Theodorescu, *op. cit.*, p. 216.

[359]*Op. cit.*, p. 226.

[360]*Op. cit.*, p. 227.

[361]Neta-Marinescu, *op. cit.*, p. 210; also, Theodorescu, *op. cit.*, pp. 228-230.

the *Liga* in Bucharest, donating 10,000 of his own books. He even donated Romanian books to Romanians in the United States, to encourage them to keep their Romanian traditions.[362] By subscription and donations (which Iorga duly published in *Neamul Românesc*), Iorga built a statue to Cuza-Vodă who established Romanian unity, and unveiled it in Iaşi in 1912.

After his break with the Conservatives, Iorga wished to found a Nationalist Democratic Organization to translate his *Sămănătorist* philosophy into practical politics. Elected as an independent candidate, his nationalism excluded all other ideologies and parties with their *Politicianism*. He failed to appreciate the importance of allies in achieving goals; alliance requires compromise. By 1908 his ideas about his own party — and its program — were maturing. Finally, in April 1910, Iorga founded the *Partidul Nationalist Democrat*. The program, adopted at the first party congress, echoed *Sămănătorism* and also *Frăţia Bunilor Români*. Elected on the party's platform in Galaţi (with A.C. Cuza elected in Iaşi), Iorga led the party. Dimitrie Munteanu-Râmnic (Iorga's far-way relative, and a former student) was to become his faithful lieutenant until the very end. Support came from Moldavia, Oltenia, Galaţi, Brăila, and Ploieşti, especially where overwhelming Jewish presence generated anti-Semitism; in Bucharest and in Wallachia the party had less support. Iorga began to have conflicts with Cuza because of Cuza's excessive, racist anti-Semitism. Iorga was ready to admit any Jew who identified himself with Romania, *Sămănătorism*, and the party's platform; Cuza vetoed this and enforced anti-Semitic exclusivism.[363] Iorga was not philo-Semitic at the time, but he did not share Cuza's hatred of Jews.

---

[362] *Neamul Romnânesc*, 5 March 1908; also, Neta-Marinescu, *op. cit.*, p. 212; and Theodorescu, *op. cit.*, p. 229.

[363] *O viaţă de om*, vol. II, pp. 163-164. Iorga pointed out that "there are no damned nations," and "to hate the Jew because it had no chance to become something different is both childish and barbaric." Petre Judea: *Nicolae Iorga în viaţa politică a României*, (Bucureşti 1990), p. 66.

The fact remains that the new party was the first Romanian political party with an open anti-Semitic program. Besides Iorga and Cuza, the party's leadership consisted of Leon Cosmovici, Vasile Kogălniceanu, (the son of Mihail Kogălniceanu), C. Sumuleanu, and Ion Zelea Codreanu, the father of the future founder of the Iron Guard. The Nationalist Democrats proposed mild agrarian reform, revision of the 1864 Cuza land reform, colonization on government lands, measures against alcoholism, the nationalization of insurance companies, universal vote for Romanians; foreigners (Jews) were to be expelled from villages, and no Jews were to serve in the Armed Forces; there were no provisions for industrialization. (It is questionable whether Iorga desired it.) Further, the party proposed educational reforms and the re-establishment of national unity (an idyllic union between the landlord and the peasant). These proposals were considered compatible with democracy. But then, it was a "nationalist democracy..."[364] In foreign policy, national unity headed the list; "dangerous alliances with great powers" (Romania's secret alliance with Austria Hungary and Germany) were to be avoided; friendship with Balkan nations encouraged; and demands made for "frontiers that befit Romanian history, Romanian tradition, and Romanian rights.[365]

Even though the masses were politicized only after the First World War, the Nationalist Democratic Party never became a mass party; it consisted mostly of intellectuals, professors, *lycée* instructors, attorneys, priests, engineers, students, and the readers of *Neamul Românesc*. The party centered around Iorga. As Iorga's granddaughter wrote: "It was called always "the party of Iorga" — its members: "Iorghists" (...) a party' which exists in his shadow."[366] The Bu-

---

[364]*Neamul Românesc*, 19 April 1910. In Poland, the "National Democratic Party" of Roman Dmowski ("Endecja") found its strong authoritarianism, brutal anti-Semitism and obscurantist Catholicism no obstacle in calling itself democratic. Dmowski was unscrupulous and unprincipled. Thus, he was more successful in politics than Iorga was.

[365]*Neamul Românesc*, 13 January 1913.

[366]Bianca Valota Cavalloti, *Nicolas Iorga* (Napoli, 1977), p. 81, and Frasin Munteanu-Râmnic to the writer in 1984.

charest political establishment did not consider the challenges a threat; Take Ionescu's Conservative Democratic Party, founded after he left the Conservative Party in 1907, seemed a more substantial opponent. Iorga attacked "Tachi-Mochi" (Jewish capitalist influence and Take Ionescu) regularly. Nicolae Filipescu, the leader of the Conservative mainstream could live with that — and the Liberals could too.

More importantly, the Bucharest political establishment recognized Iorga's shortcomings as a politician, and foresaw the pattern which would evolve: Iorga was an excellent lecturer and animator. Beyond that he was a historian. Politics demands close to a total commitment, the kind he never wished to give. He was more a historian than a politician. And there was his temper, his naiveté, and his personality, which assured Iorga's failure as a politician.

He became a full member of the Academy in May 1911. Eligible since his election as corresponding member in 1897, the intrigues of his adversaries key him out; it was only when the Academicians "tired of these intrigues" that the door opened.[367] Xenopol received his former student into the august ranks; over the years he had found it difficult to maintain good relations with Iorga, but he set their differences aside, praising Iorga's contribution to history, expressing only doubts about Iorga's "activities in the domain of literature and politics."[368] Iorga's entry speech, "Two Concepts of History," is the concise expression of his views on the nature of history and the historian's role in politics. According to him, "the duty of the historian is to be a tireless animator of national traditions, to be a witness for the necessity of national unity that transcend borders and classes. The historian must be a preacher of national solidarity, and must discover ideas which give a direction to the nation, setting an example for the youth." During the discussion period, Xenopol burst with admiration about the quality of his former students accomplished work.[369]

---

[367] *O viață de om*, vol. II, p. 44.

[368] *Generalități*, p. 98.

[369] *Op. cit.*, pp. 77-98.

It was during this month that Iorga wrote his historical play, *Michael the Brave*. Besides his university lectures, he traveled to Transylvania to lecture during sessions of the Romanian Cultural Society ASTRA. Thanks to his history of the Romanian army,[370] Iorga would be named professor of history at the Romanian Military Academy. The old king appreciated Iorga's work on the Romanian army so much that he sent the son of his nephew, Prince Carol, to Vălenii, and later to the University of Bucharest to audit Iorga's lectures. This was the start of an unfortunate relationship between Iorga and his student, and future king.

Iorga wrote some of his best works between 1900-1914. During these years he established his reputation.[371] *Scurta istorie a lui Mihai Viteezul* (Bucureşti, 1900) led Academicians to attack Iorga, claiming that he had "insulted the memory of Mihai Viteazul"; actually, he intended to glorify him. In *Istoria Literaturii Române in secolul al XVIII-lea* (2 volumes, Bucureşti, 1901), a pioneering work on eighteenth century Romanian literature, he resurrects many nearly forgotten works. *Istoria lui Mihai Viteazul pentru Poporul Românesc* (Bucureşti, 1901) is a popular version of Iorga's earlier work on Michael the Brave. *Braşovul şi Românii* (Bucureşti, 1905) treats Romanian contacts with Braşov, a Western city situated on the edge of Transylvania, a point of communication between Romania and Transylvania. The city has had a Saxon character, even given the traits of its Romanian population, and was a center of commerce and fertile soil for German and Hungarian culture.

Karl Lamprecht wanted to publish a series of histories of European nations; he asked his former student to write Romania's history. The result was *Geschicte des Rumänishen Volkes in Rahmen seiner Staatshildungen* (Gotha, 1905), in which Iorga sketched Romania's Geto-Dacian past and the medieval period in

---

[370]*Istoria Armatei Româneşti*, vol. I (Vălenii-de-Munte, 1910), relates the history of the Romanian army until 1599; the second volume (1919) brings the history up to the present.

[371]Theodorescu's two volume bibliography records Iorga's accomplishments only up until 1934. The first is *Bibliografia istorică literară a lui Nicolae Iorga,* (Bucureşti 1935); the second is *Bibliografia politică, socială şi economică a lui Nicolae Iorga,* (Bucureşti, 1937).

an attempt to establish Romanian continuity in Transylvania. It was well received by Western historians. Well-organized and documented, Iorga added a characteristic closing chapter on contemporary Romanian politics, writing more as a journalist than historian. With devastating irony, he criticized political opponents and Politicianism. He duly sent the two volumes to the Royal Palace. The old king was so angry that he did not even thank him.[372]

Next came *Inscripţii din bisericile României* (Bucureşti, Vol. 1, 1905, Vol. 2, 1908) and *Istoria românilor în chipuri şi icoane* (2 volumes, Bucureşti, 1905). This is a metaphor only. The book covers a very different subject. In the first work Iorga discusses Romanian church inscriptions, the second reconstructs Romanian history from pictures and icons. *Istoria universală* (Bucureşti, 1905) is his earliest attempt to discuss history in the broadest fashion. *Sate şi mănăstiri din Romania* (Bucureşti, 1905) seeks to establish Romania's organic development and territorial continuity through a study of villages and monasteries. *The Byzantine Empire* (London, 1907) resulted because his fame as a Byzantinist had reached England. Brown, a well-known Byzantinist and author of *The Republic of Venice*, had recommended that Iorga write this book, published in English. *Istoria literaturii româneşti in veacul al XIX-lea*, 3 volumes (Bucureşti, Volume 1, 1907, Volume 2, 1908, Volume 3, 1909): unfortunately, Iorga's treatment of Romania's literature after the Junimea Society suffers from his emotional involvement with *Sămănătorism*. Iorga's literary criticism and history after this massive work, would be but ironies, dictated by his *Sămănătorist* views. *Geschichte des Osmanischen Reiches* (5 volumes, Gotha, 1908-1913) deals with the history of the Ottoman Empire from its rise until the Balkan Wars and collapse of the empire. This work was inspired by Lamprecht's seminal *Geschicte der Europaischen Staaten und Geschichte der Ausser-europaischen Staaten*, along with other German works; documentary sources came from Iorga's research in Venice, Ragusa, and all over Europe. His accomplishment is

---

[372] *O viaţă de om*, vol. II, pp. 90-91. The secret police (the Siguranţa) file on Iorga summarized: "Nicolae Iorga is at the heading all activities whose goal is nationalist *Arhivele de Stat*, Bucureşti: Fond direcţia Poliţiei şi Siguranţei Generale, Dosar No. 39/1908, File: 11.

admirable (given Iorga's inability to read Turkish). His great feeling for the subject, his keen understanding of the *Pax Ottomanica*, and his grasp of the reasons for the empire's fall, make this one of his greatest works. The Turks admired it, and Turkish delegations often called on him. *Istoria Românilor* and *Istoria Românilor pentru poporul românesc* (Vălenii-de-Munte 1908) were popular versions of Romanian history (often re-issued). They would be adapted as textbooks, and smuggled into Transylvania and Bucovina. *Der lateinische Westen und der Byzantinische Osten in ibreti Wechselbeziebungen wabrend des Mittelalters*, Berlin (1909), Iorga, an established Medievalist, discussed the dilemma of the Eastern Latin (of nominally Orthodox faith and of Greek origins). The work is objective, many-sided, and informative on the medieval controversy between the Byzantine East and the Latin West, with instructive comments on contemporary aspects of the problem. *Carol XII, Petru cel Mare și țările noastre* (București, 1910) discusses the fateful consequences of Peter the Great's arrival at the Dniester River in pursuit of Charles XII, and of Charles XII's invasion of Russia at the beginning of the eighteenth century. Translated into Swedish, Iorga established relations with scholars in Scandinavia.

Francisc Ràkòczy al II-lea (București, 1910), is dedicated to the Hungarian national hero Francisc Ràkòczy II, who, after the Hapsburgs liberated Hungary from Ottoman domination and treated Hungary as a conquered land, and taught the Hapsburgs a lesson. Iorga details Ràkòczy's appeals to "aristocrats and commoners," and the uprising. The work is factually reliable and well-documented; he does not neglect the role of the Romanian inhabitants of Hungary in Ràkòczy's uprising. His admiration for Ràkòczy's personality, struggle, and his goals is evident. In *Breve istoria dei Rumeni* (Bucharest, 1911), Iorga appealed to the Italian public ("Latin brothers") to realize the extent the Hungarians Magyarization threatened Latinity, emphasizing the perceptions of Italians who traveled through Romania and Transylvania, and using much Italian documentation. *Oameni cari au fost* (Vol. 1, Vălenii-de-Munte, 1911) was the first volume of four containing Iorga's portraits of celebrated men, leaders, personalities, and contemporaries. He included journalistic obituaries and recollections. *Chestiunea Rhinului* (Vălenii-de-Munte, 1912), written on the eve of the Great

War, analyzed the problems surrounding the Rhine. For him (as for Napoleon), the Rhine is the geopolitical line from which Europe is ruled, the backbone of Europe, separating two cultures, two concepts of humanity and nation. In *Acţiunea militară a României în Bulgaria cu ostaşii noştri*, (Vălenii-de-Munte, 1914), Iorga acts as an apologist for Romanian military action, explaining the "bloodless" march of the Romanian armies into Bulgaria during the Second Balkan War to counter the charges of "a cowardly triumphal march." *Chestiunea Dunării* (Vălenii-de-Munte, 1913), describes the rich set of historical, ethnic, and political questions that arise around the Danube. Needless to say, Iorga emphasizes the Danube's southern stretch. In *Auf und Niedergang des Turkischen Herrschaftgebietes in Europa* (Gotha, 1913), written at the behest of Professor Lamprecht, Iorga explains the two Balkan Wars, which lead to the collapse of Ottoman rule in Southeastern Europe. *Două tradiţii istorice in Balcani, a Italiei şi a Românilor* (Bucureşti, 1913) explains much of Iorga's political thought and activities. He hoped for a solidarity between Latin nations working for Romania's benefit. Could such an alliance between Italy, France, and Romania be contracted? He hoped Italian influence might substitute an Austro-Hungarian and Russian one. Serbia would accept it, and it would be in keeping with Roman-Venetian traditions. Iorga did not show much sympathy for Croatian aspirations; or the Croat character of Dalmatia, or Italian designs on it. Even after Mussolini became the patron of Hungarian revisionism, Iorga cherished the notion of Romano-Italian cooperation. But Italy was weak and unreliable: Iorga seems not to have taken to heart Gregorovius' descriptions of the Italian political types: Machiavelli, Cesare Borgia, and the condottieri.

As for the Balkan Wars of 1912 and 1913, Iorga had not approved of Italy's invasion of Libya. Neither had the Romanian public. Iorga was strongly pro-Serbian,[373] (even more pro-Montenegran; indeed, he considered the Montenegrans a martial people). When Konrad von Hötzendorf, Chief of Staff of the

---

[373]*O viaţă de om*, vol. II, p. 181. On 5 October 1908, after the annexation of Bosnia-Herzegovina, he wrote an editorial in *Neamul Românesc*: "Tragic Serbia."

Austro-Hungarian Empire, visited Bucharest in 1912, Iorga argued it could only mean that "Hötzendorf (has come) to review a satellite."[374]

From 1912 on, Iorga's relations with A.C. Cuza began to deteriorate; Cuza founded his own newspaper *Unirea* (in Iaşi), and seemed ready to start his own party.

With Bulgaria's attack on Serbia, the Second Balkan War started. Romania had been neutral until then, and Iorga was considered a friend of Bulgaria. Balkan nations (including Turkey) banded together to shear off some of the territory Bulgaria had acquired during the first Balkan war. When Bulgaria was defeated, Romania saw an opportunity to acquire the territory Russia denied her in 1878: the Silistra "quadrilateral." Iorga was permitted to wear a uniform and went to northern Bulgaria to participate in what Romania's enemies called a "cowardly triumphal parade,"[375] in Prince Brâncoveanu's car. He traveled through northern Bulgaria in the company of Aristide Blank. The Bulgarians he conversed with thought of Bulgaria only in terms of the San Stefano treaty, meaning Greater Bulgaria.[376] The new Liberal government of I.C. Brătianu promised a sweeping agrarian reform (a fact almost ignored by Iorga) and limited electoral reform.

When the Peace Conference convened in Bucharest Iorga met Nikola Pasič, the old Serbian statesman, who told him: "You are young and will see the rise of a Greater Romania; I will not see the rise of a Greater Serbia." Iorga also met the Greek statesman Venizelos, whom he considered left by the Venetians in Crete.[377]

In 1913, the last World Historical Congress before the outbreak of the War convened in London. The Prime Minister at the time, Maiorescu, was petty enough to deny Iorga permission to participate as a Romanian delegate. Iorga

---

[374] *Neamul Românesc*, 20 November 1912.

[375] *Supt trei regi*, p. 175.

[376] *O viaţă de om*, vol. II, pp. 140-145.

[377] *Op. cit.*, vol. II, p. 198.

went anyway, and later recalled the Congress' charged atmosphere and every-one's forebodings.[378] He delivered two papers, one on "The Necessary Bases of the New History of the Middle Ages," and on "Byzantine Survivals in the Ro-manian Countries."

In October 1913 Iorga traveled to Belgrade to present a bell that had be-longed to Karagheorghe Petrović to King Peter I of Serbia. He congratulated the king on the acquisition of Macedonia. The king answered: "What is all that com-pared to Bosnia and Herzegovina?"[379]

In 1914, Iorga was one of the founders of the *Institutul de Studii Sud-Est Europene*; in 1915 he published *Revista Istorică* for this institute. He believed, since the Balkans developed under Macedonian, Roman, Byzantine, and Otto-man rule, the peoples of the region developed similar administrative, political, social, and religious institutions. Thus, one cannot understand the history of any nation in Southeastern Europe, if one considers it isolated from the history of the region, as a whole. Unlike the similar institute in Vienna, which (as Iorga saw it) trained imperialist proconsuls to rule the Balkans, he conceived of this institute teaching mutual love and understanding to the Balkan peoples.[380] Iorga's pro-Serbian, and hence anti-Austrian and anti-German activities met with the old king's disapproval.[381]

In the summer of 1914, the nineteenth century and with it a way of life was coming to an end. Iorga felt vague premonitions, but hoped also for a new be-ginning. No one, least of all Iorga, could know what lay in the offing; no one could foresee that the magnificent edifice that was Western Civilization had a weak spot that Gavrilo Prinčip would strike with a bullet.

---

[378] *Op. cit.*, vol. II, pp. 124-126, and 186.

[379] *Op. cit.*, vol. II, pp. 201-203. And also in his *Clopotul dăruit de Caragheorghe, întemeietorul Serbiei, satului Topola* (Bucureşti, 1913).

[380] *Generalităţi*, p. 94.

[381] *O viaţă de om*, vol. II, p. 204.

Chapter IV

"In Expectation that the Scriptures Would Be Fulfilled"[382]

If I penetrate into the Romanian ancestral soul, I find there the command of national instinct, and I see the Gates of Heaven open up to us; a superstitious fear tells me to close my eyes: it is too beautiful! Destiny has chosen this generation to carry out the greatest deeds.... It will carry out the task of centuries, and such beautiful times are on their way that foreseeing them mesmerizes me.

— Take Ionescu

Iorga considered that the Sarajevo murder "by a Serbian fanatic" dashed all hopes that Franz Ferdinand would stand up against the Hungarians in Transylvania.[383] This became the end of the nineteenth century. It had lasted practically until 1914: a hopeful age, which started maybe with the *lumières* of the Enlightenment, and was born out of philosophy. A series of tragedies started, one inexorably leading to another; and these sequences are by no means finished. After that shot in Sarajevo, as Winston Churchill said, "events passed very largely outside the scope of conscientious choice. Governments and individuals con-

---

[382]*O viață de om*, vol. II, p. 311. Iorga placed this inscription on Michael the Brave's catafalque.

[383]*Neamul Românesc*, 22 June 1914. Attention should be paid to the dating; until 1919, the dates of Romanian newspapers reflect the old Orthodox calendar, consequently 22 June would be 5 July.

formed to the rhythm of the tragedy, and swayed and staggered forward in hapless violence on an ever-increasing scale, till injuries were wrought to human society which a century will not efface, and which may conceivably prove fatal to the present civilization."[384] The first reaction of Iorga "the man of the nineteenth century" was naive: since the Sarajevo act is reprehensible, there should be an investigation, and "the rest should be fought out between the Viennese and Belgrade newspapers." But he also warned that nobody should forget the "number two item on Tisza's program," namely, Romania.[385] Although nobody foresaw where the Sarajevo bullet would lead to, very few people knew the designs of Count Berchtold, Count Hoyos, Konrad von Hötzendorf, and General Potiorek. On the other hand the Serbians remembered their past glory, which touched Iorga and others like Leopold von Ranke. The Germans were forced at Versailles to sign Article 241, accepting the guilt for unleashing the war. There were more guilty ones, but not Serbia, fighting for its life. German guilt was that of omission, not of commission. The Kaiser gave Vienna a kind of a carte blanche; he would repent later at leisure for this. Vienna hoped for a Serbian-Austrian-Hungarian conflict. This was not to be. The Balkans were considered vital, the General Staffs took over from the diplomats, and after the first shots were fired, all the Powers were sucked into the conflagration much against their own will. But everybody was counting on a short glorious war in the style of the "Charge of the Light Brigade." Neither Iorga nor anyone else foresaw in the initial enthusiasm[386] of mobilization the "Iron Man" — a full-fledged mecha-

---

[384]Winston Churchill, *The World Crisis, 1915* (New York, 1929), pp. 1-2.

[385]*Neamul Românesc*, 20 July 1914. Iorga's profound hostility towards Count Istvàn Tisza had two grounds: Tisza's determination not to make concessions to the Romanians; and Iorga's mistaken belief (held together with many Hungarians) that Tisza was responsible for the war. As a consequence, Tisza would be shot to death by a Hungarian at the outbreak of the October (1918) Revolution. Iorga later discovered his misjudgment of Tisza's role and he made amendments. *Neamul Românesc*; 28 September 1919.

[386]Iorga commented: "The power which was not a state, but wanted to destroy states, and the force that was not a nation, but wished to destroy nations, is defeated. It is socialism! Its deserters are under different flags." *Neamul Românesc*, 17 August 1914. Iorga was as enthusiastic about this development as Lenin was disgusted by it.

nized war. Iorga felt that there was serious trouble in his nineteenth century paradise: "That ignoble war, this cannibalistic dance, which turns us either into mentally deranged people, or into terrorists. It will cause immense losses to human culture."[387] When the war would be over, its material damage could be repaired. Even lost life could be replaced; but the moral damage, the discredit it brought to nineteenth century values, the discredit it brought to the intellectual was another matter.

Amidst tragedy, Iorga also saw opportunity. Despite his profound aversion to war, he wrote that Romania must be ready for opportunities to assert its "national rights."[388] And he was fretting for France and Serbia. "France must not perish!" because this would be a moral catastrophe for humanity. Romania must help France, even if only with a gesture. He asked, "Why do we love France? Do we love it because of upper class luxuries; or because of Latin brotherhood, or our readings in the French language, French literature? To a great measure this is true; but this is not all, because all want to conquer; France wants only to live."[389]

In Romania, the feelings of the old king were on the side of the Central Powers. Despite the old king's feelings, Ion I.C. Brătianu kept Romania neutral. This was decided by the Crown Council in Sinaia on 4 August 1914. There was a pro-Central Power faction like P.P. Carp, a Bismarckian, pro-German boyar, and Sturdza, not so much pro-German as anti-Russian. Although the return of Bessarabia was almost impossible, the acquisition of Transylvania and Bucovina might become practical. Romanian public opinion was in its majority pro-Ally from the outset. Although it was anti-Russian in the meantime, no Romanian wanted a war with Russia. Iorga considered Russia so powerful, that even after its defeat at Sebastopol, it was courted by the Great Powers.[390]

---

[387] *Neamul Românesc*, 27 July 1914.

[388] *Ibid.*

[389] *Neamul Românesc*, 27 July and 17 August 1914; and *O viață de om*, vol. II, p. 180.

[390] *Supt trei regi*, pp. 180-210.

But King Carol died on October 10, 1914 and with him a restraint passed away. The new king was Ferdinand, his nephew. The new king was a weak, irresolute, sickly man given to sudden rage. Many educated Romanians nicknamed him "Fritz." Reminded by high German officials of his "duty" or "honor," he quickly retorted that duty and honor "are also known in Romania, but it is also known how they must be understood, without foreigners needed to interpret or to interfere with them."[391] His wife. Queen Marie, an English princess, was strongly pro-Allied, anti-German, and anti-Austrian. The Austrian ambassador. Count Ottokar Czernin, complained once that he did not feel popular enough in Bucharest society, asking Queen Marie to make him more popular; she answered: "It is terribly difficult to make an Austrian popular in Romania."[392] Count Czernin saw that it would be Queen Marie who would govern King Ferdinand; moreover, he realized that she would be a deadly enemy. The queen always wanted Romania to enter the war on the Allied side.

A few words about the Prime Minister, Ionel Brătianu, the son of one of modern Romania's founders, and Iorga's relation with him. Iorga uttered copious opinions about Brătianu. He felt a tremendous hostility towards him. Iorga was wrong in his treatment of Brătianu. But compared with Brătianu, Iorga was a better, more moral human being (both in public and in private life). Something more than incorruptible; a good family man, husband, father, and a good son to his mother, good-hearted and charitable. These qualities were not cardinal virtues of Ionel Brătianu. Iorga was a patriot, he always managed to put himself in second place behind Romania and had a love for the peasantry. As far as Iorga the intellectual goes, there is simply no room for comparison. Brătianu was a textbook example of an Oriental despot. Proverbially arrogant (like the whole family), Iorga rightfully referred to Brătianu's father as a "tyrannical vizir." This arrogance was prevalent in Brătianu's style, even in his voice, which demanded respect from above and was accustomed to being obeyed (for generations).

---

[391]*Op. cit.*, p. 201.

[392]*Op. cit.*, pp. 199-200.

Brătianu did not have much social conscience, he felt a birthright to the peasant's toil, sweat, even to the peasant's life. And, like Oriental despots, he assimilated his self-interest with that of Romania. For his kind, this was not contradictory, but rather complementary. He did for Romania only good if this good served also him and his clan. Iorga was a better human being, but in one aspect: Brătianu was a statesman. And this cannot be taken lightly.

Brătianu, like many representatives of his class, possessed of long, not always edifying but instructive historical experience, was subtle in his judgements (and in his judgement good faith was not a major commodity), and showed astonishing realism! As Iorga wrote, "Brătianu was inaccessible (after the First World War broke out) and he worked like an engineer in total silence, but with a secure touch."[393] From the beginning Brătianu had plans to bring Romania, on the side of the Allies, into the war. He stretched out secret feelers. Since the Central Powers could offer only Bessarabia, he opted for Transylvania and Bucovina. Although Brătianu and the Liberals were traditionally anti-Russian, he knew that the acquisition of Bessarabia was an almost hopeless undertaking. He also knew that only the disintegration of the Russian Empire could return it; if not, Russia could always take back the province (like it did in 1878 and also in 1940 and in 1944). The Russians always considered that there was more room in the other direction; to reunify Moldavia under Russian rule. Even during the First World War, as the publication of secret treaties by the Bolsheviks shows, the Sturmer-von Jagow negotiations foresaw a further partition of Romania. Transylvania and Bucovina were more realistic propositions. Transylvania especially, which is so important for every Romanian (and for every Hungarian too). Nicolae Titulescu demanded to strive "for Transylvania and three times for Transylvania!"[394] So did Take Ionescu and Nicolae Filipescu. Within the *Liga Culturală*, Iorga asked for action. For Brătianu the only question was: when to enter on the Allied side.

---

[393] *O viață de om*, vol. II, p. 214.

[394] The Iorga family to the writer.

The first year of the war brought a lot of movement on the fronts. Iorga's brother-in-law, Alexandru Bogdan, died late in 1914, mobilized in the Hungarian Army. In the fall of 1914 there was the "Lemberg Momentum," when Russian armies took this important city with most of Galicia, penetrating into Hungary. But Hindenburg won at Tannenberg. The Germans almost took Paris, but they were stopped at the Battle of the Marne. During the winter of 1914-1915, the Serbians liberated their country. In the spring, Italy entered the war on the Allied side; the Allies tried to land in the Dardanelles. Late in 1915 Bulgaria entered the war on the side of the Central Powers. In the West everything settled down to a deadly trench warfare; there was stalemate, and the "All Quiet on the Western Front" atmosphere ensued, surrealistically described by Remarque. During it, huge armies faced each other, and month after month and year after year destroyed each other hopelessly and systematically with artillery, poison gas, barbed wire, and machine guns. Ultimately victory or defeat was more a product of the mathematics of cannon fodder than of leadership, skill, or courage. For France and Britain it was the Western Front which mattered. Everything else was a "side show," including Romanian neutrality. Brătianu knew the egotism of the Great Powers, how they use little nations as pawns only, and how the pawns' fate is to be taken. But he also knew that a pawn can check a king; and when it reaches the eighth square, it becomes a queen. He weighed all of this when he asked the price for Romania joining the Allies. He never for a moment considered joining the Central Powers. Brătianu emerged as a statesman of some magnitude.

Brătianu was measured, slow, sullen, and statesmanlike in foreseeing the role for Iorga, and dealing with this "firebrand." Iorga said "Brătianu's political game is more able than beautiful." And again "Brătianu lacked the generous sincerity, the noble convictions without which one cannot be a true politician."[395] Unfortunately, politics is made more of necessity than out of sincerity. Iorga was too deeply anchored in *Sămănătorism*. With all his Romanian and world historical studies, Iorga was astoundingly "un-Romanian" in politics. His

---

[395] *O viață de om*, vol. II, pp. 213 and 292.

Sămănătorist views overshadowed his natural Romanian instincts, even his knowledge of Romanian historical experience. One can find little in Iorga's politics from the first lesson of Romanian history, namely that inflexibility is not very helpful for survival. Besides differences of temperament and personality, Iorga's hatred for Brătianu and his whole clan was based on his *Sămănătorist* outlook. For him, Brătianu and the Liberals were destroying a Romania based on organic peasant development. This was ever present in Iorga's mind. In sum, Iorga was subjective when he described Brătianu, especially when he wrote his Autobiography in 1934.[396] Brătianu was unflinchingly pro-Ally, despite certain risks for himself. When a separate peace treaty was concluded in 1918, he was threatened with being put on trial, as the one who was responsible for the war. Iorga knew that. Nevertheless, he remained anti-Brătianu. When Goga suggested (in the spring of 1917, during the Russian anarchist disorder in Iași) that it might be a good idea to level Iorga's house in order to open a defensive perimeter for Prime Minister Brătianu's residence, Iorga promptly retorted: "Why not the other way around?"[397] Iorga's opinion of Brătianu provides a good example of the extent to which he was able to lose perspective when he — allowing himself to be carried away by his emotions — was dealing with his contemporaries either in history, politics, or in literature. Brătianu was more reasonable towards Iorga. He, like the rest of the Bucharest establishment — Aristide Blank, Take Ionescu, Constantin Argetoianu, or the future King Carol II — considered Iorga like a first class race horse difficult to handle. Sometimes Iorga could help in winning some (not all!) choice races, but after the race was over one had to put Iorga back "into his place," into the stable (The Academy). Any trap Brătianu or the Bucharest political establishment would set for Iorga, he

---

[396]Just before the fall of Bucharest, Iorga had a conversation with the Minister of Defense, whom he considered a defeatist. Iorga advised Brătianu to remove him. Brătianu calmly asked him, "Do you know anybody better who could replace him?" Iorga was even more unreasonable when he misconstrued some remarks of Brătianu. Brătianu expressed (an alleged) regret that no separate peace was possible. Later, with the Germans advancing, Brătianu mocked at Iorga asking: "And what do you think about the chances of an Allied victory now?" Iorga assured him that he had always believed in an Allied victory; only he could not predict the time. *O viață de om*, vol. II, pp. 234 and 281.

[397]*Op. cit.*, vol. II, pp. 243-244.

was likely to walk straight into. During Romania's neutrality, Brătianu accomplished the difficult task of controlling Iorga. It was not easy.[398] The difficulties started right away. Iorga wrote a blistering editorial "Not with Austria-Hungary!"[399] (Iorga always wrote, during crisis times, several editorials daily, reprinted in the mass circulation daily *Universul*.) The instrument for Iorga to reach the broader public was the *Liga Culturală*. He had left it in 1912-13 because of the intrigues of *Politicianism* but now he returned.[400] When Iorga came back, the head of the *Liga Culturală* was Father Vasile Lucaciu, a refugee from Transylvania. Iorga became Acting Secretary General of the *Liga*. Other refugee intellectuals poured in, including the Goga brothers, Octavian and Eugeniu. Besides the refugees, there was Nicolae Filipescu, Barbu Ştefănescu-Delavrancea, Stelian Popescu, and others; but nothing matched Iorga's inspiration or appeal to the masses, especially the younger generation and the student body.

The Romanians in Transylvania were divided. Iuliu Maniu took a neutral position and was drafted. Vaida, as Iorga called him, "the old believer in Vienna," took a pro-Austro-Hungarian position; so did the Church hierarchy. This included the future Patriarch of Romania, Miron Cristea.[401]

Iorga returned to the *Liga Culturală*, chastened by Brătianu. The so-called pro-Entente "National Action," paralleled the activity of the *Liga*. In 1915, A.C.

---

[398]*Op. cit.*, vol. II, pp. 214-215; also, Şeicaru, op. cit., pp. 61-62; and Mme. Liliana Pippidi-Iorga confirmed to this writer that Brătianu had imposed heavy restraints on Iorga. Brătianu considered Iorga "a dangerous man" — "whose activities must be always supervised." Actually, this supervision of Iorga (during these years of Romania's neutrality) was entrusted to I.G. Duca. (Petre Ţurlea, *op. cit.*, pp. 90, 389). In his *Memorii* (Bucureşti, 1931), in the first volume, Iorga explained: "During the period of neutrality, I avoided the haste (inherent to demagoguery) of those who were suggesting entering the war prematurely."

[399]*Neamul Românesc*, 20 July 1914.

[400]Theodorescu, *op. cit.*, p. 235.

[401]*Supt trei regi*, p. 191; and *Neamul Românesc*, 17 August 1914. A few months before the war, Iorga organized with students a violent reception for the pro-Austro-Hungarian Bishop of the Romanian Church in Transylvania, V. Mangra.

Cuza joined "National Action," while Iorga denounced it for its "hasty" irresponsibility.[402] During the whole duration of neutrality, he toned down his activities within the Nationalist Democratic Party to insure "national unity." As he explained later: "To make politics in such a moment seemed to be nothing less than criminal because all forces should be applied for a last desperate effort of defense."[403]

Iorga's relationship with Cuza deteriorated even further, with Cuza attacking Iorga in the Assembly. The majority of the Party supported Iorga. Although Cuza still contributed a few articles to *Neamul Românesc* until 1916, when Iorga arrived (as a refugee) in Iaşi he did not receive any comfort from his former friend.[404] Both Cuza and Ion Zelea Codreanu (who exchanged his theologian's rag with the folkloric cloth of a Bucovinian peasant) exploited Iorga's national-unity stand to take over the Party (Iorga dissolved the Party when Romania entered the war). Iorga considered this an "usurpation."[405] He still refused many an opportunity to hold lectures, or to address meetings, in the same vein of restraint. But as the situation within Austria-Hungary evolved, it was not easy for Iorga to maintain such an aloof attitude. In 1915, the major Budapest newspaper *Pesti-Hirlap* wrote: "If Romania betrays, the Romanians in Transylvania are our hostages." The Romanian minority politician Ştefan C. Pop filed a protest. Colonel Fischer, in charge of security in Bucovina, said: "In Bucovina I know Germans, Jews — and traitors."[406] Yet, withdrawn from the all-out "struggle," Iorga dedicated himself to his university lectures, to his work at the Academy, participating in the session of the Chamber. He organized help for Romanian prisoners (of the Austrian Army) now in Russia. Writing his editorials, he always warned against demonstrations, violence, and impatience. His journalism was surprisingly toned down but unequivocal. Iorga stood behind France and (as he called

---

[402]*O viaţă de om*, vol. II, p. 214; also *Supt trei regi*, p. 202.

[403]*O viaţă de om*, vol. II, p. 248.

[404]*Op. cit.*, vol. II, p. 244.

[405]*Memorii* vol. II, pp. 130-132; and *O viaţă de om*, vol. II, p. 248.

[406]*Supt trei regi*, p. 197.

it) "magnificent" Serbia. He condemned the wanton artillery bombardment of Belgrade and made Tisza responsible for it. When during the winter of 1914 the Serbian army cleansed the country from the occupiers, Iorga remarked: "and the Lord descended from his throne and lifted up the humble one." There followed a sympathy campaign for Serbia within the framework of his *Institutul de Studii Sud-Est Europene*, and in its journal (which began its appearance in 1915), *Revista Istorică*.

Iorga stood behind Belgium and King Albert I. With Albert I he would conclude a relationship which lasted for a lifetime. He was horrified by the burning of the Louvain library by the Germans, and by the shooting of civilians by the German army while they were advancing across Belgium, France, and Serbia. The beginning of modern warfare methods was difficult to swallow for a man of the nineteenth century. He considered the burning of the Louvain library not to be like the work of Napoleon, but that of Attila the Hun. The destruction of the Cathedral of Rheims and the use of the "Grosse Bertha" were for him the incarnation of Nietzsche's spirit, that of the "blonde beast."[407] Iorga considered German technology a "civilization which dishonors and destroys civilization itself." He saw with horror the emergence of the twentieth century man which he called a "new species." In conversation with the German commander, General von Bissing, Cardinal Mercier of Louvain reminded him that he faced the judgement of history. Bissing answered: "But Monsignor, we shall win the war, and we shall write history."[408] Iorga's love for France and aversion towards Germany had cultural roots, like his feelings towards Russia. They would last a lifetime. In 1915 he wrote: "The national monarchy of Germany tries to get as many slaves as possible for the prosperity of the dominant race." And again, speaking about German socialism, Iorga considered the German worker to be embourgeoised; he is "a boyar"; and his high living standard needs slave labor. So the German worker is against "inferior races" whom he needs only in the

---

[407] *Neamul Românesc*, 24 August 1914.

[408] *O viață de om*, vol. II, p. 219.

capacity for slaves for his culture.[409] For Iorga, a devout monarchist, personally devoted to King Ferdinand and Queen Marie, it was difficult to-accept that the Romanian Royal Dynasty was of German origin. He wrote articles, lectures, and a book about the "Latin Ties of the Royal Family," emphasizing the relations between the Romanian Royal Family and the Beauharnais and Murat families. The book is a good example of the politicized "contemporary histories" written by him. Can the Hohenzollerns be considered Latins? The facts which Iorga presented in his study are irrefutable; the impression which he tries to create is trivial. Iorga knew that European Royalty was so thoroughly intermarried that it became practically one family.[410] During these two years of self-restraint, many Romanian nationalists (especially in Transylvania!) were asking the embarrassing question: "What is he waiting for?" Iorga condemned the *"Capșa* patriotism,"[411] fulminating against the opportunist "strategies" of the politicians and opportunists in the Capșa. He asked angrily: "Maybe the achievement of national unification is meant for another, a worthier generation?"[412] Iorga even withdrew from Bucharest spending his time in Vălenii. There, correctly evaluating the Romanian unpreparedness and disorganization, he repeated daily to his family: "Entry into the war will be a disaster!"[413]

During these two years of neutrality he worked a lot. The works that he produced are mainly connected with the events occurring, supportive of the Romanian position or of Romania's relations with its allies. From 1914 to 1919 we see little scholarly research or contribution to the historical sciences. He usually presented in his books historical background to national goals. In his *Politica*

---

[409]*Neamul Românesc*, 20 December 1915; and *Neamul Românesc*, 13 January 1917.

[410]*O viață de om*, vol. II, pp. 288-290; and *Neamul Românesc*, 18 November 1916.

[411]The "Capșa" was a popular coffee and pastry shop of Bucharest high society. Vexed by the crowds sitting there and discussing political events, Iorga dismissed them as frivolous, characterizing their opinions as "Capșa crowd opinions."

[412]*O viață de om*, vol. II, p. 218.

[413]The Iorga family to the writer.

externă a regelui Carol (Bucureşti, 1916), Iorga describes foreign policies during the reign of King Carol I, presenting valuable documents and arguments to illustrate the previous 40 years of Romanian foreign policy problems, especially concerning the wars of 1877-1878, the Berlin Congress, and its aftermath. This work grew out of his university lectures. His *Dreptul la viaţă al statelor mici* (Bucureşti, 1916) restates his beliefs that every nation, big or small, is an organic living entity, indestructible, fitting into the hierarchical order of the world, with inalienable rights. His *3 Maiu 1915* (Vălenii-de-Munte, 1915) celebrates the Assembly of Transylvanian Romanians in Blaj in 1848. *La question roumaine et Autriche et Hongie* (Bucarest, 1915) presents the question of the Romanian majority in Transylvania and Bucovina and its fate under Hungarian or Austrian rule, as does his *Histoire des Roumains de Transylvanie et de Hongrie* (2 volumes, Bucarest, 1915-16). His *Carpaţii în luptele dintre Români şi Unguri* (Vălenii-de-Munte, 1915) describes the Carpathian Mountains and the role they played in the struggle between Romanians and Hungarians. Here the Carpathians are presented not so much as a geographical barrier, but as a backbone of the Romanian majority on both sides of the range. His *Serbia eroică şi martiră (The Heroic and Martyred Serbia)* (Vălenii-de-Munte, 1915) gives beautiful, evocative historical images of Romania's Western neighbor's struggle for survival. In his *Popoare turanice parazite* (Vălenii-de-Munte, 1915), Iorga offers an unflattering image of the "parasitic Turanic peoples": the Hungarians, Turks, and Bulgarians.

After the war started, *Neamul Românesc's* anti-Semitic campaign decreased. We read stories about alleged Jewish disloyalty towards Romania, Jewish sympathy towards the Central Powers, Jewish espionage or economic sabotage, or Jewish mockings of Romanian soldiers, etc. One must give a warning: in Eastern Europe the spreading of unfounded anti-Semitic rumors, slanders, and false accusations has such a tradition that they should be taken with more than a grain of salt! Nevertheless, during the First World War the Transylvanian Jews and those of Bucovina were behind the Central Powers, their homeland; the sympathy of East-European Jews toward the Central Powers needs some explanation. The First World War was not the Second; the position of the Jews during the Second World War was unequivocal. It was a question of life or death. But during the First World War, Jews in France, England, Italy, Belgium, and in the United States were patriotic citizens, supporting the struggle of their countries. This was also true in Serbia, Germany, and Austria-Hungary. The Jews in Bulgaria have rendered a good account of themselves, and, in Turkey, Jews traditionally supported the Ottoman government. The position of the great Jewish masses in Eastern Europe was more complex. In Russian-Poland, the Western part of Russia, and, unfortunately, also in Romania, there were strained relationships between the Jews, the bureaucracy and the people. For these "Pale of Settlement" type of Jews, Germany and Austria always represented a higher culture, and, before Hitler, much better treatment. During modern times, if the East European Jewish masses looked for Western culture, they looked to Vienna and Berlin. When they arrived in France, England, or especially in the United States, in the congenial atmosphere there they went through a rapid, successful assimilation; in the West, there was a different kind of chemistry which facilitated it. But in Eastern Europe the Jewish masses continued to live within the incongruent, hostile atmosphere, and in almost total isolation. Paris, London, or New York were far away; if Jews looked for culture and values, they more often than not looked to Berlin, wherefrom the *Haskala*, the Enlightenment of the Jews originated, and to Vienna. They looked to these centers of culture for inspiration rather than to the "unspoiled peasant" and the world of *Sămănătorism*. They spoke Yiddish, a German dialect. During the 1950s, the Jewish leader Nachum Goldmann, paraphrasing Goethe, spoke about a "schizophrenic affinity" between Germans and Jews. He explained this attraction between two peoples mutually enriching each other, which ended when one set out to exterminate the other. This affinity remains something of a mystery. But it is an essential ingredient in the alchemy which permitted Western civilization to proceed towards the Enlightenment. We need mention only Moses Mendelsohn. These are some of the reasons for the Jewish attitude during the First World War. But the headlong clash with the local Romanian nationalists, and also with Nicolae Iorga, should also be considered inevitable and understandable.

This attitude prevailed into the Hitlerian era. Professor Raoul Hilberg explains in his monumental work *The Destruction of the European Jews*, when the Nazis arrived in Eastern Europe, the Jews there were "blocked by psychological obstacles" to face up to the danger. Everything that was good for the Jews had come "traditionally from Germany, and everything bad came traditionally from Russia." As one Nazi bureaucrat said: "The Jews seem to be remarkably ill-informed about the German attitude towards them, and what we have in store for them." Hilberg continues that during the First World War the Jewish masses looked to the advancing German armies as "quasi-liberators."[414] So, we may understand Jewish loyalty towards the Austrian authorities in Bucovina. In Hungary (and Transylvania), the Jews assimilated unreservedly and showed loyalty. Between 1914-1918, the attitude of the East European Jews was radically different from that during the Second World War.

Although Iorga rarely generalized, he remarked more than once that "the Jews in Bucharest await with flowers" the arrival of the Germans; or "the Jews are happy about every Romanian defeat" at the hand of the German army. Later (in his evocative style), he foresaw the Jews greeting the German troops with flowers in their hands, giving welcoming speeches in "jargon" (that is to say, in Yiddish).[415] Iorga, like many other Gentiles of the region, faulted the Jewish soldiers for not showing courage. As he put it, "they had not shown much heroism since the Old Testament." Did Iorga (or the other critics of the East European Jews) expect the non-assimilated, terribly mistreated "Pale of Settlement" Jews to fight heroically for their tormentors? Or to fight and die for his *Sămănătorist* ideals? What about Jews fighting in the French, English, Italian, or American armed forces? (For that matter, in the German or Austro-Hungarian armed forces?) Could Eastern Europeans not discern the reasons for this different Jewish bearing? (Iorga did not live long enough to see the rise of the Israeli Defense Forces.) Even during the First World War, Iorga saw the different attitudes of the French and Italian Jews, and called upon the Romanian Jews to

---

[414]Raoul Hilberg, *The Destruction of the European Jews* (Chicago, 1961), pp. 206-207.

[415]*Supt trei regi*, p. 233; *O viaţa de om*, vol. II, p. 244.

emulate them. When the question of giving citizenship rights for the Jews in France and Italy came up, Iorga answered: "When they will show the same love for our people as the Jews of France and Italy show towards the French and Italian peoples, then they will get citizenship rights." He considered that the Jews in Romania "ask for everything and give nothing in return," although he saw that this situation was also the fault of the Romanians. Commenting on the Italian Jews, Iorga says: "They are only Italians of Mosaic confession; they do not know any other tongue, no other traditions, and no other dress than Italian, and they have no relations, past or present, with Italy's enemies."[416] One feels the complexity of this grave problem. Could not Iorga see why the Jews were refusing to identify with Romania? Yes, he saw it, and he would change his attitudes completely after 1918. But, as an Eminescian nationalist, when push came to shove, Iorga perceived right and wrong in the sense of Eminescu's "Supreme Law."

Until August 1916, Brătianu kept Iorga tactfully and successfully under control, despite Iorga's pro-Serbian and pro-French stance. When Italy joined the Entente, Iorga exulted. According to him, Italy had risen to a stature greater than life. "*Sacro egoismo*" was celebrated, the triumph of the national idea "against Parliament, party politics, and maybe against others, too." Then Iorga wrote mockingly: "Bah! Here in Romania, they cannot do that!"[417] Warsaw fell to the German army. Iorga wrote: "That one is only defeated who acknowledges defeat," because defeat is a psychological phenomenon. He remembered Napoleon's campaign and concluded that Russia was invincible.[418] Despite his hatred of Russia, Iorga always had a healthy respect for it. When Bulgaria attacked Serbia, Iorga wrote with contempt: "Only diplomatic relations remain." Romania has but one duty: "To be ready."[419]

---

[416]*Neamul Românesc*, 10 January 1916; 14 August 1916; and 16 October 1917.

[417]*Neamul Românesc*, 10 May 1915 and 24 May 1915.

[418]*Neamul Românesc*, 2 August 1915.

[419]*Neamul Românesc*, 11 October 1915.

Iorga had to relate and to investigate the Armenian massacres. He had close ties with the numerous Armenian communities in Romania. He described the Turkish massacres of Armenians in 1915. He told of people driven into Mesopotamia, orphaned children wandering for months without their parents, and other horrors which accompanied the massacres. Iorga knew the local German consuls knew every detail, and kept their silence.[420] *Neamul Românesc* constantly reproduced the articles of the Scottish historian R.W. Seton-Watson. Later, when Romania intervened in the military conflict, Seton-Watson asked the Allies "to save Romania." Iorga reflected: "After what Romania did for the common cause, she deserves it."[421] Seton-Watson would be an important advisor at the Peace Conference.

In the first number of *Neamul Românesc* in 1916, Iorga editorialized "The Decisive Year."[422] Finally, in August, Brătianu called Iorga into his office to announce to him Romania's military intervention. In hindsight (in 1934), Iorga mocked Brătianu's self-confidence and proverbial arrogance, describing him: "I never saw him so dominating, dominating over himself, over the king, over all of us, over destiny itself. These are the kind of people for whom the human soul, that human soul which is above scheming, is something which only poets or the naive ones can take into consideration."[423] This description reflects more on Iorga than on the patriotism of Brătianu. After his announcement, Brătianu lifted the ban he had imposed on Iorga, even proposing that he publish a paper for the front soldiers. The time of restraint was over. For Iorga, this moment was a transcendental experience. This agnostic could get close to the metaphysical only if he was touched by (what he considered) the ultimate truth: the nation. Here are some excerpts from his editorial:

"The hour has arrived for which we have waited for more than two centuries, for which I have lived my life, a goal for which I have worked, wrote, and

---

[420] *Neamul Românesc*, 12 October 1916.

[421] *Neamul Românesc*, 27 November 1916.

[422] *Neamul Românesc*, 3 January 1916.

[423] *O viață de om*, vol. II, pp. 225-227.

fought, and of which I was always dreaming." Then he made the annunciation: "We demand the right of life for ourselves!" He continued: "Those midnight tolling of our bells, which express our joys and our sorrow" (bells proclaimed mobilization and war throughout the country). "What can one not endure for the coming of such an hour? It came. It would seem that it brought even into the air of our country a deep silence, since a holy chalice full of blood and tears has been lifted up for blessing." Iorga evoked the sacred memory of martyrs and heroes who fought and fell during the long suffering for the coming hour of liberation.[424]

Since Romanian intervention came relatively unexpectedly, there were early successes. The Russian Army covered Romania from the East and North-east, Bucovina was occupied by the Russians. Austria-Hungary was busy elsewhere, and the few units in Transylvania were over-extended.

There were no German troops in the area but they would come; Germany declared war on Romania. The main Romanian effort was directed towards Transylvania. Braşov was taken. Weak Hungarian forces were available for defense only. Iorga reported from "the Romanian Braşov" and considered the liberation of it like the liberation of Alsace-Lorraine, or the Danish lands robbed by Prussia in 1864.[425]

By the early fall of 1916, the Romanian Army suffered a costly defeat at Turtucaia on the Bulgarian shores of the Danube. The Danube was dominated by the Austro-Hungarian fluvial warships. Iorga never harbored doubt about the righteousness or the outcome of the struggle. When the Hungarians accused Romania of treachery he retorted: "The barons of Budapest speak about treachery." Well, the answer: "We shall take Transylvania; it is ours!" A Romanian paper in Braşov (after the recapture of the city) called Romania the "hyena of war." Iorga considered that "the only possible answer" to this kind of journalism could

---

[424]*Neamul Românesc*, 21 August 1916.

[425]*Neamul Românesc*, 3 September 1916. At the Versailles Peace Conference, Denmark would refuse to reannex territories inhabited by Germans. Not even Hitler would touch the border. Danish restraint paid off.

be "the firing squad."[426] By November the military situation began to deteriorate radically. Bulgarian and Turkish forces with tough German command under Field Marshal A. von Mackensen invaded Dobrogea. German and Austro-Hungarian forces under E. von Falkenhayn (who had failed at Verdun) were attacking Oltenia from the Banat. Iorga tried to raise the spirit of the refugees: "You have come to your own home," trying to help them feel at ease in Bucharest.[427] But it was the Germans who counted, with their modern, mechanized, disciplined, and battle-tested force. Field Marshals von Falkenhayn and von Mackensen struck across the Danube from Bulgaria straight on Bucharest. German airplanes began to bomb the city. Iorga protested against these cruel, wanton, and indiscriminate bombings which caused many civilian victims, among them women and children.[428]

Yet, he considered it shameful to go into an air-raid shelter,[429] preferring to work in the Library of the Romanian Academy during the raids; it was during the bombing raids that he did his research for his coming book *L'Histoire des relations entre la France et les Roumains* (Iaşi, 1917). By early December, catastrophe had befallen the underdeveloped army of Romania. Iorga in his memoirs unjustly chastises Ion I.C. Brătianu, Vintilă Brătianu, and Ion Duca for the "unpreparedness." He missed the point. This catastrophe was typical for an underdeveloped nation meeting the modern war machine of an industrialized Great Power. Here heroism is pointless, there is no "stalemate"; when the "Iron Man" meets the flesh and blood man, the outcome is a foregone conclusion. Such conflicts would be repeated again during World War II and after. The late twentieth century conclusion of underdeveloped nations is guerilla warfare. Guerrilla warfare is the weapon of the weak, but it is not a weak weapon. The traditional (irrational) system of underdevelopment brings other woes to the surface: the

---

[426]*Neamul Românesc*, 22 September 1916 and 6 February 1917.

[427]*Neamul Românesc*, 12 November 1916.

[428]*Neamul Românesc*, 3 November 1916.

[429]*O viaţă de om*, vol. II, p. 233.

lack of technology compounded by easygoingness, disorganization, and the corruption of traditional societies. After the blow is delivered by the industrialized Great Power, the inaptitude to come to terms with modern challenges brings demoralization. Iorga described well these symptoms, but he did not analyze correctly the roots of the problem.[430] He foresaw this in his self-imposed Vălenii exile from 1914 to 1916. He always repeated to his family: "An entry into the war will be a disaster."

A military mission was sent by France under General Henri Berthelot to straighten out the Romanian war effort. His first remark was: "You are admirably disorganized!"[431] So the Romanian army had no choice but to fall back to Moldavia near the Russian border. According to Iorga, if one said to the Russians that Romania was an ally, they retorted: "We are not the allies of Romania; we are the 'protectors' of Romania."[432]

When Predeal on the Austro-Hungarian border did not answer the telephone call of the station-master, Iorga evacuated his family from Vălenii-de-Munte to Iaşi.[433] Not much later, Vălenii fell to the invader. The Germans and the Hungarians were less than enthusiastic about Iorga's cultural bulwark there. They thoroughly plundered it, and they placed a board designating it *Schweine-amt* (an "office for Pigs"); Hungarians even scribbled on the trees *Éljen Magyarorszag*, "Long live Hungary!" The devastation was nearly complete; Iorga, still living in the nineteenth century, faulted the officers that they did not apply the minimum solidarity which was obligatory among every intellectual.[434]

---

[430] *Op. cit.,* vol. II, pp. 229-235.

[431] *Op. cit.,* vol. II, p. 218.

[432] *Supt trei regi,* p. 234.

[433] As Mr. Frasin Munteanu-Râmnic recalled, the Iorga family left Vălenii in Prince Barbu Ştirbey's car, drove to the Munteanu-Râmnicu in Ploieşti, found shelter for one night, accommodating themselves with all the children and Mme. Iorga (for some of the children there was room available only on the floor of the apartment). Iorga's smallest daughter Alina (two years old) was especially troublesome. The next morning, they continued their journey towards Iaşi.

[434] *O viaţă de om,* vol. II, pp. 236-240.

Iorga always vowed that he would be the last one to leave Bucharest, and did exactly that; he left, disguised as a monk, and arrived after a long, tiresome journey to Iaşi. On the way, Iorga was passed by the fleeing Royal train, as Iorga put it, "as a last manifestation of the catastrophe."[435] As he alighted in Iaşi, Iorga saw Russian soldiers marching through the streets "with their long overcoats sweeping the dust. Oh, how many times shall I see the long, sloppy, Asiatic procession of these young soldiers drafted almost yesterday, dangling along with their slow rhythm, tired, without will or energy. Yet, they were singing their broad, sad songs, which sounded as if filled with all the sorrow of the *Steppe*, songs cutting through an ever colder air of the fall, which soon was to turn into snow storms, our last defense against the coming enemy invasion."[436] And the typhus epidemic was also spreading.

Iorga tried to interpret the mystery of the unfriendly Russian neighbor. Iorga, "the fighter," now inspired by the fulfillment of the nationalist dream, did not (or could not) understand that the Russian soldier had ceased to understand the sense of the war, and had but one desire: to go home. The terrible winter of 1916-1917 fell like an Apache on the Moldavian countryside, isolating, even in Iaşi, family from family, fighting parties from fighting parties, and the country-side from the town. Within this snow cover, there was misery, despondence, defeat, a ravaging typhus epidemic. The situation was dramatic: one and a half million refugees, a million Russian soldiers; lack of food, lodging, and oil, and 100,000 dead from typhus. The Bucharest elite (that part of the establishment which fled) became in Iaşi even more tightly knit. Politics became even more a family affair. Brătianu moved into a house next to Iorga. Occasionally, Iorga sent his children over to his foe for the latest news.[437] The whole establishment became a "one home, one family affair." Stere, Tzigara-Samurcaş, Marghilo-man, and others remained back in Bucharest "to keep a line open," following a long Romanian historical tradition. Iorga had little understanding for their place

---

[435] *Op. cit.*, vol. II, pp. 241-243.

[436] *Op. cit.*, vol. II, p. 243.

[437] *Op. cit.*, vol. II, p. 291.

in Romanian history, a surprising lack of relativism for the greatest Romanian historian. It was the renowned Romanian historian and academician Andrei Oțetea (the Director of the Nicolae Iorga Historical Institute in Bucharest), who in 1967 (when Romania liberated itself again from the national enemy) mockingly told this writer: "We Romanians are great patriots; but then, we are in a very, very unfortunate geographical position. We have to act in the national interest, and sometimes we even have to sell our country to our enemies; but," he admonished, "we never make a delivery after the sale." Although it makes this writer uneasy – like those Westerners should feel who later justified Yalta, or supported Ceaușescu.

Iorga would attack Stere and Tzigara-Samurcaș for their collaboration with the Central Powers for decades. But they have their place in Romanian history. They are no Roland or Bayard, the *"chevalier sans peur et sans reproche."* Nor was there much room in Romanian history for such attitudes. It was Iorga who tried to act like those shining knights, with little practical result. Stere, Tzigara-Samurcaș, or Marghiloman would serve Romania, and ultimately prevail in the framework of the historical tradition as Professor Andrei Oțetea explained it. George Enescu, the great maestro, also came to Iași to comfort and to uplift his people.[438]

Creating a new army was the task of the French Military Mission, and that of General Alexandru Averescu and General Constantin Prezan from the Romanian General Staff. But, as Iorga put it, "creating a new spirit" fell upon others; the lion's share, without much exaggeration, on Iorga.[439] At Easter, Iorga propounded his belief. In an editorial, "Two Words about Easter," he explained: "Easter is the feast of Resurrection, and we guard it in our lives only in the measure of the immortality that the Almighty has bequeathed — on nations."[440]

But now, on 14 December (or by our modern count, 27 December) of 1916, the deputy Iorga rose in the Chamber (now in exile in Iași) in answer to the

---

[438] *Op. cit.,* vol. II, p. 249.

[439] *Ibid.*

[440] *Neamul Românesc,* 3 April 1917.

address of the Crown. With his speech, he was rising to the peak of his career.[441] He proudly noted that the king overcame his German origins, and he demanded more than once during his speech the enacting of a land reform. Then he continued: "In our past, many of us have suffered; if we have become something during the ages, we have not done so because of our ancestors' triumphs, but thanks to their sacrifices; and all the powers we have now are nothing but the emanation from their sacrifices transformed into energy." Iorga remembered that when Prince Gheorghe Ştefan was advised to flee his menaced country, he cried out: "I would be rather eaten alive by the dogs of this land than to abandon it!"[442] As the situation worsened, there was a big rush in the Chamber: "let's go to Odessa!" Dr. Constantin Angelescu asked Iorga how to handle this. He answered, "With a company of soldiers; it is not constitutional, but it will be historic."[443]

Iorga concluded his address with rousing words. He reminded his audience that Romania was many times invaded in the past, yet, "in the corner into which we were pushed back, we always preserved the precious seeds of our faith and of our hope. This time too we shall witness the darkness of foreign despotism pass away from us and we shall be able to repeat the words of Petru Rareş, the son of Ştefan, who said 'We shall become again that which we were before! And much more than that!"[444] His speech had a great effect; the whole country thanked him for it, with the king and queen leading the homage. It was printed and disseminated among the trenches of the hard pressed, tired, bleeding, yet still fighting soldiers.

Iorga wrote during this period some of his most beautiful articles, writing with love about the suffering of soldiers on the front, even about the severely

---

[441]This was the unanimous opinion of the Iorga family.

[442]The suggestion that the Bucharest establishment should be eaten by Romanian dogs rather than to abandon the country did not please everybody: those who planned exit to Russia asked Iorga to strike the passage from the reprint of his speech. Iorga refused. *O viaţă de om*, vol. II, p. 254.

[443]*Memorii*, vol. I, p. 16.

[444]*Discours prononcé à la chambre des députés de Roumanie* (Iaşi, 1917).

tried horses, mobilized for the Romanian military. Once he saw a young group of refugee peasant lads. Iorga asked them, "Where are you from, lads?" The answer was: "From Olt, from Râmnic, etc.," areas now under occupation. He asked them: "Did you flee from the enemy?" The answer came promptly: "No! We came to fight!"[445]

Iorga quickly reestablished *Neamul Românesc* in Iaşi. For the first time, 5,000 copies were printed daily, on orders of the king, and at the cost of the State. Iorga remarked: "Finally the time has come when my words were not only blown into the wind."[446] He made tremendous efforts, despite being ill with severe intercostal pains. His collaborators were Vasile Bogrea, who (after the death of the actor Liciu) was the only friend Iorga had left. Beyond Bogrea, there was Alex Cusin, a capable, loyal collaborator. There was also the Transylvanian priest and poet Ion Agârbiceanu, Dimitrie Anghel, and Alexandru Vlahuţă, also the young Nichifor Crainic and Aurel Metroniu. Iorga's journalism was always political. When Tsar Nicholas's Patron Saint day came on 6 December, Iorga wrote: "The ruler of the half of two continents, a noble and good man, a delicate soul and a wise ruler, inspired by noble ideas.... He came to us in 1914, breaking a long ice" (Romanian-Russian relations), concluding: "Long live the Emperor Nicholas, a powerful friend of Romania, today and tomorrow!"[447]

Was this article a tribute to an ally? A concession to Brătianu?[448] It sounds too good to be true; Iorga tried to be "expedient" for Romania's sake. What he thought about the Russian presence emerges when he describes the Orthodox Church service on Nicholas II's name day. Even the way of the incantations in low keys of Russian Orthodox traditions (according to Iorga) "seemed for us,

---

[445]*Neamul Românesc*, 16 December 1916.

[446]*O viaţă de om*, vol. II, pp. 261-262.

[447]*Neamul Românesc*, 7 December 1916.

[448]Mme. Liliana Pippidi-Iorga to the writer.

despite of our common Orthodox faith, like a foreign invasion, an insulting foreign domination, which weighed heavily on our souls."[449] He constantly complained about the Russian behavior, raping girls even younger than 10 years of age, pillage of Romanian property, clashes with Romanian military and civilians. With the general revolutionary mood and spreading anarchy, these incidents would increase steeply.[450] Iorga concluded: "Everyone knows that the Russians behave today as a people as they acted yesterday as a State."[451] Iorga remained with his family. His oldest son, Petru, a professional officer, often passed through Iaşi, almost always visiting his father.[452]

In the beginning of 1917, Brătianu offered Iorga a government post (since there was a conservative-liberal "National" government formed). Iorga rejected it, saying: "I cannot associate myself with a policy which I fought against for years." He assured Brătianu that under the present circumstances there was no time for politics; he would support any national government, be it Conservative or Liberal.[453]

Meanwhile, Iorga continued his work on the lines of a politicized history, to explain and interpret Romanian national goals. He brought with him the manuscript of his *L'histoire des relations entre France et les Roumains* from Bucharest, to be published in Iaşi, where he would also write and publish his *Histoire des relations Anglo-Roumaines* (Iaşi, 1917). Analyzing Anglo-Romanian relations (as described by English travelers), Iorga concluded with the hope that the world's greatest power, England, would honor the sacrifices which fourteen million Romanians brought for the common cause. In his *Relations des Roumains avec les Alliés* (Iaşi, 1917) he analyzed Romanian relationship with the Entente. But there were limits to Iorga's expediency. In his *Histoire des Russo-Roumains*

---

[449]*O viaţă de om*, vol. II, p. 252.

[450]*Memorii*, vol. I, pp. 41 and 78. These passages represent only a few of Iorga's complaints about the behavior of Russian soldiers.

[451]*Op. cit.*, vol. I, p. 56.

[452]*O viaţă de om*, vol. II, p. 266.

[453]*Op. cit.*, vol. II, p. 269; also, *Supt trei regi*, p. 239.

(Iaşi, 1917), he described the unhappy relations between Romania and Russia. From the historical point of view, Iorga's analysis is irrefutable. Şeicaru expressed the desire that this book by Iorga should become a textbook in Romania. The problem was in the political sphere. Iorga remembered that when the Spanish Ambassador asked Russian diplomats about Iorga's evaluation of the Russo-Romanian relationship, they answered that this was written "from the Romanian point of view." Iorga answered: "I wonder what they would have said if I had really written from the Romanian point of view?"[454] Brătianu was angry. Iorga later told Şeicaru: "The events bore out that I was right." He continued that "it was not the politician who was vindicated, but the historian. Not the kind of politician who is a tributary to the immediate present." Şeicaru correctly asserted that it was precisely this supremacy of the historian over the politician which made it so difficult to take Iorga's political activities seriously.[455]

The problems in Russia, accentuated by the misconduct of the war effort and war impact on the population, led to the February Revolution. The Tsar was forced to abdicate. Iorga considered this positively but he was rather apprehensive. "Romania cannot remain indifferent," but expressed "best wishes for Russia," noting that the morale of the Russian soldiers was good.[456] At least it was so for the time being. The Romanians had few contacts with Russian troops. As Iorga remarked, only Poles came to his house "wearing the uniform of the Tsar." He remembered them, "high-ranking officers did not desire anything more in the interest of their nation than the fastest and total destruction of the army in which they were forced to serve."[457]

Another visitor came to Iorga's house in Russian uniform. A Bessarabian soldier, Buzdugan, who would become an important source of information. Buzdugan was a self-made poet who published in a Chişinău newspaper. He explained to Iorga that it was chimeric to expect the Russian soldiers to fight for

---

[454] *Memorii*, vol. I, p. 31.

[455] Şeicaru, *op. cit.*, pp. 86-87.

[456] *Neamul Românesc*, 2 March 1917.

[457] *O viaţă de om*, vol. II, p. 252.

the bourgeois of London or Paris. Then he attacked King Ferdinand; Iorga made it clear that he was not only a monarchist but also a personal friend of the king. All this did not prevent Buzdugan from later becoming an under-secretary in a Ministry during the reign of Carol II.[458]

By March and April the disintegration of the Russian Armed Forces started in earnest. Officers were disrespected, then they were demoted, later they were killed. Amidst this general breakdown, something infinitely more serious happened. Buzdugan came to Iorga with the news: Christian Rakovski, freed by rebellious Russian soldiers from prison, was addressing the crowds, Iorga rushed down with Buzdugan, and caught Rakovski still speaking. Iorga was optimistic; according to him, Romanians looked at Rakovski as an animal who had escaped from his cage.[459] But Buzdugan brought more ominous news; Russian units stationed outside Iaşi planned to arrest the Romanian Royal Family. They were under the influence of the anarchist student Rashal, and his girlfriend. Rashal came from St. Petersburg, where he distinguished himself by throwing Russian Navy' Officers into the boilers of a warship and cooking them alive.[460] With his detachment, Colonel Gheorghe Rascoviceanu, a determined Romanian officer, saved General Shcherbachev, the commander of the "Russo-Romanian Front" from being "arrested" (murdered in cold blood).[461]

Iorga became alarmed at the news of Buzdugan. These anarchist elements were worse than the Bolsheviks; so he impetuously decided to take action. First he tried to communicate the news to the political leadership, but he found complete disarray and incompetence. As Iorga recounts, I.G. Duca said: "to arrest a popular ruler in the center of his capital city!" repeating this sentence in an effect-seeking way, "as if Duca would address the Chamber or a meeting and, after

---

[458] *Op. cit.*, vol. II, pp. 270-271.

[459] *Op. cit.*, vol. II, p. 272.

[460] *Op. cit.*, vol. II, p. 284.; also, *Supt trei regi*, p. 242.

[461] *Ibid.*; Dimitrie Munteanu-Râmnic was with his family in Iaşi. He saw Colonel Rascoviceanu calming the rebellious Russian soldiers.

pronouncing his sentence, he would wait for an outbreak of a resounding applause."[462] Then he turned to General Petalá to inquire whether he would order the guards to open fire on the Russians if they moved on the Royal Palace? The General answered that he could not give such an order and the Romanian army could not move on the Russians, not even on disorderly Russian elements influenced by anarchists. Now Iorga decided to rake resolute actions. Since he did not hope for anything from Romanian politicians or even the Romanian Army, he visited foreign diplomats. The Italian Ambassador, the Baron C. Fasciotti, gave a mouthful of Machiavellian answers: Rakovski was the kind of person whom one should either shoot or win over. The Romanian government could not accomplish either of these feats. But Fasciotti promised Iorga that yes, he would intervene. He received similar assurances from Saint-Aulaire, the Ambassador of France. The English Ambassador, G. Barclay, was not very helpful. The United States Ambassador, Charles Vopicka, remained in Bucharest where he offered services to Romania, the value of which Iorga thought could not be overestimated. The American Embassy in Iaşi was in the hands of the Secretary, Andrews. Andrews immediately agreed to do what he could, and he proved very helpful.[463] Then Iorga went quickly to the Royal Palace and advised the king to leave Iaşi immediately (Queen Marie was nursing the wounded and typhoid stricken soldiers). The king's departure was made under the pretext of his reviewing troops. It was not to seem to the Romanian Army that his departure was flight. The king was very sad; Iorga saw that he had the fate of Tsar Nicholas II before his eyes. The king said "Well, I shall leave; I am useless here anyhow." Then, Iorga met with some politicians, and they decided to go to appeal to the Russians in person.[464] On 21 March undisciplined and rebellious troops, under

---

[462]*O viaţă de om*, vol. II, pp. 272-273.

[463]*Op. cit.*, vol. II, pp. 273-274.

[464]*Op. cit.*, vol. II, pp. 275-276.

"Bolshevik" leadership,[465] liberated Rakovski from a Romanian prison. The Russian command (the "Stavka"), General Shcherbachev and General Golovin (on 22 March) disapproved and tried to restore discipline. The Russian commanders called the attention of the soldiers to the fact that "Rakovski was arrested by an Allied government for his pro-German demoralizing activities"; consequently, those who freed him "were under the influence of foreign agents."[466]

But the Soldiers' Council (Soviet) continued to foment anarchy. General Prezan, the Romanian Minister of Defense Vintilă Brătianu, and the Chief of Staff of the Romanian Army, General Cristescu, appealed to the Romanian army the same day. They explained that, since the enemy was unable to break Romanian determination, it was trying to subvert the Romanian army from the inside. Foreign agents had liberated Rakovski; the Russian allies would fulfill their dudes in an exemplary way and all rumors about a separate peace were false. The appeal ended: "We cannot allow the Germans to break our will. Fulfill your duties and continue the struggle!" The Romanian Labor Party (a group of dissident Liberals under George Diamandy) aimed to the Soldiers' Soviet in Socola, asking them to stop interfering in Romanian internal affairs.

The Soldiers' Soviet (from Socola) sent a bombastic answer: Point 1: all rumors about the possible Russian show of force or any demonstration in Iaşi on 23 March are false. No Russian troops stationed in the Iaşi, Vaslui, or Socola area will participate in such demonstrations; Point 2: contrary to Tsarist Russia, the new revolutionary Russia does not intend to interfere with the internal affairs of other countries; Point 3: the Russian Army, based on discipline emanating from authority, not on authoritarianism, is healthy; Point 4: all rumors which indicate that the Russian Army is weak are false. This new, democratic Russian

---

[465]Iorga believed the rebellious Russian soldiers (and student leader Rashal) were Bolsheviks or Bolshevik-influenced. It is unlikely that Bolsheviks started such large-scale activities as early as the end of March 1917, before the summer. Various actions — including murder — in March 1917 were more likely carried out by anarchists than by the disciplined, purposeful Bolsheviks.

[466]*Neamul Românesc*, 23 January 1932.

Army is stronger than ever. The world will see what this new Russian Army "based on democracy" is worth; and soon enough.[467] But in the atmosphere of general breakdown and anarchy these words had little to do with reality On 23 March, some rebellious Russian units appeared in Iaşi; they menaced King Ferdinand.

There was no time to waste. Iorga wrote in Russian and in Romanian a direct appeal to the Soldiers' Soviet at Socola. "To our brother citizens of the NEW RUSSIA!" Iorga explained that Romania "sincerely welcomed the Russian Army to fight the German, Austro-Hungarian, Bulgarian, and Turkish autocracies which wish to subjugate mankind." He continued: "We have shared with you everything we have. Now we have almost only the last piece of bread left, but, according to the custom of our fathers, we are sharing with you, who are our guests, that too.... Now you have become free and you wish to help us achieve our internal reforms and obtain our citizen rights. But you must understand that the right of ever)' people to be master in his own house is beyond discussion." Then, in capital letters and in bold print: "WE ROMANIANS WISH TO BE MASTERS IN OUR OWN HOUSE TOO!" Further, "This war has found you Russians together with us (i.e., Romanians) on the eve of the realization of those reforms of which we have always dreamed during the last fifty years of our constitutional life. Now this hour has arrived; in a few days, the Romanian Chamber will discuss projects about an agrarian and electoral reform, and, with these reforms, all of us in our country shall participate in the process of restructuring our lives and becoming free citizens. If there are still obstacles in the way of this, we shall remove them by our own efforts. Your duty, the duty of the citizens of the New Russia, and the duty of your soldiers consists of contributing to the liberation of our land and to help to re-establish those rights which were trampled down by the Germans and Bulgarians. Only this way can you give us powerful support and contribute to the common cause of liberation. Our public symbol, our spokesmen are not those few German

---

[467]*Neamul Românesc*, 25 January 1932.

agents who gave a chance to the Socialists (that is, by liberating Rakovski), but our beloved king who started the reform by giving the land to the peasants!"

"He who opposes Him obstructs the realization of those very democratic reforms which He intends to carry out, which he desires more than anything." Now in capital letters: "No true Democrat, no true Revolutionary will make any violent attempt to thwart this process against the will of our country and our people. The liberty of every people, may it be small or great, has to be respected by every other people, if that other people is truly free. Long live Russian-Romanian unity!" The appeal was signed by "The President of the Nationalist Democratic Party, Professor Nicolae Iorga."[468] Although during his whole appeal he adhered strictly to the Romanian raison d'état, on the basis of what we know by now about Iorga's ideas it seems he was also sincere. We are faced with the quintessential Iorga, who, without abandoning his principles, was ready to cooperate even with Russian revolutionaries.

To what extent did his appeal calm the spirits? Iorga thought that his appeal was well received by the Russians.[469] There was also the powerful intervention of foreign embassies, Iorga's resoluteness, and the very fickle nature of the prevailing revolutionary anarchy. But perhaps the most important factor was that Russian revolutionary seeds had fallen on a dry Romanian rock; and the agrarian reform, and the enfranchisement of the people made this rock even more solid. But it became clear to everybody that for immunizing the Romanian spirit from revolutionary contagion, and the general uplifting of morale, more than just words were necessary. According to Iorga's own account, the next important step was his improvisation. When he returned from Socola, Iorga (urged by Barbu Ştirbey) wrote, on the streets of Iaşi, the proclamation about the agrarian reform and the enfranchisement of the peasantry on the palm of his hand, telling the people that "Stephen the Great also gave land to his soldiers." On this same memorable day, 23 March 1917, by nightfall the appeal was carried to *Monitorul Oficial*. Buzdugan, the Bessarabian — and also the Secretary of the United

---

[468] *Neamul Românesc*, 26 January and 27 January 1932.

[469] *O viaţă de om*, vol. II, p. 275.

States Embassy, Andrews — assured Iorga that the Russians would remain quiet and there would be no repetition of the events in St. Petersburg or otherwise.[470]

Problems not resolved in decades, let alone in centuries, were resolved in a few hours. Even women were to be enfranchised, because (as Iorga put it) they had shown understanding and courage, both in struggle and in politics.[471] But according to Iorga, all this was not easy to legislate. Brătianu told him: "The landlords will revolt!" Whereupon Iorga retorted: "Then one will have to shoot the landlords for the peasants' sake like one shot before the peasants for the landlords' sake." Iorga impressed upon the king that he should approve the fait accompli, saying: "Either reforms will be carried out with the king, or they will be carried out against the king." He added that he eased his mind and saved his soul by telling this to the king.[472] There was no time for pursuing class interests and playing the games of *Politicianism* the hour was too serious for that. Thus, the crisis subsided. Ion Mihalache later qualified the agrarian reform as a kind of a "safety valve" for the ruling class. It certainly worked. Not only did the Romanian peasant soldier remain steadfast amid the daily demoralizing spectacle of the Russian Army's dissolution, but this peasant soldier remained steadfast during the whole revolutionary upheaval between 1917 and 1920, Romania being surrounded by Communism and Civil War in Russia, Hungary, and a leftist upheaval in Bulgaria. The Romanian peasant soldier would be instrumental in crushing the Hungarian Soviet.

And how did the war go in Romania (and elsewhere)? While the disintegration of Russian forces increased, a new French-trained and equipped Romanian Army was ready by the late spring of 1917. According to Iorga, not only

---

[470]*Op. cit.*, vol. II, p. 276.

[471]*Neamul Românesc*, 20 June 1917. Iorga was not always in favor of women being enfranchised. In 1907, he wrote a report on the suffragettes in England with little sympathy. Having described the demonstration, he concludes: "The more disgusting ones among them were naturally apprehended by the police." *Neamul Românesc*, 8 February 1907. Thus, like another "man of the nineteenth century," Woodrow Wilson, Iorga changed his opinion on women's vote.

[472]*O viață de om*, vol. II, pp. 277-278.

were they French-trained and equipped, they looked French, and (as he put it hopefully) even the spirit with which they were imbued seemed to be French. General Berthelot and his staff seemingly did a good job. This Romanian Army was not inconsiderable; it was a force of 300,000 now also psychologically fortified by the king's declaration of an agrarian reform and enfranchisement.[473]

The front line was unchanged. Only Moldavia was still in Romanian hands. The great event was the United States of America's entrance into the war. Iorga, an almost unreserved admirer of the United States, had reason for celebration. He editorialized: "The America of Lafayette comes to the aid of martyred France." America would put its industry at the disposal of the Allies. In another editorial entitled "The Mission of America" he expressed a high opinion about American war aims, above all President Wilson's championing of the principle of self-determination.[474] On the Western front the entry of the United States could not have come at a better moment. By this time, the French soldiers had had enough. Mutinies and disobediences occurred. Iorga was well-informed, because the Romanian censor transmitted to him every copy of neutral Danish and Dutch papers.

During this spring Iorga wrote an article entitled: "How Empires Are Made and Undone." He expounded his belief that all empires are of a transitory nature, including the present Russian, Austro-Hungarian, Ottoman, and German Empires; only states based on the nation endure, because they are the product of an organic process, rather than an artificial gathering in. In another article he expressed his opinion again that "nations cannot be destroyed." This is a faith which Iorga proclaimed during his life to the very end.[475]

By this time many articulate officers on the front, both professional and mobilized ones, looked increasingly to Iorga for leadership. Șeicaru remembered his visit to Iorga's home in Iași during September of 1917.

---

[473] *Supt trei regi*, p. 243.

[474] *Neamul Românesc*, 22 and 26 March, 23 June 1917.

[475] *Neamul Românesc*, 8 and 9 May 1917, and 22 June 1917.

He explained to Iorga the psychology of the trenches, and described the conditions: disorganization, low quality of supply, the profound corruption, and the absence of the most elementary honesty of those who were leading. He continued: "Iaşi is a different world, for which the war did not exist. Iaşi does not live in the world of expectations and ideals of those in the trenches. Those who live within the relative comforts and security of Iaşi think 'the hell with us in the trenches!'" And he warned how easy it would be for the youth to identify all evil with one person, concluding his expose: "We identify all this evil with Ion Brătianu!" During this memorable encounter there emerged the Maurasian difference between the *pays légal* and that of the *pays réal*. Şeicaru remembered Iorga listening to him without interrupting once, deeply moved. He brought with him also hundreds of letters from the trenches written to Iorga. (In this way the letters remained unseen by the military censor.) He handed them over to Iorga. The letters described abuses, corruption, incompetence. At that point Iorga got up and showed Şeicaru a sack full of other hundreds of letters, which officers on trips of duty in Iaşi left at his place, telling the same story. Then Iorga rose and answered, explaining that he was aware of everything, and that in Russia revolution opened the gates to anarchy. Germany would certainly take advantage of that. He was aware of the terrible shortcomings of the Brătianu government, yet, and here Iorga raised his voice high as if he wished that it could be heard where the trenches were dug: "Yet, I do not care who carries the banner of our country; I see only the flag and I only defend the flag of our country."[476]

A great chance was taking shape for Iorga, namely to become the leader and spokesman of that generation which was to emerge from the trenches. A generation which began to look to him for leadership because of his utter sincerity, honesty, and incorruptibility (known to everybody in the country and not

---

[476]Şeicaru, *op. cit.*, pp. 52-54; also, *Memorii*, vol. I, pp. 137-138. This writer has read dozens of letters in Iorga's correspondence from the years 1917 and 1918. They reveal the characteristic conditions in the Armed Forces ruled by "oriental despotism": arbitrariness, corruption and cynicism resulting in inefficiency, egotism and incapacity. The soldiers paid the price for all this: having lost confidence in superior authority figures, these letters give indications of developing selfish, but self-preserving attitudes, caring only for themselves, and (maybe) for their friends.

a major commodity amidst the leadership of contemporary Romania). They looked towards him because he was a firebrand fighter as well as an orator and animator of unparalleled erudition. Iorga the historian-politician could become a great political leader! Unfortunately for Romania, he would miss this chance.

As summer came, the Romanian army started an offensive at Putna. It would have been successful but for the Russian army. Kerensky might have inspired the Russian army by his fiery speeches, but there was an enormous anti-war sentiment among the Russian people, carefully fostered by the Bolsheviks. The front in Bucovina fell on 21 July 1917. Cernăuți was lost, and the news unleashed a panic in Iași. Brătianu advised Iorga to send his family to Odessa. Iorga, after long soul-searching, decided to evacuate his family from Iași: "This was the most difficult decision of my life."[477] He had no intention of leaving. Odessa began to play the role as a prospective fallback capital (although, according to Iorga, some of them would have preferred Kharkhov because it was about a thousand miles farther away). Gold bullion and some historical relics were also sent to Russia for safekeeping.

By the end of July, in the Southern part of the front, the Romanian army started a sweep against the enemy forces at Mărăști. It was rather successful; nevertheless, the Germans attacked in strength at the end of July, in the area of Mărășești. The greatest battle of the Romanian campaign ensued. There was fierce fighting, and shattering Romanian losses during the hand-to-hand combat; but the Romanians stood their ground. There was uncertainty and anguish in Iași because military bulletins and other news filtering out were scarce. Iorga's oldest son, Petra, was fighting in the first line of battle. During these days of anguish, sometimes dark, unconfirmed news came out from the storm of iron and fire. Other times, comforting news brought hope. Finally, by the beginning of August 1917, the Battle of Mărășești was over. The Romanian Army had stood its ground. Iorga (and many Romanian historians) called the outcome a Romanian victory,[478] which is somewhat exaggerated. Yet, if a small underdeveloped

---

[477]*Memorii*, vol. I, pp. 76-82.

[478]*O viață de om*, vol. II, pp. 280-288; also, *Memorii*, vol. I, pp. 80-92.

country is capable of holding its own against the onslaught of a strong, industrialized power's well-equipped, battle-experienced armed forces, in that case it has held more than its own. The worsening situation within Russia cast deep shadows on the Romanian scene. By September 1917, Kerensky (Iorga called him a "democratic Napoleon") declared Russia a Republic. Iorga supported him,[479] but did not understand fully the desperation behind his measures. Iorga's hopes were not directed towards the Hast, but towards the United States. He editorialized: "The United States, this gigantic tree society," continuing to describe what he called "the glorious American experience" starting with the Pilgrims, then arriving at the conclusion: "The United States has proved that liberty is not a goal but the very condition that man should fulfill his supreme mission."[480]

At this time, Iorga showed a great deal of sympathy for Zionist aspirations. He welcomed the entry of General Allenby's forces into Jerusalem. General Allenby was no Godefroy de Bouillon; he came to the Jerusalem of David and Solomon. Iorga explained his sympathy: "As being a nationalist, he cannot do otherwise."[481]

In the fall, the situation in Moldavia became desperate. The Romanian army was impervious to the anarchy within the ranks of the Russians, but not to the consequences of the disintegration of the armed forces of its principal ally. Finally, Russian units left over were chased out by the Romanian Army. Departing Russians showed their depravity and lack of discipline, committing a lot of crimes.[482] Iorga remembered that false, fantastic rumors swept in and hung like a dark cloud over unoccupied Romania.[483] By the end of October, Iorga announced in his paper that the "Maximalists" (as Iorga called Lenin and his party)

---

[479] *Neamul Românesc*, 8 and 9 September 1917.

[480] *Neamul Românesc*, 13 and 19 November 1917.

[481] *Neamul Românesc*, 1 December 1917.

[482] *O viață de om*, vol. II, p. 283.

[483] *Memorii*, vol. I, pp. 160-162.

were in control in St. Petersburg. The historian understood the developments and the acceleration of the revolutionary process. He concluded that, in defeating Robespierre, the French Revolution could conserve and hand down to posterity those achievements which Robespierre hated so much. He warned: "Hungry mobs always consider the government guilty, and the opposition to be the salvation.... Every revolution has its own Robespierre; there is but one solution for this, this is what historical experience teaches us."[484]

Lenin started negotiations for a separate peace. The Russian defection made Romania's position untenable. With Bucovina and the Carpathian range now in the hands of the Central Powers, and Germans moving into the Ukraine, Romania was encircled. Ultimately, Lenin's policies forced the Romanians to abandon the struggle.

Could not Romania have followed the example of Serbia, to make a last desperate stand? Iorga was always inspired by Serbia and by Montenegro even more! So he opposed the abandonment of the struggle. But Iorga's *jusqu'au boutisme* was not the position of the Romanian government. The Serbians, their king, and their leadership fought their way through Albania to Corfu. Geography and the situation during the fall and winter of 1917-18 did not leave such a way out for the Romanians. Also, Serbian history and tradition in the struggle for survival differed from that of Romania. But Iorga was opposed to negotiating with the Central Powers, as Marghiloman and others started to do. He called them "Our Ghibellini."[485] King Ferdinand (especially Queen Marie) opposed stretching out peace-feelers; yet the negotiations went on. They started during the winter at Buftea (at the headquarters of the Supreme German Commander, Field Marshal von Mackensen); they were continued in Focşani, where an armistice was concluded on 11 December 1917.[486] Iorga explained that General Averescu, who went to Focşani, did not represent the Romanian nation.

---

[484]*Neamul Românesc*, 30 October 1917 and 2 November 1917.

[485]*Neamul Românesc*, 31 January 1918.

[486]*O viaţă de om*, vol. II, pp. 286-287.

As in February, the peace treaty with the Central Powers was just about concluded, Iorga concentrated his attention on hope: he celebrated George Washington's birthday and ridiculed the Romanian position, namely that Romania was returning "to neutrality." He asked: "Are there two different Romanias?"[487] He wrote another editorial: "Are we going to Canossa?"[488] The partisans of the separate peace treaty (above all Constantin Stere) in Bucharest and those in Iaşi, not directly involved in the peace negotiations (like V. Madgearu, I. Mihalache, or the Brătianus), fared badly in Iorga's biography, as far as their role during these negotiations is concerned.[489]

By the spring of 1918 a peace treaty was signed. Dobrogea was ceded to Bulgaria, and large strategic strips of territory within the Carpathian range were ceded to Hungary. The new government in Bucharest under Alexandra Marghiloman (according to all indications) was as convinced about an Allied victory as Iorga was; they concluded this peace treaty as a kind of re-insurance treaty; and as they saw Romania's interests and historical tradition, they did not have much of a choice.

But in the spring of 1918, the eyes of many a Romanian politician were turned towards Bessarabia; this was the time to move on this ancient Romanian land and bring it back (as the Romanians say), "into the mother homeland." The spring of 1918 offered opportunities opening up across the Prut.

During the revolutionary upheaval of 1917, the Bessarabian population formed a Moldavian Autonomous Republic within the framework of the Russian Democratic Republic. But with the Bolsheviks starting a heavy-handed centralization, the Bessarabian *Sfat* (meaning council or Soviet in Romanian) became uneasy. At this point, with German consent, Stere traveled to Chişinău, and had himself elected as the president of the local Moldavian *Sfat*. With the Ukraine declaring its independence, somehow Bessarabia remained dangling in the air.

---

[487]*Neamul Românesc*, 11, 16, and 17 February 1918.

[488]*Neamul Românesc*, 11 February 1918.

[489]*O viaţă de om*, vol. II, p. 264.

Iorga, the Moldavian, did not want to stay out of this process. He sent his political lieutenant, Dimitrie Munteanu-Râmnic, to Chişinău to further the process by now well under way.[490] The Moldavian *Sfat* was induced to call in the Romanian Army which entered Chişinău in January 1918. The local *Sfat* voted on 27 March 1918 for the unification of Bessarabia with Romania with stipulations of autonomy, which would never be honored. According to Iorga, it was France that facilitated the entry of Romanian troops into Bessarabia,[491] but he never explained how France facilitated this. Under the circumstances, it seems most likely that Iorga simply could not bear to admit that Bessarabia was returned to Romania with German help.

In Bucharest, the Marghiloman government had to continue to enact a comedy according to history's textbook. Iorga did not make politics during the war, much less did he participate in the tragic-comedy of a collaborating government; he remained in Iaşi. The Marghiloman government, in order to obtain legitimacy, held elections under enemy occupation. Cuza was elected, and he strongly attacked Brătianu in the parliament.[492] After the elections, the Marghiloman government continued its policies on the lines as described before. To please the Germans, it began to make noises addressing the king, that he should "finally make the redeeming gesture" (that he should abdicate). It went on to demand (or promise) that Brătianu and the others "responsible for the war" would be tried. Finally, the Romanian Chamber resolved this problem with an intelligent compromise: it enacted a law that granted amnesty to Brătianu and to all the politicians who were "responsible" for starting the war against Germany.[493] The former Austrian Ambassador, Count Czernin, returned to Bucharest; now he could play the role of "pro-consul," to which he always aspired. General Berthelot and the French military mission had to leave Iaşi. When they departed, the king, the queen, and, of course, Iorga said goodbye to them at the platform of the railroad

---

[490]*Op.cit.*, vol. II, pp. 300-301.

[491]*Neamul Românesc*, 2 April 1918.

[492]*O viaţă de om*, vol. II, p. 303.

[493]*Memorii*, vol. II, pp. 30-36 and 62.

station. The farewell of the Royal couple was especially warm. These are the small gestures which make Royalty so attractive.[494] The king never ratified Marghiloman's re-insurance peace treaty; nor did Brătianu or the Liberals. The Royal couple withdrew to Bicaz, into the forests of the Carpathians.

During the whole spring and summer of 1918, Iorga's position remained inscrutable as far as the "Ghibellines" in Bucharest were concerned. He was joined by those, like Take Ionescu, who were ready (as they put it) to retreat all the way to Port Arthur, rather than abandon national dignity.[495]

Prince Carol did not help soothe the pain and the humiliation of his parents. Giving a good insight into his character, he left his suffering country, dressed in the uniform of a Russian officer, with the dancer Zizi Lambrino for Odessa, where they married. After this rash act, he was apprehended and, as punishment, secluded until the fall in the Bistriţa Monastery. Carol was Iorga's pupil. He received the best education possible, not only from Iorga. The problem with him was not how he was brought up, but rather how he aimed out. The scandal had a shattering effect on the already hard-tried Royal couple. Iorga commented that Prince Carol committed "an act which should be committed but only once." In his newspaper, Iorga wrote that "he does not wish to judge him, only to love him." The rest of the article puts the blame on the prince's entourage rather than on him.[496] But the Royal couple considered it necessary that Prince Carol's image should be polished up by a man whose honor was beyond question. So Queen Marie asked Iorga to write a book about Prince Carol which would accomplish just that.[497] In the little book *Prinţul Carol pentru cine nu-l cunoaşte şi totuşi îl judecă* (Iaşi, 1918) (*Prince Carol, for Those Who Do Not Know Him, but are Ready to Condemn Him*) Iorga described how the Transylvanian people

---

[494] *O viaţă de om*, vol. II, p. 296; and *Memorii*, vol. II, p. 40.

[495] *O viaţă de om*, vol. II, pp. 286-287 and p. 295.

[496] *O viaţă de om*, vol. II, p. 310; and *Neamul Românesc*, 12 September 1918.

[497] As Mme. Liliana Pippidi-Iorga explained, Iorga did not feel enthusiastic about exonerating Prince Carol. But the king, and especially Queen Marie, insisted, so he undertook the task.

loved Carol during his visit. He also described Carol's participation at Iorga's Summer University in Vălenii-de-Munte.

The summer of 1918 was hot and long. Iorga constantly received news from occupied Romania about the general depravity, demoralization, and the plunder to which the Germans and the Austro-Hungarians subjected it. From April 1918, at the request of the Central Powers, a censor was installed in Iaşi for the Romanian press. We see many of Iorga's articles censored with large blank spaces. He managed to bypass the censorship by writing historical allegories relevant to contemporary developments.[498] More important were some of Iorga's works. They were politically motivated, nevertheless, are interesting and valuable. His *Cugetarea şi fapta germană* (Iaşi, 1918) (*German Thought and Action*), contrasts systematically the loftiness and idealism of German philosophy with German political and military actions. He tried to find an answer to the contradiction and to explain how a people constantly engaged in abstract, idealistic thought might, in the next moment, be ready to submit to the most thoughtless and regimented military action. According to Iorga, it was a confrontation between the spirit, thought, common sense, and the fist. This dominated the life of the German people which showed a great spiritual complexity. Another interesting book is *Originea şi desvoltarea statului austriac* (Iaşi, 1918) (*The Origins and the Development of the Austrian State*). Iorga followed the growth of the Austrian State and Empire which occurred in a casual conjunctural fashion, almost without any organic development. Yet, a culture and a way of life was established during Hapsburg domination. Iorga did not fail to point out the importance of the universal character of Catholicism in this process or that of the Papacy, concluding that there was no European state which was as important as was the Hapsburg Empire. The Papacy had kept a watchful eye on Vienna during the last 500 years, intervening immediately when it felt that its position or the Catholic character of the Hapsburg domains was challenged.

But the war still continued on the Western front. The Germans, concentrating their best forces, started a last effort during the summer of 1918. They did

---

[498]*O viaţă de om*, vol. II, p. 298.

not succeed. By the end of September Bulgaria asked for an armistice, to be followed by Turkey. Starting from Salonika, the Serbians and their French allies pushed relentlessly to the North. The victorious advance did not go unnoticed either in Iaşi or in Bucharest. By the end of October the Austro-Hungarian Empire disintegrated.

The historians I. Nistor and I. Flondor, both Bucovinian Romanian nationalists and friends of Iorga, assumed the leadership in Cernăuţi, counterbalancing some feeble Ukrainian autonomist moves. They invited the Romanian Army and on 16 November 1918 Bucovina was united with Romania. Iorga hailed in an editorial: "The Moldavia of Stephen the Great has risen again."[499] Then suddenly Woodrow Wilson's picture covered the front page of *Neamul Românesc*, presented by Iorga as the "hope of humanity." He continued (perhaps a little too idealistically) to describe disinterested American motives, arriving at the conclusion that the role of the United States would be "arbitration and the establishment of an eternal peace," the goals of President Wilson. Iorga made a naive historical analysis of the American role in Cuba, the Philippines, and in Mexico — an analysis which Professor Bancroft could not have written differently — and described finally Wilson as a "Professor of History and a quiet Academician."[500] One can only remark with melancholy at the end of the twentieth century that President Wilson, like Iorga, and the founder of Czechoslovakia, another university professor, T.G. Masaryk (who visited Iaşi during 1917 and was a friend of both Woodrow Wilson and Nicolae Iorga) were typical "men of the nineteenth century" All three of them would face a different world than the one which they desired or envisioned for mankind.

Just before Armistice Day, Romania theatrically "re-entered" the World War on the side of the Allies, and General Prezan ordered the Romanian Army to liberate Transylvania. A few days later Germany asked for an armistice, and

---

[499] *Neamul Românesc*, 26 October 1918.

[500] *Neamul Românesc*, 16 October 1918.

Iorga could editorialize: "France Leads!"[501] With the Romanian Army penetrating into Transylvania, let us examine Iorga's position. He commented during the summer of 1917, when Tisza and his government fell in Budapest, that even after his fall he was determining the policies of the Hungarian government. He considered Tisza the greatest enemy of the Romanians and absolutely inflexible on the Transylvanian question. As Iorga commented: "In vain does the sociologist Professor Jàszi protest." In August 1917, it appears that Iorga exchanged some messages with Professor Jàszi: "Is it possible to have an understanding between the Hungarians and the Romanians?," Jàszi asks. Iorga commented, as we said before, that Professor Jàszi was "a White Raven." Answering him, Iorga wrote that he considered peace between the Hungarians and the Romanians possible, if not so much as an inch of Romanian inhabited land remained under Hungarian rule. "Then there will be peace between the Hungarians and the Romanians, as there was peace 400 years ago." Professor Jàszi thanked Iorga for his comments, but said in his answer that "for the moment he cannot publish them." "And," Iorga commented, "he did not publish them!" But in November 1918 Jàszi was not only a University Professor, but the new Minister of Nationalities of the new democratic Hungarian government. In a message to him, Iorga remained as inflexible as ever: "If every nationality will be content with its territory, we shall love the Magyars!"[502]

This was not only Iorga's position, but of the overwhelming majority of Transylvanian Romanians, indeed, the position of the whole Romanian nation. The problem would be how to implement this principle that "every nationality should be content with the territory it inhabits!" Large, unruly, dissatisfied chunks of Hungarians would be incorporated into the Romanian state and into the other Successor States.

On 1 December 1918 delegates of the Transylvanian Romanians gathered in Alba Iulia, the capital of Michael the Brave. During a huge Popular Assembly, they proclaimed the unification of Transylvania with Romania. "The Scriptures

---

[501]*Neamul Românesc*, 14 November 1918.

[502]*Neamul Românesc*, 10 July 1917, 14 August 1917, and 27 October 1918.

Were Fulfilled..." In a few months a dream was realized, something which, during the months of humiliation of the spring and summer 1918, nobody could possibly foresee. The unification was orchestrated and carried through by the leader of the Transylvanian Romanians, the great democrat Iuliu Maniu. Iorga described him in his paper, explaining that Maniu came from the glorious atmosphere of the Uniate Ecclesiastical Center of Blaj, and he carried within himself the spirit of it. Iorga continued that all Hungarian hatred and abuse against Maniu could not change his spirit or detract from his positive qualities. Because "in Transylvania everybody knows for the last twenty years that if there is talk about somebody without fault whose road is straight and righteous, one has only to look where Iuliu Maniu is going." He concluded by remembering that Maniu carried out the great act of Alba Iulia in a military demobilization suit.[503]

The Romanian national dream was fulfilled. Iorga was certainly one of its chief architects. Would he rush now to Bucharest to take advantage of the dazzling opportunities like everybody else did in Iaşi? By November and December practically nobody of importance remained in Iaşi. The political establishment had left. As Iorga remarked, Iaşi became a quiet provincial town again. But Iorga was no politician. He did not "hurry" to Bucharest. He expected to be invited, because of his past merits. He would be absent during the return of General Berthelot and the victory parades. Nobody called Iorga back; Queen Marie alone invited him. Iorga answered that "he is too busy with his newspaper" (with the armistice Brătianu ended subsides for Iorga's *Neamul Românesc* immediately). Iorga remarked that "he has no room among the victors of today who were the traitors of yesterday." Brătianu, now the leader of the country, considered him the last person he wanted to see. As Iorga commented: "The gratitude of the world is not something on which one can count upon."[504]

---

[503] *Neamul Românesc*, 18 December 1918.

[504] *O viaţă de om*, vol. II, p. 313; *Memorii*, vol. II, pp. 120-121.

Chapter V

The Uncertain Triumph

"I want to make only that music which I myself like, or no music at all."

— Bismarck

Bismarck knew that politics were the art of the possible. No greater contradiction could be imagined than there was between *Realpolitik* and *Sămănătorism.*

In 1918 Romanian dreams seemed to be fulfilled beyond the wildest expectations of nationalists. Take Ionescu saw the gates of heaven open up, yet he was too superstitious to look inside (because "the sight was too beautiful). Now we will take a look. The interwar period, despite its shortcomings, was the happiest period in Romanian history.[505] Although not everything was going for the best, in the early years there was a general optimism. Yet, Marshal Foch remarked (when they showed him the text of the Versailles Peace Treaty in 1919), "This is not a peace treaty; but an armistice for 20 years!" Clemenceau, the very architect of it, was pessimistic about the chances of peace by 1929.

The Versailles Peace Treaty was much criticized and much of the criticism was justifiable, not to the extent to which the losers or Hitler or the Soviets condemned it; nevertheless, there were shortcomings. The Hungarian-Romanian

---

[505]Recently even Romanian communist historians showed more positive perspective of the interwar period. See Mircea Muşat and Ion Ardeleanu, *România după Marea Unire* (Bucureşti, 1976) and *De la statul Geto-Dac la statul naţional-unitar* (Bucureşti, 1983).

controversy over Transylvania was as acute as ever. Yugoslavia and Czechoslovakia no longer exist. But in Versailles, for the first time, the borders were settled more or less on the basis of self-determination. This was also the cardinal principle of President Wilson. To put it more exactly: how would these people think to determine their future in 1918. The former empires, which ruled over these areas, were multinational states. This resulted in great waves of migrations and population transfers. Drawing of boundaries on ethnic lines became problematic, Iorga was an almost unconditional admirer of that other man of the nineteenth century, President Wilson.

We shall divide the interwar period into two parts. The first, from 1918 until 1930. During these twelve years, the two predators, Germany and Russia — now called the Soviet Union — were prostrate. There was hope for democracy and economic ascendancy. After this came the second different phase: the depression, and the return of Carol II to Romania. Germany under Hitler and Russia under Stalin recovered, challenged the Versailles Settlement, and set out with other regimes like Fascist Italy to destabilize the Versailles System. The world was returning to international anarchy. By 1940 Romanian national unity was forcibly ended.

In 1918, all this was far away. Besides achieving national unity; Romania embarked on the hopeful era with an agrarian reform, the most sweeping one in post-war Europe, doing justice to more than 80% of Romanians: the peasantry. United Romania (called "Greater Romania") started its new life with a democratic constitution and universal suffrage.[506] Endowed richly with resources, it was referred to as "a beautiful marriageable girl with a rich dowry." What more could a nation wish for? Unfortunately, this rosy picture had little to do with Romanian reality. One should remember Oscar Wilde's aphorism about dreams. Accordingly, there are two kinds of tragedies. One if they remain unfulfilled, and the second comes when they get fulfilled. This seems to be true in Third

---

[506]The new constitution left a strong royal prerogative intact. The constitution could be suspended partly or fully by the sovereign. *Politics and Political Parties in Romania* (London, 1936), p. 9. As a consequence, Romania lived many times under martial law, censorship and police brutality.

World nations, and Romania was, more than anything else, an underdeveloped nation. As in many Third World countries, Romania's most important goal — called "national unity" (today they call it "national liberation") — was achieved. The almost insoluble problems were considered secondary ones during this struggle for national liberation. Now these problems came painfully to the fore, and Romanians learned that national unity was no panacea; it would add new problems to the well-known old ones.

National unity was achieved at the cost of including minorities — called *nationalitățile conlocuitoare* ("nationalities which live with us") — which made up about 30% of the population. Before 1918 (with the exception of the Jews), there were practically none. Of these minorities, the Hungarians and the Jews were the most numerous, strategically placed, and problematic. Together they made almost two-and-one-half million, a not inconsiderable 15% of the inhabitants. The key to the minority problem was Transylvania; there Hungarians and Jews were identical, a discontented minority, not even making the pretense of accepting Romanian rule. Encouraged by Hungary, they were just biding their time.[507] Besides them, there were Ukrainians, Bulgarians, and Lipoveni (Russian old believers) in Moldavia and in the Danube delta. There were about half a million Germans, Saxons of Transylvania, and Swabians in the Banat. The Saxons reconciled themselves to Romanian rule; the Swabians in the Banat were less conciliator; though there were no particular problems with German minorities until the rise of Hitler. There were also small numbers of Greeks, Armenians, or Tartars in Dobrogea, where Aromanians (Romanians from the Greek areas) would settle; some Serbian pockets remained in the Banat, and Austrians and Poles in Bucovina. Gypsies were to be found all over the country.

They say that national security is for the nation like cancer for the individual; until it is there, one cannot think of anything else. The national security of Romania was well taken care of as far as Hungarian and Bulgarian revisionist

---

[507]Recently, a cousin of this writer, twelve years his senior, remembered how the Hungarian and Jewish children gathered (during the interwar period) in the forest to play. Often these children pronounced a memorialized text starring with proclamation of loyalty to "thousand years old Hungary," and ritually ending with a devastating curse "on Bucharest."

claims. Russia was a different matter. But Romania was part of the French alliance system and had a definite role to play in it, and in the "cordon sanitaire," isolating Soviet Russia.

The sweeping agrarian reform was enacted in Bessarabia in 1917 and 1918. It was easy to enact an agrarian reform in Bucovina and in Transylvania. Most of the landowners were not Romanians. Finally in 1921 the land reform was enacted in the Regat. There farmers had no experience in farming their homesteads. They lacked modern know-how, and credit to help them on their feet. Agrarian credit was the main topic of interwar political demagoguery. Instead of helping new individual farmers, the Liberals in the early 1920s started a program of forced industrialization, the cost of which the peasantry was to bear.

In 1918 the prestige of victorious France (and of the other victorious democracies) was so great that all new nation-states of East Central and Southeastern Europe adapted democratic systems; as did Romania. All these changes were codified by the new constitution in 1923. But the establishment of a working democracy is more difficult than that. In this area the conditions for democracy only existed in one country: Czechoslovakia, especially the Bohemian part of it. There democracy would work. In the rest (especially in Romania), democracy remained, to quote Maiorescu, a "form without foundation." As Iorga would put it, democracy was not "organically" based on the traditions of the country. There was no historical precedent for democracy in Romania; its first trial, the Depression, and the rising tide of Fascism swept it away. Romania had no native middle-class, no living standard to check political demagoguery, no educational level to help voters understand issues; finally, there was no experience in self-government. It should not be surprising that in Romania these new democratic institutions produced strange, un-Western results. But in 1918, everybody looked forward towards the future with great expectations, Iorga included.

In an editorial, Iorga again reiterated the role he foresaw for historians who, according to him, had to get out of their Ivory Tower to assume a political role. Under the title "The Historian and Politics," Iorga explained that history never repeats itself, like the same tree never breeds the same leaf; but there is similarity between event and event, revolution and revolution, conquest and conquest.

Thus, nobody can explain or forewarn about coming events better than the historian. The historian descends from the past into the present. Unlike politicians, the true historian is not led by petty and sordid passions and interests. As far as literature goes, he should use his voice against "models," set by the disastrous imitations of fashion of writers who follow examples which do not derive from the native environment. The historian should remind everyone constantly that art and literature are but manifestations of the nation. It is his moral duty to see to it that this should remain so, since only evildoers dare to ignore these rules. In his work the historian constantly follows the achievements and misfortunes of his nation's past, and thanks to this, he turns into a kind of "elder." Thus it is his duty to speak up on current issues. "Doing this he does not exceed his duties, rather he fulfills them to the end." Iorga remembered Professor A.D. Xenopol differentiating between his historical, literary, and political activities. "I do not see any discrepancy between them." Then he continued: "I believe that in our not yet stabilized society, where people sunk from the easy enthusiasm of unification into the search of an easy, cheap material gratification of life, the historian must remain a tireless reminder of national traditions, bear witness in foreign countries to the unity of our nation, witness a national unity which reaches across class lines, and advocate ideas which we must follow in order to lead the youth to follow the right way in the right direction." But when Iorga wrote this in 1921, in his own words: "I was politically an isolated man."[508]

The ideas Iorga propounded were the same he offered in his speech ten years before, when he became a member of the Romanian Academy. But the world had changed since then; Iorga did not change. He reiterated in 1928, and again many times after: "The politics of Nicolae Iorga is logically complementary to his cultural concepts," continuing that people in bad faith may say that there is Iorga the historian, a man of culture, and Iorga the politician. This is simply not true.[509] But by 1921 Iorga's political chances were gone despite of his Prime Ministership in 1931 and the role which he would play during the

---

[508]*Neamul Românesc*, 2 January 1921; also *O viață de om*, vol. III, p. 65.

[509]*Neamul Românesc*, 16 February 1928.

Royal Dictatorship. Everything he did politically after the immediate postwar years would be but one missed opportunity.

By the fall of 1918 the signs of war-weariness surfaced powerfully, accentuated by a severe drought, coupled with cruel German and Austro-Hungarian exactions and hunger.[510] There were the Soviet activities next door, Bessarabia was in a ferment. There were leftist disorders in neighboring Hungary and Bulgaria. Finally pent-up fury erupted in the fall of 1918. Iaşi became the center of leftist disorders. Later, it would become the birthplace of the Romanian extreme right. The period between 1918 and 1921 would be a period of leftist disorders throughout Romania. On 13 December 1918 there was a leftist demonstration in Bucharest before the National Theater, which turned into an insurrectional procession, marching towards the Royal Palace with the cry "Long Live the Republic." There was a mass shooting of demonstrators. Similar outbursts occurred in Iaşi and elsewhere.[511] On 12 November 1918, King Ferdinand reaffirmed the pledges concerning universal suffrage and an agrarian reform.

After Romania's re-entry into the war in November 1918, the king dismissed the collaborating Marghiloman government, and appointed General C. Coandă as Prime Minister. Since he was French-educated, he was the logical person to deal with General Franchet d'Esperey and General Berthelot. In a few weeks, Ionel Brătianu became Prime Minister again. During the fall of 1918 General (later Marshal) Prezan gave orders to the Romanian Army to advance into Transylvania. Since the Dual Monarchy had collapsed, a democratic government was formed in Hungary' under Count M. Karolyi; the Minister of Nationalities was Oskar Jàszi. He tried to stop the nationalities from leaving the fold of historic Hungary, with democratic promises, but he failed. Despite this, Jàszi's personal credentials were impeccable. It was Hungary that had a credibility problem with its nationalities and with the Romanian nationality in particular. The Romanians preferred unification with their kinsman. In mid-March of 1919 Colonel Vyx handed a note to Karolyi in which he notified him that the

---

[510]*Supt trei regi*, pp. 298-308.

[511]*O viaţă de om*, vol. III, p. 22; and *Memorii*, vol. II, pp. 134-135.

demarcation lines which denoted the advance of Czech, Romanian, and Yugo-slav troops (in many cases were drawn across unequivocally Hungarian inhab-ited areas) were to be considered as provisional boundaries. In this desperate moment the only possibility left was to appeal to the international solidarity of the working classes. Karolyi handed power to a Bolshevik agent, Bela Kun, who established his regime on 21 March 1919, and vowed to re-establish the territo-rial integrity of historic Hungary.[512]

At first, the Entente (even France) was reluctant to grant Romania such large chunks of territory, especially in view of the separate peace it had con-cluded with the Central Powers. But Brătianu pointed out to Clemenceau that if Romania would not have concluded a separate peace, there would be no Roma-nian Army at the disposal of the Allies now.[513] And this Romanian Army was needed during the spring and summer (and later). It was used to crush the Hun-garian Soviet. The C.F.R. (Romanian railroad) workers, Ploieşti oil workers, and other Romanian workers organized sympathy strikes for the Bela Kun regime.[514] The Romanian Army entered Budapest on 4 August 1919. Iorga would not hide his intoxication by the hour. He editorialized: "The Romanian Army in Buda-pest: The Atonement." He knew Budapest well, and wrote: "What can we say about Budapest?" describing magnificent public buildings, bridges, broad boulevards, he advised the Romanians to learn from the enemy.[515] According to Iorga, Romanian forces were welcome. Hungarians were happy to be delivered from Bolshevik terror, and Romanians behaved in Budapest in an exemplary fashion. Iorga's son, Petru, a professional officer, entered Budapest with the Ro-manian troops, and wrote numerous letters to his father from there.[516] This is one reason why Iorga should have known better. The behavior of the Romanian troops in Budapest was not impeccable and the plunder was great. This was the

---

[512]*Supt trei regi*, p. 310.

[513]*Memorii*, vol. II, p. 111.

[514]*Op.cit.*, p. 232.

[515]*Neamul Românesc*, 9 and 10 August 1919.

[516]*Supt trei regi*, p. 316; BAR *Corespondenţa lui N. Iorga*, vols. 283, 284.

opinion of the American General Hill Bandholtz, although his reminiscences are questioned by many, and of the head of the Italian Mission in Budapest, Colonel Romanelli. Compared to the plunder carried out by the Central Powers in Romania, the actions of Romanian troops in Budapest could be considered something like peanuts. Iorga remembered that Romanian forces recovered from the Hungarian National Archives (among other things) certain documents taken by the Hungarians from the library and the archives of the Romanian Academy and National Library.

As far as politics go, during the spring and summer of 1918, Iorga clashed with A.C. Cuza in Iaşi. Cuza left the National Democratic Party and became one of the co-founders of the "People's League" of General Averescu. But he had disagreements with him (mainly about the lack of anti-Semitism in the program), and ultimately came back to the National Democratic Party. Iorga remarked, "Cuza is not sincere."[517] The Bucharest Peace Treaty obliged Romania to grant citizenship for Jews. Only Cuza and Ion Zelea Codreanu voted against this provision, Iorga would not run during this Central Power-sponsored election. By this time he had changed his stand on the Jewish question. The government in Iaşi also foresaw Jewish emancipation after the war. Conflict over the Jewish question between Iorga and Cuza would become more obvious during the coming months, and would be the single most important reason for the break between them. During the last months of the war Iorga constantly complained about usurpation, especially "the usurpation of the Party in Bessarabia" practiced by Cuza and Ion Zelea Codreanu; their "provocative attitudes," etc.[518] It was critical that Iorga sought support within the Party, and reshuffled his support for the showdown, in other words, that he reorganized the Party for the new era. The more so, since he declared that his Party was "a democratic party of the left," demanding a sweeping land reform, universal suffrage, etc. But it was this critical need for party organization in politics that Iorga did not understand.

---

[517]*Memorii*, vol. II, pp. 130-132.

[518]*Memorii*, vol. II, pp. 267, 271, 273; also, *O viaţă de om*, vol. III, p. 3.

Many supporters left him during these months and afterwards, not only Cuza and Ion Zelea Codreanu, but even his own brother-in-law, Ştefan Bogdan, who joined the Liberals.[519] Was it Iorga's lack of understanding of what a party machine meant in politics, or was it (according to his family) his disgust during the fall of 1918 towards the "Eventualists" and "Conjunctualists" and their success in dirty politics? Tactical errors could have been repaired. In Bucharest much larger possibilities opened up for Iorga than his confrontations with Cuza, or petty struggles about anti-Semitism, or egos. These greater opportunities and more lofty demands called for Iorga's return, in voices louder and louder. Others, much less meritorious in the achievement of national unification than Iorga was, were fighting their way towards the pork barrel. Revolting to Iorga, that is what politics was and is all about.

Finally, at the end of December, Iorga returned from Iaşi to Bucharest. He had nothing but contempt for a city which lived under enemy occupation, calling it "the city of shame." He remarked on the attitude of the inhabitants, the "insolence of which only a whipped slave can demonstrate."[520]

Since his home in Vălenii was badly damaged, he took for himself a modest residence, and his first action was to assure the reappearance of *Neamul Românesc*. The paper — as always — was in deep financial trouble. Finally, by late 1919, from public subscription, Iorga could afford a worthy residence on the Chaussé Bonaparte. He was close to his fiftieth birthday. Queen Marie was a great help; she supplied him with oak bookshelves for his beloved books. As Iorga recalled, "After forty-eight years I have a roof over my head."[521] France also remembered: in 1919 he was decorated with the Legion of Honor.

On the other hand, Iorga's virulent attacks on Professor A. Tzigara-Samurcaş (whom he accused of collaborating with the Germans), resulted in Tzigara-

---

[519]Şeicaru remembered, and his reminiscences were confirmed by the Iorga family, about Iorga's disregard for and the inconceivability to understand the function a party is playing within political activity. Şeicaru, *op. cit.*, pp. 50-51.

[520]*O viaţă de om*, vol. II, p. 315.

[521]*Op. cit.*, vol. III, p.6.

Samurcaş challenging Iorga to a duel! Since Iorga had no idea about dueling, it was Pamfil Şeicaru who took his place.[522] Brătianu and his clan dominated the Royal Palace. Brătianu, whom Iorga called the political "Engineer," began to put his talents to work. He decided to put the "racehorse" (Iorga) back into the stable. To wit, Iorga was not invited to accompany the Romanian delegation to the Peace Conference, a bitter humiliation for the fighter who had such a part in the establishment and the intellectual underpinnings of Greater Romania. Alexandru Vaida-Voevod, and the Transylvanian politicians who recently united Transylvania with Romania were shocked; they were not used yet to the petty party interests and *Politicianism* in Bucharest. They would learn.

On the Hungarian side every intellectual was mobilized to participate in the Hungarian Peace delegation. There was Count Pál Teleki, the great geographer, Count Albert Apponyi, an excellent diplomat with a great versatility of foreign languages, and above all, the historian Sandor Domanovszky. Iorga was a match for them in erudition, and, above all, a fighter. It was Iorga who had traveled for years on train, carriage, and on foot through every corner of Transylvania, Bucovina, and Bessarabia, and written enough to show Romanians the true dimensions of their nation. The Transylvanian leaders did not want to believe that Iorga would be ignored, so they called on him. Şeicaru was present. They came in January 1919 to the editorial office of *Neamul Românesc* on a cold winter day. Şeicaru described the two little rooms containing Iorga's desk. The machines of the printing press were next to his desk, and there was an iron stove which was sometimes too hot, but more often too cold; "the whole redaction had the aspect of a romantic press of the revolutionary era." Vaida-Voevod, P. Mihaly, Şt. Ciceo-Pop, V. Goldiş, and Aurel Vlad filed in. Vaida spoke first. "His Transylvanian accent gave authority to his words." Vaida asked Iorga to write up the memorandum which the Romanian delegation would present. Iorga asked, "Why do you ask me? Ask Brătianu! I was useful during the years of neutrality, and during the war, now I am good for nothing. You ask me to write up a memorandum to present the cause of the Romanian nation? Did you ask

---

[522]*Op. cit.*, p. 12.

permission from Brătianu?" They answered all in concert that since they had the mandate of the people of Transylvania through the *Consiliul Dirigent*, they did not need the permission of anybody. But Iorga was angry. "You think that if I am not worthy to participate in the Romanian delegation at the Peace Conference, it will be all right to ask me to write up a memorandum?" He continued in his customary style alternating violent phrases with scathing, ironical ones, and despite the intervention refused his cooperation.[523] Thus (as Şeicaru put it), Brătianu's pettiness prevailed. This writer disagrees. Pettiness is not the word to describe an Oriental despot. Oriental despotism always seeks a kind of natural coincidence between personal and national goals. Brătianu knew that Iorga's absence in Versailles was a formidable absence, but all Hungarian eloquence would not prevail against self-determination and the validity of the secret treaties.

To what extent were Wilsonian principles applied here? The Peace Treaties left about three million Hungarians (which now became the largest minority under foreign rule in Europe) under a foreign rule, which they loathed. And more than half of these Hungarians were living in regions where a 20 or 30 miles shift of the border would have incorporated two out of three of them into a Hungarian state.

Yet, the situation in Transylvania was different. Cluj and the Szeckler region, also other large Hungarian islands within the Romanian (or Germanic) majority were isolated from Hungarian inhabited areas. It was impossible to include them into Hungary without depriving as many Romanians of their right to self-determination. This was done in 1940, when Transylvania was partitioned by the Diktat of Vienna.

Would the Hungary of the interwar period have satisfied itself with self-determination, leaving to Hungary only those territories which had an unequivocal Hungarian majority? This writer, educated in Hungary, has doubts. The general spirit was: "*Nem! Nem! Soha!* (No! No! Never!) Never will Hungary accept the Versailles Settlement!" The general idea — "Justice for Hungary!"

---

[523]Şeicaru, *op. cit.*, pp. 56-57; also, *Memorii*, vol. II, p. 147.

— was not self-determination, but, as the songs expressed it: *"Mindent vissza ami a miènk volt!"* ("We want back everything that was ours.") All the history books, geography lessons, all the maps circulating, and the general spirit of education reflected these demands. It was the spirit of Hungarian interwar foreign policy. It is this track of revisionism which led Hungary' towards alliances with Mussolini and Hitler, and ultimately into a sordid doom. One incident can give food for thought. Masaryk was the only one who in 1930 made a gesture towards Hungary, trying to return some purely Hungarian-inhabited areas. Despite his admiration for Masaryk, Iorga warned that such a gesture would open a Pandora's box, since he believed that integral revisionism and not self-determination was the Hungarian goal; he wrote: "The Hungarian goal is to restore "Hungary as it was and as Hungary cannot be."[524] One can muse on what the result was of Masaryk's offer. The Hungarian government never took him up on it, and democratic Czechoslovakia remained the most hated country in the eyes of the Hungarians among all the succession states. Ultimately, Iorga was justified: "Peoples of the new national states have no desire to re-enter the 'Apostolic prison' of old Hungary."[525] (By 'Apostolic" Iorga meant the traditional character of the Kingdom of Hungary).

Iorga, with a sense for history, should have made allowance for the impact of events on the Hungarians — the shattering blow, the shock of losing a 1,000 years old patrimony! And not only for the ruling classes! Fighting against the Versailles Peace Treaties, Hungarians were united from the ruling classes to the Social Democratic (and even the illegal Communist) Party. The loss of two-thirds of historic Hungary and their relegation from a position of European importance (the Hungarian element dominated the Austro-Hungarian Empire) to relative insignificance, and all this in the name of "self-determination" — so

---

[524]*Neamul Românesc*, 8 October 1930.

[525]*Supt trei regi*, p. 351. Even Count I. Bethlen, the most formidable (and anti-Nazi) statesman of Hungary during the interwar period, engaged in his memoirs in a facetious justification of the Hungarian attack on Yugoslavia in April 1941, *Bethlen Istvan emlekirata, 1944* (Budapest, 1988).

cynically applied! It was because of this failure of self-determination for Hungarians, that Hungarian revisionism would become so strong. Iorga maintained that not self-determination but "restitutio ad integram" was the Hungarian goal. Versailles was the place to try it out! This did not happen.

As for internal Romanian politics, with the distribution of the large estates, the Conservatives were no significant force in postwar politics. The almost unchallengeable leader was Brătianu. He had essentially two goals: to restore the Liberal establishment (under his leadership) in the new constitutional system as much as possible; and to keep power for himself and his family. At the beginning of 1919 he left with the Romanian delegation for the Peace Conference. Brătianu always considered Iorga "a dangerous man." He was just about the last person to whom Brătianu would give gratuitous publicity as a member of the Romanian delegation. At the Peace Conference, a dispute arose between Romania and Yugoslavia over the Banat. In 1916 the hard-pressed Entente gave Romania the whole Banat as a prize for its entry into the War. At Versailles different boundaries were presented to the Romanian delegation. The French and the English were the most favorable to Romanian demands, American boundaries were less favorable, and the Italian line was the least favorable one.[526] But all the boundaries drawn by all the Great Powers left Transylvania entirely (Cluj, and the Szeckler region included) within Romania. The differences which arose concerned how far west Romania should reach, and the disputed matter of the Banat. If in 1916 the Allies promised the whole Banat to Romania, now they were increasingly taking into account the magnificent Serbian war record and the numerous Serbian populations in the western part of the province. There was also the ignorance of the statesmen (like Lloyd George) about ethnic (and other) factors. The decision affecting two allies was not easy. Brătianu was intransigent. He demanded the Danube to be the boundary between Yugoslavia and Romania to avoid clashes; he wanted the whole Banat or nothing; he would not accept partition.[527]

---

[526] *Erdély tôrténete*, (3 vols.), Budapest, 1986, vol.3, p. 1730.

[527] *Supt trei regi*, p. 313.

Iorga was a friend of the Serbians; yet he often proclaimed, "every nation to its holy confines." What were the confines of different nationalities in such a mixed region as the Banat?

Clemenceau became angry, especially with the Romanians, and the Powers presented Romania with an ultimatum. Clemenceau's indignation was synthetic. He should have known integral nationalism was a one-way street, and should have remembered what was promised to the Romanians in 1916. Finally, in July 1919, the Banat was partitioned between Romania and Yugoslavia. Brătianu refused to sign the treaty. Nevertheless, the partition turned out to be successful and held fast for the last 70 years.[528] The walk-out of Brătianu from the Peace Conference led to his resignation and a government under General Arthur Văitoianu was formed to run the first elections under universal suffrage in Greater Romania. Held in the beginning of November 1919, these were the first free elections. During the voting there were many strikes in progress. All this did not interfere with the freedom of the elections. Iorga still ran on a common list with Cuza within the framework of the Nationalist Democratic Party. General Averescu's People's League abstained from the elections, Iorga's party received 5.7% of the vote and sent 34 deputies to the new Assembly. The party' program advocated national solidarity, supposedly to run across class lines. Most of those who voted for the Democratic Nationalist Party did so for personal reasons: it was "Iorga's party..." The elections, like the other rare free elections of Greater Romanian history (in 1928 or in 1937) led to significant shifts of the political forces.

On 20 November 1919, the National Assembly was opened by King Ferdinand. Election results made the formation of a broad coalition mandatory. This was the National Democratic Bloc (the "Bloc"), consisting of the Peasant Party of Mihalache, the Peasant Party of Inculeț, Iorga's Party, Maniu's Transylvanian Nationalists, and the Bucovinians. The unofficial head of the "Bloc" was Iorga.

---

[528]During April 1941, the Nazis offered the Yugoslav Banat to Marshal Antonescu. Antonescu, not wishing to spoil relations between the Romanian and Serbian peoples, firmly declined the offer.

Unfortunately, the heterogeneous "Bloc" lacked cohesion. Vaida-Voevod presented his government in the Palace on 1 December 1919.

In the coming days, Professor Iorga was elected by acclamation as the Speaker of the First Assembly of Greater Romania. Originally, Maniu's Transylvanian Nationalists and the Liberals would have preferred the Transylvanian politician Goldiş as speaker; but the Peasant deputies' enthusiasm carried Professor Iorga to the speaker's seat.[529] Iorga went personally (as a gesture) to the Văcăreşti prison, and liberated the writer Tudor Arghezi, who were incarcerated for misbehavior during the German occupation.

What were the chances for the Vaida government? What chances did democracy have? These years (until the winter of 1921) were marred by continuous leftist disorders. There was even a short-lived socialist boom. No wonder the Palace and the Camarilla were frightened; especially of two key members of the Vaida government, and the *Consiliul Dirigent* (the Governing Council) of Transylvania. The most objectionable person for the Palace was the Minister of Interior (a key ministry in every revolutionary situation), Dr. N. Lupu (General Averescu, who was the Minister of Interior originally, resigned in mid-December). Şeicaru said about Dr. Lupu that it was "bad enough if a minister acted in a demagogic way, but even more dangerous if a demagogue became a minister." Dr. Lupu was quite inconsistent, and he would change his positions radically in decisive moments. Professor Cuza called him, with one of his aphorisms, "a socialist sui generis."[530]

Amidst constant strikes, upheavals, and disorders, Dr. Lupu liked to preside over negotiations with striking workers. The king became increasingly worried

---

[529]Within Iorga's correspondence there is a document from the Hungarian Ministry of Interior, showing Vasile Goldiş quite compliant with the Hungarian authorities during the war. BAR *Corespondenţa lui N. Iorga*, vol. 281, doc. 149. Politicians keep files on each other. Vasile Goldiş's abject submission and cooperation with the Hungarians emerging from these documents contrasts with the words he spoke at Alba Iulia. Şeicaru counted 300 deputies in this National Assembly who were Iorga's students, thus "Iorghists." Şeicaru, *op. cit.*, p. 62. See also *Memorii*, vol. II, p. 303.

[530]Şeicaru, *op. cit.*, pp. 63-65; also *Supt trei regi*, p. 335.

and asked Iorga to "stop Lupu." The *Siguranța.* (State Security) entered the intrigue, of course, with unfounded accusations. By mid-February 1920 Lupu reported to Iorga that the king had ordered that machine guns be brought to the Cotroceni Palace, in expectation of a coup attempt by him. The Camarilla paid the police to bring Lupu farther into discredit before the Palace.[531] King Ferdinand, thanks to the Liberal agitation, considered Lupu as a kind of a Kerensky, always keeping the fate of Tsar Nicholas and his family before their eyes.

The task of Dr. Lupu was to bring together the administration of the Old Romania with the divergent new provinces, an exceptionally difficult task even under normal conditions; but conditions were far from being normal. Dr. Lupu was singularly unfitted for this task. The Palace's fears were exploited by the Brătianus and the Liberal press.

The other key personality who contributed to the failure of the democratic Vaida government was the Minister of Finances, Aurel Vlad. A Transylvanian, a banker from Oraștie, having a patriotic background, he was quite incapable of organizing the finances under such turbulent circumstances. It was pivotal to bring the finances of this newly unified state into order. But the Liberal Party traditionally controlled finances. What the country needed was a financial expert of stature, a technocrat. Vlad was not the one. His personality was uncontrollable, his gestures on the floor of the Assembly evoked more ridicule than respect. The most powerful voice in the National Assembly belonged to deputies of the newly founded Peasant Party constituted in 1919, and their leader, a school teacher and former student of Iorga, was Ion Mihalache. The king and the Liberal establishment distrusted both the Peasant Party and Mihalache, who even at Royal receptions symbolically wore his peasant attire. Mihalache was an honest and convinced democrat. This did not stop King Ferdinand from making incessant jokes in bad taste about Mihalache's peasant "shirt," or from worrying about his party.

Beyond traditional politics there was something else emerging, as much in Romania as elsewhere in Europe. From the terrible ordeal of the First World

---

[531]*Memorii*, vol. III, pp. 323, 326, 335-338, 340-344.

War, awakening from nineteenth century idealism and crushed dreams, and from sufferings (the "All Quiet on the Western Front" spirit on the side of the defeated ones), a "lost generation" emerged. In which direction they would go was not clear at this point. They were neither on the left, nor on the right.

There was also in Romania such a generation emerging. Let us call them the "Trench Generation." The articulate ones among them were grade school or high school teachers, priests, civil servants, attorneys, physicians. They were all "Iorghists" before the war, readers of *Neamul Românesc* and during the Iași times all looked to Iorga for leadership. The peasants were not demi-slaves anymore. They were proud veterans, knowing that the welfare of the country depended on their sacrifice. Now owners of their own land, they were people who had proven themselves, and had been promised the right to participate in politics. Both the inarticulate and articulate Trench Generation experienced the corruption and hypocrisy of the ruling classes during the war. Now they all hoped for something radically new in Greater Romania.

We should remember the visit of Șeicaru in 1917 to Professor Iorga's Iași home, expressing the hopes of this generation to him. And there were also the letters that many wrote to Iorga from the trenches. These voices were full of hope; maybe because the war in Romania lasted a shorter time than in the West, these people were less in the soul-destroying atmosphere of the trenches than their counterparts on the Western Front. Romania was on the winner's side; there was the dazzling prospect of Greater Romania. During this time this Trench Generation believed in democracy, in equal rights for the minorities, and a better future. How unfortunate that this life-giving faith they brought from the bloody storm of war would not last. The majority of these people did not wish to return to the social inequities, and the corruption of the Romania of old; to fraudulent politicianism; to a Romanian reality where there were 1% privileged and 99% terrorized. But that was what Brătianu wished to update, and for the restoration of which he was working: to restore within the changed circumstances the old political system (and his power), resembling the pre-war politicianism as closely as possible.

Within this Trench Generation at this point everyone of consequence was a "Iorghist." In the freely elected Assembly emanating from the elections of November 1919 there were at least 300 deputies who were formerly Iorga's students. And Șeicaru counted (even in the 1930s) 36% of the governing National Peasant Party's deputies in the Assembly who were formerly Iorghists.[532] Now the Trench Generation looked to Iorga, who they considered rightfully a "fighter," an intellectual giant, something more than incorruptible (a rare phenomenon in Bucharest). They were looking to his ardent patriotism, and they knew that he was a sworn enemy of the restoration of that Romania which Brătianu represented.

Iorga possessed all the qualities his partisans in the French Generation endowed him with, except for one: he was no politician. Because of this the Trench Generation's expectations would be disappointed. Greater Romania would remain an underdeveloped nation, divided by classes, where the old system would eventually be restored by the Brătianus. Some new, formidable difficulties were added to the existing woes. Iorga would not or could not assume the leadership offered to him by the Trench Generation. It is here where Iorga missed the opportunity to become a political leader of consequence, the leader of a Romanian renewal, to take over the ship of state, to do what he wanted all his life, to help with his honesty and his energy to create a new Greater Romania.

Why did this happen? Mostly because of Iorga's personal qualities; above all, because he was no politician. After missing the opportunity to become the articulate, almost irresistible firebrand-spokesman for the Trench Generation, Iorga returned to the establishment. Thus Iorga allowed the restoration of the Liberal system by Brătianu.

Nevertheless, during 1919-1920, Iorga was almost in a revolutionary mood, in consequence of Brătianu's treatment of him. The tone of *Neamul Românesc* was distinctly of the radical left. Here is an article of his, reflecting this. Writing about "La douce décadence" of the "haute société," dismissing their pretense of

---

[532]Șeicaru, *op. cit.*, p. 62.

being an elite, Iorga has the following things to say: "These people of high society take only privileges but no responsibilities. They are not the products of history, but of good investment and scandalous luck. They have but one desire: to be seen and heard of. The English aristocracy died during the war at Ypres; not these." Then Iorga hits home. "*L'Indépendence Roumaine* (the Liberal paper) just loves them."[533]

Nationalism has two faces: if in Iorga's nationalism traditional conservatism won out, there were personal reasons: his *Sămănătorist* dream world. No wonder that during these months even Christian Rakovski approached Iorga from Moscow, trying to bring him into the Third Internationale.[534] Marxist socialism remained alien to Iorga. *Sămănătorism* was supposed to answer all the needs of Romania. Communism based on Russia gave (like to many of his countrymen) an ultimate touch to the monster. He wrote a series of editorials during these months calling the Soviet system in Russia an "anti-social socialism."[535]

During these postwar years Iorga damaged his political career almost beyond repair. What were the reasons for this? This writer, after his numerous interviews with the Iorga family (and others who knew him), can forward the following answers: besides Iorga's personality; his ego, and his naivete, there were his *Sămănătorist* concepts. It was a social, political, and national declaration of faith from which "he never parted for the rest of his life." All this led in politics to an attitude which the seasoned and knowledgeable journalist of the Bucharest scene, Şeicaru, called "the fanciful, whimsical zigzags of Iorga's fanciful, whimsical, capricious attitudes." (*Zigzagul fantezist al atitudinilor lui fanteziste*).[536]

Iorga did not understand that for channeling the Trench Generation's (or any potential) support one needed a party. Despite his oratorical and animating

---

[533] *Neamul Românesc*, 13 March 1920.

[534] Professor Iorga answered these approaches in a scathing article, referring to the Marxists as "Tov", instead of calling them "Tovarăş." *Neamul Românesc*, 6 November 1919.

[535] *Neamul Românesc*, 20 August 1919.

[536] Şeicaru, *op. cit.*, p. 49.

talents, he did not understand the role of a party in politics, and what the party machine was supposed to do: to articulate and to carry into practice ideas by influencing public opinion and maintaining day by day contact with supporters. Şeicaru was present in 1918 in Iaşi when Iorga addressed the leadership of the National Democratic Party: "I need no party, it only bothers me; it imposes sacrifices I cannot make. You are free to go wherever you wish." And they went, even his brother-in-law, Ştefan Bogdan. Şeicaru was right, that no devotion can resist such treatment.[537]

The leadership of the Nationalist Democratic Party was always a small coterie of mediocre people around Iorga (and he recognized their limited capabilities). Now, as the break was about to happen within the party (with Cuza), they became smaller. From 1920 on, the party would receive just about one percent of the vote.

The Liberal Party was under the leadership of the Brătianu clan, and it was the enemy. Iorga understood this correctly. But the Liberal Party had organization, experience, determination, and the Royal Palace behind it. It could control and reward the bureaucracy and the repressive apparatus; finally, the Liberal Party understood Romanian reality better than Iorga did, and it had a concept. Iorga would have had to borrow a chapter from Hitler's book; that knowing his weakness he should have looked for potential allies. In his Nationalist Democratic Party, the party program still stood on the basis of *Sămănătorist*, there were no great issues attacked. It dwelled on the problem of alcoholism, but did not even notice that Romania had the highest infantile mortality rate in Europe. It did not even present a gradual approach to social reform; instead, it propounded cultural nationalism, which would lead to a cultural revolution. It hoped to change man instead of institutions. The only great change — Iorga's complete abandonment of anti-Semitism — led to a rupture with Cuza. Cuza understood only the Jewish question. Anyone who opposed Cuza in this was in his eyes a Jewish agent.[538] Consequently, Cuza, C. Sumuleanu, and Ion Zelea

---

[537] *Op. cit.*, pp. 50-51.

[538] *Supt trei regi*, pp. 319-324.

Codreanu, the inflexible core of anti-Semitism within the Party convoked a Party Congress on 9 April 1920 in Iaşi. Despite the solidarity of Iorga's friends, the Congress excluded him from the Nationalist Democratic Party.[539] Since Iorga did not dissolve his own Nationalist Democratic Party, Cuza and his supporters founded the *Partidul Naţionalist Democrat din Romania de sub şefia lui A.C. Cuza* ("The Nationalist Democratic Party of Romania under the leadership of A.C. Cuza") or *Partidul Naţionalist Democrat Creştin* ("The Christian Nationalist Democratic Party"). But there was little hope for this new formation. Cuza was still a deputy, yet wished to retire from politics rather than abandon his anti-Semitism. So, the Nationalist Democratic Party continued under the leadership of Iorga, with his newspaper, *Neamul Românesc*.

It became clear that Iorga needed a much greater vehicle and a powerful ally. Who could this ally be? Was it General Averescu's People's League? There was little chance for understanding since it became clear that Averescu's People's League was little more than the interposition of Brătianu in his progress to regain power. In 1918, Iorga was quite friendly towards General Averescu. Perhaps jealous of the support that the peasants brought to Averescu, Iorga wrote a devastating editorial entitled "Chanzy." Always looking for parallels in history, he reminded Averescu of the French General, Chanzy, who during the Prusso-French War of 1871 made a successful counterattack, but after the war was modest enough to refuse any political role.[540] This editorial spoiled relations and possible collaboration with Averescu.

The greatest chance for political action was offered to Iorga by Ion Mihalache and his Peasant Party. Mihalache's concepts were democratic. At this time, Iorga was also devoted to democracy. The cooperation would have been logical. Later, if Maniu's Transylvanian Nationalists had joined, this would have become a force of great consequence.

But Iorga's *Sămănătorist* views were incompatible with a party based on a class, even if that class represented more than 80% of the Romanian people!

---

[539] *Memorii*, vol. III. pp. 5 and 9.

[540] *Oameni care au fost*, vol. II, p. 398.

Iorga was for national unity on the basis of *Sămănătorism*. There was also to be considered Iorga's ego and his deep devotion to the dynasty, which made this natural political union problematic, even if Mihalache offered Iorga the presidency of the Party. The numerous negotiations between Mihalache and Iorga were not leading to any result.[541] Iorga soon attacked Mihalache in his *Neamul Românesc* as the "Gaius Gracchus of Topoloveni." But the most important obstacle of this hopeful union was a personal one: Iorga's insurmountable hatred towards Stere. He referred to Stere as "odious man," the "most filthy one among men."[542] His personality conflict with Stere, a long-standing advocate of peasant rights, overrode any political consideration and destroyed any chance of a political alliance. Iorga carried on his campaign regardless of the political costs to himself or others for years and caused great damage to any chance for a positive evolution in Romanian politics. Consequently, this promising alliance with the Peasant Party did not come about in 1919, neither did it later. Iorga's hostility towards Stere, step by step ruined the chances of the opposition.[543]

This was not the fault of Mihalache. Iorga was inflexible. He always said that he did not want a party based on class, thus, anyone who agreed with his program could enter the Nationalist Democratic Party; consequently, there was no need for him to found a new party. It was Mihalache's fault that his Peasant Party and the workers (under Socialist leadership) could not establish a common front. Brătianu continued to exaggerate and exploit leftist excesses. Bucharest

---

[541] *O viață de om*, vol. III, pp. 13-16; p. 39. Also, *Supt trei regi*, p. 326.

[542] *O viață de om*, vol. III, p. 65. Iorga wrote a book about Stere, entitled *La traison de Stere*, (Bucarest, 1921), a good example how Iorga could lose both perspective and control of himself when his personal feelings were involved. Trying to discredit Stere, he forgot about the decisive role Stere played in convincing his Bessarabians to vote for the return of Bessarabia into Romania. Iorga conveniently forgot that Stere began to collaborate with the Germans only after the infamous Stürmer-von Jagow negotiations became public knowledge. He accused Stere of "*lèse-majestè*," forgetting that King Ferdinand decorated Stere for his merits in the return of Bessarabia.

[543] Professor Iorga continued his campaign against Stere haunting every politician (among them, Maniu) to force them to recognize publicly that Stere committed "*lèse-majesté*," which Iorga succeeded in achieving, but caused so many confrontations, as Șeicaru put it, "as if possessed by a demon's instinct of destruction, Iorga also succeeded in tearing apart the opposition federation's chances for success." Șeicaru, *op. cit.*, pp. 68-69.

was full of rumors. Bucharest was the city of colorful, but very irresponsible rumors which made governing problematic.[544] King Ferdinand told Iorga that as long as the Peace Conference was in session, it was good that the prime minister was a Transylvanian (namely Vaida-Voevod), leading the Romanian Delegation at Versailles.[545]

By the spring of 1920 it became clear that the democratic government was not able to cope with the problems. So the Brătianus moved in with the aid of proxies and their influence in the Palace. Brătianu foresaw the future self-destruction of Iorga in the political sense. His appraisals were to be proven cruelly accurate.[546]

The postwar upheavals in Romania were similar to those prevailing in the rest of Europe during these years. So, statesmen hurried to fix the boundaries and to overcome revolutionary fervor (the Russian example in view). This process meant in practice a return to the establishment. However, in Romania this left out the Trench Generation. Such "back to normalcy" in Romania meant the restoration and the consolidation of the old political system and its expansion to the newly won territories. From now on Brătianu and the political establishment engaged in continuous self-congratulation, something like this: "It is we who created Greater Romania, it is our merit, it is our achievement." Thus they left a lot of hopes unfulfilled, and grave problems unresolved.

Iorga was left somewhere in between the expectations of the Trench Generation and self-congratulating complacence. He remained a man of the nineteenth century, enveloped in his *Sămănătorist* dreams but he also looked at the

---

[544]The first three volumes of Iorga's *Memorii*, dealing with the war and the immediate postwar period, are full of references to rumors. Marshal Antonescu expressed his opinion about the "rumor mill" in his book *Pe marginea prăpastiei* (Bucureşti, 1941), pp. 190-193, saying that "out of 1000 of such rumors, 999 are false...." And Sir Reginald Hoare, the British Ambassador, said: "If even' half an hour a rumor is launched — one is bound to arrive to exaggerations."

[545]*Supt trei regi*, p. 330.

[546]Şeicaru, *op. cit.*, pp. 49-71.

interwar period as a fulfillment, not a challenge, and he saw not with the eyes of a new type of nationalism to emerge. The 13th of March 1906 was far away.

The pretext used to do away with the freely elected National Assembly was ignoble. The Palace arrived at the conclusion that, since General Averescu abstained from the elections, the Assembly was not representative. This idea, without constitutional foundation, emanated from the Camarilla: the Brătianu clan, Ion and Vintilă Brătianu, and the brother-in-law of the Brătianus, Prince Barbu Știrbey, and several important bankers. So, while Brătianu denounced Averescu's party publicly, he saw possibilities in a future Averescu government and a greatly increased representation of the Liberals in the new Assembly. General Averescu, the head of the People's League (now the People's Party) was of peasant origin. He was not for the Camarilla; Averescu refused to court them. He was an upright man and spoke his mind freely even before royalty. In Iorga's opinion, Averescu was "totally inexperienced" where governing and politics were concerned.[547] Averescu did not need a great deal of experience; the political establishment and the Palace had all the political skill and experience, the organization and *politicianism* to put to Averescu's and his party's disposal. And let us not forget the predatory, effective, mass-circulation Liberal press. So, on 13 March 1920, we witness the dissolution by Royal decree of the Assembly, with the pretext that Averescu and his party did not participate in the elections. When the Royal Edict was read in the chamber, the deputies greeted it almost unanimously with a violent demonstration; many leaped to their feet and sang "Deșteaptă-te, Romane!"

A few days before the dissolution, Iorga, acting with unusual political dexterity, introduced the bill of the agrarian reform. Mihalache, the Minister of Agriculture, hesitated, but Iorga understood that time was not on their side. In his last speech as speaker (answering to threats about the possible establishment of a dictatorship), he warned the king: "The blood will spatter the walls of the Royal Palace."[548]

---

[547] *Supt trei regi*, p. 341.

[548] *Op. cit.*, p. 339; also, *O viață de om*, vol. III, p. 37.

On 13 March 1920 General Averescu was entrusted by the king to form a government. This government promised new elections, reassured the Palace and the establishment, and served (not for the last time) as an interposition for the Brătianu clan until they were ready to assume power directly. The peasantry considered Averescu, in Iorga's words, as a kind of god, kissing his feet when he appeared among them.[549] Rarely in Romania were sincere hopes so cruelly deceived as the Averescu regime deceived them. For an opener, the elections held were as corrupt as any. As a result, his "People's Party" swept the elections. To conciliate Iorga, they left him an unopposed seat in Ismail where he was duly elected.

The first act of the government was to do away with the Transylvanian *Consiliul Dirigent,*[550] *The Consiliul Dirigent* was in no small measure responsible for the failure of the democratic experiment, and there were various reasons behind the failure of Transylvanian politicians. Nevertheless, it is questionable whether throwing into the dust all the promises to the Transylvanians about preserving their autonomous status in Greater Romania was the remedy to these failures. The government of General Averescu, who had so brutally put down the Peasant Uprising in 1907, also enacted an agrarian reform, watered down from that which Mihalache and the Peasant Party proposed. But despite its shortcomings, the Agrarian Reform Law of 1921 finally distributed most of the great landed estates, even in the Regat, to the peasants. Another much needed measure for unification, a financial reform, was also enacted. The former antagonist of Iorga, now a political ally, Take Ionescu, entered into the Averescu government as Foreign Minister. This gave some political opportunity to Iorga, who was more and more isolated. Cuza was elected in Teaca during the Averescu-managed elections on his sterile anti-Semitic platform.

In the background Brătianu was preparing his return. All this flouting of the democratic process seemed to be justified, since leftist disorders increased during 1920; on 9 October 1920 there was a General Strike (ultimately aborted),

---

[549] *Memorii,* vol. II, p. 332.

[550] *Supt trei regi,* pp. 371-372.

and on 9 December a deranged Jew planted a bomb in the National Assembly which killed and maimed several deputies. It should be symptomatic of the prevailing anarchistic spirit that newspaper vendors hawked the papers with outcries: "They began to finish off the rats!" meaning the politicians.[551]

During this time the sinister Constantin Argetoianu made his debut as Minister of Interior. He would become Minister of Interior several times, always excelling in the work of repression and intrigue, in which this Phanariot despot was at his best. Argetoianu outlawed the First Congress of the Romanian Communist Party and then he turned on Iorga's role in public life, calling his *Neamul Românesc* "that ignoble paper, an organ of anarchy." When Iorga protested, Argetoianu promised Iorga "to put a fist through his mouth.[552]

After the dissolution of the Assembly in March 1920, Iorga was considered the spokesman of the "United Opposition" — called also the "Federation." Actually, there were two oppositions: the Liberals (pretending to oppose Averescu) and those removed from power by the coup of March 1920 (The "Federation"). If opposition to the coup could not coalesce, that was mainly because of Iorga's continuous, apolitical hostility towards Stere. By the end of 1921 this sterile hostility succeeded in wrecking the "Federation." The Liberals continued (during the Averescu government) to arbitrate the political process. If Iorga was the head of the opposition, he was the most loyal opposition to the Crown. Iorga never drew conclusions from the fact that the main backer of Brătianu was the Crown. Iorga was no doctrinaire monarchist (like Charles Maurras). His support for the monarchy, especially King Ferdinand and Queen Marie, and later for King Carol, rested on an emotional rather than doctrinaire basis, like 90% of his politics, even his Romanian nationalism. Iorga was all too many times carried away by his personal feelings. The king was a weakling; Queen Marie, despite her human weaknesses, took a sincere, and also very ambitious interest in Romania. But many aspects of her human weaknesses made her increasingly insupportable. There was a Canadian Colonel Boyle, who was very intimate with

---

[551]*Supt trei regi*, pp. 355-356.

[552]*Op. cit.*, p. 356.

Queen Marie, with free access to the Palace. He was accused with amassing fabulous wealth, although many people in Romania dispute this, and not even Brătianu dared touch him. He interfered in Romanian internal politics.[553] By 1922 he was back again and continued to interfere (even with Crown Prince Carol). Not everybody was so tactful about Colonel Boyle as Iorga was, although he was also outraged. For instance, Argetoianu was not so charitable; nor were some important people around him.[554] Crown Prince Carol, after his escapades during the War, seemed to settle down, and married a Greek princess, Helen. Shortly after, a boy was born named appropriately after the first unifier of all Romanian lands, Michael the Brave (Mihai Viteazul). Iorga liked his former student, but his love towards Carol was misplaced and ultimately would prove to be fateful.

Iorga was loyal towards the Palace because he considered the Crown a bulwark against the egotistic *Politicianism* of the political parties. The question was raised: was Iorga a Monarchist or merely a Palatist? He answered that he was neither, but a "Regalist!" He explained that he tried to be a disinterested servant of the Crown for the common good. The Crown was the symbol of the nation. In an editorial entitled "How to be Loyal to the King," he wrote: "In face of the Crown, he maintains the following principles: 1) One should not flatter the king; 2) One should not insult the king; 3) The king should be enlightened; 4) The king should be protected when he makes a mistake; and, finally, 5) The king should be exalted when he does a great deed."[555]

So far so good; the problem was in a different sphere. The Dynasty was, since it arrived in Romania, always tied with the Brătianu clan. Brătianu's father brought the Dynasty to Romania in 1866. It was Brătianu's father who gave the predecessor of King Ferdinand the necessary guarantees during the anti-Prussian

---

[553] *Memorii.* vol. III, pp. 178-181.

[554] *Op. cit.*, vol. II, p. 302; also, *O viață de om*, vol. 1, p. 33. Argetoianu had some reliable information about Queen Marie, surprised in embarrassing intimacy with Colonel Boyle. Argetoianu, "*Memorii* (Fragments)," *Magazin Istoric*, vol. 1 (1967), no. 4, pp. 82-85.

[555] *Neamul Românesc*, 15 October 1922; and *Neamul Românesc*, 1 November 1927.

mood in 1870. The Brătianus gave the king all the support during the dark days in 1917 in Iaşi. And during the postwar leftist disorders, the Brătianus again bolstered the king's self-confidence, authority, and power.

From all of Iorga's writings (public and private), one can see that he had constant contact with the Palace, was invited by the king, queen, Prince Carol, and even by Prince Nicolae, and he considered them personal "friends."[556] In Iorga's mind, the king was the historical personage; the others were a low "Capşa Cafe Crowd."[557] How might he oppose Brătianu and be for the king? What was the logic in Iorga's dialectics? In politics, often Iorga had his own logic. Emotions, sentiments (especially when it came to the royal family), and desires were accepted for realities.

In December 1921, Take Ionescu — at the personal request of the king — made an attempt to form a government (since Averescu resigned) and during these few weeks Iorga had another political chance; his attempt failed. Maniu was consulting with Iorga to assure a parliamentary majority to the government in the chamber.[558] By January 1922, Brătianu formed a government. This signaled the end of postwar ambiguity. Stabilization was accomplished. Iorga called this system the "disguised dictatorship of Brătianu."[559]

By 1922, the king, the queen, even the Princes Carol and Nicolae were against Iorga, proposing that "one should send Iorga back to his scientific occupations." Iorga wrote desperate letters to them, but to no avail. King Ferdinand told Stelian Popescu "Iorga is such a superior man, that it is because of this it is impossible to cooperate with him politically." Another time, King Ferdinand opined that Iorga, "besides his undeniable qualities, is also rude."[560] Iorga's lack of political talents were also clear to the enemy. Wrote the *Berliner Tageblatt*:

---

[556]Iorga's *Memorii*, and the volume *Supt trei regi*, and also *O viaţă de om* carry numerous references that Iorga considered the members of the royal family his friends.

[557]Mme. Liliana Pippidi-Iorga to the writer.

[558]*Memorii*, vol. III, p. 243; also, *Supt trei regi*, pp. 365-368.

[559]*O viaţă de om*, vol. III, p. 78.

[560]*Memorii*, vol. III, pp. 262, 265, 271.

"Iorga is the chief instigator of anti-German feelings in Romania," but saw a silver lining: "but he's a man without any political sense or political skill."[561]

By 1922 Iorga's political chances diminished. He did not assume leadership of the "French Generation," nor did he rally meaningful allies. During the coming two decades, people (especially intellectuals) listened to Iorga with respect. Every foreign intellectual ritually called upon him while visiting Romania, like almost every foreign ambassador. Royalty constantly invited him to the Palace, yet with few deputies in the Chamber and without any money (in the "Paris of the Balkans" one needed money to make politics) Iorga was weightless. Politicians who were "Iorghists" before bowed out gracefully, to quote Şeicaru, "they abandoned Iorga with the pain we feel when we leave the love of our youth."

Iorga remarked that he heard many times "across his shoulders" people calling him "an idealist, a visionary," in political circles.[562] His personality', in addition to all, assured a chronic instability in his politics; neither friendships (with a few exceptions) nor hostilities showed consistency.

With Brătianu's return to power there was a Romanian version of "back to normalcy" The victory of *Suprafanarul* (as Iorga called it) was achieved. *Suprafanarul* it might have been; the legend of the mythical, sacrificial lamb, *Miorița*, and the rueful, sad, love songs, the *Doina*, might be (according to S. Mehedinți) the greatest Romanian contribution to world folklore and culture, yet Romania lived in the twentieth century. Iorga's *Sămănătorism* lacked what Brătianu and his system had: a twentieth century concept, called *"prin noi inşine"* ("we shall do it by ourselves"). Brătianu meant that Romania would industrialize by her own effort without any recourse to foreign loans.

Iorga took a stand against *"prin noi inşine."* He said he was for inter-national exchange, etc. (he missed deliberately or otherwise the point of the Liberals, who did not want to put the development of the economy under foreign

---

[561] *Op. cit.*, vol. III, p. 151.

[562] *O viață de om*, vol. III, p. 210; also, Şeicaru, *op. cit.*, pp. 50 and 71. In addition, the Iorga family always emphasized this to the writer.

control). With his *Sămănătorist* ideas, Iorga wished to preserve the agricultural character of Romania?[563] Despite the several books he had written on commerce and industry, Iorga had little understanding of what burdens a modern capitalistic economy places on agriculture, especially during the transition from a traditional to an industrial economy, Iorga saw effects, but did not really understand the causes: how protectionism impoverished about 80% of the Romanian population, but which was necessary in order to industrialize forcibly and rapidly. However, there was no systematic plan to implement the industrialization. The burden for the rapid industrialization was placed squarely on the peasantry.[564]

Under such circumstances, the "Liberal System" did not look at the Constitution and universal suffrage as something sacred, but rather an obstacle which should be outflanked and bypassed. However the Constitution and universal suffrage would ultimately become an insurmountable obstacle. The mainstay of the "Liberal System" was the Crown, the bureaucracy, police (both uniformed and the dreaded *Siguranţa* then there was that old Liberal mainstay, the big banks; also their press and the Liberal party-machine. In 1926 (imitating the Acerbo Law in Italy), the Liberals introduced a system by which the party that received 40% of the vote automatically received a majority of seats in the Chamber, and those with less than 2% did not receive any. This was meant to reduce the number of splinter parties and help the development of a healthier, possibly two-party system. In practice the electoral abuses were constant. Laws stayed on the books, the government did pretty much what it meant to do.[565]

---

[563]*Neamul Românesc*, 2 November 1921.

[564]A revealing item: in 1923-1924, the government spent six hundred million lei on the all-important cooperative movement, the success of which could have largely decided the issue of the agrarian reform. In the meantime private banks received seven and a half billion for the same period. Henry Roberts, *Romania: Political Problems of an Agrarian State* (New Haven, 1951), p. 127.

[565]A good insight into the conditions which prevailed during these years is: C. Costa-Foru, *Aus den Folterkamern Rumäniens* (Vienna, 1925).

One can follow the parliamentary life of this period from the Parliamentary Diaries. They give ample (if not very edifying) proof of the standards within the Chamber, one of the lowest in recorded history. The real issues disappeared in a constant flow of personal attacks, "justifications," "explanations," slanders, and mud-slinging. If Iorga was used to silence and respect in the classrooms, he had a crude awakening. In the Chamber, interruptions were rather the rule than exceptions, and most of them were not exactly respectful ones. Rude expressions were freely flying, directed against Iorga, like "Ocnaş" ("jailbird") or "Mojic" (a crude, uncouth peasant), or simply because of Iorga's emotional nature, "epileptic," and advice to "choose between an insane asylum or the can."[566] Some politicians, like A.C. Cuza, loved this atmosphere; Cuza felt comfortable there with his witticisms and aphorisms. Even Iorga adjusted to the Chamber, and he gave as well as he received. He was still elected to the Assembly, and participated in its work, but he was always busily preparing his university lectures or coming publication — and when did Iorga not have a publication coming? — following the debate with half-ear, ready to use his biting language.

The opposition always promised to "clean up the mess"; but they did just the opposite. They held public meetings in Bucharest, then loyally marched to the Royal Palace and sang "Traiască Regele" (the Royal anthem), shouted several times "Down with the government!" and dispersed peacefully.

In *Neamul Românesc* Brătianu was always depicted with a fez or a turban, and referred to as "Pasha" or "Vizir." Every semblance of the promised autonomy for Transylvania, Bessarabia, and Bucovina disappeared amidst multiple abuses; Balkan Liberals (and Romanian Liberals in particular) were always centralizing. This is what Romania was like for most of the 1920s, despite the democratic constitution, universal suffrage, and its Napoleonic Code.[567] It was Jean-Jacques Rousseau who wrote in his Social Contract about the importance of

---

[566]*Memorii*, vol. III. p. 94.

[567]Iorga held a series of political lectures at the Sorbonne in which he violently criticized the Liberal System. But his book *Formes byzantines et réalités balcaniques* (Bucarest, 1922) deals rather with the Middle Ages in Southeast Europe.

"virtue" of the government: "The institutions are never better than the people who man these institutions and make them function and work."

Nevertheless, the Liberal System was not unprincipled. The general idea not inline" was not rejected entirely even by Iorga. Even such a self-confessed economic ignoramus as Iorga grudgingly referred to Vintilă Brătianu, who was responsible for this *"prin noi înşine"* concept, in the following terms: "Vintilă Brătianu gave a good speech befitting a financial bureaucrat."[568]

Some experts fault the Brătianu system, that it carried out industrialization but did not achieve results like those of Switzerland, Denmark, Holland, or even the Bohemian part of Czechoslovakia, because there, industrialization could be carried out "without a rupture." If rupture could be avoided in those countries, the mentality of those peoples should partly explain why. Furthermore, there was more time to carry out this transition. The fashion in which Romanian industrialization was carried out was objectionable. Foreign capital was also angry. They did not receive the "dowry" of the "rich marriageable girl" they hoped to have married at Versailles.

And what was the reaction of the people to this democracy? The overwhelming majority never really understood what democracy was all about, much less the implications of forced industrialization. They understood that their misery did not come to an end, there was no millennium, and the "system" continued to spell misery. In the immediate postwar years most of the articulate public opinion vaguely believed in democracy, Iorga also believed in democracy. He wrote to Romanians in America that it was the duty of all Romanians there "who still have a Romanian soul" to help and to defend democracy in Romania.[569] The realities meant a rude awakening for most Romanians.

In October 1922, in Alba Iulia, where Michael the Brave united all Romanians, the solemn coronation of King Ferdinand as King of Greater Romania took place. Iorga was there, together with lots of Balkan royalty, and foreign

---

[568] *O viaţă de om*, vol. III, p. 74, also, *Memorii.*, vol. IV, p. 113.

[569] *Neamul Românesc*, 14 September 1920.

guests (Marshal Foch and Petain of France). After all, Romania was a kingpin of the French alliance system. Maniu who, after Iorga prepared the union of Romanian intellectually, became the very architect of Greater Romania, was absent to protest the Liberal abuses of Romanian democracy. Iorga disagreed: "National unity must remain beyond party dispute."[570]

Where would Romania go? To the left, or to the extreme left? Iorga's philosophy was resumed in *Sămănătorisim*. He dismissed the foundation of the Third Internationale as a "useless experiment."[571] The Socialist prosperity of the postwar years was over by now; they would never mobilize the Romanian masses again; Democratic Socialists in Third World countries (in Balkan countries in particular) never got a real chance. Problems were too urgent for Democratic Socialism; many thought that a more radical Marxism was necessary to appeal to the masses. In 1921, the Romanian Communist Party was founded, but communists had little to offer a country with 80% peasants. The Comintern forced on the Romanian Communist Party a platform which demanded self-determination for Transylvania, Bessarabia, Dobrogea, and Bucovina, thus the dismemberment of Greater Romania. This proved to many Romanians that the USSR was still Russia and the number one national enemy. Despite the desperate economic and social situation, the communists could not have the appeal they had in Serbia, Greece, and even in Bulgaria. In 1924, the government outlawed the Communist Party. Few ethnic Romanians shed tears, even if such an action violated the principles of democracy. Communism meant high treason for most ethnic Romanians; the Romanian Communist Party went underground with about a thousand members, never becoming a party of any consequence during the interwar period. We see few ethnic Romanians amongst its members, but a great number of so-called "hostile" nationalities: Hungarians, Ukrainians, and many Jews.

From 1920 on, Iorga never wavered. Long before Stalin made out of the Comintern a section of the Soviet People's Commissariat of Foreign Affairs,

---

[570]*Neamul Românesc*, 4 January 1923.

[571]*Neamul Românesc*, 6 March 1920.

Iorga regarded the Soviet Union as the successor of Tsarist Russia, bound on expansion, hegemony, and domination. The Soviet Union's refusal to recognize the return of Bessarabia into Romania had something to do with this.[572] Iorga was from Moldavia, which had long experiences with Russia. But there was also something that Dr. Samuel Johnson would hardly approve of: Iorga had a sense, an intuition in history. This also marked his other works, not only about the development of Communism in Soviet Russia. It is this sixth sense which made Iorga's works so valuable. Here are some quotations he penned 60 or more years ago about Russian Communism when few people doubted (even inside the Kremlin!) that Russia was not following a truly internationalist proletarian course. Tactical steps were only a temporary retreat, which at the next favorable occasion would be made up for by moving at least two steps ahead. When during the early summer of 1920, after the successful Soviet sweep into Poland, the Russians presented their peace conditions, Iorga commented, "The Bolshevik metaphysics of Lenin, Trotsky's rhetoric, the popular education plans of Lunacharski, the 'new' diplomacy of Chicherin and Krasin are only ways and means of cheating. The basis of Soviet politics remains an all-powerful instinct of conquest, force, and that of domination."

In 1929, the Soviets forced a weak China to reinstate conditions, prevailing under the Tsar, to recognize Soviet ownership of the Manchurian Railroad System. Commented Iorga, "The Soviet regime resembles the devil Nicholas I and his grandma Catherine II." In the spring of 1940, Iorga attacked Peter the Great. It was he who brought Russia into the West, built Petrograd, plagiarized from the West. Russia's entry into Europe became a curse for the West and (according to Iorga) also for his own people. It was not based on organic development "because before that, Russia belonged to Eastern Byzantium and elsewhere." And, when the Soviets forcibly overtook Bessarabia, Iorga commented on the Soviet

---

[572]During 1919, Vaida-Voevod and the Soviet People's Commissar of Foreign Affairs, Chicherin, negotiated for a settlement over Bessarabia but they never managed to arrive at an agreement. *Politics and Political Parties in Romania*, pp. 311-314. With the Soviets consolidating their position, they never found it necessary to recognize the return of Bessarabia to Romania.

Union being "a nationalist hegemony with social pretenses."[573] (Mao Ze Dong's definition of the Soviet Union was a "hegemony based on Socio-Fascism," not far from the one of Iorga.) Iorga mourned the death of the Ukrainian nationalist leader Petliura: "Petliura was a friend of Romania, a friend of our country."[574] A nationalist Ukraine between Bessarabia and Russia as a buffer zone would have been convenient for Romania and Poland, as it is in our days. Even more stunning were Iorga's reminiscences from the World Historical Congress in Oslo in 1928. Meeting Mme. Kollontay and other Russian historians, Iorga remembered their "bourgeois charm," "their impeccable French language and pronunciation," then: "Perhaps neither war nor revolution can defeat Soviet Russia; maybe *embourgeoisement* can."[575] When Lenin died, Iorga commented that the Tartar Khan of Russia had expired.

The mourning reminded Iorga of the sorrow displayed by nomads when their spiritual and military leaders expire. Then he commented on Lenin's "horrible errors," and concluded that "maybe his comrades did not mourn him so much as the civilization he destroyed."

How different was Iorga's farewell to President Wilson! "The whole world salutes the noble figure of the dead Wilson." He continued that all national states thank only him for their existence, but Wilson's work was still unachieved and unfinished.[576]

Iorga loved the United States almost as unabashedly as the late George Meany did. In 1921, a letter arrived to Iorga from America from "The Society of Friends of Roumania," and the Secretary General of this society was none

---

[573] *Neamul Românesc*, 20 July 1920; 28 July 1929; 20 March 1940 and 29 June 1940.

[574] *Neamul Românesc*, 7 June 1926. Iorga was no friend even of a separate Ukrainian history. He wrote with anger with the renewed Ukrainian historian. Professor Khrushevski, whom Iorga considered to be "learned, but confused," who wanted to add to the volume organized by Professors Lamprecht and Tille a chapter about, as Iorga put it, "non-existent Ukrainian history." *O viață de om*, vol. II, p. 88.

[575] *Neamul Românesc*, 14 August 1928.

[576] *Neamul Românesc*, 8 February 1924; also, *Neamul Românesc*, 20 and 21 February 1924.

other than the young John Foster Dulles.[577] Iorga took a stand against American isolationism. "American participation in world affairs is mandatory both for peace and civilization." Then again: "One should change the League of Nations' statutes so the United States could enter because, without America, we could not have achieved in Romania what we have." Commented Iorga during the disarmament talks of 1922: "America, the Living Conscience of the World." Then he adds: "Will a new faith emerge from the United States? We hope it will." When Colonel Lindbergh crossed the Atlantic, Iorga commented that everybody was thinking about money and here we have a hero not wishing to become a hero, without even knowing that he was "a worthy symbol of his country."

But Iorga's sincere friendship towards the United States had limits. He had no patience with fog philosophers like Senator Borah of Idaho. As Prime Minister in 1931, Iorga did not consider it beneath his dignity to comment on Senator Borah's statements to Pierre Laval of France (to whom Senator Borah said that the Versailles boundaries should be revised since they were established by force). Prime Minister Iorga had something to say: "I can send two maps to Senator Borah: one as the United States was in 1776; and another as its boundaries are today." He concluded: "As long as the United States's boundaries will remain where they are, we shall remain within our boundaries of today."[578]

What were the opinions of Iorga on the multiple problems facing Romania?

Economics was as important for the success of Greater Romania as anything. It was also the key to the success of democracy. But Iorga was no economist. As far as democracy goes, under the impact of the performance of democracy he would become increasingly uncertain whether it was the ideal form of government for Romania. This would become pronounced during the 1930s.

What about youth? That is: the future? Since the question of youth and the student body would be so intrinsically interwoven with the minority issue (especially with the Jewish minority, and the Hungarians), we shall consider the

---

[577]BAR *Corespondența lui N. Iorga*, vol. 292 (1921), doc. no. 88.

[578]*Neamul Românesc*, 21 October 1921, 30 January 1921; 5 January 1922; 8 June 1927; and 4 November 1931.

problem first. The slogan of the Nationalist Democratic Party was: "Romania for Romanians and for all Romanians." But these were slogans of 1910; realities now were different.

Iorga theoretically divided minorities into two groups. The first had "historical rights," such as the Szecklers in Transylvania or the Saxons. The second had "contractual rights," this group included minorities which were "brought in," like Ukrainians, Jews, and Austrians. He was not consistent in his definitions. Sometimes he said that "Romania was quite kicky, having German, Latin and Slavonic symbiosis of culture on its territory." Later he forgot the minorities for which Romania should feel lucky. Sometimes Jews were considered a minority which had contractual rights. Other times he considered that Jews had neither historical nor contractual rights.[579]

More realistically, Iorga saw the solution to the minority problem through the establishment of a prosperous economic commonwealth in Greater Romania, based on its rich resources. Minorities would be happy because of "a strong economy."[580] But the Third World economy of Romania was not strong enough. Only the potential was strong.

Of all the minorities, the Hungarians were the most troublesome. In Cluj, a Hungarian stronghold, this writer heard many times, of friends of the family: "They will never accept being ruled by those who were their servants and coachmen before." Iorga understood this. He commented that "In Cluj there is a society present that does not like us, and cannot like us, but maybe it can be induced to respect us." Iorga considered Târgu Mureş "that great Szeckler city." Or Satu Mare "this foreign center, this foreign bulwark." Then Braşov: "Braşov seems for me stranger than ever." He did not hesitate to condemn the poor show Romanian rule demonstrated in this Saxon center.[581] In Trei Scaune County, the Szecklers — according to Iorga — were showing an "Asiatic" hatred towards Romanians. For years Bishop Majláth did not take the seat offered him in the

---

[579]*Memorii*, vol. IV, p. 68; also, *Neamul Românesc*, 21 March 1923.

[580]Theodorescu, *op. cit.*, p. 291.

[581]*Neamul Românesc*, 25 May 1921; *Memorii*, vol. II, p. 313, vol. III, pp. 313-315.

Romanian Senate. Iorga commented in the 1930s: "In Transylvania, the Jews remain Hungarians, the aristocracy closes its doors to us."[582] After the war, Iorga had good intentions toward the Hungarians in Transylvania, both Christians and Jews, in the framework of Greater Romania. Yet, when realities of Hungarian revisionism within and outside Transylvania began to dawn on him, he arrived at a pragmatic conclusion: Hungarians in Transylvania should renounce revision, then they can receive rights and acceptance "in proportion" to their loyalty and their acceptance of Greater Romania.[583]

The Romanians did not go so far in their forcible Romanianization campaign as the Hungarians had. Nevertheless, they took quite a few measures to assure their domination, measures which did not correspond to the image of Elysian perfection they tried to project about Transylvania, Iorga never raised an objection against these measures. More disquieting are certain writings of his about the Szecklers, to whom he granted "historical rights." Iorga analyzed some Szeckler origins, names and institutions, and arrived at the conclusion that Szecklers were but Hungarianized Romanians; consequently, the road should be open to lead them back to their Romanian origins.[584]

The Saxons, an ancient German community which was quite hostile towards Hungarian rule (their Assembly in Mediaş, in January 1919, joined Greater Romania), also had, according to Iorga, "historical rights." Iorga addressed the Saxons in 1925 in Sighişoara (a German town which looked as if it would have been transplanted straight from the Mosel region from where the Saxons originated). He lectured Saxons about "real, true, Romanian and Saxon culture in Transylvania," and took a stand against modernism in Romanian literature, especially the trends of the Transylvanian writer Lucian Blaga, and also some new Saxon literary schools. Then followed an attack against the "impossible ideal of Pan-Germanism," to be completed by a condemnation of "racism

---

[582]*Supt trei regi*, p. 375.

[583]*Neamul Românesc*, 24 March 1928.

[584]*Neamul Românesc*, 13 December 1927.

and racial theories." Iorga concluded praising the influence of the natural environment and popular literature (*Sămănătorism*), saying that, if Saxon intellectuals accept these premises, "on such basis we can have an understanding."[585] Iorga remained awesomely consistent.

During this period, Jews rather than Hungarians caused most upheavals in Greater Romania, and they put the democratic system on trial. Iorga welcomed the numerous Jews. He was never an intransigent anti-Semite. If we agree in the kind, the degree becomes significant. Iorga always wished to see Jews at his Summer School at Vălenii; he treated Cuza's "doctrine" (his intransigent anti-Semitism) with irony and contempt. Everything is relative; even anti-Semitism. Even during his anti-Semitic period, Iorga's bark seemed to be much worse than his bite. By 1918, Iorga's anti-Semitism was gone.[586]

By 1920, in an attack on Cuza, Sumuleanu, and Ion Zelea Codreanu, Iorga said that "...I have not represented this kind of policy for years. Hating the foreigner (the Jew) just because he is a foreigner is incompatible with my conscience... Therefore, I consider the political antics of Professor Cuza and the outbursts of Mr. Ion Codreanu (in that sense) quite repulsive."[587]

Not long ago, a French journalist made the following statement: "*Le racisme est la haine de l'autre; l'anti-sémitisme est la haine d'imperceptiblement autre.*"[588] The Jew might be only imperceptibly different in the West. In Romania, the Jew was greatly different from the majority. And by 1919, Romania had

---

[585] *Memorii*, vol. V, p. 15.

[586] Amidst Iorga's correspondence twelve documents relate to cruelties committed against Romanian POWs in the Austro-Hungarian prison camp at Ostffyasszonyfa. Hundreds of former inmates signed, testifying under oath, telling about cruelty and mistreatment committed by Hungarian and especially by Hungarian Jewish officers, sergeants, and enlisted men. Full names and ranks are indicated. If one takes into consideration the feelings of Hungarians and Hungarian Jews, and Romanians harbored at that time, most of the accusations were not inventions. More significantly, Iorga struck out every anti-Semitic reference before he submitted the document for publication. BAR *Corespondenţa lui N. Iorga*, vol. 279, docs. 15-27.

[587] *Neamul Românesc*, 8 April 1920.

[588] *Le Monde*, 27 September 1987.

about 800,000 Jewish inhabitants. Their number almost quadrupled after 1918. Romanian treatment of Jews did not have a very good reputation. The majority of these newcomers were quite unfriendly. During the fall of 1918 Iorga noticed that Jews from certain areas fled before the arrival of Romanian troops in Bucovina, although, he wrote, "nobody was bothering them." Heavily Jewish-populated Cernăuți, according to Iorga, remained "a foreign city." He saw everywhere Franz Joseph I and other Hapsburg pictures. The old "Moldavian Cernăuți" survived only in marginal slums and poverty at the edge of the city.[589] Nor were the numerous Jews of Bessarabia friendlier.

But the Jews of Transylvania showed the greatest hostility, but not on a Chasidic platform! Most of these Jews were assimilated, and had been for decades in the forefront of forcible Magyarization. They were feeling (like their counterparts in Bucovina) quite unhappy about the arrival of the corrupt, Jew-baiting Romanian officials from the Regat.

In 1923, Iorga's friend, the Minister of Education, Dr. Constantin Angelescu, offered (on the principle of divide and rule) Jewish rather than Hungarian schools in Transylvania. The Jews quickly answered with a petition: "We are Hungarians of the Jewish faith; we were born into the Hungarian language, we grew up with the Hungarian language, with it our own Hungarian soul is related. Our state of mind and our spirit is tied with that of St. Stephen, St. Ladislaus, and we are in a moral community with them. Do not relegate us to the Zorobabel of Jerusalem!" Iorga commented: "If we hunt for their souls, it is more than a savage act: it will be the lowering of our national dignity." Then with some bitterness: "Why do not the Romanian Jews of the Regat, who lived longer perhaps among us than Jews lived amongst the Hungarians in Transylvania, demonstrate the same kind of devotion towards Romania as the Jews of Transylvania demonstrate towards Hungary?"[590]

---

[589] *Memorii*, vol. II, pp. 121-122; *Supt trei regi*, p. 375. Also, *Neamul Românesc*, 12 May 1921.

[590] *Neamul Românesc*, 20 September 1923.

But Romania was now part of the "Versailles System," and Iorga understood that 1918 was not 1878. Every Versailles Treaty required something very different than the Berlin Congress. There was article 60 of the Romanian Peace Treaty, which not only demanded equal rights for every nationality, but nationalities, if discriminated against, could appeal to international bodies and to the signatory Powers (the League of Nations included) for redress. And for the Jews, there was the powerful Alliance Israelite in France, always ready to step in.

Iorga also understood the needs of Greater Romania for internal peace. He took many strong stands against anti-Semitic hate-mongering, demagoguery and violence (especially by students), warning that "in Greater Romania only love can accomplish something."[591] Being in steady contact with Western intellectuals (many of them Jewish) and travelling frequently to the West, he understood that Romania's vital integration within the Versailles System would be difficult if the anti-Semitic barbarism which prevailed in Romania before continued. Consequently, he was for acceptance of the numerous Jewish minority and their integration into the Romanian society; he wished to improve their social stratification — in other words, to transform the Jews into full-fledged, patriotic, useful citizens, as he saw happening in Western countries. One can only reflect that, if demands of morality and those of humanity go hand in hand with those of political expediency, then suddenly everything will go in the right direction.

The Jews in the Regat responded with enthusiasm. There was less Jewish enthusiasm for assimilation in Transylvania, in Bucovina, and Bessarabia. Iorga perceived the difference. When the central Romanian Jewish organization, the "Jewish Union of the Land," wanted to change its name to "Union of Romanian Jews," he protested. According to him, the culture of the Jews of the Old Romanian Kingdom was different from the culture of the newcomer. The Jews in the Old Kingdom were Romanians, while those in Arad "were still dreaming about the return of the Hungarian Hag." And the Cernăuți Jew was still weeping about the fall of Austria. The culture of the Chişinău Jew was Russian.[592] There was

---

[591]*Neamul Românesc*, 15 December 1922.

[592]*Neamul Românesc*, 22 February 1923.

another problem: practically no Jew — neither recent arrival or otherwise — showed interest in *Sămănătorism*.

Iorga, belaboring anti-Semitic excesses almost on a daily basis, with the usual steadfastness asked Jews to abandon the ghetto, to come out of their isolation, and abandon their (Yiddish) language.[593] Commenting on "anti-Semitic disorders," Iorga maintained that "in Greater Romania, although the Romanian element should be dominant, there must be room for other nationalities. The Jews must not be mistreated." He reminded people that he was also an integral nationalist, but had learned that Romanization could not be achieved by force. He asked the Jews not to wave the Zionist flag or sing the Zionist Anthem (after raising the Romanian Hag and singing the Romanian Anthem). The same advice was given to the Saxons in Transylvania as far as Germany was concerned. Iorga found no historical tradition for such Jewish or German nationalism.[594] When the ugly anti-Semitic manifestations increased, he made a major statement. Concerning the Romanization of the cities, Iorga maintained that Jewish retail trade elevated prices through their status as middlemen. He did not consider this a legitimate fruit of work, adding that, if a Romanian retail trader did this, he would consider it equally offensive. Then (considering that this was said in 1924) Iorga attacked Jewish intellectuals for sticking with their German culture! "Why do they adhere to German culture? Does the German past with its attitudes towards the Jews deserve it? No! The Jewish intellectuals are kissing the whip and the feet of their tormentors." While Iorga's instincts can once more amaze the reader, he failed to understand his own ideas manifest in Jewish attitudes towards cultural nationalism, based on the organic roots, of 1,200 years of Ashkenazi (German-Jewish) culture. And he failed to understand or accept the German-Jewish cultural symbiosis. Iorga pointed out: "There are Romanian-Jewish patriots too. Romanian Jewish students (of Iorga), who accomplish good scholarly work in Romanian history, and other proofs of the right Jewish attitude towards Romania, etc." But Iorga looked at Zionism as some kind of romantic

---

[593] *Neamul Românesc*, 12 July 1924.

[594] *Neamul Românesc*, 31 October 1922.

utopia, an impossible dream. We remember Iorga's enthusiasm for Zionism in 1918, but then he did not have the task of transforming a million Jews into Romanians. Thus, the "Supreme Law" was entering the scene. "How can European Jews show an interest in an Asiatic country?" (The answer is: to realize the utopia in building a twentieth century Western industrial democracy in surroundings as alien as a hostile planet).

Iorga saw the solution of the Jewish problem not only in welcoming their assimilation, but in the social and economic restructuring of the Jewish community.[595] In the Moldavian town of Roman, many Jews came to Iorga's lecture in 1923. (This was new, and happened all over Romania.) He lectured about the difference between Latin nationalism, with its inclusive diversity, and German "pagan" nationalism. He attacked Zionism, an "impossible dream after 2,000 years." Jews should abandon the idea of "two fatherlands," they should not seek salvation in the new democratic constitution, "they should find a way to the heart of the Romanian people. The road is not closed."[596]

Iorga's correspondence shows him to be in permanent contact with Jews, above all with intellectuals who turned to him as a protector on any occasion of anti-Semitic discrimination. On 26 February 1929 Iorga made an interpolation in the Chamber about an illegal transfer of a Jewish mathematics professor, motivated by anti-Semitism. Cuza's embryonic LANC daily, *Apărarea Națională* ("National Defense"), took note: "Iorga the Upholder of Kikes," explaining that "Iorga has nothing better to do than to inquire into the allegedly unjust transfer of a qualified Jewish mathematics professor," quoting Iorga that "all good elements of the didactic corps are driven away." The article concluded: "As you can see, what keeps Iorga busy is supporting Kikes in Romanian faculties."[597] This writer could bring up dozens of such examples. Iorga also carried on correspondence with a "Jewish intellectual of German culture from Cernăuți," who

---

[595] *Neamul Românesc*, 22 November 1924.

[596] *Memorii*, vol. IV, pp. 68-72.

[597] *Egalitatea*, București, 8 March 1929; *Apărarea Națională Iași*, issue 10, 3 March 1929.

had an abiding interest in Romanian literature.[598] Or with a Hungarian Jewish notable from Carei in Transylvania, to whom Iorga sent materials about his stand on the issue of anti-Semitism.[599] Not surprisingly, he developed close contacts with the Sephardim, the Latin Jews, who invited him to their Synagogue services, celebrating the anniversary of the establishment of Greater Romania.[600]

He also had contacts with the chief Ashkenazi Jewish Rabbi of Romania, Chaim Schor, corresponding about the Bible, the Talmud, the Shulhan-Aruch, and other Jewish religious literature. Other times Rabbi Schor sent his greetings to Iorga on the day of his patron saint, Saint Nicholas.[601]

During these years Iorga received many letters from Zionist organizations. The Zionists perhaps thought that as a nationalist he would have understanding for their endeavors. When Zionism disrupted the assimilation process of the numerous Jewish Community, sympathies were over, Iorga now maintained that Zionism was false, because "one cannot live in one country and love another." As far as the Old Testament was concerned, the present day Romania was as far from Numa Pompilius or the Horații and Curiații as Jews were from the Maccabeans.

Iorga always said that, if Jews wanted better relations with the Romanian people, this must be resolved within the heart. It could not be legislated. When during the late summer of 1929 bloody disorders broke out in Jerusalem, Iorga commented that there was nothing to be expected from Palestinians who always remained barbaric, but Jerusalem was also holy to three religions. He questioned further the value of romantic Zionism, while expressing deep sympathy for the Jewish faith and for Jewish tragedy through history. It becomes clear he did not consider Zionism a product of organic development. There was no historical precedent nor tradition for it. (Apparently, the longing of Jews for 2,000 years

---

[598]BAR *Corespondența lui N. Iorga*, vol. 283 (1919), doc. 340.

[599]BAR *Corespondența lui N. Iorga*, vol. 313, docs. 508 and 509.

[600]BAR *Corespondența lui N. Iorga*, vol. 289 (1920-1928), doc. 55.

[601]BAR *Corespondența lui N. Iorga*, vol. 307, doc. 182 and vol. 324 (1925), doc. 435.

did not impinge on the consciousness of Iorga.) Iorga repeated his cardinal principle: "A Zionist Jew in Romania betrays both of his countries." When the Jewish minority appeared in the Assembly as an ethnic political party ("the Jewish Party'"), Iorga was outraged, "How do they dare claim to be Jews who became assimilated? How do they dare come here with their disgusting Galician names forced upon them by Emperor Joseph II?" (...) "Do these Jewish minority parties dare claim perhaps the highly-placed French and Italian Jews, too?"[602]

Unfortunately the situation in Romania bore no resemblance to the situation of the Jews in France and Italy. In Romania the Jewish Community (like the Jews of Eastern Europe) constantly appealed to the League of Nations, demanding rights guaranteed in the Versailles Peace Treaties, Iorga condemned this invitation of foreign interference into the affairs of Romania, yet the barbaric excesses committed against the Jews which the Romanians were not able to handle made such interventions mandatory.

Here we should reflect on an instructive parallel. Although the Alliance Israelite forced the victorious Romanian state to keep anti-Semitic excesses under control, and enforce civil rights for the unassimilated Romanian Jews (many of them barely able to speak Romanian), when the Alliance Israelite offered its services to the Hungarian Jews they refused. It was not in Hungarian Jewish tradition to look to foreigners for help against compatriots. V Vázsonyi, the leader of Jewish masses, answered in 1924: "The Treaty of Versailles is a sorrow for our nation, it cannot become the source for our rights." The Alliance Israelite drew its conclusions and broke with the Hungarian Jewish communities, thus excommunicating them from world Jewry. The Hungarian Jews were undeterred. Vázsonyi reiterated the Jewish position: "Our foreign coreligionists do not understand us either, we are Hungarians, first and above all. We are not Hungarian Jews, but Jewish Hungarians."[603]

---

[602]*Neamul Românesc*, 21 March 1923, 12 September 1929, 31 October 1922, 25 February 1923, and 18 December 1928.

[603]Leva Jeno, *Fekete Knoyv a magya-zsidosag szenvedeseirol* (Budapest, 1946), p. 8.

Iorga would have agreed in one thing with the Zionists: the Zionist Jew who does not go to Israel is "a traitor" to both of his countries. He said he wished the Jews "to enter into the spiritual fortress of the Romanians," the fanciful *Sămănătorist* views of Iorga about Romanian reality. The Jews of Romania had different experiences with the sordid realities. But even if Romanian reality had followed the best examples of Christian tradition, Zionists would have answered: to abandon Jewish history, tradition, achievements, and great Jewish contributions to humanity in general and to the Christian West was unacceptable. Zionists would never accept that, even in exchange for the best Western Christian tradition, all Jewish past should be discarded. Only then would a patronizing, graceful "acceptance" follow, for which the Jews were supposed to be grateful.[604]

Such could not be the view held by Iorga, who envisioned "the unspoiled Romanian peasant" within a *Sămănătorist* setting. Despite similarities, Iorga bore little resemblance to Charles De Gaulle, who could speak about France as a mystical ideal, but could be realistic (even cynical) about Frenchmen. De Gaulle loved France more than he loved Frenchmen.

Iorga's opposition to anti-Semitism brought about his break with Romanian students and the rising "New Nationalism." Indeed, his position on the Jewish question and his break with A.C. Cuza became his nemesis.[605] Cuza showed in his anti-Semitism a consistency unusual during the interwar period in Romania. Since the Jews had been granted citizenship, Cuza had become even more obsessive in his anti-Semitism.[606] The assimilation of the Jews for a doctrinaire anti-Semite remained an anathema. How can one desire the assimilation of a

---

[604] Abba Eban, *The Story of the Jews* (New York, 1968), passim.

[605] On 16 March 1920, Cuza addressed a note to Iorga written on a menu (maybe Cuza had a brainstorm while dining at the Hotel Boulevard): "Cuza for Iorga." Then, "Cuza is the landmark by which the distance can be measured which Iorga has covered since he entered the political struggle and where he is today." There is no signature, but Cuza's handwriting is unmistakable. BAR *Corespondenţa lui Nicolae Iorga.*, vol. 284, doc. 162.

[606] Iorga remembered with great irony how "Professor Cuza was wringing in despair his hands" in the Assembly while it was discussing equal rights to the Jews. *O viaţă de om*, vol. III, p. 36.

race whom their prejudices make out a diabolical, absolute evil? Would any nationalist desire that such an element should become a part of the warm, life-
giving body of the nation? The unsolved problems, coupled with the alienation
of youth, would give Cuza during the coming years a chance to work for his
ideas.

Many of the young people (all too many students, both on university and
high school level) found the road to the traditional left blocked, but not because
leftist politics were incompatible with anti-Semitism. There was the platform of
the Comintern. Nationalist Romanians would not accept the dismemberment of
Greater Romania. There was also the anti-peasant attitude of the communists.
Many of these young students came from peasant stock, and they had to look
only across the Dniester to get a good idea what sufferings the communist system imposed on the peasantry. Many of these young students were religious.
Atheism was not much help in gaining their allegiance. Last, but not least, there
was a deadly efficient secret police, the *Siguranţa*, which held more than its own
in comparison with any other secret police.[607]

The painful forced industrialization was felt by the many students of peasant origin. With postwar illusions dissipated, the road to the left blocked, yet,
the unsolved problems awakening a strong sentiment, the radicalism of the
youth went to the right. This was the way to register a protest without becoming
an atheist, or a traitor. Identical evils existed in Serbia, Greece, and Bulgaria
(without the existence of a disproportionately large Jewish community). The
youth of Serbia, Greece, and Bulgaria could go to the left for answers, and channel efforts into more sane channels.

Jews became an easy target for students; above all, Jewish fellow students.
Jewish students were rarely admitted to Romanian universities before 1918.
Many of them city-dwellers, they were better prepared for studies and for the
mentality of modernization than the peasant students were. Now young Jews

---

[607]The illegal Communist Party was not unattractive for Jewish and (to lesser extent)
Hungarian youth.

entered the university in masses to better themselves through education, this always being an effective Jewish weapon in advancement.

With the establishment of Greater Romania, the Romanian government wanted to create, almost overnight, a solid Romanian middle class. Thus, the government encouraged enrollment in the universities. This was done in a chaotic, haphazard Romanian fashion, without any preparation or the establishment of an infrastructure. The underdeveloped Romanian state soon had an almost equal number of students as Great Britain. Most students avoided those professions the developing Romanian state so badly needed. The majority took up law which would grant them administrative posts and security with it. Since Jewish students had no chance of entering the administration, they took up medical studies, law, and engineering. Here they clashed with those Romanians who entered similar fields.

There was no preparation as far as dormitories, student restaurants, lecture halls, etc., to handle this influx of students, and this increase occurred also in high schools. Under such circumstances Jewish students had definite advantages. Contrary to students who came from the provinces and felt themselves alienated in the big cities, Jewish students in their majority had their families and homes. Jewish students had to rely less on the chaotic, Third World conditions created by government negligence. Many Jewish students had an intellectual tradition which enhanced their studies.

The abominable living conditions for students became one of the main reasons for their radicalization. Iorga condemned student radicalism (which he labelled "anarchy") but remembered how much he suffered as a scholarship student. Now he vividly described the conditions in student dormitories, the lascivity, filth, and the miserable quality of food.[608]

The disproportion between Romanian and Jewish students (even in the better high schools) was striking. Here are statistics presented by Corneliu Zelea

---

[608]*O viață de om*, vol. III, pp. 204-207.

Codreanu, the future Captain of the Iron Guard (used with reluctance, but no other statistics were available. Even if partly true, they point to the essence of the problem.)

In 1920, at the University of Cernăuți:

Number of Students

Confession	Faculty of Law	Faculty of Philosophy
Orthodox (Romanians, Ukrainians, Others)	237	174
Catholics	98	n/a
Lutherans	26	n/a
Other	31	n/a
Jews	506	574

In Bessarabia, in elementary schools the proportion of Romanian or other nationalities and Jews seems to be much more balanced. In the cities, Jews are disproportionately represented. An entirely different situation emerges in the high schools and professional schools.

Bessarabia, Number of Students

Confession	High Schools	Other Schools
Orthodox Christian (Romanians, Ukrainians, Russians, Other Slavs)	1,535	690
Jews	6,302	1,341

Private High Schools in the Old Kingdom

City	Romanians	Jews
Bucharest	441	781
Iași	37	108
Galați	190	199

University of Iași

School	Romanians	Jews
Medical School	546	831
Pharmacy	97	229
Philosophy	1,073	421
Law	1,743	470

The only improvement in the balance between Romanian and Jewish students was in the Faculties of Law and Philosophy, these were the training grounds for administrative jobs or sinecures. The Jews tried to go into the professions, but the Romanian economy did not provide sufficient opportunities. The disproportion of the Jewish students made Codreanu ask in horror: "Shall we have an intelligentsia from this kind of element?" (meaning the Jews?).[609]

In the 1920s, it was not the number of Jewish students which ignited the radicalization among students but the disorganized and unplanned increase in

---

[609]Zelea Codreanu, *op. cit.*, pp. 75-78. Not only in Romania was there protest against compering Jewish intellect. Quite a few Ivy League colleges maintained a quota (a "Numerus Clausus") where Jewish students were concerned. And even if the Jew graduated, he had great difficulty in finding employment reaching English, Speech, or History. Perhaps because of this the Jewish literary movement flourished in New York City. Jews with English rarely found employment. When Iorga visited the United States, he was surprised finding out about these conditions. When he visited these colleges, he naively inquired about this unofficial but effective "Numerus Clausus." Ignoring even more naively how our system works, Iorga was uneasy about the ambiguous answers. See *Americani și Romani din America.*, pp. 314-315. Perhaps Iorga read the Marquis de Cusrine who said: "to lie in the letter of the law is more revolting than to proclaim the most audacious tyranny."

student numbers. There was a determination to create an ethnic Romanian middle-class quickly. The poet-politician Octavian Goga assessed the results in 1925. Describing these jacks-of-all-trades who emerged from the faculties, who did all kinds of shoddy business, Goga elaborated on the essence of the problem: "These are carnivorous birds who, as if by tacit consent, prepare the doom of our country. They create a disgusting atmosphere, a pestilential stench of carcasses. Unfortunately, there is, for the salvation of these corrupt creatures, a theoretical justification which has achieved the strength of a dogma, namely, we should base our national life on this dubious scum of our towns. The well-known policy that we should create quickly and at any cost a steady bourgeoisie. But because in our great haste we could not wait for the slow process, we replaced the citizen with the scoundrel."[610] These would be prophetic words. How disillusioning that a decade later most of the articulate support of Goga would come from this element.

It is in this that the roots of the phenomenon (which Armein Heinen fittingly called) "New Nationalism" are to be found.[611] It was a twentieth century nationalism only vaguely resembling its predecessor, nineteenth century nationalism. This "New Nationalism" rose out of the overburdened Romanian faculties to symbolize the dashed dreams so many people placed in Greater Romania. They introduced twentieth century methods into the "nationalistic struggle." When in 1923 (in a protest against the naturalization of the Jews) the *Liga Apărării Naționale Creștine* (the League of National Christian Defense) was formed by Cuza and Codreanu, Codreanu's first speech reflected this: "To arms!" The essence of "New Nationalism" was a "direct action," adapted from the Italian Fascists. The LANC was (according to Codreanu) not a hateful political "party" but a movement, a combat organization.

If there is practically nothing between thinking up an action and carrying it out, this is a "Magna Carta" for violence. Violence was not unknown in Romania and the Liberal establishment employed it often, thinking that the ruling class

---

[610]Octavian Goga, *Mustul care fierbe* (București, 1925), pp. 44-45.

[611]Heinen, *op. cit.*, p. 99.

had a monopoly on it. For the first time "New Nationalism" successfully challenged this monopoly with dire consequences.

On the more shadowy side we see amidst nationalist students in Romania symptoms more familiar today than scores of years ago. The "professional students" emerged creating the impression of a strange mixture between a tape recorder and gangster. Yet, these students were the product of unresolved problems and legitimate grievances. Some of them were intellectuals, but most were pseudo-intellectuals — superficial, incapable of rational thinking — yet they wished to voice opinions on almost every subject despite that they were quite ignorant and half-educated. Beaumarchais said: "It is not necessary to understand an issue in order to be willing to argue about it." Torn out of their patriarchal environment, they rarely graduated; after one or two years at the university they left and added to the increasing number of unemployed half-intellectuals. Not only were they unemployed, but they were also unemployable, because of their great numbers. These malcontents were in a much more explosive mood than the peasantry. At the university they were made aware of their grievances, and became militantly discontent.

Romania did not resemble the West with enough room for the "old" and the "new" intelligentsia to live together, but rather the Third World colonial situation. The new intelligentsia emerged for the purpose of challenging the old one, which was also the ruling class. Since the old system was restored by Brătianu, these students fought the ruling class (with its economic backbone, the Jews, protected by the Constitution and the Liberal establishment) which blocked the future of the new, emerging intelligentsia.

As for the overproduction of pseudo-intellectuals, Iorga did not worry about it. He would answer *L'Indépendence Roumaine*, "which worried about the emergence of an intellectual proletariat," explaining that he did not wish to be lectured by anybody as far as the universities go. The degree merely verified the work accomplished; it was no claim for a job.

"If we have too many attorneys, let us create conditions for their employment." For Iorga, the more students enrolled in universities, the better."[612]

Here we have an example of Iorga's economic thought and sociological awareness. It seems strange that the very Iorga, who wished to promote education in Romania and its future, did not realize the lack of technical orientation in this swollen, student body! There were dangers inherent in the great numbers of liberal art graduates, and the lack of professionals on whose emergence the economy and development of Greater Romania depended! Iorga was oblivious to the alarming increase of the pseudo-intellectual rift-raff. His example, Eminescu, was aware of this problem and he constantly spoke about the "proletariat of the pen." Strangely Iorga never launched a serious literacy campaign, though more than 50% of the population were illiterates.

By the late fall of 1922, student bitterness led to a general student strike.[613] This right-wing student movement coincided with a similar anti-Semitic student excess at Hungarian, Austrian, Polish, and Lithuanian universities. "Numerus Clausus" severely restricted the enrollment of Jewish students. The government, aware of article 60 of the Versailles Treaty and its international implications, could not grant a "Numerus Clausus."

Could Iorga have offered to the youth a practical alternative? It was difficult to find such an alternative; yet, if Iorga had shown more political skill, and had assumed the leadership of the "Trench Generation," perhaps with a strong hand he would have been the man to offer an alternative. What would the Iorga of 13 March 1906 have done? Even then Iorga did not wish to become a revolutionary. But the situation of 1922 did not resemble 13 March 1906, and, as a nationalist, he could not confront Romania with the world. Neither did Iorga

---

[612]*Neamul Românesc*, 20 March 1929.

[613]Within Iorga's correspondence from this period is a tasteless postcard the students sent to the "former Apostle," depicting Romania in the form of a naked body of a beautiful woman, tortured by a Jewish hand complete with Stars of David. The hand is dressed in ritual Jewish praying shawls. Among other things, the text contains accusations that there are two and a half million Jews in Romania. "The Romanian people are unaware of the extent of the Jewish danger." BAR *Corespondența lui Nicolae Iorga*, vol. 304 (1923), doc. 101.

resemble the young firebrand he was twenty years before. He was often re-minded of his role in March 1906; Iorga explained that there was no similarity between the movement of 1906 and that of 1922. For him the issue now was not the Romanian language, but dead and maimed bodies at the universities, and the unacceptable demand for a "Numerus Clausus," a demand incompatible with democracy.[614] More could have been achieved to harness the indignation of this student and youth movement into a positive direction.

In 1922, Iorga was still part of the opposition, but within the establishment. Unfortunately, he was out of touch with the new Romanian reality and the emerging "New Nationalism." He, like Hindenburg and Horthy (even, in a sense, Petain in France), and like many other nineteenth century nationalist lead-ers, allowed the youth to slip through his fingers. He was repelled by the mani-festations of this "New Nationalism" and the radicalization of the student body.

Iorga editorialized about "The Seduction of Youth": "There are some par-ents who have no more common sense than their children do." When violent student disorders broke out in Oradea in 1927, he wrote: "Who is guilty? The parents are."[615] During the student disorders in Oradea (and Cluj), Romanian students mishandled Mr. Weiszlovics, a Hungarian-Jewish nationalist, owner of the famous Oradea Hotel, "The Black Eagle." This and other devastation and pillaging in these two Hungarian-inhabited cities were considered by Iorga "only the product of a lack of education."[616]

When, in the Assembly in 1927, Cuza demanded in the name of the students the introduction of anti-Semitic legislation, the Minister of Education addressed the student body in a patronizing vein: He, as Minister of Education, was not

---

[614]*Neamul Românesc*, 15 December 1922. A memorandum to Iorga in March 1923 by the leadership of his Nationalist Democratic Party explained that the Party was losing and lacking support because of three reasons: it supported the government's position within the National Assembly on too many issues; the Party was isolating itself from other opposition parties; but perhaps the most important reason was Iorga's hostility towards the student movement. BAR *Corespondența lui Nicolae Iorga*, vol. 304 (1923), docs. 35 and 36.

[615]*Neamul Românesc*, 12 October 1923; also 16 December 1927.

[616]*O viață de om*, vol. III, p. 79; and *Memorii*, vol. V, p. 263.

about to deal with "minors" as "equals." The Chamber applauded.[617] Iorga became even clearer in his *Neamul Românesc pentru Popor* (distributed among the literate peasants of the villages), Iorga expected that students would now return to their peasant homes, so he addressed their parents, explaining that in Oradea, dangerously near to the Hungarian border, overzealous students caused great disorders. "Parents should not listen to the nonsense that students have to say when they come home for Christmas. Parents should tell their children that we, the older ones, created Greater Romania and we did not found our country and make it great with the help of disorder and pillage."[618] It is what we call "the generation gap!" Regardless of the rights and the wrongs, there is a certain patronizing, self-congratulating attitude of the older generation which exacerbated "New Nationalism" even more. But one should not judge Iorga or his contemporaries; the interwar period was the happiest period of Romanian history. No wonder Iorga or his contemporaries were "taken in by it." The tragedy was that he, as many other intellectuals of the older generation, was out of step with the problems, yearnings, and ideals of most of the students, even if history vindicated the suspicions and doubts of his and that of the older generation. Iorga advised Romanian students to compete with Jews in the faculties in the fields of intellectual endeavors and to overtake them rather than to attack them physically.[619] He was naive; all too many students, representatives of the "New Nationalism," considered the introduction of a "Numerus Clausus" and the beating or chasing of Jews out of the university (in certain instances not hesitating to cripple or kill them) more expedient than Iorga's suggestion to "overtake" Jewish students in their studies! The same brutality occurred in the high schools, and from there it spilled out into the Jewish ghettoes, shops, or to innocent Jews on the streets, synagogues, etc., keeping the country in ferment. "Students" were leading these activities. And because Romania was poor, the trash of the cities often joined in.

---

[617] *Op. cit.*, vol. V, p. 195.

[618] *Neamul Românesc Pentru Popor*, 16 December 1927.

[619] *O viață de om*, vol. III, p. 90.

Yet, the success of the LANC or Codreanu (he was acquitted by juries even though he committed first-degree murder) cannot be explained by anti-Semitism alone. It should be considered as a volcanic outbreak of protest against the "Liberal System." "New Nationalism" considered Liberal practices and the "system" which emerged from them to be immense hypocrisies.

Codreanu shot the brutal Police Chief of Iaşi, Manciu, point-blank, only to be acquitted by a jury later. Iorga was outraged.[620] One should not think about those seated on the jury as bloodthirsty beasts! This acquittal was proof of the people's hatred towards Brătianu's bureaucracy and police brutality One should also understand the culture of the area, which does not consider a murder committed for a political cause without any motivation of personal profit to be equivalent to a killing motivated by personal gain. This was what Codreanu explained to the jury.

The foundation of the LANC under the leadership of Ion Codreanu (the father of Corneliu) and A.C. Cuza, both brothers in arms of a younger and a different Iorga, happened in the spring of 1923. Young Codreanu's closest associate was young Ion Moţa, the son of an Orthodox priest from Transylvania, with whom Professor Iorga corresponded, and was closely associated with during the struggle against the Hungarians.

Cuza and young Moţa traveled in September 1925 to Budapest, to participate in the anti-Semitic World Congress, which the leading Hungarian racist, Gyula Gömbös, and T. Eckhardt convoked in the Hungarian capital. Considering Hungarian-Romanian relations, this Romanian participation (in opposition to Brătianu's Liberal system) seemed to be bordering on treason, and so was incredible for this writer that he doubted his Hungarian sources. Yet, he confirmed the participation of Cuza and young Moţa from Moţa's own correspondence.[621]

---

[620]*Supt trei regi*, pp. 380, 387.

[621]Szokoly Endre, *És Gömbös Gyula, A Kapitány* (Budapest, 1960), p. 234. Also: Ion Moţa, *Corespondenţa cu Serviciul Mondial*, Biblioteca Verde (Roma, 1954), p. 46.

All this anti-Semitic violence heavily tainted Romania's image. After all, this happened long before Hitler, but protests impinged little upon the consciousness of "New Nationalism." Iorga wrote: "They could not care less about the reputation of our country."[622]

Iorga did not give up considering his relations to the student body too important. Again and again he tried in vain to reason with the students, like in Timișoara in 1922. He concluded: "They are against the future, their parents, their country, and against the national interest." Wrote a Hungarian Jew from Timișoara: "Professor, you saved the honor of Romania."[623] These students had another message: an indirect, effective attack on the whole Liberal system, using Jews as scapegoats. There was plentiful proof that local Liberal officials exploited anti-Semitism in heavily Jewish inhabited cities like Vaslui or Dorohoi.[624] Iorga commented: "Everyone seems to be an anti-Semite."[625] He noted with disgust: an anti-Semitic club was installed just in front of the Royal Palace in Bucharest. He also knew how Liberal ministers encouraged the anti-Semitic student movement with monetary donations.[626] Thus, *Politicianism* was at work one more.

Gradually, all too many students rejected Iorga. The time of the "Apostol" had passed. All too many letters written to him now bear the sad inscription "*Fostului Apostol*" ("to somebody who used to be an Apostle").[627] In early 1923, he held a lecture at the Ateneu. As he left in the company of the Minister of Education, Dr. Angelescu, he was met by a violent student demonstration. (Iorga was forewarned that Cuza and Sumuleanu had come to make the arrangements

---

[622]*Supt trei regi*, p. 379.

[623]*Memorii*, vol. IV, pp. 44-45. Also, BAR *Corespondența lui Nicolas Iorga*, vol. 304, doc. 22.

[624]*Memorii*, vol. IV, p. 93, and vol. 5, p. 51.

[625]*Op. cit.*, vol. IV, pp. 46-47.

[626]*O viață de om*, vol. III, p. 189. Also, *Memorii*, vol. V, pp. 39 and 61.

[627]BAR *Corespondența lui Nicolac Iorga*, vol. 287, (1920). There are all too many letters addressed to Iorga in this vein.

for this anti-Iorga outrage.) He confronted the students. As he commented, had he shown any hesitation, it would have "only encouraged this kind of insolence." Iorga walked up to the menacing crowd and said: "Happy are those parents who gave birth to you!" Dr. Angelescu tried to reason with the students. Ultimately, he (like Iorga before) was drowned out by an indiscriminate hollering and whooping. Iorga stopped his lectures at the university. He only returned to the university in June for examinations.[628]

From December 1922 on, Romanian universities celebrated every year (in December) a so-called "Student National Holiday" in memory of the student General Strike of 1922. For this yearly "student holidays," military and police had to be mobilized to protect synagogues, Jewish property and lives. The Romanian archaeologist Vasile Pârvan told Iorga: "The students say you are in Jewish pay." Then Pârvan concluded: "Our generation does not understand us anymore."[629]

In December 1924, during the "Second Student National Holiday," professors left the auditoriums under loud outcries of "*Jos Jidanii!*" ("Down with the Kikes!"). Iorga was ashamed. These scenes occurred before the visiting French university professor, Mario Roques, whose lectures were "tolerated for the time being."[630]

As time advanced, all too often universities had to be under military occupation and not only during the "Student National Holiday." All this resulted in beatings, mayhem, broken windows, ugly scenes in parks, where women were sometimes publicly whipped, people entering Jewish restaurants and leaving their bills unpaid, unspeakable scenes occurring with Jews thrown from moving trains. Sometimes students were egged on by their schoolteachers, even by police officials to go even further.

---

[628]*Neamul Românesc*, 9 February 1923; also, *O viață de om*, vol. III, pp. 90-91; finally, *Memorii*, vol. IV, pp. 50-51.

[629]*Op. cit.*, vol. IV, p. 55.

[630]*Op. cit.*, p. 190.

Jews were subject to degradation and continuous mockery, an omnipresent characteristic of East European anti-Semitism: their accent was imitated; so were their mannerisms, religion, and dress. In one word, their humaneness. Anti-Semites in Eastern Europe did not learn that whatever the "Pale of Settlement" Jew had become (thanks to centuries of un-Christian degradation and persecutions), one would not change him by mocking.

The situation of the Jews in Romania after citizenship was granted to them deteriorated rather than improved, with students mainly responsible for these excesses. The majority of Romanians (especially the peasantry) were too good to participate in this. In most cases they were neutral, but under such circumstances neutrality' is a zero quantity which helps the stronger in an uneven struggle.

Apart from foreign reactions (Romania was part of the civilized Versailles System), perhaps the saddest effect of all this was that it administered a disastrous setback to everything Iorga worked for, especially to integrating the Jews into the framework of Greater Romania! These happenings reinforced the historic Jewish "fear" of Gentiles and this old Jewish fear is difficult to explain. It manifests itself sometimes even in the West. The slowly rising Jewish confidence and willingness to assimilate within the Old Kingdom was gravely damaged; it undermined beliefs in Iorga's promise. The process could not take off. The large Jewish communities of Transylvania, Bucovina, or Bessarabia shrugged their shoulders:

"I told you so! Nothing should be expected from the Romanians!" And during the 1930s Jewish hope would be gone forever. The Jews withdrew within the framework of the Kahal, the Jewish Community, and into religion. Iorga remarked, "The Jewish phalanx is within the framework of the religion like the Armenian."[631] Romanian Jews in their majority closed themselves in within the framework of the ghetto and continued to have little in common with the traditional spirit of the country. They felt unwelcome, only tolerated until they paid

---

[631]*Neamul Românesc.* issues between 12 and 22 August 1937, appearing under the series "Judaica."

their bills or gave a bribe. Gandhi, the champion of non-violence, used to say, "Non-cooperation with evil is a duty." The "Pale of Settlement" Jews never assimilated to a non-Western environment. A product of history, their mentality was capitalistic. The older generation was fatalistic, but the young people rarely wanted to live as their fathers did. Thus, many Jews turned towards Zionism or Communism for answers. At that point, they clashed with Iorga and his Romanian nationalism. Almost a million such Jews were too much for the country to absorb. This affected Iorga's attitude, too, as time passed by.

We remember Codreanu's fear about the great number of unassimilated Jewish students at the universities.[632] On the other side of the coin, Jews took a look at students for whom the beating up of a Jewish female student passed as a heroic deed and could rightfully ask themselves: shall we have a bureaucracy which will rule over us from this element? Should we assimilate, becoming like them?

Where did all this commotion leave Iorga? In an uncomfortable position. The students were circulating leaflets claiming that "Iorga is in Jewish pay," calling him "a characterless person," "he should be liquidated."[633] Students maintained that Iorga received immense amounts from the Jewish banker Aristide Blank. With this we arrive to the perhaps most painful episode in Iorga's life: the "Blank Affaire."

Aristide Blank, President of the Banque Marmorosch Blank & Co., headed the largest financial institution of Romania, which financed the Old Romanian Kingdom decades before the First World War. He had close relations with the Liberal Party; the Brătianus, Al. Constantinescu (the future president of the National Bank), etc. Aristide Blank did his best to get along with every political party. He was, according to that knowledgeable cynic, Argetoianu, "the most dangerous man (Argetoianu) has ever met." Argetoianu considered him perceptive, intelligent, and remembered that during the years in Iaşi. Blank pretended

---

[632]Codreanu wrote: "Not only that the Jews are unable to create Romanian culture, but they will falsify even the culture which we have." Codreanu, *op. cit.*, pp. 75-78.

[633]*Memorii*, vol. IV, pp. 56 and 82.

to suffer from an incurable asthma to avoid military service. He quickly recovered once the armistice was concluded. His policy was to buy everything and everyone around the king. It takes one to know one. Argetoianu was not motivated by anti-Semitism. He spoke about the industrialist Nicolae Malaxa (an Orthodox of Greek origin) in more devastating terms, and he referred to the three financial advisors of King Carol II as the "three crooks."[634] Iorga thought Blank became "interested in Romanian culture" as a "kind of Maecenas."[635] Blank was no Maecenas. Iorga knew that Jews in the West traditionally supported culture generously. Vienna Jews led Viennese culture to unprecedented flourishing. Jewish finance supported almost every artistic manifestation in the West, even in neighboring Hungary. But in the incongruent atmosphere of the "Pale of Settlement" (including Romania), a similar phenomenon never got a chance.

Iorga and his cultural nationalism would have been better off without the support of Blank, who was making politics. Iorga found our later that Blank also financed the newspaper of Iorga's archenemy, Stere, and supported the Peasant Party with donations. Moreover, Iorga did not know in his naivete (but Argetoianu knew it, as did Codreanu) that every politician of weight was on the payroll of Blank, receiving millions of lei, like Titulescu (with 19 million lei), Grigore Filipescu (with one and one-half million lei), etc.[636] Later, during the reign of Carol II, Blank would finance Carol, by buying villas for his mistress, etc.

Blank always prepared an account of the amounts he spent for printing Iorga's books, helping Iorga's schools abroad, his son's study, etc. When in 1926 Argetoianu (at that time associated politically with Iorga) found out about this, he loyally resigned from the Board of Directors of Blank's bank. On another occasion, Blank offered Iorga the presidency of the Peasant Party and, in case of Iorga's reluctance, promised that he would publish the files concerning

---

[634]Constantin Argetoianu, "Memorii," *Magazin Istoric*, No. 2, (May 1967), pp. 66-70.

[635]*O viață de om*, vol. III, p. 9.

[636]*Memorii*, vol. II, p. 321; also, Codreanu, *op. cit.*, pp. 373-376.

the support given to Iorga's son, Mircea. Whereupon Iorga threatened to take Blank to court.[637]

How naive Iorga was getting involved with such a man! With Iorga now at loggerheads with Cuza and the students, and deadly opposed to the Liberal system, all this was bound to get a public airing! Thus, the Liberal Party hatchet man, Alecu Constantinescu, came up to Iorga in the Assembly with a file trill of documents of Blank's contributions to Iorga's cultural activities. Iorga, self-righteously (and naively), rejected this "crude blackmailing attempt."[638]

This writer saw all the relevant documents in the Romanian archives (Iorga was innocent enough to keep them). Blank contributed to the following cultural activities of Iorga: the establishment within the *Liga Culturală of the Teatru Popular*, to Iorga's Romanian Schools in France and in Italy; to the printing of certain of Iorga's books serving Romanian culture abroad; to his lectures at the Sorbonne; finally, to the transfer of funds for Iorga's son Mircea, who studied in Italy, and later for getting him a job as an engineer at Cugir industrial complex. Iorga's newspaper always published the contributions of Aristide Blank to Romanian culture. The documents date from July 1920 to October 1924.[639]

The sums which emerged from these documents are significant, Iorga's bank account (on 15 March 1919) carried a balance of 7,230 Lei — next to nothing.[640] During the Averescu and Brătianu regime, Iorga could not hope for help for his cultural activities from the state, much less for the eternally troubled finances of his *Neamul Românesc*. And cultural activities were the "raison d'être" of Iorga's existence.

An instructive document dating from July 1920, written to Iorga from the *Liga Culturală*, notifies him about the catastrophic lack of funds.

---

[637]*Memorii*, vol. IV, pp. 212, 220-221.

[638]*O viață de om*, vol. III, pp. 92-93.

[639]BAR *Corespondența lui Nicolae Iorga*, vol. 284, docs. 142, 143, 144; vol. 285, doc. 12; vol. 290, doc. 127; vol. 291, doc. 28; vol. 294, doc. 4; vol. 300, docs. 167, 168; vol. 305, docs. 20, 138; vol. 306, docs. 55, 78; vol. 309, docs. 3, 4, 396, 548; vol. 314, doc. 143.

[640]BAR *Corespondența lui Nicolae Iorga*, vol. 278 (1919), doc. 519.

There is no money for group travel, for any of the *Liga Culturală's* activities in the newly acquired territories. "With the present railroad ticket prices," the *Liga* could not undertake a thing. They were asking Iorga's possible intervention for a 75% reduction of railroad ticket prices and for other benefits for the *Liga*.[641]

In view of documentary evidence, how true are the charges that "Iorga sold out to the Jews, to Blank, to Jewish banks," etc. — and "he is in Jewish pay?" These charges seem exaggerated, even false. If one looks at Iorga's endeavors, these charges become grotesque politics. One of Iorga's shortcomings in politics was that he had no money. In the case of Blank's contributions, documents show that Iorga accounted for Blank's help. He did not spend any of it on his politics — let alone on himself. The only exception: he accepted Blank's help to transfer (his own) funds for his son, studying in Italy, and it could seem objectionable that Iorga agreed that his son should work at one of Blank's subsidiaries as an engineer, even if Mircea Iorga was qualified.

But contemporary Bucharest was so far removed from Puritan ethics! It was Iorga who came close to Puritanism — so, relativism is in order. The more, because corruption of all kinds was so prevalent, starring with the Crown (and from the Crown downwards). Those who now accused Iorga besmeared a man (proverbially clean) that "he sold out to the Jews..." Then the "*Mahalaua Bucureșteană*" as the Iorga family called them to this writer,[642] starred exaggerating Blank's contributions 10, 20 or more times than the real amount. And due to Iorga's political stand, these attacks came as much from the Liberal establishment as from A.C. Cuza and the anti-Semitic student movement. Iorga soon found himself between a rock and a hard place. In vain he made gestures, bequeathing his Bucharest home to the Romanian people! All these gestures did no good. The Liberals, Cuza, and the students (even the democratic economist, Virgil Madgearu) could not resist the political capital to be acquired by engaging

---

[641]BAR *Corespondenţa lui Nicolae Iorga*, vol. 284 (1919-1920), doc. 142.

[642]*Mahalaua* (Turkish word) means a town borough, but in Romanian means the scum of Skid Row. However *mahalaua Bucureșteană* refers not to destitute people but rather society, gossiping in an irresponsible fashion.

in such mudslinging.[643] Since Bucharest and its politicians were so corrupt, everything was believable. Iorga was unlike them. But why should Brătianu, Cuza, other political enemies, or the radicalized student body, with its low morality (and poverty), accept the truth? Was it not more convenient to say that the "Teacher of the Nation," the (former) "Apostle" sold out to Blank?

The Bucharest rumor-mill began to spew out even more fantastic tales: the accusation was made that he "sold out to other Jewish banks, too" (like those of Berkowitz, Loewy, and Braunstein), and that he was also a member of the Board of Directors of these banks.[644]

All this was totally unfounded. The Liberal establishment fostered these accusations with vengeance. However the pivotal role was played by A.C. Cuza, who hoped to assure his political comeback by appealing to this suddenly rising anti-Semitism among students.

Cuza started his regular attacks on Iorga and his connections with Aristide Blank in the National Assembly. Here he could use, at leisure, his famous aphorisms and vituperations. These attacks started by the end of 1920, increased by 1921, and from then on they went on and on. They seemed to have followed a rather monotonous pattern and ended with "Iorga is financed by Blank!"[645] Cuza wanted to develop the greatest political mileage out of the rise of anti-Semitism among students.

In the exchanges with Iorga, Cuza did not hesitate to hit below the belt. He called Iorga a *iepuraș* meaning a kind of "rabbit-monger." What he had in mind was Iorga's father, who during the last days of his coma imagined that he had a bunch of rabbits roaming around within his head, Iorga did not talk to Cuza for months. Cuza seemed unperturbed. He remarked to Șeicaru that "he does not understand the oversensitivity of Iorga, who is showing 'the symptoms of a male menopause' because of a harmless joke." In his memoirs, Iorga never became

---

[643] *Neamul Românesc*, 6 December 1924.

[644] *Neamul Românesc*, 16 February 1923.

[645] *Memorii*, vol. III, pp. 92, 97, and 112-113.

specific about the incident, speaking only about an "immense scandal provoked by Cuza in the National Assembly," adding "Cuza was attacking me all day."[646] This writer may only add that if everything is said, writing the biography of somebody is not the best among all available formulas for exorcism by the means of writing history.

Iorga answered Cuza (and the LANC) in style: "The Party which desecrates synagogues, seduces minors, and whips women in public acts so heroically in the public gardens." After which, Iorga reaffirmed that Jews would be welcomed, despite the outcry of Cuza, in the Nationalist Democratic Party and at the school at Vălenii as well.[647]

Later, Iorga put his personal feelings in the case of Cuza ahead of political considerations. He liked his old comrade in arms, would restore an acceptable kind of relationship with Cuza, and as Prime Minister he made Cuza a Senator. This relationship, not so warm anymore, rested more on personal sympathy than on political compatibility, lasted almost until the very end.

William Oldson said about Iorga: "He was not only an anti-Semite, but militantly so." And, "Iorga was to remain an anti-Semite all his life." Finally, that "Iorga is never really humane or liberal when it really counts, when the rights of others have to be balanced against the claims of Romanian nationalists."[648] One should remember that Iorga never was a Liberal, but a Romanian nationalist, who wrote, thought, and acted (and was murdered by the Legion) before the Holocaust. The Holocaust occurred after Iorga was murdered. His life and activities, his hostility towards racism (that of German racism in particular) give a key to what his position would have been had he lived. If anyone wished to study the sincerity of "revisions" on the Jewish question, one could always parallel the sincerity of Iorga's with that of Gömbös in Hungary. There is no room for a retrospective view of history; only for relativism. Only impostors

---

[646]Șeicaru, *Un junimist antisemit*, A.C. Cuza, p. 7. All this was confirmed to the writer by the Iorga family. Also, *Memorii*, vol. III, pp. 45 and 49.

[647]*Neamul Românesc*, 1 August 1923.

[648]Oldson, *op. cit.*, pp. 85, 87-88.

give the pretense of reality to their images of the past. One should once more remember Oscar Wilde's remark: "If one tries to reduce truth to facts, one deprives the truth of all of its intellectual content."

It was Dr. Moses Gaster, Iorga's former opponent, now a friend and intellectual associate, who told Iorga (at a reception at King's College at Cambridge in 1930) regarding his kindness towards the Jews: "I assure you, wherever you will go in life, if you will run across a Jew, he will be grateful to you."[649]

Iorga did not abandon politics. Since Brătianu kept him out of power, he could dedicate himself more to his professional activities. This was refreshing, compared with Iorga's relations with the *Suprafanarul*! These scholarly activities during the first ten years of the interwar period were immense, fitting into the framework of the "Versailles System." In Romania, he resumed his university lectures. In 1928 he became the Dean of the Faculty of Letters; later the President of the University of Bucharest. He held numerous lectures at the Romanian Academy and at other institutes of higher learning, at the *Liga Culturală*, and different Romanian organizations. Then there were schools which Iorga established in the two Latin countries which he cherished the most, France and Italy. During the late 1930s, for reasons of Geto-Thracian archaeology, he attempted to open an institute in Albania.

The school in France was located in Fontenay aux Roses, near enough to Paris for Romanian students and scholars to make it to the Sorbonne, the museums, the archives. The Romanian House at Fontenay aux Roses served as a residence, a warm community and intellectual brotherhood, where lectures and exchanges took place, with Iorga at the center of activities. This Romanian House was presided over alternately by Iorga and Vasile Pârvan. It was Romanian state property and opened in 1922. Aristide Blank contributed greatly to its establishment. The inside was decorated by Romanian art and frescoes in the *Sămănătorist* tradition. It had a good library. Deserving students received state scholarships for their stay.

---

[649] *Memorii*, vol. V, p. 394.

The other Romanian center Iorga opened in 1930 was in Venice, a town he loved. The *Casa Romena di Sua Eccelenza* Iorga housed students of art, but not artists alone. It had a good library. It was mainly financed with subscriptions in the daily *Universul,* and contributions from the National Bank of Romania. Its interior decoration represented beautiful examples of Romanian folklore. Many foreign visitors enjoyed the warm Romanian hospitality there.

During the 1930s Iorga played an important role in the establishment of a Romanian school in Rome. His purpose: "to counterbalance the Hungarian influence in Mussolini's Italy with appeals to 'Latin solidarity,' and to "have a Romanian cultural presence in the two great Latin capitals."[650] The school in Rome was not to be such a "one man show" of Iorga as the other schools of his were.

His summer university reopened at Vălenii-de-Munte in 1921 as "The Summer University of Professor Nicolae Iorga," functioning until the summer of 1940.

Romania now had numerous minorities. Iorga welcomed at Vălenii Hungarian and German students from Transylvania, and also Jewish students. But Jewish students never came; they could not feel at ease in this progressively poisoned atmosphere among Romanian students. Only Jewish scholars and professors invited by Iorga came, like the philologist Dr. Moses Gaster.[651] The instinctive absence of Jewish students is as sad as it is significant. Iorga would have welcomed them, to assimilate and imbue them with his cultural nationalism! Iorga would have considered it to be his mission to receive Jews with their Hungarian culture from Transylvania, and those with their Austrian-Germanic culture from Bucovina, and the Jews with Russian culture from Bessarabia, to familiarize them all with his cultural nationalism! Jewish students saw the limits of equality, still rejecting assimilation and a Romanian nationalism based on

---

[650]*O viață de om,* vol. III, pp. 55-58.

[651]*Neamul Românesc,* August and September 1921, and *Neamul Românesc,* 1 August 1923.

Sămănătorism. This was the consequence of the anti-Semitism spearheaded by the students.

The *Liga Culturală*, after national unity was achieved, became less significant than before. Iorga set new goals: to raise the cultural standards of the peasantry, to encourage excursions in the countryside, promote folklore, etc. The Liga was to become instrumental in the cultural collaboration with minorities, to organize congresses, exhibitions, and the issuing of folkloric yearly calendars, "The Calendars of Romanian Patriotism." The two innovations Iorga brought to the *Liga Culturală* after the war were his *Teatru Popular* and his Missionary School.[652] Regrettably, Iorga never organized an all-encompassing literacy campaign.

Now for the first time, many Jews came to the meetings of the *Liga Culturală*. Iorga asked them to be patriotic Romanians, and disapproved of anti-Semitic excesses.[653] In November 1929, the *Liga Culturală* received new headquarters in Bucharest.

The Missionary School was to offer national and moral education for women. After that, they were expected to return to their villages and work on raising moral and patriotic standards, disseminating knowledge, and strengthening the family. According to Iorga, the school was "to form a new Romanian soul with the help of women."[654] This endeavor was not a great success. Although the Missionary School was opened in August 1922, in November 1923 only one female student participated.[655]

During the first decade of the interwar period Iorga organized several international congresses and participated in others. As a renowned Byzantinist, he realized now an old dream: convoking in Bucharest the First International Congress of Byzantine Studies, in April 1924. A review, *Byzantion* was launched,

---

[652]Theodorescu, *op. cit.*, pp. 270-271.

[653]*Memorii*, vol. IV, pp. 14-15.

[654]*O viață de om*, vol. III, pp. 178-183.

[655]*Memorii*, vol. IV, p. 106; also, Theodorescu, *op. cit.*, p. 286.

which became an informative journal for Byzantine history. Many renowned Byzantinists participated. After the Congress, Iorga showed them Romania. The Second International Congress on Byzantine Studies took place in Belgrade during the spring of 1927. After the Congress, Iorga brought many foreign participants as guests to Romania and, of course, to Vălenii.

The World Historical Congresses resumed their work in April 1923 in Brussels, with the animosity of the war still lingering on. Only the historians of the victorious countries were present (Iorga remarked: the Congress took place "without the participation of our enemies").[656] Iorga lectured about "Danubian Romania and the Sixth Century Barbarians," and the Thracian elements in Romanian folk art.

The next World Historical Conference took place in Oslo in August 1928. Iorga met numerous historians, among them H. Koht, the Norwegian humanist and historian, and future Foreign Minister. German and Soviet historians were also invited, Iorga considered the Soviet historians "quite mediocre" and managed to clash with them on more than one issue.

The following World Historical Conference took place during the spring of 1930 in Cambridge, England. World Historical Conferences were (and are) quite politicized, therefore, Iorga always considered them important. He could always be (before the representatives of his profession) the spokesman of Romania.

During the interwar period, Iorga gave numerous lectures abroad. His lectures fell somehow into the pattern of the Versailles System and allowed him to further pursue his lifelong endeavor: to show Romania to the world and to establish for his country's history a place in world history. From 1921 on, he lectured at the Sorbonne regularly.[657] He was often invited to other French higher institutions of learning like the College de France. He also returned to his Alma

---

[656]*O viață de om*, vol. III, p. 120.

[657]Characteristically, Iorga noted that a French colleague at the opening lunch, "had good words to say about our country." *Memorii*, vol. III, p. 108.

Mater, the Ecole des Hautes Etudes. He was in permanent contact with a pleth-
ora of scholars and statesmen, from all political convictions. In 1923, he visited
Charles Maurras, the editor of the *Action Française*. Iorga found him "almost
deaf, a very kind person." Maurras spoke to him about a French aristocrat, a
descendant of a Romanian boyar family.[658] *Neamul Românesc* praised Leon
Daudet, a militant journalist of *Action Française* considering him "not only a
great journalist, but a great French writer."[659] Daudet, the son of the great writer
Daudet, apparently inherited some poetic imagination. But how could someone
consider him a great French writer? Reading his articles, his style was sometimes spectacular, always violent, but most of all it would seem that Daudet gave
a new meaning to vulgarity.

During 1928, a French Assumptionist Priest (the Assumptionist Order was
known for its extreme anti-Republican reactionary views) and historian suggested that Iorga lecture in Vălenii about Constantinople and the Turks in the
Balkans.[660] But the meaning of these contacts should not be exaggerated. Iorga
was in permanent contact with historians and politicians across the entire political spectrum, also with Henri Bergson, who sent Iorga a circular about possible
world cooperation among intellectuals.[661]

When Iorga was the Speaker of the Assembly, he expressed his views on
the foreign policy goals of Greater Romania, outlining long-term strategy. This
strategy suffered little change for the rest of his life. For him the past, the present,
and the future of Romania formed an organic entity. There were certain permanent, unchanging, and unchangeable factors in history, thus foreign policy followed from it with an ironclad consistency. Geographical and ethnic conditions
have their implications. (He brought up Britain as an example.) In the present,
Romania was supposed to follow the lead of its strongest ally, France, and keep
close relations with Italy. Commercial relationships should serve to strengthen

---

[658]BAR *Corespondența lui Nicolae Iorga.*, vol. 305, doc. 117. Also, *Memorii.*, vol. IV, p. 77.

[659]*Neamul Românesc*, 26 January 1928.

[660]*Memorii.* vol. V, p. 244.

[661]BAR *Corespondența lui Nicolae Iorga*, vol. 305, doc. 325.

the "natural" (Latin) relations with these countries. Built on these relations, Romania should orient its policy toward the Balkans and the prolongation of the Balkans, the Middle East. He concluded that "Romania must do the utmost to conquer influence in the Near East, and with our strength (which depends on us) we shall put this influence to the service of the West, with which our physical structure (Latinity) and our soul are inextricably tied."[662]

As for practical matters, with allowances for Iorga's likes and dislikes, he tried to uphold the "Versailles System," which was a "French alliance system." Iorga loved France; for him it was ideal that Romania's position should be tied with that of France. During the 1920s such Romanian foreign policy seemed to be justified. With Germany defeated and Russia prostrate, France was the strongest power on the European continent. But there was something artificial about this, and how illusory this was became clear during the next decade. Despite Iorga's long stays in France, he did not notice the terrible impact the War had on French psychology. Once more Iorga took his desires for realities. Despite his early failure politically at home, Iorga continued his efforts to serve Romania abroad. He thundered his incomparable anathemas whenever the Versailles System was as much as criticized, let alone challenged.

During the interwar period, that very Iorga who studied and received his doctorate from German universities never visited or lectured in Germany once! Except for a short visit after the war to Vienna, he never visited any Austrian higher institution. Hungary was completely off limits. Not because of any Hungarian restriction placed upon him, but because of his refusal to go there.

Iorga's antipathy and suspicion towards the former Central Powers, Germany in particular, was (to use Iorga's term) "organic." Once when he had to cross Germany (because of geography) on his way to Scandinavia, he found Germany "sad," and had the impression that "the Germans tried to make gestures towards people to seem to be amiable."[663]

---

[662]*Dezvoltarea politică a poporului românesc (Conferința ținută la Ateneul Român în Noiembrie 1919)* (București, 1919).

[663]*Memorii*, vol. V, p. 99.

Iorga gladly visited Yugoslavia, Czechoslovakia, and Poland; these countries were part of the Versailles System. He considered Poland, even Finland as natural allies, facing the Russian menace.[664] He worried about Russia, mainly because of Bessarabia. Iorga always insisted that the Romanian government should seek Soviet recognition for the return of Bessarabia to Romania.[665] Beyond Russian expansionism which Romanians were quite familiar with for the last two hundred years, there was the Communist regime. Iorga hated it and spoke about the "crazy ideas of tyrannical Bolshevism." To the French press, he said that "Bolshevism simply did not go down with us in Romania; it is incompatible with Romania's Latin character and way of thinking." Yet when the Romanian secret police arrested and brutally tortured Communist students, Iorga immediately protested.[666]

Russia for Iorga always remained Russia. Of all the new territories, Bessarabia was in the greatest danger. Iorga understood this. How could Romanian policy and Romanian politicians follow such a foolish policy in Bessarabia, allowing this most dangerous irredenta to become the most misgoverned province?

When Bessarabia voted to return to Romania, a great deal of autonomy was promised. This was never honored. Instead, there was almost unlimited police brutality, misgovernment, corruption of all sorts, neglect and lack of development, all accompanied by anti-Semitic persecutions of the numerous Jewish population.

Iorga saw this. He wrote: "Never was a policy so blind in the face of such a great menace." Invited in 1928 to the military parade on the tenth anniversary of Bessarabia's return to Romania, he wrote: "What did I see in Bessarabia? A splendid military parade, and poverty and neglect, villages without electricity

---

[664]*Neamul Românesc*, 17 May 1922.

[665]*Neamul Românesc*, 3 November 1920.

[666]*Neamul Românesc*, 6 January 1921; 26 January 1921; 15 February 1928.

and light; this is what I saw, and it is my duty before my conscience to say so."[667]
He was in the position to know. Since the beginning of the century he had had
contacts there. Among them, nobody seemed to be as sympathetic as was Paul
Gore. From the year 1905, he emerged as a quiet hero, a non-violent fighter.
When Gore died in 1927, Iorga dedicated a moving obituary to him, remembering how he witnessed under the whips (the dreadful *nagayka* of the Russian police) to his belief in his nation.[668] No hatred can be detected in Gore's correspondence towards other nationalities in Bessarabia, not even towards Russians.

After Bessarabia returned to the "Mother Homeland," a chastened Gore
wrote to Iorga, after the war, as the head of the archives in Chişinău. He asked
for Iorga's help to prevent the loss of some important historical documents from
abuses and neglect. When Iorga met Gore in 1919, he impressed Iorga as a pessimist.[669]

Iorga saw Gore shortly before his death. By this time Gore was very dissatisfied; he told Iorga: "Those who hated us before, now have contempt for us."
The peasants were poorer than ever, and many received no land. Iorga could
never bear too strong a criticism of Romania (with the exception of his own).
He concluded: "What a disastrous influence of Russian Hamletism!"[670]

The Soviets knew the situation and provoked border incidents constantly.
They established across the Dniester the Moldavian Soviet Socialist Autonomous Region as a kind of magnet. In 1924 they staged disorders in Tatar-Bunar

---

[667]*Neamul Românesc*, 26 February 1924; also, *Neamul Românesc*, 6 May 1928. Iorga had
tenuous contacts in Bessarabia; in his correspondence after the war we find constant
reminders of the abuses. BAR *Corespondenţa lui Nicolae Iorga*, vol. 273 (1918-1928), docs.
309 and 528 (this letter notifying Iorga of especially ugly abuses). And then there is
document in volume 285, number 216, and many others.

[668]*Neamul Românesc*, 11 December 1927.

[669]BAR *Corespondenţa lui Nicolae Iorga*, vol. 282, doc. 441; *Corespondenţa lui Nicolae
Iorga*, vol. 304 (1923), docs. 28 and 29.

[670]*Memorii*, vol. V, p. 168.

and Nikolayevka. According to Iorga, Rakovski founded the Moldavian Autonomous Soviet Region in order to make some inroads into Romania; and then in
October the uprising occurred.[671]

Rakovski was somebody Iorga "loved to hate." Nevertheless, a whole town
does not rise up without reason. Iorga placed too much guilt on the Communists.
He saw the whole Tartar-Bunar incident as a continuation of the Tsarist policies.
He wrote: "Now they do not come with Church flags, the images of saints, the
bones of the martyrs, but on motorboats with pistols to kill."[672] The USSR now
demanded the Slav inhabited regions of Bucovina too. For Iorga everything was
clear. They were trying to use Communist ideology to restore Russia as it was.[673]
That might have been true, but this made Romanian misgovernment even more
reprehensible.

Iorga wrote (in 1921): "The Bolsheviks in Moscow are finding out that nations are a reality, a truth, and a great indestructible reality."[674] But Stalin did
not believe in the indestructibleness of a nation. Once, annoyed during the Second World War with Hungarian behavior, he casually remarked to President
Benes: "The Hungarian question is only a question of the availability of cattle
cars." The time would come when Stalin would get a chance to try out this
method in Bessarabia, changing the "great, indestructible reality."

What did Iorga think during this decade about Europe and the world?
When, after the trial of the War, the idea of a United States of Europe emerged,
Iorga was favorable in principle. He considered economic cooperation between
European states mandatory for such an end, and that would be difficult to
achieve. The example of the United States was based on a common path and
hard work, but Europe was burdened with its past. Disarmament was no abstraction for Iorga, yet he asked: "Does it have teeth?" There were revanchists full of

---

[671]*Op. cit.*, vol. IV, p. 184.

[672]*Neamul Românesc*, 22 September 1924.

[673]*Neamul Românesc*, 22 November 1921.

[674]*Neamul Românesc*, 3 December 1921.

hate, and others, who wished to plunder. Iorga concluded: "With disarmament one does not achieve social justice; but with social justice one may arrive at disarmament."[675] His suspicion of Germany was overwhelming. When at Rapallo the Soviets concluded an agreement with Weimar-Germany Iorga was outraged. "Two predators understand each other; they remain what they always were, and they hope to restore their empires and hegemonies." A few months later Walter Rathenau was murdered by the Nazis. Iorga commented: "The Beast is Rising Again," and he felt that every civilized person regardless of his political opinions must rise against this monster. During the "Beerhall Putsch" and the years after it, Iorga did not pay much attention to the Nazis. (His newspaper misspelled Hitler's name as "Hittler"). In 1928, when there was talk about an Anschluss and Mussolini opposed it, Iorga agreed; he pointed out that the treaties must be respected, and "not letting the Germans arrive at Innsbruck will prevent the Hungarians from coming to Oradea."[676]

As far as Hungary was concerned, Iorga's feelings were those of many Romanian intellectuals: both Hungary and Romania, being two non-Slavic and non-Germanic nations placed among Slavonic and Germanic peoples, he would have liked close Hungarian-Romanian collaboration, but on the basis of the status quo. According to Iorga, Romania's logical ally was Hungary, but this collaboration was made impossible by the Hungarian attitude. Then he repeated his old dictum: "Each people has to live within its own ethnic confines." And, "By following the dream of restoring Hungary to what it was, the bands of Horthy are destroying the Hungary which can be!"[677]

Iorga did not worry about Austria. He dismissed Charles of Hapsburg with his restoration attempts as the "degenerate Hapsburg," directing his hatred on

---

[675]*Neamul Românesc*, 25 September 1929 and 27 March 1921.

[676]*Neamul Românesc*, 21 April 1922, 8 July 1922, and 14 August 1928.

[677]*Memorii*, vol. V, p. 213; also, *Neamul Românesc*, 7 December 1923.

Horthy's system and its "white terror." Captain Gömbös was, for Iorga, "Chief of the Hungarian racists."[678]

If Iorga had any contact with Hungarians, they were Hungarian Jewish intellectuals of democratic convictions. Finally, he could meet Hungarian Jews other than nationalist zealots. In November 1920, Iorga met Oszkàr Jàszi in Bucharest, another man of the nineteenth century, now hopelessly out-distanced by events, who wanted to turn Transylvania into a kind of "Eastern Switzerland." Iorga and Jàszi had long-standing contacts. Now Jàszi came to Bucharest and met Iorga to have a talk "as democrat to democrat." He explained that he was for Karolyi's republic, but set against the Bela Kun regime (many of whose leaders were Professor Jàszi's former students), which tolerated him; but the Horthy regime wished to murder him. Jàszi pointed out that the present Hungarian regime was fomenting a murderous anti-Semitism against small Jews while the Jewish capitalists were the very mainstay of the system. Terror squads riled and fomented an irresponsible revisionism. Under their rile, Hungary perished. Jàszi asked Iorga to intervene in France for Hungary. Iorga found him very sympathetic and considered Jàszi "enthusiastic as only a student could be."

The Horthy regime put Jàszi on trial in absentia. Iorga commented: "The Hungarian government — this pompous, feudal outfit — ordered the arrest and the imprisonment of Professor Jàszi," concluding that Jàszi's only sin was to exercise his academic freedom. Then Iorga resumed: "How fortunate it is that Professor Jàszi is residing in a country (the United States) where nothing but honest work is respected, and found for himself bread and shelter!"[679] Other Hungarian Jewish intellectuals in exile also came to Iorga. In April 1920, a Hungarian democratic journalist in exile came, his recommendation being that "he was a follower of Jaszi."[680] Iorga corresponded with the renowned Hungarian

---

[678]*Neamul Românesc*, 23 March 1920 and 28 July 1928.

[679]*Memorii*, vol. III, pp. 83-84; and *Neamul Românesc*, 10 July 1929.

[680]*Memorii*, vol. III, p. 130.

democratic writers in exile, G. Bölöni and Jenö Gömöri, and even received letters from their wives.[681] Iorga's relations with Italy before Mussolini marched on Rome (and after) are instructive. The evolution of this relationship is interesting, especially how it would evolve during the following decade. We know how much Latin brotherhood counted for him. Nothing can be found in Iorga's writings about Mussolini's background. He never mentioned that Mussolini was a Marxist, a very radical Socialist. Following the events in Italy, Iorga was informed of the developing "anarchy." His correspondence also shows he was aware of the brutal Fascist methods.[682] He did not like them. Yet, when Mussolini took power, Iorga editorialized that Mussolini saved Italy from a Bolshevik dictatorship. Iorga, not unlike some Italian Liberals (Giovanni Giolitti and others), considered the Fascists a positive, temporary, phenomenon. They hoped for the strength of *transformismo*). Neither Iorga nor the others recognized that they were dealing with an entirely new, twentieth century phenomenon.

Soon, Iorga changed. By 1925 he thought that "Mussolini was preparing for himself a Caesarian throne of dictatorship." From then on, he refers to Mussolini as the "Italian dictator," who attacked parliamentarism. His conclusion: "Parliamentarism is a nineteenth century institution which one should update, and not destroy."

Iorga did not like Mussolini's advocacy of Hungarian revisionism nor his policies. He quoted Mussolini: "Hungary's body was cut", and reproached Mussolini for his designs on French and Yugoslav territory. Iorga understood: to this, Mussolini will need Hungarian and Bulgarian help. He concluded: "We in Romania wish the great Latin nation well." But Iorga feared that Mussolini was upsetting the Versailles System.[683]

---

[681]BAR *Corespondența lui Nicolae Iorga*, vol. 287, doc. 61; vol. 301, doc. 262.

[682]Iorga's correspondence during 1922-1924 leaves us reassured that he knew what the Fascists were up to.

[683]*Neamul Românesc*, 4 November 1922, 10 February 1925, 21 November 1925 and 17 June 1928.

Iorga took a strong stand against the minuscule Fascist parties of Romania which tried to imitate Mussolini, calling them *maimuțolini*, ("those who are aping Mussolini"). Fascist splinter groups were violently anti-Semitic. Iorga reminded them that "the Romanian Fascists should keep in mind Jewish participation and leading Jewish roles in Fascist Italy."[684] Iorga did not consider it to be beneath his dignity to write on this subject to Brătianu. On 11 October 1923, Iorga called them the "gang which calls itself *Fascia Română*, that attacked and killed people who did not agree with their anti-Semitic scandals, they carried out in continuity a shame for Romania." They constantly menaced Iorga's paper's editor, A. Cusin, and another, a Jewish journalist from *Adevărul*, Mr. Rosenthal, and they threatened Iorga's life. Because the police did not take action to end this behavior, Iorga brought to the prime minister's attention these conditions and felt that if these Fascists carried out their threats, Brătianu would be responsible for the breakdown of law and order also.[685]

Iorga often traveled to Italy. He had plans to establish his school at Venice, and later in Rome. Mussolini, the skillful opportunist, knew Iorga's importance in Romania as far as culture was concerned. Knowing Iorga's love for Italy and his ego, he invited him to Florence in May 1925. Later, he was received by Mussolini for a long personal audience.[686] Then two events occurred. In 1927 Mussolini recognized the return of Bessarabia into Romania. In this very year Mussolini also began his systematic encouragement of Hungarian revisionism. It may be (as the Iorga family remembered it) that Iorga hoped that with his deep love for Italy and now having established a meaningful relationship with Mussolini, he could counterbalance the Hungarian influence in Rome! If there were a Romanian to accomplish such a fear, it would be him! Everything else fell on the ground; Iorga wanted to serve Romania. So, by approximately 1928, we see Iorga slowly coming around on Fascism in Italy — in public at least.

---

[684] *Neamul Românesc*, 28 August 1925. Iorga disapproved even Crown Prince Carol's adhesion to the Fascist movement. *O viață de om*, vol. 3, p. 92.

[685] Pippidi-Iorga Archives.

[686] *Memorii*, vol. V, pp. 25 and 189.

He rarely discussed Fascist ideology or Fascist practices. Iorga remembered Mussolini's promise that "Fascism was not for export." This effort of his (together with other "zigzags of his fanciful, whimsical attitudes, produced by his fanciful, capricious fantasies") was but one to which he stuck with stubbornness to the end.

It is interesting from the perspective of more than three score of years to read Iorga's views about other international issues, Iorga, the nationalist, did not sympathize with empires, or with colonialism. Yet his displeasure was tempered by his concern to uphold the Versailles System. Furthermore, his nationalist sympathies distinguished between distinct, definable nations and those which were nor. When the Greeks began to move into Anatolia inhabited by ethnic Turks, Iorga took a strong stand against this move, and when the Turks defeated the Greeks, he did not like that either. He spoke about the "fanatic Albanian, Mustapha Kemal," and he sadly considered the Greek defeat "the last chapter of Xerxes." He thought the establishment of a Greece on two continents was not possible, regardless of whether it was good for civilization or not. He was appalled by the uprooting of the Greek population of Asia Minor, this being in Iorga's eyes a most terrible attempt on the organic development of a nation. He misunderstood Mustapha Kemal's policies and spoke about a "Pan-Islamic victory." More importantly: "The breach of treaties encourages the breach of treaties elsewhere. Our attitude follows from this."[687]

Irish inflexibly demanded the establishment of an Irish Free State, Iorga was opposed to it. Then Iorga raised the central issue of every nationalistic movement: "Will there ever come a time when a people limits its ambitions to conform to the common interests of human civilization?" Iorga explained that the Irish did not safeguard their national language, traditions, etc., and Iorga had little tolerance for such a kind of nationalism.[688]

De Gaulle sharply criticized the pretension of those who spoke about the Algerian nation. He reminded them that the Berbers of Algeria were never able

---

[687]*Neamul Românesc*, 9 August 1921, 15 and 22 September 1922.

[688]*Neamul Românesc*, 11 September 1921.

to establish a state with definite boundaries, or a common national language, culture, and tradition. When De Gaulle spoke for the first time about the "Algerian nation," thus according them this supreme distinction, everybody familiar with De Gaulle's thinking knew that the independence of Algeria was near.

This is what Iorga had to say about the British domination of India: "The values of British domination in India may be questioned. The Soviet exploitation of the situation may not be questioned because the Soviets and Communism have no answers for those suffering millions."[689]

It must have been a great dilemma for him when the people in the Rif under Abd el Krim rose up against French and Spanish colonialism. Strangely, Iorga considered the whole uprising manipulated by the Germans. He also condemned the French Communist Party, which broke the ranks of national unity by supporting the insurgents. So much for Iorga's editorializing as a politician. What the historian felt, maybe remembering Posada, becomes clear: "A new era is starting in colonialism. The natives must be allowed to participate in running the respective countries." And then: "The hour of the heroic defenders of the Rif has not come yet."[690]

One cannot help but see that beneath Iorga's pro-French sympathies lies the Romanian, who has known so much oppression and foreign domination, and the struggle for liberation. And Iorga showed this as much as he dared.

What emerges from this? The same thing as always. Do you wish to know Iorga's position? Ask first what is Romania's interest. After that, you may ask about many other things; but do not forget to return to Romania's interest.

Even the honors and decorations, even honorary degrees awarded to him, seemed to fall into the pattern: the framework of the French Alliance System, the Little Entente, and Iorga's Pan-Latin solidarity. Iorga became Doctor Honoris Causa at the University of Strasbourg in 1920, of the University of Lyon in 1923, of the University of Geneva in 1926, and of the University of Wilno in

---

[689]*Neamul Românesc*, 28 July 1928.

[690]*Neamul Românesc*, 2 June and 21 August 1925.

1929; finally, of the University of Oxford in 1930, and also of the Protestant Faculty of Theology at the University of Paris in 1926. He became a corresponding member of the Institute de France in 1919, of the Historical Academy in Stockholm in 1923, of the "Reale Istituto Veneto" in Venice in 1928; Full Member of the Polish Academy in Krakow in 1923; and an Associate Member of the Academy of Letters and Sciences and Art of Lyon in 1923; Corresponding Member of the International Academy of Letters and Sciences in Naples in 1921, and of the Geographical Society in Lisbon in 1926.

Although Iorga was on the road often, he never traveled so much as he did during the 1920s and the 1930s. He did not bury himself so much in archives and libraries as he did before; yet he did not miss a single opportunity. He paid an extensive visit to Greece. Iorga visited the other two great Latin brothers: Spain and Portugal. He went to Spain in January 1927 and again during March 1928; he participated in the World Conference on Spanish History in November 1929. Iorga visited Catalonia and made numerous contacts with Spanish historians, and was received by King Alfonso XIII.

Iorga liked Spain and admired the people. He spoke about the "aristocratic dignity of everyone" in Spain, a country he considered to be "the most honest and polite country in the world." He was deeply affected by the "gaiety" of the Spanish people. He visited Portugal several times during 1928. Apart from going to the World Historical Conference in Oslo in 1928, he traveled to Scandinavia in 1926. As always, he put every experience into book form.[691]

Iorga continued to publish his *Neamul Românesc*, propounding his faith and opinions on daily issues, and his views about literature and art. His style did not change, nor did the financial problems of the newspaper. In the 1920s, *Nea-*

---

[691]The most important of Iorga's numerous travelogues of this period are: *Câteva zile prin Spania* (Bucureşti, 1927); *O mica ţară latină: Catalonia şi expoziţia din 1929* (Bucureşti, 1930); *Ţara latină cea mai departată în Europa: Portugalia,* (Bucureşti, 1928); *Ţari scandinave: Suedia şi Norvergia* (Bucureşti. 1929); *În Serbia de după război* (Vălenii-de-Munte, 1927); *Privelişti elveţiene* (Vălenii-de-Munte, 1930).

mul Românesc was suspended more than once and submitted to censorship during martial law. For a while *Neamul Românesc* was forbidden to call itself as such; it could not call itself the "Romanian Nation," but only *Neamul*.

As far as Iorga's editorials go, he remained a political "fighter" on a day-by-day basis, and showed spontaneous reaction rather than reflection. One of the permanent features of *Neamul Românesc* had been Iorga's violent attacks against prevailing corruption, which carried a strange mixture of the benevolent anger of a father seeing that his children do not live up to his standards of *Sămănătorism* and the cultural revolution supposedly emanating from it. The violence of Iorga's attacks, sadly, equaled their futility. Another permanent feature was the condemnation of alcoholism, Iorga's correspondence showed that he was in permanent contact with every anti-alcoholic league the world over.

Beyond corruption and alcoholism, Iorga the puritan carried out a relentless struggle against pornography. His paper carried on a crusade against political manifestations he contemptuously always referred to as "anarchy." Although he was not exactly of a serene temper himself, he hated anarchistic, disorderly, lawless manifestations. As these manifestations came from students on the radical right, his attacks only added fuel to the fire. He also carried out a relentless struggle against the prevailing bad sanitary standards in Bucharest and Romania. Not even his *Sămănătorist* love could stop him. Anybody who has lived in that part of the world can understand him. If one stays there permanently, the filth is not so offensive; but returning from the West, the lack of sanitary standards becomes irritating. Iorga remembered Marshal Lyautey, who liked Romania, but told Iorga that Romanians "are filthy."[692]

Iorga continued to issue his *Neamul Românesc pentru Popor*. The first thing that strikes one is the language of *Neamul Românesc pentru Popor*, a simple, beautiful Romanian which peasants speak. The tone is rather paternalistic. During these interwar years, Iorga rejected anti-Semitism, yet, in *Neamul Românesc pentru Popor* we can detect warnings to the peasantry against parasitic Jewish activities within the village.

---

[692]*Neamul Românesc* , 7 April 1921.

According to Iorga, the peasantry needed protection. However Iorga spent most of his columns on other problems affecting the peasantry. Unfortunately, *Neamul Românesc pentru Popor* did not reach many peasants, not even in Moldavia where the problem was most acute. Violently anti-Semitic Cuzist and Legionary newspapers putting the blame on the Jews for every existing and non-existing evil were more accessible. And more than half of the peasantry were illiterate.

As far as Iorga's participation in political life during the Liberal system goes, he considered himself politically speaking a "dead man." And small wonder. Even in 1928, he considered any participation in a national government only if it had the following attributes: the least egotism possible; the government should consist of men of experience; they should be wise men; they should also occupy posts for which they are qualified; finally, they should all be devoted to the needs of the country.[693]

It was not Iorga who had the political skill to bring such a government about, and to make it work. If he was a "fighter," his struggles in politics resembled Don Quixote fighting against windmills, without any moderating influence of a Sancho. Once, Iorga was invited to the Royal Palace, but those who invited him never thought about how he would get home in the ice-cold winter night. He hailed a taxicab and asked about the fare. The cab driver answered: "You have done enough for Romania, why shouldn't I do something for you?"[694]

"Nevertheless, Iorga never ceased to believe that the country would call upon him, as he said: "Power has to be given to me in order that I should be able to work for Romania." This became an ever-recurring hope.[695] This idea to be there when his country needed him and to serve his country never abandoned him; it remained with him until the Legionary terror squad fetched him. In 1922,

---

[693] *Neamul Românesc* , 12 June 1928.

[694] *Memorii*, vol. V, p. 163.

[695] There is ample proof to be found. For example in the fifth volume of Iorga's memoirs, from March 1925 until June 1930, pages 262, 278, 286, 287, 303, always waiting for his country to call upon him.

the years of Liberal domination, stabilization, and forced industrialization commenced. Because of the difficult economic situation and disregard for the youth, the years passed under the specter of constant anti-Semitic demonstrations. No national holiday, no memorial or religious service was off limits for the "New Nationalism." Iorga remembered students in Blaj who, during the commemorative services of a Transylvanian National Holiday in May 1925, smeared swastikas on church walls. He also noted the "powerlessness of the government."[696]

The "Roaring Twenties" were roaring elsewhere. The Liberals, who wanted to carry out this forced industrialization "by our own means alone," had made both the peasants and foreign capitalists unhappy, Iorga noticed only symptoms; he did not seem to have understood the causes: the prevalence of capitalist interest of industrialists set against agrarian interest, etc. His *Sămănătorism* stood always for the agrarian interest, Iorga's economic ignorance is pervasive; even if he wrote some good descriptive books about the Romanian economy, commerce, or industry in the historical perspective, these books are good only as far as statistics and the description of conditions go. The conclusions which Iorga drew were not realistic.[697]

In 1925, after careful preparation, the Brătianu clan arranged the exile of Crown Prince Carol and his renunciation of the succession. Carol, after his marriage, started his escapades again, which would become the favorite topic of the Bucharest rumor mill and the foreign press. Zizi Lambrino left Bucharest with Carol's child, Mircea, and settled in Paris. She sued Carol for child support. All this "made the day" for the Paris papers. Generously hating everything German and Prussian, they editorialized about Zizi Lambrino under the title "Mme. De Hohenzollern," airing every sordid derail.[698] At that time his behavior was startling, today, we know better. Carol, despite his looks, charm, and intelligence, was a sick man. His sickness was as much of a psychological as physical and

---

[696]*Memorii*, vol. V, p. 23.

[697]*Istoria comerțului românesc* (București, 1925); and *Istoria industriei la Români* (București, 1927).

[698]*Le Matin*, Paris, 5 March 1926.

pathological (or sexual) nature. Thus Carol as a sick man would deserve our sympathy if only he would have drawn some conclusions from his condition, which he did not. It is during the early 1920s that Helena (Magda) Wolff (alias Lupescu) entered his life. Since Carol would never abandon Mme. Lupescu, the Camarilla and the Brătianus organized a smear campaign, which disgusted Iorga, who refused to acknowledge irrefutable facts about Carol. King Ferdinand and Queen Marie knew the situation more intimately. The king considered Prince Carol "a rotten branch of the Dynasty which must be broken off in order to save the crown."[699] Queen Marie is the image of the mother in despair: "He becomes more and more intolerable; so much so that we frequently ask ourselves in all seriousness whether he is in full possession of his senses? What curse lies on the head of this poor boy? Why is he destined to sow the seeds of his own destruction around him? What is wrong with him? It is a very tragic sight to see those, one after another, who believed in him and consider him a victim to slowly understand the truth which his father and I have always known."[700]

At Sinaia, the Crown Council of 21 December 1925 removed Carol from succession. This would be called "The Act of 4 January" (because this is when it was published). Succession was handed down to Prince Michael. Until he came of age a Council of Regency was to exercise the Royal Prerogative.

But Iorga liked Prince Carol and this emotional consideration carried everything before it. Iorga kept a very good relationship with Princess Helen, who, after Carol was exiled from the country, remained at the side of her son. Queen Helen often visited Iorga's school at Vălenii-de-Munte, and invited Iorga to her residence.

Iorga was invited to the Crown Council that sent Prince Carol into exile. When Brătianu arrived, Iorga felt an overpowering hatred. He did not keep his

---

[699] *Însemnările notiţe ale lui A. Călinescu*, Entry from January' 1926; also, Al. Gh. Savu, *Dictatura regală* (Bucureşti, 1970), p. 33.

[700] Arhivele Statului, Bucureşti *Arhiva Istorică Centrală; Fondul Casa Regală* (Regina Maria), V, 5072, also, *Magazin Istoric*, vol. 2 (1968), nr. 9, p. 22.

tongue in check when he spoke to King Ferdinand. Iorga expressed his disagreement with the exile of Prince Carol; then he turned on the Brătianus. The king told him that "they are my advisors!" Retorted Iorga, "And the whole country fails to understand why you do not discard them!"[701]

When Prince Michael became king, Iorga wrote: "Carol should come back to the country, to be at the side of his wife and son. This became an article of faith for my conscience."[702] The Romanian people, in their majority deeply religious and monarchist, ardently wished for the return of their "Dream Prince," Carol, who would make their lot better.

Iorga, during all these years (from 1922 until 1928), remained in opposition, hoping for a political comeback. In May 1924, he fused his party with Argetoianu's People's Party. Iorga, in his naivete, considered this a durable arrangement. For Argetoianu, it was a temporary step on the chessboard of *Politicianism*. The name of the new party was *Partidul Naţionalist al Poporului*, with Iorga as president. But Argetoianu kept all the real power.[703]

Much more promising might have been the negotiations which Iorga started during the spring of 1923 with Maniu's Transylvanian Nationalists, and later Mihalache, the head of the Peasant Party. Iorga showed great sympathy to Maniu's party as Speaker in 1919. Both Maniu and Mihalache tried their best to win over Iorga.[704] Iorga and Argetoianu negotiated the possible union — mainly with Maniu — during the whole year of 1924. Other attempts were made early in 1925. Their aim was to form a "democratic, cultural, non-revolutionary, Monarchist party of the Left."

There were ideological conflicts. Iorga never deviated from *Sămănătorism*. Therefore Maniu presented in May 1925 the following conditions for unification with Iorga and his party: there would be no fusion of party organizations; no

---

[701]*O viaţă de om*, vol. III, pp. 106-107; also, *Memorii*, vol. V, p. 87.

[702]*O viaţă de om*, vol. III, p. 191.

[703]*Memorii*, vol. IV, pp. 156-157.

[704]*Supt trei regi*, pp. 399-402; also, *Memorii*, vol. V, p. 17.

change in the program of either party; and no commitment undertaken for any future government. Iorga insisted that he would not join any party based on class, instead, he would always support the idea of "national unity." But in early 1925, Iorga and Argetoianu came close to achieving a fusion with Maniu. Argetoianu even formulated an agreement, the "Ten Points of Fusion." There were personality conflicts between Iorga and Maniu: should Iorga become party president? (Maniu once conceded to Iorga the presidency, then withdrew his offer.) Should there be two party presidents? And there were also disputes concerning *Neamul Românesc*.[705] And the problem of Iorga's hatred of Stere arose again.

All this dampened Maniu's enthusiasm for a political union with Iorga. By 1926 Argetoianu abandoned Iorga and sided with Maniu, later with the Liberals, and in 1931 he formed a government — with Iorga.

During the interwar years, all over East Central and Southeastern Europe democratic peasant parties emerged. They were also pacifist, and formed a kind of a "Green Internationale" (as a counterpoint to the Red Internationale). For Iorga's *Sămănătorism*, such a development had no "organic" precedents and he did not hide his antipathy. Yet, if Iorga had achieved union with Maniu's Transylvanian Nationalists, and Mihalache's Peasant Party, this alliance would have become a formidable force! It could have challenged the Liberal System Iorga hated so much! In the spring of 1925 (without formal union), this "United Opposition" demanded the demise of the government and new elections.

King Ferdinand, always sickly, by 1925 became gravely ill. Queen Marie, then on a visit to the United States, returned to Romania. During her visit, she seemed to have a good time; but not the kind befitting crowned monarchs.[706]

---

[705] *Memorii*, vol. IV, pp. 207-208.

[706] As for Balkan nations, we conveniently forgot about them — except when we were honored with the visit of one of their royal rulers, in which case we were treated to an amount of scandal which might have shown us (but failed to do so) that any money we might sink into those countries was lost the moment it has left our shores..." Professor Van Loon was referring to Queen Marie's visit. Hendrik Van Loon, *The Story of America* (New York, 1946), p. 368.

Brătianu, in view of the storm of disapproval, decided to hand over power to Marshal Averescu in April 1926. King Ferdinand played a political game in this transition: he had already designated Averescu as Prime Minister, as well as every member of his cabinet, and had them waiting in a room of the Royal Palace to lay down their oath; meanwhile he pretended to consult with the head of every political party, as if he were still undecided. Iorga and his political ally Maniu were also invited to the Palace for consultation. King Ferdinand refused to see Iorga and Maniu together; he received them separately. After this comedy was over, on the streets the political leaders could hear the newspaper boys hawking extra editions, announcing the formation of the Averescu government.

The Averescu government was an "interposition" placed by Brătianu into the power vacuum until he and his Liberal system got a respite. The Liberal establishment and great finance continued to arbitrate the situation. Iorga na-ively remarked that he could imagine the long face Maniu made after the king made him go through a *"journée des dupes"* (referring to the historical precedent in Paris when everybody expected Cardinal Richelieu to fall from power).[707]

By 1926 Marshal Averescu was an admirer of Mussolini. After his appoint-ment, in April 1926, under the new, proportional electoral law corrupt elections followed. The Averescu government received its majority regardless of the pop-ular will.[708]

By the end of 1925, for both Maniu and Mihalache, the fusion of their par-ties became a necessity — regardless of Iorga's *Sămănătorist* "zig-zags" or his hatred of Stere. After running on a common list during the elections of 1926, the Peasant Party and the Nationalists of Transylvania united in October 1926, forming the National Peasant Party — which became one of the "Traditionalist" Parties of Romania. Iorga lost his last real democratic chance in politics.

---

[707] *Supt trei regi*, pp. 401-403; also, *O viață de om*, vol. III, p. 136.

[708] *Memorii*, vol. V, p. 232. Frasin Munteanu-Râmnic, barely in his teens, was with his older brother placing electoral posters of Iorga's party in Ploieşti. They were arrested, taken to the police station, hung up by their feet and brutally beaten.

Averescu's government was in power from April 1926 until June 1927. The Camarilla was not yet ready to surrender power. With the resignation of Averescu, Prince Barbu Ştirbey formed a transition government, referred to as "the impartial solution." Finally the real power in Romania, Ion I.C. Brătianu, returned as Prime Minister on 22 June 1927.

Formidable cracks were opening in the "Liberal system." The mainstay of the Brătianu system was the Crown; King Ferdinand died on 20 July 1927, less than a month after Brătianu returned to power. And barely four months later, 24 November 1927, Brătianu himself passed away. Thus the road had opened for great changes.

At the death of King Ferdinand, Prince Michael, six years old, was proclaimed king. Iorga remembered Maniu telling him he considered this "the first day of the Romanian Republic, since Michael will never reign." A Regency was formed of the Patriarch, Miron Cristea, Prince Nicolae, the younger brother of Carol, and Gheorghe Buzdugan, the Chief Justice of the Supreme Court. When Buzdugan died in October 1929, Vaida proposed Iorga take his place. But Iorga opposed the Regency. So Constantin Sărăţeanu, another high dignitary, became Regent instead. Within this Regency not everything was going for the best. As the Patriarch explained to Iorga: "The country does not work because Prince Nicolae is smoking cigars, quarreling with Sărăţeanu; and I, a priest, can only try to reconcile them."[709] Iorga took an open stand against the Regency, considering it "harmful."[710]

With the Brătianu clan still holding on to power, Vintilă Brătianu became Prime Minister from December 1927 until November 1928.

During the summer of 1927, at Iorga's Summer School, Mihai Manoilescu, a renowned economist who started his political career under Maniu in demo-

---

[709]*Supt trei regi*, pp. 398 and 436.

[710]*Neamul Românesc*, 6 September 1927.

cratic ranks and later became the ideologist of Corporatism and Fascism in Romania, lectured on the "false legality" prevailing in Romania.[711] He met Carol in exile and brought letters from Carol to the different party chiefs. Apprehended by the police, the letters were found, and he was put on trial.

Manoilescu's trial took place in November 1927. The trial showed that many a young officer within the armed forces were supporting the man whom they called "Carol II." Iorga testified that "Manoilescu had the right to bring letters to Romania from the oldest son of King Ferdinand." The trial ended with an acquittal.[712] A young officer in the Romanian Air Force, Colonel Paul Teodorescu, was also arrested because of his contact with Prince Carol.

The final blow to the Liberal system was given by the immense popular gathering convoked to Alba Iulia by Maniu and Mihalache during May 1928. Hundreds of thousands went to participate in the anti-Liberal rally. Iorga refused to go;[713] his refusal was based on the growing animosity between himself and Maniu, as well as on his hatred of populism. Iorga remarked later that the meeting in Alba-Iulia was held in "the best Transylvanian revolutionary tradition." This was not meant to be a compliment.

The assembled mass of humanity wanted to march on Bucharest, which fortunately did not take place. The mass rally at Alba Iulia was a volcanic outburst against the Liberal system. Iorga would have been able to live with that, but his conflict with Maniu and, above all, the disapproval of the Palace influenced him. He wrote an editorial entitled "Politics and Masses." He explained that a nation has a soul, a conscience, consequently it takes action. The masses have instincts and passions; these are primitive and savage instincts and passions which are supposed to satisfy appetites and interests. Iorga asks, "Should it be

---

[711]*Memorii*, vol. V, p. 240.

[712]*Op. cit.*, p. 255; also. *O viață de om*, vol. III, p. 259; finally, *Supt trei regi*, p. 416.

[713]*Supt trei regi*, p. 422.

allowed that such a 'gathering' should impose itself on the nation's elite, selected during the ages? No, a state cannot be run in such fashion!"[714] Iorga's aversion towards Populism did not change.

By the fall of 1928, the Liberal system collapsed. Thus we would have the second free elections in Greater Romania. Iorga's party was now running in electoral alliance with Averescu's party. The results were devastating, not only for the Liberals, but for Iorga and Averescu. Maniu received almost 80% of the vote. The results represented for Iorga "the tenacious ideological abstraction of free elections."[715] It is no surprise since the elections were a defeat for *Sămănătorism* and a victory for the peasant democracy Maniu and Mihalache stood for.

Maniu formed his government on 9 November 1928. He assumed office with a characteristic declaration: "Our first aim will be to give to the principles of the constitution their real meaning, and to impart a character of strict legality to the working of the administration."[716] But Iorga had doubts. He considered the Maniu government a risky experiment, because the tasks were overwhelming and the people who assumed power and promised to fulfill their mandate were inept. In the end, the innocent majority suffered; their guilt was credulity. Iorga also condemned "the childishness of universal suffrage at a time when real men are needed to solve problems."[717]

Maniu had a lot in common with Iorga. Both were of irreproachable integrity, both lacked political skill, and were inflexible in their ideals. Maniu would be as inflexible in his faith in democracy and Christian morality as Iorga was in his *Sămănătorism*. Both were Romanian patriots and nationalists. What a pity for Romania that these two men could not find a common platform! However

---

[714]*Neamul Românesc*, 2 August 1928. Iorga spoke to his family with contempt about the popular following of Maniu calling them "a low crowd," consisting of "waiters" and similar people, etc.

[715]*Supt trei regi*, p. 418.

[716]*The Times*, London, 12 November 1928.

[717]*Neamul Românesc*, 11 November 1928.

there was this difference: Iorga was by nature a fighter, and Maniu was much more resigned and passive.

Iuliu Maniu came to power with the ardent support of the over-whelming majority. With about 80% peasants, the hope for a peasant democracy inspired the people greatly. The man who stepped to the helm of the Romanian state was incorruptible: a convinced democrat and a patriot. His leadership was to prove that those qualities were no panacea for the ills that blacken small and underdeveloped countries. For a starter, the disorders of Romanian universities and high schools did not stop, but continued to keep Romanian schools in a ferment, and spilled over into the streets of towns. "New Nationalism" did not consider the abuse of democracy a tragedy; it did not believe in the constitution and in a solution within the framework of it. Since its proponents were ignored, and outside the political establishment, they freely abused democracy which they did not understand, and consequently, could not respect. It was a rule of politics that no extremist group would moderate its position before it were taken into account.

It was not students or the "New Nationalism" that presented the challenge to the fledgling Romanian democracy, but the oncoming Great Depression. It was the misfortune of Romanian democracy to come to power a few months before the crash on Wall Street. Black Friday arrived on Wall Street. Iorga, in his *Neamul Românesc* did not even take note of it. His cultural nationalism (like De Gaulle) paid little attention to economic realities. This is regrettable because it was to be the Depression which would have the greatest effect on Iorga's coming premiership.

The advent of the Depression can be considered a watershed within the interwar period. The first half of the "armistice of twenty years" was over. When the economic crisis broke out from Wall Street onto Main Street and beyond, the implications for the world and Romania were great.

Early in 1930, Iorga undertook an important journey; he traveled to the United States, where he visited until April. Always an admirer of America, he never ceased to emphasize his gratitude to President Wilson for his principle of self-determination, which made Greater Romania possible.

Before Iorga's departure, Vintilă Brătianu — in the best tradition of *Politicianism* — started mudslinging: "Who is paying for Iorga's trip?" Iorga instantly rendered a penny-by-penny account: Romanian-Americans who had invited him paid his expenses.[718]

Finally, in January 1930, Iorga and Mme. Catinca embarked on a ship for New York. They arrived there a few months after the Wall Street Crash. Iorga almost ignored it. His accounts rarely touched upon the darkening economic scene. If Iorga came to visit the communities of Americans of Romanian descent, his visit became more than that. He visited the United States from coast to coast, held several lectures at different universities, and met important Americans.

Since he landed in New York, it was the Romanian Jews who gave him a warm reception. Iorga encountered warm feelings for Romania among them, expressed in a good, articulate Romanian language. He visited Columbia University and met Mr. Ochs-Sulzberger (of the New York Times) at a banquet which Mr. Sulzberger had organized in Iorga's honor.[719]

We will describe Iorga's visit to America only in very broad outlines. From New York he traveled to Washington, D.C., where he held a well-attended lecture (in English) at Georgetown University. Then he proceeded to Indiana Harbor, with a sizable community of Romanian-Americans. Here he met an old friend, Mr. Vopicka, the U.S. Ambassador in Romania during the War.

Chicago being nearby, Iorga visited this "Castle of Steel" as he called it. He arrived in the "Land of Lincoln" on February 12; Iorga had an almost metaphysical admiration for Lincoln's life, work, and ideas and an interest in Lincoln's death. (Unfortunately, Iorga did not come to Chicago at the best moment. Apart from the Depression, these were the years of Prohibition, gangsterism, etc.).

---

[718] *Neamul Românesc,* 10 January 1930.

[719] Iorga considered the powers of the "Fourth Estate" to be "ridiculous," and disliked the American popular press, the tabloids exposing divorces, sex scandals, and violence.

He took an interest in the fate of American Blacks. Iorga never visited the Deep South, nevertheless, he knew about the humiliations and sufferings of the Blacks there. He listened to Black Spirituals and felt the voice of human pain arising from them. Interestingly, when Iorga asked an American intellectual for a possible solution, the answer was "By the year 2000, maybe..."

After Chicago, Iorga went to the Romanian-American communities in the industrial heartland: Cleveland, Akron, Youngstown, Campbell, and Detroit. Then the Iorgas traveled by train to California. Iorga fell in love with San Francisco instantly. He visited the University of California in Berkeley, traveled to Los Angeles and San Diego (meeting President Calvin Coolidge), and wound up his Californian visit at Pomona University.

From California, the Iorgas returned to Washington, D.C., where Iorga noted with satisfaction how many titles of his were listed in the catalogue of the Library of Congress. From Washington, Iorga made excursions to Mt. Vernon, Gettysburg, and Baltimore.

During the whole trip, Mme. Catinca was her usual self: she supported Iorga's efforts during the strains of the journey in every way, and did this in her self-effacing manner. The Iorgas returned to New York, where they participated in the St. Patrick's Day Parade. At a time when Iorga was trying to uphold Romania's image abroad, the "New Nationalism" of Romanian students embarrassed him. News of violent anti-Semitic outbreaks at Romanian universities marred the rest of his visit. Iorga held a lecture at Columbia University, and visited Harvard (and New England) before ending his American visit.[720]

Iorga made the strange remark that he did not find a single sympathetic Romanian American. In his reminiscences, one can find references to sympathetic Romanian Jews, but none towards Romanian Gentiles. What is the explanation?

---

[720]All impressions of Iorga about the United States can be found in his autobiography, *O viață de om*, vol. III, between pages 378 and 388; his *Memorii*, and in two books dedicated to the United States and his activities in our country, *Americani și Romani din America* (Vălenii-de-Munte, 1930), and *My American Lectures* (București, 1932).

Iorga, in his *Sămănătorist* naivete, did not understand that these people (from the Old Kingdom, Transylvania, or Bucovina) did not look back at their village with his *Sămănătorist* love!

Most of these Romanians had lived in grinding poverty, and the daily humiliations inherent in it. A peasant from those villages, walking behind his ox or mule in the fields from daybreak to sunset for next to nothing, collecting dung, and all this amidst abuses inherent in living under the thumb of the landlords, considered his arrival to the United States and the chance to work for decent wages as an industrial worker a definite step forward. *Sămănătorist* idealized view of the Romanian village meant much for Iorga, but little for these people! They knew different Romanian villages. Iorga remembered what a heartbreak it was for him when these Romanian Americans intoned the Romanian National Anthem in his honor. In vain did he call upon them to return home: "Do not allow yourself to get lost among strangers! We shall find work for you!" These Romanians (like most poor immigrants) had found a new home and they wished "Good Speed! — Good Riddance!" to the world they left behind.

All this upset Iorga. He did not believe in denationalization processes, much less in breaking organic ties with the native soil. But then, he did not believe in sociology either. Iorga could not understand what made these Romanians quit their native villages.

The Statue of Liberty made deep impression on Iorga. He saw it from the distance; he called the Statue of Liberty "commanding, with an imperial gesture of redemption; it is impressive." What a pity that Iorga never crossed over to take a closer look, to read the poem of Emma Lazarus, and to think about the meaning of it! If he would have done so, he could have shown more understanding towards those Romanian Americans he disliked. Despite Iorga's love and perceptive insights about the United States, there remained a lot which he idealized or failed to understand (including some basics which made the United States what it became). This becomes even clearer if one reads the books he wrote about his visit after his return, and his numerous lectures.

After returning from the United States in April 1930, he went to Oxford to receive his honorary degree. From there he went on to Cambridge to participate in the work of the World Historical Congress. There Iorga reminded Soviet Historians that Russia still had not returned all Romanian cultural relics evacuated there during the First World War for safe-keeping.[721]

As for Iorga's relationship to literature during this period, there is little change to be found. This literature had to consist of "healthy currents," and only those works could be considered to be as such which fell in line with the ideas of Iorga. It followed that the so-called "unhealthy currents" (although, Iorga found worse adjectives for these trends) had to be unmasked and fought.

This is a leitmotif of the history of Romanian literature that he published in Bucharest in 1929, *Istoria literaturii româneşti*. It would seem as the years went by, far from opening up, that he became more and more entrenched in his literary conservatism, and militantly so. Iorga made sure (because of his hatred of Futurism) that the Romanian Academy would not receive Marinetti, despite the fact that Marinetti stood close to the Italian Fascist power structure. Enrico Corradini was welcomed by him; Iorga called him the "Roman Eagle of Mussolini," and explained why he was so enthusiastic about Corradini's visit: "To spire Gönös and Ludendorff."[722] If one considers some of Corradini's writings, one may understand why Mussolini liked him. Corradini must have been a great help in covering up the ideological nakedness of Fascism. In Fascist sloganeering, one can meet Corradini's ideas: "*Vivere pericolosamente.*" "If a hundred Italians would be ready to die for Italy, that would give Italy a new life." And his ever-recurring ridicule and contempt for the sanctity of human life! Iorga detested Corradini's ideas. He wrote just a week before the outbreak of the Second World War: "Is war a sign of vitality?" "On the contrary, it is a sign of depravity, of a desperado, and a lack of respect for humanity."[723]

Iorga assured the appearance of journals which were the standard-bearers of his *Sămănătorist* credo. In March 1919 *Ramuri* reappeared and continued to be published, with interruptions, after Iorga's death, until 1944. In January 1928

---

[721]*Memorii*, vol. V, p. 393.

[722]*Neamul Românesc*, 29 January 1928.

[723]*Neamul Românesc*, 23 August 1939.

Iorga founded a new literary journal called *Cuget Clar*, meaning "Clear Thought." It continued to April 1936, and reappeared under the name *Noul Sămănător*. The main collaborators were Iorga himself, and the *Sămănătorist* writer N. Batzaria. Romanian literary critics had doubts about Batzaria's talents. His merit was to be able to follow flawlessly the *Sămănătorist* line. And there was Ion Brătescu-Voineşti. The first issue explained that it was meant to be a cultural and literary publication for schools, youth, and library committees of schools, to become an instrument to safeguard the moral standards of the people, "menaced by monstrous writers and appeals to bestial appetites."

During these years, a memorable incident occurred. It was the beginning of a sad controversy which arose between Iorga and another great representative of the Romanian spirit, Mircea Eliade. Eliade was a young student of the faculty of philosophy at the Bucharest University. He became later a religious philosopher, perhaps the best interpreter of Orthodox Christian mysticism. Eliade searched common traits between all religious beliefs, trying to find common denominators for universal mysticism. Thus, he became an expert on Hinduism, on religions of pre-Columbian America, and the best interpreter of the mysticism around the Romanian legend of the mystical lamb: *Miorița*.[724]

At this time Iorga considered Mircea Eliade a "*băieţaş*" (a "kid"), furthermore, "with a false mysticism which replaces definite religious and useful human ideas." This "kid" dared to criticize Iorga in university papers, "in a bad French language," etc.[725] Iorga added an editorial in his *Neamul Românesc*, without mentioning Mircea Eliade by name, but it was clear to everybody about whom he was talking.

What has really happened? Apparently, more than one factor was involved. There was Iorga's "ego," his temper, his lack of feeling for pro-portion; but Iorga's well-known horror of religious mysticism and even greater disdain for

---

[724]It is disturbing that some scholars consider Mircea Eliade an ideologue of Romanian Fascism. See Titu Georgescu, *Nicolae Iorga impotrivă Hitlerismului* (Bucureşti, 1966), p. 21.

[725]*O viață de om*, vol. III, p.150.

the abstract also played an important role. The whole incident took place between 1925 and 1927, concerning about six articles, also critical reviews of Iorga's books and historical method, written by Eliade in university journals and Bucharest newspapers. Before, Eliade was a great admirer of Iorga, of his activity and personality. He did not admire Iorga so much for scholarly achievements, rather Iorga's dynamism, energy, output, and his "cosmic force." About Iorga's scholarly, political, and literary activities Eliade was critical. During later articles his critical attitude hardened. Admiration was proportionately decreased. The climax was reached by Eliade's review of Iorga's *Essai de synthèse de l'histoire de l'humanité.*

What did Eliade object to? We see the usual charges against Iorga's method: too much haste in his work, also he did not look for the right French expressions to express what he wanted to say, thus confusing readers; inaccuracies were pointed out, which were increasing rather than decreasing (something Eliade hoped for). Then he went on to suggest that Iorga was not studying his sources, but just reading titles of the chapters of books he quoted (or sometimes reading only the indexes); so, he was following his historical instinct rather than doing research. There was an accusation of superficiality; Iorga disappointed Eliade. "Iorga does not change his historical method." He concluded his review of the first volume of Iorga's *Synthèse* with the hope that, since the next volume will deal with Iorga's field, Byzantine and Medieval History, he should do better.[726]

The consequences of this iconoclastic review by a nineteen year-old student were portentous. A university in Romania does not bear any resemblance to an American university. The faculty closed ranks: "How does a student dare to attack in such fashion a world-renowned scholar?"

Vasile Bogrea answered Eliade in a biting article, putting him "into his place," rather than refuting his charges. Mircea Eliade answered, explaining that

---

[726]*Tricolorul* (Toronto), vol. 2, 1982 nr. 3 (November); also, Mac Linscott Rickets, of Louisburg College in North Carolina, who did many studies and translations of Mircea Eliade's work; to his work this writer is indebted for much information about the Iorga-Eliade conflict.

he was no "Iorghist." Born in 1907, he went to school under German occupation. He was not like his father's generation, which considered Iorga as a prophet of nationalism. He reminded Iorga that he lost touch completely with Mircea Eliade's student generation.[727] Iorga was very sensitive about Eliade's articles, not only because there was truth in them, but also as they appeared when the university was in turmoil by student protests, many of these directed against the "former Apostle." Iorga was incapable of taking criticism, from anybody, and his relations with Mircea Eliade were spoiled for the rest of their lives.

Iorga commemorated the fortieth anniversary of the death of his mentor, Eminescu, in 1929. He continued also to write theatre plays on the same lines as before. During these years, he published many works on history and on politics (attacks, responses to attacks, and counterattacks on his enemies; also his opinions on different political or ideological matters, usually in pamphlet form). He wrote quite a few textbooks for schools of Greater Romania, and translated his works on Romanian history into French, Italian, English, and also into German, and republished old books, depending on their actuality.

Like almost all of Iorga's intellectual activities to strengthen, uphold, and justify the existence of Greater Romania, he made a gigantic effort to enhance the Romanian image abroad. Iorga published beautifully printed and illustrated books (mostly in French) about Romanian popular art, architecture, icons, etc.

If there were few new contributions by Iorga during this decade, he used the materials he accumulated and his knowledge. Because of the pressures of his superhuman effort, we see the same faults as before: inaccuracies and minor mistakes. Perhaps there was more of this than before.

---

[727] *Ibid.* Mircea Eliade revealed in his second (posthumous) memoirs that he did not "lose touch" with his student generation... Led by his mysticism and quest for answers, he joined (under the guidance of his mentor, Nae Ionescu) the Legion during the 1930s. Both were arrested during the Royal Dictatorship. Carol demanded that they denounce the Legion publicly, which they refused. Eliade was saved by the intervention of A. Rosetti (the militant democrat), who assured his release and appointment to the Romanian Embassy in London in 1940 — just in time for a new life, and to avoid the sordid Legionary doom. Mircea Eliade: *Memoires II: Les moissons du solstice* (Paris 1988), passim.

Iorga's works before the First World War were very accurate. There was one talent this writer considers cardinally important for a historian: the instinct for historical events, (both past and present) and conclusions to be drawn for the future. This instinct and the capacity to analyze history never abandoned Iorga.

During this decade he wrote several history books for the high school curriculum. Since the unification, Iorga wrote or re-wrote or republished several works about the lives and deeds of great national heroes in order to inspire the public. Iorga wrote no less than seven volumes about Michael the Brave, seven volumes about Tudor Vladimirescu "the Defender of the Poor;" two volumes on Kogălniceanu; one volume about Cuza-Vodă, Constantin Brâncoveanu, and Constantin Cantemir.

Iorga posed an interesting question: was there such a thing as a Byzantine Middle Age?" (*Y a-t-il eu un moyen âge Byzantin*? Bucarest, 1927). And there were a series of lectures and debates: "Is there such a thing as a history of Transylvania?"[728]

The major undertaking of Iorga during this period was to write a universal history, or (as he would put it) The History of Humanity. He would try to integrate the history of mankind and to find a place in it for the history of Romania. According to Iorga's historical philosophy, each nation's history forms part of universal history. Consequently, there must be common manifestations within the history of humanity. He explained that he tried to follow in a "synthetic, organic fashion" the great current of universal history, trying to "recapture the atmosphere of the times because if this is not done, everything written down about history may be considered accurate, but never the truth."[729]

The result was his *Essai de synthèse de I 'histoire de I 'humanité* in four volumes (Paris, 1926-1928). Iorga always considered the writing of a synthetic universal history to be the coronation of his efforts as a historian.[730] To write a

---

[728] *Memorii*, vol. IV, p. 180.

[729] *O viață de om*, vol. III, p. 8.

[730] Mme. Liliana Pippidi-Iorga to the author.

synthesis of the history of humanity was an overwhelming task, even for Iorga, and according to professional opinions it was not his most successful endeavor. One should keep in mind the enormity of the task. Few historians would undertake it. Iorga seemed to be aware of the magnitude of the task, which he continued until the last hour of his lifespan.

After the war, Iorga wrote a great deal about the histories of Romania's neighbors, the Hungarians, the Bulgarians, the Eastern Slavs, and the history of Albania. His writings about Hungarian and Bulgarian history were contributions to Helmolt's *Weltgeschichte*, volume number 4. "Die Madjaren" (vol. 4, pp. 445-487), (Leipzig, 1919). Iorga's Hungarian history provoked a storm of fury.[731] His other contributions to Helmolt's *Weltgeschichte* were about Bulgarian history: "Die Bulgaren," Helmolt's *Weltgeschichte*, volume 4, pages 363-395, (Leipzig, 1919); and finally, "Albanien," Helmolt's *Weltgeschichte*, volume 4, pages 433-444 (Leipzig, 1919). Iorga also wrote a more voluminous history of Albania: *Brève histoire de l'Albanie et du peuple albanais* (Bucarest, 1919). He saw Albania as a kind of "balcony on the Venetian Sea," (the Adriatic Sea). Whatever sympathy Iorga felt toward Italy, he always recognized that the long eastern shore of the Adriatic is inhabited by Slavs and Albanians, who are most unhappy about Italian pretensions. In his book, he gave some good samples of his "zig-zags," naivete, and dreams. He advised the Albanians "because of the lack of population to draw on the vitality of the neighboring Aromanians," and "to choose Italian patronage," which would not become so abusive as the

---

[731] A Transylvanian-Hungarian newspaper (the *Brassói Lapok* of 2 May 1924) savagely attacked Iorga's book. The paper could not understand why on earth the Germans entrusted Iorga with such a task. Hungary is a Western, not a Balkan country; consequently Iorga cannot understand Hungarian history! They belabor minor inaccuracies (dozens of them are quoted); then comes a book review of Iorga's other publications. His Ottoman History is not appreciated; better sniff appeared in the German language before him. Iorga should recognize that Hungary belongs to the West, it is not artificially French, like Bucharest. Iorga had no understanding of Hungarian history. He writes propaganda, not history, the work of a politician, not of a historian. And, lest we forget, Professor Title, the editor of Helmolt's *Weltgeschichte* considered Iorga "a traitor and an enemy of the Germans." Theodorescu, *op. cit.*, p. 295.

(former) Austrian one. Moreover, Italian patronage for Albania "would not lead to enslavement or denationalization."[732]

The sad thing was that Iorga was not joking. He had sympathy for Albanian past because of Thracian origins (Iorga had some traceable Albanian ancestry himself) and an even deeper sympathy because Albania was struggling for national self-assertion. For Iorga, every nation was sacred. He had an immense historical knowledge, but to know does not necessarily mean to foresee things to come. And when Italy swallowed Albania, Iorga was very unhappy.

When Iorga wrote his *Scurtă istorie a slavilor răsăriteni: Rusia și Polonia* (București, 1919), he feared, as always, that people would not read it. It is a pity if they did not. This work goes to the root of the Polish-Russian controversy, explaining that, although the Russians and the Poles were of the same stock, their roads parted when the Poles accepted Christianity from Rome, and the Russians from Byzantium. Through this they developed in very different cultures and worlds, and this ultimately led to an almost insurmountable hostility.

As far as Russian history is concerned, Iorga, contrary to recent Soviet historical theories, believed in the "Norseman theory." He did not appreciate the incapacity of the Slavonic inhabitants of Western Russia to form a state and their turning to the organizational skill of the Norsemen, Iorga's *Drepturile românilor asupra teritoriului lor national unitar* (București, 1919) tries to prove that the Romanians have historical, ethnical, and economical rights over the territories which were "gathered in."

Iorga published a lot in foreign languages about Romanian history. His *Kurze Geschichte des Rumanischen Volkes* (Brașov, 1921) presented his interpretation of Romanian history in German for every German-speaking person. His *Histoire des roumaines et de leur civilization* (Paris, 1920), *Les latins de l'Orient* (Paris, 1921), *History of Roumania* (London, 1925) addressed the Francophone and the Anglophone public. These works, hastily written for the sake of political expediency, left a lot to be desired, Iorga knew it.

---

[732]*O viață de om*, vol. III, p. 9.

Iorga's *Correspondence diplomatique Roumaine sous le roi Charles I-er* (Paris 1923) is a major work which contains valuable archival materials. Because of the Soviet claims on Bessarabia, he deemed it necessary to present the background of the war of 1877-1878 based on diplomatic documents, and to show how the Russian government pleaded to Romania to ally itself with the Russian war effort, allowing the Russian troops to pass through Romania, giving guarantees concerning southern Bessarabia. Iorga showed how the Russian government broke its promise. This book was his complement to *Politica externă a regelui Carol I*, (Bucureşti, 1916). Then, he wrote his *Brève histoire de la petite Arménie* (Paris 1930). This book grew out of the memorandum Iorga prepared for the Armenians during the Peace Conference.

The political pamphlets Iorga wrote during this period show his disgust with *politicianisim* and *Suprafanarul*, kept alive by a pseudo-democratic process and the political parties, as reflected in *Din originile politicianismnlui român* (Bucureşti, 1928). Finally, we can witness a sad, decreasing faith manifested by Iorga in the possibility of a Western-type democracy solving the problems of Romania. Although he would conserve his respect for democracy to the end, it began to dawn on him that Western-type democracy might work in the West, but it could not answer Romania's problems: *Originea şi sensul democraţiei* (Vălenii-de-Munte, 1927) and his *Evoluţia ideii de libertate* (Bucureşti, 1928).

Iorga's personal life from July 1919 until February 1920 suffered three great losses. In July 1919, his brother-in-law, Ioan Bogdan, died. He was followed in November by his faithful *Sămănătorist* follower, the Transylvanian poet Al. Vlahuţă. In February 1920, Iorga's teacher and mentor, A.D. Xenopol, passed away.

Iorga's family life remained as clean as ever. Mme. Catinca stood her ground to assist her husband as a most efficient personal secretary, accompanying him during his travels, taking care of the numerous children, and looking out for Iorga's aging mother. During short separations, Mme. Catinca wrote several letters to "Nicu" which show warmth, love, and an exemplary family life.[733] There was little contact between Iorga and his brother Gheorghe.

The Iorga family continued to give a great amount of money to charities, but very discreetly, only discernible through Iorga's correspondence. Beyond charities, Iorga had a deep concern: the veterans of the Great War. He used his influence and did the utmost for veterans, but inconspicuously.

Iorga remained somehow aloof from everybody except his family; he remained the East European intellectual, and one must live there to understand what this means. His temperament was almost incompatible with democracy. He agreed with the necessity of criticism in theory. In practice, his ego was incapable of accepting criticism. Once he wrote an editorial: "Who Has the Right to Pass Judgment on Me?" He explained that in a democracy everyone has the right to judge everyone else. He disagreed with this and retorted: "Not so!" Only people with a certain standard have the right to criticize him. Criticism must not become a "free for all."[734]

The Depression hit the Romanian scene hard, since people (especially the peasantry) had not recovered from years of hardship endured during the forced industrialization effort of the Liberals. Could Maniu's democratic constitutional government have survived the economic crisis? The answer became academic: on the morning of 7 June 1930, at 5 a.m., Puiu Dimitrescu awoke Iorga with the news that Prince Carol had landed with a private plane in Transylvania.[735] The next day, Carol II ascended the Romanian throne.

---

[733] BAR *Corespondența lui Nicolae Iorga*, vol. 277 (1919), doc. 194.

[734] *Neamul Românesc.*, 26 February 1928.

[735] *Memorii*, vol. V, p. 398. Puiu Dumitrescu was a deceitful person. He would be the core of the first Camarilla after Carol's return.

Chapter VI

The Struggle toward Tragedy

"The best lack all conviction, and the worst are full of passionate intensity"

— Yeats, 1939

The 1930s were a time of despair for intellectuals. W.H. Auden called it the "Low Decade." Iorga referred to it in 1932 as "a Witches' Sabbath of mankind," adding that "not even in the dark Middle Ages found mankind itself so low as now."[736]

Iorga entitled the third volume of his autobiography dealing with the inter-war period, "*Spre înseninare*" ("Towards Serenity"), towards the clear, sunny uplands. This was the wishful thinking of a man in his 60s after a struggle of a lifetime. But this was not to be. On the contrary, never in his life did he experience such great challenges both politically, and in his scholarly work, or did he engage in such a frantic activity, as he did between 1930 and 1940.

If Iorga was in Romania among his contemporaries, one of the best of humans, he did not befit the second half of Yeats' dictum. He never lacked convictions, although they were not always to be the best ones. This "low decade" threw down the gauntlet to Iorga's world. It finished off the last remnant of the

---

[736]*Memorii*, vol. VII, p. 12.

nineteenth century, with little room left amidst the new "ideologies" for a humanitarian outlook.[737] With the rise of Nazi Germany and the Soviet Union, the world of the "Versailles System," only tenable while Germany and Russia were prostrate, was demolished. Greater Romania was eventually torn apart. Iorga saw it coming. He bore animosity towards any manifestations of German and Russian recovery.

This decade would sound the death knell to Iorga's illusions of a *Sămănătorist* world. Even in literature, *Sămănătorism* became irrelevant, challenged more than ever. As for the writing of history, until now (in Romania) Romanian history was pretty much what Iorga said it was. For the first time, young historians of the "Şcoala Noua" (the "New School" of history) would challenge Iorga. He would not take these challenges gracefully.

Iorga's solutions to the Jewish and other minority problems were strongly challenged both from the outside, and by realities which developed inside Romania. The youth, and much of the student body slipped away from the former "Apostle" in this grueling volcano of a decade, resulting in political challenges to which he did not always offer the best answers, if he offered constructive answer at all.

Nor were these challenges the only ones facing him. Finally, between 1931 and 1932, Iorga, the historian-politician, who considered anything less than a political stand a "desertion, a treason to the cause," would become the head of the government under very unfortunate circumstances. It would not be the best chance for him to prove that he could serve his country. The unfortunate situation greatly contributed to his failure. He wished always to serve his country with the people behind him. But Iorga would not become prime minister by the will of the Romanian people. Nor would his government leave behind a good impression. This would become an anti-climax to the great chance he missed after the Great War, to become the uncontested leader of the elite emerging from

---

[737]Like De Gaulle, Iorga hated ideologies. Wrote he: "Ideologies are fallacies. They lead straight into an abyss!" *Neamul Românesc*, 19 December 1939.

the trenches, and the chance to lead Greater Romania towards a national, cultural, and social renewal. After the failure of his government, Iorga did not quit politics until his untimely death. He would continue to hope that his country would call upon him. In 1938, during the Royal Dictatorship, of which Iorga would become one of the most illustrious (and the most unfortunate) mainstays, he would become Minister of State, the President of the Corporate Senate, and a permanent Crown Council member.

Iorga was never passive about anything. He took up these challenges. But he unwittingly fought within the framework and (as it unfortunately seemed) also in the defense of a discredited king and establishment.

Iorga took an unequivocal stand against the left, which was identified as the national enemy number one. But he had to take a stand against a much greater challenge rising from the radical right. It would be during this final decade of his life that Iorga would undertake his most superhuman efforts in the defense of Romania. He took his stances against Naziism and Communism. Above all he would stand up for the values of a nineteenth century understanding of the Western world.

Also, during this fateful decade Iorga would commit his worst errors of judgment and show the greatest inconsistencies, politically, personally, even in historical sciences and literature. The vehemence of Iorga's stances in his political journalism, trying to "square the circle," to justify his positions, remind us of Şeicaru's reference to the "zigzags" of Iorga's fantasies, reveries, and his whimsical, fanciful conclusions. Were these inconsistencies based on immorality? No. They become consistent if we keep in mind that Iorga tried to defend Greater Romania within the framework of his *Sămănătorist* ideals. Greater Romania and *Sămănătorism* were the foundations of his world. For him they were the pinnacle of morality and of conscience. Were these premises possible? Were Iorga's positions serving Romania? Iorga sincerely believed so. He was not self-seeking in his stands, as so many others in contemporary Bucharest were.

During this decade the pressures on Iorga's world were almost unbearably great. Could anybody have saved, or served during these years in any way, when everything was out of the control of Greater Romania? Was there a constructive alternative? Nothing is easier than to apportion praise and blame half a century after. Ultimately, the conjectures of all these pressures led to the fall of Greater Romania. Iorga did not survive his raison d'être. A few months before its end he arrived fighting to the tragic end of his own road.

The "low decade" started in Romania with the fading of the democratic experience. When Maniu took power, a widening Depression was casting deepening shadows across the vulnerable, underdeveloped economies of East Central Europe in general, and of the Romanian economy in particular. Depression also cast shadows on Romania's newly restored democratic institutions, which were fragile at best. It would be the Depression which would help the rise of the irrational activism of Fascism and Nazism almost everywhere. Fascist tendencies would become an almost irresistible force in Romania. Yet Maniu and Mihalache would still have formidable support.

As if economic depression, increasingly discrediting democracy would not have been enough, the Low Decade (in June 1930) brought back a befitting person: Prince Carol. If Maniu and Mihalache were the symbols of integrity, constitutionalism, democracy, and the hope of the Romanian people for a better future, Romania's only other public symbol, King Carol II, would in the coming decade do his best to create just the opposite impression. Perhaps it is no exaggeration that Carol was the most corrupt crowned head of twentieth century Europe. No other king abused the sincere devotion of his people so unscrupulously as he. The other cardinal sin of the country, violence, was the answer of the Legion to Carol's corruption, and the unhappy country found itself caught between the two.

In a few days, Prince Carol would become King Carol II of Romania, and he would rule over Romania until September of 1940. We saw that his mother, Queen Marie, thought that Carol was bound to destroy himself. Queen Marie was wrong. The destructive blow came from the outside. Since Iorga's association with King Carol would prove to be fateful to Iorga, let's take a closer look at Carol.

The student of Iorga both at the University of Bucharest and at Vălenii-de-Munte, we saw Iorga's relationship with him during the War, and saw that at the request of Queen Marie, Iorga even wrote a book to exonerate Carol of his misdeeds. However, more important (for such a very individualistic human being as Iorga) was that Iorga liked Carol. He always disapproved his exile, as much as he disapproved of the Regency. He maintained contact with Prince Carol during his exile, closer than Manoilescu did. But since Iorga had close contacts with the palace (especially with Queen Marie), and with Carol's brother Prince Nicolae, these contacts were ignored. Iorga didn't bring messages from Carol to political parties, and more importantly, Iorga had no political clout. Although he took stands against the Liberal Party and the National Peasant Party, politically speaking Iorga was in the political wilderness. He was a lightweight; he had a great deal of scholarly prestige, so they ignored his ties with Prince Carol.

Iorga was an appointed Senator, regardless of whether his party got the necessary two percent to be represented in the Chamber. From the Senate, Iorga participated in political life.

Carol II was a Hohenzollern; a strange Hohenzollern indeed. Bismarck said: *"Wir sind nicht in die Welt geboren um glücklich zu sein, sondern um unsere Pflicht zu tun."* What did happiness or duty mean to Carol? Argetoianu, with his peculiar sense for historical analogies, pointed out once in a press interview (which Iorga disapproved very much) that Prince Carol resembled the young Frederick the Great.[738] One can muse about the road the Hohenzollern dynasty covered in Romania from the first Carol to the second. Was this descent due to the *"douce decadence"* which prevailed in Bucharest?[739] Yet, there were antecedents. There was Carol's stay at the Military Academy of Potsdam, where he auctioned away the beautiful Romanian folkloric articles Queen Marie sent him in order to offer gifts to his comrades in arms. And there was the scandalous relation with Zizi Lambrino during the tragic months of Romanian defeat during the War. There were the accusations about corruption in which Carol became involved before his exile. Of course, the Bucharest rumor mill was not always

---

[738]In January 1932, Argetoianu compared for the Parisian daily *Liberté* the youth of King Carol "with the youth of Frederick the Great." *Memorii*, vol. VII, p. 299.

[739]Nothing can be more descriptive dealing with this period than the novel of Petru Dimitriu, *The Prodigals* (New York, 1963).

reliable. But we saw the opinions of his parents. Apart from deceit and his greed for money, Carol was lascivious, very vain, and disloyal. And all these qualities blossomed luxuriantly in the Byzantine atmosphere of the Palace intrigues. Perhaps the best explanation of the phenomenon is that Carol was a sick man. Argetoianu remembered that as the Minister of Interior, he knew about Carol's escapades five times a week in a little black car (Marshal Averescu was aware of these escapades also). Thus Carol (leaving with his trusted driver) picked up whores around the Royal Palace and took them back to the Palace, paying them 500 lei, after which the prostitutes reported to the Police Prefect of Bucharest, Colonel Gavrilă Marinescu (the confidant of Carol), and there they received 5000 lei with the understanding that they would keep their silence. After a while, Colonel Marinescu obligingly filled the streets around the Palace with the kind of prostitutes which pleased. As Argetoianu called them the "proper" whores for the daily walks of His Majesty "to satisfy his masochistic rites."[740]

And there was Magda Wolff, alias Lupescu, a liaison which would be more endurable. The tale of love between the grandson of Queen Victoria and Tsar Alexander II of Russia and the daughter of the ghetto of Iași would read like Cinderella if only it had not cost so much bloodshed in Romania. Mme. Lupescu (or as Carol and her flatterers called her *Duduia*) was as cold, calculating, and selfish as Carol was. She was the most influential royal mistress of the 1930s and the most hated person in Romania. Although it is hard to imagine a more astronomical difference between the backgrounds of two humans, she and Carol possessed in their distance a harmony, a deep sympathy for each other. This may be the reason for the strange fact that after their meeting in 1925 they stayed together through thick and thin, and only the death of Carol in 1952 separated them.

Apart from Mme. Lupescu's indirect, negative, but effective meddling in politics, the presence of a Jewish mistress at the side of their king, who drove away their Queen Helen, had a profound effect on the deeply mystical, religious, and anti-Semitic Romanians. The "Jewish female serpent" became a symbol of

---

[740]"Memoriile lui Constantin Argetoianu," in *Magazin Istoric*, vol. 1 (1967), nr. 2, p. 76.

absolute evil, a viper that would choke off their country. When Carol, looking like a blond Siegfried, descended from the sky in Transylvania in 1930, the people worshipped him. Millions of Romanians were so happy to have their dream prince back that they knelt in the dust before him. But Carol was always in a hurry. There was a bridge party at the Aleea Vulpache (the home of Mme. Lupescu in Bucharest); or a deal to be concluded with Colonel Gavrilă Marinescu, or with Max Auschnit. In vain did his people proffer their love before the gate of his Palace. The king was interested only in such treasures he could touch. And the cold winds blowing from Moldavia scattered the despised love of the Romanian nation.

When Carol abandoned Princess Helen and his son Michael, the Brătianus had a presentiment. In retrospect, Carol's exile was justified, despite Iorga's many times proclaimed hatred of this arrangement; but Iorga was no politician and the Brătianus were. Iorga, because of his personal love for Carol, and his hatred for the Brătianu clan, with his well-known stubbornness, refused to face facts. The facts were staring straight into his face but Iorga refused to admit that he was wrong. He had chosen not to remember certain things which have happened in the past, and he would overlook things which would happen in the future.

The Liberals deferred to the dynasty. Because of their respect, they didn't force the truth about Carol (of which they were aware) out into the open. But the Brătianu clan — Constantin, Vintilă, Ion, and also Prince Barbu Știrbey deadly opposed Carol's ascending the throne.[741] Few even among the initiated knew the extent of Carol's problems. Iorga wrote it all off as Carol's "youthful escapades." Carol knew much better Iorga's character than Iorga knew Carol's. Carol knew Iorga's vanity, instability, and his proclivity for flattery. Iorga always wrote that Carol must assume his place on the side of Princess Helen and

---

[741] As Mme. Lia Brătianu related to Iorga's lieutenant, Dimitrie Munteanu-Râmnic (and he remembered it to his son, Frasin Munteanu-Râmnic), Gheorghe Brătianu, siding with Carol after his return, was practically disowned by the rest of the Brătianu clan. Also, as the story went in the Bucharest gossip-mill, Carol, after his return, found Prince Barbu Știrbey in the apartments of Queen Marie. Carol made a scene. Carol, who worshipped his mother before, could not accept that Queen Marie was also human.

his son. This was for Iorga "an article of faith." Before many members of the Bucharest establishment, Prince Carol was the one "who was wronged" (that is: by the Camarilla). The Romanian people were the last ones to know the truth. The people were deeply monarchical and naive; twentieth century *politicianism* was inconceivable for them; ardently wishing Carol's return, the average Romanian expected a fairy-tale salvation, to rectify Liberal misgovernment and to fulfill the unfulfilled dreams of the establishment of Greater Romania.

Carol's brother, Prince Nicolae (one of the Regents), was busy with his mistress, Miss Doleti Dumitrescu. When Carol arrived, his brother received him with an embrace. The National Peasant Government welcomed Carol's return under three conditions: he must observe the Constitution, reconcile with Queen Helen, and Mme. Lupescu was supposed to stay abroad.[742] The Armed Forces did not represent any obstacle; the younger officers, like Colonel P. Teodorescu, Colonel Gavrilă Marinescu and others looked forward to Carol's return, perhaps hoping for promotion, which was altogether humane from them.[743]

Carol was a believer in fascism. He returned with a firm intention to wreck the Parliamentary System. As early as 1925, Carol traveled to Italy (with Argetoianu's help) to familiarize himself with the workings of Mussolini's government.[744] If Carol had doubts, the workings of democracy in Romania coupled with the effects of the Depression offered an impulse to turn Romania into a fascist, authoritarian state under him. As Carol saw it, "the reason for the political and spiritual crisis of Romania is to be found in the spell of Western ideas and reforms (which) were the product of a different tradition (and of a different) economic, historical, national, geographical, and moral conditions." Carol went on to explain that with the Parliamentary tradition Romania adopted all the heritage of the bourgeois revolution of 1789, without having a bourgeoisie. Then

---

[742]Corneliu Coposu, a close associate of Maniu, remembered this in a debate with Vlad Georgescu. *Românul Liber*, (London, March 1986).

[743]Dimitrie Munteanu-Râmnic always reminded Iorga that the young officers supported Carol. *Memorii*, vol. V, p. 241.

[744]Iorga referred then ironically to this as "the passion of the Crown Prince." *O viață de om*, vol. III, p. 105.

he continued: "Our political life must pay for this original sin of lies, and this original sin encompasses all spheres of (our) public life, culture, civilization, national economy, administration, all resemble a distorted framework not fitting into the essential, to the content of those truths which come from the distant past, from the depth of our very existence."[745]

There was a lot of truth in Carol's quasi-Junimist analysis, but did his wrecking of the Parliamentary System and his corrupt "personal regime" offer a better alternative? Thus Carol wanted to establish a fascist system from the outset, a popular movement, with the youth especially under his leadership. He did not want a Mussolini-Victor Emanuel arrangement.

What chances did democracy have in Romania? The Romanian people were not ready for democracy. There was no democratic tradition, rather a tradition for Proudhon's dictum: the Romanian people reacted more to the realities of power than to any "social contract." Carol, and also *politicianism* understood this. The result was the performance of Romanian pseudo-constitutionalism. The youth not only didn't understand democracy, but many of them, especially the educated ones, identified its performance with the political establishment. Since the youth was left out, they turned against this political establishment, searching for something radically new.

Iorga increasingly lost faith, not in democracy, but in the relevance of Western democratic institutions to Romania's problems.[746] By now Iorga thought that the right of people to participate in politics presupposed: 1) knowledge of a large outline of the world, and 2) the understanding of the day-by-day issues. Thus, he concluded that "universal suffrage was never a blessing from heaven in Romania."[747] He was no ideologist. Beyond *Sămănătorism* he didn't believe in ideologies. He was no economist, nor a sociologist. Iorga, a

---

[745] *Enciclopedia României*, vol. I, p. 937, Bucureşti, 1939.

[746] *O viaţă de om*, vol. III, p. 226.

[747] *Neamul Românesc*, 18 February 1938.

romantic, impulsive historian with excellent instincts, saw the spectacle and performance of democracy in Romania.

Carol was proclaimed king and his son, Prince Michael, became the "Great Voievod of Alba Iulia."[748] There was talk about a transitory period of a regency. Iorga recommended a government under Marshal Prezan.[749] There was a continuation of a National Peasant government instead under G.G. Mironescu. Mironescu was replaced soon enough by Maniu as prime minister.

The economics of the National Peasants were more liberal than those of the Liberals. They enacted a law allowing peasants who benefited from the land reform to sell their homesteads. They suspended the xenophobic *"Prin noi însine"* laws which barred foreign investments, and stabilized the Romanian Lei. These measures didn't get a chance because of the Depression. Grain prices collapsed together with Romania's international credit. The Romanian people which elected the National Peasants, with a landslide majority of 78% of the vote, were deceived again. As Iorga said: "for the people, the government is always guilty, and the opposition the savior..." Time was running out for democracy in Romania.

Carol returned on an airplane, because he wanted to avoid possible difficulties on the border. Maniu could have ordered Carol's arrest. What stopped him was the agreement concluded with Carol, agreeing to Maniu's three conditions. Maniu did not wish to risk a civil war either. In Bucharest, Carol reaffirmed to Maniu once more his intention to respect the constitution, to reunite with Princess Helen, and not to allow the return of Mme. Lupescu. Maybe he thought (like Henry IV of France) that, if Bucharest "was not worth a mass," it is worth a promise or two. As Carol saw after his arrival the support for his return, he began to renege on his promises fast enough.[750] On 12 August 1930,

---

[748]Coposu credited Iorga with creating the title, Iorga in his political diaries angrily rejected this. *Memorii,* vol. VI, p. 2.

[749]*Ibid.,* pp. 2 and 4.

[750]Coposu, *op. cit.*

Mme. Lupescu came back also, using a passport of the wife of the economist Mihai Manoilescu.[751]

With the return of Carol, Iorga saw an opportunity "to serve Romania." The Liberals were gone with the exception of Gheorghe Brătianu, the only Liberal who became a Carolist and who was because of this excluded from the Liberal party. Brătianu now founded his own Liberal Party called the "Gheorghists" or "Neo-Liberals." Vintilă Brătianu died at the end of 1930. The others of the clan were disoriented, and Duca later concluded a deal with Carol. Iorga saw the Palace open to his influence.

Iorga established close ties with Carol. He said once to Frasin Munteanu-Râmnic, "Listen, dear: when I am with the king, what do you think? Do I speak up or wait until the king will ask me?" For him, the king was a "historic personage." The others were the "Capşa Crowd." For Iorga (since democracy did not work), the goal was "national unity," to prevail above all against "the political parties" which Iorga hated as De Gaulle did. This supreme goal could be achieved only by gathering around the king. Iorga felt that his role was to bring this about. Did Iorga's ego play a role in this line of thinking? Or was his ambition "to serve Romania"? Iorga did not follow any personal ambition; his "ego" was to serve Romania the only way he could, and that was his way.

Maniu and Mihalache developed during the coming years into an obstacle for Iorga, and this led to a vicious hostility. We saw Iorga's apotheosis of Maniu in 1918. That was the unpolitical image of the greatest Transylvanian of the twentieth century. There was a cooperation possible between these two honest men and true patriots. But there were obstacles, Iorga's culture was mainly French, based on a Latin and Byzantine Greek background; Maniu's background was German from Transylvania, and he was Uniate, Iorga came to emphasize Maniu's "odious, sub-German, Hungarian culture," and his K.u.K. and Transyl-

---

[751]Argetoianu commented, when he found Carol awarding Manoilescu "The Order of the Crown of Thorns": "The order *'la couronne des putains'* would have been more appropriate." "Memoriile lui Constantin Argetoianu," in *Magazin Istoric.*, vol. I (1967), nr. 2, p. 74.

vanian Catholic background. He considered Maniu's Christian morals and constitutionalism as "hypocrisy." Once Maniu was seated next to Vera, the wife of his son Mircea, with Mircea at her side. He took a slice of orange and by mistake put salt on it instead; when he tasted it, Maniu allegedly remarked, "I am punishing myself this way." Commented Iorga: "Maniu is a Jesuit, a hypocrite."[752] Iorga abused Maniu in his biography, almost daily in his *Neamul Românesc* and elsewhere, always mocking Maniu's Hungarian education; for him Maniu was a Hungarian nobleman (a *nemes*) from Badacin (Sălaj country), a Transylvanian, a puritan, a K.u.K. officer; he elaborated on Maniu's alleged contempt for the "Byzantine Regat." He reminded Maniu that he never traveled in the world except as a K.u.K officer, and that he withdrew to Alba Iulia like Mohammed withdrew into Medina. He also belabored Maniu's "vulgar, wine-ridden red nose." According to Iorga, "Maniu wanted to become the president of a solemn and inoperative republic," with Mihalache in the shadow of Maniu's stiff elegant collar from Budapest.[753] When Maniu said that in a democracy "the king reigns, but he does not rule," Iorga retorted: "This is against the tradition of Romanian history. Romania has always had rulers." We see the evolution of Iorga's thought towards a medieval authoritarian *monarchy*. To Maniu, the people of the Regat (and other Transylvanians) were "a blend between an Orthodox Greek and a non-believing Gypsy girl." Finally, Iorga administered to Maniu the ultimate insult, speaking about him "as a foreigner." Iorga explained that this "foreigner" conducted politics in Romania since 1918. He was actually not even a bad patriot, although Catholic. But not a Catholic like Innocentiu Klein, who turned Catholicism into a weapon of the oppressed. Maniu, because of his Calvinist education in Zalău, entered the Budapest University where he studied too much the law of Werböczy. He would remain a foreigner forever, and looked

---

[752]Argetoianu commented, when he found Carol awarding Manoilescu "The Order of the Crown of Thorns": "The order *'la couronne des putains'* would have been more appropriate." "Memoriile lui Constantin Argetoianu," in *Magazin Istoric*, vol. 1 (1967), nr. 2, p. 74.

[753]*O viața de om*, vol. III, pp. 13-14, 20, 27, 39, 193 and 242.

upon the Regat as a foreigner, without having the ability (only *Sămănătorism* can give) to love and understand Romania.[754]

Maniu was very passive, and rarely answered Iorga. In the chamber, Professor Madgearu, (and also Mihalache), tried many times to throw in Iorga's face his connections with Aristide Blank. Maniu referred once to the four chairs Iorga occupied at the university, whereupon Iorga retorted (as a representative of the work ethic): "he hopes to get even more chairs and cam even more money honestly."[755]

One can only say that during this confrontation Maniu was more dignified, and Maniu was right. How right he was would be proven during the Crown Councils of 1940 where Iorga had finally to see Carol for what he was. And it would be the personal intervention of Maniu with General Antonescu (who had a great respect for Maniu, despite political differences) which will assure for Iorga a Christian funeral.[756]

In 1934, Iorga wrote a pamphlet about Maniu. He applied *politicianism* at its worst. This pamphlet is by no means superior to the one Cernăianu wrote about Iorga. Through 45 pages, Iorga repeated all he had said about Maniu before, and added more. King Carol must have loved it. Iorga emphasizes that "he is not presenting the case as a politician, but as a chronicler." Iorga's opinions about Maniu are not exhaustive. He describes Maniu as an "effete dandy," accusing him of not defending Romanian interests in the Hungarian Parliament, mentioning ambiguous connections with Blaj banks, and condemning his "fanatical devotion to a Democratic Internationale." Iorga ended all this with an

---

[754]*Isprava.* pp. 23, 58-59, 71-72.

[755]*Neamul Românesc*, 4 May 1931.

[756]Mmc. Liliana Pippidi-Iorga to the writer, and similar findings of Scurtu and of Şeicaru. Wrote Maniu to Antonescu: "It was my appreciation of his scholarly and national merits which held me back from answering his continuous attacks (against me)." *Curierul Românesc*, June 1991.

almost American public relations touch: "I believe that I have convinced you!"[757] Maniu had become one of the people whom Iorga "loved to hate."

In October 1930, Maniu resigned because of Mme. Lupescu's return to Romania. Professor Hugh Seton-Watson gave a classic definition of Maniu's political error: "Bourgeois sexual morality is probably less esteemed in Romania than anywhere else on the continent. It was not the dictatorship."[758]

Thus Maniu left the field open to Carol. The new prime minister, G.G. Mironescu (from Maniu's party) was no match for the king. Queen Helen left Romania in July 1931. Thus, the rule of Carol started in earnest.

Mme. Lupescu was referred to as the "Romanian Pompadour." She was a motherly figure who put up with and advised Carol during his aberrations and business activities. She became irreplaceable. Iorga never mentioned her, although he made indirect puns, stigmatizing the situation in the Palace during his lectures. To his family he made devastating comments about her presence, but Iorga never took note of her presence when he visited the palace. Now even the anti-Semite Goga was making curtsies before Mme. Lupescu; otherwise, one couldn't survive politically. Only General Antonescu had enough character not to do that, which became his undoing. Cuza, with his fanatic anti-Semitism, kept a conspicuous silence. One may ask about that proud "Republic of Letters": How many people of character inhabited it? Argetoianu didn't talk about the order of "Crown of Whores;" he joined the crowd fawning on Mme. Lupescu and the power and influence she yielded. Crown Prince Mihai loved his father and he also liked Duduia although, some newer revelations: Mircea Ciobanu: *Convorbiri cu Mihai I al României* dispute this. Whatever Carol did as king or husband, even his enemies conceded that he was a good, loving father.

Carol proclaimed himself to be "the first peasant, laborer, and the first civil servant of his realm." But he was no economist in the middle of a Depression.

---

[757]N. Iorga, *Istoria unei legende: Iuliu Maniu*, Vălenii-de-Munte, 1934

[758]Hugh Seton Watson, *op. cit.*, p. 04

His Camarilla advised him to cope with the crisis on an "ad hoc" basis. Unfortunately, Iorga was no economist either.

This first Camarilla (always identified with its core) was led by Puiu Dumitrescu. Its other members Felix Wieder, Alexandru Mavrodi, and Nicolae Tabacovici, were financiers. Besides these wheeler-dealers, there was the obscurantist philosopher Nae Ionescu, and Aristide Blank, to whom Carol would listen spellbound even after his advice failed to produce results. Blank offered a villa to Mme. Lupescu and another villa to Prince Nicolae. And there was also the industrialist of Greek origin, Nicolae Malaxa, and the neo-Liberal economist, Mihai Manoilescu, a defector from Maniu's party. In the background was Mme. Lupescu. Real decisions were made in her salon during bridge parties.

Although Carol had definite plans to install a fascist authoritarian regime under his leadership, he had to wait. We see between 1930 and 1933 a period of instability. Between 1933 and 1937 there was a stabilization, a hardening of the personal regime of Carol, in view of the increasing challenge of the radicalism of the Legion. During the winter of 1937, thanks to the conjecture of the international situation and internal pressures, we see a convulsion, before Carol could arrive at his ultimate conclusions; from February 1938 until September 1940 he updated the system, and established a pseudo-fascist dictatorship. Stability would be re-established. Fascist trappings (insincere ones), his army and police did a good job of keeping the system going. Iorga had a definite and unfortunate role in the first and last phase of Carol's rule.

There were about ten months between the return of Carol and Iorga's premiership. When Carol returned, Iorga didn't rush to Cotroceni Palace to greet him despite of his devotion. As President of Bucharest University, Iorga had legal reservations. He nevertheless welcomed Carol's return: "he hopes that the old Prince Carol returns, and as far as the other Prince Carol he does not want to remember that one."[759] He continued to express futile hopes that King Carol and Princess Helen would reconcile. Although Iorga had maintained good relations

---

[759]*Neamul Românesc*, 8 June 1930.

with both of them, Carol and Princess Helen visited Iorga's Summer School at
Vălenii-de-Munte during the summer of 1930 separately.[760]

Meanwhile, the Depression widened. Iorga analyzed modern life and realities: "The Agony of Industrial Economics." He did not understand that, despite
a rich harvest and a tremendous industrial production, people still went hungry
and naked, concluding that human labor turned against human happiness, this
being the result of the French Revolution, eighteenth century philosophy, and
also of Cartesian logic. The individual was set free with savage appetites, and
his incapacity to adapt or foresee. "The individual's folly, destroying raw materials, will lead not only to the destruction of civilization, but to worse things. An
answer must be found collectively, but not the Russian way. Mankind must find
an answer (Romania in particular) without prejudicing anyone, without imitating carelessly alien forms."[761] Whether Iorga considers economy or society, he
remains first and foremost a historian.

As the Depression's effects struck, there were demonstrations all over the
country. The most violent disorders occurred in the mining region of Petroșani,
where soldiers killed striking miners.

Iorga was approaching his sixtieth birthday. His enemies did not want to
let the anniversary pass. An attorney, Constantin Cernăianu (whom Iorga qualified as being "a religious agitator"),[762] wrote a pamphlet about Iorga, "the idol
of the Romanian nation." This was the most detailed and malicious attack ever
written against him. As we know, Iorga's Orthodox piety left a lot to be desired.
His qualified attitude towards Orthodoxy added to Mr. Cernăianu's ravings.
Cernăianu's study was dedicated "to the Romanian Orthodox Church, and to the
Romanian Nation." He pointed out that since he was serving the Orthodox faith,
he must raise doubts about Iorga's Orthodox devotion. He brought many quotations from Iorga to substantiate this charge. Supported with quotations from

---

[760]*Neamul Românesc*, 18 June 1930, and 22, and 22 July 1931, and *Memorii* vol. 6, pp. 13-
14.

[761]*Neamul Românesc*, 22 June 1930.

[762]*Memorii*, vol. VI, p. 58.

Iorga's critics or enemies like Eugen Lovinescu or Mihail Dragomirescu, Cernăianu attacked Iorga's scholarly works, personality, and temperament in denigrating fashion. Every conflict (and Iorga had many) was amply discussed in a one-sided manner, Iorga's positions in literature was not forgotten. His *Sămănătorist* views, even his clashes about literature with his brother-in-law Gheorghe Bogdan-Duică, were amply mentioned. Due attention was paid to his controversy with Maiorescu.

The problem with Mr. Cernăianu's pamphlet was how he presented it. He offered extrapolations of Iorga's changes on different issues, like the Jewish question, Maniu, his different works on Michael the Brave, his changing personal relationships, etc., etc. Mr. Cernăianu even questioned Iorga's patriotism. His argument rested on Iorga's statement in Athens, where he dared to remember before a Greek audience his Greek origins. Doubts were voiced over Iorga's loyalty to king and Dynasty. Iorga's ups and downs on the political scene, his changing relationships with Dr. Lupu, Vaida, Goga, Maniu, and Argetoianu were carefully fostered, and his changing relations with Cuza were not forgotten. Cernăianu even quoted Constantin Sion's pamphleteer-exaggerations in his *Arhondologia Moldovei* to taint Iorga's family.[763] Iorga answered the pamphlet in the usual fashion, with a lawsuit for slanderous libel.

The Vienna newspaper *Welt am Montag* wrote about Iorga that he received a bribe from Deterding. Iorga answered this charge promptly with a slander suit. The Bucharest Liberal Newspaper *Viitorul* took the side of Tzigara-Samurcaş in his continuing conflict with Iorga. Iorga answered these articles by theatrically resigning from the presidency of Bucharest University. The matter was duly transferred to the courts.[764]

---

[763]C. Cernăianu, *Nicolae Iorga — Neamului Românesc: Antologie pentru posteritate*, (Bucureşti, 1931).

[764]*Neamul Românesc*, 4 March 1931; *Memorii*, vol. VI, pp. 7-8, 396.

Iorga remembered the Depression Christmas of 1930: "There is a snow, mud, and morass on the streets. People seem to be destitute, sad and poor, and they have no faith in the future."[765] A sad omen for his future Premiership.

Although Iorga's 60th birthday was in June, anniversary celebrations started in March. The speaker of honor was Argetoianu. These were the preliminary stages of the formation of a Iorga government, the public relations build-up could not wait. Argetoianu, through meetings and addresses, carefully fostered and eulogized Iorga.[766]

By April 1931, Carol's plans were maturing. Carol's first move towards the establishment of a personal dictatorship was to establish "a government above parties." First he sought under Nicolae Titulescu a government of "national concentration." Titulescu did not belong to any political party; he was the greatest Romanian diplomat during the interwar period, president of the League of Nations. There was intense (although, civilized) animosity between Iorga and Titulescu. Iorga refused to enter a Titulescu government. Thus, Titulescu left for London to become Romania's ambassador.[767] From there, he would work hard on discrediting (the future) Iorga government.

A week of negotiations preceded the formation of the Iorga government. Carol considered it expedient to cover-up his dictatorial ambitions with Iorga's prestige. Also, the king considered Iorga to be easier to manipulate, than Titulescu. With the destitution of King Alfonso XIII of Spain during the same days as a somber backdrop, on 18 April 1931, Nicolae Iorga became prime minister of Romania.[768]

The government had many names: The "Iorga-Argetoianu" or the "King's Government." Titulescu wanted to form a "Government of National Concentration," above parties to deal with the depression. The government of Iorga would

---

[765]*Op. cit.*, vol. VI, p. 38.

[766]*Neamul Românesc*, 6 March 1931. Since months, Iorga was approached by the king about forming a government.

[767]*Memorii*, vol. VI, p. 74.

[768]*Op. cit.*, pp. 79-85.

also be called the "government of technicians." Iorga said: "I was prime minister in Argetoianu's government," perhaps the best definition.[769] Iorga was prime minister, and reserved for himself the portfolio of Education; he was (temporarily) also his own Minister of Interior. He ran his Ministry of Interior through his lieutenant, Dimitrie Munteanu-Râmnic. Argetoianu was to become the Finance Minister and the "pro-tempore" Foreign Minister; Mihai Manoilescu, the Minister of Commerce and Industry; G. Ionescu-Sisești, the Minister of Agriculture; C. Hamangiu, the Minister of Justice, and General C. Ștefănescu-Amza, the Minister of Defense. With Argetoianu and General Ștefănescu-Amza being the men of Carol, the control of the king was decisive. Iorga's party remained practically unrepresented.

When his government fell, Iorga remembered that on the way back from the Black Sea, "a sympathetic girl" asked him: "Are you the former prime minister?" Iorga answered, "Yes, unfortunately." The girl retorted, "The most unpopular man in Romania." After the fall of the Iorga government, even in Vălenii the slogans of the coming elections (in July 1932) went like this: "Iorga ate our salaries and pensions, and took the bread from our mouths." And even Mme. Catinca was exposed to vulgar abuse by the mob during a train ride. And C.C. Giurescu, certainly not without malice, wrote to a friend, "Iorga was the most ridiculous prime minister and minister of instruction ever in office in Romania."[770]

After he missed his chance to become a Tribune for the "French Generation," the former "Apostle" of youth finally saw his lifelong vision fulfilled. He was called upon under extremely difficult circumstances to help his country. Before his appointment Iorga said to King Carol, "I will serve Your Majesty only with ideals I believe in," later he referred to his government as "an unsupported and a misunderstood undertaking," and remarked: "If I would have had a powerful party, or a courageous, intelligent nation behind me, things would

---

[769]Mme. Liliana Pippidi-Iorga to the author. Maniu warned Iorga: "Argetoianu will lead you without you even noticing it!" in vol. VI, p. 87.

[770]Basil Munteanu, *Correspondence* (Paris, 1979), p. 436. Also, *Memorii*, vol. VII, pp. 8, 12, and 21.

have gone differently."[771] Iorga had none of those. Even if Iorga would have had the support he desired, his position would have been extremely precarious. But Iorga was no politician, no economist, and his personality and temperament disqualified him. His prime ministership would be an echo of his former failures in politics. He was made prime minister by Carol only because of exceptional circumstances. If not for those, Iorga probably would have never become the head of the government. Carol made Iorga the head of the government because of the Depression and his own ambitions which he could not accomplish right away.

By the spring of 1931, the Depression (like the cause of it) was out of the control of the National Peasant Government. Between 1929 and 1932 national income dropped in Romania by 45%, export revenues fell from 29 billion lei in 1929 to 14 billion, even though exports increased from seven million metric tons to eight million, reflecting the drop of prices of agricultural products. Imports fell from 1,102,000 metric tons in 1929 to 450,000 in 1932. State revenues declined from 36 billion lei to 18 billion, despite the fact that the petroleum exports preserved an active balance of trade. The consequences of the economic crisis were disastrous, especially for the peasantry. By 1932, the debt per hectare of arable land reached the figure of 6,585 lei.[772] Romania reacted with demonstrations, strikes, and a general breakdown of law and order. Banditism was rampant, not even public order could be upheld.[773]

In King Carol's long-standing dictatorial ambitions, democracy, Maniu, and Mihalache had no place. Iorga agreed with the king as far as Maniu and Mihalache were concerned. For Carol, the national emergency seemed a good pretext to do away with democracy, and Iorga was to serve as an instrument in

---

[771]*Memorii*, vol. VI, p. 31; also, *Memorii*, vol. VII, p. 25, and *O viaţă de om*, vol. III, p. 247.

[772]Roberts, *op. cit.*, p. 176.

[773]The extent of the social dissolution can be vividly felt from Iorga's political diary. Foreigners compared Romania with Mexico, and cars close to Bucharest were ambushed by hungry bandits. *Memorii*, vol. VI, pp. 30, 60, 90.

this transition. Carol could use him because he knew Iorga. The king was showering on Iorga orders and decorations. He was appealing to Iorga's sense of duty, to his ego, even flattering his family.[774]

Thus, the transition towards the king's personal regime started behind the impressive facade Iorga gave to the new administration. The appointment of the government seemed to be a decision made by the Camarilla.[775] Iorga became prime minister, but Carol wouldn't trust his quixotic statesmanship. First, he tried to impose Iorga-Titulescu as a *homo regius*, then the king imposed Argetoianu (as Minister of Interior) in the capacity of *homo regius*.[776] The Foreign Minister would later be D.I. Ghică.

Since the role of Argetoianu would be decisive (he headed key ministries: The Interior and that of Finance), let's take a closer look. Besides King Carol II and Cuza, Constantin Argetoianu was the most unfortunate associate of Iorga. The clashes and reconciliations with him reflect the unfortunate instability of Iorga's personality.

The culture of Romania was Byzantine, so was her political culture.[777] This was the celebrated *politicianism* which Iorga contemptuously referred to as *Suprafanar*, feverish changing of sides, eternal "realignments," accompanied by intrigues and connivings, motivated rarely by ideals but convenience. Incessant

---

[774]According to Bucharest society he must be "asphyxiated" by now under the weight of orders. *O viață de om*, vol. III, p. 246. King Carol tried to flatter Iorga by giving orders to Mme. Catinca, which by the way were well-deserved.

[775]Argetoianu protested against the Bucharest notion that "his government was formed in the salon of Mme. Lupescu," saying that he met the lady in 1934 for the first time. "Memoriile lui Constantin Argetoianu," in *Magazin Istoric*, p. 73. But such were the practices of the Camarilla it was not necessary to meet Mme. Lupescu personally to receive the stamp of approval out of her salon. Goga was also strongly opposed to the formation of a Iorga government. *Revista de istorie și teorie literară*, București, No. 3, 4 (1985), no. 1, 2-3, 4 (1986), finally, nos. 1-2 (1987).

[776]Carol liked to impose a *homo regius* to the Ministry of Interior. Later, he imposed Călinescu on Goga (as the king put it) "to prevent stupidities." Scurtu, *op. cit.*, p. 388.

[777]See Iorga, *Formes byzantines et réalités balcaniques* (Bucarest, 1922).

repellent combinations, reflecting only one principle: unprincipledness and opportunism.

If Iorga made politics, thus, participated in this process, to what extent was this motivated by his Nationalism based on the albatross of *Sămănătorism*. Or, was it the result of his temperament, ego, and personality? Was it because Democracy in the 1930s became more and more irrelevant to Romania's problems?

Iorga still believed in his *Sămănătorist* answer — with a stubbornness only Eminescu's "Supreme Law" could imbue him with. The Great Depression discredited democracy economically. The quest for easy answers would contribute to the rise of a "Fascist Rainbow" all over Southeast Europe. Within this "Fascist Rainbow," the frenzied, unprincipled fluctuations of politics in Romania would increase in a runaway fashion.

All this was not a monopoly of Romanian politics. In Italy they called it *transformismo*, introduced by A. Depretis. Later Giovanni Giolitti led it to a flourish. You could say this is what politics are all about. In Washington, they call it "situation morality." But in Romania, the degree of this kind of politicking reduced political and constitutional life to a sterile agitation. Franz Borkenau explains that whether in Latin America, Russia, Spain, Poland (or for that matter in Romania), the precondition (and not the only one) for a working democracy is the existence of a middle class, or the only substitute, a strong, self-confident, land-owning peasantry. If it is absent, there will be futile convulsions, after which the choice will lie between a leftist or a reactionary dictatorship.[778]

Nevertheless, Argetoianu should occupy a special place. Constantin Argetoianu originated from a powerful boyar family from Oltenia. He was the study case for an Oriental despot: skillful, brutal, in addition completely uninhibited, devious, and cynical. Those who remember him recalled the "balancing act of Argetoianu": the more devious Argetoianu became, the more sincere he

---

[778]Franz Borkenau, *The Communist International* (London, 1938), pp. 110-112.

pretended to seem. He spoke the softest at his meanest; and smiled before pouncing. And there was Argetoianu's corruption, too much even for the Carolist decade.[779] He was a firm believer in Totalitarianism.

When we call Argetoianu corrupt, perhaps we are off the mark, because of how we imagine unselfish service to the commonwealth. Oriental despotism considers corruption a kind of accessory to office, like the official limousine, or the expense account. These things might seem terrible in countries which have known equity, but not so terrible in countries which have never known it. Argetoianu never shared Iorga's *Sămănătorist* dream world. More importantly, Argetoianu, as the Minister of Interior and Finance, knew everything about power. He knew what power meant, knew how to obtain power, how to hold onto it, how to use power, and knew how to abuse it. No wonder Argetoianu caught the eyes of Prince Carol early. With Argetoianu's help Prince Carol traveled to Italy to familiarize himself with the workings of fascism.[780] Argetoianu suggested to Carol very early that establish a totalitarian dictatorship, "long before the rise of Mussolini, or even Hitler."[781]

How could Iorga work with such kind of a "*homo regius*"? Not well.[782] The problem of this "government of technicians" in the middle of an economic crisis was that the prime minister was no economist. Unfortunately, Argetoianu was

---

[779]The father of this writer (when Argetoianu was the economic czar) managed to get Argetoianu's permission for the purchase of a considerable amount of lumber for his furniture business, in return for a formidable bribe. Many years later, with Witold Sworakowski, a Bucovinian Polish aristocrat and businessman (the Assistant Director of the Hoover Institute), this writer managed "to compare notes." Sworakowski remembered that a similar business venture needed Argetoianu's approval, his family had resorted successfully to a bribe — which Argetoianu managed to increase substantially during the negotiations.

[780]*O viață de om.* vol. III, p. 105. Iorga knew (as early as 1924) that Crown Prince Carol "showed sympathy and confidence towards Argetoianu." "Memoriile lui Constantin Argetoianu." in *Magazin istoric*, vol. 1 (1967), nr. 4, p. 66. These feelings were not reciprocated. Argetoianu refers amply to Carol's disloyalty, inconsistencies, and sexual perversions with cynical contempt. "Memoriile lui Constantin Argetoianu," *Magazin Istoric*, vol. 1 (1967), nr. 2, pp. 73-75.

[781]*Op. cit.*, year no. 2, issue no. 3, March 1968, p. 70.

[782]Iorga in his *Memorii* (between 1932 and 1938) never missed an opportunity to make a contemptuous remark about Argetoianu.

no economist either. Later (in July 1931), Manoilescu, one of the good Romanian economists during the interwar period, left the government and became president of the National Bank.

Iorga wanted his lieutenant, Dimitrie Munteanu-Râmnic, as Minister of Interior, but Carol felt more secure with Argetoianu. Argetoianu began to complain that "nobody wants to entrust him with the Ministry of Interior." During the talks he did not hesitate to pretend to cry. Tears are always a proof of sincerity. He continued to beg Iorga to appoint him as Minister of Interior: "He's no such monster, and if he doesn't get the Ministry of Interior, he will resign from the government!" So, Iorga gave Argetoianu the post. Iorga thought, that with Dimitrie Munteanu-Râmnic as First Secretary of the Ministry of Interior he would have control. Iorga was disabused soon enough. Argetoianu demanded the transfer of Munteanu-Râmnic to the Ministry of Instruction. "Let him work under Iorga!" Iorga flatly denied the request. Argetoianu launched a number of intrigues against Iorga, while reassuring him that "Iorga shouldn't believe for a moment that he (Argetoianu) would engage in intrigues against him."[783] Two of Argetoianu's letters that Iorga managed to get hold of will follow: the first a memorandum, handwritten and signed by Argetoianu, written on the stationery of the Ministry of Interior, not dated, from the (office) of the Minister.

The letter concerns scandalous data about Ş. Meteş (a Transylvanian intellectual, a friend of Iorga), whom Iorga appointed to a post. Argetoianu instructs the journalist to attack Meteş because of his legal problems, promising (the journalist) evidence about his disreputable affairs with a Bank. This, and the fact that Meteş was sponsored by Iorga was to be carefully fostered in the article. Hamangiu (Minister of Justice, and also close to Iorga) was to be attacked in the press also, because of some shoddy dealings with the Blanc Bank. And the articles should emphasize repeatedly the closeness of these people to Iorga.

The second memo written by Argetoianu is also undated, but the Iorga family assured the writer that both memos were from a time when Argetoianu passionately denied his guilt in any press campaign directed against Iorga. Although

---

[783] *Memorii*, vol. VI, pp. 94-98, 158 and 179.

unsigned, Argetoianu's handwriting is unmistakable. Written also on the stationary of the Ministry of Interior, it comes from the office of the Minister:

Here Argetoianu instincts several hatchet-journalists to start another campaign against Iorga, Meteş, Munteanu-Râmnic, Hamangiu, and other friends of Iorga. Sources (where to pick up ammunition for the campaign and where to obtain help from similar-minded journalists) are indicated. Argetoianu was to be kept abreast, and to proofread the article(s) before they went into print. The articles were to be placed on the first or last pages of the paper(s). Cernăianu was to be contacted; Iorga's appointments and policies were to be attacked; great urgency was advised. Argetoianu assured everybody that all expenses would be taken care of.[784]

The press campaign against Iorga got underway financed with funds of the Ministry of the Interior. Iorga considered Argetoianu's behavior with his colleagues "brutal." When Iorga admonished him that "the glass is full!" Argetoianu duly shed rears to show his sincerity."[785]

Iorga kept the Ministry of Public Instruction for himself, hoping to do something decisively new for Romanian education. Beyond that, Iorga's role was reduced to that of decorum. Manoilescu informed him that there was no money to pay the salaries of the public servants.[786]

Foreign reactions to Iorga's appointment were mixed. Some were favorable, especially those of intellectuals.[787] Reactions in France, and from democratic quarters were not so good, especially after the elections which followed.

---

[784]Iorga-Pippidi family archives.

[785]*Memorii*, vol. VI, pp. 173-177, 311, 318.

[786]Iorga, *Doi ani de restaurare*, p. 21.

[787]Iorga received enthusiastic telegrams from Marconi, and President Masaryk, who wrote: "How good that after the Great War some professors survive!" Iorga, *Credinţa mea*, Bucureşti, 1931, p. 169. Gheorghe Brătianu, of the Şcoala Noua, wanted to support Iorga; because of this scholarly controversy he was not able to do so. The scion of one of the Hungarian aristocratic families in Transylvania, Bishop of Alba-Iulia, Count Kàroly Majláth, also sent his greetings to Iorga. BAR, *Corespondenţa lui Iorga*, vol. 369, doc. 156.

Elections were held because the government could not govern with a chamber of Maniu's supporters. In Romania a new government always brought new elections, with plenty of fraud and violence. Frequent new elections discredited democracy even more.

Iorga was crisscrossed the country during the campaign. In the Jewish center of Iaşi he lectured Jews "to find the road to the heart of the Romanian people." In Chişinău, he called on Jews to abandon the ghetto, restructure themselves socially and professionally, and send their Rabbis for education to French Rabbinical Seminaries. Unfortunately, conditions in Bessarabia were not like those of France. During his campaign, Iorga called for national unity, which should transcend class.[788]

There was little pretense that the elections would be free. Iorga pro-claimed to his inner circle: "Gentleman! This will be a very narrow chamber!" Argetoianu would take care of that. He knew how to adulterate the electoral process by more than one means.[789] Iorga was allied with the Liberals now under Duca, with whom he later diverged, and formed the so-called "National Union." The German Party and the Ukrainian Party, and the anti-corruption league "Vlad-Ţepeş," also supported Iorga.

---

[788]Iorga, *Credinţa mea*, pp. 81, 99, 125.

[789]R.W. Seton-Watson (whom Iorga called "a friend") and others in the West called these elections "a prostitution of electoral methods," adding that Romania was in the hands of a clique, Iorga pointed out that he was a member of this "clique," and asked Seton-Watson to remove his name from the sponsors of the *Slavonic Review* There would also be a quarrel between Iorga and the Carnegie Foundation. The Carnegie Foundation explained to Iorga that Seton-Watson was free to express any view he chose. In Romania, many politicians sent telegrams to Iorga, like Grigore Gafencu, Dr. Lupu, P. Halippa, and D. Ioaniţescu, and also Gheorghe Brătianu, complaining about the brutal methods employed against them. Characteristically, complaints were not addressed to the source (Argetoianu), but to Iorga, considered to be something very different. Iorga uniformly answered (his answers noted on the back of each protest telegram), that "he cannot in a few weeks change the political morality of the country like this since time immemorial." Unfortunately Iorga showed (a kind of) solidarity with Argetoianu's methods. *Memorii*, vol. 6, pp. 113-118; also, pp. 203 and 208. Also BAR, *Corespondenţa lui Iorga*, vol. 362, doc. 164, and vol. 371, docs. 184, 185, 186, 187, 226, 227, 228, and *Doi ani de restaurare*, p. 53. If Iorga called his party "a monarchist party of the Left — now he clearly calls his government "a government of the Right" "but not a retrograde one." *Neamul Românesc*, June 18, 1931.

Argetoianu assured the desired results. The elections took place in the beginning of June. The National Union received more than 40% of the votes, and consequently assured for itself a comfortable majority. Many mandates of the "National Union" were filled on the corporate principle. After the election, the Communists, campaigning in "The Bloc of Peasants and Workers," were eliminated administratively by a vote of the Chamber, which invalidated their mandates. All this was an anticlimax to Iorga's repeated promise that he would accept power only if the people stood behind him.

Iorga made his literary discovery Sadoveanu a senator. He restored personal relations with Cuza, making him a senator also. He even made a deputy out of his brother Gheorghe.

The program of the Iorga government was ambitious in its educational reforms. They were undone by the Depression and lack of funds, Iorga had to enact a moratorium for the indebted peasantry. The Depression-ridden economy got worse as time advanced, but Romania's chief ally, France, was still prosperous. Would France help? Would the League of Nations (under French influence) help Romania? It would not be easy to obtain such help.

Things went badly for the Iorga government in France and the West. Much of the French press was hostile; Foreign capital was outraged because of the moratorium, fearing for their investments. Titulescu continued his skillful snipings against the Iorga government. However the most forceful opposition to the government in the West came from democratic circles, exacerbated by Argetoianu's conduct of the elections.

Argetoianu traveled to France as Minister of Finance. He found in Paris hesitations, doubts, stiff conditions, and questions. He broke out: "We were under Turkish domination, we were under German domination, now we are under the domination of foreign banks! Tell us, for how much did you buy us?" The answer was sobering: the French called the Romanians "ingrates!"[790]

---

[790]*Op. cit.*, p. 59.

Iorga was his own Minister of Public Instruction. He wanted to reform grade schools, which he hoped would become "the soul of the village," follow the spirit of Spiru Haret, and above all, remain faithful to *Sămănătorism*. In the high schools, Iorga wished to make the obtaining of a Baccalaureate straight-forward but more difficult. His draft law proposed that the directors of the high schools be elected and supervisors would come from the universities. He made new dispositions about high school curricula, new schedules and criteria for awarding grades. In the university Iorga stood for absolute autonomy.[791] All over Romania he wanted to organize libraries and museums in order to educate the public. His law stipulated, "All urban and village communes are obliged to organize a library and a museum."[792]

Unfortunately, this would be undone later, since there were no means to finance it.[793] There was not even money to pay teachers.[794] Argetoianu, behind Iorga's back, was cutting that money which was left over for education.[795] After Iorga's fall his educational laws would be undone by his friend, Dr. Angelescu.[796]

Iorga paid attention to the education and schools of Romania's minorities. During the electoral campaign in Cluj he said: "I will be (the Minister of Public Instruction); I will have approved every request from minority schools, because it is my conviction that every parent has the right to bring up his child in the way he wishes. But there is also another consideration: the state will also have the

---

[791]*Memorii*, vol. VI, pp. 126 and 133-134; also, *O viață de om*, vol. III, p. 255.

[792]Theodorescu, *op. cit.*, p. 274.

[793]Shortly after the downfall of Iorga's government, V.V. Hanes proposed to undo all of Iorga's educational reforms. *O viață de om*, vol. III, p. 256; also, *Memorii*, vol. VI, pp. 370-373.

[794]*O viață de om*, vol. III. p. 255. D. V Țoni, a former supporter of Iorga, head of the Teacher's Association, would, because of his protests about salary cuts affecting teachers, become one of those whom Iorga "loved to hate."

[795]*Memorii*, vol. VI, pp. 189 and 199.

[796]*Op. cit.*, vol. VII, pp. 156 and 176.

right to select those which will work for it."[797] The implications are far-reaching and clear. Iorga insisted that minorities should be proficient in Romanian, and should be loyal to Romania. Iorga was close to Dr. Angelescu, and Hungarians of Transylvania hated both of them, accusing them of attempting to Romanianize the Hungarians of Transylvania through education. How short are some memories! Few Hungarians remembered the Apponyi educational laws.

Dr. Constantin Angelescu, Romania's Ambassador in the United States during the war, exerted a powerful influence in America for the Romanian cause. He became a Liberal politician and pursued the old Liberal policy of secularizing and centralizing education. These were also Iorga's goals.

Dr. Angelescu became Minister of Education during the 1920s, and his measures met strong resistance especially in Transylvania. The loudest protests came from the Romanian Orthodox and Uniate Churches — which refused the Liberal state's intrusion into their prerogatives in education, which throughout Transylvania was strongly denominational.

The Hungarian and German Churches were traditionally bulwarks of nationalism and most schools were denominational. Thus the names of Dr. Angelescu and Nicolae Iorga were held up for execration. It seems both Iorga and Angelescu wished to achieve three goals: to secularize, Romanianize, and finally to centralize education throughout Romania. To consider their policies merely as anti-minority would oversimplify the issue.

Iorga established within the Ministry of Public Instruction a department for minorities headed by the Saxon intellectual Rudolf Brandsch. Brandsch's assistant was a Hungarian, Dr. Árpád Bitay.[798] Bitay, Iorga's favorite Hungarian intellectual, showed interest in Romanian culture and the common Hungarian and

---

[797]Iorga, *Credința mea*, p. 196. Dr. Angelescu was responsible for undoing Iorga's gestures towards the minorities. But Transylvanian-Hungarians put the blame on Iorga. As one of them wrote, during his administration, not a single Hungarian textbook was allowed to be printed. Lajos Gáldi, "Iorga," *Magyar Szemle*, no. 40. pp. 40-47.

[798]*Memorii*, vol. VI, p. 91.

Romanian past in Transylvania. But Bitay was rather unhappy with Iorga's preference for Brandsch to head his department of minorities, since the number of
Hungarians was almost four times larger than the number of Germans. Iorga's
preference followed from the decision taken by the Saxon Assembly early in
1919 in Mediaş to join Greater-Romania voluntarily. Iorga's position should be
clear, and identical with the Romanian position. Minorities can receive rights
and favors in proportion to their loyalty to the Romanian state.

After becoming prime minister, Iorga would continue his lectures in Romania, his lectures at the Sorbonne, at his schools in France and Italy, and elsewhere.[799] Many politicians (including Şeicaru) disapproved. Politics are a full-
time job, and a prime minister of a country in deep crisis cannot afford such
distraction.

The students during the Depression were ever ready to erupt. Iorga was the
President of Bucharest University. In 1930 and 1931, the "Student Day" (the
commemoration of the Student Strike of 1922) was duly celebrated, with an anti-
establishment undertone. The slogan was "Long Live Cuza!" The 13 March
1931 (the anniversary of 13 March 1906) ended also in outcries, "Long Live
Cuza!" Cuza despite his reconciliation with Iorga was never a restraining influence.

Yet when, in 1931, Iorga asked troops to use their firearms if necessary to
stop the university violence, anti-Semitic papers made the accusation that he
"wishes to shed blood!" During February 1932, the association of "students and
patriots" demanded a Cuza government and "the massacre of Jews." Finally,
disorders widened into a general student strike whereupon Iorga, on 15 March
1932, ordered the university be closed.[800] The Legion was behind these university disorders. It would be during the years 1932-1933 that the Legion would
make its decisive breakthrough into Romanian politics.

---

[799]Iorga resumed his lectures practically the day after his appointment as prime minister.
Memorii, vol. VI, p. 89 and 401.

[800]*Op. cit.*, pp. 34, 57, 64, 302, 305-307, and 354-357.

Iorga also had problems with communist students, calling themselves an association of "poor students." He promptly notified the police. C.C. Giurescu played an active role, asking for actions against the leader of the communist students, a certain Peretz.[801]

In July 1931, the most important banks in Romania declared bankruptcy. The first bank was the Banca Generală a Țării Românești, followed by Banca Berkovici, and Banca Franco-Română, finally Blank's Banca Marmorosch-Blank & Co. According to Iorga the cause of the failure of Blank was his expensive "love life," and his financing of politicians. It was suggested that the Blank Bank be bailed out. Iorga was deadly opposed. Liberals explained: "Iorga tries to ruin the Liberal banks."[802]

By February 1932, there were 300,000 unemployed in Romania.[803] This figure tells only part of the story. In a traditional society most of the agrarian unemployed do not make the statistics. The government was near insolvency. Salaries remained unpaid for months. Iorga instructed Argetoianu that for the coming Christmas the salaries must be paid. Argetoianu obligingly lied that he was doing just that. There was not a word of truth in it. When Iorga found out that people didn't even receive their Christmas paychecks, he confronted Argetoianu. Argetoianu's cynical answer was: "Of course, for the holidays everybody wants a little more money."[804]

During the spring of 1932, a new scandal rocked the Palace, centering around Prince Nicolae. Iorga liked Prince Nicolae too, who was an intelligent, yet irascible young man. If any car stood in the way of his sports car while driving the streets, he didn't consider it beneath his dignity to slap and kick the driver or pedestrians in public. His escapades were notorious. He fell in love with Miss Doleti Dumitrescu, the daughter of a viticulturist from Tohan in Buzău County.

---

[801] *Ibid.*, pp. 52-54.

[802] *Ibid.*, pp. 157, 169, 207-209, 240, also: *O viață de om*, vol. III, p. 253.

[803] *Memorii*, vol. VI, p. 314.

[804] *Ibid.*, p. 257; also, Mme. Liliana Pippidi-Iorga to the writer.

The *primar* (head of the village) married them, causing a scandal. He promised to leave Romania, but broke his promises to Iorga and Argetoianu. After this morganatic marriage Iorga and Argetoianu took responsibility before the king (and the Queen Mother) that he would leave the country. Carol, whose private life was not above reproach, was not tolerant with the love life of his younger brother. Queen Marie was furious. Argetoianu recalled the scene in Cotroceni Palace (Argetoianu remembers, in the very salon where Queen Marie was found in the arms of the Canadian Colonel Boyle). Queen Marie was uncontrollable, making hysterical outbursts, crying, laughing alternately. She called Prince Nicolae "ce misérable." Afterwards, she turned to Iorga and Argetoianu and cried out, "Vous êtes misérables aussi!" Finally she threw herself into Iorga's arms (but as Argetoianu remembers, she became irritated by Iorga's beard, and also by Iorga's cheap tie). Iorga pushed her away gently and told her: "Well, my lady, there is nothing left to say after the reception you offered to the representatives of the government of the country." Iorga and Argetoianu left; on the way out they decided to forget about the whole incident entirely.[805]

Nicolae was not charitable about his brother's love life either. More than once he referred to Carol's Palace as "Palestine."[806] Prince Nicolae would establish ties with the Legion to assure succession for himself in case his brother be overthrown. Prince Nicolae visited Iorga at home. People heard a very heated exchange as Iorga, in a crying voice, tried to convince Nicolae to annul his marriage in the national interest, or leave the country without delay.[807] A few months later, Nicolae left for Malta, and was seen together with Queen Marie in Belgrade and elsewhere, both being unwelcome and behaving scandalously.

---

[805]"Memoriile lui Constantin Argetoianu," in *Magazin Istoric*. vol. 1 (1967), nr. 4, pp. 82-85.

[806]The antics of Prince Nicolae were well-known. Because of this, and his connections with the Legion, the Crown Council in April 1937 deprived Prince Nicolae of all rights as a member of the Royal family.

[807]Mme. Liliana Pippidi-Iorga and Frasin Munteanu-Râmnic, who were both present at home during this passionate exchange, to the writer.

Iorga followed the Romanian foreign policy of the interwar period inflexibly, demanding respect for the existing treaties and the maintenance of the status quo. But Western platonic sympathies were with Maniu and democracy. With Iorga as prime minister, his editorials became synonymous with Romanian policy. Editorialized Iorga: "With France! On the side of France!"[808] Did this demonstrate his overwhelming sympathies for France? Or his cardinal principle: "Romanian foreign policy must be identical with that of her strongest ally?" Iorga didn't get along with Ambassador, Gabriel Paux, who later became the French ambassador to Austria (at the time of the Anschluss), and an ardent Gaullist. Paux sympathized with Maniu and democracy.[809]

In Paris, Iorga met Briand and Laval. In 1932, the Versailles System was still not shaken. With Hitler gaining strength, the French tried to establish a "Danube Union," (the idea of A. Tardieu), an alliance between Austria, Hungary, Czechoslovakia, and Romania, to prevent the Anschluss.[810] France opposed an Austro-German customs union. Iorga kept the line open to Poland and to Czechoslovakia. He met Marshal Josef Pilsudski, and Foreign Minister, Colonel Josef Beck, his old friend Professor Masaryk, and Foreign Minister E. Benes. Iorga also conferred with E. Venizelos.

Bulgaria followed a pro-Italian policy. Iorga, during a conversation with the Bulgarian ambassador, made the following statement: "Italy took the place of Austria in the Balkans. I love Italy, but I love above all the autonomy of my country." He met the representatives of the Armenian community in France. He considered the Armenians as a "friendly minority." Nevertheless, Iorga made it clear that Romania could offer the Armenians only moral help, because good relations with Turkey were in the Romanian national interest.[811]

---

[808] *Neamul Românesc*, 7 October 1931.

[809] Paux, was referred to by Iorga as "a proconsul." *Memorii*, vol. VII, p. 55.

[810] *Doi ani de restaurare*, p. 107.

[811] *Memorii*, vol. VI, pp. 42 and 282.

During these years there was some hopeful development between Romania and Hungary. The former Hungarian prime minister, the great statesman Count Istvàn Bethlen, (a scion of a great Transylvanian family), visited Romania, and tried to find some accommodation in this age-old quarrel. They agreed that the Russian danger represents a menace for both countries, but ultimately failed to come to meaningful agreement about Transylvania.[812]

With the USSR there was no real movement on Bessarabia during the Iorga government, although some fruitless negotiations were undertaken. A few years before, in a polemical article in the *Revue Slave* (Paris, 5th year, vol. 2, April 1928, p. 141), Iorga answered the Soviet historian Adamov, mockingly reminding him that since the USSR cannot be nationalist, it cannot invoke rights to Bessarabia based on diplomatic or military actions. Then Iorga explained that "the Soviet author manifestly demonstrates the nationalist and annexationist tendencies of the Tsars." Further, Adamov was ignoring the fundamental documents relating to Bessarabia, used by Rakovski and "the venerable Karamzin." Iorga pointed out that Adamov ignored his works, or if he took note, he misquoted them.

During Iorga's government the horrors of the collectivization of agriculture in Russia reached their peak. *Neamul Românesc* carried a kind of a diary of these horrors, daily reporting how peasants tried to flee across the ice-bound Dniester River, only to be shot down by border guards. They were left wounded to die on the ice, occasionally devoured by straying dogs before the eyesight of Romanian and Russian villagers. No help was offered on the Russian side or permitted from the Romanian side if they were lying on the Soviet half of the ice.[813] Romania protested to the League of Nations without result. Iorga paid a memorable visit to political prisoners in the Văcărești Prison accompanied by the sister of Mme. Catinca. They entered a prison cell where the inmates were communist women. (As Iorga recalls: "all of them were ugly Jewish women"). They were

---

[812]*Ibid.*, pp. 250-251. It was Count Hunyadi who championed the Hungarian-Romanian rapprochement. Iorga remarked that it is fitting that somebody bearing the name Hunyadi should be the champion of such reconciliation. *Neamul Românesc*, 14 April 1932.

[813]*Neamul Românesc*, 11 and 15 March, 8 April 1932.

intellectuals speaking several languages. When Iorga told them about the scenes on the ice of the Dniester River, the women quickly retorted in the classical Stalinist fashion: "That's the way one arrives to victory!" When Iorga answered that one should achieve victory with one's own sacrifice, not sacrificing others, bringing up the sacrifice of Christ, he was answered with mocking laughter. At this point, Mme. Lucia said that they may laugh over the sacrifice of Christ, but their laughter did not stop Christianity from enduring for 2,000 years. Iorga said that they may believe what they wish, but they should behave in an orderly fashion.[814] As Iorga told an American audience: "I cannot be certain that Bolshevism will never reach London or New York, but I am sure it will not get there by the way of Romania."[815]

In February 1932, Iorga celebrated the 200th anniversary of Washington's birth. He convoked a large meeting in the Ateneu, where, before the Ambassador of the United States, he paid tribute to the "citizen general," presenting George Washington as an example to be followed by any young Romanian.[816]

Iorga took constant stands against the legalization of gambling, abortion, and against concessions of telephone services to be given to a foreign (American) company.[817] He remained incapable of taking criticism, even during the years of Depression. Any criticism was considered by him "a press campaign against Iorga."[818] Two incidents deserve mention which took place in the Black Sea resort of Mangalia where Iorga acquired a modest home. When Iorga moved in, some people near his home suggested that it was bought out of bribes, Iorga remembered with indignation that these remarks from the gutter were uttered "within the earshot of my children!" Also in Mangalia, a delegation of unemployed called upon Iorga. Some yelled that they were desperate. Iorga, with his

---

[814]*Memorii*, vol. VI, p. 387.

[815]Iorga, *My American Lectures*, p. 79.

[816]*Neamul Românesc*, 24 February 1932; also, *Memorii*, vol. VI, p. 328.

[817]*Memorii*, vol. VI, pp. 10, 11, and 335.

[818]*Isprava*, p. 3.

temper, retorted that in that case they shouldn't have come to his home but should have continued to walk straight into the sea behind it. He was oblivious to what would happen when the media got hold of such remarks. When the media did get hold of it, he was surprised that it made such a big deal out of it.[819] Iorga should have understood that such remarks, whether uttered sincerely or unwisely, tend to weigh as a millstone around the neck of the politician. But then Iorga was no politician.

Iorga, as always, spent almost anonymously a great deal of his modest means on charities. He wasted a great deal of time answering almost every letter addressed to him during his time as prime minister. He looked personally into every request or grievance of any veteran.[820] A special light military plane brought daily his correspondence from Bucharest to Mangalia. Iorga never realized how much better his efforts would have been served if he would have appointed a trusted subordinate, and not wasted his time as prime minister.

Iorga first offered his resignation to the king in February. It was rejected. The end of the Iorga government came during May 1932. By then, Duca's Liberals had broken their alliance with Iorga. A French expert, Charles Rist, had been appointed to study Romanian economy. Iorga knew Charles Rist; he was the son-in-law of Iorga's professor, Gabriel Monod, from the *Ecole des Hautes Etudes*. Rist arrived in Bucharest at the beginning of May. The remedies offered by him were drastic. He did not bring loans from France or the League of Nations, but demanded drastic budgetary reductions. Iorga found this unacceptable. He wanted to cut salaries proportionately. Rist told Iorga that if salaries were not paid, one would see the consequences. Iorga retoned, "Anything will be better than the death of the patient." A few days later, Iorga found out that, thanks to another deception by Argetoianu, not even the salaries of the soldiers and army officers were paid. Since Carol went along with the remedies offered by Rist, Iorga resigned at the end of May 1932.

---

[819]*O viață de om*, vol. III, pp. 188 and 252.

[820]Iorga's correspondence for the years 1931 and 1932 show examples for his well-meaning but time-wasting efforts. BAR, *Corespondența lui Iorga*, 1931-1932.

Thus, on Iorga's advice, though not by choice, the king returned to the political parties.[821] The following months were a time of sad failure in Iorga's life. The king tried to sweeten it by offering Iorga a Ford (1932 model) as a birthday gift. It was a small consolation.[822]

Iorga was bitter. During these months, he churned out several books telling his life story and his side of the story concerning his administration and the aftermath. These books served the purpose of justifying how and why he had failed. The most important was Iorga's autobiography, *O viață de om așa cum a fost* ("A Life of a Man as it Was"), written in a beautiful Romanian. According to Mme. Liliana Pippidi-Iorga, Iorga wrote this book in response to an opportunistic biography written by Barbu Theodorescu, his librarian (an expedient admirer).[823] Mme. Catinca did not like this adulatory and selective biography, neither did Iorga. Mme. Catinca (more than Iorga) disliked Theodorescu. Iorga was more tolerant. He knew that Barbu Theodorescu was a flatterer, who occasionally stole books and documents from his library to sell; he made a living off Iorga. Later he became an opportunistic servant of the Communists. Apart from this, his personality was insufferable. He never allowed people to talk during a conversation His last adulatory biography of Iorga appeared in 1968. After the appearance of Barbu Theodorescu's Iorga biography in 1933, Mme. Liliana overheard more than once Mme. Catinca saying to her husband: "Do you really want that your life story left for posterity should be this one, written by him?" Thus, as on so many other occasions, Iorga acted on Mme. Catinca's advice.

In three months (from June to September) he wrote his *O viață de om așa cum a fost*. During the same months, Iorga wrote a parallel biography concentrating on politics, *Supt trei regi* ("Under Three Kings"). About his administration and the aftermath, Iorga wrote three books: *Credința mea* ("My Faith"), a collection of the speeches Iorga gave during his electoral campaign, and the program he intended to carry out. The story of the Iorga government was *Doi ani*

---

[821]*Memorii.*, vol. VI, pp. 380-384, and 400-413.

[822]Iorga always sat in the front next to the driver, and made a point of picking up hitchhikers.

[823]Barbu Theodorescu, *Nicolae Iorga* (București, 1933), and the other edition from 1943.

de restaurare ("Two Years of Attempted Restoration"). His third book, *Isprava* ("a tricky business, a tricky fear") referred to the aftermath, the return to the rule by parties. The books showed that Iorga was devastated by his failure. He was perhaps down, but he didn't consider himself to be out. This fighter didn't intend to write an apology it was rather to be a bulletin about his coming campaigns. But there was another result: by 1933 Iorga had lost even more faith in the relevance of democracy to the solution of Romania's problems.

The king's first attempt to establish a personal regime failed. Carol decided on a retreat, there was a return to the political parties, the system Iorga hated so much by now. Universal suffrage meant the return to power of Maniu's National Peasant Party.

On 6 June 1932 Vaida-Voevod formed a government, to be followed on 20 October by Maniu. But Maniu's integrity and constitutionalism was an anathema for Carol, he would resign. On January 14, 1933, a government was again established under Vaida. It lasted until the Neo-Liberal restoration in November, Iorga ridiculed the leadership of the National Peasant Party, which he now considered to be worse than the Liberals. Vaida became the "Pest (Budapest) adventurer"; "They dared to abuse His Majesty by name." "To humiliate the Crown, this is the most ardent desire of Mr. Maniu, the constitutional dictator of Romania." But Iorga continued menacingly: "The Crown has prerogatives!" Once the Vaida government fell, Iorga rejoiced. "The collapse of an adventure."[824] King Carol could live with that. It was Iorga who ran the danger of becoming a kind of respectable "hatchet man," for Carol. The elections were (even according to Iorga) cleaner than usual, but four elections in little more than five years weighed heavily on the Romanian scene. Iorga, still running within the framework of the "National Union," won 2.28% of the vote (5 mandates). Shortly after, Iorga's party reverted to its old name: The Nationalist Democratic Party.[825]

---

[824]*Neamul Românesc*, 14 June. I July, and 18 October 1932. Also, 10 January 1933.

[825]Argetoianu's Agrarian Party kept lingering on without significance.

Maniu and Carol could not get along. An ugly incident developed between Carol and the Minister of Interior, Mihalache, involving Colonel Gavrilă Marinescu, the legendary Police Prefect of Bucharest, appointed personally by the king, for obvious reasons. It was not a misplaced confidence. Colonel Marinescu took care of the king's business, his "extracurricular activities," to the satisfaction of His Majesty. Every prostitute, every gambling den, every shoddy dealer paid him a tribute in Bucharest, and after that Carol got his cut. When Mihalache (technically Colonel Marinescu's superior) tried to remove him, he flatly refused to quit, pointing out that the king appointed him, and he would obey only the king. It was Mihalache who had to resign.

This was not a confrontation between Colonel Marinescu and Mihalache, but a government standing on constitutional integrity and the kind Carol stood for. Iorga squarely sided with the king. Editorialized Iorga in those days: "In the system of universal suffrage, Mr. Mihalache is a truly great man." As rumors about Colonel Marinescu's dealings multiplied, Iorga wrote a devastating editorial entitled "Holy Filth." Feeling perhaps the incongruity of his role, Iorga started by explaining that the place of Colonel Marinescu was in the barracks, and that of Iorga at the university. Never taking a stand as to whether the charges levelled against Colonel Marinescu had bearing, Iorga concluded suggesting to Marinescu that he rent a cesspool, so all the pigs might dwell there at leisure.[826] One can only say again, that here were not the words of Iorga, the man with irreproachable integrity or the historian. This was Iorga the politician. And Iorga the politician was dead wrong again.

Meanwhile, the economy still did not improve. Iorga described the prevailing hardships in shattering words.[827] There were two more salary cuts (as high as 15%) for the public employees in 1932 and 1933, and two more moratoriums on agrarian debts in October 1932 and in April 1934. Control on foreign currency exchanges and severe import restrictions were enacted again and again. Only after 1935 would there be a very slow improvement.

---

[826]*Neamul Românesc*, 18 January 1933 and 6 March 1934.

[827]*Neamul Românesc*, 18 December 1932.

This was a worldwide phenomenon, not something Romania could change single-handed. The crisis would soon bring Hitler to power. Closer to home it would bring about the collapse of parliamentary trappings all over the "No Man's Land of Europe" with the exception of Czechoslovakia, where democratic institutions rested on sound foundations. The Depression would seed doubts even in solid parliamentary democracies in the West like France. Iorga quoted A. Tardieu, who emphasized the breakdown of parliamentary democracy. Wrote Iorga: "Not a miserable one says this like me, fighting for these (democratic) ideas here, abandoned in his fight from above and from below, but a French democrat, an incontestable democrat like Mr. Tardieu!"[828]

During March of 1933, the Skoda-Seletzky Scandal, an ugly revelation of corruption, espionage, and greed reaching high into the National Peasant government erupted. Iorga suggested that even Maniu must have been involved, but this was never proven. All this added to a demoralizing effect, ravaging even that little faith which was left in democracy. Soviet Communism was never so popular as during the 1930s. This might be true for the West, further away from Stalinism than Romania or Poland was. In Romania, it is hard to believe that even the genius of a Romanian Lenin could have dissipated the widespread antipathy. The genius of Mme. Ana Pauker certainly did not.

Romanians drew their conclusions in different ways, but the prevailing resentments against the political establishment ignited by unresolved problems exacerbated by the Depression, created a great deal of radicalism. By February 1933 formidable disturbances of the radical left took place. Leftist disorders on a large scale were a rarity in Romania. The workers of the oil industry in Ploiești struck, and strikes spread to the C.F.R. (the railroad marshaling yards) at the Grivița workshops in Bucharest. There were mass shootings of workers, martial law was declared. The brutality of the measures can be put at the doorstep of Vaida. But sustained Communist radicalism was inconceivable. Radical protest will come from the radical right — with sincerity and energy, but not in a con-

---

[828]*Neamul Românesc*, 7 February 1933.

structive fashion. In Romania, like almost everywhere in Europe, the right profited from the Depression politically (except in such remote places as Serbia or Greece). It would signal the breakthrough for the Legion.

Since the Legionaries would take Iorga's life, let's take a closer look at them. The only fascist movement founded under a holy icon, the Legion of the Archangel Michael was an original fascist movement. This movement introduced to Romania "New Nationalism," and took the struggle outside the Romanian political establishment.

Though very young at the time, this writer remembers well the turbulent days of the autumn of 1937, when the most hotly contested elections of the interwar period were being fought in Transylvania. As a child of eight, I visited with my parents some relatives and family friends in a village deep in the Apuseni Mountains, the heart of Romanian Transylvania, home of the *moți* and the birthplace of the legendary Avram Iancu. In the evening, when the intelligentsia gathered in the salon of the owner of the local saw mill (a Hungarian Jew), the venerable dowager duchesses of village society discussed but one thing, the visit of Codreanu, the dreaded Captain of the Iron Guard the next day. There was simply no limit to the abuse these ladies and gentleman, Hungarians of the Christian and Jewish faith, heaped on him.

One of the ladies who had seen him in Târgu Mureș the year before spoke of him as if she had seen the monster's head, but dared not describe it. Something of an adventurer by nature, I decided I must take a closer look at this fabulous being, whatever the cost. The next day, I proceeded to carry out this decision. My best friend, the son of the local Orthodox priest, older than I by four years, provided some pieces of peasant costume, and two conspirators headed towards the church yard, where the Legionary meeting was to take place.

The little square before the church teemed with peasants dressed in their colorful Sunday best. Many of them had walked dozens of miles to get there, and there were many, too many gendarmes from the local gendarme station. The Prefect of the district of Turda had, as officials of corrupt regimes often do, administered the pin-prick to exasperate rather than a blow to crush. He had forbidden Codreanu to speak, but had not outlawed the meeting itself. And a crowd of simple miserable peasants swelled until the churchyard could hold no more.

There was suddenly a hush in the crowd. A tall, darkly handsome man, dressed in the white costume of a Romanian peasant, rode into the yard on a white horse. He halted close to me, and I could see nothing monstrous or evil about him. On the contrary, his childlike, sincere smile radiated over the miserable crowd, and he seemed to be with it, yet mysteriously apart from it. Charisma is an inadequate word to define the strange force that emanated from this man. He was more aptly part of the forest, of the mountains, of the storms on the snow-covered peaks of the Carpathians, and of the lakes and rivers. And so he stood amid the crowd. He had no need to speak; his silence was eloquent. It seemed to be stronger than us, stronger than the order of the Prefect who denied him speech. An old whitehead peasant woman made the sign of the cross on her breast and whispered to us, "The Emissary of the Archangel Michael!"

Then, the sad little church bell began to toll, and the service, which invariably preceded Legionary meetings, began. Deep impressions, created in the soul of the child, die hard. In more than half of a century, I have never forgotten my meeting with Corneliu Zelea Codreanu.

The Legion and Corneliu Zelea Codreanu remain inseparable; he dominated the Legion even from beyond the grave. He was a Moldavian, like Iorga, born in Huși, in 1899, the son of Iorga's comrade in arms, Ion Zelea Codreanu, with whom Iorga (together with A.C. Cuza) had founded the Nationalist Democratic Party. The family originated from Bucovina. Zelea became the Romanianized version of Zelinski, a Ukrainian name. The mother of Codreanu, Elisabeth Brunner, was of ethnic German origin. Nevertheless, both father and son became sincere Romanian nationalists. Thus, the father Romanianized his name from Zelinski to Zelea and added Codreanu ("forester") to it, the profession of their ancestors.

During his youth, Corneliu, as the son of Iorga's prominent comrade-in-arms, was nurtured on *Neamul Românesc* and *Sămănătorul*, and Iorga's nationalist dreams. When the war broke out, young Corneliu, barely 17, volunteered, and marched alongside his father, a Romanian officer, into Transylvania, only to be returned by the commander because of his youth.

After the war, his father's (and Cuza's) political path separated from Iorga. Corneliu followed in his father's footsteps. In 1919, he enrolled at the University of Iași. Iași during these months was the center of leftist disorders. In addition, next door in Bessarabia, the Bolshevik menace was a tangible thing.

During the coming few years, Iași would become the center of the Romanian right. Young Codreanu contributed his share to this. When he entered the University, he started his political stand right away, as the protegée of Cuza and Sumuleanu. He would supply to Cuza's party, moribund after the break with Iorga, a lifeblood.

Since there would be little change in Codreanu's basic ideas and since his ideas would be decisive for the Legion (the Legion was a "leadership movement," where only the ideas of the leader count), let's consider them. The leitmotif of his ideas was a nostalgia for a pre-industrial past, gravely menaced by the realities of the twentieth century. He thought on the lines of integral nationalism, synonymous with Orthodoxy and with the "authentic Romanian," the peasant. By definition of the Legion, "Eminescu was the great precursor of the Legionary movement."

Codreanu was a monarchist to the end despite the bitter conflict with Carol II later. Since his nationalism was synonymous with Orthodoxy (or rather, with Orthodox mystique), he thought about the nation as a whole, with great emphasis on peasants and workers. One of the basic components of Codreanu's ideology was anti-Semitism, which he considered synonymous with anti-Bolshevism. There was an elitist trend in his ideas. Not that Codreanu would have looked down upon the lower classes! What he tried to accomplish was to elevate the lower classes, not levelling society to standards in which the Romanian lower classes were forced to live.

Codreanu was an activist. From its beginnings, the Legion believed in "direct action," all too often hasty direct action. But these were young people indeed. For them, the most important thing was to act.

By 1921 and 1922, calm was settling down on Iaşi. Codreanu went to Germany to continue his studies. Then he received news about the Romanian student body starting a strike, demanding a *Numerus Clausus*. He promptly returned, and assumed the leadership of this movement. What all too many students found offensive was the new constitution, enfranchising the Romanian Jews. The result was in March 1923, the foundation of the LANC (the National League of Christian Defense) in Iaşi. New recruits also came. Some Romanian splinter fascist groups joined up, but perhaps the most important recruit was a young student, Ion Moţa, who brought over the *Acţiunea Românească* ("Romanian Action"), with obvious Maurasian inspirations. Ion Moţa became the ideologue of the movement, his importance being only second to that of Codreanu.[829] But the "Liberal System" was in place; this meant "back to normalcy."

This was not what the youth expected from Greater Romania. The answer was the rise of a "New Nationalism." An unbridled violence and counter-violence came in the form of "direct action." Jews were attacked in Iaşi and elsewhere. The police prefect of Iaşi, Manciu, used brutal means in repressing them. He was shot by Codreanu; there was a wide-ranging plot to kill all Jewish leaders, etc. When put on trial, Codreanu and his companions were enthusiastically acquitted by the jury. The acquittal was not so much proof of anti-Semitism, but a protest against the existing Liberal system.

They represented a quest for social justice, based on Orthodoxy. The Bible has enough dynamite to blow up any social system. This kind of "archangelic socialism" when applied to practical issues was meant seriously, thus it became a challenge to the establishment. This brought inevitably a confrontation with Cuza. Codreanu saw it all coming. There was a generation gap between Cuza and his generation. Beyond that, Cuza was a good bourgeois; he wanted a party within the framework of the establishment. Codreanu wanted a movement to challenge the establishment. The inspiration for Codreanu was not the sterile anti-Semitism of Cuza, but *Gândirea*, ("The Thought") of the young religious

---

[829]The father of Ion Moţa was Iorga's companion in the struggle for the unification of Romania, the Orthodox priest from Orăştie, Transylvania.

philosopher Nichifor Crainic, and the religious philosopher Nae Ionescu and his journal *Cuvântul* ("The Word").

In 1927, as a result of some of his "direct action," Codreanu was in the Văcăreşti Prison. In the prison chapel, he received inspiration from the Icon of the Holy Archangel Michael, and he named his movement The Legion of the Archangel Michael, formally seceding from the LANC of Cuza. Within it he founded a combat organization, the Iron Guard, "against Jewish communists." In reality, it was intended to defend the movement against the repressive apparatus of the establishment.

What did Codreanu's movement stand for? Codreanu emphasized that his organization was no "party." Political parties became odious, with their unkept promises, politicking and corruption. Codreanu said that his organization was a "movement." When people asked for his "program," he rejected the concept with indignation as something synonymous with unkept programs. His movement "has no program, but faith!" His movement's Orthodoxy meant an *a priori* conflict with Iorga. If Iorga's relation with Orthodoxy was maintained through the nation, for Codreanu it was the other way around. Iorga's nationalism was based on *Sămănătorism*. But for Nae Ionescu or Nichifor Crainic, *Sămănătorism* was "not Orthodox enough." The Legion was permeated with Orthodox mysticism, not the nationalist "mystique" of Iorga.

The view of Romanian history was for the Legion a constant, unending passion. There were only two colors in it: black and white. That was their view of the world too. Sacrifice was something central. Thus, the strong death cult within the movement. Some people dismissed this as morbid. Maybe it seemed such from the vantage point of Mme. Lupescu's salon. But her salon and that Romania which surrounded her salon was in astronomical distance from that of the Romanian peasant. The Legion represented an almost evangelical protest against the gaps which existed between the two. The main program of the Legion was to create *omul nou* (a "new man"), who would bridge the gap between Codreanu's ambition and Romanian performance. In contemporary terms we would call this a cultural revolution. For the long term, the goal was the reward: salvation, the resurrection of Romania through Legionary victory. The Legion was to be everything that the present-day Romania was not: absolutely honest, rejecting the all-pervasive corruption of the establishment. Codreanu hated every form of venality with a passion.

More than half a century later (if one ignores the Legion's actions later), it is not easy to condemn the Legion's ideas. If only all Legionaries had been like Codreanu, Moța, or the Transylvanian Ion Banea were! Codreanu had no respect for democracy, equality, or for political parties, elections, *politicianism*, or "party programs." The Legion was anti-Semitic, but Codreanu was not rejecting the Jews on the basis of racism. Orthodoxy excluded any racist approach. Yet, Codreanu's anti-Semitism was pathetic. It bares every mark of Hitler's pathetic anti-Semitism, without racism. In their black and white view, the Legion extolled the Romanian nation, its two-millenia history. When Karl Marx envisioned a society outside the nation, when Albert Einstein pulverized time, or when Sigmund Freud exculpated sin with the subconscious — no wonder they obsessed the likes of Codreanu or Moța! Thus Jews had to become the absolute evil. They were imbued with satanic qualities by Romanian anti-Semites who saw them as poised against their dream world. Jews were also regarded as representatives of a detested "bourgeois world," and the twentieth century.

Here is a sample of the Legionary daily, to show to what extent the Legionaries hated the bourgeoisie. "There can be no place for the bourgeoisie in Legionary terminology, not only in linguistic sense, but because of a more imperative and rational cause, the ethical sense of the Legion. The bourgeoisie is nothing; it is a way of life hostile to Legionary existence: individualism. The Legion will resolve radically the problem of the bourgeoisie. By its very name the Legion of the Archangel Michael is at loggerheads with bourgeois individualism."[830]

The Legion flatly rejected the twentieth century in the name of God, Christ, and Orthodoxy, conducting an unrelenting struggle against (what they considered) evil. They almost always made correct appraisals of the Romanian situation. Only their goals were absurd which these realistic methods were supposed

---

[830]*Buna Vestire*, 10 January 1941.

to serve. Legionary terror squads recognized evil so, after committing violent acts, usually gave themselves up to expiate for the transgressions, committed in the name of a higher goal.

However, believers should not take it for granted that good ends can be achieved with evil means. The Legion appealed to the disoriented, bewildered, neglected young Romanians enrolling, out of proportion, to universities. It appealed also to their parents, and to many honest Romanians, bewildered by the realities of Greater Romania and the twentieth century. It appealed to the most dislocated segments of Romanian society under strain economically and psychologically. Later many peasants would come, disillusioned with Romanian democracy. Young intellectuals came for the same reasons: they were ready to try something radically new.

Little good could come in the long run from the Legion's Manichean view of the world. Was the Legion a precursor of those movements in the Third World today which generated strikingly similar responses to the challenges of the twentieth century in Iran, Kampuchea, or elsewhere? Today these movements determine the surface of our earth.

The Legion made up for its lack of education, power, financial means, its understanding of twentieth century realities, and finally, for its lack of discipline, with religious fanaticism and enthusiasm. The Crown, the political establishment, and the police bullies had everything the Legion lacked with one exception: both parties had an equal disposition to brutality and a lack of scruples. After 1933 the battle between the Romanian establishment and the Legion started. It would rage for the rest of the decade like an elemental storm, and the Legion would ultimately be consumed in it.

To what extent was the Legion inspired by Iorga's nationalism? This writer had a long talk with an elderly Hungarian pastor in Transylvania. I mentioned working on Iorga's biography, and Iorga's assassination by the Legion. The pastor retorted: "It served him right! He seeded Romanian nationalism, so, his chickens came home to roost!" Then: "Iorga reminded him on the Zauberlehrling of Goethe." Professor Jean Ancel (a native of Iaşi) of the Yad Vashem Institute in Jerusalem, also offered me his opinions about Iorga. They were more balanced and moderate than those of the Hungarian pastor, nevertheless, almost identical. While recognizing Iorga's intellectual greatness he said: "Although he changed his position on the Jewish question, it was he who created Romanian nationalism, inspired it, and he ultimately became the chief inspiration of the Legion."

Both opinions came from those considered by "the New Nationalists" as "hostile minorities." Arnim Heinen, in his monumental work, rejected the opinions of this writer, that the Legion might have had some populist inspiration, which all fascist movements had. Heinen thought that the inspiration of the Legion came straight from Iorga and Cuza. With all due respect, populism considers the nation a whole. It welcomes even the upper classes, provided they see the light. Populism rejects industrialization, and wants to establish the new, just social order around the peasantry. I had this in mind when I drew the parallel. Besides (as Heinen pointed out), I am in good company. Two experts on Romania, Henry Roberts and Stephen Fischer-Galați arrived at similar conclusions.

In my opinion, Iorga's nationalism resembles the "New Nationalism" of the Iron Guard, like Karl Marx resembles the stone-age Marxism of the Khmer Rouge, or that of the "Shining Path" in Peru. Or, like the liberalism of Thomas Jefferson or Alexis de Tocqueville resembles the liberalism of that Washington "apparatchik" Hubert Humphrey, whose enthusiasm was as systematic as his smile was.

The Liberals (or the National Peasants) wanted to make a direct transition to Western parliamentary democracy. Iorga's *Sămănătorist* approach (following Junimism, although less rationally than Maiorescu) suggested a more gradual, selective adaptation of Western institutions rather than the shock treatment of the Liberals.

The Legion became the nemesis of the hasty adaptation of the last sixty or seventy years, and its conclusion was a categorical, almost evangelical rejection of all that the Western industrial way of life stood for. Nae Ionescu and Nichifor Crainic rejected rationalism, rejected positivism, and there was no question of selective adaptation of Western values. For the "New Nationalism" Western culture and the "Romanian being," steeped in Orthodoxy, were incompatible. This "absolute" was the very essence of Codreanu. Like Islamic fundamentalism's (based on a similar failure to adapt Western institutions) rejection of the Shah's policies in Iran, the Legion considered Western values in Romania, to be nothing short of cultural rape.

No wonder that we hear the outbursts of Iorga against the "occult *Mioriţism* and *Sophianism*" and Orthodox mysticism of the Legion! Iorga was a romantic, but no abstract mystic. His nation was an "immense being" tangible and rational. Iorga's "*Sămănătorist* Man" is not identical with the "New Man" of the Legion. Consequently, the similarities between Iorga's nationalism and the "New Nationalism" of the Legion are superficial, but differences are basic.

First (during the spring of 1931), Codreanu welcomed Iorga's appointment as prime minister, because of Iorga's honesty. Codreanu's respect for Iorga's integrity was sincere.[831] But the by-election of Neamţ, and the violence of Tutova, where Argetoianu employed all the brutality for which he was renowned, disabused him. Then came the disorders caused by the Legion in Maramureş, Bessarabia, and in the Moţa region. This led to the dissolution of the Legion by the Iorga government in the spring of 1932.[832]

For Iorga, violence trailed the son of his erstwhile comrade-in-arms (Iorga considered him Ion Zelea Codreanu's "violent, mediocre son"). In 1931, besides the violence mentioned before, there was an attempt on a Jewish journalist, on a Secretary in the Ministry of Agriculture, and more. But Iorga never mentioned how greatly the Legion was provoked by the "forces of order!" The Legionaries were not representing Iorga's generation — or his "cultural nationalism." They were mostly in their 20s; nor were they part of the political establishment. Their very raison d'être was to challenge it. With organic development being the cor-

---

[831]Heinen, *op. cit.*, passim. Iorga was not unknown to the son of Ion Zelea Codreanu. He wrote in a Legionary circular: "His Majesty placed in his wisdom to the helm of the country a man of exceptional honesty." *Legionarii II*, No. 4, 20 May 1931; also, Heinen, *op. cit.*, p. 214, footnote.

[832]Iorga was less appreciative of Codreanu than Codreanu was of Iorga. *Memorii*, vol. VI, pp. 170, 352-358.

nerstone of Iorga's philosophy, the Legion and its activities became inconceivable for him. In 1934, the Transylvanian Orthodox Church spoke up against the Uniates.

Iorga, pointing out that he was Orthodox, took the side of the Uniate Church. In Bucovina on the other hand, the Uniate Church was strongly infiltrated by Ukrainian nationalists. Iorga took a stand against the Uniate Church of Bucovina. Neither stand had anything to do with faith, only to the extent to which it served as a vehicle of Romanian nationalism.[833]

As for Legionary mysticism, Iorga always showed a healthy abhorrence of everything abstract. He was a Latin rationalist, and explained the Legion's mysticism: "Codreanu was a Slav."[834] Iorga's "ego" did not allow any challenge from the "New Nationalism." In his eyes, he was instrumental in building Greater Romania and its nationalism was to be based on *Sămănătorism*. Iorga rejected Legionary violence as "anarchy," and he hated anarchy. He was also the protector of the Versailles System, and devoted to France politically and culturally. After the rise of Hitler, Iorga would turn with hatred towards the German orientation of the Legion.

He was deeply resentful of the challenge that the Legion represented, Iorga's hatred, fueled by his personality, became irreversible. It continued relentlessly until the Legionary Death Squad fetched him.

During the coming years, Vaida hoped to find common ground with the Legion. Even Averescu did. Even Carol would try to co-opt the Legion, but the Legion would remain inflexible. There was no co-opting by the establishment. Instead, it stood for radical social reform and social justice.

How different the Legion's nationalism was, two examples will show. Pacifism was inconceivable for Codreanu. He proclaimed not to be interested in peace, but in war (against evil). Thus, Iorga remembered: French pacifist intellectuals arrived in Bucharest, and were received promptly with a "direct action"

---

[833] *Neamul Românesc*, 3 November 1934 and 31 January 1937.

[834] *Neamul Românesc*, 7 April 1934.

by the so-called "Anti-Judeo-Masonic Committee" (of Legionary inspiration and membership). As the couple left their hotel, in Iorga's words: "they were ambushed by three brutes who spat on Mme. La Fontaine's dress," etc. Iorga and Argetoianu visited the La Fontaines to apologize, resorting to what Iorga considered a white lie. They explained, "those who committed the outrage were Bolshevik agents coming from Bessarabia," and their apologies were accepted. As Iorga explained: "he had to say this to save the face of the country."[835]

On 30 January 1933, the noisy torchlight parade passing under the Brandenburg Gate announced the *Machtergreifung* of Hitler. The great drama of the Christian West had begun, and the man who came out of nothing would lead Europe towards tragedy.

Iorga had no illusions. His first editorial (after Hitler's seizure of power), "Naziism on the March," spoke of Hitler's aggressive naiveté. Hitler was, for Iorga, "the chief of all discontents, and the symbol of all hopes of the German people." Financed by heavy industry, some naive illusionists hoped, Hitler would proceed "to put to death the Jews, take the Polish corridor, and the Rhineland."[836]

Where would Hitler go? Would he be co-opted? Or would Hitlerism become only a passing phenomenon? Stalin thought that. From now, because of the way Nazis conducted politics (especially in Romania, with her oil, her long border with the USSR, and large German and Jewish minorities), Nazi foreign relations and meddling into Romania's internal affairs would become inseparable, even complimentary. By now, many Romanian supporters of democracy abandoned it. Manoilescu, Vaida, Ghelmegeanu, A. Călinescu, started out in democratic ranks. It was surely something more than just opportunism which made them to come over to authoritarianism. From 1933 on the Legion was steadily advancing, despite the systematic repression.

---

[835]*Memorii*, vol. VI, pp. 195 and 198.

[836]*Neamul Românesc*, 8 February 1933

In the beginning, the establishment showed sympathy and made efforts to co-opt the Legion. Vaida, as Minister of the Interior, allowed a Legionary' construction project at Vişani, then later forbade it. Averescu visited a Legionary construction site, the future "Green House." So did Italian Fascists. But the Legion would not turn to Mussolini. Italian Fascists were never anti-Semitic enough for Codreanu. The kind of anti-Semitism the Legion was looking for they would find in Berlin. If quite a few politicians sympathized with the Legion, that was because its youthful idealism. The Legion lived the lives these people remembered from their youth. Now they could not live such lives. They were too comfortable and corrupt, and had too much vested interest in the existing mediocrity. But many young Romanians were touched by the Legion. In 1935, Gheorghe Furdui, the Legionary student-leader, was elected as President by the Student body of Bucharest. In October 1935, another Legionary, Traian Cotigă, became the president of the Students of all Romania.

Carol was temporizing. He would approach the Legion more than once to co-opt. But in the black and white world of the Legion there was no room for "co-option." In April 1933, Codreanu sent his greetings to Hitler to express the solidarity of the Legion after the reaction of the world to the beginnings of anti-Semitic excesses. In May 1933, a new wave of anti-Semitic disorders hit the Bucharest University. Iorga commented on the disturbances fomented by the Legion, asking, "Is this the authority of the state?" In the future, Iorga would often refer to the Legion as "Hitler's agency."[837] Finally, the real problem, the over-production of unemployable pseudo-intellectuals was recognized by Iorga.

Iorga would continue his stand against Naziism. "For Hitler, only the needs of the day exist." What Hitler wants is "Lebensraum" Wrote Iorga about the first Nuremburg rally in 1933: "They sound like the trumpets of the Apocalypse — it is on its way."[838]

---

[837]Iorga continued his outbursts against the Legionary uniforms appearing on the streets of the country. *Neamul Românesc*, 17 February and 30 July 1933.

[838]*Neamul Românesc*, 14 April and 12 September 1933.

Hitler's rise to power caused a strong reaction amongst the German minorities of Southeastern Europe; Iorga was perturbed by the Saxons and the Swabians. Jickeli, the Transylvanian-Saxon leader called on Hitler. The Lutheran Bishop Glondys was attacked by Iorga because of his "Pan-German" and anti-Versailles stand. Iorga called him "Glondys, an old enemy." The Catholic Bishop of Timişoara, Pacha, called also on Hitler. This seemed to Iorga as a "Sudeten" type of movement,[839] which he considered unacceptable and disloyal. Iorga noted with fury a parade in Sibiu with "Heil Hitler!" greetings, and noted Saxons displayed the Swastika in Braşov.[840] Iorga wrote to a Romanian intellectual, Toma Cornea in Sibiu; praising his remark that he prefers a Jew to a Hitlerite Saxon, Iorga said: "You see the danger where it really is." He continued that he was as much against a "Mussolinite, as against a Hitlerite dictatorship, and their influences on the Romanian nationalists."[841] Iorga remembered a German Jew, arriving to England, who considered anti-Semitism in Germany a passing phenomenon, proclaiming that he still considers himself a German. Not everybody was so hopeful. The old friend of Iorga, Professor Tiktin wrote to him in despair, telling about his sufferings, and asking for Iorga's help. Being now over 80, he regretted having lived so long. Iorga immediately stepped in to help, trying to mobilize King Carol, and to find for Tiktin a position at his institute in France.[842]

After Hitler's arrival to power, the king and the political establishment consulted with Romania's allies. Their purposes seemed to coalesce. The stabilization of the internal situation in Romania became mandatory; The new prime minister designate, Duca, traveled to France, which was worried that after the rise of Hitler, the whole unstable "No Man's Land" of Europe would slip into fascism. Duca was glad to give the necessary assurances that the Romanian political establishment was in control. This was the kind of language Paris wanted

---

[839]*Neamul Românesc*, 29 March 1933 and *Memorii*, vol. 7, pp. 39, 46, and 146.

[840]*Neamul Românesc*, 14 October 1933 and 3 February 1934.

[841]*Arhivele de Stat Bucureşti*, Fond Nicolae Iorga, Dosar 4, F. 18.

[842]*Memorii*, vol. VII, pp. 85 and 94.

to hear. In December 1933, for the fifth time in six years, elections were held in a violent, corrupt fashion, with two goals: a violent crackdown on the Legion, and on the National Peasants. The result was a foregone conclusion. But Duca would hardly enjoy his triumph. On 29 December 1933, he was murdered by three Legionaries. The three became a Legionary legend, the *"Nicadori,"* a name formed by the initials of their first names. Iorga called Duca's murder an "odious crime."[843] Martial law was once more declared, and a violent repression of the Legion started. After a transitory Liberal government, in the beginning of January 1934, Gheorghe Tătărescu (the brother of Ştefan Tătărescu, the fascist leader) formed a neo-Liberal government. His government would bring stability to the Romanian scene for almost four years.

The new prime minister was an enigmatic and versatile character, cooperating with Carol, the Iron Guard, the Nazis, and finally with the Communists, yet, he died in the terrible Communist prison of Sighet. Now he stated a move towards Corporatism and fascism. The Liberals drew some conclusions from their failure in the late 1920s, coupled with the experiences of the Depression. The new Liberal policy was to be very un-Liberal. It meant forced industrialization (emphasizing heavy and armament industries) to be financed not through private banks as in the 1920s, but by the National Bank. Most of the new industries were in private hands, like Max Auschnit, Nicolae Malaxa, Mihai Constantinescu, Dimitriu Mociorniţa, and the king, who was the Royal industrialist (supported by the excellent business talents of Mme. Lupescu). They were protected from foreign competition by high tariffs, capital was mostly domestic. All this put a heavy' burden on the shoulders of the peasantry. Manoilescu, the President of the National Bank, leader of the "National Corporalist League," was the ideologist of this program. He knew that such burdens could never be accepted voluntarily by the people, especially in the fashion the industrialization was to be carried through. The necessary coercion was proposed in the framework of a cooperative fascist state.

---

[843] *Neamul Românesc*, 2 January 1934. But Iorga understood the terror directed against the Legion "did not destroy the roots of the evil," see *Istoria Românilor* (Bucureşti, 1939), vol. X, p. 487.

But the ultimate consequences of this policy (called "neo-Liberal") were not realized until 1938, and only because of the dangerous growth of the Iron Guard competition. The agrarian scissors were set at an angle of 59.4% as late as 1940, and the living standard was 33% to 64% lower than it had been in 1916. Romanian living standards were the lowest in the Balkans. The government promulgated ever-improved moratoriums on peasant debts, but it applied its repressive apparatus for the collection of taxes, with a ruthlessness the Romanian lands had not seen since the Phanariot rule. Many of the poor had their last belongings taken away to be sold at public auctions. A typical announcement from the official paper, *Monitorul Oficial*, about a coming auction is instructive: "On 11 September, there will be a public auction of two shirts, three cracked cups, a damaged glass, a thimble, two crutches with the names of Costache and Gradu engraved on them, a reel of threads, the saucer bottom of a damaged glass, and a purse with the content of two lei in it."[844]

As a stark contrast, Bucharest was rebuilt. New boulevards opened, high rises rose, almost baby-skyscrapers. Bucharest turned into a typical Third World capital, an abyss separating it as always from the misery of the countryside. The real power rested with the king, and with the "Second Camarilla" usually identified by its core: Ernest Urdăreanu. This was to be the industrializing Camarilla. New members included the Jewish industrialist Max Auschnit, and others.

Iorga would become increasingly identified with this Camarilla. To what extent, "in spite of himself"? Corruption and cynicism were also on the increase; the most prestigious general of the Armed Forces, Ion Antonescu warned like Cassandra in vain about the unpreparedness and corruption within the Romanian armed forces.[845]

With Hitler's arrival to power, the world (and Iorga) was approaching collective tragedy at an ever faster pace. We shall consider Romania's foreign relations, and Iorga's reaction to the coming ordeal. Hitler set into motion a process to carry out his plans laid out in *Mein Kampf*. Iorga foresaw it, writing that

---

[844]Roberts, *op. cit.*, p. 80 and Lebedev, *op. cit.*, p. 16.

[845]*Memorii*, vol. VII, p. 208.

Germany was not happy with the borders which were the outcome of the War. She was ready to start another, even more terrible war. The steps would be the annexation of Austria, the destruction of Czechoslovakia, then Hitler would try to get hold of the Polish corridor. When Hitler promised "25 years of peace," Iorga answered: "He doesn't believe Hitler, but in *Mein Kampf*."[846]

The rise and the appeal of Naziism was not the problem of Romania alone. Much of Europe emerging from the Depression was dazed by the lure (or fear) of fascism here, of Communism there, and lost its patience with democracy and its slowness in resolving problems. Europe, in many cases headed by old men, now offered to the dynamism of "young" fascist leaders, more than one opportunity. Hitler and Mussolini did not intend to miss any of these. But Hitler, a product of the First World War, kept a watchful eye on the United States. Also in 1934, he cracked down on the leftists within his party during the "Blood Purge." Commented Iorga: "General Schleicher was shot," then, "some of the close friends (of Captain Roehm) were found in the company of young boys with special morals" (Iorga could not resist a pun on Symbolist literature he hated so much) "who were not even Symbolist poets." Then he concluded, "and so, the Nazi ship of state is steering towards those thousand years which Hitler just proclaimed yesterday."[847] At the death of Field Marshal Hindenburg Hitler proceeded to promote himself to "Führer und Reichskanzler." Iorga wrote a blistering editorial, "Führer und Verführer": "Will Adolf I cross the Rhine, invade Poland, and annex Vienna? Or will God's blessing save us from the catastrophe he is preparing for us?"[848]

With the enactment of the Neutrality Act in the United States, Hitler felt easier. He proclaimed rearmament, reintroduced the draft, and allotted 90 billion Marks for the purposes of German rearmament. In 1935, a referendum in the Saar region was another victory for Hitler. Iorga, not happy about the outcome,

---

[846] *Neamul Românesc* 23 January, 31 March, and 11 April 1935.

[847] *Neamul Românesc*, 3 July 1934.

[848] *Neamul Românesc*, 4 August and 5 August 1934.

understood: "The voice of blood is stronger than any consideration, and this intimate moral element reaches beyond any material advantage." But he was also worried that this happened "two steps away from Metz."[849]

Then, in March 1936, Hitler made his move: the occupation of the Rhineland. France was before elections; there was a "caretaker" government. France was also divided, but she couldn't have moved without England, and England was not about to move. Commented Iorga: "A treaty' was broken again, and we have the reality of Hitler's assurances of '25 years of peace,' and 'respecting boundaries.'" He concluded that, "Treaties in Berlin have the value of a piece of paper."

With the occupation of the Rhineland, the credibility of the Little Entente was destroyed, and the defenses of France (and the defenses of Romania) were swept away. But in England, the prime minister, Stanley Baldwin, also read *Mein Kampf*, and he commented, "If Hitler moves East, I shall not break my heart."[850] The policy was more accentuated under Neville Chamberlain, hoping to deroute Hitler toward the East. France, more exposed to a possible German attack, could not act alone. As for the French upper classes this writer remembers from his childhood the atmosphere among friends of the family in Blois, Tours, and Orléans (and *patisserie* sweets practically melting in the mouth). Those who were present during afternoon outings remarked, that the air of the Touraine is "so sweet that it puts one practically to sleep..." The mood was consecrated by the phrase: "Better Hitler than Blum!" The counterpart of these people in England knew that even if the English would win the coming war, the British Empire would not survive. Appeasement became the order of the day.

Iorga would support appeasement (since the "appeasers" did not wish to upset the status quo in Romania, and a destructive war between Hitler and Stalin would not have broken Iorga's heart either). It did not work out that way. The

---

[849]*Neamul Românesc*, 19 January 1935.

[850]Robert Keith Middlemas and John Byrnes, *Baldwin* (London, 1969), p. 947.

succeeding events of 1936 would open the road towards the Hossbach Conference.

During the French elections (which the Popular Front won), Iorga was apprehensive. After Leon Blum became prime minister, Iorga commented with satisfaction that he sounded in Geneva like Laval before. Blum spoke for peace, the inviolability of frontiers, and respect for treaties, Iorga added, "One cannot imagine how power transforms." Yet, as French enterprises were occupied by workers, he deplored the excesses. "Enough is enough!"[851]

If the upheaval was manageable in France, it brought civil war in Spain. Iorga was always mistrustful about the temperament and maturity of the Southern fringe of the European continent. He approved A. Salazar in Portugal, and welcomed by General I. Metaxas in Greece. When the Spanish Republic was proclaimed, Iorga gave a warning: a republic demands a middle class and a few intellectuals cannot replace it. When this will become manifest, anarchy will take over. Five years later when anarchy broke loose, Iorga wrote: "Spanish Fascism will try to enslave thought as any dictatorship does." But Iorga was appalled by the spectacle of unfolding horrors. He commented that Soviet influence doesn't explain it. National character is the explanation. But he asked: "What was education doing in Spain?" When Franco made his *pronunciamento*, Iorga commented, "It is deplorable for the army to intervene in politics, but if politics become a sport for murderers, this intervention becomes mandatory."

As anarchists went rampant in Catalonia and Barcelona's churches were burning, Iorga called them "the most deranged example of human degeneracy," and asked if people were outraged about the flames consuming the cathedral in Rheims, why are people silent now? Never approving Spanish fascism, Iorga (with a significant nuance), nevertheless clearly stated that: "I am with the Spanish Army!" Yet, as Iorga saw it, the real background to the Spanish Civil War was: "Two peoples, the Germans and the Russians, who hate each other with passion. Both were "odious dictatorships." Both dictatorships were "socialist ones." He didn't understand why Spain offered her territory and her army "to be

---

[851] *Neamul Românesc*, 9 and 18 July 1936.

the terrain to display these fierce hatreds." (Iorga failed to comment on the nefarious role the "Latin brother," Fascist Italy, played in the Spanish tragedy during the Civil War.)[852]

And with this we arrive at Iorga's relationship with Mussolini. When the Austrian Nazis assassinated Dolfuss, Mussolini sent Italian troops to prevent an Anschluss. Iorga was in agreement. He commented that "Dolfuss's crime was that he wished to keep Austria out of the clutches of German imperialism," and "his murderers were sent from there where one more killing doesn't really matter." But Mussolini was bound on unlimited expansion. The next prospective victim was to be Albania. When in 1934 Mussolini sent his fleet on a demonstration before Albania, Iorga protested, (as he put it) despite his sympathies towards "Latin" Italy.[853]

A few months later, came the assassination of King Alexander I of Yugoslavia, and French Foreign Minister Barthou. Iorga knew that both were irreplaceable in a stand against Nazi and Fascist aggression in the Balkans. But, like the rest of the world he directed his fury on Hungary, and not on the real culprit: Italy. Iorga attacked Gömbös, the prime minister of Hungary, writing: "the world opinion rejects terrorism, and Gömbös and his friends will find this out soon enough."[854] In the increasing controversy between Mussolini and Yugoslavia, Iorga was in a dilemma. He had to support the Little Entente, he was friendly towards Yugoslavia and had to uphold the Versailles System. Yet, he felt a strong Latin solidarity towards Italy.

While following an unbroken line of hostility against Hitler and Germany (it was a rarity that Iorga could establish even civilized relations with visiting Germans, diplomats included), he had good relations with the German chargé Pochhammer, the exception rather than the rule. In other instances, he was not

---

[852]*Neamul Românesc*, 18 April 1931, 29 May, 23 July, 22 August, and 10 December 1936, and 19 February 1937.

[853]*Neamul Românesc*, 4 July 1934 and 2 August 1934.

[854]*Neamul Românesc*, 11 and 12 October and 27 November 1934.

only unfriendly, but rude with visiting German diplomats, even with scholars if they supported Naziism.[855]

The evolution of Iorga's position towards Italian Fascism was complex. We saw his hostility towards Fascism during the 1920s. Iorga's temperament was too individualistic to find accommodations with any dictatorship. But, if Iorga was so hostile towards Hitler, how could he find a compromise with Italian Fascism?

First, although Iorga was (partly) educated in Germany, and spoke a good German, yet, he was a Latin, deeply rooted in French culture, also, a true friend of France, with everything this implied culturally. German actions (between 1914-1940) did not help. Then, Iorga for a long time considered the Versailles System menaced more by Germany and Hitler than by Mussolini, despite Mussolini encouraging Hungarian revisionism since 1927. Iorga read *Mein Kampf*, perhaps more carefully than many others did. Hitler's ideas about "superior nations" and nations "with the lesser cultural significance;" Hitler's quest for "Kultur," his racism, and the lack of respect and the fate he reserved for small nations were repellent for Iorga. Iorga remained very consistent, always repeating that he wouldn't believe any peace pledge made by Hitler, but "I believe in *Mein Kampf*" Did Mussolini respect small nations more than Hitler did? Iorga would stand up for Albania and other small nations in the future, and for Romania in the face of Mussolini. Yet, Iorga overestimated the sentiment of Latin solidarity which meant so much to him and so little to Mussolini. Iorga was also influenced by his subjective love for Italy. The rude awakening would come in the spring of 1939 when he had to face facts. Mussolini was full of contempt towards the

---

[855]*Memorii*, vol. 7, pp. 229-230. This was true for Gamillscheg's visit in 1934 He had close professional contacts with Gamillscheg before; now, not only did Iorga avoid any contact, but managed to be studiedly rude. The Nazi's answer was coming. Gusti was awarded a "kudo" by the University of Leipzig in 1935. When suggested that the same honorary degree be awarded to Iorga, the Nazi cultural hierarchy refused. The president of Breslau University even suggested that the degree Iorga earned at the University of Leipzig be taken back. The Charge d'Affaires Pochhammer (later the German Ambassador, Dr. W. Fabricius) opposed this, pointing out that, although Iorga's attitude was "far from friendly towards Germany and the Nazi regime," he is not someone to offend. Auswartiges Amt, Politiches Archiv, Bukarest Botschaft, 1934-1936.

"brotherly," "sisterly," "brother-in-law" nations, dividing the world into totalitarian and democratic nations instead. A deeply hurt Iorga warned him: One kind of leader wants expansion and war; the other kind want peace. But even in totalitarian countries people want peace regardless of their leaders. In peacetime, their desire for peace can be suppressed. "But, when there is war?... Here is the risk!"[856]

Iorga, in one of his zigzag type of political fantasies envisioned a common "Latin destiny" in which Italy and France would unite in love. Once more, he took his own desires for reality. But there was something else. Since 1927, Mussolini supported Hungarian revision. Influenced by his ego, Iorga thought that his personal diplomacy as a Latin, supporting Mussolini, might counterbalance much of the Hungarian influence in Rome. Thus, he may "serve Romania." Iorga considered this his "mission," and (like many others did in contemporary Europe) hoped that Mussolini would counterbalance Hitler. His personal opinions about Mussolini or Italian policies were by no means identical to statements Iorga pronounced between 1935 and 1940. However in 1934, according to Iorga, Mussolini was wonderful, his concepts were "Roman" concepts. Iorga would sooner have seen Hungarians try to fulfill their revisionist dreams with the help of Hitler rather Mussolini. He pointed out that Mussolini is one thing, Hitler another. Some people mentioned them together but this is wrong. Mussolini was a fighter of the First World War, a capable orator and intellectual, a powerful thinker who created something out of nothing. Hitler was none of these. Hitler had no relation to culture, no talents, or achievements. Thus, "only barbarians can confound Mussolini with Hitler." During the first meeting of Mussolini and Hitler in Venice, Iorga benevolently agreed that Mussolini, as an ancient Roman *dux gentium*, received Hitler and didn't ascribe any greater significance to their meeting.[857] This was the hope of other Conservatives during the period in Austria, Hungary, and in Poland. Iorga was for a strong alliance with the Western democracies and as close as possible relations with the United States, and he

---

[856]*Neamul Românesc*, 14 April 1939.

[857]*Neamul Românesc*, 27 March 1936, 26 April 1933 and 22 June 1934.

hoped lining up with Italy against Nazi Germany. So were some Western states-men. In trying to smith an alliance with Italy, one must keep in mind Italian weaknesses and her unreliability. During Mussolini's time, Fascist parades pre-sented Italy as a kind of superpower. Mussolini was making great noise on the international scene. He was a "showboat" (what the French call "vedette") with his charades, grandstanding, and dramatic gestures. What came out of this at the moment of truth? Gregorovius described the political Italian as the composition of Cesare Borgia, the Condottieri, thinking with the mentality of Machiavelli. Iorga imputed to Mussolini the qualities of Caesar, but history shows something different.[858]

Mussolini could find support for his ambitions only with Hitler and not the West. Iorga began to realize this, even in his paper. During the fall of 1936, the Axis came into being. But in those months Iorga again gave proof of his naivete. When during September of 1936 the Byzantine Conference took place in Rome, Iorga was greatly flattered that Mussolini came, and called him aside: "Venga Iorga."

Iorga wrote to Cuza, starting his letter by pointing out that he did not like to talk politics with him (because of Cuza's unequivocal Hitlerist line and his own opposition to Naziism). He continued, praising Mussolini and remembering how "Mussolini, in variance with your German" (Hitler) had called him aside,

---

[858]Iorga spoke about "Mussolini's modesty'" and Mussolini's "fighting corruption in Italy." *Neamul Românesc*, 3 November 1936. The Italian ambassador wrote reports from Moscow, Mussolini didn't look into the reports for three years. Yet, almost even' day he found time to scrutinize press photographs and documentary movies about himself, and gave detailed orders about poses in which the Duce was to appear. Denis Mac Smith, *Italy: A Modern History* (Ann Arbor, 1969), p. 465. Concerning Mussolini fighting corruption, Smith said that corruption became "normal, unconcealed, regulated, and even taxed." Page 397. Iorga expressed his conviction about Mussolini's modesty'. Nicolae Iorga, *Idei asupra problemelor actuale* (Bucureşti, 1935), p. 108. One should remember the melodramatic scene between him and Emil Ludwig, when the Duce remembered how he was wounded during the War.

"Venga Iorga!" He asked Cuza naively whether Hitler was ready to talk so nicely to Goga, as Mussolini had to him?[859]

A few weeks after the "Venga Iorga" encounter, Mussolini endorsed Hungarian revisionist claims in the strongest manner. Iorga reacted against this very strongly.[860] He expressed his wishful thinking: "Never to do any-thing against France, and never shoot on an Italian soldier."[861] One cannot help remembering Goethe: "Du meinst zu schieben, aber du wirst geschoben!"

Iorga saw the relations between the Romanian right and Naziism and Fascism correctly: "Our right is Hitlerist, not Mussolinite." The problem would arise when Mussolini became a "Hitlerist." Iorga tried to suggest that the noise of the Romanian right would help only Hungarian revisionist designs.[862] For Mussolini (spoken to his son-in-law, Count Ciano), smaller nations were only "pawns" on international chessboard, and we know the fare of which is to be taken.[863] Iorga dismissed Mussolini's support for Hungarian revisionism cleverly, saying. "Mussolini is smart saying these things, and the Hungarians are stupid believing it."[864]

In November 1932, France and the USSR signed a non-aggression pact. After Hitler came to power, the Little Entente was formalized, to be followed a year later (in February 1934) by the Balkan, pact.[865] In June 1934 the Little Entente (including Romania) established diplomatic relations with the USSR. The architect of this was Titulescu.

---

[859]*Memorii*, vol. VII, pp. 356-361, and also, BAR, *Corespondența lui Iorga*, vol. 103 (1936) Doc. 1.

[860]*Memorii*, vol. VII, pp. 366-368.

[861]*Op. cit.*, p. 155.

[862]*Neamul Românesc* , 3 March 1937.

[863]C.A. MacCartney, *October Fifteenth* (Edinburgh), vol. 1, p. 346.

[864]Iorga, *Pentru Italia și ce ne leagă cu Italia* (București, 1935).

[865]In an editorial (*Neamul Românesc*, on 14 February 1934), Iorga expressed doubts about the Balkan pact: it would not be the "Ghazi" (Ataturk) who would defend Timișoara and Oradea against Hungarians, and deplored the absence of Bulgaria.

Iorga considered reestablishment of relations with Russia natural, "provided the Russians are sincere." He welcomed the French Foreign Minister Barthou to Bucharest in the only serious French attempt to counter Nazi expansion to Southeast Europe.[866] Iorga could not bring himself to show trust towards the USSR, and continued to reject any pretense of proletarian internationalism as a motivating force in Russian policies. He saw there always integral chauvinism. Way ahead of many contemporaries (even many communists), Iorga wrote: "he is not against communism, not against the Russian people," but against the Mongolian crudity and "the Russian leadership whose methods remain unchanged, regardless of the regime."[867] Iorga was always looking at Russia through historical experience. So he opposed the policies of Titulescu (personal animosity weighing heavily), in his attempts to conclude a defensive alliance with the USSR without Russians renouncing their claims to Bessarabia. Although even if Romania had become the ally of Russia, this wouldn't have stopped the Russians reannexing Bessarabia. The Russians always imposed their will when they were "in the driver's seat."[868] By the fall of 1936, Titulescu's concepts were discredited. The power shifted with the German occupation of the Rhineland, and Titulescu overplayed his hand in Spain.

Mussolini now started a war of plunder and conquest in Ethiopia. The evolution of Iorga's position is interesting. Iorga, the nationalist, the anti-colonialist, took his first stand politely but unequivocally against the Italian ambitions. As he explained, the Italian youth is wonderful, but Iorga regretted every drop of blood spilled in Ethiopia in vain, since colonialism was a thing of the past. After the Italian invasion, when Hungary lined up with Italy, Iorga made a 180 degree sharp turn. From then he fully supported Italy "to counterbalance" Hungary. Romania and its Foreign Minister, Titulescu, demanded and supported sanctions in the League of Nations. Iorga took a strong stand against this, suggesting that

---

[866]*Neamul Românesc*, 12 June 1934, 22 June 1934.

[867]*Memorii*, vol. VII, p 41.

[868]The French ambassador in Romania during the War, St. Aulaire, remembered how Brătianu dismissed all Russian guarantees to Romania — now an ally — and categorically insisted on unequivocal French and English guarantees instead.

Romania could not deny history, or the ties of blood. He qualified Romanian policy as insanity. In many articles Iorga took an ugly anti-Ethiopian stand. He explained the Axum Empire as a mixture of Jewish and Byzantine influences, declaring that Ethiopians have no claim to be a real nation, and have no claim to a fatherland. Iorga organized public manifestations where he was the chief orator. The title of his address was "Long Live Italy!" There was no thought given to Ethiopian self-determination, there was a lot of talk about Italy's "civilizing mission" and "Ethiopian barbarism". Iorga failed to mention the Italian methods of fighting, the use of poison gas, and Mussolini's son's celebrated letter to his father describing the bombing of defenseless Ethiopians: "that my bombs opened as a flower." Iorga took stands even against France and England opposing Italy. He gave support to anti-English/Egyptian nationalism, and decried "the young Eden" who (instigated by Sir Samuel Hoare) dared to take a position against Italian policy. Further nonsense followed, Iorga comparing the backward English colonial methods in Cyprus with the (allegedly) wonderful Italian colonialism in Rhodes. Iorga saw behind it all the City of London, concluding: "one can obey conquerors, but no one listens to profiteers?[869] The sobering up came when an Italian journalist Zingarelli, known for his rudeness, attacked Iorga on the pages of *La Stampa*. Zingarelli did not go in for gratitude but flatly identified Iorga with the official Romanian position. Cads like Zingarelli or Virgilio Gayda distinguished themselves (on Mussolini's personal orders) in the press gallery of the League of Nations, booing Haile Selassie during his speech. Iorga did not give up. He answered Zingarelli that he (Iorga) never attacked Italy or Italian policy.[870]

Hungarian revisionism was encouraged by these events. The Rome Protocols were signed by Italy, Hungary and Austria, putting Austria — what an outcome for the heirs of Metternich — under Italian protectorate.

---

[869] *Neamul Românesc*, 8 March 1935, 6 July, 19 and, 23 October 1935, 19 November 1935, and 15 May, 25 September, 6 October, and 6 Dec 1936.

[870] *Neamul Românesc*, 13 January 1937.

On Hungarian revisionism (especially on the issue of Transylvania), the Germans were more understanding than Italy, because Hitler needed oil. Hitler personally reassured Gheorghe Brătianu and told the Hungarians that they should seek revision in Czechoslovakia. "That should be sufficient for one Hungarian generation." Iorga took note of the German position, writing that Berlin gave a setback to Hungarian revisionism. This was a credit to Alfred Rosenberg, the Nazi ideologist. Iorga continued explaining that Berlin corrected the errors of Rome, saying that he (Iorga) would have rather had it the other way around, but this may be as well for the world.[871]

The other important neighbor, Poland, figured prominently in Iorga's interests. Iorga didn't like Poland's delusions of grandeur. He (like many others) reserved a special dislike for Foreign Minister Colonel Beck and his erratic policies, who according to Iorga "did not trust the Romanian army.[872]

Let's take a look at Iorga's relation to internal developments during these fateful years. As the whirlwind unfolded, Iorga considered the king a mainstay of stability. Increasingly so, as the destabilization of international situation was complemented inside Romania by right-wing radicalization, Iorga repeated incessantly, "I am for the king." Iorga (like any nationalist) hoped to bring about national unity around the king, continuing to take stand against political parties, and the Legion. He continued to hope that he would be called upon "to serve Romania." On 6 June 1936 Iorga met the visiting Benes, and asked him to tell the king: "Romania needs a government of national unity, and only Iorga can form such government, but Iorga is not disposed to do so. Thus, the king should not change the government for the time being."[873]

With democracy unworkable, radicalism on the right (which meant the Legion and Hitler), and radicalism on the left (meaning Stalin), Iorga became an unreservedly conservative nationalist, to preserve his world of the nineteenth century and also Greater Romania. However, this involved contradictions. Iorga

---

[871] *Neamul Românesc*, 19 November 1936.

[872] *Memorii*, vol. VII, pp. 109 and 110.

[873] *Op. cit.*, p. 344.

was anti-Nazi, always "on the side of France, with France," but also for appease-ment. He continued to hope for a strong Italian stand against Germany, and for a chimeric Italian-French ("Latin") cooperation. He never abandoned an even more chimeric hope, to use Mussolini against Hungarian revisionism. So, his fanciful, sentimental "zigzags" would continue. Even Iorga's Nationalist Dem-ocratic Party continued to exist, even if he was not elected anymore. The Senate seat was automatically accorded to him; Iorga was listened to with respect, after all he was the "Teacher of the Nation." He also continued his war against Stere, asking once more in 1934-1935 the Senate to try Stere for treason he (allegedly) committed during the War.[874]

Meanwhile, the Legion was gaining ground. The method of the Legion was now, as Codreanu put it, "silent work." Iorga continued to oppose the Legion, referring to it contemptuously as "Codreni" ("the Codreanus" — Corneliu Zelea Codreanu, his brothers Decebal and Horia, finally, the father, and also the daughter, Irredenta Codreanu). There was in Romanian politics a general turn to the right. Vaida seceded from the National Peasant Party and founded his *Frontul Românesc*, with an authoritarian program.[875] The fusion of Cuza's Na-tional League of Christian Defense with Goga's Agrarians in 1935 was of more consequence.

The new party was authoritarian, of the fascist mold, directed against mi-norities, especially against Hungarians, and strongly anti-Semitic. The new Na-tional Christian Party reflected the Christianity of Cuza. For this former atheist, Christianity was meant to be anti-Semitic. The party emblem, the swastika, was an old Cuzist symbol of international anti-Semitism. The membership was re-cruited amongst Romanian establishmentarian bourgeois, interested in Jewish property. Thus, Goga and Cuza, while adapting fascist trappings updated the establishment. The newspaper closest to the party was *Porunca Vremii* ("The

---

[874]Iorga saw Brătescu-Voineşti in the chamber "arm in arm" with Stere. He promptly warned Brătescu-Voineşti "whether he was aware with what a monstrous being he was walking down arm in arm?" *Memorii*, vol. VI, p. 1.

[875]Vaida's *numerus valachius* was directed more against the Hungarians than against the Jews.

Command of the Times"). The most important Cuzist journalist, Ilie Rădulescu, was a worthy representative.[876] Goga, as a student at the Budapest University, was (as many Transylvanian Romanians) influenced by Karl Lueger and Georg von Schoenerer's ideas from Vienna (many of the most zealous Hungarian chauvinists in Transylvania were Jews). Goga the poet was a different person from the politician. Goga's poetry has one suggestion, one insinuation: Transylvania. But Transylvania does not manifest itself through Goga's poetry as it does in the works of Coşbuc or Slavici. For this writer, a Transylvanian himself, Goga's poetry sounds, even in California (where he is writing down these lines), even today, like a call from across the Carpathians, resembling Transylvania with its haunting beauty, calling to fulfill the Romanian destiny.[877]

However, Goga the politician did not resemble the young idealists of the Legion. There were no reformist delusions, no "archangelic" quest for social justice. Those Romanian middle-class and lower middle-classes which followed the Goga-Cuzists focused attention mainly on one thing: Jewish property, commerce, and jobs. But they wanted these things within an updated Romanian establishment. That was their *Porunca Vremii*. Their relationship with the Legion was predictably a bad one. For the Legionaries, they were but a bourgeois outfit; Codreanu called them "the other face of the government."[878]

Until now Goga had been ambiguous and opportunistic on the Jewish question, Iorga did not share the violent stand of this new party against minorities, nor did he share the pro-Nazi dedication of the Goga-Cuzist outfit. The Goga-Cuzists (and not the Legion!) were to become the Nazi agency in Romania. The

---

[876]*Politics and Political Parties in Romania.*, p. 171. Horia Sima referred always to the *Porunca Vremii* to Antonescu as a "blackmail paper," and Giurescu's opinions about Ilie Rădulescu's journalism and corruption were devastating. Munteanu, op. cit., p. 446.

[877]Goga was a lyrical fascist. When he found out that during the Dolfuss Putsch three Austrian Nazis cried out before their execution "Heil Hitler!" Goga remarked ruefully, "If only three men would die in this fashion for me!" *Memorii*, vol. VII, p. 273.

[878]Corneliu Zelea Codreanu, "Circulari, Scrisori, Sfaturi, Gânduri" (in mimeographed form), p. 5.

newest research of Heinen established these connections on the basis of materials found in German archives, between the Goga-Cuzist party and the different *Nazi Dienstrtellen*. We have proofs of Nazi money flowing into the coffers of the Goga-Cuzist party; sums; and also the names of the intermediaries. The most important figure was Cuza's cousin, the sinister Radu Lecca, who was very close to King Carol. He enjoyed virtual immunity (contrary to Codreanu, sent to jail because of allegations of contacts with the Nazis, never proven). Radu Lecca was a worthy representative of the regime's political underworld. Through him, Carol kept a line open to the Nazis.[879]

These Cuzist connections with Hitler should not surprise. Academician Andrei Oțetea recalled to this writer the enthusiasm of Cuza after Hitler took power. He said, "It is my LANC that took power in Berlin!..."

Was Iorga aware of this?[880] Iorga was too naive for that. He maintained a sentimental relation with Cuza, and was glad that this old relation (if not on political, but human level) was re-established. He felt sympathies towards Cuza even across the continental dividing line of political differences, which Iorga never forgot.[881] Cuza was less sentimental than Iorga.

While Iorga was intervening with the king and everybody he could think of for German-Jewish scholar Tiktin, now persecuted by the Nazis, Cuza was pursuing his relentless tunnel vision of anti-Semitism. He tried as early as 1932 to

---

[879]Heinen, *op. cit.*, pp. 331-339. Radu Lecca would become during the Second World War the infamous "General Commissar of the Jewish Question." During the summer of 1942 he traveled to Berlin to organize the deportation of the Romanian Jews to the killing centers in the East. Only the alertness of Dr. Willy Filderman and the cooperation of Queen Helen and that of King Michael, also the negative stand of Antonescu prevented this.

[880]Mme. Liliana Pippidi-Iorga assured this writer that Iorga had no idea about the disreputable connections between Goga and Cuza and the Nazis, and if he had heard about it he would not have lent credit to it.

[881]Iorga's correspondence between the years 1931 and 1936 render proof of his joy that good relations with his old friend were reestablished. When Cuza became the member of the Romanian Academy, Iorga editorialized: "His deductions represent his weakness, but fortunately these do not penetrate into his heart." *Neamul Românesc*, 31 May 1936.

convince King Carol to take measures against the Jews. He proposed the deportation of all Jews, sometimes to Uganda, also to Madagascar.[882]

Yet, Iorga's naivete, with ties to the king, would prefer the Goga-Cuzists to the Legion, or to Maniu. One doesn't see in the orientation of either Codreanu or of the Goga-Cuzists any preference of Mussolini over Hitler. Was this line a realistic alternative for Romania? Both Goga-Cuzists and Legionaries wanted political power so ardently that they preferred not to read Hitler's *Mein Kampf* or to investigate the theories of Rosenberg. With democratic politics and economics discredited, the German and Italian example seemed to offer more hope. Iorga saw what this would mean for the existence of Greater Romania for the long run; but for that considerable proportion of Romanian youth which sympathized with the Legion, with anti-Semitic Germany on the rise, when this burgeoning, young, authoritarian Germany was compared with the decadent "Jew-ridden" Western democracies, it was clear where the choice would lie. Yet, many Romanians continued to believe in Maniu and in Mihalache and the hope for a peasant democracy. They continued to believe in Christian morals and constitutionalism which Iorga ridiculed on behalf of King Carol. However, what were the alternatives for those who did not want to follow Maniu? Or the Cuzists? For the youth they were no alternative. The Legion was more dynamic and popular. The king failed to co-opt the Legion; he did not worry about the Cuzists.

By 1936, both Iorga and much of Romania were finding themselves in utter political confusion. Western democracy became irrelevant. As Iorga the historian saw it, democracy in Romania was not the product of an "organic" development. No wonder it could not work! In this growing confusion, as early as 1933 Iorga made a quest for a "creative regime." He explained that he didn't care whether this creative regime was based on one man or on parliament.[883] He would even support appeasement if it would preserve stability internally and

---

[882] *Memorii*, vol. VI, pp. 30, 35, 62, 259, 362, and vol. VII, p. 299.

[883] *Neamul Românesc*, 20 September 1933.

externally would guarantee the continuation of the Versailles system. This was not to be.

In the spring of 1937, Chamberlain, the architect of appeasement, became prime minister of England. Iorga would support his appeasement with reservations; Iorga could sacrifice a lot in order to appease Hitler as long as no sacrifices were demanded from Greater Romania. Wrote Iorga: "Chamberlain comes from another age," continuing that Chamberlain believes that "if mankind is not good, it can be seduced to become good" through peace, quiet, and a balance of armaments and power. Consequently, Chamberlain is like the men of Geneva. Iorga concluded with a somber intuition: "The shadow of sadness will descend on the last days of Chamberlain, when he will realize the tragic futility of his illusions."[884]

Chamberlain and Iorga will die almost simultaneously. Iorga assassinated by a Legionary terror squad, Sir Neville Chamberlain passed away mercifully, a few days before Birmingham, which his family ruled for generations, was blitzed by the Luftwaffe. Chamberlain's appeasement was no match for Hitler's Nietzschean and Stalin's hardline policies.

Until 1929, Iorga had a monopoly on history writing in Romania, more so as far as Romanian history was concerned. He directed the historical section of the Romanian Academy. The challenge came in 1929 from Sibiu, at the congress of history teachers of Romanian high schools, which Iorga was naturally invited to preside over. P.P. Panaitescu, a historian, in his speech, threw down the gauntlet: the old generation of historians was a romantic generation. They sacrificed the truth for national considerations, which made sense before the realization of Romanian national unity. But now, these falsifications, useful in those times, must stop; from now, one must follow a road of unadulterated objectivity. For

---

[884] *Neamul Românesc*, 21 March 1937.

this purpose, a new (historical) journal will be created to become the instalment of this struggle.[885]

This speech was the founding stone of the "New School" of Romanian history. The battle would last almost until Iorga's death. The "Şcoala Nouă" published its own historical journal, *Revista Istorică Română*. The directors were Gheorghe Brătianu, P.P. Panaitescu, Scarlat Lambrino, and N. Cartojan.[886] The confrontation between Iorga and the New School of History increased; the climax would be reached in 1936.

The protagonists of this confrontation were (besides Iorga) C.C. Giurescu (1901-1978), PP. Panaitescu (1900-1967), and Gheorghe Brătianu (1898-1953). There were some less important young historians, and one older historian participating in this confrontation: Demosthene Russo. Some of these young historians also became politicians, like Gheorghe Brătianu, or C.C. Giurescu, who became a "Gheorghist" Liberal deputy, and later a high official during the Royal Dictatorship.

All three protagonists — Panaitescu, Giurescu, and Gheorghe Brătianu — had been Iorga's students. Two of them (Panaitescu and Giurescu) attended Iorga's school in France, and all three had previously published in Iorga's *Revista Istorică*. Gheorghe Brătianu maintained with Iorga the most civil relations. Although Brătianu was a pillar of the *Şcoala Nouă*, he pointed out that "it was Iorga who went into the forest and felled the trees and cleaned away debris by the dint of his unlimited energy, and plowed the land and sowed it, so that the others might reap."[887]

Gheorghe Brătianu, the son of Ion I.C. Brătianu, received an excellent education. He became professor at the age of 25. After Carol II returned, he would

---

[885]Iorga remarked that P.P. Panaitescu spoke up "against falsifying history." *Memorii.*, vol. VI, p. 52. Also, Iorga, *Şcoala Nouă de Istorie: o lămurire definitivă* (Bucureşti, 1936), p. 8.

[886]*Memorii*, vol. VI, p. 320.

[887]Gheorghe Brătianu, *Nicolae Iorga: Istoric al Românilor* (Bucureşti, 1944); Iorga, *Trei Cuvântări*, p. 67.

be the only Brătianu who sided with him. He formed his own "Gheorghist Liberal Party" in 1930. Brătianu was a medievalist; a Byzantinist. So he and Iorga shared a common interest. Brătianu always wanted to know more about the "riddle of history" the Romanian people represented. He worked feverishly to investigate the almost millenary, non-documented period of Romanian history. But contrary to Iorga, Brătianu recognized the importance of social sciences, and tried to reject nationalist romanticism, giving priority to sources and documents. He would die tragically in the special prison for the former Romanian political leaders in Sighet in 1953. His death remains unexplained to this day.

The second protagonist, C.C. Giurescu's family originated from Moldavia. Giurescu would become one of those whom Iorga "loved to hate."[888] Or rather (Iorga knew the difference), Iorga nourished his contempt against Giurescu.[889] Iorga reminded Giurescu that he had "a good memory," and his contempt was not helpful for setting a serene tone for his debates with the "Şcoala Nouă." It was never pleasant to be at the receiving end of Iorga's temper.

Giurescu's father was a professor at the University of Bucharest, and took antagonistic stands against Iorga. He died during 1918. Iorga, as a gesture, became the protector of the younger Giurescu, who, under Iorga's sponsorship, became a historian, and studied at the University of Bucharest. After, Iorga took him to his school in France. Giurescu became a professor of Romanian history at the University of Bucharest in 1927, at the age of 25, due to Iorga's help.

---

[888]Iorga wrote to Basil Munteanu: "I have no time for hatred." If it only would have been so! Munteanu, *op. cit*. p. 356.

[889]Iorga, even at the meeting of the *Liga Culturală*, repeatedly referred to C.C. Giurescu's initials pronouncing it as "Caca," resuming this denigration even in publications. See *O Şcoală Nouă Istorică*, Bucureşti, 1936, pp. 6 and 28. The son of Giurescu, Dinu Giurescu, told the writer that after I.D. Ştefănescu (a professor of art) returned from a visit with King Albert, he described how the king had recalled with shock that when Iorga visited him, he abused Giurescu in a volcanic outburst.

Giurescu's inaugural address at the University was already a gauntlet thrown down to challenge Iorga.[890] Iorga promptly labelled this a scientific "aggression."[891] Not that Giurescu would have resembled a Bayard, *"le noble chevalier sans peur; sans reproche."* As we saw, he denounced Communist fellow students at the University of Bucharest, although this did not stop him serving the Communists later. He always knew to serve his own ends. As a student of Iorga at Vălenii, he wrote with ridicule about Mme. Catinca more than once, and spoke with disdain about Iorga, but pointed out: "I sure insulted Iorga — in thought..." He boasted about his crude anti-Semitic acts in the Chamber in Bucharest. According to Giurescu, the Jews wished to "colonize Bessarabia." Giurescu, as a deputy, "quickly intervened and prevented this." He wrote: "I wonder what kind of eyes the 'Jidani' (Kikes) will open" following his intervention? Another absurdity was — according to Giurescu — that Jews wanted to export good earth out of Bessarabia to the Promised Land. Again Giurescu managed to cut this short.

But the key to Giurescu's character is a letter he wrote to his friend, Munteanu (a professor of French Literature, and not a fan of Iorga). This letter discusses Giurescu's coming marriage. It is edifying; the lack of space prevents reproducing it in full. He notifies Munteanu about his coming marriage. His future wife, the daughter of Professor Mehedinţi, "is 22 years old, healthy, and serious. She has got quite a deal of money, too, and this fact is no obstacle either." Then Giurescu explains that he kept the engagement secret even before his best friends, because "the professors at the university would have made, I am sure, my career more difficult if they would have known about my marriage beforehand, and whom I am going to marry." Then: "You and Nandriş always considered me a rationalist, who is fireproof from an internal spiritual life or

---

[890]Paul E. Michelson, "Interwar Romanian Historiography in Transition," *Etude d'Historiogarphie*, (sous la direction de Lucian Boia), Université de Bucarest (Bucarest, 1985). pp. 227-240.

[891]*Memorii*, vol. VI, p. 333.

romantics." Giurescu rejects this notion, asserting he is a "sentimental being in a rational disguise."[892]

Why did young Giurescu keep his engagement secret? There were not very commendable reasons for this, connected with his coinciding appointment to the chair at the Bucharest University. One couldn't find similar manifestations of character in Iorga. On the contrary, Iorga was ready to take any risk regardless of the cost, if he thought he was right.

The third important member of the New School of History was P.P. Panaitescu. He became a Legionary, but this posed no obstacle to his serving the Communists later. The Communists needed a specialist in Slavic Studies.[893] There was perhaps another factor which made Panaitescu's metamorphosis easier. He never engaged (at least in his writings) in anti-Semitic polemics. Paul E. Michelson considers his historical works original and controversial.[894] This writer would consider them more original than controversial, especially his interpretation of Michael the Brave, or of that other short flash on the Romanian scene, that democratic firebrand (another historian-politician) Nicolae Bălcescu.

Panaitescu brought back to Romanian historiography something missing since Bogdan passed from the scene: A thorough knowledge of Slavonic languages, from the crucial Old (Church) Slavonic, through Polish and Russian, to Serbo-Croatian. He was also a student of Iorga in Bucharest, and at his school in France, and studied at the Jagiellonian University of Cracow. He became a lecturer of Slavic history at the University of Bucharest in 1927, thus resurrecting the heritage of Ioan Bogdan. Panaitescu always demanded objectivity with-

---

[892]Munteanu, pp. 410, 417, and 443.

[893]Dinu Giurescu recalled that during the Royal Dictatorship, Călinescu asked his father (C.C. Giurescu) whether he should send Panaitescu to a concentration camp. Giurescu advised against it. Dinu Giurescu remembered when the Legionaries took over, his father did not find support from Panaitescu, who became the Legionary President of the Bucharest University.

[894]Michelson, art. cit.

out concession to nationalist romantics. As the worthy successor of Ioan Bogdan, he demanded that, "Slavic influences in Romanian history should not be
de-emphasized, and the Latinization over-emphasized."[895]

Their stimulating historical journal, *Revista Istorică Română*, published articles by historians representing a wide range of points of view. Many historians
who contributed were sympathetic to the Legion. Besides Panaitescu, Radu
Vulpe, Vladimir Dumitrescu, and other Legionary historians wrote in *Revista
Istorică Română* (among them, the unfortunate Vasile Cristescu, who was executed together with other Legionary intellectuals during the rampage following
the assassination of Călinescu).

The stage for the showdown between Iorga and the "New School of History" was set. What was involved in this confrontation? There was the generation gap. Gheorghe Brătianu asserted that he and his generation were formed by
the First World War (and not by the nineteenth century). Consequently, "even
our historical perspective could not be the same."[896] Giurescu wrote that: "In the
Academy the section of history is still terrorized by a gerontocracy."[897] It is not
difficult to guess whom Giurescu had in mind. And, we remember the opening
address by Panaitescu at the Congress in Sibiu in 1929. Panaitescu expressed a
wish "to make Romanian historiography more Western and less Balkanic because this more Western and less Balkanic history reflects another generation."
Iorga replied: "as if history would be the property of a certain generation!"[898]

Iorga's views of history rested on organic development. Therefore, the past
could not be described in a mechanical way, to register a series of events and
dates only. Iorga, a romantic nationalist, and a "fighter," considered Romanian
history an unending struggle for the preservation and development of national

---

[895] *Ibid.*

[896] *Ibid.*

[897] Munteanu, *op. cit.*, p. 450.

[898] *Neamul Românesc*, 16 May 1936.

character; part and parcel of his cultural nationalism, upholding national ideas and values, and the national language.

Giurescu remembered that Iorga, in his presence (and also that of Gheorghe Brătianu and Grigore Nandriş) in 1927, when the question of historical veracity came up said: "What good does the truth do for if I have to defend interests of my country?"[899] Whatever one might think of Giurescu's trustworthiness, the remark sounds like something Iorga might say. It fits squarely into the Eminescian "Supreme Law."

The first number of *Revista Istorică Română* in March 1931 answered Iorga, demanding "a strict adherence to the truth," pointing out that between patriotism and truth, there can be no contradiction.[900]

Besides different approaches to history, and the generation gap, there seemed to be other factors involved: who should be appointed to which chair; conflicts concerning research grants and monies; there was a question of prestige; and finally, acquiring standing as a historian. Between Iorga and Giurescu there was also a personal matter concerning Iorga's family. This perhaps more than anything accounted for the extreme bitterness of the controversy.

Given what we know about Iorga, it is no surprise that a clash with his ego and vanity became inevitable if one dared to disagree with him over his interpretation of Romanian history, the basis for his cultural nationalism. Iorga's character was not a conciliatory one. He could not leave unanswered a challenge to his monopoly on the interpretation of Romanian history; consequently, a "struggle" had to ensue. Although between Giurescu and Iorga there was no political difference: both supported King Carol.

---

[899]Munteanu, *op. cit.*, p. 442.

[900]*Revista Istorică Română*, no. 1 (Bucureşti, 19 March 1931). Quoted also by Michelson in his article.

Others (like D. Russo) joined the confrontation because of personal grievances or opportunism. According to Iorga, Russo resented that he was not made the president of the Byzantine World Congress in 1924.[901]

The merits of the "New School of History" were defined by Michelson: 1) The productive debate of historians representing the New School of History was initiated by throwing down the gauntlet to other historians; 2) *Revista Istorică Română* "set new standards for historical publications in Romania"; 3) the monographs of the new historians were a real contribution, and "stimulated equally important efforts in these respects by their opponents"; and finally, 4) the call of the historians of the "New School" against "nationalist excesses" and for "methodological objectivity." Michelson explains that these efforts "while they were not always consistent..." helped the maturation of Romanian historiography.[902]

This writer can but register his opinion. *Revista Istorică Română* was a valuable journal, Panaitescu made contributions to Romanian historiography with his original approach, and his knowledge of Slavic languages and Slavistics. Brătianu was an expert in Byzantine history. Giurescu's contribution to Romanian historiography was called by Michelson, "a hallmark," which goes perhaps too far. Giurescu did not offer the intellectual horizon of Iorga. His knowledge of universal history was limited, and he had no profound knowledge of the history of Romania's neighbors. He had limited capacity to write comparative history. He was the historian of the Old Kingdom; his knowledge of Transylvanian history was rather limited. Giurescu certainly was a hard worker, and managed to write a good historical synthesis. But, if we scrutinize all the editions of Giurescu's *Istoria Românilor* (*History of the Romanians*) we can find some disturbing passages too. While describing the rule of Mihai Racoviță in Moldavia, he had this to say: "And, motivated by his greed (Mihai Racoviță) did not meet out to several Jews a punishment which they well-deserved — (who committed on Easter Day of 1726 in Onițcani a ritual murder — killing a little child,

---

[901]Nicolae Iorga, *Un om, o metodă și o școală* (București, 1940).

[902]Michelson, *art. cit.*

five years old). Instead of hanging them — as they would have deserved — they were incarcerated instead, and paid (to Mihai Racoviţă) several sacks of money later. Meanwhile, the boyars in Istanbul were alerted (about the incident) and they obtained from the Vizier a "Firman," ordering (the Jews) to be released, and the guilty got away." Giurescu continued describing the incident: "...the Jews complained — because they considered themselves slandered and despoiled," etc.[903] It would seem that, at this point, the "New School of History" — avowing a ritual murder charge — returned to the Middle Ages.

Iorga always maintained: "A nation is not just a piece of territory or a state or an economic necessity; nor is it a product of treaties (which created it), but a nation is a soul, an elemental, almost mystical being."[904] In his anti-Cartesian lecture, held at the height of his confrontation with the New School, he confronted the Sămănătorist spirit with that of Junimism, the rationalist spirit of his old foe, Maiorescu: "Should one interpret history with a formal, naked rationalism which is emptied of spiritual life or content? Or with the national soul, representing the truth?" Iorga continued, that "this is the bottom line which inflames public debate today!" According to Iorga, Giurescu, Panaitescu and the other representatives of the "New School of History" are the lineal descendants and commit the same errors committed by Maiorescu and his partisans 50 years ago. Then Iorga concluded his address: "It will be forever the question: Are you with Iorga, or with Maiorescu?!"[905]

Ion Dimitrescu pointed out: "for Professor Iorga, everything is either white or black." He explained that Iorga's critics did not attack his works so much than the blind enthusiasm of *Neamul Românesc*, and the initiatives of the

---

[903]C. Giurescu, *Istoria Românilor*; vol. 3, part 1, 2nd Ed. (Bucureşti, 1944), p. 231. Since Giurescu's *Istoria Românilor* sold several editions, it is important to keep in mind this 1944 edition appeared during the Antonescu regime in 1944, This unhistorical passage was conveniently removed in other editions.

[904]Iorga, "Rumanische Seele," Ernst Gamillscheg, ed., *Von Leben und Wirken der Rumanen*, Heft 1, Iena-Leipzig, 1933, p. 1.

[905]*Neamul Românesc*, 17 May 1936.

Sămănătorul. But details and little mistakes should not detract from the prestige of Iorga's works. Let's not harp on petty details.[906]

The first edition of Giurescu's *Istoria Românilor* consists of three volumes. The first volume (Bucharest, 1935) discusses Romanian history' from the beginnings until 1432. The second volume (Bucharest, 1937), from Alexander the Good until Michael the Brave. The third volume (Bucharest, 1942) continues Romanian history from 1601 until 1821. Giurescu also wrote a comprehensive Romanian history, *Istoria Românilor: din cele mai vechi timpuri până la moartea regelui Ferdinand* (București 1943).

Panaitescu's work about Michael the Brave was the main point of friction with Iorga (P.P. Panaitescu, *Mihai Viteazul*, Bucharest, 1936). Panaitescu also presented valuable documents about Michael the Brave. *Documente privitoare la istoria lui Mihai Viteazul* (Bucharest, 1936). Iorga attacked Panaitescu's conclusions on the origins of Michael the Brave. Panaitescu maintained that Michael the Brave was not the son of Pătrașcu the Good (a prince of Wallachia), but the illegitimate son of a "racheriță" (a saleswoman of plum brandy). Remarked Iorga: "How nicely Professor Panaitescu democratized the origins of Michael the Brave! So, Michael the Brave fell out from beneath a drunk plum brandy saleswoman to the floor of an inn. Maybe he was also drunk from plum brandy and was not really wounded when leading to victory his soldiers in the battle of Calugăreni."[907] Panaitescu remembered that Iorga did not always show Michael the Brave in a positive light, calling him a condottieri, and critical of his behavior in Transylvania. Panaitescu asked whether Iorga would be happier proving that Michael the Brave was the bastard son of a prince, rather than an innkeeper woman selling plum brandy.[908] There was no law assuring lineal succession in the Romanian principalities, and a lot of controversy about Michael the Brave's origins, activities, motives, and his contacts with the Constantinople

---

[906]*Curentul*, 17 May 1936.

[907]*Neamul Românesc*, 16 May 1936.

[908]*Universul*, 13 May 1936.

Greek power-structure; or whether he was an instrument of the Boyar oligarchy of Oltenia. Iorga had less problems with the medievalist Brătianu on any level.

The answer of Iorga to the New School of History came in a monumental work: His *Istoria Românilor*, in 10 volumes, (Bucharest, between 1936-1939). In answer to charges that he wrote history on "intuitions," and did not substantiate his statements with documents, these 10 volumes carry the heaviest possible documentation. In vain did Giurescu mock the work in advance! Wrote Giurescu to Munteanu (imitating how Iorga pronounced the letter *r*), "Ei Drrhagha, this Bolshevik generation is so impertinent." "But I will "schrrie" (that is: scrie = write) ten volumes of Romanian history," adding: "God save us from that what that's going to be!" On another occasion, Giurescu threatened to turn Iorga's ten volumes "into the laughter of the turkeys."[909] Iorga's ten volumes are a sum-total of the work of a lifetime, and Şeicaru is right: "This was the most beautiful gift Professor Iorga could bequeath on his nation."

The title of Iorga's ten volumes was the same as Giurescu's, not by accident. The historical journal of the "New School of History," *Revista Istoria Română*, was the same format printed with the same title letters as Iorga's *Revista Istorică*. There was a battle here, a challenge to Iorga.

In these ten volumes, Iorga tried to make amendments for his *Histoire des roumains et de leur civilization* (Paris, 1920) and his *A History of Roumania: Land, People, and Civilization* (London, 1925). These two volumes, written after the War hastily for political reasons, were attacked by the "New School of History" because of inaccuracies. Unfortunately, they were also read by others, and not to the benefit of Iorga's scholarly reputation. Iorga tried to correct this.

Iorga's conflict with the "New School of History" degenerated. This can be explained partly with cultural factors, and with Iorga's uncontrollable temper. Iorga himself called it *perseverare diabolicum*.[910] And when it got to the "popular press" of the Strada Sărindarilor, they considered it such a sensational story

---

[909] *Şcoala Nouă de Istorie: o lămurire definitivă*, p. 14; and Munteanu, op. cit., p. 443.

[910] *Neamul Românesc*, 16 May 1936.

that they drove several coaches and chariots across the dignity of academe, letting attorneys pick up the pieces. E. Condurachi commented: "The reviews of Professor Giurescu's *Istoria Românilor* surpassed everything known in book reviews." (Iorga called the historians of the "New School of History" "wild asses"). Condurachi remarked that "this is an extremely rare metaphor on the pages of universal historiography."[911] Worse was to follow. Iorga, the eternal student, concocted from Giurescu's and Panaitescu's initials four-letter words which he used on a number of occasions, even in addresses to public meetings.

A more moderate view was presented by Ion Vlădescu. Vlădescu showed that Giurescu followed the theses expounded by Onciul in 1899 without mentioning him either in his bibliography or in footnotes. Dealing with Serbian and Bulgarian forms of architecture (which early Romanian churches follow), Giurescu doesn't mention definitive works on the subject which he follows almost to the point of plagiarizing. Further, he is skilled in passing historical opinions which displease him. Wrote Iorga: "Panaitescu lowers himself to the level of any Giurescu!"[912] During the spring of 1936, Iorga didn't consider it beneath himself to send through General C. Ilaşievici a message to the king: The king may support the publication of Giurescu's *Istoria Românilor* with his own money, but not with the funds of the Royal Foundation, because, if so, Iorga would not accept invitations to the Palace anymore. In vain did Gheorghe Brătianu try to conciliate.[913] This time Iorga had no luck with strong-arm techniques. Not only was Giurescu's work published by the Royal Foundation, but he was appointed to handle all monies for the Royal Foundation. Giurescu, Panaitescu and Iorga continued exchanges in the Bucharest dailies, answering each other through intermediaries like Stelian Popescu. Wrote Iorga: "I prefer not to answer Professor Giurescu; his courage to negate and to justify and the vulgarities of

---

[911]*Adevărul*, 10 July 1935.

[912]*Neamul Românesc*, 16 May 1936, and *Adevărul*, 24 June 1935.

[913]*Memorii*, vol. VII, pp. 262, 263, and 274.

his attacks make any discussion impossible. And the former Prefect (collaborator with the Germans) Tzigara-Samurcaş, and Panaitescu follow him."[914] In April 1936, Iorga made a characteristic gesture: he resigned the chairmanship of the Romanian Committee of Historians.[915] According to reliable sources, Carol enjoyed this conflict between the historians greatly.[916] But this exchange of vindictives was started by Giurescu long before 1936. Giurescu compiled a 122 page list of Iorga's minor errors, which was sold (in book form) at a time Iorga was prime minister by the Liberals at the entrance of the University of Bucharest.[917] Iorga answered Russo with a devastating pamphlet as late as 1940.[918]

Finally Iorga, true to himself, answered with slander suits and other lawsuits: that Panaitescu violated the obligatory secrecy handling documentary evidence; charges accusing Giurescu with plagiarizing the works of Onciul, and references to Giurescu's mistakes (he called Alaric "Atanaric"). Iorga wrote to the Dean of the University, that if the Dean would not handle this within the framework of the University Disciplinary Procedure, then Iorga would turn to the Minister of Education.[919] These slander, plagiarism, and other lawsuits were always considered by Iorga always "the only way."[920]

What conclusions can we draw about all this more than a half a century later? Can we accept that history is nothing, just dry facts? A kind of telephone directory with names and addresses and numbers? Should intuition (or, as Wesley put it, an "inner light") play no role in writing history? In his *Generalităţi*,

---

[914]*Universul*, 14 May 1936.

[915]*Memorii*, vol. VII, p. 329.

[916]According to Dinu Giurescu, who heard it from his father, C.C. Giurescu.

[917]*Revista Istorică Română*, vol. 1 (1932), nr. 4, 1932, quoted also by Michelson in the article referred to; also, *Memorii*, vol. VII, p. 69.

[918]Iorga, *Un om, o metodă şi o şcoală*, passim.

[919]*Universul*, 23 May 1936.

[920]*Neamul Românesc*, 16 May 1936.

Iorga wrote, "I wish I would have had a greater poetic talent in order to be able to approach more closely and better the historical truth."[921]

The New School's accusations concerning Iorga's lack of documentation can be dismissed as unsubstantiated. Concerning Iorga's conclusions, his recapitulations of the past, and his reconstructions of history, Iorga presented an unparalleled quantity of materials, substantiating these honestly. If anyone wishes to interpret those materials differently, he can suit himself. To emphasize Iorga's numerous small mistakes seems a petty exercise. Descartes, or Dr. Samuel Johnson, are not an absolute key, even concerning Wesley, let alone in understanding Iorga, or any romantic nationalist historian. To understand Iorga one should not use the method of Dr. Samuel Johnson but rather another professor of history, Charles De Gaulle.

Shortly before his death, at the session of the Romanian Academy, Iorga spoke on this subject. He again drew parallels between his opposition to the Junimea Society and his problem with the "New School of History." He recalled the Junimea Society in Iași during the 1870s, a small intellectual literary club around a literary journal, *Convorbiri Literare*, and noted that real changes in culture do not come from the education Maiorescu received in the Theresianum! They come from the people and the land — people of peasant origin — like Eminescu was. Xenopol, like Eminescu, studied in Berlin. Nevertheless, they brought home many things and managed to achieve a synthesis between studies abroad and reality at home. A Romanian synthesis. By the 1870s, there was a different message to the *regulamentul organic*. It was the youth of Transylvania which brought it in literature, about the peasant. The last product of this true synthesis was Eminescu. Iorga concluded that he found it his duty to say this because, for many decades, he had researched the Romanian past, thought, and society. And as far as the results of Iorga's lifework, "they (Iorga had the New

---

[921]*Generalități*, p. 348. Iorga also lectured about the "anti-national rationalism." His lecture was held at the peak of the controversy on 13 May 1936. *Memorii*, vol. VII, p. 339.

School of History in mind) could not oppose but words and interests which one could ignore with a smile."[922]

The other professional conflict Iorga had in the late 1930s was between him and Hungarian historians, particularly Sandor Domanovszky. Domanovszky criticized Iorga's historical method in a major work, *La méthode historique de M. Nicolas Iorga* (Budapest 1938). The book started as a critical study of Iorga's *Geschichte der Madjaren*, and a review of Iorga about a monograph, Domanovszky's *Geschichte Ungarns* (Munich-Leipzig 1923), which appeared in the Revue *Historique Sud-Est Européenne* in Paris in the January-March issue of 1936. Domanovszky developed an erudite polemic with Iorga about Hungarian and Romanian history, and the history of Transylvania. Domanovszky subjected Iorga's approach to historical research to criticism over 350 pages or so. Domanovszky's book was put free of charge at the disposal of any foreigner requesting it. Iorga quickly reflected that Domanovszky and Antal Bella, the "so-called historians" from Budapest wrote about a probable infiltration of Romanians into Transylvania starting during the 12th century. Such theories "served revisionism, not history." Further (according to Iorga), Domanovszky wrote almost 400 pages on these subjects, Iorga considered that "less money should be sufficient for this purpose." As for Domanovszky's criticism of Iorga's historical theory and methods, he reminded Domanovszky that his teachers were Xenopol, Monod, and Bemont, and also German professors. There should be no reason to question his competence, Iorga found it rather offensive that Domanovszky qualified the descendants of King Decebal as "migratory shepherds." And he concluded (as usual) that this is "a Hungarian scientific aggression!"[923]

First, let's take a closer look at the evolution of Hungarian-Romanian relations during the interwar period and the fate of the Hungarian minority. The

---

[922]*Academia Română: Memoriile Secțiunii Istorice*, Seria 3. vol. 19-14.

[923]*Neamul Românesc*, 16, 17, and 21 August and 2 September 1938, and Iorga, *L'origine et la patrie première des roumains— réponse à une agression* (Bucarest, 1938).

real issue hiding behind this historical-scientific debate was Hungarian revision-ism. Hungarian revisionist hopes, encouraged by Mussolini's oratory before, were even more encouraged by Hitler's successful challenge to the status quo.

Already in 1920, after Hungary signed the Peace Treaties (in Hungary they were called the "Trianon Treaties," because they were signed in the Trianon Palace), a competition was announced for a Hungarian prayer. In the selection of the results the Hungarian Academy of Sciences was instrumental, and the winner, called "Hiszekegy," ("I Believe in One"), was recited by every school-child daily. This writer remembers the text vividly:

I believe in One God,

I believe in One Fatherland,

I believe in One Eternal Divine Justice,

I believe in the Resurrection of Hungary,

Amen!

During manifestations or sport events the orators always included refer-ences to the territories "torn away" from Hungary, and the crowd answered re-soundingly: *Mindent Vissza*! ("We want back everything'") The center of these activities was the government sponsored Revisionist League with branches all over the countryside. Hungarian historians and geographers played a prominent role. Money came from both public and private sources. The mail of the Revi-sionist League traveled abroad in the Diplomatic Poche. The slogan of the Re-visionist League was: "Justice for Hungary!" To this justice songs, sporting events, Trans-Atlantic flights, and the Hungarian success at the Olympic Games were dedicated. Many important Hungarian cities erected Revisionist statues.

The revisionist struggle was led by the Hungarian Academy of Sciences, with professors of economy, geography, and above all, the professors of history playing prominent roles. They were the initiators. These historians, geographers and economists tried to prove how well the Slovaks lived in Hungary, and that there was more danger for their national existence from Czechs than historical Hungary; Czechoslovakia had no right for existence, it was an artificial state.

Other Succession States received similar attention.[924] Older Hungarian historians, like J. Holub, I. Kiss, and the great Henrik Marczali, and younger ones, Gyula Szegfü, Bálint Hóman, and above all, Sandor Domanovszky, were in the forefront of this activity.

A few words about Hungarian-Romanian relations before the bitter debate between Hungarian and Romanian historians erupted during the second half of the 1930s. Like the USSR which never recognized the right of self-determination for the territories lost by the Czarist Empire (and refused to recognize the return of Bessarabia to Romania), or the Bulgarians who would not acquiesce in the loss of the Silistria Quadrilateral (Southern Dobrogea), Hungary never recognized the Trianon Peace Treaty as a final word. This, and the fate of the Hungarian minority in Romania dominated the relations between Hungary and Romania.

The approximately 1,700,000 Hungarians in Transylvania didn't even make the pretense of accepting the rule of the Romanian majority. Let's take a look at the position of the formidable Hungarian minority, the largest and the most irreconcilable in Greater Romania.

Before the War, Hungarians of Greater Hungary considered themselves "the nation of the state" (*államnemzet*). Although they permitted for the nationalities the use of the vernacular at home, in education, the courts, administration, army, or even the railroad network, everybody was supposed to speak Hungarian. Iorga considered the Romanians as the "dominating nation," yet conceded (vaguely) that "there is room for other nationalities."

In Greater Romania, Romanians comprised 70% of the population. Since both Hungarians and Romanians, once establishing their nation-state, considered themselves in a dominating position, the interpretation of their rights which derived from this differed rather in degree than kind.

During the 1920s the Romanians left a lot of elbow room for the nationalities. As the years passed two factors hardened the Romanian attitude (towards

---

[924]Ferenc Glatz, *Trianon és a magyar töréenelemtudomány, Történelmi szelme* (Budapest, 1978), nr. 2, p. 411.

Jews and Hungarians in particular): The Hungarian refusal to accept the status quo, and Hungarian hopes for a revision being generously encouraged from Hungary. With Right Radicalism rising inside and outside Romania, which in Romania also took the form of a ruthless twentieth century "New Nationalism," advocated by Vaida, Goga, and the Legion, life was not becoming easier for Hungarians. Let's consider also the omnipresent, unpleasant, Oriental corruption. All these factors were on the increase by the late 1930s, and there was also the increase of right-wing violence. All this was not directed against Hungarians alone. These were unfortunate characteristics of Romanian life and government. Yet, the Romanian position became clear. As long as the Hungarians were biding their time, and hostile to the idea of living in a state governed by a Romanian majority, why on earth should the Romanians make meaningful concessions to them?

In Cluj, a magnificent city of almost purely Hungarian character, and in the Szeckler Land, (also in other ethnic Hungarian areas), all too many times a whole generation grew up without even speaking Romanian. The Romanians demanded the double acid test before granting full-fledged rights: The command of Romanian, and loyalty.

And then there was another problem. Except the heavily Hungarian-populated border areas, much of Transylvania's Hungarian minority lived far from the border, embedded among Romanians. If anybody thought about including these areas into Hungary, it would lead to injustice as the Diktat of Vienna did in 1940. The Romanians foresaw this. In 1924, Dr. Angelescu, the Minister of Education, established so-called "cultural zones" (mostly in the western part of the Crişana area, along the Timişoara-Satu Mare railroad, and along the Szeckler borderlands). Here, the Romanian state offered 50% higher salary for Romanian schoolteachers, and gave them extra land and many other benefits. There was an effort to Romanianize these areas slowly, through education. In the economy, the Hungarians (and Hungarian Jews who dominated the economy) were quite irritating for Romanians. Most of the Hungarian schools were denominational, and this was natural, since the Transylvanian churches were always the best vehicles of nationalism. But during the interwar period we saw a decrease of Hungarian students in better high schools and Hungarian student enrollment at the universities.

This was also true of the economy. There was a slow, yet unmistakable Romanianization. It never reached the proportions of Hungarian pressure exerted before the war on Romanians; nevertheless, these pressures increased during the 1930s, with Vaida's "Numerus Vallachicus," directed more against Hungarians than Jews, although in Transylvania this difference didn't seem great. Goga was temporarily more against Jews than Hungarians. (As Iorga put it, "Goga wishes the minorities to disappear," because, according to Goga, the nationalities "have no vitality." Iorga was against this polity of Goga.)[925] This hardening line against Hungarians was not inspired by Maniu whom the Hungarians hated so much and not by the Romanian left. This campaign was mainly inspired by the "New Nationalism." By the late 1930s this opportunistic campaign got rough. It seemed to be a profitable undertaking. This was the time when the exchange took place between Transylvanian Hungarian Bishop S. Makkai, and the writer, S. Reményik. Their essay-titles became a slogan: Wrote Bishop Makkai in 1937: "Nem lehet!" ("It is impossible!"). He explained that in Transylvania, for the preservation of Hungarian identity whether national or cultural one, the Hungarian minority needs cultural and economic autonomy; without such autonomy the identity of the Hungarians would be endangered. The Transylvanian-Hungarian writer S. Reményik answered Bishop Makkai with his essay entitled meaningfully: "Ahogy lehet!" ("As much as it is possible!"), namely, that as much possible under the circumstances should be preserved of Hungarian identity in Transylvania. By the late 1930s a Transylvanian-Hungarian identity began to develop, not synonymous with the identity of Hungarians outside Transylvania.

The Depression, which hit the Southeast European countries indiscriminately, opened the eyes of these nations. All of them faced the same kind of

---

[925]Iorga strongly opposed Goga's anti-Hungarian and anti-minority attitudes. See Iorga, *Ideea asupra problemelor actuale*, p 95.

problems. We spoke about Count Bethlen's attempt. The mayor of Bucharest, Dobrescu, visited Budapest; there was talk about a visit by Prince Nicolae. Count Hunyadi spoke in the Hungarian Parliament about the possible anti-Bolshevik common front. But in Hungary the Transylvanian aristocracy (by definition Hungarian) had a lot to say: Bethlen, Count Teleki, Count Csàky, Count Bànffy, and many others. These aristocrats preserved a certain idea and nostalgia towards a very specific Transylvania, which had proven insurmountable.

We saw the significant visit of Count Bethlen in Bucharest. By 1933 Count Bethlen lectured in Cambridge about turning Transylvania into a kind of a "Eastern Switzerland" (which meant an independent Transylvania in practice). Iorga swiftly rejected this, asking how can one create Switzerland without Swiss spirit?[926] Nor did Iorga leave it at that. He wrote two pamphlets about Count Bethlen's address. His pamphlets were also a challenge to Lord Rothemere, the proprietor of the London *Daily Mail*, the most important convert for Hungarian revisionists in Britain, Iorga called the Hungarian government "the feudal regime in Budapest." More significantly, answering Hungarian charges that the Romanians infiltrated Transylvania during the thirteenth century, Iorga maintained "one does not colonize (during the Middle Ages) any foreign element anywhere without issuing them a 'charter' first."[927] Yet, when the great Hungarian composer, Bela Bartok, a great collector of Hungarian and Romanian folk music (who originated from Arad county) came to Bucharest, Iorga was overjoyed. Here Romanian-Hungarian cooperation went hand in hand with Iorga's *Sămănătorism*. Iorga wrote: "There must be another way than hostile usurpation!" Then he tried to offer some alternatives. "Now, when the Saxons of Transylvania are transformed into the Eastern sentinels of Pan-Germanism, Hungarian and Romanian popular understanding becomes mandatory. It is because of this that the visit of Bela Bartok is so important for us!"[928]

---

[926]*Neamul Românesc*, 6 December 1933.

[927]Iorga, *Rèponse aux conferences domnées à Cambridge par le Comte Bethlen* (Bucarest, 1933), and *Seconde rèponse au Comte Bethlen* (Bucarest 1933).

[928]*Neamul Românesc*, 25 February 1934.

Iorga always tried (unsuccessfully) to balance Mussolini's pro-revisionist policies with a kind of a "personal diplomacy."[929] But, it was the rise of Hitler which encouraged the Hungarian articulate public opinion in its revisionist hopes. It was from Hitler that these Hungarians expected the destruction of the Versailles System; it was from Hitler that all too many Hungarians expected the overthrow of the European status quo. For many Hungarians (regardless of Jewish loyalty to Hungary), like too many Romanian anti-Semites, there was a difference: Berlin was anti-Semitic and Rome (at that point) was not. A revision achieved with the help of Nazi Germany (according to this school of thinking) would combine a pleasant thing with a useful one (meaning the acquisition of Jewish property). After 1936, a doctrine was coined by the illustrious medieval historian (who became an Imrèdist-fascist politician), Bàlint Hóman: *Magyar-nèmet sorsközosség* (*The Common Hungarian-German Destiny*). According to him, there is a common destiny between Hungary and Germany, a common destiny between the former Central Powers. Hungarian revisionism stands or falls with the success and the survival of Hitler's Germany.

The consequences of this "Common Hungarian-German Destiny" are known. Hungary joined the Axis, broke its treaty of ''Eternal Friendship'' with Yugoslavia and attacked that country; then Hungary declared war on the USSR and on the Western Allies; finally, when the Imrèdists arrived in power during the spring of 1944, Hungarians, with Eichmann's cooperation, deported their Jewish population to Auschwitz — becoming the only European government hilly aware of what the fate of the deported would be. More than half a million of them perished practically a few weeks before the collapse of Naziism in Hungary. Iorga opposed this kind of nationalism with vehemence and consistency.

With imminent German menace hanging over Austria and Czechoslovakia, the debate about revision became sharper. Historians were leading it. What could Hungarian revisionist arguments be based upon? Upon self-determination? By no means.

---

[929]*Nicholas Iorga, Former Prime Minister of Romania to Benito Mussolini, Head of the Italian Government* (Bucharest, 1937).

Hungarian revisionism also used a geographical argument, the natural geographical unity of the Carpathian Basin around Hungary.[930]

The third revisionist argument followed from the second: the economic unity and advantages of Greater Hungary based on the Carpathian basin. By the late 1930s one could go a long way to prove the economic advantages of Czechoslovakia, of Greater Romania, and Yugoslavia. If there were advantages to the Hapsburg Empire as an economic unit, this was not necessarily true about historic Hungary.

The argument of Hungarian historic rights over the Carpathian basin remained. Today the decisive argument is self-determination (although the outcome of the Yalta Conference put it between parentheses). Yet, if one reads the traditional interpretation of Hungarian history, a feudal aristocratic interpretation, the political concepts of which became increasingly difficult to implement during the twentieth century, the basis of it was the existence of the "historical Magyar state," with "historical boundaries," which encompassed the Carpathian Basin looking back to a thousand years of history. Transylvania was lying within the Carpathian Basin, and, according to Hungarians, Transylvania belonged to Hungary' for a thousand years. As for the Romanian majority, they began to arrive into Transylvania at the end of the twelfth century at best. They could only thank for their settlement to the benevolent tolerance and hospitality of the Hungarian kings and rulers of Transylvania.

Iorga was in his element. He had to reaffirm for the Romanian majority also their historical rights. Iorga, the historian-politician par excellence, took over the command in the counter-attack, on what he considered "a scientific struggle against Romanian rights."[931] Accordingly, Iorga argued that Transylvania was

---

[930]Iorga referred to this, remarking that Hungarians imagined the Carpathian basin "secluded Elysian Fields," adding that geography must be no obstacle to national self-determination.

[931]Iorga, *Lupta științifică împotriva dreptului românesc (Conferința la adunarea "Astra" la Abrud la 1 Septembrie 1938)* (București, 1938).

never really under Hungarian domination, except the years following the *Ausgleich*, from 1867 until 1918 (he pays little attention to the period from 1050 A.D. until 1526).

According to Iorga, the ancestors of the Romanian people have a continuity of 25 centuries in this area and in Transylvania, Iorga always emphasized "his respect for the Hungarian people, history, and achievements." Nevertheless, his respect for Hungarian history is limited. He respected Ràckòzi and other Hungarian national heroes, but sometimes speaks very negatively about Hungarian contributions to history. But even if Iorga showed respect for Hungarian achievements in history, Hungarians in general, and the Hungarians in Transylvania in particular, did not want Iorga's respect. What they wanted (like the Romanians!) was Transylvania.

Iorga's historical theory on Transylvania follows the lines of Xenopol's "Dacia Traiana" theory. We can call it the Daco-Roman theory; Xenopol established the basis for it; Iorga evolved it further; and Pârvan gave archaeological substantiations. It goes back to Geto-Dacians which lived on the lower Danube and elsewhere centuries before Christ, engaging in agriculture and in trade. At the beginning of our era Dacia, under King Decebal, irritated the Roman Empire too much from across the Danube. So, Emperor Trajan built his famous bridge across the Danube at Drobeta (Turnu-Severin) and after overcoming a valiant resistance, defeated Decebal and his people. The testimony of his triumph can be seen on Trajan's Column on the Forum of Rome. But it was neither triumph, nor defeat, rather it was the painful birth of a new nation.[932] Theses and antitheses resulted in a synthesis. The remote province of the Roman Empire (Dacia), reaching up to the Black Sea (where Ovid and many others were sent into exile), became a kind of Siberia for Rome; those in disgrace or unwanted in Rome were exiled in great numbers to this province. According to Latin tradition, always profoundly non-racist, these exiles, as well as the officials or the military stationed there intermarried with the autochthonous Dacians, mainly in Transylvania. When in 271 Emperor Aurelian withdrew the Roman legions and much of

---

[932]Iorga, *O călătorie în țara Hațegului* (București, 1906).

the population left with them, there was already a new nation in the making. Under such circumstances the population never withdrew completely when the Roman legions left. Domanovszky strongly criticizes Iorga's conclusions that a substantial part of the population of Dacia remained, not accepting the sources and historical methods by which Iorga tried to substantiate it. Further, Domanovszky sees little likelihood of a synthesis between the native Dacian and Roman population.[933]

For the coming centuries, during the great migrations, this area was one of the most turbulent of Europe. Any historical document which would unequivocally prove the continuation of the Romanian element is missing. It is here where Iorga's theory about the "organic" evolution of history becomes helpful. Accordingly, during this period the Romanian element withdrew into a kind of "Popular Romania," hid in the forests, became shepherds, engaged in agriculture, in one word, they became survivors. As Eminescu said: "The forests are the best friends of the Romanians." Anyhow, their survival amidst the storms of the migrations, and their emergence in large numbers later was and remains a mystery. It was best expressed by the Romanian medievalist Gheorghe Brătianu in the title of his book: *Une énigme et un miracle historique: le peuple roumain* (Bucharest, 1942). Iorga went beyond that: "a miracle which we made by ourselves."

Domanovszky's position is based on the lack of documentation for almost 1,000 years. But then there is one medieval document available: the writings of the anonymous notary of King Bela III of Hungary during the twelfth century, the famous 'Anonymous." His writings are controversial, and relate (among other things) to how the Hungarians penetrated from the plains in (or about) the end of the tenth or eleventh centuries into Transylvania. A Romanian (Latin) leader (or prince, chieftain), Menumorut, according to Anonymous' writings, resisted fiercely when the Hungarian tribes tried to penetrate into Bihor and Transylvania.

---

[933]Iorga, *O călătorie în ţara Haţegului* (Bucureşti, 1906).

Those who in Hungary question the authenticity of Anonymous, think of him as a typical medieval notary, telling fairy tales like so many medieval notaries told. Some think Anonymous confused Menumorut's followers with Bulgarians. Some compare him to the Nestor's Chronicles of Kiev Russia.

The Hungarians penetrated into Carpathian Basin in 895. Anonymous wrote his chronicles more than two hundred years later. Neither the Primary (Nestor) Chronicles nor Anonymous were naive. Both served dynastic aims. Such type of medieval chronicles cannot be taken literally, yet they almost always contain a lot of truth. Since one has no other source to rely upon, a historian cannot ignore them.

The position of Hungarian historical research is that when the Hungarians penetrated into the Carpathian basin Transylvania was quasi-empty, with no Romanians there. Romanians infiltrated into Transylvania from the Balkans as Vlach migratory shepherds starting at the beginning of the thirteenth century, and this infiltration continued on and on. They could multiply because the Hungarians fled, defending the West against the Tartar and later Turkish hordes. Hungarians were replaced by the fecundity of these infiltrating shepherds.[934] After Versailles, this debate sharpened, because the Hungarians had to rely almost exclusively on historical rights. So historians came to the fore in the struggle for revision, and were led by Sandor Domanovszky.

Domanovszky was born in Sibiu, Transylvania. His father was professor at the Juridical Academy there. Domanovszky taught from 1909 at the Budapest University as a Medievalist. During the peace negotiations he formed part of the Hungarian delegation as a historical expert, very close to the great Hungarian geographer (and future prime minister), Count Pàl Teleki. Domanovszky was also the Hungarian delegate in the International Commission of Historians. He took a commendably strong stand against the anti-Semitic disorders by fascist students at the Hungarian universities after the War.

He founded practically single-handed Hungarian economic and social history. Domanovszky always emphasized a dispassionate, painstakingly precise

---

[934]Domanovszky pointed out the strong pro-Hungarian stance of Michelet about this.

and critical study of medieval documents. For him, the document was every-thing. Consequently, he could feel nothing but horror at Iorga's "organic" theo-ries, "intuitions," or worse, his "instincts," "historiology," let alone his "recon-struction of history." He was a very different personality to Iorga. He spoke lit-tle, and what he said, he said slowly and softly.[935] If one may draw a parallel, Domanovszky was more like Maiorescu. He was an anathema to Iorga's per-sonality and concept of how history was to be written. Yet, Domanovszky would not hesitate to quote Michelet's romantic definition of Hungarian history, "Hun-gary, the defender of the West against the victorious Crescent (Turks)."

But Domanovszky continued his criticism of Iorga saying: "Iorga's mani-fest error lies in the system he applied. This was the reason for his manifestly false interpretation of historical sources, his hiding of important facts or his triv-ialization of the real significance of the facts." Or elsewhere: "In order to be able to hide truth, the Romanian author (Iorga) preferred to resort to his own arbitrary and artificial hypotheses." More importantly, Domanovszky maintained that "in order to ascertain the spirit of a scholar, his faculties of synthesis should be even closer scrutinized than his way of using documents." Iorga's *La place des ro-mains dans l'histoire universelle* (vols. 1 and 2, Bucharest, 1935) especially the first volume, was something "bizarre," because (while speaking about the foun-dation of the Romanian Principalities across the Carpathians) it maintained that "no other people created a durable state in Southeast Europe." Consequently, Iorga denied the national character of other states around the Romanians.

Here we shall consider only the main points of Domanovszky's debate with Iorga: Domanovszky writes: "He is establishing his thesis on the basis of an a priori" Or, "His political prejudices are guiding his research." Finally: "Iorga's method and approach to history should not be called a scientific method in the true sense of the word," because, according to Domanovszky, there can be nei-ther historical instinct, nor historical intuition used to fill a hiatus in history where there are no documents. However instinct or intuition are considered by

---

[935]F. Glatz, "Domanovszky Sàndor helye a magyar történelemben," *Szazadok* (1970), no. 2, Budapest, 1978, pp. 211-234.

some historians as of the greatest value to historical scholarship (and not only of Iorga's historical scholarship). Domanovszky copiously quotes Iorga's errors, rather petty ones, the product of Iorga's haste.[936] He opened his criticism of Iorga's historical method and work by saying "Iorga's works on Hungarian history are created by passion, frill of intentional errors."[937]

There was another curious coincidence. The overwhelming majority of prominent revisionist Hungarian historians originated from territories lost to the Successor States, with many relatives left behind. Many archivists shared this fate. This added to their bitterness. These people lived for a long time in poverty as refugees. They were not only a willing audience, but potential supporters for an integral revision.[938]

Iorga's reaction, because of his devotion to Romania made sure that even scholarly debates concerning Romania were not conducted on the level of the Olympus. They resembled rather East European political journalism with Iorga's personal touch. He carried on exchanges in such fashion with Gyula Kornis, a professor at the University of Budapest. Kornis was an articulate revisionist. The whole exchange was conducted in a sardonic tone. Iorga was surprised that Kornis wished for an Italian meditation between "the Hungarian owners of large estates and the Romanian people." Concerning the overwhelming Hungarian character of Oradea, Arad, or Timisoara, Iorga thought that those alleged Hungarians were mostly Jewish, and the Jew eagerly learns any language of the dominant nationality. (We should remember that, concerning these very Jews, Iorga knew better). Concerning Kornis' position on historical rights, Iorga asked whether one should rebuild the Holy Roman Empire with Rome as a capital; or Spain should re-annex Milan, Holland or Belgium; or should the Ottoman Empire be re-established with Hungary a part of it? As for English and American sources supporting Hungarian revisionist claims, Iorga reminded his

---

[936]Domanovszky, *op. cit.*, pp. 58, 139-140, 143-150, 225-229, and 314-316.

[937]*Ibid.*, p. 11.

[938]Ferenc Glatz, *Trianon és a magyar törenélemírás*, p. 414.

interlocutor that the English and the Americans know as much about Transylvania as about Greenland or the Tierra del Fuego. As for the suggestion of plebiscite, Iorga asked: who should preside over it? And (since Iorga's brochure to Kornis was written in 1940) he asked whether such a plebiscite solved problems in Silesia? Then Iorga received how the Hungarians mistreated the Romanians of Transylvania, and wound up his pamphlet with a categorical refusal to consider revision in Transylvania.[939]

Iorga always resorted to a favorite of Southeast Europe, ridiculing the names of political opponents. If their origins were not of the nation which they espoused (and this was the case with all too many Hungarian historians), their names were upheld for ridicule — their former names were also ridiculed. As far as Kornis, Iorga considered that perhaps his original name was *Corniş* meaning he was Romanian. L. Tamás was reminded that a few years ago he was Tremel, a German. I. Lukinich's Croatian background was carefully fostered; so was Domanovszky's Polish background; Ferenc Eckhart preserved his German name, of which he was reminded. Bàlint Hòman was reminded of his original name, Hochman, a German.[940] And the German origin of Count Kunò Klebelsberg, the Minister of Education (the very motor of Hungarian revisionism), was not forgotten.[941]

Iorga should not hold this assimilation against the Hungarians. On the contrary! While this debate was not the time to recognize it, the Austrian historian-politician, H. Friedjung pointed out: "One should also count amongst the best political qualities of the Hungarians that they know how to attract the best sons

---

[939]Iorga, *Réflexions sur "la question de Transylvanie"— Reponse a un article de M. Kornis Gyula. Professeur de l'Université de Budapest* (Bucarest, 1940).

[940]Iorga expressed towards Hòman, a prominent Medievalist, a great deal of respect before the debate became acerbic. He showed more respect towards Hòman than toward Gusti. *Neamul Românesc*, 22 February 1935.

[941]*Neamul Românesc*, 29 March 1936.

of other nationalities and after that, they treat them with all the warmth of their temperament as brothers."[942]

The Romanian historical arguments, especially those of Iorga, make sense. The problem is the missing documentary evidence attesting Romanian presence in Transylvania for a millennium. In such a situation one has to use the evidence at one's disposal. Not admitting other than documentary evidence supports Hungarian historical claims. But no matter how objectionable it should be for a rationalist skeptic like Domanovszky, one cannot ignore the non-documentary evidences. One has to complement them resorting to hypotheses, historical parallels, and to consider organic development. The absence of written sources for a millennium does not leave us other choice. There are the writings of Anonymous, and his chronicles cannot be dismissed as medieval sagas only, or unreliable fantasies. Anonymous followed a medieval tradition, added embellishments and tables like others. But in such a case there are cores of truth. In Hungary, monuments are built to Anonymous.

Perhaps the most important evidence for Latin continuity is the Romanian language, which is a Latin language, in its grammar, structure, and vocabulary. If there are non-Latin words in it, one should consider the almost two millennia of Romania's isolation from the Latin mainstream; it is rather surprising that there are relatively so few foreign words (Slavic or otherwise) in the Romanian language, taking into account the flow of peoples who passed through this area. Romanians, although they borrowed words (and other cultural aspects) from Slavs and Hungarians and intermarried with them (even with Tartars, later with Greeks, etc.), they were never Slavicized like the non-Slavic Bulgarians or Macedonians were. The most important instrument of Slavicization, the Orthodox Church, could have become instrumental in this process (like for Bulgarians or Macedonians). Romanians used the Church Slavonic written language until the eighteenth century and the Cyrillic alphabet even longer. One should not ignore the Greek influence in the Principalities, and Hungarian, even German influences in Transylvania (or Polish influences in the northern part of Moldavia),

---

[942]Heinrich Friedjung, *Österreich von 1848-1860* (Stuttgart-Berlin, 1908), vol. 1, p 227.

Despite this, Romanians managed to safeguard their ethnic and cultural identity (even before the age of nationalism), under very severe conditions. During many centuries they did not have a state they could call their own. Their instinct for survival became an ethnic, cultural, indeed, an organic instinct, something we would call later a spontaneous national instinct. They preserved their vernacular (that most pregnant expression of national culture). Many Italian and other travelers during the Middle Ages (as Iorga has proved with documents) admired the tenacity with which Romanians clung to their language. It would also be hard to account for the fact that illiterate Romanian peasants name their sons after Roman emperors, or their daughters after Roman patrician ladies.

Hungarian historians asserted that during the early Middle Ages Transylvania was almost devoid of population, and there were no Romanians there. Romanian "infiltration" of Transylvania started around the thirteenth century. When the Hungarians penetrated into Transylvania for the first time during the eleventh century from the plains, Gyula (Gelu) was the first who later submitted to King St. Stephen and his successors. The Hungarians erected a "gyepü," (a kind of a military frontier) on the mountain crest around the Carpathian crescent and the Transylvanian Alps, in order to protect stable settlements in the interior of Transylvania from incursions from outside the Carpathian basin and to check the intrusions of semi-barbaric nomads. (There are the solid masses of Szecklers within the eastern Carpathians, another obscure phenomenon as far as their origins are concerned.) If so, how could the Romanian ("Wallachian") shepherds penetrate in such great masses through such a barrier from the South? Domanovszky argued that the Romanian "infiltration" started during the thirteenth century when the "gyepü" (defense perimeter) was already crumbling away.[943] But in the thirteenth century the Kingdom of Hungary was established firmly enough institution-wise, so the withering away of the military frontier did not make such a difference. The institutions in place could deal with numerous arrivals — if they were unwanted. The Kingdom of Hungary was a great medieval power thanks to the roads of commerce which the Hungarian kings controlled.

---

[943]Domanovszky, *op. cit.*, pp. 11-12.

Hungary was by the thirteenth century an essential part of medieval Europe, part of the medieval "ordo." In this Europe no large migrations much less their settlement could take place without a charter issued for the newcomers. Let's keep in mind that the number of these alleged Romanian infiltrators had to be large.

During the same decades when this alleged Romanian penetration started, Transylvania was also enriched by another arrival, the Saxons, who duly received a charter from the Hungarian king. This made the construction of their walled cities and fortresses possible. Jews, when they were allowed to settle in Transylvania, repeatedly received charters. So did any other settlers which arrived in larger groups. Thus the Romanians must have been there previously in one form or another. There was never a charter granted to Romanian settlers considering their entry in such numbers. Even if soon (even by the Hungarian sources) they would be recognized as very numerous in Transylvania.

Admittedly, when the Hungarians arrived to Transylvania they found there neither a state, nor cities, Latin or otherwise. But Transylvania was not empty! There were Latins (and Slavs) in the mountain-crags and within the dense forests — as the names of geographical features show. And during the centuries which followed, the Hungarians failed to assimilate them.

Thus, with the beginning of the fourteenth century a process started by which Romanian village chieftains were emancipated (assimilated). After their conversion to Catholicism they became Hungarian gentry. The overwhelming majority of Romanians were degraded into serfs. Yet they survived. The Czech historian, Professor Susta maintained that Romanians were the most Eastern of Latins, and Czechs the most Western of Slavs.[944]

Such precarious positioning taught both Czechs and Romanians to become the virtuosi of survival. The Romanian capacity for survival turns even setbacks into opportunities, and manages always to get the Romanians on their feet, sometimes escaping the capacity of Western rationalism to understand. As we saw Brătianu called his book *The Romanian People: A Historical Enigma, A Historical Miracle*. This is true, that during the Middle Ages (especially during

---

[944] *Memorii*, vol. 4, p. 80.

the Ottoman rule), numerous migrations of Balkan peoples took place, and there was a flux of Wallachians from the area of Macedonia and Albania towards "Dacia Traiana." Many of them entered Wallachia. They also came (to a lesser extent) to Moldavia. Few of these arrivals can be traced with certainty to Transylvania (arriving directly from the southern part of the Balkans). During the Middle Ages, many Romanians were to be found on both banks of the lower Danube.[945]

If the Albanian-Macedonian area was the ancestral home of the Romanians, why did their mass-movement take place in one direction, towards the "Dacia Traiana"? What attractions did these lands have for them that they came in such numbers? These lands were no Promised Land, but where serfdom awaited them. If the Romanians entered Transylvania only during the twelfth and thirteenth centuries as nomad migratory shepherds, "how can one explain the mystery," as Vasile Pârvan, the Romanian archaeologist asks ironically, that "the Romanians returned to the same lands from which they have been removed a millennium before?" Pârvan continues, "One cannot help wondering how is it, that after ten centuries, they found exactly the same place?"

If one accepts the historical theory of Romanian infiltration, one could understand that such infiltration should take place into the southern borderlands of Transylvania from Wallachia like Făgăraş or Hunedoara. It would be more difficult to explain the massive Romanian ethnic presence in the eastern Carpathians. Why does the compact Romanian population of Maramureş speak an almost identical dialect to the Romanians in Bessarabia? Thus it would seem that suddenly, by the fourteenth or fifteenth centuries, the Romanians became a majority (and much within the limits of the Roman province of Dacia) in Transylvania.[946]

---

[945]Because of Iorga's emphasis on the extent of the role Romanians played in the Bulgarian Arsenide Empire, he clashed with P. Mutafeiev. See Mutafeiev: *Bulgars et Romains dans l'histoire des pays danubiens* (Sofia, 1932).

[946]Domanovszky (*op.cit.*, pp. 82-83) maintains that the counties of Alba, Turda, Someş, and Cluj, were in the late Middle Ages still "almost entirely" Hungarian. This seems strange, because this area was the road of the alleged Romanian "infiltration." Domanovszky ignores the Romanian stronghold in the Apuseni Mountains which these counties surround.

Again, it is difficult to see how Romanians could enter a firmly established medieval great power's territory without any charter. And, entering from the south, passing through the counties of Făgăraş and Hunedoara, they continued to advance across the Transylvanian plateau almost unnoticed. And formed solid majorities in the eastern Carpathians, in Maramureş, Bistriţa-Năsăud (and beyond that, in Bucovina and Moldavia!) And, one should remember again the numbers of Romanians involved, this being accomplished about little more a century after their arrival during the thirteenth century. Such a theory boggles the imagination, and seems to lack any historical precedent. Since Domanovszky insists on documentary evidence, one might point out that this allegation also lacks solid documental substantiation.

These opinions are shared by the majority of historians except those of Hungary, Bulgaria and Russia despite the lack of 1,000 years hard documentary evidence of Romanian presence in Transylvania. There is Leopold von Ranke and others. The opinions of Hendrik van Loon are revealing. He wrote in his world history about the rise of modern Romania: "(There was) the ancient Roman province of Dacia, which had been cut off the Empire during the third century. Since then, it had been a lost land, a sort of Atlantis, where the people had continued to speak the old Roman tongue, and still call themselves Romans, and their country Romania."[947] It was mainly R. Roesler in the *Rumänische Studien* (in 1871), elaborating further theories of a Swiss historian, F.J. Sultzer, about the alleged deportation of the Dacian population by the Romans, who maintained that Transylvania was empty at the turn of the millennium; in 271 A.D. the settlers withdrew entirely (with the Legions) from Dacia; consequently, one has to look for their descendants south of the Danube. But there are strong indications that the majority of Romanians were always rural (free) agriculturists or shepherds — they had a bond with the land. Romanians were not nomads. How could they appear (as peasants) in such number in "Dacia Traiana" again?

During the long centuries of their struggle for survival, Romanians had to withdraw into a spiritual nationhood, which according to Iorga, is one of the

---

[947]Van Loon, *op. cit.*, p. 370.

fundamental human emotions. On a certain level culture replaces even nationhood. During this long period the Romanian people went through great sufferings. In the Balkans, this crossroads of history, between two continents and
worlds, many other people had to suffer. There is no place for a contest of comparative horrors. Romanian proverbs are better proofs of Romanian national instinct, than many history books: "The flood sweeps down the river bed, yet the
stones remain on its bottom." Or, "The wind bends the grass, yet it doesn't tear
it out." And the most indicative: "O Lord! Do not make the Romanian suffer as
much as he can bear!" Peoples survive fighting, others through submitting, and
some manage to do both at the right time.

These exchanges between the Romanian and the Hungarian historians in
the atmosphere of 1937 and 1938 degenerated, Iorga, of course, considered Domanovszky's guesses about Romanian origins "scientific aggressions." His answers became sardonic. Hungarian epithets concerning the Romanians of Transylvania were not flattering either. Iorga constantly referred to Hungarian culture as the "Hungarian sub-German culture," sometimes "odious sub-German
culture." When the radical Hungarian fascist movement, the Arrow-Cross,
promised to recognize the cultural autonomy of non-Hungarian nationalities
(within the framework of a Greater Hungary), Iorga rejected its *Pax Hungarica*,
asking "Is that all that a new Hungarian generation can think about and produce?" Then he continued: "And what are the guarantees that they would treat
these nationalities (in this *Pax Hungarica*) decently?"[948]

These arguments caused a great deal of bitterness on both sides, Iorga saw
it, so he published a pamphlet *Against Hatred Between Nations*. And by 1940,
he elaborated it further, translating it into Hungarian, and signing it as "Iorga
Miklos." Written in good Hungarian, it presented a popular (Romanian) history
of Transylvania. Iorga argued that common Hungarians and Romanians do not
hate each other. Only the press, schools, and the intellectuals spread it. He called
upon Hungarians and Romanians to unite against the common enemy: Russian

---

[948]*Neamul Românesc*, 8 November 1934.

Bolshevism.[949] If Iorga offered reconciliation, he envisioned it on the basis of Versailles. On this question there was a complete unity between the historians of the "New School" and Iorga.

Hungary could stand up against Versailles in unity, including Nazi sympathizers, Conservatives, Liberals, and Socialists (even the communists). This was not the case in Romania. Romanian communists were forced to adapt an absurd, un-Romanian position. At the height of the debate, in a tense atmosphere, the World History Congress took place in Zurich, during the summer of 1938. Iorga was elected as Vice-President of the International Committee of Historians (mostly due to the support of his friend, the Norwegian historian H. Koht, who was also the Foreign Minister). He received this honor with an almost childish joy, not for himself, but as a vindication for Romania. Wrote Iorga, "In Zurich Domanovszky was mortified by my election. I believe there cannot be a more complete failure."[950]

Iorga was a greater, and a better known intellectual than anybody from Southeast Europe. On this International Committee, one gave a place for a Southeast European, which was obviously Iorga. He had another satisfaction in Switzerland. Purchasing something in a shop, the shop owner asked him where he came from. Iorga answered he came from Romania, whereupon the shop owner reflected: "All! That is the country of Professor Iorga!"[951]

But, the Versailles System was crumbling. The World Historical Conference was followed by the Munich sell-out of Czechoslovakia, and Hungarian revisionism was on the march. Iorga continued "the struggle with the absurd

---

[949]Nicolae Iorga. *Contra duşmăniei dintre naţii Romani şi Unguri* (Bucureşti, 1932); reprint Nicolae Iorga. *Contra duşmăniei dintre naţii Romani şi Unguri /Against Hatred Between Nations: Romanians and Hungarians*, ed. Kurt W. Treptow (Iaşi, 1995); and Iorga Miklòs, *A nemzetek között levo gyülölködés ellen, maqyarok es romànok* (Bukarest, 1940).

[950]Iorga, *Hotare şi spaţii naţionale* (Vălenii-de-Munte, 1938), pp. 105-107.

[951]The Iorga family to the writer.

Hungarian revisionism,"[952] taking one of his fierier stands in the middle of the Czech crisis addressing a mass meeting in Abrud, in the heart of Transylvania.

The further developments (in 1940, 1944, and after 1944) are known. Those who made policies in Berlin and in Moscow must have been happy about this sterile hatred between Hungarians and Romanians, because for them the Hungarian-Romanian hatreds opened many opportunities.

There was a sad epilogue in 1986. The Hungarian Academy of Sciences published a three-volume study entitled *Erdély törtènete*, (*A History of Transylvania*) (Budapest, 1986) consisting of 2,000 pages, beautifully illustrated. These volumes contain little new concerning the Hungarian view of the arrival of Romanians in Transylvania. Arguments are the lineal continuation of arguments presented by Domanovszky and I. Lukinich a half a century ago, reaffirming the view that the Roman presence in the "Dacia Traiana" was discontinued, and Romanians appeared in Transylvania for the first time in the beginning of the thirteenth century. Iorga's works are often quoted.

Somebody of Transylvanian origin and who loves Transylvania can read these volumes of history (and the bitter debate which exploded between Hungarian and Romanian historians after the three volumes appeared) only with sadness. Despite the fact that cooperation between Hungary and Romania is mandatory, sterile debates continue. Socialism did not resolve a thing. Hungarians and Romanians do not see more eye-to-eye now than they did at the beginning of the century. They cannot agree about the past of Transylvania, about Transylvania's present, and apparently they do not agree about the future of Transylvania either.

---

[952]Iorga, *În lupta cu absurdul revizionism maghiar* (Oradea-Mare, 1930).

Chapter VII

Axis Rainbow

"Watch out my people for the dangers in the making for you!"

— Nicolae Iorga in *Timpul*, 23 May 1937

By 1937, in East Central Europe and Romania in particular, politics and the general atmosphere turned into an irrational, seething volcano. It became ever clearer that the interwar world based on the Versailles Settlement, could not last. This became manifest when those powers who established it were unwilling to sustain it. Their means were not lacking; it was rather their determination and convictions which were lacking, and more so with every' month which passed. All this was becoming complementary to the flaws within the Versailles System which the Depression accentuated. These rising doubts were encouraged by determined Nazi and Italian Fascist (also Japanese) aggression, and the disastrous policy of "appeasement."

These unhappy times would serve as a backdrop for the last years of Iorga's life, during which Naziism would march from triumph to triumph over Iorga's world. But he would keep his faith in the ultimate triumph of the West, and the defeat of Naziism.[953] He would die fighting. The tragedy was that he passed away at the Zenith of Nazi power.

---

[953] At the outbreak of the Second World War, Iorga wrote that according to his knowledge of history, "he is certain that not technology will decide the issue, but intelligence, leadership, and the enthusiasm for the cause of humanity. Only those who brought enough sacrifice for honor can master these qualities." *Neamul Românesc*, 3 September 1939.

By 1937, the Versailles Settlement was tottering. Many Romanians watched this in anguish. Others within the "No-Man's Land" looked forward to this with anticipation, like most Austrians, Hungarians, not a few Slovaks, Croats, or Ukrainians (under Polish rule); also Lithuanians, and even many Bulgarians. These people looked forward to the collapse of the interwar world, thinking little about what a Hitler or a Mussolini would substitute for it. Even people in Western Europe saw how during the Depression Italy and the USSR kept order at home (albeit with low wages!), and expanded their industrial power, while liberal economics and politics were more and more discredited. When Nazi Germany by 1937 grew into an industrial and military giant, it became clearer: the democratic states were deprived precisely by their Depression-remedies of the moral and material means and also the will to resolutely oppose the dictators. Even in the West many feared that Naziism and Fascism might be the wave of the future. But from the vantage point of East Central and Southeast Europe (also, for not a few young Romanians), the Third Reich was an oceanic wave of the present and the future combined, representing a new kind of order in Europe! Perhaps in the whole world!

Although, for all too many Romanians democracy had become identical with corruption, unkept electoral promises, and unsolved problems, some conclusions were drawn in a different manner. There were those who lost faith in democracy but remained pro-Western in the interest of Greater Romania's integrity. Iorga, the king, and many other Romanians in the leadership belonged among them.

A large group of Romanians, especially younger ones, all too many half-way-articulate students, and younger officers of the armed forces, were ready to gamble on the rising Nazi and fascist ride, and not only because of their hatred for the Jews or disillusionment with democracy. They hoped for a place for Greater Romania in the new (Nazi) order. In the short run, there was a possibility of accommodation, mainly because of Hitler's need for Romanian oil. The problems with Nazis would have emerged in the long run.

And there was the third group, the largest number of Romanians, a kind of Romanian "silent majority": the numerous followers of Maniu, who remained faithful to the hope of a peasant democracy and to a policy of close relations with the West. In Europe, the new wave was accompanied by a fashion for uniforms with a bewildering array of shirts in black, brown, yellow, etc. In Romania the colors were green and blue.[954]

All this led to the contusion and despair of intellectuals in the West, but in East Central Europe the disorientation was even greater. Let us quote an autobiographical note of the Romanian playwright Eugene Ionesco, *Les Rhinoceros*:

> Le rhinocéros, c'est l'homme des idées reçues.... Je l'avais vécu, une première fois, en Roumanie, lorsque l'intelligentsia devenait peu à peu nazie, antisémite, "Garde de fer".... Les professeurs de faculté, les étudiants, les intellectuels. — Au début, bien sûr, ils n'étaient pas nazis. Nous étions une quinzaine à nous réunir, à discuter, à trouver des arguments pour les opposer aux leurs. Ce n'était pas facile: il y avait une doctrine nazie, une biologie nazie, une ethnologie nazie, une sociologie nazie. Et puis des avalanches de discours, conférences, essais, articles de journaux, etc., toutes sortes de bréviaires, aussi simplistes. — Nous tachions quand même de trouver des arguments. De temps à autre, l'un de nos amis disait: 'Je ne suis pas du tout d'accord avec eux, bien sûr, mais sur certains points, pourrant, je dois reconnaitre que, par exemple, les Juifs...', etc. Et cela, c'était le signal. Trois semaines après, ou deux mois au plus tard, cet homme devenait nazi. Il était pris dans l'engrenage, il admettait tout, il devenait rhinocéros.[955]

Only those who lived through those fateful years, even vicariously through the daily reminiscences of parents and friends, have a true feeling for the events which occurred. Almost every few weeks some determined aggressor was "marching in" somewhere, accompanied by fiery martial music, flowers, cheers and tears, in a deceptive display of joy, with panacea and millennium. The bewildered population of the "No Man's Land of Europe" perhaps believed that

---

[954]Iorga was disgusted early with the "demagoguery of shirts," and took stand "against the uniforms and the green shirts of the Codreanu family." *Neamul Românesc*, 17 February 1933. In 1937, the government forbade uniform-wearing in public.

[955]E. Ionescu, *Les Rhinocéros*. Also, Heinen, *op. cit.*, p. 5.

their problems would be solved. Determined aggression seemed to pay. The re-occupation of the Saar, and the Rhineland, the war in Ethiopia, the Spanish Civil War, the Japanese aggression in the Far East, the occupation of Austria, the Sudentenland, Cyeszyn, Kosice, and Upper Hungary; later Prague, Ruthenia, Memel, and Albania, seemed to add to this "marching in" mood. And when suddenly the "expectations" in Danzig were not fulfilled so easily, all this irrational enthusiasm suddenly came to an end. The "enthusiasts" paid a terrible price for making Hitler (as Iorga put it) "the leader of all discontents."

When Cuzists and Legionaries celebrated Hitler's Austrian triumph, reacting to their spontaneous instincts rather than to the implications for Romania, Iorga commented: "We celebrate the triumph of others and without thinking."[956]

During the spring of 1937, an Italian paper editorialized: "Either Fascism or Bolshevism." Iorga answered that he wanted neither. Every nation should develop its own form of government, based on its national experience.[957]

By 1937, especially in Austria, Hungary, Poland, and Romania, the rise of this "marching in mood" hysteria (to which Western Europe, or the rest of the Balkans never succumbed) was accompanied by waves of public anti-Semitic savagery. Such outrages also occurred in Germany, for the first time in recent history. Iorga warned: "Even a cold man who cannot get carried away by anything is better than enthusiasm, ready to leap in a destructive manner into the darkness."[958] This new wave of anti-Semitic violence meant in Romania renewed brutal incidents at the university. All too often, students assured the participation of the shoddiest elements of Romanian society. This blossomed into savage attacks against Jewish temples and shops.[959] The harassment of Jews through bureaucratic means (asking bribes, blackmailing them, etc.) was also on

---

[956]*Neamul Românesc*, 20 March 1938.

[957]*Neamul Românesc*, 13 March 1937.

[958]Iorga, *Idei asupra problemelor actuale* (Bucureşti, 1935), p. 104.

[959]By 1937, another Romanian specialty developed. Free-lancing Cuzists and Legionary terror squads checked ID cards of passengers on trains. Those who were Jewish were thrown off the trains moving at 40 to 50 m.p.h.

the increase. All these things existed before in a manageable degree. It was the degree and frequency of incidents which, by 1937, in Romania became incompatible with civilization. All this happened despite the non-cooperation of the decent majority of Romanians. One doesn't need the cooperation of the majority to create such conditions.

Iorga blamed the twentieth century. "One must find balance between what a machine is capable of, and (the goals) that the human soul strives to accomplish. "Then again, "There is a need for a historical method (to interpret the present). We do not depict the soul of animals better than those who painted the Altimira caves. We are not morally superior to the Christians of the catacombs. Neither more disciplined than the Romans, nor are our cities superior to Greek cities. Historical method is needed to see that Russia has abandoned Marxism in favor of a primitive, ancient, Slavic collectivism." And, "Hitler is the incarnation of some savage, ancient Germanic tribalism and religion."[960] Under the title, "The Civilization of Frustration and of Waste," Iorga described how he saw modern life. Man (in the big cities) is "thrown into the chaos of an ugly, rumbling life," where the light blinds and the air is polluted by the exhaust Himes, and blackened by coal particles. Here, this miserable modern man in his abode in a corner of a blockhouse, exposed to an ever-changing and disorderly environment is laboring. His labor is draining him (from all his strengths), and forces him to take refuge in pleasures hurting his sick nerves. This martyr of an absurd civilization is alone. The family is (but) a memory. When not overwhelmed by his burdens, there is no relief in friendship, gone with old letters, or conversations about the good old days. A social life with meaningful exchange of ideas became virtually impossible. One will seek relaxation in the confusion of dances (a barbaric game of jumping up and down), to embrace people not even known to him, and stampeding in the same place to the wild sounds of Negro music.

---

[960]Iorga, *Idei asupra problemelor actuale*, p. 68; also, *Neamul Românesc*, 6 and 8 August 1935.

Children are raised amid such sick weirdos, and in time they will become even more unhappy than their parents.[961]

At a time of change which he did not appreciate, Iorga tried to remain time to himself, looking out for Romania, her welfare and interests (as he conceived these to be). All of Iorga's inconsistencies do not seem to be such if we remember: his opinions on subjects such as, art, literature, and morality, became complementary to his main concern: Romania. He supported the king (unfortunately, the king was Carol II), and the monarchy, because within this hectic turbulence he considered the king a guarantee of stability, a bulwark of national unity against the predatory political parties with their "Suprafanarul" on one hand, and the hated "anarchy" of the Legion, on the other.

During the days of the Anschluss and the hysteria we described before, Iorga commented that in these days of European upheaval "one may follow an adventurer or a monarch; I have chosen to follow the latter."[962] He supported the Western powers (especially France), and preserved his robust love for the United States. However he wished to adapt their example to Romanian conditions, rather than to copy it; and (since he saw many negative aspects of the industrial civilization), adapt it carefully. Iorga was irreconcilably set against German Naziism, but not so much against Mussolini (at least in public). He hoped that he might tilt Italian politics away from its pro-Hungarian revisionist position, and waited longingly for Mussolini's stand against Hitler.

By 1937, Iorga turned resolutely against the political parties, and consequently against democracy in Romania because of its performance. Iorga did not consider democratic institutions in Romania to be the product of an organic process. He continued to admire democratic institutions in the West (a product of an "organic" process) which were more compatible with his values than Naziism or Italian Fascism. Iorga was, by his temper, always an authoritarian; but he never abandoned his individualistic touch. Neither did he wish to force others to abandon theirs. A clean, incorruptible individual, he always fulminated against

---

[961] *Neamul Românesc*, 3 January 1936.

[962] *Neamul Românesc*, 15 March 1938.

corruption, but closed his eyes to the unheard corruption of and around King Carol, because of considerations mentioned. Iorga stood against the Legion but not so unequivocally against the Goga-Cuzists, although they were more of a Hitlerite agency than the Legion. He was sentimental enough to remember his ties with A.C. Cuza, although he always distanced himself from Cuza's pro-Nazi stand. Iorga took strong stands against Jews who refused to assimilate, and would become (during the second half of 1937) quite indiscriminate in his attacks. In parallel, he continued to hold up those Jews who assimilated or showed interest in Romanian culture as an example, welcoming them with open arms. He always condemned violence against Jews, or any other violence. Could one prevail in those times with such an individualist stand? We say "yes, but" often, but this is the recurring pattern of Western civilization. There were no "buts" left for Iorga in his stand against Hitler, or Stalin. He may have been open to Hungarian cultural autonomy (within the framework of Greater Romania, of course). He may have welcomed Jewish assimilation. However, Naziism and Russian-sponsored Communism were for Iorga criminal endeavors directed against Romania and the rest of humanity.

Iorga never wavered in his stand against any modern trend in art (especially in literature) either. These contradictions would become the reason for some of his most pathetic "flip-flops," during the last years of his life.

Time has come to examine the evolution of Iorga's relation with the Legion. Since the pervasive characteristic of the Legion was youth, let us take a look at the Romanian youth, and Iorga's ideas about this youth during the last years of his life. Thirty years earlier, Iorga was considered the leader, the "Apostle" of the Romanian student body. Since then, a lot of things had happened. Iorga was now closer to his seventies, and Romanian youth had also changed, but for one consistency: the articulate youth (or semi-articulate youth) was still against the establishment, and for radical change. One may ask some tantalizing historical "ifs": "If" Iorga had had a different personality and temper; "if" he had only been a better politician, and had assumed the leadership of the "Trench Generation;" would he have succeeded in becoming the leader of a Romanian regeneration? Could such a renewal have produced a different Romanian youth?

But this failed to happen. Iorga wrote in 1937: "We old people are left over on earth for the sole purpose to witness which road is the right road to take." Or, "It would seem that my generation is unwelcome in every possible domain. We seem to be guilty that we have been born such long time ago, and we have survived for so long."[963]

Iorga analyzed the problems of Romanian youth. He concluded that Romanian youth was disoriented, yet, there were four recognizable cur-rents: one was career-oriented. Another imbued with Messianism. A third current consisted of those whose motivation was anti-Semitism, and a fourth were in search of an idea. Iorga understood that a career is a powerful motivating force, going hand-in-hand with intellectual unemployment, and the yearning for a respectable destiny. As for Messianism, he rejected the idea that Orthodoxy should be translated into practical politics like Catholicism in the West, since in Orthodoxy, there were no Franciscans. It was because of such a futile quest that Nichifor Crainic and Nae Ionescu turned towards the Legion. Iorga advised Latins to remain rational. Codreanu (according to Iorga) was no Romanian, but a Zelinschi, a Slavic mystic. As for the anti-Semitic current, Iorga recognized the gravity of the Jewish problem, how Jews blocked the advancement of Romanians in the cities. (He made an exception for Oltenia.) He reminded the youth that he had been more radical on this issue yet advised students to keep away from the streets and not to engage in violence. Finally, in those searching for an ideal, Iorga recognized the general emptiness of present day Romanian life. He saw the youth was turning towards Hitler and Mussolini. Iorga made the understatement that he is "not a Germanophile," and assured everybody that he would always fight against any German in France or Romania, regardless of Transylvania's heritage.[964]

Iorga did not believe that "being young represents a right in itself." Rights must serve a broader segment of society than one age group. The youth still had a lot to learn and duties to fulfill, after this they could demand rights. His advice was, since "he was in the forefront of Romanian nationalism for 50 years, nay,

---

[963] *Neamul Românesc*, 23 January and 12 June 1937.

[964] *Neamul Românesc*, 7 April 1934.

since he created it," that it must remain a Romanian nationalism, and not the imitation of foreign models. "We cannot kneel before Berlin." He reminded Romanian youth of the infinite goodness of the Romanian people and asked them to abstain from violence. "The Romanian people absorbed Christianity not only aped it." "The Swastika is not the Cross of Christ."

However, hysteria, the landmark of 1937, increased with every month. "Within the convulsions, the terror and the 'hero' seeking, were those who try to 'educate heroes' or 'students who teach professors" Iorga offered an example. He advised that Romanian universities, at that time profaned and subjugated (by Naziism), should learn from the example of Lincoln. But in 1937, Romanian youth preferred to look to Codreanu, Hitler, and Mussolini for inspiration rather than to Abraham Lincoln, Iorga argued that the Romanian adolescent of the day does not reason. In Romania, which by 1937 has all too many "saviors," the adolescent goes forward, "kills, gets killed, or lands in jail." Pity for him and for Romania, which this youngster "loves, but does not know how to love." Then: "Even if the youth does not like it, the government will make foreign policy." No wonder that Iorga concluded that "it is sometimes a duty to become unpopular."[965]

All these admonitions were only the corollary to Iorga's stand against the Legion, which during 1937 exerted a powerful influence over the youth of Romania. From 1933 on, as the Legion became an important political factor, Iorga's hostility toward it increased it in proportion to its rising popularity.

After Duca's murder, Codreanu, the "Captain" of the Iron Guard, changed tactics. "Silent Work" was Codreanu's new method. Through its accomplishments the Legion wished to produce the argument which within a corrupt society is always the most powerful one: the example. The Legion organized labor camps for youngsters without any class distinctions. Among the great Boyar families sympathy for the Legion was on the increase. Battalions of "Legionary Commerce" were established to prove that Romanians are able to engage in

---

[965] *Neamul Românesc*, 14, 15, and 27 February 1937; 6, 14 and 27 March; and 27 April 1937.

fruitful commerce. A chain of "Legionary Restaurants" served the same purpose. *Buna Vestire* ("The Annunciation") was founded as a Legionary newspaper in 1937. By 1936, Codreanu had devised an ingenious means of raising funds, the "Friends of the Legion," for anyone who wished to contribute to the Legion, even anonymously.[966]

The Legion dominated the Romanian Student Congress in April 1936 in Târgu Mureş. During the Student Congress, the Echipele Morţii (the Death Squads) were born to avenge by "direct action" any treason or injustice against the Legion.

They meant business. A few weeks later, a former Legionary leader, Mihai Stelescu, tried to split up the Legion. He was lying in a hospital bed. Ten Romanian Legionary students, all members of Stelescu's own former Legionary cuib ("nest"), decided to take "direct action." They broke into his hospital room, hacked him into pieces with axes, and danced with his flesh, after which they embraced each other and cried in joy. According to tradition, they gave themselves up to "expiate." In prison, they became another Legionary legend, the "Decemviri," the "ten men."[967]

Meanwhile, the Spanish Civil War, being the dress rehearsal for the Second World War, continued. It seemed that everybody in the West had to take a stand. In Romania prominent Legionaries, I. Moţa and V. Marin, left as volunteers. A few months later in January 1937, they fell outside of Madrid. Iorga, despite his hostility towards the Legion, was moved by the "two heroic youths," who "left dirty politics and went to where people put to stake daily their lives for the ideas in which they believe in."[968]

Not only Iorga was moved. When the bodies of Moţa and Marin were buried, their sacrifice shook up this complacent, corrupt society. When the train

---

[966]Jewish contributions were mostly consequence of a crude blackmail, against which they could rarely find protection from the authorities.

[967]Iorga wrote: "How can students act in such a fashion? What youth do we have!" *Neamul Românesc*, 29 July 1936.

[968]*Neamul Românesc* ,19 Jan 1937.

carrying the bodies reached the Romanian border it was received by unprece-dented crowds. Priests blessing the coffins. In Bucharest one of the largest man-ifestations of Romanian history took place. Legionary orderlies kept exemplary discipline. There were no incidents, but the gathering aimed into a silent mani-festation against the existing order associated with the king and the system. A people discovered itself united, and in its contempt abandoned the establishment to solitude. There was no word of hate spoken. No stone was thrown, just a fervor of being shoulder to shoulder. The vast crowds administered to the estab-lishment the supreme insult: they were nothing for them, not even subject for mockery. The crowd marched by the Royal Palace. Carol was there; the songs and shouts penetrated into his apartments and awoke his savage jealousy. In-credibly, Carol wished always to be something Codreanu was, despite his pa-thetic corruption, Carol always wished to be loved by his people, especially by the youth.

The king tried to steal Codreanu's thunder by organizing his own youth movement, *Straja Țării* ("the Guardians of the Fatherland"), under Teofil Si-dorovich. Sidorovici got involved in a graft scandal, and committed suicide. His movement was a failure. Despite Iorga's respect for Moța's and Marin's sacri-fice, he was disgusted by the commotion the funeral caused among the youth. The university was empty, no classes could be held. Iorga commented that "all students are politicized," intervened before Tătărescu and the Government about the gravity of the gravity of legionary menace, asked a leave, accused Cuza in the Chamber of being against him and for Hitler, and accused the government of cowardice. The extreme right responded, saying: "Iorga has lost all touch with the youth." Legionary death sentences showered on him, and his mock "funeral" was arranged in Vălenii-de-Munte by the Legion. For Iorga, Legionary students represented nothing but anarchy and Naziism. An indefatigable advocate of the extreme right, Istrate Micescu, tried to meditate between Iorga and the Legion. Iorga's answer was: "I was never interested in the nationalism of a party!"[969]

---

[969]*Memorii*, vol. VII, pp. 292-293, 398-401, and 425.

The first attempt on Iorga's life was carried out by a crazed Iron Guardist student on 13 April 1936, and did not succeed.[970] By the second half of 1937, the establishment began to realize the challenge the Legion represented, and to close ranks. The establishment was losing patience. Non-university dormitories were dissolved. On 2 March 1937, the university would be temporarily closed, the Legion's recreation camps were forbidden, as the bureaucracy tried savagely to repress the Legion. The Legion answered in the usual manner. An attempt was made on the life of the President of Iaşi University, and other brutal "direct actions" followed.

After the elections of December 1937, Iorga would take an ever more violent stand against Codreanu, the Legion, and the Legion's pro-Nazi line.

The Legion (especially Codreanu) had Hitler's personal sympathies. Beyond German "Dienststellen," the SS might have sympathized with the Legion, while the more traditional Foreign Service preferred to conduct relations with Romania on official lines. Hitler promoted German national interests. In such capacity he tried to arbitrate between different proposals. The Southeastern part of Europe (the Nazi hierarchy called it "Südostraum") was a source for raw materials, Rohstoffzone for Hitler. (Romania had oil.) Nazi geopolitics derived from the recognition of this fact. Despite Carolist accusations that "the Legion was a German agency in German pay," there is no irrefutable proof. Arnim Heinen's study shows one can lay this accusation to rest. As Heinen stated, "Self-financing is the precondition for every nationalist extremist movement."[971] Hitler chose to woo King Carol rather than to cooperate with the Legion, despite his platonic sympathies. Because of this, he discouraged Hungarian revisionism. Carol had a good chance of becoming Hitler's Proconsul; it was because of his pro-Western sympathies that Carol missed his chance. In January 1941, Hitler,

---

[970]*Op. cit.*, p. 329.

[971]Heinen, *op. cit.*, pp. 337-342.

in German interest, gave Antonescu a free hand to annihilate the Legion.[972] In 1937 Goering stated frankly, "Without Romania, we cannot start a campaign." (Quoted by Lebedev *op.cit.*, p. 53. also by Pravda 14 May 1938). And in April 1938 Hitler repeated to the Romanian ambassador: "He (Hitler) has stated that he has only economic interests in the Balkan states, and he reaffirmed his previous promise to check Hungarian revisionist claims made to Gheorghe Brătianu." (Quoted by Professor Hillgruber, p. 118.). Iorga was less than enthusiastic about viewing Romania as a *Robstoffszone or Sudostraum*: "We are not a market, but a people!"[973]

There was a whirlwind of fascist emotions; the rising tide of Naziism brought traditional Romanian foreign policy into question; and there was the festering problem of Mme. Lupescu's presence in the Palace. How did this affect one of the central problems of Greater Romania, the presence of more than 800,000 Jews in the country, and how did Iorga's position evolve on this issue during 1937?

Iorga became the champion of Jews, provided Jews were ready to assimilate and be loyal to Romania. Yet, it was in the assimilation and loyalty of Jews to Romania that things were not going well. This was not the fault of Jews alone. By 1937 all hopes nurtured by the birth of Greater Romania were gone. In place of it the hysteria of "marching in mood" formed the backdrop to an extremely grave Jewish problem. Powerful forces within and without turned this problem into a national obsession, without offering any constructive (let alone humane) solution. Iorga quoted the Jewish statistician, A. Rupin: There were more than 800,000 Jews in Romania, the majority crowded into cities. According to Iorga, 75% of this Jewish population: — the Jews of Transylvania, of Bucovina, and Bessarabia — were hostile. Transylvanian Jews remained Hungarian, those in Bucovina remained Austrian, many of those in Bessarabia were either Zionist

---

[972]Gheorghe Barbu, Manorial Antonescu — *Le III-ième homme de l'axe* (Paris, 1950), pp. 73-105; and A. Hillgruber, Hitler, *Koenig Carol und Antonescu: die Deutsch-Rumanische Beziehungen 1938-1944* (Wiesbaden, 1954), pp.10-12.

[973]*Neamul Românesc*, 27 November 1938.

or Communist. This was too much for Romania. "It was the duty of Jewish intellectuals to recognize the problem and to decongest the cities, to decrease this number legally, humanely, and quietly."[974]

The question arises: how could this "decongestion" be carried out humanely, legally, and quietly in 1938?! With the outbreak of the Second World War, the chances for a decongestion "humanely, legally and quietly" became remote. The fact remains that if the assimilation of the Jews within the Old Kingdom was limited, in Transylvania, in Bucovina, and Bessarabia (where the majority of Jews of Greater Romania lived), lands representing an irredenta for Hungary and the USSR, the assimilation of the Jews was a failure.

Iorga's anger about the refusal of the Hungarian Jews of Transylvania to become Romanians was great. He knew also the Jews in Bessarabia. In Bucovina he was furious about the Jews of Cernăuți. Jews in this Austro-Jewish metropolis (according to Iorga) disliked even the sounds of church bells; Romanians living there had to learn German or Yiddish to communicate with the Jews in shops. If asked to be served in Romanian, they were insulted.[975] During the time he was prime minister, to his great anger a "Jewish Party" was formed. Given that Iorga wanted to make Romanians of Jews, a party, based on Jewish ethnic identity was anathema for him. But Iorga was traditionally revered by Jews because of his pro-Jewish stands (and because Jews revere intellectual giants as a second nature). Nevertheless, he enjoyed almost no Jewish support politically.

Jews were realists; they had to be if they wanted to survive. They showed no enthusiasm for Iorga's *Sămănătorism*. At the polls, most Jews voted for the Liberals, and Iorga knew it. Not that Iorga didn't make a sustained effort to attract the Jewish vote! He even published electoral pamphlets in Yiddish, pro-

---

[974]*Neamul Românesc*, 5 November 1938.

[975]*Neamul Românesc*, 9 February' 1936 and 8 June 1939. Wrote Iorga: "Our anti-Semitism consists of our right to live in our country'." In 1930, Carol explained to Iorga that he "was no philo-Semite," but used humane and economic considerations when dealing with the Jews. *Memorii*, vol. 6, p. 36.

moting the program of his Nationalist Democratic Party. He tried to form a Jewish constituency. All this did little good. The Jewish situation was so precarious that Jews could not afford the romantic dreams of *Sămănătorism.*

During the interwar years, there was another matter for Iorga and the majority of Romanians to consider: the communist sympathies of the desperately poor Jews. During the 1930s, there was often evidence of support among such desperate Jews for the USSR and Stalinism, a support as misguided as it was transitory.

Sympathy for communism based on Russia (still the national enemy number one for most Romanians) became detrimental for Romanian-Jewish relations. One should not underestimate the hatred, fear, and the suspicion Romanians feel towards Russia. Let us remember Iorga's inflexible hostility. Romanians (including Iorga) were not willing to engage in "self-criticism," or to contemplate to what extent their treatment of Jews contributed to their refusal to assimilate and desperate search for Stalinist answers! They preferred to consider Jews as a hateful, parasitic and disloyal minority, to be gotten rid of by one means or another — the sooner, the better. And now (in 1937) the excesses of the "New Nationalists" only aggravated the bad situation.

Romanian anti-Semites wildly and grotesquely exaggerated this, by considering every Jew a communist. (This was too much even for Antonescu. When in 1941 bureaucrats arrested Jewish millionaires as communists — the "Conducător" reminded them that those Jews had no interest in communism, and ordered their release.)

For the overcrowded ghetto, where the majority of the Jews lived in desperate poverty and daily humiliation, with no future to look forward to, Zionism and even communism seemed to be more of a salvation than *Sămănătorism.*[976] Add to this the many successful appeals the Romanian Jewish community made to the League of Nations (or to Romania's French and English allies). In view

---

[976]Writing in his political diary, Iorga commented about some arrested Communist activists that one could find among them "the inevitable Jews." *Memorii*, vol. VI, p. 171.

of the situation, such appeals were more than justified; but for a Romanian nationalist, appeals by Romanian citizens to foreign powers for protection seemed to be (in view of everything we mentioned before) another manifestation of hostility.

For Iorga, there were also the memories of the "Blank Affair" sordidly distorted, and permanently kept to the fore by the Cuzist reptile press and Legionaries repeating: "Iorga is in Jewish pay." The anti-Semitic hooligans had no access to Iorga's correspondence or to archives; they believed what they wanted to believe. The more, since Iorga took ever stronger stands against them and Hitler. He stood also for the establishment. Consequently they arrived at the convenient conclusion that the "Apostle," the "Teacher of the Nation," had sold out to Blank and the Jews. In the atmosphere of this increasing hysteria, it was power rather than truth that mattered. And political power rarely comes from truth, but from what mobs led by half-rape recorder, half-gangster type students, egged on by corrupt blackmail journalists, depict as truth.[977] The message was something like this: "Iorga got his share at the counter of the Blank Bank; now he wants to deprive us, with his 'Jidoviți,'[978] dogs from our share." This was the reason why he was "the defender and hireling of the Jews'" This theme would often return during the last years of Iorga's life. The devastating cumulative effects of all this on anybody (especially on Iorga!) cannot be overestimated. It became imperative for Iorga to counterbalance this outflow of filth if he wished to play a political role, which he did. During the coming election Iorga would ally himself with the king, the Liberals and Cuzists, in the defense of an establishment challenged by Maniu's supporters and the Legion. This represented a dilemma for Iorga, especially during the fall of 1937. The dilemma was accentuated during the short-lived Goga-Cuzist regime, until the advent of the Royal Dictatorship.

---

[977]They were egged on by Cuzist intellectuals like the corrupt Cuzist journalist Toma Vlădescu, attacking Iorga "in the name of the true Cuzists," writing sordid articles about the Blank affair. Iorga answered with the usual slander suit. *Neamul Românesc*, 1 June 1935.

[978]The "hireling of the Jews," who was (according to this school of thinking) anybody not an anti-Semite.

Iorga, a nineteenth century nationalist, was a stranger in the world of "New Nationalism." Yet, his anti-Semitic political beginnings were still alive. These were balanced by influences exercised on his outlook by Western culture. Yet, Iorga never attacked the big Jewish capitalists in Romania (like Kaufmann, Shapiro, Auschnit), let alone Mme. Lupescu.

The tone of *Neamul Românesc* during these last years of Iorga's life (to quote an American expression) "did not necessarily reflect the opinions of the management," but of Nicolae Georgescu-Cocoş, managing the paper for Iorga. A lot of the abominations in *Neamul Românesc* were his work.[979] One can notice the difference reading the seventh volume of Iorga's *Memorii*, regarding that period, or reading the diary of Mme. Liliana Pippidi-Iorga about what her father spoke in the family circle, and in what Mme. Liliana recalled to this writer. And one should always remember that when it came to standing in the breech, Iorga stood for Romania first putting everything to the second place, himself included. As his librarian and biographer Theodorescu put it well: *Neamul Românesc* and Iorga, the political journalist, were guided by Romania's interest on a day-to-day basis.

No Jew who identified with Romania was ever abandoned by Iorga, but praised, defended, and upheld as an example. This did not stop Iorga carrying out attacks on other Jews. Thus, during the worst times of these hysteria years, Iorga upheld Rabbi Nemierower as an example,[980] defended Sephardic (Spanish) Jews, praised Dr. Gaster, Sigmund Freud, Albert Einstein, and many others. He also deplored any Legionary or Nazi anti-Jewish atrocity.

Dr. Anna Colombo, an Italian Jewish student, came to Vălenii-de-Munte to lecture at Iorga's invitation. She remembers that in Italy she did not encounter any anti-Semitism, but the situation in Romania was a shock for her. She began to feel uncomfortable, and after her lecture she left Vălenii quickly. She returned during 1939, and Iorga promptly offered her a job as a Greek or Latin or Italian translator at his Institute of Universal History. During the interview Iorga freely

---

[979]Mme. Liliana Pippidi-Iorga and many other family members to the writer.

[980]*Memorii*, vol. VI, p. 328; also, *Neamul Românesc*, 15 January 1936.

spoke about his Jewish antiquarian friends, etc. When Miss Colombo decided to reveal (in a letter) to Iorga her Jewish identity, Iorga answered in Italian: "Signorina, I wish to be sincere also. Nobody is guilty for belonging to any nation or religion, which one ought to love. But under present conditions, considering the prevailing spirit, you will hardly find at the Institute among your colleagues the affection necessary for the achievement of a collective effort. I hope I will be able to help you otherwise. If you think I can be of any help to you, let me know. I am at your disposal. Signed, Nicolae Iorga."[981]

Miss Colombo was a Sephardic, Latin (an Italian) Jew. She had all the sympathy Iorga could muster. There was also his friend, Tiktin, the old man whom Iorga wanted to help with all his heart, and on whose behalf he mobilized the king. Yet even though Tiktin accomplished a great deal in Romanian philology and spoke Romanian perfectly, Iorga wanted to bring him to his school in France, not into Romania. In July 1939, it was impossible for Iorga to employ an Italian-Jewish young woman at his Institute of Universal History. He wished to help her, but this woman with a Western psychology and spirit decided proudly to forego his help.

During the hysteria of the fall of 1937, *politicianism* made Iorga sign his name to articles which ought not to have been written. In the second half of 1937 during this "Axis Rainbow," Iorga's journalism is characterized by an unchanging stand against both Nazi Germany and the USSR. He continued to attack Hitler, still hoping that Mussolini would turn against him. Meanwhile, Austria moved closer to the *Anschluss*.[982] During the winter of 1937/1938 the Romanian Ambassador in Vienna (just returning from his post) called on Iorga. The Romanian diplomat (like many from the Balkans) was contemptuous towards Austrians and Viennese in particular. Balkan nations do not see Austria as it is depicted through films like *The Sound of Music*. They have real impressions, not forgetting that Vienna can be very deceptive! Her cafes, theaters, princesses and

---

[981]*Toladot*, 1972, pp. 16-19.

[982]*Memorii*, vol. VII, p. 451.

waltzes, her opera — also, some of the best spirits of Europe — create an impression that life is but a continuous party. History unfortunately does not remain nice for long. It seems to have acquired such a trend since its beginnings, mining good reputations, and bringing the credulous to their senses. After the carnage of the Great War, Vienna was no longer the colorful legend she was under the Hapsburgs, but a mongrel, twentieth century metropolis.

The Romanian diplomat said: Austria is a place "where everybody is lying." Franz von Papen (the German Ambassador) "was certainly a formidable person," yet "all Austria was Nazi, and desired the Anschluss."

When E. Daladier became the French prime minister, Iorga hoped for French regeneration. Codreanu sent greeting telegrams to Hitler on any occasion of the Axis Rainbow, like Mussolini's decisive visit to Germany during the fall of 1937, and immediately after the *Anschluss*. Iorga watched the weakening of the Little Entente. He became furious about the proto-fascist comic opera staged by the prime minister of Yugoslavia, M. Stoyadinović. In the summer of 1936, Titulescu (prodded by the French) tried to improve Romanian relations with the USSR (possibly even to conclude a defensive alliance with them), Iorga remained inflexible. He explained to the king that "Russia remains Russia. There can and should be no alliance with her. If France would demand such an alliance, we should prefer to break with France rather than to accept such an alliance!" Iorga warned the king that under the party system Romania was moving towards the right "like galloping horses." He asked the king what would happen if the Legion quintupled its seats in the Chamber during the next elections?" The king answered that he did not intend to become a rubber stamp. Yet, like everyone in the Third World, Iorga admired Soviet efforts of industrialization. "I will not hide my admiration towards the experience of the USSR (during the 1930s), which I consider the vastest experience the world and humanity have ever known."[983]

---

[983] *Op. cit.*, pp. 436-437; also, *Neamul Românesc*, 10 August 1937, 29 November 1937.

Where Iorga's heart really lay, one can read in two obituaries he wrote during the second half of 1937. The first of the nineteenth century humanist intellectual T. G. Masaryk, and the other of Marshal E. von Ludendorff, the German military demigod, Hitler's companion during the "Beerhall Putsch."

In August 1937 Masaryk passed away. Along with President Wilson (and perhaps together with Iorga), he was a representative intellectual of the nineteenth century and the shaper of the interwar world. Iorga wrote, "a wise man of the world has passed away. Even President Masaryk had to succumb to the fatality of human life. An entire people is mourning the one who was its animator in hard times, and in a decisive hour became the liberating Archangel, assuring wisely order during the hard times inherent in the resurrection of a state destroyed almost a half a Millennium ago." Iorga explained that the success of Masaryk had but one secret: a deep faith in humanity and humans. This was the reason he had no opponents or flatterers. Concluded Iorga: "His death will become a transfiguration, a supreme elevation way beyond the narrow limits of life."

A few months later Marshal Ludendorff died. Iorga, who hated everything Ludendorff stood for wrote: "The Death of a Heathen: That of Ludendorff. Ludendorff did not find peace in the Lord whom he violently rejected as a Semitic intruder into the temple of his ancestors... He took his soul so thirsty of struggle, victory, and domination to the Valhalla of Odin, to reside amidst those merciless demigods." Iorga continued that the Great War for world domination (to which, according to Ludendorff, only the German race had the right) was planned, inspired and sustained by his spirit and absolute convictions: "When he realized he has failed, he did not admit mistakes... but discovered instead the unfortunate Crucified One of the Golgotha as the real culprit. But meanwhile, supported by the Aryan mythology of his ancestors another, more fortunate rival has risen who little by little pushed him aside, and became the leader of the German people. And today, the Heathen who avenged himself in this manner, is on his way on his last mission, with hands dripping of blood, and savage, icy eyes: to announce the latest triumph of Nordic demigods over the Semitic Divinity."[984] One can only once more shiver before Iorga's historical intuitions; Iorga wrote down these lines just a few days after Hitler summoned the Hossbach Conference.

With both internal and external instability, the hectic atmosphere of expectations changing almost daily had only increased by the fall of 1937. Romania was the only Balkan country left with meaningful parliamentary elections. But time was running out. King Carol and the Romanian establishment were challenged not from the left (like in Yugoslavia and Greece) but by radicalism from the right. By the fall of 1937, elections were coming up. Iorga was dubious. "There will be one more attempt to check the validity of universal suffrage."[985]

For the elections, the battle lines were drawn: On one side the king, the political establishment, the Liberals, Goga-Cuzists, and Iorga. A motley crowd opposed them: The National Peasants, the Legion, neo-Liberals, and even the Jewish party. The establishment's goal was to stop the Legion and Maniu. Dr. Angelescu and Costinescu asked Iorga to campaign for the Liberal ticket. Iorga asked Liberal politicians: "What if Codreanu campaigns with revolvers?" He received a telling answer. "We shall do the same, and we have machine guns too."[986]

Iorga, allied with the king (who, in turn, was allied with the Goga-Cuzists) tried to face up to the anti-Semitism of the Legion. This was not easy. Iorga (by political necessity) had to catch "the wind out of sails" of the Legion and couldn't go "soft on the Jews," given his record for the last 20 years. This tactic was bound to turn ugly. By the end of August, he addressed the two great minority problems: He dealt with the Hungarian minority first, in articles which also appeared in brochure form: *Hungarica*. Iorga attacked their irreconcilable

---

[984]*Neamul Românesc*, 1 September 1937, 22 December 1937.

[985]With Iorga's faith in democracy's relevance to Romania's problems shaken, some circles in Czechoslovakia expressed hope that "Romania will remain faithful to democracy." Iorga swiftly retorted: "It is up to our needs and to King Carol!" See *Neamul Românesc*, 24 November and 20 December 1937.

[986]*Memorii*, vol. VII, pp. 435-436.

hostility towards Romanian rule, Hungarian refusal to accept Romanian self-determination, and Hungarian maneuvers to revise the peace treaties. He belabored the reactionary character of medieval Hungarian institutions, attacked "the sub-German culture" of Hungarians, and reminded them of the past oppression of Romanians, concluding: "to re-establish the monstrous and impossible medieval borders (of Hungary), those people (who wish such a course) do not realize the political and social implications and the possible cost."[987]

Later, Iorga wrote a series of articles about the Jewish minority, which also appeared in a brochure: *Judaica*. The articles grew from Iorga's responses to the article of the Romanian Jewish leader, Dr. Willy Filderman, written in the daily *Curentul*.[988] Iorga answered what he considered "the 'insolences' of Dr. Wilhelm Filderman." He went further than that, belaboring Filderman's great mistake (as Iorga considered it): "Dr. Filderman has written that "there is enough room in Romania for everybody, Jews or otherwise."

Dr. Filderman could not have brought up a more unfortunate argument! He ignored Iorga's concept of "organic" development and rights of a people to a territory! Iorga answered that "Romania was not a land to be colonized, which had empty square kilometers," accused Dr. Filderman of making degrading remarks about Romania in and outside the country (Dr. Filderman was interceding on behalf of the Romanian Jews with the League of Nations and Western governments). He continued that Jews in Romania engaged in easy and profitable professions only, and did not assimilate, thus their contribution to Romanian culture was not constructive. Iorga rejected anti-Semitic violence ("broken windows") but saw the situation approaching a cataclysmic climax. He deplored the Jews who did not see it coming, and did not do something about it. He argued that the only solution to this problem was organized Jewish emigration, to decongest Romanian cities. If the Jews continued to refuse to assimilate, then the

---

[987]*Neamul Românesc*, 1-10 August (A series) 1937.

[988]Dr. Willy Filderman, the former schoolmate of Antonescu, would become the determined leader of Romanian Jews during the Second World War.

solution would be: "they will remain among themselves, and we among our-selves." As always, he made allowance for "sympathetic Spanish (Sephardic) Jews, the 'Latin' Jews."[989]

Iorga wrote a lot of truth in his articles, but only considered the situation in a one-sided way and did not offer practical solutions. As the anti-Semitic excesses increased, Dr. Filderman would intervene again in the League of Nations and appeal to French, English, and American Jewish communities, governments, and public opinion. This infuriated Iorga even more; he created a new definition: "Fildermanism."

Now Iorga (the "fighter") entered into combat. He wrote another series of articles on the Jewish question: "The Sowers of Ruin and of Desert." He accused the Jews of ecological destruction, claiming that Jewish entrepreneurs stripped Romanian forests without reforestation. Accusations of other capitalist abuses followed. Jewish capitalists cared only for money, without respect for beauty. He offered Iaşi as an example of how the Jewish population changed the character of the city and not for the better! Iorga concluded: "Jews were different in their own country. Their crude but noble monotheism elevated them way above the others living around them," remembering King David's "Song of Songs." He sadly observed that the Jews were displaced by fate from their own country, with two-thirds of them living in Eastern and Southeastern Europe, causing a problem there.

Contrary to Cuza, Iorga never considered the Jew evil "per se." He always identified difference between Jew and Jew, even while criticizing. He praised the well-integrated Sephardic Jewish community (the trouble was that amidst 800,000 Jews, the ratio between the Spanish Jews and the Jews of the "Pale of Settlement" type was perhaps one to 30). He reserved his worst for the non-assimilating Jews of Transylvania, Bessarabia, and Bucovina. Finally he arrived to his conclusion that "the Jewish question in Romania had to be solved." "After the failure of Zionism," Jews had to find a piece of land for themselves, where "these people can enter into the ranks of the great creative peoples of the world."

---

[989]*Neamul Românesc*, 12-22 August 1937, (A series).

Strangely, Iorga asserted that American Jews had shown a commendable attitude which other Jews ought to emulate.

From the distance, it is possible to maintain that the State of Israel is a reminder that Zionism did not fail. There Jews can successfully engage in agriculture, and be brave soldiers. But Iorga didn't desire the Romanian Jews to become Israelis, he wanted them to be Romanians! As for the American Jews, one should remember the beginnings of the Jewish community in the United States. An address of President George Washington should serve as an example. To the Jewish community of Newport in Rhode Island, Washington wrote: "Our country gives to bigotry no sanction, to persecution no assistance." Such beginnings led to a different Jewish community than the one of a Greater Romania. By this time, Iorga was in favor of boycotting Jewish commerce, in response to Jewish refusal to identify with Romania. "We shall boycott those who have boycotted us."[990]

All this had a touch of electoral geometry. The alliance of the king and of the political establishment with the Goga-Cuzists made Iorga's attitudes politically mandatory, Iorga's diary shows a different attitude. In November 1937, he explained to the king the impossibility of government by the National Peasants. He also warned against a Goga-Cuzist government, because the slogan: "Down with the Jews!" would not suffice to govern. He warned the king that such a government could not be presented to the allies of Romania. Such a program would inevitably lead to excesses. Nor did Iorga consider other politicians more hopeful, concluding that the king must have courage to appoint a government above politics. (Iorga meant that only he could lead such a government.)[991]

---

[990]*Neamul Românesc*, 21-30 September 1937; 16 and 19 October 1937; and 13 November 1937.

[991]*Memorii*, vol. VII, pp. 429-432.

Iorga's oldest son, Mircea (thanks to Tătărescu's intervention) became secretary of the Ministry' of Industry. Later, Mircea Iorga would make more offensive anti-Semitic remarks than his father ever did, during the unfolding electoral campaign.[992]

In the fall of 1937, as Iorga saw it, Romania's interests in the Jewish question demanded from him a kind of preemptive action. Unfortunately, within the confusing whirlwind of the second half of 1937, this great man and intellectual giant lost a lot of perspective and proportion, Iorga failed to distinguish between the secondary' and the essential. He allowed himself to be carried away, failing to draw the line between *politicianism* and honor, or even simple morality. Trying to look out for Romania first and last, Iorga made some unpleasant compromises. And in such a process, one may' inevitably' compromise oneself, despite following Eminescu's "Supreme Law."

Iorga always presented Western Jews (the Jews of France, in particular!) as an example to the Jews of Romania. In November 1937 when Iorga traveled to the Sorbonne to deliver his yearly lectures, he was treated to his own medicine: as he entered the amphitheater, Iorga was genuinely' surprised that "my Jewish friends stayed away from my lecture collectively."[993] Iorga was not unfamiliar with the maxim of Leon Gambetta: "The true democrat does not merely recognize equals, but creates them!"

But Iorga's fury was directed to Maniu and his party. He repeatedly promised Maniu that "the king would crush him." In order to check electoral abuses, Maniu and the Legion concluded an electoral alliance, Iorga attacked Maniu for trying to "mislead the good youth" (an unusually expedient epithet for the Legion).[994] There was a clear disagreement between Iorga and the Goga-Cuzists on foreign policy, and their indiscriminate anti-Semitism. Yet, both the Goga-Cuzists and Iorga stood close to the king and the political establishment.

---

[992]Mme. Liliana Pippidi-Iorga did not like her brother's politics, his thoughtless ties with the Legion, etc.

[993]*Memorii*, vol. VII, p. 432.

[994]*Neamul Românesc*, 1-3 December 1937.

Since Maniu would often be attacked, both from right and left (especially by Iorga) because of his electoral pact with the Legion, it is fair that Maniu's explanation be reproduced. Mounting the witness stand (together with General Antonescu, and with Mihai Manoilescu) in May 1938, during the trial of Codreanu, Maniu explained that he concluded the electoral pact with the Legion only to keep under control electoral abuses which the bureaucracy always employed, and he expected. Under the circumstances, it was mandatory that two entirely different political parties (his National Peasants and the Legion) should close ranks. Maniu pointed out: "I am a democrat; he (Codreanu) is for a dictatorship. I have seen what democracy has done for the peoples of France, England, and the United States. I am for an alliance with France and Great Britain. He (Codreanu) is for an alliance with Germany. He's an anti-Semite; I do not believe that persecution can solve problems." Concluded Maniu: "But I do believe that he is a man of sincerity and probity; he was never in a hurry to take power."[995] These were words worthy of Maniu. Nevertheless, to what extent must the National Peasant Party have lost confidence in itself, if ready to conclude an electoral alliance with the Legion!

The electoral pact assured a free election. The result was devastating for the establishment. It couldn't muster the necessary 40% of the votes to assure the electoral bonus. But the Legion received more than 16% of the votes, becoming the third party of the country.

Given the situation (with the Liberal party unable to continue in power), the king entrusted Goga (with barely 8% of the vote) to form a government, Iorga explained: "The Liberals could not awaken neither enthusiasm nor discipline. The other party (Maniu's party) conducted an absurd campaign bordering on 'lese majestic.' The third major party (the Legion) was lacking direction or program, it represented only mysticism and dictatorial ambition. So, the king called on Goga to form a government. We cannot deny sympathy for this government." Then he went on to praise Goga as "an illustrious poet," and describe the other members of the new government: Goga being the friend of Istrate

---

[995] *Neamul Românesc*, 26 May 1938.

Micescu, a friend of Italy, etc. Iorga found it encouraging that a defector from the National Peasant Party, A. Călinescu, had joined the cabinet. For him the new government was "an intellectual substitute for the electoral mobs." General Antonescu was minister of defense. He concluded that the king had no other choice. All new cabinet members were the king's trusted men.[996] This editorial of Iorga was politically expedient. His real opinions show something very different. Mme. Liliana Pippidi-Iorga carried a diary which she kindly put at the disposal of this writer. An entry from 28 December 1937: Goga visited Iorga and said that he planned to confiscate "the Jewish press," (the popular press of Bucharest). Iorga was less than enthusiastic. He wrote in his political diary (the Goga-Cuzists receiving only about 8% of the vote), "this should cure Goga's dictatorial ambitions." Iorga knew that Călinescu as minister of the interior (the homo) was the king's personal representative, Iorga warned Călinescu that "Goga, with his definite inclination for theatrics, was to be reined in." That was why Carol placed Călinescu into the government, and that would be exactly what Călinescu would do.

Goga said that his first act was to outlaw the "Jewish" press. In quick sequence *Adevărul*, *Dimineața*, and *Lupta* were forbidden to appear, by Ministerial Decree Law. This would become a favorite way of the Goga Cuzist government to carry out legislative measures. Another decree law dissolved the Assembly just elected. Administrative Councils were also dissolved. At that point Iorga told Călinescu (obviously transmitting messages to the king) "I cannot remain in a country where legal principles are enacted by ministerial decisions alone," continuing, "I cannot remain in a country which is governed by such means, on such basis." He concluded saying that "Cuza's doctrine has won." ("Cuza's doctrine" was how Iorga always referred to Cuza's intransigent anti-Semitism.) Iorga added that "he prefers not to enjoy such kind of rights," and wishes "to expatriate himself." He pointedly asked Călinescu to inform the king

---

[996]*Neamul Românesc*, 30 December 1937.

about this, angrily noting: "Goga has broken his word to me concerning the minorities."[997]

At the beginning of January, Cuza's son, Gheorghe, visited Iorga and assured him: "There is no need to respect the constitution, since it does not correspond to public opinion," ridiculing English demands that Romania "should respect the treaties."

The withdrawal of capital from Romanian banks started on a colossal scale, promising to bring down the Romanian economy. On 9 January 1938, Cuza visited Iorga. Feeling that his "doctrine" was being realized, Cuza was radiant. His appearance disputed his age. He was over 80. Iorga remembered Cuza was "healthy, full of energy, and in best mood." He asked Iorga to enter into the government and tried to justify the dissolution of the Assembly carried out "in anticipation." In vain, Iorga pointed out the absurdity of the measures taken.[998] When new elections were called and a violent electoral campaign got under way, despite his disgust, for the sake of politics, Iorga closed ranks with the king, the Goga-Cuzists, Vaida's party, and Dr. Angelescu's Liberals in order to stop the Legion and Maniu. Once Iorga made his choice, he began to employ his qualities as a fighter through his *Neamul Românesc*. This was to be a grave mistake.

Goga assured Argetoianu that "during the coming elections not a single Jew will be allowed to vote." He (Goga) would not recoil from employing any violence to prevent Jews from voting.[999] The king never expected or wished the Goga-Cuza government to succeed. This was to be a necessary transition to a royal dictatorship, proving that parliamentarism did not work, and there was no other alternative for the establishment and for Romania's allies. While trying to make this point, they allowed anti-Semitic excesses and corruption, which in their abominations surpassed even the National Legionary State (if we disregard the violence during the Legionary uprising). Mommsen referred to anti-Semitism as the "mentality of the canaille." The Goga-Cuzists had nothing to offer

---

[997] *Memorii*, vol. 7, pp. 442-445.

[998] *Op. cit.*, pp. 449-450.

[999] "Memoriile lui Constantin Argetoianu," in *Magazin Istoric*, vol. 1 (1967), p. 83.

even for their supporters except the plunder of Jewish property and anti-Semitic excesses. Foreign protests (he USA included)[1000] multiplied, as well as complaints in the League of Nations. If Goga or Cuza were not worried about the West, the king, Iorga, and the Romanian political establishment were. Iorga was against Dr. Filderman's interventions, not only because he believed (together with the king) that anti-Semitism was the best way to stop the Legion, but because he was jealous about Romanian sovereignty. During the Goga-Cuza regime, Iorga continued to attack the Jews of Transylvania and Bucovina because they did not identify with Romania, and continued to praise the Spanish Jews. King Carol gave an interview to the *Daily Herald* of London explaining that, although anti-Semitism was an old story in Romania, government measures only concerned the citizenship of approximately 250,000 Jews who came to Romania illegally after the First World War.[1001] A few days after, the government announced it would re-examine the validity of all Jewish citizenships and the civil rights of Jews.

The government found most of its support within the anti-Semitic bourgeoisie who felt menaced by Jewish competition. Goga-Cuzists didn't have any semblance of a social program or plan for reform, only a desire, reaching the proportions of a kind of a leprosy, to acquire Jewish property. All too many bureaucrats supported the Goga-Cuzists. The "re-examination" of 800,000 Jewish citizenships meant a boondoggle for corruption. The *lănceri* (the "lance bearers"), the militia of the Cuzist party which had a thousand members, increased its numbers within a few weeks to many tens of thousands of armed toughs. An unprecedented scandalous wave of robbery, wanton devastation, blackmail and terror descended on the country. As excesses increased, Iorga received a letter containing the accusation that "he put himself in the service of a campaign preparing a cosmic destruction." He promptly answered that "all injustice and all

---

[1000]The US ambassador, Mr. Franklin Mott Gunther, handed to Goga personally a protest from the American Jewish Communities. Commented Goga, "These are merely impudent!" Time, 24 January 1938. Yet, reliable German sources show that the anti-Jewish campaign was exaggerated on behalf of Cuza, against the will of Goga. Hillgruber, *op. cit.*, p. 16.

[1001]*Neamul Românesc*, 9 and 13 January 1938.

violence is alien to him, but he is nevertheless a Romanian." Jewish intellectuals called upon Iorga "asking for a homeland." He answered that "a homeland is a mystery, an altar; one cannot give it and one cannot divide it either." Iorga reminded Jewish intellectuals that Jews had come to Romania, and taken the wealth of the country without identifying themselves with it.[1002]

During this campaign, the great Jewish industrialists and bankers were not even mentioned, let alone Mme. Lupescu! Goga, a talented poet, but not equipped with conscience, declared himself "a firm friend of Mme. Lupescu.[1003] Nor did Mme. Lupescu (or the Jewish industrialists) intervene for the Jewish masses. It was Dr. Filderman who was fighting almost single-handed. Otherwise, "everybody was for himself, and God for all!" Goga thought about other Jews: "If the Jews are the salt of humanity, the Romanian dish is too salty." He was a poet, but as prime minister he kept the poet and the politician in different rooms, and the communicating door between the two was locked."[1004] It was during the Goga-Cuzist regime that *Neamul Românesc* reached its low point. According to the Iorga family (and if one reads Iorga's non-official opinions, the family's information is borne out), this did not reflect on Iorga, but on Nicolae Georgescu-Cocoș to whom Iorga relegated all too much power. To what depth *Neamul Românesc* had stooped one article should prove: a certain Nicolae Davidescu wrote about "The Judaic Personality of Mr. Titulescu." One may imagine its contents.[1005] Iorga's complex position during this time did no good to anyone, Romania included.

Meanwhile, by the end of January, the electoral campaign was going at full blast in the atmosphere of general breakdown and violence, despite foreign protests on the increase.

[1002]*Neamul Românesc*, 14, and 30 January 1938.

[1003]*Time*, 17 January 1938.

[1004]Hector Bolitho, *Romania under King Carol* (New York, 1940), pp. 43-49.

[1005]*Neamul Românesc*, 5 February 1938.

From the beginning of February, things were moving ahead. After the gravest electoral incidents between the lăncieri and the Legionary guards, the Legion (on Codreanu's orders) withdrew from the campaign. Early February, Codreanu met with General Antonescu. Finally (thanks to the meditation of Prince M. Sturdza), Codreanu met Goga on 8 February 1938. Perhaps they could have worked out something because both of them felt that the king was about to move. It was too late. In the atmosphere of general anarchy and breakdown, with Legionary strength increasing, the king felt his hand forced.

From 7 February on, he initiated his minister of interior, Călinescu, into his plans. At that point, Călinescu left the National Peasant Party, amidst the insults of Mihalache. On 8 February, Iorga was also initiated. And on 10 February 1938, the king announced in his pleasant radio voice through "Radio Romania": "In hard times only heroic methods can strengthen Romania, the salvation of which is our supreme law which I will obey without hesitation."[1006]

Goga, who rightfully felt himself used, out-maneuvered, and unceremoniously discarded, parted most disgracefully with a phrase which has become celebrated: "Israel, you have won!" One of the most obscene experiments in Romanian history came to an end.

In order to "save Romania," the king declared a state of siege, abolished political life and freedoms, suspended the constitution and pro-claimed a fascist corporate constitution instead. He suspended trial by jury and introduced unlimited police brutality coupled with bureaucratic excesses.

The new government consisted of a lot of worthies (nationalist worthies). The prime minister was the Patriarch, Miron Cristea, Marshal Alexandru Averescu, Alexandru Vaida-Voevod, General A. Văitoianu, G. Mironescu, and Constantin Argetoianu also participated. The minister of defense was General Ion Antonescu, the foreign minister Gheorghe Tătărescu. The most important portfolio belonged to the king's now trusted henchman, Armand Călinescu, the minister of interior. Iorga became a minister without portfolio. He welcomed the

---

[1006]Codreanu, *Eiserne Garde*, p. 447.

establishment of the Royal Dictatorship: "an old wish of the king was now to be fulfilled."

With the Goga-Cuzists gone, and no more need to toe their anti-Semitic line, *Neamul Românesc's* tone changed overnight. Iorga (perhaps more sincerely) took a stand against Cuza. "Professor Cuza should not try to disguise his ambitions" (about anti-Semitism and personal power).[1007] So, the process which Borkenau predicted came full circle. Since conditions for a Romanian democracy were lacking, the futile convulsions left only a choice between a radical (leftist) or a reactionary dictatorship. Neo-Liberalism (as Manoilescu developed his corporatist ideas) came to its logical conclusion; a fascist, (or pseudo-fascist) state under the leadership of an industrializing clique; an up-dated establishment with the king playing the role of dictator. Since the people would not accept voluntarily the sacrifices of forced industrialization political freedoms had to be done away with. But democracy was impracticable, communism unthinkable, the right radicalism of the Legion inadmissible. What seems to be so sad is how difficult it was then to find any constructive solution for Romania's problems. Iorga wished for neither the rule of the "odious" political parties, nor dictatorship. Although he now gave his support to Carol (and his prestige!), he had always declared himself to be "categorically against all dictatorships," because "all revolutionary movements, whether from the left or right, kill culture systematically."[1008]

If he expected a "creative regime," the Royal Dictatorship was not to be the one. Yet, he cooperated with it because he identified this regime with the survival of Greater Romania. Not the government but the Royal Camarilla governed. Besides Carol and Mme. Lupescu, its core was Ernest Urdăreanu (its most unpopular member), and the minister of interior, Călinescu, a real desperado, perhaps the kind of person the king needed. Călinescu was strongly pro-Western, ruthless and skillful. The king could rely upon his talents. There were the industrialists Malaxa and Auschnit (sometimes in disgrace when their interests

---

[1007]*Neamul Românesc*, 8 April 1938.

[1008]*Neamul Românesc*, 13 and 25 March 1937; also, 28 May 1939.

clashed with those of the royal industrialist Carol). There was G. Marinescu, and the sinister secret police chief, Mihail Moruzov.[1009] There were some less important members, all under the supervision of "darling Duduia." Mme. Lupescu's influence on Carol remained strong. Codreanu was right when he remarked, "Madame orders, the king wishes."

After the dissolution of political parties, Iorga thought that "time has come for reconciliation." A new corporatist constitution was drafted, Iorga was instrumental in working it out. It was put to a referendum by open ballot, and was approved by an all too impressive 99% of votes. A new "one party," the PRN (Party of National Rebirth) was formed, and, according to *Porunca Vremii*, uniforms were introduced for every functionary and profession. Predictably, only Maniu and Mihalache refused to wear the new fascist regalia. Iorga, with his abhorrence towards such theatrics, resisted wearing it, but Călinescu (Iorga's former student) knew how to make him to toe the line.[1010]

The corporate constitution had some important articles. One of them was that members of the government were to be selected by the king, and every cabinet member was supposed to have at least three generations of Romanian ancestry. This stipulation was clearly aimed at the Zelinski family.

So much for the forms. As for the foundations, it remained more of the same. Peasant misery, creating an increasing agrarian proletariat, continued. But the new industrial complexes and the I.A.R. (a Romanian aircraft industry paid for by every Romanian with an excise tax on postage stamps) guaranteed fabulous profits for the Camarilla and those few near enough to the pork barrel. Henry Roberts pointed out, in assessing the Carolist corporate state, that while industrialization in Romania was desirable, the manner in which it was carried

---

[1009]Mihai Moruzov conducted Carol's own personal Secret Police (not to be confused with the dreaded Siguranța). He looked out for Carol's business interests, personal security, and the safety of Mme. Lupescu.

[1010]As Mme. Liliana Pippidi-Iorga remembered. Professor Iorga did not want to dress up in this ridiculous fascist dress. Călinescu threatened to confiscate his beloved library. Iorga gave in and dressed up unwillingly. The next day he met journalists dressed up in the uniforms of their own journalist corporation. He addressed them: "You come in new uniforms, but still have your old moral and professional standards."

out was not. "It would appear that the Romanian people were not paying temporarily for the establishment of industries which would benefit them subsequently, but were instead being drained of their resources for the profit of a small group of industrialists, politicians, and court favorites in no way responsible to them."[1011]

Iorga continued to support the king because he didn't see any alternative. Mme. Liliana remembers in her diary an entry from 10 May (the Romanian national holiday) 1938: Mme. Liliana read "the speech made by Dad" during the festivities. She discussed it with Mme. Catinca, and noted down: "both she and Mom agreed with Dad." Iorga said during his speech "to redress the present situation, the king has to be strongly supported."

After the establishment of the Royal Dictatorship, Codreanu offered Iorga his cooperation. Were these tactics? Iorga's answer to Codreanu certainly didn't contain tactics: "I cannot have anything to do with people who operate in a criminal way, and I am indifferent whether they hate me or appreciate me." He concluded with advice that Codreanu dissolve the Iron Guard and instead set-up an anti-Communist league.[1012] On 21 February 1938, Codreanu dissolved the Iron Guard, but issued a secret circular that the Iron Guard would continue its existence and activities.

Meanwhile, Hitler came home. On 12 March, he entered Vienna in triumph. (Codreanu immediately sent his greetings to the Fuhrer.) Iorga prophesied long before: "If Vienna loses its international context, it will become a provincial town. And Vienna is Austria." Now Iorga saw the present in the perspective of the past: "And they will come, the vulgar mobs, and will not understand the tombs in the Capucines, something which they destroyed now forever."[1013] The Hapsburg tombs in the Capucines were the last thing on the mind of those "vulgar mobs."

[1011]Roberts, *op. cit.*, pp. 206-214, and also pp. 344-345.

[1012]*Memorii*, vol. VII, p. 459.

[1013]*Neamul Românesc*, 13 October 1933 and 29 March 1938.

Several hundreds of thousands of them welcomed Hitler on the large opening before the "Hofburg" with a thunder of "Sieg-Heil!" Vienna, had for so long been the powerhouse and cultural center of Central Europe — what had she become during those days! No wonder those "vulgar mobs" appreciated Hitler! He was formed by them — not by the cosmopolitan Vienna — but by the other one: the dormitory on the Meldeman Strasse. The faceless anthill of a great city of the twentieth century, dominated by lower-middle-class frustrations. The sterile frustrations of Karl Lueger and Georg V. Schoenerer (whose paper the young Hitler had hawked on Vienna streets) came now to the fore. This Vienna always rejected the humanism and universalism of the other Vienna. Now, with Hitler's help it triumphed over it, and relegated it into oblivion. Iorga was not surprised. He knew the Janus-face of this city well.

On 14 February 1938, an important Council of Ministers took place. With General Antonescu not invited, Călinescu explained the situation as follows: the king, having failed to come to an agreement with Codreanu, had decided to eliminate him. (This did not mean physical elimination yet.) Călinescu seemed to be eager towards this end. General Antonescu, the minister of defense, on the other hand was emerging as an obstacle. Călinescu explained that Antonescu had prestige, even with those officers who sympathized with the Legion. Because of this, General Antonescu participated in the government; he was a guarantee of order. But he would not allow the army to be used or manipulated, especially for political purposes. As Călinescu saw it, only if Legionary activity constituted a threat to the national security could Antonescu be moved. At the present, it did not represent such a threat. With Antonescu absent, Călinescu continued to lay out his school of thought: "If we in the present situation will proceed softly, we shall lose both authority and power." Călinescu recommended "a radical action." Iorga, Tătărescu, and other cabinet members supported his recommendation that radical action be to be taken under some "legal pretext," after which the Legionaries could be shipped off "to concentration camps like Dobrovăţ, Miercurea-Ciuc, and others." Iorga repeated enthusiastically: "Off with them to

Dobrovăț and to Miercurea-Ciuc."[1014] Although the minutes of Călinescu's diary seem to be genuine, this writer cannot be sure they are complete.

During the summer of 1985, this writer had a long interview with the engineer Traian Boeru, the leader of the Legionary *Echipa Morții* (Death Squad) that murdered Iorga. (When this writer spoke about murdering Iorga to Boeru, he protested: "No, we executed him!") Boeru told a different story. According to him, Iorga said during the Council of Ministers: "If there is a pack of wolves to be taken care of, you should aim at the leader first!" Such was the opinion also of Horia Sima about Iorga's role. (Horia Sima could not get along with Traian Boeru, and was very contemptuous of him).[1015] More importantly, such was the opinion of the Legionary rank and file, and also of the Legionary leadership, especially those with whom this writer had the chance to establish contact.

In retrospect, whether the version of the Legion is true or not is academic. The remarks sound much like what Iorga would blurt out in one of his emotional states of mind. (Whether true, or not, the Legionaries believed this.)

"The pretext" Călinescu needed was supplied by Codreanu. Iorga wrote a violent editorial accusing the Legion of subversive activities in the chain of Legionary Restaurants. Codreanu answered Iorga in two letters. Mme. Liliana noted in her diary: (entry from 27 March 1938) "Dad received a letter dated from 17 March from Codreanu," calling him an "unclean soul," and "similar epithets." Iorga answered reminding Codreanu "how much bloodshed he is responsible for," and talked the matter over with Călinescu, hoping to take Codreanu to court (for insulting an active Cabinet member). On 30 March, Iorga started a litigation "for offending a minister." This was a standard operational procedure for Iorga. Was this the nineteenth century? Or the "pretext" for which Iorga and Călinescu were waiting? Maybe both. It had fatal consequences for Iorga. Dealing with the Legion's "New Nationalism" was not the process of a nineteenth

---

[1014]The proceedings of this Council of Ministers were not seen by the writer in its original. They are from Armand Călinescu *Memoriile*, the entry dated 14 February 1938 quoted by Gheorghe Savu, *Însemări politice*, LX, No. 6 (123) June 1977, p. 59.

[1015]Horia Sima, *Cazul Iorga-Madgearu* (Madrid, 1961), pp. 17-20, 75.

century courtroom. It was more likely dealing with "death squads." The reaction of the Legion was not lacking. Here is an entry from Mme. Liliana's diary (1 April 1938): letters began to arrive claiming that "Iorga sold out to the Jews." Another letter explained that if Hitler came to Romania, "he could deliver us from the Jews." Wrote Miss Liliana: "What kind of sad and hard times we are living in" (Iorga was less concerned with his security than his family was). Iorga had some after-thoughts. As Mme. Liliana remembers in an entry into her diary from 17 April 1938: "Dad is angry, arthritic pain is tormenting him, and he sent a telegram renouncing the process against Codreanu because 'Codreanu did not render account, he simply did not know what he was doing when he sent the letter to me.'" It was too late.

A night before, Călinescu struck. Within a few hours about 30,000 Legionary homes were searched, and thousands of them arrested. Almost the whole Legionary elite was imprisoned in Jilava, Miercurea-Ciuc, Râmnicu-Sărat, Vaslui, Dragomirna, and Dobrovăț. The violent persecution of the Iron Guard was intensified during the summer and the fall; from then on the emblem of the Legion, the crossed bars of a prison, was well-deserved.

Mme. Liliana remembers under the same diary entry (17 April 1938) that Călinescu informed Iorga of the discovery of Legionary circulars calling for revolt, etc. As Mme. Liliana remembers: "It greatly surpassed everything Codreanu wrote in his letter to Dad." Iorga changed his mind. Călinescu got what he wanted from him: Iorga did not withdraw his accusations against Codreanu, and the process proceeded. Iorga launched a press campaign against Codreanu. Here we reproduce only a pale reflection of the original. Iorga wrote serials for two weeks, "how the Legion abused the Romanian people's confidence," which was looking for an "Emissary of the Archangel." Further, about Codreanu, whom "they do not understand but still love." In the same issues there were adulatory messages of loyalty (telegrams and letters) addressed to the king. Then Iorga described the little Romanian, now sadly lost in the twentieth century. He did not wish communism, but something genuine for his country. This little Romanian felt oppressed and useless, "an inert object of a life he doesn't understand." In such a void, Orthodoxy could have had a natural role, but (according to Iorga) the Orthodox faith of the Legion was a deception. Iorga thought that this lost little Romanian would have been happy even if touched by a lie. Thus, reforms must come from above, and must be inspired by loftier souls than that of the Legion. One should follow the king.

Facsimiles of Codreanu's letter to Stelescu and about the assassination of Duca were reproduced by Iorga. He referred to the Legion as being "a seditious movement," which infiltrated even the General Staff. Then Iorga laid out the Zelinski family tree: Codreanu did not have as much as a drop of Romanian blood in his veins! Iorga answered the letter of a young Romanian sympathizer of the Legion: "I want also a quick, radical improvement like you do, we only differ in our methods and leadership. You are following a man who was extolling and committing crimes. I follow the king." The facsimiles of more Legionary documents captured by Călinescu's raid were published, proving that the Legion had accepted Jewish money, followed by a list of Legionary crimes, torture instruments, and weapons.[1016]

In the entry in Mme. Liliana's diary from 19 April 1938, we read: "Walk with Dad. He knows about Codreanu's arrest." She continues that Codreanu was taken to Predeal. Next day (20 April 1938) Mme. Liliana remembered that Călinescu came to Iorga with proofs (words) which his raid had found in the "Green House" in Bucharest. They found traces of German subsidies for the Legion, and contacts with the Nazis. Călinescu said that the majority of arrested Legionaries were taken to the concentration camp of Dragomirna and Tismana. If there were Legionary connections with Nazis, or Nazi subsidies paid to the Legion, the proof has not been found to this day.

Iorga concluded his press campaign addressing the youth: "Well, kid-heroes, the new Romania is established through order, but order cannot be established except by those who keep order at home." Codreanu was sentenced to six months imprisonment for insulting Iorga. Iorga commented, "The military tribunal pronounced a sentence according to its considerations. I also had my role

---

[1016]*Neamul Românesc*, 21, 22, 27, 29, and 30 April and 1 May 1938.

in it." He explained that he was prodded into action by the "perfectly authentic" documents found in the Legion's possession shown to him. He went on, that he saw to it that Codreanu ("admired, by so many") should receive a treatment "which does not correspond to his errors soaked in blood, but to his social class." With this, Iorga "will take the Christian Communion of Easter and look forward to the Second Coming of Christ." The last of Iorga's editorials was entitled "Down with the new religion of Hate!"[1017]

But a six month prison sentence for Codreanu did not seem enough for the political establishment. In a few weeks, the Military Tribunal (well-selected) gave Codreanu a ten-year sentence on charges (Iorga, referring to Codreanu only as "Zelinski", or "the terrorist Zelinski"), of being in contact with foreign (understand, Nazi) organizations. The Military Tribunal did not present any proof to this end.

Iorga concluded that Codreanu was "no new Christ," because "the terrorist Zelinski" was responsible for three murders: Manciu, Duca, and Stelescu. Many Romanians did not agree with Iorga. Iorga concluded again: "One must sometimes enjoy the bitter pleasures of unpopularity."[1018]

Thus, the process which started Iorga's life as a politician almost forty years ago with his article in *L'Indépendence Roumaine* came full circle. Now he was committed on the side of King Carol (the updated establishment) in a showdown with the social radicalism of "New Nationalism." And he was committed irrevocably. Although Iorga never made a commitment to stand with Carol to the end, the evolution of the situation and to Iorga's well-known personal characteristics, made sure that once he was a part of the operational machine of the Royal Dictatorship, he could not extricate himself until that machine ceased to function. Iorga had therefore to reckon with all the consequences of defeat, which incidentally were bound to include not only the loss of his university position and income, but also his physical annihilation. This followed if from nothing else, from the role Iorga played in the imprisonment of Codreanu. Whether

[1017]*Neamul Românesc,* 4, 5, and 7 May 1938.

[1018]*Neamul Românesc,* 18, 19, 21, 23, 26, and 27 May 1938.

mistaken or not, the Legion believed that Iorga advised Călinescu that "if there is a pack of wolves to be taken care of, you aim at the leader first!" And for Legionaries it became mandatory to retort in kind and to see whose arm was longer. To kill somebody whom these young fanatic idealists considered primarily responsible for the imprisonment (and subsequent death) of their idolized leader was a legitimate action. If and when they got into the position to do so, they would extirpate their challenger. Iorga and his family received letter after letter full of death threats.[1019] The family lived in terror. Not Iorga, he was nonchalant about such things, and a brave man. On 30 November 1937, at the University of Paris, Iorga gave a voluminous interview. At the end of the interview, the French journalist asked Iorga to comment on the anarchy in civil war-ridden Catalonia, in which his friend, the archeologist, Professor Puig y Catafaleh, was almost murdered. Iorga answered: "Who knows? This is a menace we all face. I cannot tell how to act or what to do when you have to confront your murderers." And (as the journalist remembers) Iorga descended with good humor into the noisy lecture hall.[1020]

If Iorga took the danger in his stride, his wife and daughters (Mme. Liliana and Alina) were living in terror. And not only the Iorga family; even friends of the family and the servants despaired for his life. He was now a minister, the President of the Corporate Senate, and permanent member of the New Advisory Crown Council, with enlarged functions and responsibilities.[1021]

[1019]Iorga received a considerable amount of anonymous hate mail. This writer read these letters in the Iorga family's archives. One of the letters calls Iorga "a cynical criminal". Another said that "not being a Romanian anymore," Iorga should "get out of our country, that showered honors upon you." Another letter promised Iorga that he would be found anywhere in the world. "We swore on our lives, and shall keep our oath. Remember, you have a wife and children, the curse of the Romanian mothers will reach you! Keep this in mind, because this is the 11th hour!" Signed: "A good Romanian woman." Legionaries constantly sent Iorga pictures of the Captain, which he ripped apart in anger.

[1020]*Adevărul*, 30 November 1937.

[1021]Iorga refused to touch salaries from these additional positions and donated them to charitable causes.

By the summer of 1938, General Antonescu left the government. There were conflicts of personality and policy between Carol and Antonescu. Antonescu, a proud man of character, refused to submit to Mme. Lupescu's meddlings, and made himself a nuisance, by constantly calling the attention of the king to the state of unpreparedness of the Romanian army. Iorga was conscientious about the sensibilities of King Carol; he went out of his way "not to anger the king." When somebody proposed making Antonescu an Academician (a flattery, bordering on the absurd), Iorga opposed the move, for the sake of the dignity of the Academy, but mainly because he feared angering the king. He intervened with Colonel Urdăreanu, Professor Lepădatu, and others. He explained: "General Antonescu was a dangerous man!", reminding people of Antonescu's relations with Codreanu, etc. General Antonescu's candidacy was rejected. But Antonescu with his "long memory" would never forgive this.[1022]

During 1938, the Legion went through a nightmare. Călinescu was relentless. One should not forget the cruelty and efficiency of the torture chambers of the *Siguranţa*. Even compared with the NKVD or the Gestapo, the *Siguranţa* held more than its own. The Legionaries continued to carry out senseless outrages, very much against the will of Codreanu in prison. He felt that it endangered his life.

Right after the *Anschluss*, the Czechoslovak crisis started. From the first day of the crisis, Iorga stood up for Czechoslovakia, and wrote: "A Friend in Need." He considered Austria the springboard of Nazi imperialism towards Southeast Europe and the Near East, warning desperately about this.[1023] He did not object to Sudeten German minority rights, but the very moment Germany brought up the idea of *Lebensraum*, all rules of the game changed. Iorga was furious when the Yugoslavia of Stoyadinović remained silent. "Not even an enemy would deserve that!"[1024] On 20 September 1938, Iorga commented to his

---

[1022] Alexandri Lepădătu, *Scrieri Alese: Articole, Cuvântări, Amintiri* (Cluj-Napoca, 1985), p. 408.

[1023] *Neamul Românesc*, 30 March and 24 May 1938.

[1024] *Neamul Românesc*, 16 July and 23 September 1938.

family: "In the present, Europe is governed by outright fools or deranged, abnormal men like Hitler, Mussolini (sic!), or Stalin, or for that matter, Kemal Ataturk." And England tries to escape from it all by occupying herself with the Duke of Windsor. (Mme. Liliana's diary, entry from 28 September 1938).

Finally in Munich, Czechoslovakia was sacrificed "to peace in our times." The goal seemed laudable, and the sacrifice wouldn't have been excessive, if peace had been assured. As it happened, the visible result was the destruction of the only democracy of Central Europe, and with millions of Czechs under German yoke, the prize would be even more elusive. The failure was now aggravated by dishonor, for the West had sacrificed an ally.

When Hitler said after Munich, "he had no more territorial demands in Europe," Iorga commented, "If Munich succeeds in calming the German soul, peace is saved and the credit goes to Chamberlain. In Munich, civilization recognized the danger; maybe there is hope."[1025] The Polish foreign minister, Colonel Beck, now demanded Cyeszyn. Iorga had some premonitions: "Poland should remember Frederick II and Catherine II!"[1026] He was not always wrong about the course of events he predicted. He feared that Hungarian revisionism would be encouraged. When Hungarians began to press their territorial demands, Iorga commented, "The Hour of the Jackal." Later, when the first Vienna Diktat returned to Hungary the southern part of Slovakia, he ominously commented, "Hungary has won!"[1027] But Iorga forgot that the return of this territory was justified, forgot his own ethnic, organic principle. More than 90% of the inhabitants were Hungarians, and wanted to return to Hungary. The mistake was made at Versailles, not at Vienna in 1938.

[1025] *Neamul Românesc*, 1 and 6 October 1938.

[1026] *Neamul Românesc*, 27 September and 16 October 1938,

[1027] *Neamul Românesc*, 12 October and 6 November 1938.

Now the fate of the Carpatho-Ukraine (Ruthenia) became acute, Iorga opposed to the change of the status quo,[1028] demanded a vigilant stand against Hungarian revisionism, and the collusion of it with Nazi Germany. (Hungarian revisionism was colluding more with Fascist Italy, but Iorga preferred to ignore this connection.) The debate with Hungarian historians, was going on apace, Iorga engaged also with Lord Rothermere's *London Daily Mail* because of its support for Hungarian revision.

When the Romanian Transylvanian Patriotic Society (ASTRA) organized a gigantic meeting, Iorga was the chief orator. After a sardonic attack on Hitler's "well-known peaceful intentions," he refuted Hungarian pretensions, continuing attacks on Hungarian historians.[1029] Iorga gave other advice to Hungarians, explaining that the day would come when Hungary will recognize the real dangers threatening her from Germany and Russia, and would need cooperation with Romania.[1030]

Wrote Iorga during the fall of 1938: "Everything is crumbling away, the whole post-war world, the treaties. Let us prepare for the worst without hysteria."[1031] Another reason for his anguish was the decreasing significance of small nations, such as Romania. Finally, he was an old man, of another century.[1032]

During the fall of 1938, Carol traveled to the West, first to France and Britain. Then, on the way back, he had a long talk with Hitler. The Legion went on a rampage, murdering Professor F. Ştefănescu-Goangă, the President of Cluj University (and a relative of Călinescu) and a high police official (Colonel G. Cristescu in Cernăuţi).

[1028] *Neamul Românesc*, 13 October and 6 November 1938.

[1029] "Lupta ştiinţifică impotrivă dreptului românesc," passim.

[1030] *Neamul Românesc*, 21 September 1938.

[1031] *Ibid.*

[1032] Many times Iorga's ideas in foreign policy would seem childish. When Mussolini demanded from France, Corsica, Djibouti, and Tunis, Iorga endorsed his claims in (as he called it) "this Latin hostility." *Neamul Românesc*, 20 December 1938.

The king's answer was swift and merciless. The next day, Codreanu, the Nicadori, and the Decemviri were shot, "while trying to escape." Iorga wrote: "Grave events have come to pass." He continued that no oppressor used such hound-like methods as the Legion; consequently, conventional methods of justice do not suffice. One must go beyond laws, society has to be protected and saved. "Instead of prostrating itself (society) has to defend itself." This defense has to go beyond legalities, "through instant decisive reflexes." Then Iorga asked: "Will Romanian society understand this?"[1033]

Regardless of what Iorga has written, everything indicates that his real feelings were something very different. As Mme. Liliana remembers in her diary (the entry bears the marking December 1938): "Dad is disgusted with the murder of Codreanu, and of other Legionaries." Iorga told Călinescu the following: "I am upset, not because they were shot! But because the state has become a murderer!" He told his family that the king and Călinescu arranged these murders. The other cabinet members knew nothing about it and Iorga seriously considered resignation. During a visit of Călinescu to Iorga's home, which (according to Mme. Liliana) took place on 3 December, Mme. Liliana overheard a violent exchange between Iorga and Călinescu, and Iorga offered his resignation.

During these days, (and during the whole winter of 1938-1939) Professor Iorga had to cope with another grief: Mme. Catinca fell gravely ill, an illness which was to continue for months. Her predicament, (like anything concerning the family), was handled with the utmost "European" discretion, which did not diminish the grief of her loving husband or that of the family.

Hitler overlooked for now the murders, because he found it expedient to maintain normal relations with Romania for reasons we know, but he never forgave Carol. The restriction on the Nazi press was lifted (temporarily) and Nazi newspapers started attacking Carol and his Jewish mistress with relish. Editorialized the *Angriff* (the newspaper of the SS) "The king and his Jewish Mistress." The historical analogy was ancient Persia and Queen Esther. The Biblical story

---

[1033] *Neamul Românesc*, 4 December 1938.

had a most un-Biblical ending. Wrote the *Angriff*, "The Jews infected his country and Persia went to pieces."[1034]

By December 1938, Călinescu had become too self-centered and conscientious of his power. He had to clash with an individualist such as Iorga. Iorga wrote that "those who created Greater Romania are bound by certain memories and ideas despite some innovations" (Iorga had made a pun against the one party system of the Front of National Rebirth). After that Călinescu ordered the confiscation of *Neamul Românesc*, as Iorga angrily put it, "like a Bolshevik pamphlet." Nor did Călinescu stop. An entry in Mme. Liliana's diary (from 19 February 1939) recounts how a *Siguranţa* file was presented to Iorga with reports about Iorga allegedly committing "lèse-majesté" during his lectures. Iorga promptly demanded an inquiry.[1035]

Călinescu gave a confident interview to the *Paris-Soir*. "The Legion is an old story. The Legion does not exist anymore." Lloyd's of London thought differently. When he tried to buy a life insurance policy, Lloyd's refused to sell him one. Ultimately, it would be Lloyd's estimate which was to be proven cruelly accurate.[1036] After the Patriarch, Miron Cristea's death, on 7 March 1939, Călinescu became prime minister. Finally, the real power in the government went to the fore.

Although by now Iorga had definite opinions about what Mussolini was doing, we still see in the press a flip-flop in Iorga's attitudes towards him. Just before the War, Iorga wrote that Mussolini was "not only the man of Rome," but "a Roman." And, as a Roman, he should understand the "golden mean," and recognize certain limits. Iorga followed with great interest the increasing American attention paid to Europe. "The United States decided the issue of the First World War," and then "the idea of human solidarity, escaping a Hitler and a

---

[1034]*Angriff*, 8 December 1938, and *Time*, 19 December 1938.

[1035]*Neamul Românesc*, 17 and 30 December 1938. Iorga loved to exercise an indirect, devastating criticism of the court during his lectures. with historical parallels. No wonder that some of his lectures were interpreted in the correct way! They certainly bordered on *lèse-majesté*.

[1036]Roger-Weber, *op. cit.*, p. 556, and *Time*, 22 October 1939.

Mussolini, is central in the mind of people in Washington, and those who blackmail with war should keep in mind American public opinion." Then, "Italy today represents an imperialism without limits."

And then, we see Iorga's illusions again. Mussolini is the good guy, and Hitler the bad one, representing Nietzsche's paganism. But (according to Iorga) Hitler can do nothing if Mussolini says no. "Does Mussolini not feel to be his duty to say no?"[1037]

When Hitler marched into Prague, Iorga was shattered. With everything crumbling away, national unity was mandatory. All illusions about Wilson, Benes, the League of Nations, and Titulescu should disappear. Only force counted. Hungary asked a protectorate over Ruthenia, as if it were Syria or Palestine.[1038]

Then, the Italians occupied Albania. Iorga was very upset, perhaps because Mussolini had unmasked his real face even for Iorga. Then there was also Iorga's deep sympathy for Albania and King Zog, and he did not cherish the sight of a small nation trampled over. The entry in Mme. Liliana's diary (8 April 1939) reads: "As the Italian fleet was bombarding Durazzo and Valona, Dad was very upset. He has a foreboding about the imminent start of the Second World War." Iorga did not remain silent. He wrote that he wished to avoid talking about Albania, but could not help expressing sympathy with King Zog. There was also Iorga's fledgling institute in Santi Quaranta. But Santi Quaranta would soon be renamed as "Porto Edda," in honor of the Duce's daughter.

In the middle of March, the Hungarian army, crushing the resistance of the Ukrainian nationalists, overtook Ruthenia. Wrote Iorga; "Fire Is On The Way!"[1039] Romania ordered mobilization, which turned into a disaster showing how right the predictions of General Antonescu were. The entry in Mme. Liliana's diary (from 17 March 1939) describes the sixth Crown Council in which

---

[1037]*Neamul Românesc*, 22 August 1939; 15 July 1938; 21, 23 August, and 10 November, 1938.

[1038]*Neamul Românesc*, 16 and 17 March 1939.

[1039]*Neamul Românesc*, 30 March and 18 April 1939.

Iorga participated. Iorga described how the mobilization order was decided, but generals also spoke up during the Crown Council. They considered the defenses and the armaments of the Romanian Armed Forces inadequate. Yet the mobilization was carried out with a fanfare, and slogans like "Nici o brazdă!" ("we shall not give back as much as a furrow!") a slogan which was soon coming home to roost. During these days the Nazis took away Memel from Lithuania without ado.

Romanian diplomacy worked overtime, concluding an economic agreement with Germany (the "Wohltat Treaty"). In the entry of 24 March 1939, Mme. Liliana remembered the act of mobilization and the conclusion of the Wohltat Treaty coinciding. Also, that Iorga was displeased with the terms of the Wohltat Treaty. As he saw it, Romanian oil and raw materials would be traded for Czechoslovak armaments (the Romanian army to a great extent was armed with Czech weapons, but the factories were now under German control). He had a discussion with Foreign Minister Gafencu with no result. As Iorga concluded: "We do not speak the same language!" Parallel with the opening towards Nazi Germany, Romania obtained (together with Greece) an English and French guarantee of her territorial integrity, Iorga saw Romania between two imperialist blocks, Nazi Germany and the USSR. Romania did not ask for anything, and put its raw materials at the disposal of everybody. But, when Italy turned on France, Romania had to draw some painful conclusions. Romania was obliged to break the absolute neutrality she observed between two Latin brothers.[1040]

During the spring of 1939, Carol, who had the chance to become a German pro-consul in Romania, definitely missed it. Hitler moved now to destroy Poland. As early as 2 April, Iorga considered it his moral duty to line up on the Polish side. During the coming weeks Iorga emphasized Polish historic and economic rights in Danzig, which he called "Gdansk."[1041] He reminded Colonel Beck that almost ten years ago he had addressed Iorga demanding that Romania "bring sacrifices for European peace" (to re-establish good relations with the

---

[1040]*Neamul Românesc*, 17 June 1936 and 16 April 1939.

[1041]*Neamul Românesc*, 2 April and 16 May 1939.

USSR without settling the issue of Bessarabia). Iorga (and Romania) did not give similar advice to Colonel Beck, "now that his dreams are collapsing."[1042] Meanwhile, the Western powers were negotiating a possible defensive treaty with the USSR and cooperation against Nazi Germany. Iorga always saw the difficulty of such an alliance.

And, on 23 August 1939, the shattering news of the Nazi-Soviet Pact arrived. Ultimately, this pact would decide the fate of the "No Man's Land of Europe" for almost the rest of the century.

Iorga didn't seem so alarmed in his first reaction as Romanian articulate public opinion was. He wrote: "So Russia concluded a commercial treaty with the Reich like we did; as of now Russia apparently does not wish to get into the war.... So let us calm the agitated souls." But a week after the treaty was concluded, war broke out. Within two weeks Germany and Russia partitioned Poland for the fourth time. Iorga somehow followed Dr. Samuel Johnson's dictum: He began "to substitute imagination with the real thing what was there." Finally, he found the pertinent historical parallel in a blistering editorial entitled: "Tilsit." As Iorga wrote, "the shadow of Tilsit is haunting." And added, "will the division of Europe last this time?"[1043] A good example of Iorga attempting to career his political journalism to "daily needs", and to assure calm amongst those intellectuals who looked to him for guidance.[1044]

The great Peloponnesian War of European civilization was on hand. Romania's official position was neutrality in practice, with a pro-Western tilt. But Iorga was never neutral. From the very first day, he showed strong support for England and France.

[1042]*Neamul Românesc*, 25 August 1939.

[1043]*Neamul Românesc*, 24 August and 11 October 1939.

[1044]Mme. Liliana Pippidi-Iorga and other members of the Iorga family explained that Iorga often wrote editorials much in spite of himself, to keep in line that intellectual public which relied upon him for political guidance.

On 15 September, the Soviets fell on the back of the still desperately resisting Poles. Romania proceeded to abrogate a treaty with Poland concluded exactly for such an occasion. Iorga did not comment. Instead, with tens of thousands of Poles (the government of Poland included) fleeing to Romania, he wrote: "Let us open our hearts to the Polish refugees."[1045]

Then, the Iron Guard carried out its feat. On 21 September 1939, it ambushed Călinescu's car in Bucharest and shot to death their implacable enemy. They went to the headquarters of Radio Romania, broke into the studio, and announced in trembling, triumphant tones: "The Iron Guard killed Călinescu! The murder of the "Căpitanu" has been avenged!" After that, in true Legionary tradition, they gave themselves up in expiation.

Neamul Românesc appeared in a black frame. Wrote Iorga, "a man who has sacrificed everything for the quiet and the peace of Romania was murdered yesterday by fanatics who were following him for a long time. The country will pass judgment on the deed." He continued: "Even until the last moment of his life (Călinescu) thought to keep Romania out of the war, and keep her intact. If anyone follows a different goal, he is against everything we believe in!"[1046]

The country might have passed judgment over the murderers of Călinescu, but the king and the Camarilla substituted for it. And the fury of the oligarchy knew no bounds. Călinescu was the strong man, the king's most trusted advisor, executioner, friend, and administrator. He proved to be irreplaceable. The oligarchy was in position to show its resentment. The very day of the murder, his assassins and their accomplices were shot on the spot of the murder and left there to rot for days. But that was not all. In every county, a certain number of Legionaries had to be executed, or hung from telegraph poles or lamp posts. Their bodies were to be displayed in such a state for days, for the education of the people. It is impossible to tell how many Legionaries perished. It is reasonable to assume about 250 or 300. But it was not the quantitative side which hurt the Legion. When the regime's terror squads burst into the concentration camps,

---

[1045] *Neamul Românesc*, 6. 7, and 20 September 1939.

[1046] *Neamul Românesc*, 23 September 1939.

they shot Clime, the T.P.T. leader, Polihroniade, the Legion's foreign policy expert (who had earned the dubious fame of being the Romanian Goebbels), Prince Cantacuzino (Jr.), the brilliant attorney Tell, the comrades-in-arms of Moța in Spain, Totu and Dobre, and perhaps the most admirable man in the Legion after Codreanu, the Transylvanian, Ion Banea, the professor of engineering Ionică, the poets V. Cadru and C. Goga, the student leaders Furdui and Cotiga, Antoniu and V. Rădulescu, and the youth leader Istrati, to name only the most outstanding. This blood-letting was considered by some Legionaries a terrible thing, but (as some of them commented) it also got the Legion out of a critical situation, and uplifted it. Others might agree with the sour appraisal the writer heard in contemporary Romania. After these massacres, the Legion was "like a potato, the best part of it was under the earth." The Iron Guard would find itself leaderless when it had to face the responsibilities of power, to live up to the high ideals it had set out to accomplish.

Iorga did not mention the massacres, although, according to his family, he was very upset about the methods used by the regime. After Călinescu's murder, a transitory government was formed under General G. Argeșanu, in order to organize the bloodbath. Then, for about two months, Argetoianu became prime minister. Finally, the versatile Tătărescu formed a government. This was the time of the "Phony War," by which Iorga was not deceived. He was in anguish for the fate of small nations.

Just when the Second World War started, Iorga wrote a telling article reaffirming his faith: "Our Glorious Nineteenth Century." In the article, he remembered that, in 1901, some Frenchman said that it was a stupid age, and now everything would be different. Iorga explained that one can see how things turned out to be different. One sees confusion and degradation; a degradation of all sentiments, and the rise of superstitions, of craziest mysticisms, paralleled with the most crude cult of the machine permeating the moral order with brutality, and trampling down everything, laughing triumphantly over the hecatombs of dead, killed with the most perfect and sophisticated tools of destruction.

Yet, those who managed during those "stupid times" (the nineteenth century) to receive their education were shaped in a religion which was a faith in man. The awakening nations and doubting souls were exposed to enchanting literature and works of daring philosophers. Iorga concluded: "and as long as we are still alive, we, brought up during those times, will remain proud that we belonged to that proud century, the creations of which are in our days trampled upon by the barbarians."[1047]

With the start of the Second World War, Iorga resumed his ideas concerning the role of small nations, and the dangers in store for them. He drew an unmistakable line between his concept of nationalism as opposed to theories about *Lebensraum* and racism. If ever a line could be drawn between Iorga's nationalism and the "New Nationalism" of the Nazis and Fascists, Iorga drew it. He emphasized, "we are a small nation," and set out to defend the right of small nations to exist in an age when this became increasingly anachronistic in Europe. He wrote: "Not small nations, but sacred nations, and original civilizations!" He asked: "Can nations and peoples be destroyed? Nations are organic forms of mankind!" Imperialism is destroying small nations. He found the establishment of the "Czech Protectorate" offensive. But Iorga continued that one can add to the Behemoth size and body, but it will not be able to carry the load. During the fall of 1939, Iorga started a serial in his *Neamul Românesc*, 8 October 1939, taken over by other great dailies, entitled: "The Origins of the Small States." Iorga also started a series of speeches on the Romanian radio about "The Future of Small States." The essence was that practically four states are running Europe, but the nationality principle must be safe-guarded. Nevertheless, small states should trust no treaties, only themselves.[1048] Iorga always looked forward to a time when small nations might align themselves against the power of large states.

Iorga editorialized: "Our thoughts go out to the small nations," like Holland, Belgium, and Scandinavia." Belgium was created by European interests,

---

[1047]*Neamul Românesc*, 8 October 1939.

[1048]*Neamul Românesc*, 27 August and 16 October 1938; also, 9 September, 12 and 31 October, and 10 December 1939.

and thanks to the existence of it, "neither France nor Germany is there." He looked forward to the solidarity of "small nations" in the coming onslaught.[1049]

Iorga drew the line between his nationalism and a nationalism he considered incompatible with humanity, against the inhuman nationalist extremism represented by Hitler and the Legion. He pointed out that their spirit is incompatible with the spirit and the thought of the Romanian peasant. Even the mysticism of the Legion was pathetic and sick. A condemnation of the so-called "new empires" followed, which were founded without humanity, right, and even without understanding. If Napoleon was a genius, modern technology was no substitute for it. For Iorga, real nationalism did not manifest itself through race, but through a spiritual condition for which only noble souls had the instinct and consciousness. True nationalism represented duty and sacrifice. According to Iorga, this nationalism was defensive, the other (the "New Nationalism") was suicidal. Condemning the German occupation of Slovakia and the Hungarian occupation of Ruthenia, "the murder of nationalism," he asked: "By whom is this murder of nationalism carried out? By an imperialist nationalism!" Iorga hated the idea of Lebensraum, even autarchy: "No nation has enough raw materials. This is a savage kind of nationalism!"[1050] The Nazi idea of *Lebensraum* was hateful for Iorga. He posed the question: "Lebensraum?" Then he answers, "We shall defend our borders and independence against everybody, even against every advice!" Then again: "Is 'living space' an excuse for plunder and conquest?" He answered his own question: "Living-space is given to a nation in consideration of each other, without trampling over the borders or opening wounds. Old noble nations acted in such fashion, and they became great!"[1051]

Some people might have considered racism as a kind of "command of our times." For Iorga, racism stood without foundation, and put in question the right

---

[1049]*Neamul Românesc*, 30 November 1938, 23 June, and 14 November 1939, and 28 January 1940.

[1050]*Neamul Românesc*, 2-12 June 1938; also, 23 March, 26 April, and 22 June 1939; finally, 14 January 1940.

[1051]*Neamul Românesc*, 18 March and 14 June 1939.

of nations to have independent nation-states. Consequently, racism was an aberration.[1052] Iorga maintained that the "conquerors of today" have more in mind than conquest. They wish to finish with certain races and nations. This explains their theories about the existence of superior and inferior races, and this was a logical outcome of their aberrations. But Iorga brought up many examples as proof that this was bound to fail. In an editorial, "Non Salutant Morituri!," he turned around the gladiators salute. Those little nations supposed to die do not salute great nations which condemn them to death! Then, as a jab to the idea of *Lebensraum*, Iorga opined, "the Romanian majority of Transylvania also demands a 'living space.'"[1053]

Iorga wrote a blistering attack against racism, pointing out that all ideas about "superior races" started with Gobineau's ideas. Gobineau considered those which were not superior races to be "cultural garbage," who should work for those who were superior. Gobineau suggested that they should be exterminated for the benefit of all and quickly. But history proved something very' different. People need certain conditions to be able to rise. If there are riches available, people can develop and raise themselves through technology'; if not, they' need leadership. But, "if a people is constantly stigmatized as inferior, would it be surprising if it would fail?"[1054]

Then, the Soviet Union attacked Finland. With this, a dilemma which haunts every small nation arose. "Should it act like Hácha or like Mannerheim!"[1055] Iorga had decided the answer a long time ago. For him, Finland set the example. "Feeling menaced by Soviet imperialism which follows the footsteps of Czarist imperialism, Finland mobilized under the leadership of Mannerheim, the founder." And the Finns mobilized, not only the army but also their

---

[1052]*Neamul Românesc*, 19 January 1940.

[1053]*Neamul Românesc*, 25 and 28 April and 5 May 1939.

[1054]*Neamul Românesc*, 9 December 1939.

[1055]Even Antonescu faced this dilemma before he went to see Hitler for the first time. He told his entourage, "Either I will return in the guise of Hácha or in the uniform of Mannerheim." Barbu, *op. cit.*, p. 76.

spirit. Because (as Iorga pointed out) without the spirit, all mobilization remains a dead letter, and all the Skoda ammunition works and all the fortifications will not suffice. He concluded: "Hardly-won independence, dignity, and liberty has to be defended."[1056] According to Iorga, Finland had all the sympathy of the world, "the small nation and its great civilization." He stood up for Finland in his editorials almost daily, calling on Sweden and other countries to help Finland "in the name of humanity."[1057]

During the "Phony War," Bucharest was a "living center," the "Paris of the Orient." The awakening would come soon and it would be rude. For the time being, Bucharest was the capital of the Balkans. "*Douce décadence*" was sweet indeed; there was a lot of money to be made by those who had "influential connections." Party followed party, orgy followed orgy. King Carol decided to enlarge his palace, and block after block was condemned on the Calea Victoriei to make place for it. Mme. Lupescu's brother, Constantin (Shloim) made millions on the project. Survivors of the Iron Guard found it expedient to sit out the storm. A law was passed promising the death penalty for anyone leading a political organization from abroad.

Iorga observed this mood and was revolted. In an editorial, "Belligerents and Neutrals," he pointed out that Romania is technically neutral, but not in sentiment, and assured everybody that the atmosphere of Bucharest, with all the corruption prevalent doesn't have anything to do with the spirit of the Romanian people. It was revolting.[1058]

He rejected also the ubiquitous Nazi-Fascist charges that England and France were "plutocracies," explaining that whatever wealth England and

---

[1056]*Neamul Românesc,* 22 October and 3 December 1939.

[1057]*Neamul Românesc,* 15 February 1940.

[1058]*Neamul Românesc,* 31 March 1940.

France had, came from their national character, mentality, and genius. Iorga violently rejected the notion that there was any confrontation between "poor nations" and "plutocracies."[1059]

By the spring of 1940, a certain uneasiness swept over Europe and Romania. Everybody felt that the "Phony War" would end. In the end of March, the Soviet People's Commissar of Foreign Affairs made a speech, pointing out that the question of Bessarabia was still unresolved. The king and the political establishment felt uneasy, especially about the Legion. By April, the king and Tătărescu made serious overtures towards the Legion, aiming at a reconciliation.

By the beginning of April, the "Phony War" was over. Hitler broke the neutrality of Denmark and Norway. There was little chance for resistance in Denmark, but in Norway the situation was different. Iorga turned in an editorial to his friend, the historian-politician, Professor H. Koht, (the Norwegian foreign minister) in pain. When the King of Norway became the spirit of resistance, Iorga greeted him as "a true descendant of the Vikings."[1060] And in a few weeks, the fateful morning of 10 May 1940 dawned.

Literature was for Iorga, as he used to say, "the mirror of the nation's soul." From the time of *Sămănătorism* until the end of his life, literature had become a major battlefield for him — and an all-important one — fought by Iorga with a closed mind. Anything which wouldn't fit into his "nationalist realism," shaping and forming the Romanian national soul along *Sămănătorist* lines (showing Romania "not how it was, but how it should be") or any new "unhealthy current" (coming from outside or inside Romania) which might interfere with the educating process of cultural nationalism and the formation of a *Sămănătorist* man was to be exposed, condemned, and possibly extirpated from Romanian literature. It was not granted free access to the Romanian soul, if Iorga could do something about it. Literary criticism was the least constructive amidst his manifold activities.

[1059]*Neamul Românesc*, 14 April 1940.

[1060]*Neamul Românesc*, 13 and 18 April 1940.

E. Lovinescu (no friend of Iorga) was right pointing out that "Mr. Iorga, powerfully endowed with talent and the best intentions, (despite all this) has become the most powerful obstacle to the natural development of his nation's literature."[1061] Iorga's intolerance towards modern trends in literature was not new, but during the 1930s it was getting worse.[1062] But he would continue his life struggle against "the ambitious vulgarity of ultra-modernism" (meaning everything in Romanian literature after Eminescu) and covering approximately the same timespan abroad. In literature he has proven himself the most conservative. Indeed nothing — as G. Călinescu pointed out — impinged on his consciousness that was new.

But from 1920 on, modernism in art was marching from victory to victory in the Western world. Not only in literature, but also in music, in the plastic arts and in architecture, although these seemed less important for Iorga. There was Picasso in Paris, Kandinsky in Weimar, Stravinsky in Paris and Schoenberg in Vienna. The functional buildings of Gropius and Le Corbusier rose. For Iorga, not even Enescu or Brâncuşi could awaken the interest and passion he felt for literature.

In literature, Iorga continued to oppose any modern trend (like symbolism, futurism, or surrealism). He would even oppose realism, with the same "nationalist realist" vigor that the Soviets opposed true realistic literature (despite the great traditions in Russia) when truly realistic literature interfered with their propagandistic dream world. Both the Soviets and Iorga — in their respective ways — wished to show their readers not how things were, but how they should be. So, he would fight Lucian Blaga, who wrote a cosmic, philosophical poetry, searching for answers to the great questions of mankind. Iorga already found

---

[1061]E. Lovinescu, *Istoria literaturii române contemporane*, (Bucureşti, 1900-1937), p. 20.

[1062]After Duca's murder, Iorga did not consider it incongruent to turn to the king and explain that "it is crazy modern literature which is responsible for this kind of outrage." *Memorii*, vol. VII, p. 123.

these answers in *Sămănătorism*. He could not but oppose Blaga's abstrac-tions.[1063] Iorga was very upset with Liviu Rebreanu's realistic description of a Transylvanian village in his novel *Ion*, pointing out that Rebreanu presented the life of Transylvanian peasants — but "in the form of showing the ashes, the lowest residues of the human spirit." Rebreanu presents "about 80 actors, with rapes and murders, these manifestations presented in a coarse fashion, resembling a kind of a rotten carcass which somebody rattles by his foot. This is (Rebreanu's) realism of savage authenticity, the basest in the zoological life of our nation. This is (how village life looks like) to the author, observed in some accursed corner of Transylvania, presented like an incontrivable testimony of inferiority, in the cold style of a police report, registering the different infamies occurring within the police precinct." Iorga asks in despair, "where is the noble Transylvania of Slavici or Agârbiceanu?" Rebreanu's *Ion* reminded him of the stench arising from Zola's *La Terre*. Even the anti-Hungarian struggle of the Romanian peasantry does not redeem Rebreanu for Iorga. Rebreanu transgressed against Iorga's "nationalist realistic" rule. He showed in realist (according to Iorga in a demoralizing) fashion, the villages as they were, abandoning the primary function of literature (according to Iorga) to educate, to show the village in the *Sămănătorist* ideal, how it should be! Lovinescu was right, that Iorga's literary criticisms are "either vague aesthetic principles or ethical and nationalistic considerations."[1064]

Positivism did not fare better with Iorga than did Descartes. Gheorghe Bogdan-Duică, his brother-in-law (a Professor of Literature at the Bucharest Uni-

---

[1063] The Iorga family recalled that Iorga visited Switzerland with Mme. Catinca. Lucian Blaga received Iorga (with whom he entertained friendly relations). They walked the streets together, and Iorga wanted to go to a used book store. He asked Blaga and Mme. Catinca to wait. Suddenly, he turned back, warning Blaga mockingly: "Well, on my return, I hope to find my wife in good mental health."

[1064] E. Lovinescu, *Titu Maiorescu și prosperitate lui critică* (București, 1943), p. 214.

versity) was a positivist. Far from the relations Iorga maintained with Ioan Bogdan, because of his literary controversy with Bogdan-Duică, they were barely on speaking terms.[1065]

Iorga's feelings towards Lucian Blaga, Rebreanu, Gheorghe Bogdan-Duică, Marinetti, Verlaine, Rimbaud (and other symbolists), were all pale reflections of what he felt against Tudor Arghezi, the prominent Romanian representative of modernism. Tudor Arghezi occupied a place in his pantheon, among those whom he "loved to hate."

Tudor Arghezi (1880-1967) was one of the greatest Romanian poets and writers in modern times. Born as Ion N. Teodorescu, he started his career (as Iorga contemptuously remarked) as an "Orthodox ex-monk." He started to publish in 1896, in an Orthodox paper, *Liga Ortodoxă*, under the title "Din ziua de azi" ("From the Day of Today"), signing "Ion Theo." Tudor Arghezi went from post Symbolism to religious mystical fear, then a cosmic current, developing into a poetry of humor, that of the absurd. Yet, it remained always a fusion between traditional and modern trend.

He showed a daring realism, detailing the promiscuity and misery of some aspects in Romanian life as they existed on the outer margins of contemporary society. Arghezi introduced in Romanian literature the aesthetics of the ugly (*inter alia*, he upset Iorga describing cats making love on a tree). We understand the hostility, Iorga with his "nationalist realism," would feel towards Arghezi's art. These were "unhealthy currents" if there ever were some!

Tudor Arghezi founded in 1928 a literary paper, *Bilete de Papagal* ("The Notes of a Parrot"). It appeared in a small size with ostentatious colors. As suggested by its name, the "Notes of a Parrot" was young and disrespectful, writing about sacred things in a profane way, things which Iorga dared to approach only with *Sămănătorist* love. Iorga explained that Arghezi looks at everything and sees reality only through an interaction of a moral and intellectual insanity. But

---

[1065]When Professor Bogdan-Duică died, Iorga received condolences. He commented: "They apparently were unaware how relations were really between us two." *Memorii*, vol. VII, p. 186."

humans can live only in a state of sanity — and that is valid also for Romanian society.[1066]

All this preoccupied Iorga. Would Romania and the world go in such a direction?[1067] Commented Iorga on Arghezi's *Cuvinte Potrivite* ("Suitable Words"), "It encompasses everything that can be considered to be the most obscene of ideas, and the most vulgar the form of expression of these ideas goes." But Arghezi's volume was a success, appreciated by Tudor Vianu and Mihai Râlea. Their comments were taken up by Iorga: how did they dare call Tudor Arghezi "our greatest living poet since Eminescu," or "the king of new poetry?" Commented Lovinescu in his *T. Maiorescu și prosperitatea lui critică* (București, 1943, p. 210): "What a low kind of literary' criticism!" But Iorga would pursue his attacks on Arghezi with unabating violence. Tudor Arghezi hit back at Iorga in a cheap way. Exploiting the prevailing anti-Semitism in 1937, he reproduced (in his *Notes of a Parrot*) the electoral leaflet, in which Iorga appealed to Jewish voters. He wrote Iorga's name in Hebrew letters, then rewrote it in reverse in Romanian (Latin) alphabet, "Agroi," appealing to the basest anti-Semitic sentiments.[1068] Not to be outdone, Iorga replied with a punch beneath the belt. After the establishment of the Royal Dictatorship, on 15 February 1938, he complained to Călinescu about "the intolerable insults of Tudor Arghezi."[1069]

Iorga continued to write plays on the same lines as before, which awakened little interest. Staged by the *Liga Culturală* in the Teatru Popular, presented also (because of Iorga's clout) in the National Theatre. Often tickets had to be given

---

[1066] *Neamul Românesc*, 17 January 1937.

[1067] Iorga protested to King Carol personally that Tudor Arghezi's volume, *The Annunciation Graveyard* should not be published with the money of the Royal Foundation, because it is "vulgar!" *Memorii*, vol. 7, p. 342. Fortunately, Iorga's intervention remained without success.

[1068] *Bilete de Papagal*, no. 243.

[1069] *Memorii*, vol. VII, p. 459.

away. Iorga did not accept the shift of artistic values which occurred after the War. His younger son, Ștefan, wrote poetry, published in *Neamul Românesc*.

After a pause, Iorga's major literary criticism was his *Istoria Literaturii Românești Contemporane* (București, 1934). Volume one on the period 1867 to 1890, volume two from 1890 to 1934. It reads more like a polemic on modern literary currents than a review of Romanian literature. In the preface, Iorga explained that after "all too long," hiatus, he would deal with the development of Romanian literature, "with its development, and not with its presentation". Because history, and consequently the history of literature, "was not a chronological enumeration, but an explanation. People and their works enter the scene and retreat from it, according to their role within the organic development, they intervene or stand by and leave the scene they have influenced, withdrawing from the stage little by little until they vanish. Such kind of presentation is necessary nowadays more than ever before." The respected literary critic Pompiliu Constantinescu commented: "Mr. Iorga affirms an idea in which he did not believe, in the sense that he did not respect it." And within the same preface we shall see a remarkable change of tone: "And (through Iorga's work) one will be able to observe the futility of the caprices of certain paper boats whoever set them afloat. These (paper boats) will (be able to) sail, guided by their childish authors within the shallow waters at the edge of the sidewalks; yet, when the stream gets stronger and deeper, they will capsize. Certain (new) fashions conquer as easily as short time they last. The daring insolence of their pretenses helps them as little as the vehemence of polemics do. Nor will the docile acceptance by a temporarily stupid public do any good. Because there is an iron rule in literature, also in art present, as at the foundation of all human society, and one cannot escape from this rule: everything that is for humans must remain human. And what is human, regardless of the form, must preserve its basic human structure." Iorga concludes in his vintage style: "Any detailed observations, comments, or criticisms — as always — I will register gratefully. But if the one (who presents them) criticisms has no upbringing or manners, I will send out somebody to collect the best from the mud of insults, and (I will make sure) that they will be used. I did so in the past, and I will do it also in the future." Commented Pompiliu Constantinescu: "All this should seem very promising as far as the serenity of the scholarly approach or the understanding (of literature) goes."[1070]

Iorga celebrated the fortieth anniversary of Eminescu's death (1929) belatedly, as prime minister, writing a two volume appreciation of Eminescu's poetry, *Poezia lui Eminescu* (1931-1932, Bucharest). He also continued to publish his literary journals, *Cuget Clar, Noul Sămănător, Neamul Românesc Literar,* to keep up the *Sămănătorist* creed.

Beyond modern trends in literature and art, Iorga always showed antipathy toward ugly aspects of modern civilization. He foresaw the ugly evolution in sports, so far from the classical ideal of *mens sana in corpore sano*. He foresaw also the politicization, commercialization, brutalization and dehumanization of sports. Therefore, he wanted to separate sports from the university and higher education. During the Berlin Olympics of 1936, he thought something was missing: harmony and serenity, which opposes violence. What Iorga saw instead was a brutal passion, a desire of profit, and an ugly exhibitionism, amidst the hysterical howls of the mob. "God is missing, God, Zeus, stayed on the Olympus." He asked later mockingly, that sportsman pretend to raise moral and cultural standards? These sportsman of today are not those of antiquity! The broken noses, and torn apart heads testify to this. "Let them stay away from academe and universities!"[1071] Three or four score years later, one can only say that Iorga had not seen anything yet.

As far as Iorga's historical works during the last decade of his life are concerned, we shall consider the most important ones only. It was the historical trio of Xenopol, Pârvan, and above all, Iorga who established Romania's place in historiography. Xenopol was founder of the Daco-Romanian theory, Pârvan supplied archaeological foundations, and Iorga made the contributions which established Romania's place in universal history.

[1070]Iorga, *Istoria literaturii românești contemporane* (București, 1934), vol. 1, preface. Also, Pompiliu Constantinescu, *Vremea,* 14 October 1934. Also Iorga, *op. cit.,* pp. 155-168.

[1071]*Neamul Românesc,*12 August 1936 and 26 May 1939.

After a lifetime of research, teaching, and historical experience, Iorga undertook writing a Romanian and world historical synthesis. Many historians attempt this, but it remains most difficult, even for somebody with Iorga's stature. This does not concern Iorga's most important work during the decade: the resumption of the work of his lifetime, and an answer to the *Şcoala Nouă's* attacks, was his *Istoria Românilor* in ten volumes, published between 1936 and 1939. Within these volumes Iorga restated almost everything he said on Romanian history. It can be considered a nationalist and patriotic interpretation of the Romanian past. These volumes show how the Romanian past looked to Iorga. Yet, Iorga presents a remarkable portrait of princes and voievod, at his evocative best. Iorga tries to find a place for the Romanian experience within universal history. According to him, Romanian history can only be understood if seen in a larger framework than Dacia. He remains faithful to his principle: geography, nature, and even climate play a role in shaping the "soul" of a nation. (These ideas can be found in his *Generalități*, too).

Iorga describes the distant ancestors of the Romanians before Rome, and present longer than Rome. They became integrated into the future Romanian nation during this formative process, and held fast in this land, which received (according to Iorga) relatively little from the Slavs around. These Romanians were located between Slavic peoples through "Eastern Rome" (Byzance). Because of a steady contact with Byzance these Romanians preserved ancient Rome, and safeguarded the Roman heritage. Representing thus a moral balance, the Romanians helped the consolidation of nations living around them.

The first volume is entitled *Ancestors Which Preceded the Romans*; the second, *The Mark of Rome*, then comes *The Founders*; and (more importantly), the fourth called, *The People of the Land*, being the most controversial of all, because it deals with the undocumented millennia of Romanian history. The "people of the land" survived in this turmoil of great migrations and barbarian onslaught, withdrawing into forests, into the high mountains, forming a kind of "popular Romania." The fifth volume is *The Knights*, dealing with the high and late Middle Ages, the emergence of the Romanian Principalities, and of Iancu de Hunedoara in Transylvania, etc. Volume six, *The Brave Ones*, with the six-teenth and seventeenth centuries. Volume seven, *The Monarchs*, and volume eight, *The Reformers*, represents Iorga's all-too favorable view about the Phanariot period. For Iorga, the most important contribution of the Phanariots was that they did not disrupt organic development, and did not cause a deplorable rupture.

This "rupture" is dealt with in volume number nine: *The Revolutionaries*, the antecedents of 1848, that revolutionary year, and the consequences. The final volume consists of two volumes, bringing Romanian history up to the mid-1930s. The first part is entitled *The Unifiers*, in which Iorga deals with the process and the personalities who brought about the national union. The second part, *The Integrators*, describes "the integrators."

Writing about himself (and his brother-in-law, Ioan Bogdan), and his good friend, Professor Onciul, Iorga remembers that "Bogdan, Onciul, and Iorga," one of them at the university of Iaşi, the other at the University of Vienna, and he himself at universities and archives all over Europe, went to work and dug out every document for the benefit of their nation, brought the documents home, and let them be known to the rest of the world. It was in this way that they fought for the integration of Romania.

Iorga also started a French translation of his *Istoria românilor*, but it was never completed. Critics of these 10 monumental volumes maintain that Iorga did not analyze his facts carefully enough; but since protagonists of the *Şcoala Nouă* accused Iorga of writing only on intuition without sufficient documentation, within these 10 volumes Iorga accompanied his conclusions with the heaviest documentation. Iorga supplied thousands of documents he gathered during his research. Within these 10 volumes we can find also minor mistakes, which would be carefully fostered by his opponents. They rarely dispute Iorga's conclusions, even rarer do they detract from the monumentality of his works.

During this period, Iorga wrote his *La place des Roumains dans l'histoire universelle*. He wanted always to interpret Romania for the Romanians; show Romania to the rest of the world; and to find for Romanian history a place within world history. The first volume is *Antiquité et le Moyen Age* (Bucarest, 1935);

the second, *Epoque moderne* (Bucarest, 1935); the final volume, *Epoque contemporaine* (Bucharest, 1936). This trilogy is the enlargement of Iorga's *Trei lecții de istorie despre însemnatatea românilor în istoria universală* (Vălenii-de-Munte, 1912) in which at the beginning of the century he tried to place Romanian history within the framework of mankind's experience. According to Iorga (in these three volumes), Romanian culture is a synthesis, and as such it is ready to offer and also to receive creative impulses. Historical immobility is as alien to Romanian culture as to other European cultures. Yet, while Romanian culture is flexible, it remains original and it cannot be conceived outside Romanian society. It has also great vitality, and a contemporary character. It is a culture of action, capable renewing itself through its vitality.

After a lifetime of research, travel, of writing history (and sometimes making history), Iorga moved to writing a synthesis of world history. Iorga said, in his "Concepția umană a istoriei" (Iorga, *Conferințe și Prelegeri*, vol. 1, București, 1943, pp. 7-15), that when writing history one should feel above all a human being, shape himself in order to be able to reconstruct the past. One must think and live a lot (there is no suitable substitute for personal experiences). Since this is not easy, without these qualities one shouldn't write history. After his *Essai de synthèse de l'histoire de l'humanité*, writing historical synthesis would become Iorga's main occupation. During the last years of his life, he founded his Institute for the Study of Universal History. Iorga's method of historical analysis, his historiology, would take its definite forms by the last decade of his life.

Iorga was above all a medievalist, a Byzantinist *par excellence* of world renown, always trying to go beyond Byzantine history. He would emphasize his own ideas about certain aspects of it. There were three phases of Iorga's development as a Byzantinist. His first works were outlines with no crystallized opinions (like his Byzantine history published in the English language in 1907).

Then came a period with Iorga searching, with his questions still unanswered. At the end of his life, Iorga seemed to have found an answer to what Byzantium was, and presented a synthesis of Byzantine history.

It was during Iorga's work as a Byzantinologist that he won for himself and for Romania numerous faithful friends among foreign historians, who disseminated knowledge and friendship for Romania the world over.

For Iorga, the understanding of Byzantium was indispensable for understanding Romanian history. His *Istoria vieţii bizantine* three volumes (Bucharest, 1934), and the French translation, *Histoire de la vie Byzantine* (Bucarest, 1934) is one of Iorga's most successful historical synthesis. According to him, Byzantium was a double synthesis of the West and the East, the West represented by the Roman Empire and Hellenism, and the East by Orthodoxy and Asia.

His other work, *Bizanţ după Bizanţ* (Bucureşti, 1933), was the translation into Romanian by Mme. Liliana Pippidi-Iorga from *Byzance après Byzance* (Bucarest 1933) of her father, and the French translation, *Byzance après Byzance* (Bucarest, 1933), is a logical extension of this school of thought: the presence and "posthumous" (after the fall of Byzantium) continuity of Byzantine ideas and institutions within the Romanian Principalities were the continuity of the Roman empire. Thus, the Roman-Byzantine past was perpetuated within the Romanian Principalities, and the Principalities succeeded to preserve Roman-Byzantine (that is, European) values during the long Ottoman domination. Iorga tried to explain how this "Christian republic" faced up to the Ottoman Empire. He underlined the survival of Byzantine institutions, values, and culture in the Romanian Principalities. Continuing his earlier works, Iorga also wrote studies like *France de Chypre* (Paris, 1931) or *Rhodes sous les Hospitaliers*, (Bucarest, 1931).

He wrote many political-historical works during this period. In this sense, he wrote, as prime minister, *La vérité sur le passé et le présent de la Bessarabie* (Bucarest, 1931), and *La Bessarabie et l'œuvre des Roumains* (Bucarest, 1932). They were the work of the politician and not the historian. They exaggerate the positive aspects of Romanian rule in Bessarabia, although it points out correctly that, whatever the Romanian administration was like in Bessarabia, the province belongs ethnically and historically to Romania. His *Comment la Roumanie s'est détachée de la Triplice* (Bucarest, 1931 and 1932) is about Romania's "renversement des alliances" during the First World War.

In his *Originea și sensul democrației* (Vălenii de Munte, 1932), one can feel Iorga's disillusionment with democracy in Romania. Another book on this subject is *Definiția noii stări de lucruri in România* (Bucharest, 1939), Iorga's speech before the Corporate Senate on 28 June 1939, an expedient justification of the Royal Dictatorship, The book is an example of Iorga's public thinking. As far as his real ideas, we know better.

Iorga collected his lectures at the outbreak of the Second World War entitled *Dezvoltarea imperialismului contemporan* (Bucharest, 1940). These volumes are a perspective and interpretation of imperialism from the Middle Ages until the "new imperialism" of Emperor William II of Germany. For Iorga, Bismarck was "a man of peace" who, since Germany was saturated, was opposed to the open-ended adventures of the young Kaiser. But reading Iorga's interpretations of imperialism, one senses once more how much Iorga was the product of the nineteenth century.

Iorga continued to participate in World Historical Congresses: in Warsaw in 1933, and Zurich in 1938. From Iorga's memoirs one gets the impression that World Historical Congresses somehow consist of 50% history and 90% politics.

He had an almost permanent seat on the International Historical Committee, automatically the choice for the seat reserved for Southeast European (and also European) history. Iorga made the most of it, capriciously, when he saw the interests of Romania (or his ego) challenged. At the last World Historical Congress before the War, in August 1938 in Zurich, Iorga was elected vice-president of the congress.

The World Conference on Byzantinology, which Iorga brought to life in 1924, continued. Byzantinists met in Athens in 1930, and again in Sofia in August 1933. Because the Bulgarian historian P. Mutafeev (with whom Iorga had acrimonious debates) presided over the historical section, Iorga refused to participate.[1072] The last World Congress of Byzantinology took place in Rome in September 1936 and Iorga was there.

He continued to receive a flow of Doctorates Honoris Causa. In March 1932, a kudo from the Comenius University in Bratislava, January 1933 from the University of Rome. February 1933 Iorga became member of the Institut de France, and in 1939 Doctor Honoris Causa of the University of Algiers. He became the corresponding member of the Stanislas Academy of Nancy, of the Slavic Institute in London and in Prague, an associated member of the Society of Byzantine Studies in Athens, finally of the Academy of History in Santiago, Chile. King Carol continued to shower orders and medals on him. In 1936, on Carol's personal intervention, another "cordon" of the Legion of Honor was awarded by France to a faithful friend.

As within the "Low Decade," crisis would follow crisis, Iorga's activities would increase proportionately. Although crisis always had a stimulating effect on him, the amount and scope of his activities from 1930 to 1940, make it hard to imagine that just one man could have accomplished it. Iorga continued to lecture regularly at the Bucharest University, and taught classes at the Military Academy, also at the Commercial Academy. He would continue as a guest lecturer yearly at the Sorbonne, and the College de France. He was continuing to lecture at his schools in France, Venice and in Rome. The organization of his School of Archaeology in Santi-Quaranta (Albania) got underway.[1073] Iorga's Summer University at Vălenii continued until the fateful summer of 1940. Iorga did not abandon his "Missionary School for Women."[1074]

[1072] *Memorii*, vol. VII, pp. 181 and 185.

[1073] *Op. cit.*, vol. VII, pp. 373-374. The Iorga family recalled that Mussolini made a gesture after the occupation of Albania and allowed Iorga to continue the organization of his school there. Iorga preferred to pass on the honor.

[1074] Queen Helen offered a home for the missionary school. *Memorii*, vol. VII, p. 96.

In April 1937, Iorga founded his Institute of Universal History in Bucharest. Lectures would begin in May 1937 with a series entitled "The Human Concept of History." The lecture was a manifesto against modernism, the assault by modern life on a daily basis against the individual in more than one form. Iorga demanded "the preservation of the human character of human life, because beyond that there is only something inferior, deserving our contempt." He continued lectures at this institute until the spring of 1940 dealing with the fate of the Baltic States and Silesia.

Iorga continued his activities within the *Liga Culturală*. He would continue to lead his Nationalist Democratic Party until February 1938 when the Royal Dictatorship dissolved all political parties. He remained the editor of *Neamul Românesc*, also *of Neamul Românesc pentru Popor* and *Neamul Românesc Literar*, although the post of the "administrative director" was taken over by Nicolae Georgescu-Cocoş, a very different pair of shoes to Iorga. An ambitious man with few scruples, he always followed the "command of the times." This slogan of proto-fascist opportunism from the political underworld of Southeastern Europe describes the problem. Although Iorga was quite unhappy about the tone of his paper under Cocoş management, in the political whirlwind, he did not take action against it.

After Mr. Cocoş arrived at the paper, every Jewish briber, every Jew caught with a false passport, every Jewish counterfeiter apprehended, and every anti-Semitic manifestation in Romania (or abroad) received attention on its pages, despite Iorga being very unhappy about this.

He also wrote many editorials for other mass-circulation dailies, such as *Curentul*, *Universul*, and *Timpul*. Starting in 1934, Iorga, an inspiring orator, began to use the media. He started weekly radio addresses, called *Sfaturi pe întuneric* ("Advices into the Darkness"), which also appeared under the same title in book form. Seen from the perspective of half a century, his conclusions were often faulty. But these radio addresses were meant for a short-term effect. Here again, the opinions voiced by Iorga during his radio addresses were sometimes markedly different, the product of expedience to those voiced in his diaries and within his family.

Beyond political journalism, Iorga continued his *Revista Istorică* and his *Revue Historique du Sud-Est Européen* and would play a leading role in *Buletinul Comisiei Monumentelor Istorice* and *Buletinul Comisiei Istorice*. He would also continue to address numerous audiences in Romania and abroad on many occasions. During his numerous travels he never missed a chance to do research.

His private life — in strange contrast to the Carolist regime he supported so wholeheartedly — remained exemplarily clean. In 1933, Iorga's brother, Gheorghe, passed away. A much greater loss (during the spring of 1934) was the passing away of his mother, Mme. Zulnia, in her 90s.

Shortly before Stere's death — since he had got into a major conflict with Maniu, and wrote several violent articles against the leader of the National Peasant Party (which pleased Iorga greatly) — Iorga relented in his implacable hostility against him.[1075] And Iorga continued to take to court anyone by whom he felt insulted or slandered.

[1075]Mme. Liliana Pippidi-Iorga to the author.

Chapter VIII

The Tragedy

*"Our nation was established on crossroads of tempests —
which keep here roaring since ages and continue to roar where
riches are so tempting and roads of hosts pass (...) We are so
few amidst the many! (...) Every other nation would have quit
and dispersed (to the four corners) of the world. But we have
stood fast!"*

— Iorga at the outbreak of the Second World War

*"They cut down that mighty old pine, for it cast too deep (a)
shadow..."*

— Before his assassination, Iorga wrote down these lines.

The dawn of 10 May 1940 became a turning point for Greater Romania and unleashed a sequence of events which led to Iorga's doom. The 10th of May 1940 ended for a long time a world in which Europe played a decisive role. France would be "weighed in the balance" and she "would be found wanting". Temporarily Britain would become the spokesman for Europe. After the collapse of the unhistorical Nazi Reich, decisions would pass to the non-European superpowers, until the fall of the USSR, with Europe — inevitably — torn between them.

It would be forlorn to ask about Greater Romania the usual excruciating "ifs": what "if" Romanian policy had not overestimated French strength? Or, "if" Romanian policymakers had not underestimated the might of Nazi Germany? What "if" Romania had had better leadership than the Carol regime could offer? What "if" Romania had at the helm, a statesman with the stature of Ion Brătianu? Even "if" all the "ifs" had been resolved in a positive sense — they could not have tilted the balance. Because, as Iorga pointed out, the cardinal tragedy of this unfortunate land: her geographical position would have remained.

With the invasion of Scandinavian countries the "Phony War" came to an end. As Mme. Liliana remembered, Iorga was militant, but also very apprehensive of the approaching trial, and he submerged into a defiant, somber mood.

Then on 10 May, the axe fell. Hitler broke the neutrality of Holland, Belgium, and Luxembourg. His armored columns were advanced. While Rotterdam burned, they broke through the French defenses at Sedan, and in no time reached the Channel. After Dunkirk the fate of France was sealed.

After the German breakthrough, Iorga asked "what humanity could expect" following a victory by totalitarianism? "A 'New Order' of chains?" "Will they be able (...) to keep mankind enslaved?" With every day such a victory became more probable. As the tragedy of the Christian West evolved, he wrote an editorial entitled "Prayer." Appalled by the destruction of European civilization, he asked: "Who could possibly accept the enslavement of his own nation and that of humanity?"[1076] Iorga, "the fighter," refused to accept the thought of surrender!

With the Germans "closing the ring," Iorga wrote that "the solution for France is a proud 1792!" Unfortunately, the France of 1940 was far from that of 1792. He was deeply hurt by the capitulation of King Leopold III of Belgium, and remembered that "sovereigns capitulate like Napoleon III did, but the peoples do not." He reminded the king of the Belgians that his father did not capitulate — "and the Belgian people did not complain about the untold sufferings it had to undergo." For Iorga, Cardinal Mercier became the "moral head of state" in Belgium. And Iorga reached out to small nations. The defeated Luxembourgers (annexed by the Reich) were reminded that their way of life "cannot be oblit-

---

[1076]*Neamul Românesc*, 16, 23 and 25 May 1940.

erated — it is not German!" Or to the Swiss; "Switzerland; a small, proud country!"[1077] Meanwhile, Mussolini (to paraphrase Roosevelt) "stuck his dagger into the back of her neighbor." Iorga was hard-headed and naive enough to consider the Italian move the consequence of "France voting in the League of Nations for sanctions against Italy during the Ethiopian War."[1078]

Then, Paris fell. Crack SS divisions goose-stepped down the most beautiful avenue of the world, passing the Eternal Flame under the Arc de Triomphe. Iorga, like most intellectuals, was in a deep sorrow. He was searching for words; they didn't come easily to him. "Paris has fallen... Paris, a sacred city for all humanity... but Paris remains (deeply engraved) in our hearts..."[1079]

Four days later, Marshal Petain asked for an armistice. Wrote Iorga: "The Tragic Finale." He said that "his hands tremble" while writing down these lines, and he doesn't dare to judge Marshal Petain, "the most glorious of French soldiers. Only time will pass judgment over his terrible act." Iorga, the nationalist fighter, looked far and deep: "but the army is not the nation, in this terrible moment one must retreat into (the realm) of spirit, because one cannot destroy the foundations of spirit, which is "a quest for freedom and justice."[1080]

On that same day, the radio address of another nationalist historian-politician answered Iorga, like an echo, as in a dialogue:

"Les chefs qui, depuis de nombreuses années, sont à la tête des armées françaises ont formé un gouvernement. Ce gouvernement, allégant la defaite de nos armées, s'est mis en rapport avec l'ennemi pour cesser le combat.... Mais le dernier mot est-il dit? L'espérance doir-elle disparaître? La defaite est-elle définitive? Non!... Quoi qu'il arrive, la flamme de la résistance franiçaise ne doit pas s'éteindre, et ne s'éteindra pas!...la France a perdu la bataille — mais la France n'a pas perdu la guerre! Les gouvernants de rencontre ont pu capituler, cédant à la panique, oubliant

---

[1077]*Neamul Românesc*, 28 May and 1,14, and 29 June, and 25 August 1940.

[1078]*Neamul Românesc*, 14 June 1940.

[1079]*Neamul Românesc*, 16 June 1940.

[1080]*Neamul Românesc*, 20 June 1940.

l'honneur, livrant le pays à la servitude. Cependant rien n'est perdu. Rien n'est perdu parce que cette guerre est une guerre mondiale."[1081]

In the end, Charles De Gaulle (and Iorga!) will be among those vindicated before history.

Iorga, at the age of seventy, saw his world crumbling away around him. But he was not giving up. Finding the historical parallel, he wrote about "Cannae of Ancient Rome and the Modern Cannae." He reminded his readers "how tough the English were," expressing his "faith in them."[1082] During the coming weeks, Iorga increasingly placed his hopes in the United States. His paper reported every speech of President Roosevelt and every increase in U.S. armament. News of the increase in interventionist mood within the United States was carefully (and hopefully) fostered.

King Carol hastily transformed his FRN into a totalitarian "Party' of the Nation," taking three Legionary cabinet ministers into his new government, one of them being Horia Sima, the "Commandant of the Legion." The prime minister was engineer Ion Gigurtu, a friend of the Axis, and the foreign minister Mihai Manoilescu. This would not alter the arrangements of the Nazi-Soviet pact; it was (as Manoilescu called it) "the government of Royal Despair."

With the collapse of France and the retreat of the British from the Continent, the sword protecting Greater Romania had fallen. A tense week followed. Everybody felt the approaching tragedy.[1083] Mme. Liliana remembered her father's mood: tense, defiant, and combative. Iorga was preparing for 25 June (Tuesday evening), a commemorative session honoring his beloved professor of the Institut des Hautes Etudes, Charles Bémont.

On the morning of 25 June, an ominous procession of dusty, muddy cars arrived in Bucharest, full of well-to-do Bessarabian Germans. The German Consul in Chișinău and Cernăuți warned them to get out while they could. During

---

[1081]Charles De Gaulle, *Mémoires de guerre. L'appel*, pp. 331-332.

[1082]*Neamul Românesc*, 26 June 1940.

[1083]Even Horia Sima had forebodings: "The whole world is going topsy-turvy. It is possible that our country will meet with misfortune." *Time*, 1 July 1940, p. 25.

the afternoon, Iorga was convoked to the Crown Council. Here he found out that Stalin had cashed his last promissory note from Hitler, Bessarabia, and more than that.[1084] The Soviet ultimatum was terse and unequivocal, demanding the transfer of territory within the shortest time-span. As Iorga told his family, the Crown Council was held with all "worthies" of the realm. The king and the majority decided to yield. There seemed to be no room for resistance after the Chief of Staff, General F. Ţenescu, explained that Romania had no military aviation deserving the name.

At that point, an exchange took place between Iorga and his sovereign. He asked the king: "What has become of all the money of the 'Aviation Fund' for which each Romanian paid when he bought a postal stamp? Funds which Your Majesty was to administer personally?'" The king retorted: "Professor, do you know how much a military aircraft costs?" Iorga had no idea, so the maneuver of the deceitful king succeeded. Iorga fell into an embarrassed silence.

Yet, Iorga wanted to fight the Russians. When the king and the others told him that this would lead to defeat, and the Russian occupation of the country, with his deep faith in his cultural nationalism, Iorga retorted: "At least under Russian rule we will remain united!"

But this was the spirit of the nineteenth century faith. Iorga had no idea about Stalin's methods. The Soviets knew that people's "organic" ideas change slowly, so they changed their residence. What good does cultural nationalism achieve in face of mass deportations, executions, and mass replacement of the native population with non-Romanians?

Thus, the intellectual and political leaders issued a solemn protest (small nations often have no other recourse). They referred to Bessarabia as "Eastern Moldavia" reminding the world that this land dominates the mouth of the Danube, bearing the name of the "Basarab Dynasty," and tied with the ancestors of the Romanians for more than 2,000 years.(...) Further historical facts endorse the Romanian character of Bessarabia, which even the Russians respected until

---

[1084]Not only Bessarabia, but also the northern half of Bucovina and the Herţa district of Moldavia, which never belonged to Russia before.

1870. The year of 1918 brought self-determination to this land. The declaration demonstrated that Northern Bucovina was never Russian. Further, it was pointed out that there were no negotiations; the brutal ultimatum denied self-determination to three million Romanian peasants. Romania solemnly declared that it refused to recognize such international lawlessness, and this document was "signed by the founders of self-determination in Greater Romania." Everybody worth his salt in public life signed the declaration, Iorga included.[1085]

Mme. Liliana remembered the session in the memory of Professor Bémont was to start at 7 p.m. Iorga was always punctual — but this time he didn't arrive even by 9 p.m. from the Crown Council. The audience waited for him in silence. The rumor-mill created a nervous uneasiness. Finally, shortly after 9 p.m. Iorga's car came to a halt before the Institute, Iorga mounted the staircase shaken, with red eyes, and as one of his students remembered, he announced in a shattered voice, "Our borders have been violated!"[1086] Then he shortened his commemorative address, because, as he explained with tears in his eyes: "During these moments terrible things are prepared against us... We will have to suffer as we have suffered before, but (ultimately) we have prevailed throughout our history."[1087]

Iorga now started a sweeping press campaign. His *Neamul Românesc* appeared in black frame and he started his articles: "The Truth about the Past and Present of Bessarabia." He idealized the conditions in this most misruled province, flatly contradicting his previous repeated accounts about conditions there, and even more his own correspondence. He would answer every Soviet attack, refuting Soviet accusations (metaphors of Trotsky and Rakovski) about Romanian "Boyar rule." Iorga was right, asserting: "This is only a preliminary demagoguery," next comes the "Kolkhoz" and Moldavians will soon understand this.

____

[1085]From the Pippidi-Iorga archives.

[1086]From Academician Cornelia Bodea.

[1087]Nicolae Iorga, "Un profesor francez — Charles Bémont," *Conferința la Institutul de Istorie Universală, iunie 1940, București*, Vălenii-de-Munte (1940).

Iorga could have added: With the Kolkhoz will come the NKVD, mass deportations and executions. In one of his articles, Iorga, in contradiction to his former position, praised King Carol for ceding the province without a fight. Here Iorga the politician was talking again, not the historian or the human being.

Iorga was more on the mark concerning ridiculous Soviet assertions about "the Moldavian language," which Romanians "persecuted," and Russians "(allegedly) saved." He rejected assertions about a so-called "Moldavian language." When the Soviets congratulated themselves that they re-established the "brotherhood" between Russians, Ukrainians, and the Jews in Bessarabia, Iorga swiftly reminded them of the "brotherhood of the Kishenev pogrom" in 1903.[1088]

He made repeated appeals to the population of Bessarabia and the Northern Bucovina that, if anybody should get hold of his *Neamul Românesc*, they should spread it. Little did he know about the efficiency of the NKVD! He thought he was dealing with the Austro-Hungarian police, or the Tsarist "Okhrana."

The secessions, with hundreds of thousands of Jewish inhabitants, brought the Jewish issue to the fore again. During the havoc created by the short time limit of the Russian ultimatum, and the disorderly Romanian retreat, many things happened which ought not to have happened. The Jewish and the Slavic population, in their elation at the departure of the Romanians, and remembering two decades of abuses, treated the retreating hapless Romanians in a manner which was to cost them dearly a year later. They were soon to be acquainted with the NKVD — and other blessings of Soviet power. There is no need to elaborate on the Jewish problem again. Conditions beyond the control of either Jews or Romanians created a conflict. There was no immediate constructive solution for the all too numerous Jewish community. The first choice for Jews would have been neither Communism nor Iorga's *Sămănătorism*. They had a Western, capitalist mentality. For the time being, the arrival of the Soviets seemed to be better for the majority of desperately poor Jewish masses than the terror they experienced before, and the terror — which was to come! History

---

[1088] *Neamul Românesc*, 2, 4. 5, 11, 12, 20, and 24 July 1940.

plays strangely with its participants. In East Central Europe, many of the persecuted Jews, with a profoundly capitalist mentality, would rally to the Communists, not by choice but for self-preservation.[1089] They would be no different
to the Arabs of Nazareth (in Israel), who staunchly elect Communist deputies,
or blacks in South Africa which give their support to the Communist dominated
African Nationalist Congress. All too many Jews in this area (especially the
young without a future) had little to lose when the Soviets arrived.[1090]

But that was the Jewish side of the coin. On Iorga's side, (so deeply hurt in
his national pride and by the denial of self-determination for the Romanian majority) there was fury about Jewish disloyalty and preference for a Communism
based on the national enemy number one. Iorga always maintained that Romanians had "organic rights," and the Jews had "no organic rights." Every minority
had rights in proportion to its loyalty. So, with his temperament, he more than
once denounced in his editorials the "joy" the Jews demonstrated when the Soviets arrived.[1091] After all, he wanted to turn Jews into Romanians. He had even
welcomed the translation of the "Protocols of the Elders of Zion" into Romanian. He forgot his own obituary dedicated to Bjornstierne Bjornson (a defender
of Romanians), whom Iorga loved: "the defense of the truth is one of the most
undeniable rights of a great writer."[1092] Iorga even welcomed the "Jewish Stat-
ute" mildly limiting the rights of Jews in Romania, hastily enacted by the opportunistic king. A few days later, as so often before, he regained his composure:
Jews have also good or bad sides like other nations do. They are intelligent,
show solidarity, but by dominating Moldavian cities they became a problem.

[1089]Bessarabian Jews explained to this writer the choice: "The communists take our property,
but leave our lives intact; the Nazis and Legionnaires take both our lives and our property
away."

[1090]The staunchly anti-Communist former Chief Rabbi of Romania, the distinguished scholar
Alexandru Safran, maintains that the majority of the members of the illegal Romanian
Communist Party in 1940 were Jewish. Alexandru Safran, *Memorii* 1940-1947 (Jerusalem).

[1091]*Neamul Românesc*, 12 July 1940.

[1092]*Neamul Românesc*, 30 July 1940 and Nicolae Iorga, *Oameni care au fost*, vol. I, p. 388.

The greatest problem was (as Iorga explained) that Jews showed sympathy towards that state where they could obtain more power, the USSR, and that could not be tolerated.[1093]

A long hot summer followed with Hungary and Bulgaria pressing their claims. Iorga opened his Summer School at Vălenii for the last time, held in an atmosphere which was palpable. The Hungarians mobilized 400,000 soldiers on the Romanian border. The USSR began to make noises that she considered the settlement reached in June "unsatisfactory," Romanian territorial concessions were "insufficient." The Russians were aiming at the whole of Moldavia. During August, Hungarians and Romanians tried to settle their differences through negotiations without result. The Germans got deeply worried about the possible pretext for Russian involvement, threatening their oil. Hitler warned the Hungarians. In a note the Nazis explained that the Hungarians could not count on German support against Romania, adding: "one can see the beginning (phase) of such a war, but not the course it might take."[1094]

Carol asked Hitler and Mussolini to arbitrate between Romania and Hungary, which turned into the Vienna Diktat. The Romanians harbored illusions of making "minor concessions." Iorga proposed an exchange of populations "along the future borders." However, the Romanian delegation was shown a map drawn out by the Nazis and the Italian Fascists which cut Transylvania in half. When Foreign Minister Manoilescu saw the partition map, he fainted. Hungary received 43,000 square kilometers with roughly 2.5 million inhabitants. The majority were Romanians, because it was the numerous Jews which held the balance for Hungary — that before 1944. It was an unimaginative solution, but Ribbentrop explained its intrinsic value: "The basic idea of our actual policy towards Hungary and Romania is to keep two irons in a red-hot state, and to

---

[1093] *Neamul Românesc*, 11 and 15 August 1940.

[1094] Macartney, *October Fifteenth*, vol. 1. pp. 415 and 419 n.; also, *Allianz Hitler-Horthy-Mussolini — Dokumente zur Un qarischein Aussenpolitik 1933-1944* (Budapest, 1966), pp. 263-265.

shape them according to German interests — according to the development of the events."[1095]

Mme. Liliana remembered that it was two subsequent Crown Councils which deliberated the acceptance of the Nazi partition plan. At first, Iorga wasn't present, when everything (the compliance with the Vienna Diktat) was accepted. For formality's sake, the king invoked a second Crown Council. A special train was sent for Iorga, who was resting at Băile Herculane. Dinu Brătianu was also brought to Bucharest; there were many non-Crown Council members present at this second Crown Council, among them Horia and Decebal (Codreanu's brothers), whose presence Iorga protested against promptly, but unsuccessfully. The second Crown Council (like the first), was dominated by the fear of Russian invasion in Moldavia. Because of this, Iorga, after a bitter address about the Vienna Diktat (which will be "a triumph for the Hungarian grófs" (counts), and other Hungarian feudal landlords), advised acceptance. Iorga wrote later: "The choice was to lose 1,100,000 Romanians — or the whole of Moldavia." He continued that the state is one thing, the nation another, concluding: "It is the nation which enters now to the forefront." The next day, Iorga wrote that the Romanian people were "embarking on a journey on a path full of wolves."[1096]

The effect in Romania (especially in Bucharest) was indescribable. Bitterness filled the heart of the people. Within two months Romania had lost large territories where the majority of the inhabitants were Romanians. In Bucharest on that 30 August it was not unusual to see people weeping in public. The mood was a revolutionary one. The system that abandoned one-third of the territory without firing a shot, had surrendered millions of Romanians to a foreign yoke (for yoke it was to be, and of the most onerous kind) — that system had to go! Great crowds gathered around the statue of Michael the Brave shouting for one man, Maniu: "Let us fight! Give us Maniu!" The great daily *Universul* came out with a sweeping editorial about "ten years of tyranny under which the young

---

[1095]See *La Roumanie pendant la deuxième guerre mondiale* (Bucarest, 1964), p. 15; also. *Les archives secrètes de la Wilhelmstrasse* (Paris, 1954), vol. 5, Book 1, p. 376.

[1096]*Neamul Românesc*, 3 and 4 September 1940.

nationalist generation was murdered in a cowardly fashion, and billions embezzled under the pretext of rearmament." The fact that the censor allowed this to be printed made it an open call to revolt.

If the mood was a revolutionary one, nobody called for Iorga. The tragedy was that he was identified with the discredited regime. The dilemma of Romania was the eternal dilemma of small nations: "Hácha or Mannerheim?" And this question was not resolved until Carol called on General Antonescu. Antonescu had been exposed to indignities from the Camarilla since his disgrace in 1938. He was put into solitary confinement in the Bistriţa Monastery and only the speedy joint intervention by the German Ambassador Fabricius and Dr. Neubacher before Carol (on Antonescu's behalf) saved his life. But now, he was released. Carol did not choose to fight, and the military withdrawal from Transylvania was not easy. There was little likelihood that Carol's orders would be obeyed. He wanted to use Antonescu's prestige to carry out this feat.

Some hours after the pro-Maniu demonstrations (the grand old man did not answer the call of the street, he was not the type who would become a revolutionary leader), other songs were sung, and other crowds filled the streets. They wore green shirts, and marched on the Elisabeta Boulevard towards the Royal Palace. They sang about the Căpitanul, about death and resurrection. Their sad refrains were the expression of the sorrow and frustration of a whole generation. "Give us the king! Give us Lupescu! Do not let them get away with their money!" The Legionary revolution had begun. Legionary detachments distributed in the barracks Horia Sima's leaflets containing invectives against the king and Mme. Lupescu. Attempts were made to seize public buildings in Bucharest, and the telephone exchange and other government installations in Braşov and Constanţa were in the Legion's hands by 3 September.

This supplied General Antonescu with arguments, when asking Carol for dictatorial powers. The king yielded. Then Antonescu went further, demanding Carol's abdication. A disgusting wrangle followed, mostly about financial questions: how much gold, jewels, and Rubens and El Greco pictures would the king take with him? How much pension would he receive? Carol decided to leave

Romania. The king, Mme. Lupescu, and Urdăreanu decided to make their disgraceful exit for all practical purposes on a treasure train. The treasure train started a long torturous journey through the Legionary-infested countryside. What followed was like a Wild West story as the Legionaries made attempts to catch up with the train. Finally, in Timisoara, several miles short of the Yugoslav border they succeeded; but the garrison of Timisoara and the rail workers still considered Carol, whether worthy or unworthy, to be their king. They led the train safely through the hail of Legionary bullets to Yugoslavia.

On 6 September 1940, the same day Carol made his exit with his retinue, the Hungarian army began the march into Transylvania amidst the great rejoicing of the Hungarian and Jewish population, and the proud, tormented silence of the Romanians. The first thing the Hungarians did was to undo the Romanian agrarian reform.

As the Romanian army fell back, the country held its breath. What would Antonescu do next? Would he (as some expected hopefully) "pull a De Gaulle"? Not even Maniu wished for that. Yet, on whom could he base his government? On Maniu? That was impossible — the Germans would never accept it. On the Goga-Cuzists? Goga had been close to Antonescu, and it was his widow, Mme. Veturia Goga, who both then and after the fall of the Legionary state was the "grande dame" of the regime, trying to dissipate Hitler's doubts about from Antonescu's pro-French and pro-English past. Although Goga-Cuzists would play a decisive role in Antonescu's regime later, at that point it was impossible for Antonescu to snub the Legion. Nor could he turn to the Romanian army for support at that time, although no other officer could match his prestige. An army can afford to be beaten and still remain a decisive force; there are examples for that — for instance, in Weimar Germany. But an army that retreats without firing a shot at the three arch-enemies of the country cannot have realistic pretensions to power. So the Legion (or what was left of it) remained the logical choice. It was avowedly pro-Nazi, and its mystical Christian-Socialist ideas fortified by its martyrdom made it popular in those desolate days. So General Antonescu (he would later promote himself to Marshal, and became the *Con-*

ducătorul or Leader) formed on 6 September 1940 a government with the majority of portfolios being Legionary. On 15 September 1940, he proclaimed the National Legionary State.

Antonescu was no friend of Iorga. Iorga was a pillar of the Carolist regime, and had some personal conflicts with Antonescu. In his editorials, Iorga, nobly, but unwisely, still defended Carol: Carol was a "good king" and "was loved by the Romanian people." Iorga maintained that King Carol "worked for the good of the country (sic!)." Accordingly, it was the circumstances which made him unpopular.[1097]

The Russians, during September, provoked ominous border incidents within that Russian priority, the Danube Delta. The Hungarians also made it clear that they did not consider the Vienna Diktat the last word in Transylvania. Antonescu had to preserve the existence of the Romanian state, and there seemed to be no other protector in sight than Nazi Germany. So, Antonescu accepted a German-Italian guarantee, for the territorial integrity of rump Romania, and he requested a German "military mission." By mid-October strong German formations entered Romania.

Iorga hated Hitler and Naziism too much to bring his position around. He had too much dignity for that. But for Antonescu, Iorga's ferocious anti-Nazi, anti-German attitude was embarrassing! Added to this were Iorga's close relationship with Carol and the role he played during the Royal Dictatorship, his hostility towards the Legion and the worst liability of all, the fact that the Legionaries considered Iorga the cardinal culprit in the death of their beloved leader. The result was that Iorga was now for all practical purposes proscribed.

Violent press attacks on Iorga started immediately, carried out at the moral and intellectual level of the Strada Sărindarilor. It is interesting that not the Legionary press but the press of the Cuzist bourgeoisie were leading these assaults. Press attacks were spear-headed by the dregs of Cuzist journalism, like I.P. Prundeni, and Ilie Rădulescu, director of the Cuzist daily, *Porunca Vremii*. Horia Sima detested him and his paper. Rădulescu had previously adulated Iorga

---

[1097] *Neamul Românesc*, 8 September 1940.

and King Carol in a nauseating fashion. He was firmly against the Legion, and wrote about "our great Iorga" (...) "his great soul," calling him "Apostle, a brilliant writer and a political inspiration." He considered that "no love (shown by) our country could be considered enough towards Iorga." With the advent of the National Legionary State, Rădulescu changed his tune and ripped into the defenseless Iorga. Iorga now became "not only the moral author of the persecution of the Legion — but an enthusiast of crime, of killing without a trial — Iorga is a professor who rejoiced when students dropped dead under the hail of bullets, etc." The references to Iorga as *dascălul neamului* (the teacher of the nation) were always made in ridiculing quotation marks, and always more contemptuously. Rădulescu remembered how wickedly he had been persecuted by Iorga, he, the poor man, returning from Berlin in 1939, expressing his enthusiasm for Naziism! Iorga "subjected him to mockery and the brutality of the censorship!"[1098] The other Cuzist journalist, Mr. Prundeni, did even better.

Iorga fought back, reminding these people of articles they had writ-ten before. Wrote Iorga: "A man of convictions, Mr. I.P. Prundeni." He reminded Prundeni how he had saluted "the patriotic gesture" of students joining Carol in 1940, quoting verbatim, "No need to talk about the Legion — the king will receive his prodigal sons." Then Iorga quoted Prundeni in his new position: "The murderous state has collapsed — above its mins rises the Legionary State." And: "The Green Shirts mean discipline — under these shirts vibrates the love for our country, and (this love) is complemented by feelings towards our nation." Other quotations follow, Prundeni praising Codreanu's "martyrdom and sacrifice."[1099]

Cuza and his son (although Cuzists were not loved by the Legion) had great influence over *Porunca Vremii*, but they never lifted their finger to stop this campaign against Iorga. They never expressed indignation over the mud-slinging against an old friend, now abandoned and lonely.

Iorga's son, Mircea (egged on by Georgescu-Cocoş), tried to stand up against this campaign, but his method was flawed. The Iorga family was not

---

[1098] *Porunca Vremii*, 3 September 1937 and 15 and 18 September 1940.

[1099] *Neamul Românesc*, 29 September 1940.

kind in judging Mircea's moves. Mircea was too ambitious, he wanted to take over his father's party, and had some Legionary ties, the value of which he over-estimated.

He and Georgescu placed an article in *Neamul Românesc* in a forlorn attempt to re-write history. Accordingly (supported by alleged testimonies), Iorga sent a telegram to the military tribunal, in which he withdrew his complaint against Codreanu five days before the trial. Others testified how much Iorga was outraged by Codreanu's murder, and that three days after Codreanu was shot, Iorga had a violent confrontation with Călinescu. The witnesses testified in what depressed state Călinescu left Iorga's home.[1100]

This was an exercise in futility, since Iorga's editorials at that time told a different story. Mme. Liliana (and others) remember how much Iorga hated all this; he considered it "stupid! worse than stupid, futile!" All this was undertaken without Iorga's knowledge. He did not want to knuckle under pressure.

Mircea always assured the Iorga family "not a hair on father's head will be touched or bent!" (Thanks to his Legionary contacts.) When Mircea gave his assurances that not a hair on his father's head would be bent, and maneuvered with his articles, the Legionary Death Commando which would kill Iorga was already formed.[1101] The leader of the Death Commando was the agronomy engineer Traian Boeru, who came from Hârşova in the Dobrogea, and was the Legionary director of the Institutul National al Cooperaţiei, an agricultural co-operative.

[1100] *Neamul Românesc*, 2 October 1940.

[1101] All "Echipa Morţii" ("Death Commandoes") were numbered; this writer could not ascertain beyond reasonable doubt the number of Boeru's Death Commando. Some other sources slightly differ about the names of Boeru's Death Commando. This writer decided to rely on the names obtained from Traian Boeru and some other Legionaries. The number of Legionaries varies between the number of five mentioned by the Iorga family, and Mr. Boeru. Sometimes the number is given as seven, or even eight (by Horia Sima). Was the driver included? Did one or two Legionaries separate from the Death Squad after they assassinated Madgearu? Did all of them proceed to Sinaia to murder Iorga?

I had a chance to arrange a long interview with Boeru in 1985, in a sanatorium retirement home in Garmisch-Partenkirchen in Bavaria, a few weeks before his death. It is from Boeru that I received the names of the death commando of which he was the leader. Boeru — because of the opprobrium of Iorga's assassination — had made futile attempts to deny his own participation in the assassination. The other important member of commando was Ștefan Cojocaru. He nurtured a limitless admiration and love for Codreanu, and was psychologically incapable of overcoming the pain of Codreanu's disappearance. Then there were Ion Tucan, Nicolae Iorga (this strange coincidence of names between victim and assassin will become quite important), and a certain Schweninger, whose first name Boeru did not remember — he was of German ethnic origin.

None of these people had an education deserving of the name, not even Boeru was an intellectual. The driver of the car in which the death commando made its forays was Ștefan Iacobuță, a professional driver of the agricultural cooperative. All of them were Legionaries employed by the cooperative. Thus, they could plot conveniently. The car was an official vehicle registered to this cooperative, a black Buick, and bore the license plate 6211BR.

Boeru recalled that the article Mircea Iorga placed in *Neamul Românesc* worked on the Legion like trying to feed broccoli to a hungry tiger. He commented: "It was a record in the domain of the ridiculous and the contemptible." The next day, the Legionary daily, *Buna Vestire*, gave a swift retort — (Boeru claimed that it was he who placed the article). The article explained that "the Legion refuses the adroit and skillful moves of *Neamul Românesc*" and continued that the Legion is not "skillful" or trying "to be adroit...," It concluded in an ominous tone: "The day of reckoning and that of assuming responsibility has arrived rather than the days of skillfulness and craftiness...."[1102] Clear enough.

The same death commando also prepared the assassination of Virgil Madgearu, an old democratic foe of the Legion from Maniu's party. There was never any doubt why they went after Iorga; Horia Sima argued: "It is well-known why." The Legion considered him directly responsible for the death of

---

[1102]*Buna Vestire*, 4 October 1940.

Codreanu. But why after Madgearu? Because of his former stands against the Legion and mutual threats and counter threats. Now Legionary threats had to be carried out. The Legion were also against Madgearu because of his (alleged) Hungarian origins.[1103]

Only a few days after the Legionary takeover, Bucharest had gone through an almost 180 degree change of course. Foreign policy had no other alternative than a complete German-Italian line. Antonescu understood the present needs of Romania that way. The only protection he could envision for Romania now was a German-Italian guarantee. Later Romania would join the Tri-Partite Pact between Germany, Italy, and Japan. Neither of these were his choice, but this robust patriot understood that he could not always do what he would like to do, not even do the right thing, but only what he could do in the moment.

Antonescu's strict military sense of law, order, and discipline, was inconceivable to the revolutionary dynamism of a movement emerging from the nightmare of Carolist torture chambers. And Antonescu was rather unsure (considering his long pro-Western past) that the Germans would support a stand against the Legion. The Germans kept everybody (Antonescu and the Legion included) guessing for all too long whom they would support. Later at the end of January 1941, Hitler would be forced to defend German interests: "Ruhe in der Rohstoffszone!" This meant oil, food, and the security of the strategic area, the staging ground for his attack against the USSR. For these purposes Antonescu and the updated old order were the guarantee — not Legionary anarchy and experiments in "archangelic" social revolution.

Meanwhile, all Germans — not surprisingly — on all levels, be it the conservative career diplomat Ambassador Fabricius, or on the "W" (Wirtschaft) level of Dr. H. Neubacher, be it the SS or the SD, deeply resented Iorga. Boeru's death squad (as Antonescu later noted: "he became painfully aware of the fact")

[1103]Sima, *Cazul Iorga-Madgearu*, pp. 17 and 20.

obtained arms from the Germans with which they would murder Iorga and Madgearu.[1104]

In September 1940, the Legion finally arrived at power when it was the least ready. With the best of its leaders — according to the irreverent jokes — under the earth like potatoes, its new commander, Horia Sima, would offer a third-rate leadership. The Royal Dictatorship did a good job. Few of the "Old Guard" Legionaries were still alive. Now hundreds of thousands of opportunists joined the movement — looking forward to opportunities for the expropriation of Jewish properties. Old Legionaries contemptuously referred to them as "Septembrists." This diluted Legion was basically interested in power, vengeance, and enrichments. Some old Legionaries initiated policies towards social revolution and transformation, frightening the establishment even more. The frightened bourgeoisie went into opposition, Jewish capital fled, and prices of basic commodities skyrocketed.

The Legion organized its own "Legionary Police" which would be in the forefront of anarchy, pillage, murder, and disruption. Their targets were Jews, foreigners (the foreign embassies never ceased to protest!), even Cuzists.

Antonescu tried to lift up the spirit of his people. There was a public atonement for the sins of the past, parades were held, and the return of the much-wronged Princess Helen (now called "Regina Mamă," the mother of King Michael. During these parades in the colorful cavalcade of uniforms, peasant costumes, and Legionary green shirrs, there was one discordant clement — a large aggregation of relatives of murdered Legionaries dressed in black, their loved ones still unavenged. This large group ominously foretold things which would come to pass.

[1104]Hillgruber, *op. cit.*, pp. 116-117. The acquisition of arms from the Germans was confirmed by Boeru to this writer. But this doesn't point to German guilt in Iorga's assassination. Although the Nazis were not unhappy about Iorga's murder, the Legion had its own voluminous accounts to settle with Iorga, and (as Boeru pointed it out) in early October 1940, the Germans sent light arms to other Legionary units too (Death Squads or otherwise).

Antonescu refused any form of anarchic vengeance. Retribution was to be taken by legal means, and moved in that direction in a cumbersome manner. If not yet avenged — murdered Legionaries were exhumed almost daily, and solemnly reburied. A foreign diplomat called the Legionary regime "régime des marches funèbres." The most important exhumation, that of the Căpitanul Codreanu, and his reburial, was set for 30 November (on the second anniversary of his murder).

Never was a movement dominated so much from beyond the grave as the Legion. Everywhere huge billboards went up bearing Codreanu's likeness, with one thing written on it: "Corneliu Zelea Codreanu — Prezent!" And there were many billboards corresponding to the death cult of the Legion. *"Trăiască Moartea! Trăiască Biruinţa Legionară!"* (Long Live Death! Long Live Legionary Victory!) But for a conservative military man like Antonescu, it was the preservation and assurance of life rather than death which was the primary task of government. He complained to Sima ever more often that "he cannot live in anarchy!"[1105]

By the end of September, Bucharest became increasingly unbearable for Iorga. His teaching positions were taken away, his Institute of Universal History was hampered in its activities. Only *Neamul Românesc* remained, and here Nicolae Georgescu-Cocoş became more and more uncontrollable.

As Legionary anarchy became more radicalized, Iorga wrote an editorial "The Shadow of Robespierre." He warned that "every revolution has a Robespierre," the incorruptible, cold, sharp, crude, and domineering Robespierre. The next day Prundeni answered: "Yes! Iorga is right, there cannot be a revolution without Robespierre." Prundeni explained that Iorga cannot oscillate with impunity between A.C. Cuza and the counter of Aristide Blank's Bank, where he receives his money. Iorga is "guilty of civil murder." The article reminded Iorga of the fate of Fouché and Danton ascending the guillotine together with Marie

---

[1105]The Legion's reaction to Antonescu's criticism of Legionary anarchy was characteristic: They pointed out that, "they shall not force Antonescu to live in anarchy," and formed a Death Commando to assassinate him at a later date. Barbu, *op.cit.*, p. 66.

Antoinette and Louis XVI. (The ignorance of this pseudo-intellectual is remarkable, lumping Napoleon's police chief, Fouché — who did not ascend any guillotine — together with French royalty and Danton). Iorga gave a dignified answer to these howls: "Because of the situation, Iorga thinks that he should keep certain opinions to himself — opinions which should be well-known to everybody who read his articles (in the past) and followed him."

On 11 October, Iorga wrote his farewell. He thanked Georgescu-Cocoş for his help (that Georgescu-Cocoş who defied him on so many occasions). Georgescu-Cocoş later became a follower of Antonescu and Nazi Germany. He was a crude man who tried to take over *Neamul Românesc*. As the Iorga family explained to the writer, it was mainly because of him that Iorga decided to close down his newspaper. Iorga's last words on the editorial page became celebrated: "When there is a defeat, the flag is not surrendered. It will be wrapped around the heart."[1106]

Iorga left for Vălenii, where he hoped to find peace and security. Mme. Liliana stayed behind to continue her study and work. She went often to Vălenii to see her parents. Mme. Catinca's sister, Mme. Lucia Bogdan, came to stay with them; so did Iorga's youngest daughter, Miss Alina.

Iorga moved to Vălenii to find peace, and, like the hero of antiquity who leaned on mother earth and gained a new-found strength, he hoped for regeneration. His dedication to Vălenii as a kind of *Sămănătorist* village was much like De Gaulle's to Colombey les deux Eglises to which De Gaulle retired on every possible occasion. But here comparisons stop. The constituents of Colombey voted a solid 100% for De Gaulle, as a result he left in his testament instructions that he should be buried there. Iorga was not so lucky. Vălenii had become a Legionary stronghold! Iorga's bust was destroyed by the inhabitants, and he underwent constant provocations. The people there spied on him (according to engineer Boeru, even for the benefit of his Death Commando). Especially bothersome was the Legionary Primar (village chief), the notorious Gheorghe Dinescu.

[1106]*Neamul Românesc,* 19, 26, September, and 11 October 1940; and *Porunca Vremii,* 20 September 1940.

But Iorga's printing press was located there, and now, without any adequate financial means, he was not able to pay the salaries of the workers.

Iorga continued his work on his universal history, and left his house rarely. To walk in Vălenii represented no fun, despite the extraordinary beautiful "Indian summer" which prevailed so long.

On the night of 9-10 November 1940, a violent earthquake shook eastern Wallachia, Bucharest included. Since the whole Teleajen Valley (where Vălenii is) is situated over a seismic fault, the village suffered extensive damage. Although neither Iorga nor anyone in his family were hurt, his house was ruined and became uninhabitable. As Iorga was standing before the ruins of everything he built during a lifetime, his unbroken bearing surprised friend and foe; Mme. Catinca resembled a rock next to her husband. The Iorgas moved over to Mme. Lucia's damaged but habitable house temporarily. To Iorga's joy his printing press survived the earthquake.[1107]

But there was a corollary to the earthquake developing within the ranks of the Legion. Legionaries, with their "death cult" — as Mr. Boeru explained it to the writer — considered the quake as "a warning, a punishment from God, because the Legion failed to avenge their martyrs." Mr. Boeru remembered that "there was always a clamor in Legionary circles that Iorga was responsible for Codreanu's death." After the quake, this clamor was swelling, as the reburial date of Codreanu was approaching.

This reburial date was 30 November. The "Death Squad" (under Mr. Boeru) accelerated preparations. After all, as Mr. Boeru remembered, Codreanu had ordered two days of vengeance for the long sufferings — once the Legion arrived in power. And the "Căpitanul" could not be put to rest unavenged.

Iorga's child-like psychology and naivete got the better of him. Like a child, he did not realize the danger. This unawareness of danger was as childish as Iorga's innocence and capacity to fury. Sometimes, as Mme. Liliana remem-

---

[1107]Lepădatu, who visited the Iorgas after the earthquake, remembered vividly the scene. Lepădatu, *op. cit.*, pp. 412-413.

bered, when Iorga was informed about continuous Legionary outrages and murders, he broke out: "They will kill me!" But this was a passing phenomenon. Mme. Catinca was fatalistic — but not her sister, Mme. Lucia! She was the most aware of the danger, and did her best to nudge Iorga and convince him to leave the country, to go to Italy, to his school in Venice.

Iorga did not for a moment seriously consider this. He said, "My country might still need me! If the moment comes, I wish to be at hand to serve my country!" One can feel his totally disinterested love for Romania, for which he was ready for any sacrifice. It was said that one can only be crucified in his own faith.

This writer asked Mme. Liliana and other members of the family whether Iorga thought about going abroad to found a Romanian representation or government in exile in the West. After all, he was a more portentous choice than those (Tilea, Davila, and others) who tried to keep open the lines to Romania's Western friends. The answer received was a short one: "This did not even come up-ever!"

Other friends of Iorga saw the danger too. As Mr. Frasin Munteanu-Râmnic remembered, his father, Dimitrie Munteanu-Râmnic dismissed the light-hearted assurances of Iorga's son, Mircea, asked, and received an audience in mid-October with Antonescu. He made an appeal to the Conducătorul, reminding him of Iorga's great services, and asked a 24-hour gendarmerie protection for him. Antonescu — it is alleged — answered in his monosyllabic soldier fashion: "I'm sorry — I cannot do a thing. Iorga went just too far in his animosity toward the Legion."[1108]

What was Antonescu's motive for his refusal? Personal animosity? Antonescu was famous for his vindictiveness and long memory. Or, because in mid-October he was still not feeling secure about the German stand towards the Legion — which by then Antonescu heartily detested? Or was it the overwhelming

---

[1108]Other members of the Iorga family, not on friendly terms with Mr. Frasin Munteanu-Râmnic, doubt such a meeting between Dimitrie Munteanu-Râmnic and General Antonescu took place. To this writer, the version of Mr. Frasin Munteanu-Râmnic seems to be plausible.

German hostility towards Iorga? It might have been all three of these reasons —
they don't exclude each other.

A few days after the quake, the Iorgas moved to their undamaged house on
the Strada Codrului in Sinaia. It must have been a relief after the Legionary-
infested atmosphere of Vălenii. Mme. Lucia stayed in Vălenii. Iorga and Mme.
Catinca together with their servant, Aneta Cazacu, were later joined in Sinaia by
their youngest daughter, Miss Alina Iorga.

In Sinaia, Iorga continued to work on his universal history.[1109] Besides historical work, he wrote two plays, on historic lines as usual. One was "Bayazid,"
supposedly depicting the Ottoman Sultan, who, after many successes, was defeated and imprisoned in a cage, a historical allegory to Hitler and how Iorga
hopefully foresaw his fate. "Tamerlane," the Life and Deeds of a monstrous,
cruel, Oriental tyrant, was a none too subtle allegory to the life and activities of
Stalin.[1110] These plays show Iorga's political concepts during these dark days.
He never believed in the durability of the Nazi-Soviet pact, nor did he doubt an
ultimate Allied victory over Naziism. This was based as much on historical
grounds as Iorga's belief that it was an inevitability, for the benefit of humanity.

With the advent of the National Legionary State, financial difficulties descended on the Iorga family. The Legionary minister of education and cults,
Traian Brăileanu, did his petty best. He dismissed Iorga from his reaching positions, terminating his salaries immediately. He withdrew from Iorga even the
railway pass due to him as a senator, and every other benefit he had enjoyed.
The new Legionary president of the Bucharest University was the representative
of the Şcoala Nouă, P.P. Panaitescu. Panaitescu, in a vindictive fashion, did his
best to aggravate Iorga's financial situation in every way.

Many "worthies" of the old regime were, during those days, under investigation for their malversation of public funds. Since Iorga was incorruptible, and

---

[1109]*Materiale pentru istoriologie umană* (unedited fragment published by Liliana N. Iorga,
foreword by D. M. Pippidi, Bucureşti, 1969). Also, the last poetry written by Iorga, *Ultimele*,
(Craiova, 1968).

[1110]Mme. Liliana Pippidi-Iorga to the writer.

had no sense for financial matters, he had no "reserves" accumulated, like so many others had! With the cessation of his first paycheck, financial difficulties started right away. These difficulties were tangible, but what worried Iorga more was that he had difficulties paying his workers at his printing press. "Those unfortunates must be paid! — Come what may!" This is what Iorga repeated almost monotonously. Yes, but how?! In strongly Legionary Vălenii, the Legionaries exerted unpleasant pressures on Iorga because of these unpaid salaries (even if the workers at Iorga's printing press were decent, and patient), Iorga hoped to raise money by selling portions of his library. Although this was his most cherished possession, he was ready to part with it for his workers' sake — it soon became clear what the relative value of his library was. The "market value" of his library would not even scratch the surface of his financial problems.

And what was Bucharest high society doing? Iorga's numerous acquaintances, people whom he could consider his friends? That society which fawned upon him a few weeks before? Did they try to help? As written in the Scriptures: "There was a new king in Egypt — and no one remembered Joseph any more... Did Cuza try to help? No, he left Iorga to his fare as he did during the war in Iaşi. During numerous interviews, the Iorga family was very bitter recalling these last weeks of Iorga's life. They remembered that the Iorga family was almost alone in these hours of need, mocked, proscribed, abandoned, with one exception: Dr. Constantin Angelescu. For him, Iorga did not become an "unperson." By mid-October (when it became clear that Iorga could not raise any substantial amount of money by selling portions of his library) Dr. Angelescu loaned to Iorga 50,000 lei (about $220-525 U.S. Dollars in those days) to pay the outstanding salary of workers in his printing press.

But how to go on from there? Especially after the catastrophic earthquake? Iorga wrote in the beginning of November another letter to Dr. Angelescu — asking not for money, but for help and intervention to secure a loan through the Banca Românească. Dr. Angelescu's answer was delayed because of the disorganization caused by the earthquake. Because Dr. Angelescu's answer was symptomatic of the times and of Iorga's state of mind, this writer will verbatim reproduce it. Since the answer was delivered to Iorga the morning he was abducted and murdered by the Legionary terror squad, the letter was in his pocket when his murderers opened fire on him, and is riddled with bullets:

Dearest Professor Iorga,

I'm answering the letter you sent me through Mr. L. Vasilescu, dated 20 October. It was handed to me only four days ago. The great misfortune (that is, the earthquake) which came to pass last night prevented me from answering before — this misfortune placed another sorrow on our hard-tried country.

You accuse me that I have forgotten you — like almost everybody else did. Please, believe me that this is not so.

During the almost forty years I have known you, you had ample opportunity to see the manifestations of my friendship, the admiration I feel towards you as a human being, a man of culture, and a scholar. (There is a large bullet hole in the letter, making words indiscernible) ...which did such a great service to our country and nation, and after such a long time, I'm not about to change my opinion (about you) — because (such a change) would not be consistent with my character and my feelings.

The (present) misfortunes are transitory. I'm certain that you have borne them with serenity and courage — and I'm convinced that you will do so in the future.

The very day I received your letter I went to the Banca Românească, but despite my insistence I could not get satisfactory results, because under the present circumstances the bank refuses to make loans. Farcaş will inform you about every detail.

I believe that an intervention with Cancicov, who is a minister now, may favorably resolve the issue. I instructed Farcaş that he should place at your (a large bullet hole makes a word also illegible) the sum you asked for.

Ask Farcaş to transfer the money.

I will ask for intervention (in your favor with Cancicov).

Send my respectful greetings to Mme. Iorga, please receive my friendly greetings, (signed) Dr. Angelescu.[1111]

This letter was recovered from Iorga's dead body riddled by bullets. Somehow these bullet holes, tearing into the text, give posthumous testimony of Iorga's poverty and incorruptibility, rare qualities amidst the manifold corruptions of Bucharest high society, which now turned its back on the "Teacher of the Nation."

The Iorgas were now living in their little villa in Sinaia. But by the last week of November, things were beginning to move (as far as the plans of the "Death Squad" were concerned). As Mme. Liliana remembered (although she was staying in their Bucharest residence, she spoke almost daily with Mme. Catinca on the telephone), two or three days before the "Death Squad" struck, some of the squad members (or if not Death Squad members, some other Legionaries) came to "survey the terrain" around Iorga's villa. Legionaries crawled around the house and told people, "they came to finish off Iorga."[1112] The neighbor next door (Ion Pascariu) heard their boasting, after which the old man warned Iorga, offering to hide him with some of his kin. Iorga thanked him, but seemed unconcerned. Yet, he spent a very unpleasant, sleepless night. The following morning, noticing Mr. Pascariu from the window, he yelled down: "Hey you!" Waving his finger admonishingly, Iorga continued: "You sure gave me a good scare yesterday! You see, nothing has happened, everything will be all right! Thank you, though."

The next day, at noon (on 25 November 1940) Mme. Liliana came to celebrate the Day of St. Catherine, the name's day of Mme. Catinca. If Iorga had a favorite child, she was the one. Mme. Liliana wanted to see her parents on their anniversary. She didn't divine she would see her father for the last time. She returned to Bucharest. The next day, 26 November, passed quietly.

[1111]Pippidi-Iorga archives. Mr. Cancicov was a financial expert. Mr. Farcaș was the financial administrator of the Iorga estate.

[1112]The Legionaries could get away with it. The brother of one of the "Death Commando" members, Ştefan Cojocaru, was (how convenient!) Paul Cojocaru, the Chestor (Questor) of the Legionary Police in Ploieşti, the seat of Prahova County, to which Sinaia belonged.

Then Wednesday, 27 November 1940, dawned, a foggy, crispy day. The beautiful Indian summer seemed to be over. The night of 26-27 November proved to be a portentous night in Bucharest. The Legion went on a rampage in the Jilava Prison where the "worthies" of the Royal Dictatorship were detained: Moruzov, the head of Carol's personal secret police, Colonel Gavrilă Marinescu, Victor Iamandi, the minister of justice during the outrages against the Legion, General Ion Begliu of the Gendarmerie who organized Codreanu's murder, General Argeşanu, who organized the bloodbath after Călinescu's assassination, and dozens of high officials and officers of the police and the gendarmerie. A few feet away from their cells, Codreanu, the "Decemviri" and the "Nicadori" had been buried in the courtyard, acid poured over their bodies. The Legionary Death Squads burst into the cells and murdered the prisoners in cold blood; then they lined up at the grave of Codreanu and saluted: "Căpitanul, we have avenged you!" There was more on the way. In Bucharest, the Legionary Death Squads fetched Argetoianu, Tătărescu, Ghelmegheanu, General Iliaşevici, Gigurtu, and dragged them to the Prefecture. Only the speedy intervention of a pro-Antonescu official in the Ministry of Interior (Colonel A. Rioşeanu), and more importantly, the intervention of the German Ambassador Fabricius, and of Dr. Neubacher, and their transfer into German premises saved their lives.

Did Iorga know about these happenings? No. Only a few hours passed between the horrors in Bucharest and Iorga's abduction, and the news could not have reached (considering the complete news blackout) Sinaia. Reconstructing Iorga's last day, it would seem he was quite happy. The morning mail delivery brought a letter from his friend Constantin Angelescu. He was relieved, knowing he was not completely abandoned, and the letter promised relief for his financial problems.

But by noon the black Buick of the Agrarian Cooperative, with its by now famous license plate 6211BR started out. The driver was Ştefan Iacobuţă, and the huge American car (so different from the small European compacts) was full of armed Legionaries.[1113]

The car drove first to Iorga's Bucharest residence on the Șosea Jianu, looking for him. But Iorga was in Sinaia.[1114] Boeru's "Death Squad" had two goals: to murder Iorga and Madgearu. After not finding Iorga, they drove to Madgearu's residence and (as Mr. Boeru explained it to the writer), identifying themselves as the Bucharest "Legionary Police," asked Madgearu to come with them "for interrogation." Madgearu did not offer resistance; they drove him to the Snagov forest and murdered him with multiple shots around 3:40 p.m.[1115]

From Snagov, they drove straight to Sinaia with a short stopover at the Legionary Police in Ploiești. One of the Death Squad members, Ștefan Cojocaru, checked with his brother Paul; it is not clear why they stopped.

[1113]It is debatable whether five legionaries entered the Iorga villa and one or two of them remained with the car in the courtyard, or only the driver, Mr. Iacobuță remained. The murders of Iorga and Madgearu were the most unjustifiable of all Legionary outrages. Mr. Boeru was attacked for it in a devastating manner even by Horia Sima. Under the burden of guilt, Mr. Boeru tried to deny his direct participation in Iorga's murder. However, he boasted after the war in Romanian circles about it. Some Romanians (very reliable and serious professionals) recalled that Boeru boasted to them: "l-am omorât ca pe un pui!" ("We wrung his neck like a chicken!") Since this writer used Boeru's account often as a source, he wishes to point out that his account is reliable only for some basic facts; the Death Commando's organization, names, route and activities. But this writer places no faith on Mr. Boeru's account about his own role. All accounts (even of other Death Commando members), of the Iorga family, and that of the official investigation contradict the role which Mr. Boeru assigned for himself much later. The new role is a product of his burden of shame. His shame was so intense that during the early 1960s a *Juriul de Onoare* (Court of Honor) was convoked by some Legionaries, presided over by General Ion Gheorghe (Antonescu's last ambassador to Berlin) to exonerate Boeru of Iorga's murder. Whatever the decision of this "Court of Honor," Boeru had many times flatly contradicted the exonerating "findings" of the court in the past.

[1114]It was never established who were the Legionary prowlers around the Iorga house two days before; were they members of the Death Commando who came to gather intelligence? Were they the local Legionaries who kept contact with the Death Commando? Were they agents of the Legionary Police in Ploiești and its "Chester" Paul Cojocaru?

[1115]This was by no means a common crime by any criteria. As the police report shows, after the assassination of Virgil Madgearu, his attaché case with 23,000 lei, his golden wristwatch, his golden fountain pen, rings, and other valuables were left behind, untouched. Mihai Stoian, *Moartea unui savant: Nicolae Iorga* (București, 1976), p. 20.

There seems to have been an argument between the Death Squad and the Questor Paul Cojocaru: Paul Cojocaru turned to the Death Squad and said, "What have I to do with it? Take him and finish him off."

They were going to do just that. Arriving at Iorga's villa around 5:30 p.m., the car parked in the garden. The Legionaries (it is not clear which members of the terror squad entered Iorga's villa, or whether all of them entered it) entered from the backside, the servant's entry. Obviously they had good intelligence about the terrain. Their leader was Traian Boeru.[1116] As Mme. Catinca later related, Iorga, Mme. Catinca, the servant Aneta Cazacu were in the villa. Miss Alina went out for a walk shortly before the arrival of the Legionaries. The Legionaries entered through the servant entrance; four or five of them (as Mme. Catinca recalled), arrived in the living room.

They met Mme. Catinca and the last act of the drama started. Their leader (Mr. Boeru) addressed Mme. Catinca: "We are from the Legionary Police and Iorga is requested to come with us for interrogation to Bucharest." She answered instinctively: "The Professor is ill." Unfortunately, at that point Aneta Cazacu entered from the kitchen, bringing a cup of tea for Iorga. Everybody followed her into Iorga's study. The Professor was sitting at his desk with the desk lamp burning, working over his universal history. As they entered, the leader (Mr. Boeru) presented the same demand to Iorga. "Good evening, Professor. We are here on behalf of the Legionary Police, and request you to come with us to Bucharest for interrogation." Iorga sized up the situation: "Is the interrogation concerning the death of Codreanu?" The leader of the death squad answered: "Yes!" Without saying a word, Iorga took his coat, dressed up, and walked out. Outside, in the living room, he requested his fur cap and his galoshes. Mme. Catinca fetched them. Now Iorga asked permission to step out to the bathroom. This request was refused by the leader of the Death Squad. Mme. Catinca wanted to accompany her husband; this request was also rejected. The Legionaries opened

---

[1116]This writer wants to point out once more that, regardless of the findings of the "Court of Honor," Boeru led the Death Squad into the premises of Iorga's villa. It is not clear how many Legionaries entered the house and how many remained in the car.

the door, Iorga walked out amidst them. His last instructions to Mme. Catinca were: "Take good care of my papers for the world history' project!"

So, here we have the tragedy. A brave and strong man, who suspected treachery, and was always psychologically prepared to face death for what he believed in, walked off between the members of the Death Commando for whom he represented the pillar of the corrupt Carolist regime, and the chief culprit in the imprisonment and murder of their leader, the beloved Căpitanul. Legionaries filled with vengeance and the mystical impulses of a Manichaen death cult.

In the courtyard, Iorga, as usual, wanted to take a seat besides the driver. This was denied. He got into the car on the back seat, pressed in amidst the numerous Legionaries. It was now that Miss Alina returned from her walk and saw her father being put into the car. She walked up and addressed the Legionaries: "Where are you taking my father?! What do you want from him?! Father is as clean as a crystal!" She received no answer. The car drove away.

They drove straight to Ploieşti. After a short stopover at the Legionary Police (it is not quite clear whether they made a stop in Ploieşti at all),[1117] at about midnight they drove to the village of Strejnic, about five kilometers from Ploieşti. One kilometer outside the village along an open stretch of the road they ordered Iorga to descend. Before shooting him, there was an argument within the Death Squad. As Boeru remembered (although Boeru pretended to know this by hearsay, because, he insisted that he was not present), the Death Squad member Nicolae Iorga asked to be allowed to fire the first shots at Iorga, and to wound him mortally because "he bears and disgraced my name." His request was granted, Then the other shots rang out.

As it was said, "The Balkans has lost its greatest intellectual."

[1117]After Iorga's murder, there were false rumors that after his abduction he was taken to the village of Teişani (next to Vălenii) interrogated, and mocked; that he was put on "trial," "judged," and was condemned to death. Other rumors related that he was physically mistreated and tortured, after being taken to the Legionary police station in Ploieşti. All these conjectures seem to be false, with the exception of passing through the Legionary Police station in Ploieşti. This was confirmed to the writer by Mr. Boeru also. With the exception of a short stop at the Legionary police in Ploieşti (it is not even clear whether Iorga left the car), the murderers proceeded to the place of execution.

Meanwhile, Mme. Catinca desperately tried to get some phone calls through to the office of General Antonescu. It was impossible to get through to the prime minister's office. After the earthquake telephone connections were sparse and malfunctioning. Mme. Catinca tried to call her son, Mircea; finally she succeeded and she told him what had happened. If Mircea Iorga was sure that "not a hair on the head of his father would be bent" — it was now too late to prove it. Mircea Iorga called General Antonescu's office, but Antonescu was not there. He spoke with Antonescu's aide, Colonel Elefterescu, who advised Mircea to call General Petrovicescu, the Minister of the Interior (a sympathizer of the Legion). Mircea did just that, and this was useless. Finally, he reached Colonel A. Rioşeanu (a pro-Antonescu official), an enemy of Legionary anarchy, in the Ministry of the Interior. Colonel Rioşeanu tried his best. They caught up somewhere with Sima, and ordered police checkpoints set up between Sinaia, Ploieşti, and Bucharest, knowing how useless this would be, since the Legionary police (and Death Squads) could not be challenged by the regular police. There was also the time factor! By now everything was over. Sima was alerted. He was very busy on that memorable day, trying to control other outrages committed by his Legion; but he drove to Ploieşti, arriving there around 11 p.m. or by midnight. He was informed by the Questor, Paul Cojocaru, that Iorga was gone, presumably dead by then.

Now Sima drove at breakneck speed from Ploieşti to Bucharest. He knew where to look for the Death Squad! He drove to the Aleea Vulpache to Mme. Lupescu's home, transformed into a Legionary stronghold.[1118] Sima's instincts were right; he found the Death Squad (Sima remembers there were eight of them under the leadership of the engineer Traian Boeru). Boeru informed him that they had murdered Iorga and Madgearu. As Sima recalled, the killers seemed to be in a state of transfiguration. A kind of otherworldly calm reflected on their faces. Boeru spoke in mystical terms about avenging the Captain, the treachery

---

[1118]The Legionaries transformed the villa of Mme. Lupescu into a kind of museum, and organized tours daily for the faithful to show this "Shrine of Evil." Beyond that, Mme. Lupescu's former residence became a hang-out for Legionary policemen, bigshots, and "Death Commandos."

of Iorga and that of Madgearu, and Codreanu's alleged order that he should be avenged. He also spoke of the "twenty years of suffering and persecution" the Legion had to endure. Sima was moved, and discarded the idea of provocation. He condoned the "revenge for three days" after which the Legion was to return to normalcy.[1119] The next morning Mircea Iorga was received by Antonescu. Antonescu had learned of Iorga's murder shortly before, from Colonel Nicolae Dragomir, the Undersecretary in the Ministry of Coordination with the Marele Stat Major (the Romanian General Staff). Colonel Dragomir told Mme. Liliana how he turned to Antonescu: "Do you know what has happened? They have killed Iorga!" Antonescu erupted: "What do you say, sir? In what kind of troubles do you get me into!"[1120] A few days later in public statements both Antonescu and Sima strongly condemned the murders and promised punishment for the culprits. This was easier said than done. Antonescu insisted during the sessions of the Council of Ministers that Sima punish the guilty. Sima retorted: "Yes, I will look into it, if there will be a thorough purge of all politicians of the old regime! Only after that would we consider to punish the murderers of Iorga and the others." This was something that Antonescu was unwilling to do.[1121]

Nevertheless, these murderous two days seemed to be a turning point in Antonescu's attitude towards the Legion. His animosity towards Legionary anarchy was maturing. He called together some of his trusted, high-ranking officers, and as Admiral Macelaru remembered, he told them that he would finish the Legion off as soon as it is practicable.[1122] As the chief interpreter of Antonescu,

---

[1119]Sima, *Cazul Iorga-Madgearu*, pp. 59-64.

[1120]This originates from the diary of Mme. Liliana Pippidi-Iorga (entry on 25 July 1943, more than two and a half years later) because only then she received this information from Colonel N. Dragomir personally.

[1121]*Cazul Iorga-Madgearu*, pp. 73-75.

[1122]Admiral Măcelaru, over 80 years old in 1985, was asked a few years ago by Romanian authorities to put his reminiscences into writing. This is an extract from his memoirs (unpublished until now, but on the record). This information was obtained for this writer by Andrei Pippidi-Iorga, the grandson of Nicolae Iorga.

Barbu remembered, after these murders, Antonescu considered his Vice Prime Minister Sima, as a "Chief of Bandits."[1123]

However, not a word was said in the press about Iorga's murder — let alone about the murder of the others — but then, in Romania, there are no "mysteries" — even if (sometimes) everything is a secret. After these events, terror struck the hearts of the people (the bourgeoisie). In spite of an official news blackout, the young Legionary rabble (boys and girls) in green shirts descended in a noisy cortege to downtown Bucharest, and with their unfailing talent for the contemptible, celebrated the murder of Professor Iorga and the others. There was also a macabre "vengeance feast" in the notorious "Green House."[1124]

In the early morning of 28 November, Iorga was lying dead on the roadside outside Strejnic. Several bullets had blown out his formidable brain. His body was discovered around 7 a.m. on that frosty morning in the heavy fog by Romanian gendarmes. Soon after, a German soldier came by with his truck. (Strejnic had become an air base for Nazi fighter planes, ready for the defense of the Ploiești oil fields.) This German soldier (or airman) had a camera, and managed to take the only picture of Iorga's bullet-ridden body. One of the Romanian gendarmes brought the news about their discovery to the authorities. Iorga's body was identified, and brought by truck to Bucharest to the cemetery of Bellu. It was deposited in the chapel of the cemetery. Mme. Catinca was notified, came, and also identified Iorga's body.

Iorga's funeral would take place the next day, on 29 November. Maniu was busy with the funeral of Madgearu, nevertheless (as we saw) he intervened with Antonescu, assuring a "Christian funeral for Iorga." There were other interventions before Antonescu for the same purpose. High-ranking officers (among them Colonel Nicolae Dragomir) and others intervened. Although a crime made an autopsy mandatory, the autopsy was foregone.

[1123]Barbul, *op. cit.*, p. 37.

[1124]Stroian, *op. cit.*, p. 5; and *Pe marginea prăpastiei*, vol. 2, p. 143.

Even if we take into account the prevailing terror, the loneliness during the funeral was remarkable. Very few people dared to come as Iorga's coffin descended into the grave, accompanied by the wafting of the ice cold "Crivăț," the wind which sweeps into Wallachia from the Russian plains. There was no speech. The Iorga family is bitter about the cowardice and opportunism of high Bucharest society at its peak, especially after the Jilava murders. The end of the road for Iorga was a sad one. Although one exception should be made: a severely tried France did not forget a friend. The presence of the French Chargé during the funeral was conspicuous. Some high-ranking Romanian officers also came, to protest with their presence against Legionary anarchy.

Besides all this, the careful arrangements for Codreanu's and the other Legionaries' reburial had been made. A solemn procession marched from the little church Ilie-Gorgani to the Green House, where the martyrs of the Legion were laid to rest. Envoys from Axis countries (with the notable exception of Hungary) participated. The perpetrators of the Jilava murders and those of Iorga and Madgearu marched along. (Boeru remembered to this writer the re-burial of the Căpitanul vividly.) There was no attempt to apprehend them. After the collapse of the Legion, they were smuggled out of Romania in German military trains (concealed by the Nazis) and taken to Germany.

When the news of Iorga's murder arrived to the Bucharest University, the dean, Alexandru Marcu, acting on the proposition of an admirer of Iorga, the Byzantinist Nicolae Bănescu, ordered that the black flag be raised over the university. When Panaitescu (the new Legionary President of the Bucharest University) saw it, he gave another proof, that when it came to cheap shots, he was still a "pro": He gave orders that the black flag be removed.

Within the Romanian Academy, the result of Legionary terror was a cowardly silence, with one exception, the President, Constantin Rădulescu-Motru, who rose and had this to say: "Nicolae Iorga is no longer with us. That is all we can say in this tragic hour for our country. It will be left for the future, with a calmer state of mind, to judge the circumstances of his death. But we, who were close enough to him, are almost incapable to collect our thoughts to say our last farewell because of the sadness weighing on us. Nicolae Iorga was the very incarnation of our nation's intellectual effort, and nobody has surpassed him until now..." Rădulescu-Motru described Iorga's manifold work and concluded: "He became a legendary figure even while he was alive, and as time goes by, his stature will only increase."[1125]

The reaction to Iorga's assassination in the rest of the world (especially in Western countries) was great. The greatest reaction was voiced — not surprisingly — in France. Despite the German occupation, Mario Roques at the Institut de France held a moving farewell speech; also Henri Focillon spoke, and Henri Grégoire in Belgium, Oskar Halecki the Pole, Vittorio Lazzarini in Italy, and many others. The international press (in non-Nazi controlled areas) took note of the murder with deep indignation. In the United States the *New York Times*, and the *New York Herald Tribune*, in Switzerland the *Basler Nationalzeitung*, in South America *La Prensa* in Buenos Aires, and newspapers in Chile and Brazil wrote eulogies describing Iorga's life, activities and accomplishments, emphasizing his pro-Allied, pro-French, and anti-Nazi stand as the reason for his murder, and rejected Legionary anarchy and bestiality. Over many universities of the Western world, black flags were hoisted.

In Hungary, the daily of the "Hungarian National Socialist Party," *Magyarország*, wrote a disparaging editorial. The editorial of the government daily, *Magyarország*, was written by Pál Szvatkó, who, with his utter unprincipledness could pride himself as being the opposite number of Mr. Prundeni and Ilie Rădulescu in Budapest. Mr. Szvatkó wrote: "In the last moment of his life, Iorga should have cried out: 'In my polemics with Hungary, I came out as second best,' and this should be engraved as an epitaph on his grave — as a punishment for those who would spread falsehoods across the map of Europe in the future."[1126] On a different level, in the intellectual journal *Magyar Szemele*, the scholar Lajos Gáldi wrote: "Iorga was an implacable enemy of Hungary, Iorga

---

[1125]Theodorescu, *op. cit.*, pp. 369-374.

[1126]*Magyarország*, 30 November 1940.

has died." The author recalled that Iorga made many pro-Hungarian gestures: the necrology written in the memory of Professor Bitay; Iorga's pamphlet "Against Hatred between Nations" (meaning between the Hungarian and Romanian nations). But reconciliation was envisioned "only on the basis of the Versailles Peace Treaty." The article concluded: "Maybe in the Bucharest anarchy a bullet will also be found sooner or later for Iorga's murderers."[1127]

The *Popolo di Roma* (a major Italian Fascist daily) was more interested in justifying "direct action," than expressing gratitude to a life-long friend of Italy. Commented the paper: "Although assassination may be illegal — it can be justified on the basis of justice and the past."[1128]

These Legionary murders were a watershed in the history of the National Legionary State. Along with the daily radicalization of the social revolution purported by the Legion, they gave direction to the Legion's enemies. Legionaries planned new, even greater outrages, particularly for the coming New Year, which the National Legionary State was to enter "purified from the putrid past." Under the impact of this, the old establishment drew together. Consisting of the bourgeoisie, the high bureaucracy, old politicians, high-ranking military officers, and the high-ranking clergy. Their leader became Ion Antonescu.

The Germans (on whom the Legionaries counted so naively) placed their hope on the old order. Germans were mainly interested in stability. By January, it became clear that such stability would not be achieved through Legionary anarchy and archangelic social experiments. Hitler met Antonescu in mid-January 1941 and told him this. After Antonescu returned from Hitler, between 21 and 23 January he moved against the Legion. His tanks crushed them in Bucharest. A few days later, Antonescu established a military dictatorship, and the National Legionary State was officially abolished.

[1127] *Magyar Szemle*, vol. XL, no. 1, Budapest, January 1941. For this Hungarian school of thinking, anybody who does not believe in the intangibility of the "Lands of Saint Stephen" is an "implacable enemy of Hungary."

[1128] *Popolo di Roma*, 30 November 1940.

The Iorga family felt easier, and yet — they continued to suffer. The Legion was gone, but German feelings against the name "Iorga" were vindictive. The Nazis were very sensitive towards any attempt to rehabilitate Iorga. Consequently, the Iorga family continued to live in a virtual isolation, on the margins of Bucharest "high society."

Mme. Catinca (as Mme. Liliana remembers) bore her pain in a proud, strong manner. She tried to overcome the loss by being with her children, yet, she seemed to prefer solitude. In her solitude, she wrote letters to Iorga. But Mme. Catinca — as happens many times after forty years of inseparable togetherness and harmony — just couldn't stand being alone. In November 1941, she quietly passed away. There were more people at her funeral than at Iorga's. Princess Helen, in a hallmark gesture of royalty, sent a crown of flowers to her grave with her name on it.[1129]

The first public requiem ("*parastas*") held in Iorga's memory was in May 1941. Many dignitaries came. Later, Iorga's Institute of Universal History was reopened, with Gheorghe Brătianu honoring Iorga's memory. He was also honored at the Academy. Nicolae Bănescu, the renowned Byzantinologist, was the speaker. German reaction was instant. In a letter of protest, Nazis remembered that "Iorga was a determined enemy of Germany and Hitler." A copy of the protest was sent to General Antonescu. Because of this, Antonescu excused himself to Lepădatu, saying: "because of other business he cannot come to the commemorative session held in the memory of Iorga." Lepădatu commented: "What cowardice! Even from somebody like Antonescu!"[1130] Yet the ice was melting.

[1129]Princess Helen deserves a note. The sister of King George II of Greece, she was staunchly anti-Nazi and pro-Allied. After her return, she stood by her young son, now King Michael. One of her great fears was during the summer of 1942, when (alerted by Dr. Wilhelm Filderman and others) she became instrumental in saving — together with King Michael and Marshal Antonescu — the Romanian Jews from being deported to Auschwitz. Later, when Romania's "renversement des alliances" approached, since it was prepared in the Royal Palace, she was the soul and the supervisor, standing by her brave, but young son. After 23 August 1944, she showed an unprecedented fearlessness, driving around besieged Bucharest with a gun in her purse, etc.

[1130]Lepădatu, *op. cit.*, p. 416

Şeicaru's *Curentul* wrote sympathetic articles about Iorga. Gheorghe Brătianu, the literary critic and writer Tudor Vianu, and others eulogized him. One may well ask the rhetorical question: where were all these gentlemen when Iorga needed them?

In Lieu of a Conclusion:
Iorga Considered at the End of the
Twentieth Century

"L'étre de l'homme est un être historique — (...) il n'y a d'existence humaine que dans l'histoire."

— Emanuel Mounier

"He was our scholar par excellence, who (...) found his happiness only in books, and had one ambition: to foster, to elevate the fame and glory of his nation."

— D. S. Panaitescu ("Perpessicius")

This chapter should serve "in lieu" of a conclusion because the ultimate conclusions must be drawn by the reader. The aim of this study was to offer a more complete presentation of Nicolae Iorga than has previously been available in the English language.

The late Vlad Georgescu was kind enough to say (after he read some chapters of this study) that it would be the first "real" work about Iorga's life, angrily dismissing the Iorga biographies in Communist Romania as propaganda. This writer would not want to go so far. To cover all of Iorga's life, work, and activities in one study is impossible. He would like to repeat a warning voiced earlier: since there is something of an elemental force permeating Iorga's life and activities — even during their conflict Mircea Eliade called Iorga a "force of nature" — this writer could only try to present a *tableau d'ensemble*, throwing light on important actions and events. Above all: presenting his life as a whole.

One must always consider Iorga within the context of his times — he was inseparable from them. We have one advantage: a perspective of "accelerated history" (as Toynbee would call it), something Iorga could not have.

I undertook this study before 1989, seemingly another age in East Central Europe, in the Balkans, and the former U.S.S.R. Few of us could foresee the sweeping changes, namely, how the region would exchange ideas of universal liberation of the "working class" with *total national sovereignty*. It is because of this that Iorga's life and his ideas became more relevant to an understanding of the region, than they had been before 1989.

Iorga's feelings for his country dominated his life and his activities. He became a historian and a politician because of his nationalism, and nationalism determined the traditional character of his politics. His journalism was a nationalist one. As a literary critic, *Sămănătorismul* became his central philosophy, based on his cultural nationalism, as were his writings and plays. Iorga the human being, the university professor, the orator, was inseparable from his nationalism, which inspired his superhuman efforts, accomplishments, errors, and led him to his doom.

This writer quoted often Dr. Samuel Johnson, Bismarck, and Charles De Gaulle. They were not chosen accidentally. They are yardsticks, and sometimes serve as opposite poles. The first one being the incarnation of rational thinking of the eighteenth century, then the architect of "Realpolitik," Bismarck, finally, De Gaulle, the romantic nationalist, but a rare species: a realistic, nationalist dreamer. Sancho Panza rarely came so often to the aid of Don Quixote as De Gaulle was helped by his realism.

Romania is a Balkan country, and the Balkans are in the headlines again. More tragic events have come to pass. They may easily spread to the South, to the East or the North. Although the worst occurred in the former Yugoslavia, Romania has a similar political culture and problems; who is to say what the future holds for Transylvania or for Bessarabia?

According to the *International Herald Tribune*, recent events in the Balkans "turned the dream of a United Europe into a nightmare."[1131] Not so. These events only show how deficient the process leading towards unity of Europe still is; how sluggish and weak Europeans still are; how comfortable they were for all too long, allowing the situation to get out of hand in the Balkans, while they could have shaped and influenced events.

The Balkans are part of Europe, and Europeans had some experience with Balkan nationalisms during the last 150 years. But the European community in its postwar prosperity ignored the contradictions of modern European social and political thought: the international law concerning the inviolability of frontiers on one hand, and the right to self-determination on the other. (Where the populations are homogenous — like in the former Czechoslovakia — self-determination is easier. In the Balkans and elsewhere, this is not so.)

The West is panicking instead of taking resolute action. Surely, East Central Europe is moving towards danger, as is the former U.S.S.R. But even this danger is preferable to the "deep-freeze" which prevailed across half of Europe during the Cold War, the hegemony of a totalitarian dictatorship, which negated and exterminated freedom, and murdered millions of human beings! We witness a revolution of freedom in this region, and a revolution is never a quiet process.

Only a strong, democratic, and prosperous United Europe can offer an alternative to what was called for a long time and pejoratively: "Balkanization." Only such a Europe can show the way towards unity and peace instead of anarchy, excessive nationalism (incompatible with humanity), and war. If Europe continues the present trends (with even ethnic groups manifesting pretensions of sovereignty), either most European states will fall apart, or the situation will become an invitation for some powerful force to stamp out brutally any national particularism and its autonomy. Such a contagion in either case will destroy for a long time the chance to see a United Europe emerging on the basis of prosperity and democracy.

[1131] *International Herald Tribune*, May 18, 1992.

The times of Iorga were even more turbulent. The cause then was also an endangered, frustrated, national self-determination. One sees and often condemns the reprehensible manifestations of nationalism, yet, one must recognize nationalism as an incontrovertible, vital political ingredient and reality, a more endurable one than ideologies. Nationalism will not go away soon — especially in the Balkans. Understanding it may help to deal with it, and might prevent some of its unsavory manifestations. If we do not reject national or religious characteristics from our world-outlook (Iorga would call it "cultural nationalism"), we can spare ourselves the spectacle, when the "rejected one returns" — with all the savagery and brutality such a "return" brings along.

De Gaulle, the visionary (called sometimes "the last survivor of the nineteenth century"), warned: "The nation is the most important reality." If so, one should search for a national self-assertion compatible with humanity.

Was Iorga's cultural nationalism compatible with humanity? Without understanding Romanian nationalism, its frustrations and insecurities, one cannot make sense out of Iorga's life. It is not easy to understand such a nationalism from an American (or a Western) vantage point. Oliver Wendell Holmes once said: "My country — right, or wrong." Justice Holmes did not have "ethnic cleansing" in mind. Neither was U.S. nationalism — protected by two oceans, sovereign on a continent, endowed with untold riches and democratic institutions — ever endangered as Romanian nationalism (or Balkan nationalisms) were. If it felt danger, it reacted against Native Americans as consistently as it did against Japanese-Americans in 1942. (Let us not forget English policies in Ireland, or other Western manifestations of nationalism.) If nationalism is such an important reality (Iorga would call it an "organic manifestation"), then it is not wise to push it into a corner with its back against the wall. If this happens, one can expect ugly reactions, and not only in the Balkans. The "organic entity" — the Nation — will defend itself.

Iorga rejected chauvinism. He always distinguished between a "defensive nationalism" and a "suicidal" one, identifying Naziism, Fascism, racism, and the Legion as such, and rejecting them. He considered these "New Nationalisms" abusive and inhumane. Iorga considered his cultural nationalism compatible with humanity, a nationalism which engaged only in legitimate self-defense. (So much for theory.) He considered Romanians as a kind of "endangered species," the defense of them (like those of family members) became a "Supreme Law" before which *everything* fell on the ground. But this Eminescian "Supreme Law" was always defensive! It was the theory serving self-determination. The difficulty arises when one tries to apply such self-determination in such a mixed region. How to go about it? Here, nationalism is not considered an extreme. Because of a torturous history, it became a condition of survival.

Ideologues and bureaucrats hate nationalism, and even many Westerners of good faith, when they watch the consequences of national conflicts on their television sets, are more likely to ask "How?" rather than "Why?"

If we look for examples of frustrated, insecure, national self-consciousness, we shall find examples in Poland, Croatia, and Serbia; and there we shall see responses strikingly similar to those of Iorga and Enescu.

Poland's heartbreaking fate of partition by her powerful neighbors found an answer, a solution, proposed by Roman Dmowski. Incidental his party was called also the "Nationalist Democratic Party" ("Endecija"). Dmowski's school of thought strongly influences politics in post-communist Poland today.

The "Endecija" rejected both the ethical framework of romantic nationalists (Miczkiewicz, Slowacki), and the empirical school of positivism. Dmowski believed in a nationalism devoid of any moral content vision of Poland, which transcended the material world. He did not believe in wrong or right in relations with other nations — only strength and weakness. No wonder the Catholic Church was worried. (Dmowski, contrary to Iorga the agnostic, professed to be a devout Catholic.) The "Solidarity" thinker, A. Michnik — while condemning Dmowski as a chauvinist-obscurantist-xenophobe — nevertheless, recognizes his "extreme realism." For the brilliant Polish historian and intellectual, A. Walicki, Dmowski was "the main theorist of political realism Poland," also of "a nationalism of the national interest."

All this resembles Eminescu's "Supreme Law." The difference rather in degree of consistency, than in kind. Dmowski was more realistic and less romantic a politician than Iorga. For Iorga, to spell out or to apply a nationalism as brutal was inconceivable. He rested with the dreams of *Sămănătorismul*.

The similarities between Iorga and the thought of another historian-politician, E Tudjman, the president of Croatia, are striking: Tudjman a believes in the organic growth of the nation; he calls the nation (which emerges from this organic process) a "collective individual" (much like the "Gigantic Being" of Iorga), and against this "collective individual," physical individuals have no standing. Tudjman maintains that only a free, sovereign nation (like a hilly developed and free human) can offer a contribution to the world. He sees "ethnic cleansing" (or the Holocaust) as an almost routine phenomenon: "Throughout history, there have always been attempts at "Final Solutions'' for foreign and undesirable racial-ethnic or religious groups, through expulsion, extermination, or conversion to the "true religion."[1132] Thus, President Tudjman put in perspective the actions of the Ustaši in 1941, the Holocaust, and "ethnic cleansing." The Serbians supply him with his own perspective. The chief advisors of Serbian Presidents Dobrica Èosic and Slobodan Milosevič are Serbian historians. Not that Tudjman condones genocide, but as a historian, he comes dangerously close to considering it as a means to create a national state in a multinational region.

How reprehensible these desperate nationalisms should be — one should not forget the hollow promises of the "Atlantic Charter" during the war — and the stark realities of Yalta and the Cold War.

And not only then. As *Time* magazine commented on the Balkan tragedy recently, "There are not a few *nostalgists* of the Cold War" who would not mind the days of Yalta to return. They dismiss the manifestations of self-determination in the Balkans as a "European scourge: Tribalism," a "Genie let out of the bottle," etc.[1133] Such "nostalgists" of Yalta are eerily reminiscent of Disraeli (not

---

[1132]Franjo Tudjman, *Nationalism in Contemporary Europe* (Boulder: East European Monographs, 1981), p. 13; and *Bespuca povijesne zbiljinosti* (Zagreb, 1990), p. 166.

[1133]*Time*, January 4, 1993, pp. 44-46.

worrying about "an ideal existence for Balkan Christians"), or Churchill's unqualified contempt for Gavrilo Princip.

Nor is this all. In an unparalleled glimpse of the making of foreign policy, the three years of negotiations (which ended the Cold War) between Bush and Gorbachev are convincingly discussed. If Bush made a definite contribution, nevertheless, he was always unreflective, a status quo conservative. Bush was extremely uncomfortable with the process of liberation in Central Europe and in the Balkans; his disposition and advice put him always one step behind the events. After a meeting (in September 1989) with E. Shevernadze, Bush, as a good "Cold War nostalgist" said to Brent Scowcroft: "Would it be great if the Soviet Empire broke up? But that is not really practical — is it?" Although not by design, Bush's instuitive opposition to democratic reform in the region helped Gorbachev believe that "by letting things be" there, the U.S.S.R. was not surrendering to America in the Cold War. Thus, both Bush and Gorbachev failed gracefully — to nationalism.[1134]

Let us keep these facts in mind, and put a moratorium on our self-congratulations about the demise of Yalta. Our indignations about the spectacles in the Balkans are also synthetic. The U.S. and the West should and could have handled the situation there differently. It could have prevented the tragedy, even after 1990. But if — (and historical "ifs" are always tantalizing) — "if" the region had experienced half a century of freedom, democracy and prosperity, like the Western half of Europe did, instead of the life the Yalta Settlement forced on the area, there is a chance that the problems of the present would have been resolved. Resolved, like the seemingly insoluble problem of Alsace-Lorraine was. But thanks to Yalta, this region had neither freedom nor democracy or prosperity.

Iorga, the historian, became a politician, "in order to prevent the evil done" to Romania.[1135] Should a historian descend from the ivory tower of academe into the crude arena of politics? His life gives no answer. Apart from the compulsion

---

[1134]Michael R. Beschloss, *Strobe Talbot: At the Highest Levels* (Little Brown, 1993), passim.

[1135]*O viață de om*, vol. III, p. 65.

mentioned above, he was singularly ill-equipped for politics. There was Iorga's personality — his apolitical principledness maintained with an inflexible stubbornness; his naivete coupled with a volcanic, uncontrollable temper and his ego — and a Romanian historian's strange lack of the renowned political instinct of his nation: inflexibility is not helpful for survival. All his greatness as a historian and intellectual, his love for Romania, even his great integrity were canceled in politics by his unpolitical personality.

Was Iorga a democrat?

His party was the Nationalist Democratic Party. One may suggest that, for Iorga, where democracy ended, nationalism took over. Iorga respected democracy and admired the political system prevalent in Romania's Western friends and allies. He knew why President Wilson endorsed Romanian self-determination. Although Iorga wished for the unity of all Romanians as equals and during the first decade of the interwar period his devotion to democracy was sincere, he did not consider Western democracy in Romania as the fruit of an organic process. The anomalies of Romanian politics only strengthened his doubts later. His frustrations are a reminder that of all the burdens the decent democrat (or even a decent human being) carries in a poor, Third World country — which Romania was then — excessive expectations can become the heaviest burden of all.

As an intellectual, Iorga was deadly set against any dictatorship. (He managed to antagonize more than once that very Royal Dictatorship, of which he was a pillar.) But Iorga's personality was authoritarian; it was incompatible with a democratic process: he was perfectly incapable of taking criticism, his party, his newspapers, his schools, and his activities were "one man shows."

One should keep in mind that democracy for many in East Central Europe means (at best!) the rule of the majority. There is little room for a "Bill of Rights," without which democracy can turn into a mob, which since Socrates has been eager to destroy those who have more brains or courage than the mob does.

He believed in the permanence and the indestructibility of this "Gigantic Being": the nation. Epictetus warned: "Do not attempt to change the nature of things!" Iorga's analysis of our world was a simple one: he saw the future path of a nation not as a repetition, but a *natural continuation* of its past course. For Iorga, the hidden cultural forces calling from the past were all-pervasive. The latest events did great justice to him.

He was not unfamiliar with the dictum of Saint-Just: "Nobody can rule guiltlessly." He also understood that the world rests on the axis of the sword, and relations between groups of men have always been power relations. However, if his cultural nationalism would only be implemented, the recognition of cultural nationalism worldwide would bring peace and understanding to the world! He was no revolutionary, for Iorga the nation mastered more than society did and maintaining order was as natural as it was essential. He hated anarchy and upheaval (admonishing Kerensky, "who hoped to change the world with one or two speeches"). Iorga rejected a deliberate social change and forced reform. The solution was gradual, organic transformation, in the framework of cultural nationalism. The perceptiveness of nationalists (like Iorga or De Gaulle) irritates both the Left and the Right. Nationalists recognize certain realities, which in an age of illusions (on both the Left and the Right), escape so many. It would seem that the rockiest road from nationalism back to nationalism leads through a Marxist "proletarian-internationalism."

Iorga's traditional politics favored national unity, unchallenged by self-seeking political parties degenerating Romanian politics into a divisive "Suprafanarul." He considered a class struggle sterile and divisive, choosing the King as symbol of national unity — even if the King was Carol II.

Much was made (even by him!) of Iorga's ignorance of economic matters, especially concerning modern economics. He did not look at the economy as the most important yardstick by which a policy or a nation ought to be measured. He ignored some economic illusions which were the foundations of Marxism yesterday, and of Liberalism in our days. For him, the nation represented truth, the most important truth. The preservation of national identity and the nation's welfare was the "Supreme Law." Historical truth made sense to Iorga, when it served Romania.

But Iorga thought a worldwide adaptation of *Sămănătorism* would resolve these contradictions. Cultural nationalism was to bring harmony to Romania and the world; thus, it was not only a nationalism which was compatible with humanity, but was the most humane idea. Although such ideas belonged to the nineteenth century, we can detect (selectively!) much in them which give us a lot of food for thought, in view of the ideologies which failed. Problems arise when we try to translate *Sămănătorismul* into practice. During the twentieth century, Iorga's ideas were utopian ones, Iorga's *Sămănătorism* could not be objective about Romania, or seriously critical about Romanian shortcomings. His periodical outbursts proved that he knew about shortcomings. However Iorga rarely pretended to be 100% impartial about Romania. His positions reflected more often Eminescu's "Supreme Law" than impartiality. This loyalty and personal matters (his ego, his likes and dislikes, and temper) could considerably sway him. He made great efforts to promote understanding of Romania in the world and he favored an international cooperation, on lines we have discussed.

He was often accused of being inconsistent or paradoxical.[1136] Paradoxes — yes. Yet there were neither inconsistencies nor contradictions in Iorga's activities — if one keeps his *Sămănătorist* faith to the fore. He was awesomely consistent in his cultural nationalism; all his seeming inconsistencies and contradictions were tactics, serving his *Sămănătorist* strategy. A much better politician than Iorga, Bismarck, retorted when he stopped the *Kulturkampf* in order not to divide the newly-established Reich, and was accused of "inconsistency," and "contradicting himself." "I will do it again!" What the architect of *Realpolitik* meant was that he preferred war against France or Austria to a civil war.

What if Iorga had had a different personality, if he had been a good politician, and not missed his great political opportunity after the war — galvanizing the expectations of the "Trench Generation" — could he have made a great impact on Romanian history?

[1136]cf. Paul Michelson, "Nicolae Iorga between Paradox and Understanding," *Romanian Civilization*, vol. I (1992), pp. 50-60.

In hindsight, at the end of the twentieth century, it would seem that the only major difference would have been how Iorga the politician entered into Romanian history. He would have left a better, more significant mark — but he could have made in Romania's internal, let alone external, predicament (geography, economy, and the international context) only little difference. Who had a constructive answer?

Did Stalin, who turned "proletarian internationalism" into a one-way street while proposing the dismemberment of Romania? Or a Western democracy and the honesty and dedication of Maniu? Did "archangelic socialism" and the "New Nationalism" of the Legion (which grew out of the insoluble frustrations) offer any answer? Did "Liberalism" and forced industrialization (from which — to paraphrase Bunuel — only a "bourgeoisie sans charme ni discretion" profited), for which 80% of the people (the peasantry) suffered hold any answer? Later this Liberalism evolved into the facistic "Neo-Liberalism" of the Royal Dictatorship.

Despite his great efforts, Iorga's most important political contribution to his country was his early recognition of Naziism and the Soviet danger. By repeating inflexibly his warnings, he succeeded in making many Romanians aware of the menace. Beyond that, neither Iorga nor any other Romanian politician could have overcome the implications of Romania's position.

After 1918, roughly one-third of the population in the new state of Greater Romania consisted of non-Romanians. Iorga welcomed them initially, considered them as full-fledged citizens of Romania and believed that their living and working together with the Romanian majority would result in a pragmatic, mutually beneficial accommodation, a "modus vivendi." In his eyes, the minorities were divided into those with "organic" rights — with rights to far-reaching cultural autonomy — and those with no organic rights. From them, Iorga demanded assimilation. In practice, this meant the old policy: Iorga granted rights to non-Romanians in pro-portion to their loyalty to Greater Romania.

Greater Romania had two major, troublesome minorities: Hungarians and Jews. Iorga was no enemy of the Hungarians as most Hungarians (especially those of Transylvania) believed, but of historical Hungary only, where Hungarians dominated an equal number of non-Hungarians, and ruled Transylvania, with its Romanian majority. He wished to farther Hungarian-Romanian cooperation — provided the Hungarians accepted the Versailles Settlement. Such cooperation was vital for Iorga. Both peoples lived in a Slavic and Germanic sea, and there was later Stalin and Hitler.

Iorga was first and last a Romanian. While conceding historical and organic rights to Hungarians, he condoned (along Romania's new, western borders) the incorporation of large Hungarian populations, which could have been easily left in Hungary. He ignored his own principle: "Each nation to itself, on the territory where it lives." Unfortunately, the majority of Hungarians in Transylvania lived far from the border, embedded amidst Romanians, Iorga knew how irreconcilably the Hungarians refused to accept Romanian rule, but hoped for the emergence of an impressive Romanian economy which would change their minds. Even in the 1920s, in a disquieting fashion, he toyed with denationalizing the Szecklers.

But an impressive economy did not emerge. The Hungarian minority (encouraged from Hungary) rejected the status quo. As time went by, Iorga hardened his stand. He did not protest against attempts of Romanization through education, and demanded the litmus test: loyalty and the command of Romanian language. Minorities were receiving rights only in proportion to their loyalty. Hungarians and Romanians were back to the old maxim: "Either we, or they!" He rejected any revision of the peace treaty on principle.

The Jewish question — especially in Iorga's native Moldavia (and in the towns) — was not a simple question for a nationalist. Such a problem was not isolated to Romania; similar challenges can be seen elsewhere when a numerous, unassimilated (and under circumstances unassimilable) middle-class lives amidst a traditional society.

Racism was a hateful aberration for Iorga, and "not part of his nature." This writer originates from East Central Europe. After reading thousands of pages of Iorga's diaries, correspondence, articles, and historical works, he never found that almost instinctive, insurmountable anti-Semitism and hatred which he knows so well from Eastern Europe, which becomes almost a "sixth sense" there and is manifested indiscriminately, when East European anti-Semites come even into casual contact with Jews!

According to Iorga, Jews had no "organic rights" in Romania, so he demanded assimilation. Assimilation is an anathema for a real anti-Semite or racist. Iorga never attacked Jews as such. Even during his anti-Semitic period we see practically no reference to the "international Jewish conspiracy," etc.! He attacked Jews only when (according to Iorga) they represented danger for his cultural nationalism. With foreign Jews (and Jewish scholars), he maintained the friendliest relations. If a Jew showed interest in Romanian history, culture, or the Romanian people, Iorga embraced him. These tendencies are in a stark contrast to the racist anti-Semitism of Germany, Austria, and Hungary against their assimilated, patriotic Jewish communities. Patriotic and assimilated communities were what Iorga wished for. Iorga would have welcomed Jews to join a *Sămănătorist* Romania. He attacked every Romanian (like Caragiale, or Maniu and others) who did not love Romania with "deep enough" (*Sămănătorist*) love. For this reason, Brătianu and the Liberals hated him with passion.

After 1918, he became the champion of the Jews (more precisely, the champion of Jewish assimilation). When he thought about Jewish assimilation, he had France in mind. Unfortunately, circumstances in Romania bore little resemblance to the conditions in France. Iorga knew that. *Sămănătorism* was inconceivable for the "Pale of Settlement" Jewish mentality, and there was also a very large number of Jews. Finally, the late 1930s, with their brutal persecutions, dissipated Iorga's hopes for a Jewish assimilation. Jews in their despair looked often beyond the borders for salvation: to Zionism (even to Communism) and to foreign (Western) interventions on their behalf. He opposed Zionism as an obstacle to assimilation, failing to see that Zionism was but the consequence of the failure of Jewish attempts to assimilate.

Branded by many as an "hireling of the Jews," Iorga lost patience. However, he did not propose persecution. Nevertheless, by 1937, with its "marching in moods" Iorga's attitudes in his editorials became questionable. He was not in an easy position. The "champion of the Jews," the "hireling of the Jews," was almost daily slanderously reminded of his connections with Aristide Blank and there were also the day-by-day considerations of "serving Romania" on the rapidly changing scene. He strongly (and unsuccessfully) opposed violence — a Holocaust-like solution was beyond his imagination.

Iorga was friendly towards the half-a-million ethnic Germans, until Hitler tried to convert them into a Nazi fifth column. Before that, he made more than one friendly gesture towards them. After Hitler arrived to power, Iorga took a violent stand against Nazi inroads into Romania, using the German minority for the purpose. The other (less numerous) ethnic groups (Armenians, Greeks, Turks, Slavs, etc.) were considered by him as "friendly minorities." They were accepted by Iorga not according to their contributions but according to their loyalty to Romania. Interestingly, Iorga had little good or bad to say about the numerous (and quite controversial!) Gypsies in Romania.

Iorga was first and foremost a historian. The politician became a poor second. His cultural nationalism dominated also his historical writings. He followed no philosophical approach or historical law; did not belong to any "historical school," all of which were considered by him to be too restrictive and rigid. He was a romantic nationalist, an impressionist, and had good instincts and great talent to recreate the event, but always on the basis of documents and facts.

He was mainly a medievalist and Byzantinologist of world fame — and, one may say, since he was a nationalist historian, fortunately so. When Iorga wrote about more modern times (let alone on contemporary events), the nationalist politician all too often took over from the historian.

In his historical writings, the facts upon which he based arguments were correct. The interpretations he gave (especially after he entered his "struggles") were another matter. The accuracy or the objectivity of works he wrote earlier are better. Nevertheless, the 50,000 documents he dug out from oblivion are there for everybody, and they may — thanks to Iorga — help themselves to these materials, and interpret them. It is in these tireless researches that Iorga made his greatest contributions.

His detractors made much from the numerous factual errors which can be found in Iorga's 1,200 books or 20,000 articles. These numbers and the zeal of the nationalist historian-politician explain the haste which caused these minor errors, having little to do with the horizons he opened.

Fortunately, Iorga's volcanic temper affected less his historical works than it did the politician, or the political journalist, or the literary critic. In his own view, Iorga's greatest contribution to history-writing was his "historiology," which he considered to be original. Mankind's experience forms (*mutatis mutandis*) one indivisible experience — consequently, in order to understand and interpret any national history (or to fill the gaps where documents are lacking!) one should look for common characteristics and experiences in the history of other nations. After rigorously scrutinizing them, the historian should comment on their role and relevance to the problem under consideration. Thus, one can explain and fill the gap which exists because of the lack of documentation. Undoubtedly, this method was helpful for Iorga to explain 1,000 years of Romanian history where solid documentation was lacking.

Iorga had a feeling, an instinct for history and had intuitions to recreate historical situations. This characteristic is difficult to define. Many a historian would dismiss it as an unprofessional, unscientific approach, and did so in Iorga's lifetime. There is little room for compromise between this school of thought, and that of Iorga, in the interpretation and the writing of history. It was Tolstoy who said in one of his hyperboles: "History would be an excellent thing — if only it were true!" Paul Géraldy warned: "La mémoire est un poète, n'en fais pas un historien!" Iorga's way of writing history is somehow vindicated by Tolstoy and Géraldy. He wanted history to be more than a list of names, dates, geographical places, and an agglomeration of facts. As he always repeated: "You are either with Iorga — or with Maiorescu!" It was in this sense the gauntlet was cast before Iorga by the scholars of the "New School of History" (and many other historians). These challenges were closer to Dr. Johnson's thinking, for whom Iorga's world would have been inconceivable.

Literature and literary criticism was all-important in Iorga's eyes, inseparable from his cultural nationalism. Consequently, it became politicized. *Sămănătorismul* was inseparable from the literary movement of the same name. He subordinated his aesthetic concepts to *Sămănătorismul's* political concepts.

(Fortunately, this is less true about Iorga the historian.) As a result, he committed his greatest errors in his literary criticism. Anything that smacked of modern trends was rejected violently. Protagonists of modern literary trends were persecuted by him as public enemies of Romania, not only his cultural nationalism. Iorga's literary criticism or literary histories dealing with subjects after the Junimea are worthless. We see here a remarkable consequence: that very Iorga for whom literature was so important contributed the least to Romanian literature.

Iorga followed consistently in literature his cultural nationalism, and the result was what Şeicaru so befittingly called a "nationalist realism." Iorga tried (unsuccessfully) to impose this "nationalist realism" — as the Soviets imposed their "socialist realism" — with the same self-righteousness as the Soviets did. Both Iorga and Stalin, in wishing to create a new man and society (one based on the *Sămănătorist Man*, the other on Marxism) failed. Neither Iorga nor Stalin worried about what this did to art and literature. On the contrary! This was the only acceptable function of literature and art! Iorga was self-righteous enough not to recognize the similarities of his attitude with those of Stalin. As time passed, he became even more closed-minded in his "nationalist realism." *Sămănătorism* was an attempt to recapitulate an ever more rapidly vanishing past — that is, to turn back the clock. The results were the usual ones.

Iorga's journalism focused on struggling for his cultural nationalism. His journalism was better than the East European journalism of the day — yet unmistakably marked by it, and he had a style unmistakably his own.

As a university professor, lecturer, and orator, Iorga's evocative talent and encyclopedic knowledge, plus his temperament assured spellbinding oratory and lectures. He was captivating to listen to, conquering the sensibilities of his audience.

One can say about Iorga the human being only the best: good-hearted and charitable, Puritan in his tastes, something more than incorruptible, with little sense of the value of money — he stood in stark contrast to his contemporaries in Romania. One should add that he was also a faithful son, husband, and a loving father. He was an exemplary patriot-citizen, putting the welfare of his country always before his own.

Despite his love for Romania, a totally disinterested almost mystical love ready for any sacrifice, *Sămănătorism* bore no tangible results, regardless of Iorga's great efforts. It did not offer a practical solution for Romania during the twentieth century. Yet, many of his ideas on cultural nationalism — considered in a selective manner and *"mutatis mutandis"* — remain quite pertinent, especially for the region. They may become even more relevant in coming decades. Therefore, historians like Dan Zamfirescu are not doing justice to Iorga when they say that "Iorga's patriotism misled some people."

Nor is it helpful to look for parallels across the Dniester: at the end of the nineteenth century the Russian government embarked on an ambitious program of modernization. This led to upheavals in rural areas. The nobility, fearing the loss of its privileges and economic power, made a bitter attempt to halt the process of modernization. It singled out the Jews as scapegoats, trying to make them out as the perpetrators of change and decay. Thus, "it were the Jews who destroyed their 'reactionary utopia' of peace and harmony in the countryside..."

This was not what *Sămănătorism* and Iorga's cultural nationalism were about. Far from trying to save class privileges by creating scapegoats, it proposed to help the peasants, create national unity, inviting Jews to join its ranks. It wished to lift up the whole nation. Iorga considered *Sămănătorism* a way of life. After the triumph of his cultural nationalism (cultural revolution), the new *Sămănătorist Man* created by it would be able to solve almost any Romanian problem.

Was *Sămănătorism* trying to turn back the clock? Modernization came to Romania not by choice (in an organic manner), as in the West, but in the form of a disruptive shock treatment, through an irritating contact with modernized states. After that Romania was confronted (like other traditional societies) with the usual unattractive choice: to refuse change and be destroyed, or to change, transform (destroy) her own way of life. No wonder some patriots and intellectuals wanted to be selective and cautious!

Iorga was not wrong about the force of nationalism, but he was not a real politician. He pursued his dream inflexibly, his inflexibility resembling De Gaulle's "envers, et contre tout." It was a forlorn effort. Vălenii, his cultural bulwark, a place Iorga considered closest to a *Sămănătorist Village*, mustered few *Sămănătorist Men*. It turned into a Legionary stronghold instead. But Iorga was unmoved.

During Iorga's lifetime, it was almost impossible for a Romanian politician to find a constructive answer, and such a situation prevailed long after he passed from the scene. Such an answer will come — hopefully — during the next century, in the framework of a United Europe. After the horrors of two World Wars, the nations of Europe have understood that only by interlocking their economies can war between them become unthinkable. This process is well advanced. Yet, the careless, unwise inaction of Europe in the unfolding Yugoslav crisis has proven that the problem goes beyond that of economic cooperation. The peoples of East-Central Europe cling to the belief — with a faith, deserving something better that they are an integral part of Europe; they try to convince Western Europe that, without them, the European community will remain a group which only defends local interests. But such a limited arrangement will neither be capable of giving identity to a new Europe, nor will it be able to assure its security.

If, on a continent so heavily burdened by history as Europe, unity should succeed, a delicate tightrope must be walked, when touching on the nation. Such a task is not for maniac ideologues or insensitive bureaucrats, but for extraordinary statesmen. A United Europe can never become a "melting-pot," trying to force the European nations to renounce their identities. It should be a "Europe of Fatherlands" instead. Such an inclusive diversity, its identity based on a new European nationalism, a voluntary cooperation, assuring freedom and prosperity for equals (similar to the system of Swiss cantons), is a nationalism not incompatible with humanity.

Self-determination is an internationally recognized right. However, just as individual freedoms are not supposed to impinge upon the freedoms of others, self-determination (the right to accede to an international status) cannot grant sovereignty to inviable entities, unable to assure security or services, or the maintenance of sovereignty for their citizens. Only an experience of centuries, a common heritage, a common reality lived together through the ages can become the justification of a valid aspiration of sovereignty.

Within a United Europe every authentic community must have an unalienable, unchallenged, right to live according to its own traditions and desires within autonomous and strongly decentralized structures. Within such a United Europe, a "suicidal nationalism" (as Iorga called the "New Nationalism" of the Extreme Right) is unthinkable; Eminescu's "Supreme Law" — even in the sense of a "defensive nationalism" as propounded by Iorga — becomes unnecessary. Iorga's hope for "a harmony among nations" can be realized. Thus, as French President François Mittérand proposed: a Europe of cultures, that is, a Europe of nations (will arise), as opposed to a Europe of nationalisms..." If such time comes, the message of his cultural nationalism will be updated, and Iorga will be recognized for more than just a world renown medievalist and Byzantinologist.

There is a long road ahead to a nationalism which is compatible with humanity, but patience, good faith and good economic policy can make it succeed within a United Europe. If European history left an ethnic picture in its wake, which in parts of the continent resembles a carnival-jacket, the answer should be Maastricht — not the tragedy of Sarajevo. For Romania, under such circumstances, an equitable solution can be found for Transylvania or Bessarabia, but it is a solution elsewhere in the Balkans too. In such a way, the contradiction between self-determination and the inviolability of borders can be surmounted. The alternative is a return to international anarchy or a brutal repression.

If such time comes, will Iorga then be considered a visionary, or "a man of the nineteenth century"? Probably both. If he had not been "a man of the nineteenth century," he could not have become visionary. Because, the more technology advances, the more some old concepts surface. Such a paradox was not envisioned either by Marx, or by Adam Smith or Diderot. For such a goal of the twenty-first century, one will have to work in a Europe (and World) where the nineteenth century is still very much present.

Iorga could not help his country during the twentieth century towards this goal. If so — why do Romanians revere his memory far beyond the respect due to an intellectual giant? Wrote a Bessarabian writer in 1989 — a few months before the rebirth of Eastern Moldavia: "Iorga is a glowing volcano. We warm up ourselves next to him — we (those) who are so far away...."[1137] During the many years I spent in Romania, I felt this devotion towards Iorga at every step. Why? After all, he didn't solve Romania's problems. Are people trying to return his selfless love for the Romanian people? Certainly so. But it is more: Romanians are aware that Iorga did not solve their problems. Yet, they also feel that his life personified them — he incarnated these insoluble problems.

[1137]Ștefan, Ștefănescu, "Nicolae Iorga," in *Studii și articole de istorie*, vol. 59 (1991), p. 108.

Epilogue:
Meeting Traian Boeru, 45 Years Later

Traian Boeru, Iorga's assassin, exercised a morbid fascination on me for more than 25 years — since I worked on the history of Romanian nationalism and the Legionary Movement.

Since I had numerous contacts in the Romanian colony of Munich (where Traian Boeru lived), I heard a lot of talk about him, overwhelmingly negative opinions. The murders of Nicolae Iorga and Virgil Madgearu were among the most notorious fears of the Legion, and Romanians of a wide range of political convictions condemned it. Even Legionaries condemned these murders.

After talking with dozens of Romanians in Munich, this is what emerged about the fate of Mr. Traian Boeru after the collapse of the National Legionary State. After January 1941, Boeru was smuggled out of Romania, like hundreds of other Legionaries, with Nazi assistance, but placed, at Antonescu's request, in Nazi concentration camps. Like the others, after Romania's successful *reversement des alliances* on 23 August 1944, he was dusted off to play the inglorious role of the Nazis' Romanian allies.

After the war — since the Legionaries were not war criminals (in spite of themselves) — it was easy for them to submerge. Horia Sima and others went to Spain (where Franco remembered Moța and Marin, and gave them asylum and a meager pension). Others emigrated to France or to South America or, like the Legionary student leader Viorel Trifa, the future "Valerian" Trifa, bishop of the Romanian Orthodox Church in America, to the United States (He was later expelled from the United States because of his past).

But Boeru remained in Germany. His wife, Mme. Olga Boeru, was not so lucky. She was thrown into the infamous prison at Mişle, and his children were denied education. But things went well for Mr. Boeru in Germany after the war.

He married a well-to-do German lady to whom he told "the communists killed his poor wife...," knowingly committing bigamy, since he was aware that his wife was alive and in prison.

With his wife's fortunes, he took advantage of the opportunities offered by the post-war German Wirtschaftswunder, and became very rich. During these years, he openly boasted to numerous, credible Romanians (who related to me) that he led the death squad and related every sordid detail of Iorga's murder, and also the murder of Virgil Madgearu. But this was also recalled by Sima, remembering that memorable day, how he apprehended Traian Boeru and his death squad, after the murder, in the villa of Mme. Lupescu.

Thanks to Legionary factionalism, and the opprobrium that had befallen the Legion because of Iorga's murder, Sima condemned Boeru, and asked: "What did Boeru want in the Legion anyhow?" (Sima, *Cazul Iorga-Madgearu*, p. 75). After all, the Legion was always supposed to be a Puritan Host!

Was this fury, or envy (because of the economic success of Mr. Boeru after the war)? Mr. Boeru certainly prospered (with his wife in prison), but "what goes up has to come down." After financial miscalculations and catastrophic investments, Mr. Boeru's enterprises were ruined.

The unfortunate Mme. Olga Boeru, after languishing many years in Romanian prisons, was released, obtained a passport, and came to Munich. She saw the bigamy in which her husband lived. As Romanians living there recalled, there was a bitter confrontation, after which Mme. Boeru committed suicide. All this only increased the ostracism of Traian Boeru among the Romanian community, but some — very few — Legionaries still sided with Boeru.

In the early 1960s, Mr. Boeru and the legionary faction around him decided to exonerate him of Iorga's murder. As Nicolae Guguianu, living in La Garenne Colombes (a close Legionary companion of Boeru), explained to me, during an interview he granted to me, the Legionary faction around Boeru contrived a "Juriul de Onoare" (Court of Honor), presided over by General Ion Gheorghe, Antonescu's last ambassador to Berlin, and others. The court exonerated him of Iorga's murder, despite all the evidence to the contrary. As the story goes, he did not go to Sinaia in person with the Death Squad, but remained in Bucharest, etc... This fiction contradicts all known facts: the results of the investigation carried out by the Antonescu authorities; the memories of the Iorga family; Mr. Boeru's own statements in Munich and elsewhere; and Sima's reminiscences. But these people have their own sort of logic, which, at times, becomes metapolitical phenomenon.

Meanwhile, as time passed, the grave financial problems faced by Boeru after his German wife divorced him, his old age, and illness all took their roll. In the late 1970s, he married for the third time (this time no bigamy was involved), a Romanian lady who emigrated a short time before to Germany. Fortunately, the German Social Security system took care of him. By the 1980s, Mr. Boeru landed in an old-age home (a Pflegeheim) in Garmisch-Partenkirchen, near Munich.

After tenuous efforts and with the help of numerous Romanians in early August 1985, on a sunny afternoon, in the company of the third Mrs. Boeru, I was on my way in my car towards Garmisch-Partenkirchen to meet Traian Boeru. I was overwhelmed by a strange feeling, after working so many years on this biography of Iorga. I was now to meet his murderer. Driving on the Autobahn, our car submerged in a sea of vacationers, all heading towards the south. New times, in a new Germany, representing a new generation.

And there was Mr. Boeru. After the formal introductions, I tried to recall the pictures I saw of him before: a young man in a smart Legionary uniform, coupled with a green shirt and cross belts. Nothing was left of that. It was a fragile, dying old man who stood before me — a ghost.

Was he a ghost of European history'? One could remember Shakespeare: "Time is a merciless collector — it does not forgive." I was warned before I arrived that Mr. Boeru had become senile. I did not get the impression of talking to a senile man. Boeru seemed quite alert.

When we talked about the murder (despite his former self-incriminatory statements to Sima and to other Romanians) he "stuck to the script" of the "Court of Honor" scenario. Mr. Boeru explained that he "knew about the preparations of the Death Squad in the agricultural cooperative, but he did not join the Death Squad. Nor did (he) participate in the execution of the plan, but neither did (he) interfere with the Death Squad." (Which is quite a statement, considering that Mr. Boeru was the head of the Death Squad.) During the conversation, Mr. Boeru preserved his calm, composed stature, and became only angry when asked about any possible German involvement in the murder of Professor Iorga. He retorted violently: "We didn't need Germans! Iorga's role in the murder of the Captain was enough!" In vain, I tried to explain the role of the king, that of Armand Călinescu, and even the approval of Dinu Brătianu — Mr. Boeru could not be moved.

I saw that it was useless to ask Mr. Boeru about anything relating to his direct involvement in the murder of Iorga. So I asked him for information, the names of the members of the Death Squad, the articles in *Buna Vestire*, and the preparations, circumstances, motives, and personal backgrounds of the Death Squad members. As long as no finger was pointed at him directly, Mr. Boeru was surprisingly forthcoming about the assassination.

We played a strange game: since he insisted that he had not been present at the murder, but knew every detail, he always pretended to remember things in a strange fashion: "Cojocaru related to me later," or "I was told by Tucan," that "Nicolae Iorga wanted to fire the first shot," etc. It was clear that Mr. Boeru had been present, only that he now related the events through the proxy of another Death Squad member.

And we spoke a lot about "the old times." Since I lived through those times as a child and wrote the history of the Legionary Movement, there were many things we could discuss. At one point, Mr. Boeru was so moved that he cried. (The third Mrs. Boeru later commented, "You even made him cry!")

Beyond hoping to get some information and to meet Traian Boeru, I came to see him to ask just one question: "How was it possible that since Nicolae Iorga was a great Romanian nationalist and he proffered such great services to Romania, how could the Legion reconcile the murder of someone like Professor Iorga with its integral nationalism?" The answer was revealing: "During the French Revolution many great men and many great patriots, who had done great services to France and to the French Revolution, were killed: Condorcet, Danton, and many others; so why should we have hesitated?"

After writing down some addresses and telephone numbers of other Legionaries who could supply me with information on the recommendation of Mr. Boeru (all of them stuck to the script of the "Juriul de Onoare," and they were careful because they knew that I had done my "homework" — and knew the subject), we descended into the garden, and took some photos together.

As the shadows grew longer, I thanked Mr. Boeru and bade him farewell. He asked me to return anytime, a return that was never to be.

We drove back to Munich with Mrs. Boeru in the starlit, clear summer night. Driving north on the Autobahn, the road was almost empty, while the opposite side was full with an endless flow of headlights. The wave of vacationers continued to roll toward the Mediterranean beaches.

The moment we left, the current Mrs. Boeru began her angry eliminations. She was no Legionary, and she said so. Moreover (while pointing out that she was no philo-Semite), she condemned Legionary methods on the Jewish question. After unloading her anger, she fell silent. Mrs. Boeru lived on the edge of Munich. When we arrived, I thanked her and said good-bye, thinking about Hannah Arendt's observation about the "banality of evil..."

In no time, I arrived to the glitter of the rebuilt Munich night, thousands of luxury' cars bearing domestic and foreign license plates, and cafes and beer halls flooded with colorful neon lights, and well-dressed people at the tables on the sidewalks. This was the Munich Gemutlichkeit... Sanity, law, order, cleanliness, and a peaceful, (almost!) "Swiss-like" Germany.

And my thoughts wandered back to another Munich I remembered well from my childhood. Munich "Die Stadt der Bewegung," full of brown shirts, grey uniforms, four-story high swastika flags hanging down from buildings, eagles, and more eagles, with the black-uniformed honor guards goose-stepping before the Feldhernhalle Monument...

Where was the present German then? As Luigi Barzini wrote so perceptively: "It did not have to be invented..." The operation after the Second World War was a simple one, the projector-beams were shifted to the European civilized aspect of Germany, which was quite easy — since the other Germany was buried under the rubble of the Reichskanzlei in Berlin (or in Munich, lying under the nibble of the Feldhernhalle Monument blown sky-high by the U.S. Army Corps of Engineers).

Mr. Boeru, by strange fortune, would get a chance in both Germanies. He forfeited those chances. He went down in history as the murderer of Nicolae Iorga, although he went to great lengths not to be remembered as such. History should not deny him this dubious distinction. Six weeks after this meeting, Mr. Boeru died in the same Pflegeheim in Garmisch-Partenkirchen.

Acknowledgments

I would first of all like to express my utmost gratitude to the Pippidi-Iorga family; to Mme. Liliana, Professor Iorga's daughter, and to Dr. Andrei Pippidi, Professor Iorga's grandson, for the information, help, advice, and the vast amount of materials that they provided to me. During my research, at a time when contacts with Western historians were not uniformly welcomed in Romania, they invited me on numerous their home and helped my work greatly. Without them my project would not have become a reality.

I would also like to thank Professor Ştefan Ştefănescu. It was his recommendation that opened the archives to me (Professor Iorga's correspondence, and other materials) and in an unprecedented, courageous manner. Professor Ştefănescu wrote on my behalf even to the C.I.E.S. urging them to allow me access to primary sources during my research.

I am thankful for the advice and help I received from my colleagues at the Institute of History bearing Iorga's name: Professors Nicolae Liu, Paul Cernavodeanu, Emil Lazea, Cornelia Bodea, Georgeta Penelea, Eliza Campus, and Florin Constantiniu.

I cherish the memory of Professor Eugen Stănescu, the deceased Director of the Institute of Southeast European Studies, who assisted me and provided me with many materials. A Byzantinist, like Iorga, Professor Stănescu generously assisted my research.

I would also like to thank Mr. Frasin Munteanu-Râmnic, the Curator of the Nicolae Iorga Museum in Vălenii-de-Munte, the son of Iorga's faithful political lieutenant, D. Munteanu-Râmnic, for the materials he supplied me with and the reminiscences he shared with me. I am also grateful to Mr. Kogălniceanu, the grandson of the founder of modern Romania, for his help, as well as the many others who helped me during difficult political times, taking great risks.

I thank the A.C.L.S., I.R.E.X., and Fulbright grant programs, which made my research possible. Last, but not least, I thank the Center for Romanian Studies for making the publication of my biography of Iorga possible.

Nicholas M. Nagy-Talavera

Index

E

F

CENTER FOR *Romanian* STUDIES

The mission of the Center for Romanian Studies is to promote knowledge of the history, literature, and culture of Romania to an international audience.
For more information contact us at
info@centerforromanianstudies.com

Check out these and other great titles at
CenterforRomanianStudies.com